DIVIDENDS
AND
DIVIDEND
POLICY

The *Robert W. Kolb Series in Finance* provides a comprehensive view of the field of finance in all of its variety and complexity. The series is projected to include approximately 65 volumes covering all major topics and specializations in finance, ranging from investments, to corporate finance, to financial institutions. Each volume in the *Kolb Series in Finance* consists of new articles especially written for the volume.

Each *Kolb Series* volume is edited by a specialist in a particular area of finance, who develops the volume outline and commissions articles by the world's experts in that particular field of finance. Each volume includes an editor's introduction and approximately thirty articles to fully describe the current state of financial research and practice in a particular area of finance.

The essays in each volume are intended for practicing finance professionals, graduate students, and advanced undergraduate students. The goal of each volume is to encapsulate the current state of knowledge in a particular area of finance so that the reader can quickly achieve a mastery of that special area of finance.

DIVIDENDS
AND
DIVIDEND POLICY

H. Kent Baker

The Robert W. Kolb Series in Finance

WILEY

John Wiley & Sons, Inc.

Published by John Wiley & Sons, Inc., Hoboken, New Jersey.
Published simultaneously in Canada.

For general information on our other products and services or for technical support, please contact our Customer Care Department within the United States at (800) 762-2974, outside the United States at (317) 572-3993 or fax (317) 572-4002.

Wiley also publishes its books in a variety of electronic formats. Some content that appears in print may not be available in electronic books. For more information about Wiley products, visit our web site at www.wiley.com.

Library of Congress Cataloging-in-Publication Data:

Baker, H. Kent (Harold Kent), 1944–
    Dividends and dividend policy / H. Kent Baker, Robert W. Kolb.
        p. cm.
    Includes index.
    ISBN 978-0-470-45580-7 (cloth)
  1. Dividends.   I. Kolb, Robert W., 1949–   II. Title.
    HG4028.D5.B25 2009
    332.63'221–dc22

                                                2008054318

Printed in the United States of America

10 9 8 7 6 5 4 3 2 1

Contents

Acknowledgments

Many people contributed both directly and indirectly to this book. I want to thank the authors of each chapter for their outstanding efforts. Janel Carpenter and Sonya Starnes from American University provided excellent editorial assistance by painstakingly reviewing each chapter and providing helpful suggestions. I also appreciate the substantial efforts of Laura Walsh, associate editor; Todd Tedesco, production editor; and Brigitte Coulton, project manager. I dedicate this book to Linda A. Baker.

PART I

Dividends and Dividend Policy: History, Trends, and Determinants

CHAPTER 1

Dividends and Dividend Policy: An Overview

H. KENT BAKER
University Professor of Finance, American University

INTRODUCTION

An assumption underlying much of the academic finance literature is that managers make decisions that lead to maximizing the wealth of their firm's shareholders as reflected in common stock share prices. As Jensen (2001, p. 8) notes:

> *How do we want the firms in our economy to measure their own performance? How do we want them to determine what is better versus worse? Most economists would answer simply that managers have a criterion for evaluating performance and deciding between alternative courses of action, and that the criterion should be maximization of the long-term market value of the firm. . . . This Value Maximization proposition has its roots in 200 years of research in economics and finance.*

The decisions of corporate financial managers fall into two broad categories: investment decisions and financing decisions (Baker and Powell, 2005). Investment decisions involve determining the type and amount of assets that the firm wants to hold, reflected on the left-hand side of its balance sheet. Financing decisions concern the acquisition of funds in the form of both debt and equity to support a firm's operating and investment activities. The right-hand side of a firm's balance sheet reflects these sources of financing.

Dividend decisions, as determined by a firm's dividend policy, are a type of financing decision that affects the amount of earnings that a firm distributes to shareholders versus the amount it retains and reinvests. Dividend policy refers to the payout policy that a firm follows in determining the size and pattern of cash distributions to shareholders over time. A company's board of directors, with the input of senior management, sets a corporation's dividend policy.

Under real-world conditions, determining an appropriate payout policy often involves a difficult choice because of the need to balance many potentially conflicting forces. According to conventional wisdom, paying dividends affects both shareholder wealth and the firm's ability to retain earnings to exploit growth opportunities. Because investment, financing, and dividend decisions are interrelated (Pruitt and Gitman, 1991), management cannot consider dividend policy in isolation from these other decisions. For example, if a firm decides to increase

3

the amount of dividends paid, it retains fewer funds for investment purposes, which may force the company into the capital markets to raise funds. In practice, many corporate managers carefully consider the choice of dividend policy because they believe such decisions affect firm value and hence shareholder wealth (Baker, Farrelly, and Edelman, 1985; Baker and Powell, 1999). In addition, many investors view dividend policy as important because they supply cash to firms with the expectation of eventually receiving cash in return. Thus, managers typically act as though their firm's dividend policy is relevant despite the controversial arguments set forth by Miller and Modigliani (1961) that dividends are irrelevant in determining the value of the firm.

Yet much academic debate surrounds the role, if any, of how dividend decisions lead to achieving the goal of value maximization. The notion that dividends affect the value of a firm's shares is not new. For example, in writing his influential but underappreciated classic, *The Theory of Investment Value*, John Burr Williams (1938) was among the first economists to view stock prices as determined by intrinsic value and to articulate the theory of dividend-based valuation. According to Williams, a stock is worth only what you get out of it. Thus, the intrinsic value, or long-term worth, of a common stock is the present value of its future net cash flows in the form of dividend distributions and selling price. Graham and Dodd (1951) also believe that stock prices reflect an intrinsic value related to dividends and earnings. Building on the beliefs of Graham and Dodd, Gordon (1959) develops a valuation model in which the only relevant variables that determine a stock's value are dividends and the discount rate.

Others are less sanguine about how dividends affect the value of a firm's shares. In their pioneering study, Miller and Modigliani (1961) (hereafter MM) provide an elegant analysis of the relationships among dividend policy, growth, and the valuation of shares. On the basis of a well-defined but simplified set of perfect capital market assumptions (e.g., no taxes, transaction and agency costs, and information freely available to everyone), MM set forth a dividend irrelevance theorem. In their idealized world, investment policy is the sole determinant of firm value. Therefore, if managers focus on making prudent investment choices, payout policy and capital structure should take care of themselves. MM's irrelevance message suggests that payout policy is an economically trivial issue that managers can largely ignore if they make sensible investment decisions. Early studies by Black and Scholes (1974), Miller (1986), and Miller and Scholes (1978, 1982) support the dividend irrelevance argument.

As DeAngelo and DeAngelo (2007) point out, MM's dividend irrelevance principle rests on an unstated assumption that forces firms to choose among payout policies that distribute 100 percent of the free cash flow generated each period by investment policy. In addition, stockholders are indifferent to receiving a given amount of cash as a dividend or through stock repurchases. Thus, MM's theory leads to the contentious conclusion that all feasible payout policies are equally valuable to investors. Yet DeAngelo and DeAngelo contend that the set of possible payout policies is not as limited as MM assume and that payout policy matters.

MM's unconventional and controversial conclusion about dividend policy irrelevance stirred a heated debate that has reverberated throughout the finance community for decades. Early criticism focused on MM's unduly restrictive assumptions as unrealistic. Consequently, if dividend policy is important to shareholders and affects stock prices, some of MM's assumptions must be wrong.

Bernstein (1992, p. 176) notes, however, that the "MM theory was admittedly an abstraction when it was originally presented," and "no one—least of all Modigliani and Miller—would claim that the real world looks like this." Although examining dividend policy in perfect capital markets can provide useful insights about the conditions under which dividends may affect stock prices, the dividend irrelevance theorem can also be misleading. As Bernstein (p. 180) notes, "The final test of any theory is how accurately it portrays the real world, blemishes and all."

Upon leaving MM's abstract world of economic theory and entering the real world, the issue of dividend irrelevance becomes more debatable. Researchers responded to MM's conclusion of dividend policy irrelevance by offering competing hypotheses about why corporations pay dividends and why investors want them—the "dividend puzzle," as Black (1976) coined. For instance, some early theories that explain the potential relevance of dividends involve taxes, agency costs, and asymmetric information. Lease, John, Kalay, Loewenstein, and Sarig (1956, p. 46) refer to these explanations for dividend relevance as the "big three" frictions and to transaction costs, flotation costs, and irrational investor behavior as the "three little" frictions. Lease et al. (p. 196) conclude, "Dividend policy *can* have an impact on shareholder wealth because of various market imperfections." Because these imperfections affect firms differently, dividend policies may vary substantially among firms. In fact, Lease et al. develop a dividend life cycle incorporating market frictions to illustrate how dividend policy differs according to the phase of that cycle: start-up, initial public offering (IPO), rapid growth, maturity, and decline.

In a much-cited article, Black (1976, p. 5) assesses the contributions of dividend researchers post-MM and concludes, "The harder we look at the dividend picture, the more it seems like a puzzle, with pieces that just don't fit together." Feldstein and Green (1983, p. 17) echo Black's sentiments, stating, "The nearly universal policy of paying substantial dividends is the primary puzzle in the economics of corporate finance." Miller (1986) also recognizes that one of the "soft spots" in the current body of theory is the preference that many corporations have for paying dividends. In fact, the surge of dividend research after MM led Ang (1987, p. 55) to observe: "Thus, we have moved from a position of not enough good reasons to explain why dividends are paid to one of too many." Despite a plethora of existing explanations, researchers developed additional theories to explain the dividend puzzle, including behavioral explanations and dividend theories involving the firm life cycle and catering theory. Empirical tests of these theories often result in conflicting results.

In a controversial paper, DeAngelo and DeAngelo (2006) claim that, contrary to MM (1961), payout policy is not irrelevant and that investment policy is not the sole determinant of value, even in frictionless markets. They point out that by relaxing MM's assumptions to allow for retention, payout policy matters. They also claim that Black's (1976) dividend puzzle is a nonpuzzle because the crux of the puzzle rests on the mistaken idea that MM's irrelevance theorem applies to payout and retention decisions, which it does not. If DeAngelo and DeAngelo's claims have merit, then MM sent researchers off searching for frictions that would make payout policy matter, when it has mattered all along.

The main objective of this book is to provide a synthesis of the literature on dividends and dividend policy that is an accessible discussion for students, managers, investors, and others interested in these topics. The book's central focus concerns how corporate decisions on distribution policy affect shareholder wealth. Using evidence from various methods, including survey research, the authors describe managers' views on dividends and how managers make dividend policy decisions. The book also documents researchers' attempts to model dividend behavior mathematically and relates dividend policy to share prices. Such attempts reflect varying degrees of success and failure.

The book concentrates mainly on dividends and share repurchases because they are the principal mechanisms by which corporations distribute cash to shareholders. Although most chapters deal with these distribution methods, others cover such dividend-related topics as dividend reinvestment plans, stock splits and stock dividends, and corporate governance. Although much dividend research centers on North American financial markets, the book also examines dividend studies from around the world. A brief of synopsis of each chapter in the book's six parts follows.

DIVIDENDS AND DIVIDEND POLICY: HISTORY, TRENDS, AND DETERMINANTS

The remaining four chapters (Chapters 2–5) of the first part of this book discuss the history, trends, and determinants of dividends and dividend policy. Understanding the evolution and trends of dividend policy provides insights into dividend decisions, as does the identification of factors influencing dividends.

Chapter 2: The Historical Evolution of Dividends

Chapter 2 summarizes the evolution of dividend policy from the sixteenth century to modern times. The first corporations were short-term ventures that ended in full liquidation. As corporations became longer lived, managers faced the issue of how to make distributions to shareholders, and numerous firm-specific policies as well as laws developed to address how much corporations could pay shareholders. From the seventeenth to the nineteenth century, managers used dividends to influence share prices and to attract new capital. In the twentieth century, researchers developed various hypotheses to explain dividend policies. An overview of recent surveys and observed firm reactions to changes in tax laws provide additional insights into current dividend policies.

Chapter 3: Trends in Dividends: Payers and Payouts

Chapter 3 reviews recent trends in dividends and dividend payers and focuses on the phenomenon of disappearing dividends, which appeared in the United States during the end of the twentieth century, as first observed by Fama and French (2001). Researchers have advanced several possible explanations for the decrease in the propensity to pay dividends. To date, there is no universally accepted explanation. While one strand of the literature questions the existence of this phenomenon, another strand argues that the phenomenon has been only temporary, as the propensity to pay dividends has been on the increase since the new millennium. Finally, although studies on countries other than the United States have observed a similar decline in the propensity to pay dividends, the magnitude of the phenomenon is much less pronounced and much more recent.

Chapter 4: Factors Influencing Dividends

Chapter 4 synthesizes the academic evidence on the cross-sectional and time-series determinants of dividends. This evidence shows that dividends are associated with several firm characteristics, such as size, profitability, growth opportunities, maturity, leverage, equity ownership, and incentive compensation. The chapter also examines the relationship between dividends and characteristics of the market in which the firm operates, such as tax law, investor protection, product market competition, investor sentiment, and public or private status, as well as the availability of substitute forms of corporate payout, primarily repurchases. These findings have several implications for existing theories of dividend policy and suggest avenues for future research.

Chapter 5: Cross-Country Determinants of Payout Policy: European Firms

Most research in dividend policy focuses on the North American financial markets and their associated regulatory environment. Chapter 5 focuses on dividend policies of European firms and other legal and regulatory regimes. It begins by examining the evolution of dividend policy to determine whether the key trends identified in the United States, such as the declining fraction of dividend payers and the concentration of dividend payers among large firms, also occur in Europe. The chapter then examines the major determinants of European payout policy, drawing largely from Bancel, Bhattacharyya, and Mittoo (2006). The chapter provides some reassuring evidence that the major factors influencing dividend policy are similar across countries. However, some country-specific differences exist, indicating that dividend policy is a complex interaction of a country's legal and institutional structure with firm characteristics such as ownership structure.

CASH DIVIDENDS: THEORETICAL AND EMPIRICAL EVIDENCE

Part II contains eight chapters (Chapters 6–13) and focuses on the critical issue of whether dividend policy is relevant or irrelevant. At the heart of the dividend puzzle is whether dividend policy affects share prices. Some believe that payout policy is irrelevant because they contend that only investment policy affects value. Thus, one dividend policy is as good as any other. Others support dividend relevance, in which case dividend policy affects value. Despite voluminous study, researchers have been unable to identify the "true" relationship between dividend payments and stock prices.

Although dividend policies may take many forms, two generic classifications are a residual dividend policy and a managed dividend policy. With a residual dividend policy, a firm pays dividends from earnings left over after meeting its investment needs while maintaining its target capital structure. This passive approach assumes that investors prefer that firms keep and reinvest earnings. A managed dividend policy is one in which management attempts to achieve a specific pattern of dividend payments. According to certain MM assumptions, a managed dividend policy is irrelevant because such a policy would not increase shareholder wealth. Thus, corporate managers who believe that dividend policy is relevant would engage in some type of managed dividend policy.

Chapter 6: Dividend Irrelevance Theory

In their pioneering work, MM (1961) show that, under certain assumptions, dividends are irrelevant to total firm value. Their work represents a radical departure from previous views of dividend policy and is one of the first to use analytically rigorous techniques to address a finance issue. In addition, the influence of dividend irrelevance theory on finance research has been profound. Researchers have attempted to find reasons that dividends exist, and the focus has usually been either on market frictions, such as taxes, transaction costs, and imperfect information, or on behavioral considerations, such as investor preferences. Despite the hallowed status of MM's work, DeAngelo and DeAngelo (2006) have attacked the irrelevancy proof as well as the related research stream that attempts to find reasons for relevance.

Chapter 7: Residual Dividend Policy

The concept of a residual dividend policy has deep roots in the financial literature and underlies important theoretical work. Among the recommendations of agency theory is a residual dividend policy specifying that managers pay shareholders the free cash flows remaining after funding all profitable investments. Empirical evidence suggests that firms generally do not follow this type of policy. Instead, firms generally maintain a smoothed dividend sequence that is as strongly related to past dividends as it is to current earnings. In addition, firms build up cash balances to fund future investments. When a funding shortage occurs, firms often use short-term borrowing rather than cut the dividend. Managers' responses to surveys about residual dividend policy generally indicate that if the free cash flow versus dividend time series appears to indicate a residual dividend policy, this is largely coincidental and not a product of the firm's intended policy.

Chapter 8: Taxes and Clientele Effects

According to tax preference theory, rational investors prefer that firms retain cash instead of paying dividends when tax rates are higher on dividends than on long-term capital gains. Thus, firms should keep dividend payments low if they want to maximize share price. Supporters of this theory also contend that investors in high tax brackets prefer stocks with low dividend yields while investors in low brackets prefer stocks with high dividend yields. These situations represent clientele effects. Studies often use variations in the tax rates on dividend income and capital gains to examine the effects of taxation on dividend policy. Given a lack of compelling tax changes and fully convincing research designs, previous studies provide conflicting results. More recent studies offer new insights by showing that a firm's ownership and governance structure affect the relationship between taxation and payout policy.

Chapter 9: Agency Costs and the Free Cash Flow Hypothesis

MM (1961) posit that dividend policy is irrelevant to firm value, but empirical evidence shows that a firm's stock price typically moves in the same direction as that of the dividend change. According to the free cash flow model, the market reacts positively (negatively) to the news of dividend increases (decreases) because the potential for managers to misuse excess funds decreases (increases). This model implies that the market reaction to dividend-change announcements is greater for firms with higher overinvestment potential than for those with lower overinvestment potential. Empirical evidence typically supports this hypothesis. Another implication of this model is that the role of dividends varies depending on the severity of the agency problem. Consistent with this supposition, studies report that variations in corporate governance mechanisms may explain the variations in dividend policies across countries. In addition, there is little evidence to suggest a relationship between dividend changes and changes in future profitability. The cumulative evidence suggests that the free cash flow model helps to explain the market reaction to dividend changes.

Chapter 10: Asymmetric Information and Signaling Theory

The basis of signaling theory is the premise of asymmetric information, where managers have access to information that the market does not. Thus, corporate financial decisions can be viewed as signaling devices that a company's managers send to investors to communicate information, which reduces asymmetries. Changes in dividend policy are one such device at the managers' disposal to communicate information to the market about the future prospects of the firm. Chapter 10 explores the research into whether abnormal returns result from various financial decisions that managers make. Overall, most empirical evidence tends to support theoretical models regarding the ability of dividend changes to affect share price. Unexpected dividend increases (decreases) are associated with significant share price increases (decreases).

Chapter 11: Behavioral Explanations of Dividends

Chapter 11 develops a behaviorally based theory for why individual investors find dividends attractive and presents a combination of anecdotal evidence and empirical evidence supporting the implications of the theory. The behavioral elements underlying the theory include self-control, mental accounting, hedonic editing, and regret aversion. The theoretical implications pertain to the impact of age, income, and retirement status on two relationships involving the preference for dividends: the relationship between consumer expenditures and the preference for dividends and the relationship between tolerance for risk and the preference for dividends.

Chapter 12: The Firm Life Cycle Theory of Dividends

The firm life cycle theory of dividends contends that the optimal dividend policy of a firm depends on the firm's stage in its life cycle. The underlying premise is that firms generally follow a life cycle trajectory from origin to maturity that is associated with a shrinking investment opportunity set, declining growth rate, and decreasing cost of raising external capital. The optimal dividend policy, derived from a trade-off between the costs and benefits of raising capital for new investments, evolves with these life cycle related changes. As the firm becomes more mature, the optimal payout ratio increases. The empirical evidence generally supports the theory in that dividend payment propensity is related to life cycle characteristics—dividend payers are mature firms with a high ratio of earned capital to contributed capital, while young, high-growth firms do not pay dividends.

Chapter 13: The Catering Theory of Dividends

Chapter 13 reviews the catering theory of dividends, which is a recent theory based on investor sentiment. Catering theory highlights the importance of investor sentiment in decisions about dividend policies. Managers cater to investor demand by paying dividends when investors prefer dividend-paying firms and by not paying dividends (or reducing the dividend) when investors prefer non-dividend-paying companies. The dividend premium captures the relative market valuation of dividend payers versus nonpayers.

SHARE REPURCHASES

Part III contains four chapters (Chapters 14–17) about share repurchases. Instead of paying cash dividends, corporations may choose to pay out earnings to owners by buying back shares of outstanding common stock. Over the past several decades, there is a growing trend for U.S. firms to use repurchases as the preferred method to distribute cash to shareholders. Companies have several methods of repurchasing stock, including fixed-price tender offers, Dutch auction tender offers, open-market share repurchases, transferable put-rights distributions, and targeted stock repurchases. Although each mechanism has its advantages and disadvantages, most companies use open-market share repurchases. Numerous studies examine the impact of repurchase announcements on a firm's stock price. The market reaction around the announcement date depends largely on the repurchase method.

There are many potential reasons for companies to buy back their own stock. Some of the more common motives for share repurchases include regulatory and tax considerations, agency costs of free cash flows, signaling and undervaluation, capital structure, takeover deterrence, and employee stock options. These motives may differ on the basis of the type of repurchase method used.

Chapter 14: Stock Repurchases: Theory and Evidence, Part 1

This chapter surveys the theoretical and empirical studies on share repurchases. In the United States, share repurchases have surpassed cash dividends and become the dominant form of corporate payouts since the last decade. The chapter provides a brief description of five major types of share repurchases and considers the motives that influence firms' repurchase decisions. Specifically, the chapter examines regulatory and tax considerations, agency costs of free cash flows, and signaling and undervaluation. The review indicates that the existing literature provides ample support for several of these motivations while others merit further investigation. Few studies provide possible explanations for the phenomenon of increasing total payouts over time that is largely attributable to share repurchases.

Chapter 15: Stock Repurchases: Theory and Evidence, Part 2

Chapter 15 continues the review of the theoretical and empirical studies on share repurchases. It provides a discussion of three other motives that influence firms' repurchase decisions: capital structure, takeover deterrence, and employee stock options. Overall, the existing research provides support for these three influences. In addition, the chapter explores why firms may prefer one method of payout to another—cash dividends versus stock repurchases.

Chapter 16: Stock Repurchases and Dividends: Trade-Offs and Trends

Corporations routinely distribute cash to equity investors in two forms: cash dividends and share repurchases. Since the adoption of SEC Rule 10b-18 in 1982, which eliminated the risk that market participants would interpret open-market repurchases as possible share price manipulation, there has been a steady movement toward open-market repurchases as the preferred method to distribute cash to shareholders. Although this chapter discusses various explanations for this trend, the predominant one is that managers believe that repurchases offer flexibility that dividends do not. The trend toward repurchases is even stronger among new firms contemplating payout for the first time. As a result, analysts must interpret per-share data and apply valuation models with care. Unlike cash dividends that tend to vary little over time, repurchases can change markedly in the short run. This makes defining what is meant by a company's "typical" payout difficult.

Chapter 17: Beating the Market with Share Buybacks

The purpose of this chapter is to provide an overview of anomalous price behavior around various repurchase methods such as fixed-price tender offers, private repurchases, and open-market buyback programs. All these anomalies allow investors to earn excess returns, that is, beat the market on the basis of publicly available information. All anomalies have a common characteristic: Markets tend to be too skeptical about the ability of managers to time the market. That is, the market questions whether managers can buy back stocks when they are cheap. The chapter provides some evidence on why such anomalies may persist despite being widely publicized in the literature.

OTHER DISTRIBUTION METHODS

Part IV contains three chapters (Chapters 18–20) and focuses on distribution methods other than regular cash dividends and stock repurchases. Occasionally, corporations issue a specially designated dividend, which management labels as "extra," "special," or "year-end." Such labeling enables a firm to increase the dividend without the implicit need to continue paying that dividend in the future. Firms often declare a special dividend after experiencing good earnings over the previous year.

Some firms issue stock splits or pay stock dividends. Both types of stock distributions increase the number of outstanding shares of stock and should cause a proportionate decline in the stock's market price. These methods differ mainly in the size of the stock distribution and their accounting treatment. According to conventional wisdom, shareholders gain no real benefits from such distributions. While both stock splits and stock dividends increase the number of equity shares outstanding, they do not provide the firm with new funds or its stockholders with any added claims to company assets. Theoretically, neither type of distribution should affect shareholder wealth. In practice, such distributions are more than merely cosmetic changes because they involve wealth effects. Empirical studies often show that a company's stock price, on average, reacts favorably to the announcement of stock splits and stock dividends. Baker, Phillips, and Powell (1995) refer to the market reaction to announcements of stock splits and dividends as the "stock distribution puzzle."

Unlike stock splits and stock dividends, a reverse stock split reduces the number of shares outstanding and increases the price per share. Although reverse stock splits theoretically are noneconomic events, they can result in material changes in stock price behavior. Stock prices generally decline with the announcement of a reverse split. Thus, engaging in reverse splits may be inconsistent with maximizing shareholder wealth and may be of questionable value to firms.

A dividend reinvestment plan (DRIP) entitles shareholders enrolled in the plan to automatically buy additional shares of a firm's stock with their cash dividends. There are two basic types of DRIPs. The most common type of DRIP is a market plan, which involves buying shares in the open market for the accounts of shareholders reinvesting their dividends. A new issue plans allows shareholders to buy new shares directly from the company. Thus, new issue plans provide firms with an alternative way to raise new equity capital without directly using the primary market.

Chapter 18: Special Dividends

Chapter 18 focuses on the use of specially designated dividends. When a firm wants to make a single large cash distribution to shareholders, special dividends can serve as a way to distribute that cash without shareholders anticipating repeated distributions. Such large cash distributions are appropriate when a firm has accumulated cash in excess of its investment needs either from continuing operations or from sale of assets. In the past, firms paid special dividends more often and in smaller amounts but now generally pay special dividends infrequently and in larger amounts. Firms also use stock repurchases to distribute large amounts of cash, but they do so infrequently. Important determinants of the choice between the two means of distributing cash are tax considerations and the firm's stock price.

Chapter 19: Stock Splits, Stock Dividends, and Reverse Stock Splits

Chapter 19 explores the costly process of altering the number of shares in a publicly traded company, akin to changing the number of pieces of a cake without changing the size of the cake. Although the act of a stock split, stock dividend, or reverse stock split is purely cosmetic, researchers observe abnormal stock market reactions at the announcement date and sometimes at the ex-date. What is especially puzzling is the positive stock market reaction to stock splits and stock dividends, as these actions are costly and offer questionable benefits to the firm. Possible explanations include the signaling hypothesis and the optimal price range hypothesis. This chapter reviews the empirical research findings and examines the hypotheses put forth in the research literature.

Chapter 20: Dividend Reinvestment Plans

Dividend reinvestment plans have gained popularity as a low-cost, convenient way to invest over the past four decades. The DRIPs may serve as a financing alternative for corporations and as an investment option for investors. The DRIPs offer both benefits and limitations from the viewpoints of corporations and investors. The chapter discusses the financial theory and empirical evidence related to DRIPs concerning the factors determining the adoption and discontinuation of DRIPs, the choice between open market and new issue DRIPs, and the implications of DRIPs for other investment alternatives to corporations and investors.

SURVEY EVIDENCE ON DIVIDENDS AND DIVIDEND POLICY

Part V contains three chapters (Chapters 21–23) that report views about dividends and dividend policy based on survey-based research. In conducting empirical research, researchers rely on the two broad categories of data, namely primary and secondary data. Most empirical research on dividends and dividend policy relies on the analysis of secondary data, such as stock prices and accounting data. Secondary data already exist and often can satisfy the research requirements of the study at hand. For the data to depict how people operate, researchers typically must gather primary data, which are data collected firsthand directly from those under study for a specific purpose. A survey is the most common method of collecting primary data.

Because each type of data collection has its strengths and weaknesses, the combination of survey and nonsurvey research can provide a potentially richer and more complete view of an issue than using a single data source. Survey and nonsurvey research are both important in their own way and can complement one another. As Bruner (2002, p. 50) notes, "The task must be to look for patterns of confirmation across approaches and studies much like one sees an image in a mosaic of stones."

Chapter 21: Cash Dividends and Stock Repurchases

Survey research focusing on dividends and stock repurchases provides important insights into management's views about their firms' corporate payout policies. Although survey findings often confirm theoretical and empirical predictions about management behavior, sometimes they refute them. For example, Lintner's (1956) classic dividend study reveals that managers believe that shareholders prefer stable dividend payments, set their dividend levels to avoid having to reverse dividend increases, and gradually increase dividends toward a target payout ratio when earnings increase. Later surveys confirm many of Lintner's findings and provide additional evidence about managerial motives for dividends.

Chapter 22: Stock Splits, Stock Dividends, and Dividend Reinvestment Plans

Chapter 22 documents the views of managers on dividend policy by synthesizing the survey evidence on stock splits, stock dividends, and DRIPs. Managers report that stock splits enable small stockholders to buy round lots more easily and to keep a firm's stock price in an optimal price range. Stock splits also increase the number of a firm's shareholders, make stocks more attractive to investors by increasing the number of shares outstanding, increase liquidity, and signal management's optimistic expectations about the future of the firm. The reasons for issuing stock dividends include maintaining historical firm practice, conserving cash, increasing the yield to stockholders, expanding the amount of equity, having a positive psychological impact on investors, and signaling optimistic expectations about the future. Finally, financial managers believe that firms benefit from DRIPs by raising equity capital through new issue plans, improving shareholder goodwill, and allowing plan participants to acquire stocks at a reduced fee.

Chapter 23: Why Individual and Professional Investors Want Dividends

Chapter 23 summarizes evidence on how individual and professional investors consider dividends in their investment decisions. Surveys of individual Dutch and Greek investors have found that most of the investors surveyed prefer dividends. Their responses are consistent with signaling theory but not with uncertainty resolution or agency theories of dividend policy. Their views of cash (stock) dividends are inconsistent (consistent) with the behavioral theory of Shefrin and Statman (1984). The chapter also presents new evidence about dividends and dividend policy from interviews with a small sample of professional investors in Canada and readings of analysts' reports. The professional investors tend to agree that their clients want dividends because of the comfort dividends provide, despite that they do not withdraw much of their dividend income. Professionals often mention that dividends provide valuable information content but view such information as less important than cash flow. In particular, Canadian analysts do not appear to incorporate dividends into their investment evaluation.

OTHER DIVIDEND ISSUES

Part VI has five chapters (Chapters 24–28) and covers other important issues related to dividends and dividend policy. Specifically, Chapter 24 is an empirical study investigating dividend initiation and firms' motivations for paying regular cash dividends to shareholders. The remaining four chapters investigate how dividend policy relates to corporate governance, regulated industries, the global perspective, and emerging markets.

Chapter 24: Why Firms Begin Paying Dividends: Value, Growth, and Life Cycle Effects

This chapter investigates the signaling, agency, and risk explanations for dividends within the context of the life cycle hypothesis, which proposes that dividend initiation conveys information about firms' transition to a slower-growth, "mature" phase. Companies initiating dividends have different characteristics, depending upon their life cycle stage. Low market-to-book (M/B) stocks display the most positive price reaction to dividend initiation announcements. High M/B firms have greater profits, cash levels, and capital expenditure but more closely resemble the low M/B firms in terms of these characteristics within three years after dividend initiation. Excess returns earned by low M/B firms are related to decreases in systematic risk, while the returns of high M/B firms are related to their greater profitability.

Chapter 25: Dividend Policy and Corporate Governance

In recent years, academics' and practitioners' interests in corporate governance have increased substantially. The extant finance literature shows that shareholder-manager agency conflicts strongly influence corporate financial policies such as capital structure and dividend payouts. However, the literature on the relationship between agency theory and a firm's dividend policy is limited but is now growing at a rapid pace. This chapter focuses on different external (e.g., shareholder rights and legal environment) and internal (e.g., managerial and block-holder ownership, executive compensation and board structure) corporate governance mechanisms that may influence a firm's dividend policy. The literature shows that these variables affect dividend policy, but considerable variations exist in the results. Given the changing business and regulatory environment, the role of dividends in mitigating the agency costs of firms appears to be an ongoing process to study.

Chapter 26: Dividend Policy in Regulated Industries

In theory, the dividend policies of regulated and nonregulated firms could differ. This chapter focuses on the research evidence on dividends for the banking, insurance, utility, real estate investment trust (REIT), petroleum, and other industries, which are sometimes identified as regulated. In general, stock price reactions to announcements of dividend changes are similar for both regulated and nonregulated firms. Management surveys and empirical studies examining dividend payout policies provide evidence that dividend policies of regulated and nonregulated firms differ, but the evidence is far from conclusive. Overall, the research findings lead to the conclusion that studies should control for regulated and nonregulated firms.

Chapter 27: Dividend Policy in a Global Perspective

Chapter 27 focuses on the role of dividends and the patterns of dividend policy across various national settings. There is now ample empirical evidence that corporate control varies substantially between the United States and the United Kingdom on one side and the rest of the world on the other side. Hence, the role of dividends as well as their level and flexibility are also likely to vary across countries. The limited existing evidence suggests that dividend policy reflects the characteristics of national corporate governance regimes and the control structure of individual firms.

Chapter 28: Dividend Policy in Emerging Markets

Chapter 28 synthesizes the extant research on dividend policies in emerging financial markets. The environments conditioning or constraining dividend payments in these markets differ from those in developed financial markets, specifically in terms of legal mandates on the amounts paid out, legislation relating to share repurchases, concentrated ownership structures, and overall macroeconomic volatility. Although the proportion of dividend-paying firms is higher in emerging financial markets than in the United States, this proportion has fluctuated considerably. The magnitude of dividend distributions, as measured by dividend payout and dividends-to-sales ratios, has in many cases become comparable to that in the United States while remaining more volatile. Macroeconomic fluctuations and ownership structure rank as important determinants of dividend policy.

CONCLUSIONS

Despite much study, researchers still do not have all the answers to the dividend puzzle. The extant literature contains various theories on taxes and clientele effects, agency costs, asymmetric information, behavior, life cycle, and catering, but none by itself fully explains dividend behavior. Some are at best second-order explanations for real-world payout policies. The voluminous body of work on the dividend puzzle suggests that solving this thorny issue has not been simple or obvious. After reviewing extensive evidence on the dividend puzzle, Baker, Powell, and Veit (2002, p. 256) conclude:

> While not fully solving the dividend puzzle, theoretical and empirical studies over the past four decades have provided additional puzzle pieces that move us closer in the direction of resolution. In reality, there is probably some truth to all of the explanations of why corporations pay dividends or repurchase stock at least for some firms.

Baker et al. (2002, p. 242) also note, "Despite exhaustive theoretical and empirical analysis to explain their pervasive presence, dividends remain one of the thorniest puzzles in corporate finance." Thus, fully resolving this enigma has eluded theoretical modeling and empirical detection, but researchers have made considerable progress.

What explains the difficulty of resolving the dividend puzzle, if such a puzzle actually exists? Why do managers choose one method of cash distribution over the other, given that dividends and share repurchases are similar but imperfect substitutes? Baker, Saadi, and Dutta (2008) suggest that two major reasons account for the inability to fully resolve these questions. First, some financial economists have been striving to develop a universal, or one-size-fits-all, explanation, despite the well-known fact that dividend policy is sensitive to factors such as market frictions, firm characteristics, corporate governance, and legal environments. In this same vein, Frankfurter and Wood (1997, p. 31) remark:

> *Dividend-payment patterns (or what is often referred to as "dividend policy") of firms are a cultural phenomenon, influenced by customs, beliefs, regulations, public opinion, perceptions and hysteria, general economic conditions and several other factors, all in perpetual change, impacting different firms differently. Accordingly, it cannot be modeled mathematically and uniformly for all firms at all times.*

As previous evidence reveals, concentrating on a single piece of the dividend puzzle at a time is unlikely to provide a satisfactory resolution because the puzzle contains many pieces. Lease et al. (2000) offer a competing frictions model that involves combining various pieces (market imperfections) and understanding their interactions. Their dividend life cycle model consists of five stages: start-up, IPO, rapid growth, maturity, and decline. According to their model, a firm should pay no dividends during the start-up and IPO stages but should pay a low, growing, and generous dividend during the three latter stages, respectively. Lease et al. (p. 179) conclude:

> *We believe that the lack of empirical support for a particular dividend policy theory is the result of problems in quantitatively measuring market frictions and the statistical complications in dealing with the myriad interactive imperfections that likely affect individual firms differently. In other words, since each firm faces a combination of potentially different market frictions with varying levels of relevance, the optimal dividend policy for each firm may be unique. If each firm has a uniquely optimal dividend policy, we should not be surprised that significant statistical generalizations still elude researchers. Current models of the impact of dividend policy on firm's values cannot fully reflect the complexity of the market environment.*

Although the model of Lease et al. (2000) provides a framework for bringing together key pieces of the dividend puzzle, it excludes other factors that may help explain differences in dividend policy such as corporate governance and legal environments. Thus, while their integrative model of market frictions represents a step forward, it is likely to be incomplete. DeAngelo and DeAngelo (2007) also present a corporate life cycle approach that provides a useful framework for understanding real-world payout policies. They show that optimal or payout decisions evolve over the corporate life cycle with a firm's ability to generate cash internally and in its scale of profitable investment opportunities.

Second, Baker et al. (2008) note that the proposed explanations rely heavily on economic modeling approaches without an in-depth understanding of how investors and managers behave and perceive dividends. Thus, the main line of research in dividends uses market data that can explain surface reality but cannot measure motivation, which is the underlying force behind generating such data. Chiang, Frankfurter, Kosedag, and Wood (2006) conclude that the cardinal thrust of academic research should turn toward learning about motivation and the perceptions underlying this motivation.

Although all the pieces of the dividend puzzle may not be in place, the following chapters feature a wealth of information that is useful in providing guidance to identify determinants of payout policy in the real world. Now, let's begin our journey into one of the most intriguing topics of corporate finance—dividends and dividend policy.

REFERENCES

Ang, James S. 1987. "Do Dividends Matter? A Review of Corporate Dividend Theories and Evidence." Monograph Series in Finance and Economics. Solomon Brothers Center for the Study of Financial Institutions and the Graduate School of Business Administration New York University.

Baker, H. Kent, Gail E. Farrelly, and Richard B. Edelman. 1985. "A Survey of Management Views on Dividend Policy." *Financial Management* 14:3, 78–84.

Baker, H. Kent, Aaron L. Phillips, and Gary E. Powell. 1995. "The Stock Distribution Puzzle: A Synthesis of the Literature on Stock Splits and Stock Dividends." *Financial Practice and Education* 5:1, 24–37.

Baker, H. Kent, and Gary E. Powell. 1999. "How Corporate Managers View Dividend Policy." *Quarterly Journal of Business and Economics* 38:2, 17–35.

Baker, H. Kent, and Gary E. Powell. 2005. *Understanding Financial Management: A Practical Guide*. Malden, MA: Blackwell Publishing.

Baker, H. Kent, Gary E. Powell, and E. Theodore Veit. 2002. "Revisiting the Dividend Puzzle: Do All the Pieces Now Fit?" *Review of Financial Economics* 11:4, 241–261.

Baker, H. Kent, Samir Saadi, and Shantanu Dutta. 2008. "Impact of Financial and Multinational Operations on Manager Perceptions of Dividends." *Global Finance Journal* 19:2, 171–186.

Bancel, Frank, Nalinaksha Bhattacharyya, and Usha Mittoo. 2006. "Do Agency Problems Explain Cross-Country Variations in Payout Policy? European Evidence." Working Paper, University of Manitoba and ESCP-EAP.

Bernstein, Peter L. 1992. *Capital Ideas: The Improbable Origins of Modern Wall Street*. New York: Free Press.

Black, Fischer. 1976. "The Dividend Puzzle." *Journal of Portfolio Management* 2:2, 5–8.

Black, Fischer, and Myron Scholes. 1974. "The Effects of Dividend Yield and Dividend Policy on Common Stock Prices and Returns." *Journal of Financial Economics* 1:1, 1–22.

Bruner, Robert F. 2002. "Does M&A Pay? A Survey of Evidence from the Decision-Maker." *Journal of Applied Finance* 2:1, 48–68.

Chiang, Kevin, George M. Frankfurter, Armand Kosedag, and Bob G. Wood, Jr. 2006. "The Perception of Dividends by Professional Investors." *Managerial Finance* 32:1, 60–81.

DeAngelo, Harry, and Linda DeAngelo. 2006. "The Irrelevance of the MM Dividend Irrelevance Theorem." *Journal of Financial Economics* 79:2, 293–315.

DeAngelo, Harry, and Linda DeAngelo. 2007. "Payout Policy Pedagogy: What Matters and Why?" *European Financial Management* 13:1, 11–27.

Fama, Eugene F., and Kenneth R. French. 2001. "Disappearing Dividends: Changing Firm Characteristics or Lower Propensity to Pay?" *Journal of Financial Economics* 60:1, 3–43.

Feldstein, Martin, and Jerry Green. 1983. "Who Do Companies Pay Dividends?" *American Economics Review* 73:1, 7–30.

Frankfurter, George M., and Robert G. Wood, Jr. 1997. "The Evolution of Corporate Dividend Policy." *Journal of Financial Education* 23:1, 16–33.

Gordon, Myron J. 1959. "Dividends, Earnings and Stock Prices." *Review of Economics and Statistics* 41:2, 99–105.

Graham, Benjamin, and David Dodd. 1951. *Security Analysis.* New York: McGraw-Hill.

Jensen, Michael C. 2001. "Value Maximization, Stakeholder Theory, and the Corporate Objective Function." *Journal of Applied Corporate Finance* 14:2, 8–21.

Lease, Ronald, Kose John, Avner Kalay, Uri Loewenstein, and Oded Sarig. 2000. *Dividend Policy: Its Impact on Firm Value.* Boston: Harvard Business School Press.

Lintner, John. 1956. "Distribution of Incomes of Corporations among Dividends, Retained Earnings and Taxes." *American Economic Review* 46:2, 97–113.

Miller, Merton H. 1986. "Behavioral Rationality in Finance: The Case of Dividends." *Journal of Business* 59:4, S451–S468.

Miller, Merton H., and Franco Modigliani. 1961. "Dividend Policy, Growth, and the Valuation of Shares." *Journal of Business* 34:4, 411–433.

Miller, Merton, and Myron Scholes. 1978. "Dividends and Taxes." *Journal of Financial Economics* 6:4, 333–364.

Miller, Merton, and Myron Scholes. 1982. "Dividends and Taxes: Some Empirical Evidence." *Journal of Political Economy* 90:6, 1118–1141.

Pruitt, Stephen W., and Lawrence J. Gitman. 1991. "The Interactions between the Investment, Financing, and Dividend Decisions of Major U.S. Firms." *Financial Review* 26:3, 409–430.

Shefrin, Hersh M., and Meir Statman. 1984. "Explaining Investor Preference for Cash Dividends." *Journal of Financial Economics* 13:2, 253–282.

Williams, John Burr. 1938. *The Theory of Investment Value.* Cambridge: Harvard University Press.

ABOUT THE AUTHOR

H. Kent Baker, CFA, CFM, is university professor of finance at American University. He has written or edited seven books, including *Understanding Financial Management: A Practical Guide* (Blackwell, 2005), and has published more than 200 articles. Baker's research has appeared in *Journal of Finance, Journal of Financial and Quantitative Analysis, Financial Management, Financial Analysts Journal, Journal of Portfolio Management, Journal of Financial Research, Financial Review, Journal of Business Finance and Accounting, Journal of Investing, Harvard Business Review,* and many other outlets. He has consulting and training experience with more than 100 organizations and has presented more than 700 training programs on such topics as asset allocation, security valuation, credit analysis, organizational change, and strategic planning. Baker holds a BSBA from Georgetown University; an M.Ed., MBA, and DBA from the University of Maryland; and two Ph.D.'s, an MA, and an MS from American University.

CHAPTER 2

The Historical Evolution of Dividends

ERIK BENRUD
Associate Clinical Professor of Finance, LeBow College of Business, Drexel University

INTRODUCTION

Although much research exists on dividend policy, most of it focuses on dividends over the past 50 years, but dividend policy has been developing over several centuries (Frankfurter and Wood, 2003). Recent observations include the fact that during the past several decades of the twentieth century, the number of companies paying dividends declined while the total amount of dividends paid increased (Fama and French, 2001; DeAngelo, DeAngelo, and Skinner, 2004). Within a year of the passage of the Jobs and Growth Tax Relief Reconciliation Act in 2003, many companies began paying dividends or increasing payouts (Moore and Kerpen, 2004). Debate continues among researchers about the importance of tax laws and other legislation in shaping dividend policy and the origin of trends in dividend policy. Understanding the factors affecting dividend policy requires an historical perspective. The purpose of this chapter is to summarize the evolution of dividend policy from early joint ventures and corporations to modern times.

A HISTORICAL OVERVIEW

According to DeAngelo, DeAngelo, and Skinner (2000, p. 353), dividend policies "are in constant flux, so that an important task of corporate finance research is to help identify the factors that shape their evolution." The history and evolution of dividend payments are inextricably linked to the corporation as a form of business. The policy for sharing profits by paying dividends was an important consideration in forming joint ventures centuries ago, as it is now in the management of modern corporations. Although studies exist on early forms of businesses resembling corporations in ancient Greece and Rome, most research on the history of corporations and dividend payments begins with the rise of commerce associated with the early European Renaissance.

Many developments that shaped policies concerning the distribution of profits occurred from the sixteenth to early eighteenth centuries. The issues of fairness, accountability, liability, and fraud were as important then as they are in today's world. The earliest versions of corporations were short-lived ventures, usually sailing and trading expeditions, which ended in full liquidation of profits and assets. The investors received proceeds commensurate with the amount they had invested.

By the beginning of the seventeenth century, corporations had become longer lived, and they paid dividends only from earnings. Initially, investors considered dividends very important. At the end of that century, however, investors began placing less emphasis on dividend payments. A period of increased speculation followed, which culminated in a major decline in stock prices in 1720 and the passage of the Bubble Act in England. The Bubble Act placed restrictions on the formation of corporations and their activities.

Corporations became important again in the early nineteenth century with an increased demand for capital from railroad and canal companies in both Britain and the United States. British investors supplied much of the capital for expansion in both countries. Eventually, Parliament repealed the Bubble Act in 1824. Corporations increased in number, and the issue of dividend payments regained its importance. The nineteenth century saw innovations such as preferred stock and efforts by management to smooth dividends. As industries continued to grow in the twentieth century, the link between dividends and share value gained attention. After 1920, managers increased both dividend payments and their practice of dividend smoothing.

Despite efforts to smooth dividends, the twentieth century witnessed considerable variability in dividend payouts (the ratio of dividends to earnings) and dividend yields (the ratio of dividends to stock price). The reasons underlying past and current trends in dividend payments are the subject of much debate and research. Today, some experts question whether dividends are really necessary. The subsequent sections of this chapter examine the historical episodes in more detail to explore how the preferences of investors, the demand for capital from corporations, and the regulatory climate played a role in dividend policy from the earliest corporations to modern times.

CORPORATIONS, RETURNS, AND DIVIDENDS BEFORE 1800

The Rise of the Corporation in England and Holland to 1720

The modern corporation finds its origin in cooperative ventures in various parts of Europe in the late medieval period (Scott, 1912; Kindleberger, 1984). Voyages during the sixteenth century increased both the demand for and the supply of capital, and these ventures led to large and long-lived entities such as the British East India Company. As businesses evolved into early forms of corporations, dividend policies also evolved.

In the sixteenth century, investors backed expeditions, which were formed as ventures in parts. The investors owned "parts" or shares in fractions of eighths, sixteenths, and the like. These organizations more closely resembled partnerships than corporations (Masselman, 1963; Beatty, 2001). The prevailing practice was to raise new capital for each trading venture, and the joint-stock companies generally did not have fixed capital that persisted beyond a given venture. At that time, the dividend payment followed a clear and basic policy, a liquidating dividend policy.

At the end of the voyage, a mass liquidation of all assets occurred, and investors received profits in proportion to the shares they owned. With the end of the joint venture, the investors and the sea captain of the sailing vessel could negotiate the details of a new venture or go their separate ways (Lease, John, Kalay, Loewenstein, and Sarig, 2000).

Although this type of dividend policy lowered the opportunity for fraud, the practice of total liquidation at the end of each venture was not very efficient. Because the investors received proceeds from both earnings and assets, they often received some of their dividends in the form of real goods. Investors adept at managing financial risks probably found the liquidation of real assets cumbersome. Furthermore, the practice lessened the opportunity to gain from the human capital built from the relationships developed in earlier ventures (Kindleberger, 1984; Baskin, 1988).

Longer-lived entities appeared in the latter part of the sixteenth century. The Muscovy Company in 1555, the Spanish Company in 1577, and the East India Company in 1601 received some of history's first recorded business charters of incorporation. In 1606, the London Company received its charter, and it later became known as the Virginia Company of London. At that time, such concepts as limited liability began developing (Beatty, 2001). Corporate managers recognized the importance of dividends for maintaining shareholder satisfaction (Frankfurter and Wood, 1997).

Laws and precedents soon developed concerning the payment of dividends. By the end of the seventeenth century, the British Parliament had passed the profit rule and the impairment rule, which essentially regulated dividend payments (Lease et al., 2000). Policies concerning dividends also developed from the practices of corporations and special corporate charter provisions (Scott, 1912). The common themes in the laws and precedents were that dividend payments would be paid only out of profits and would not be so high as to risk bankruptcy.

In Holland in 1602, the Dutch East India Company became the first permanently organized joint-stock company. Earlier joint-stock companies had charters that had to be renewed, presumably so that the government could collect additional fees (Van Loon, 1913; Kindleberger, 1984). The Dutch East India Company initially paid 75 percent of its earnings out in dividends, but the rate eventually declined. Over the first 15 years, the average payout was 25 percent (Scott, 1912). Along with the emergence of corporate entities that existed beyond the length of a single voyage and the practice of paying dividends came the practice of trading shares and, of course, stock speculation. At first, investing and trading took place in the streets of Amsterdam, and then a building was constructed for stock trading in 1613. The patterns of stock prices at this time serve as an early example of a link among earnings, dividend payments, and stock prices. Although small shareholders may not have had voting rights, as was the case in the Dutch East India Company, the generous payout policy still made the shares desirable, which supported the stock prices (Ehrenburg, 1963).

Back in Britain, investors were supplying increasing amounts of capital. Much trading and speculating in various venues occurred in London (Baskin, 1988). During the last decade of the seventeenth century, there was a tremendous increase in the number of companies issuing stock (Kindleberger, 1984). Most stock prices increased during the period, but with the increase came much volatility (Baskin,

1988). Dividend payments apparently became less necessary as is evident from the fact that the British East India Company did not pay a dividend from 1692 to 1699, and the shares were still in demand. Furthermore, the public continued to buy newly issued shares of joint-stock companies despite the suspension of dividend payments by the British East India Company (Scott, 1912).

The prices of stock in the British East India Company and most other stocks increased dramatically from 1700 to 1720. The issuance of new stock continued, and this led to speculation that culminated in what has been called the South Sea Bubble. The South Sea Company was chartered in 1711. Although it engaged in some overseas trading, the primary function of the South Sea Company was to help the British government refinance much of the huge debt it had incurred during the War of the Spanish Succession, which occurred between 1702 and 1713. The South Sea Company issued stock in return for government debt. The promise of huge profits and dividends kept the stock price going up even though the company issued more shares.

When the stock price seemed to falter, the company took measures to prop up its price. For example, in the middle of 1720, the directors promised to pay a dividend equal to 50 percent of face value, which was about 6 percent of market value. A few months later, the directors announced a lower dividend, which may have been the precipitating factor for the collapse of the shares, as the more knowledgeable speculators took this as a sign to sell and the rest of the investors soon followed (Temin and Voth, 2004).

Parliament passed the Bubble Act in the same year as the stock collapse. Although some debate exists as to whether the Bubble Act was a response to or a cause of the financial disaster in 1720, the Bubble Act placed restrictions on the activities of corporations and the trading of their shares (Hunt, 1936; Patterson and Reiffen, 1990). Despite the growth of business in England in the century after the passage of the Bubble Act, the legal framework for businesses was fairly static until the early nineteenth century (Harris, 2000).

Corporations and Dividends in America to 1800

Before 1776, corporations were not a common form of business in what would become the United States. After the American Revolution, the number of corporations grew substantially, but the development of general statutes governing corporations lagged well behind their growth. Not surprisingly, various dividend policies existed during this period of rapid growth.

The majority of corporations in colonial America were chartered towns, churches, and schools. There are only a few recorded examples of entities that resembled business corporations (Werner and Smith, 1991). Some debate exists with respect to identifying the first business corporation in America. One reason for this debate is the lack of consensus concerning the definition of a corporation. Some contenders for the first corporation are the New London Society United for Trade and Commerce (1732), the Union Wharf Company of New Haven (1760), and the Philadelphia Contributionship for the Insuring of Houses from Loss by Fire (1768). Apparently, investors did not view dividend payments as essential for corporations in colonial America because no record exists of the earlier two entities paying dividends before 1800 (Davis, 1917).

After the Revolutionary War, investment from both domestic and foreign investors increased substantially in the newly formed United States, and there were increases in both the number of firms and the prices of shares. A dramatic upswing in share prices in 1789 coincided with newspapers regularly printing stock quotes in that year. It also led to a boom and a bust from 1790 to 1792 and to legal restrictions on trading (Werner and Smith, 1991). Nevertheless, the last decade of the eighteenth century witnessed a dramatic increase in the number of American corporations, from about 30 in 1789 to slightly more than 300 in 1800 (Kehl, 1941).

Investors did not seem to mind that most new companies did not pay dividends. The eight manufacturing corporations chartered in the 1790s reinvested all their earnings. In the 1780s and 1790s, there were 74 charters issued to corporations that had the goal of developing inland navigation in the United States. The growth in travel and trade indicates that these corporations were successful in providing important services. Despite extracting tolls from travelers, the companies did not pay dividends.

In contrast to manufacturing firms during this period, financial service corporations usually made distributions to shareholders. Bank stocks generally paid and maintained comparatively high annual dividends. Insurance companies in this period paid dividends, and although fairly successful, the amounts insurance companies paid varied widely across firms and over time (Davis, 1917).

One reason that dividend payouts varied widely was that, before 1800, English and American courts had not established case precedents on dividend policy. The corporate charter provisions and the practices, which evolved in the seventeenth and eighteenth centuries, established the nature of dividends (Kehl, 1939). The charters of the Bank of North America (1781) and the Bank of New York (1784) had clauses that linked dividends to profits. In 1790, the charter for the Bank of the United States specified that semiannual dividends would be paid out of profits (Davis, 1917). The Bank of the United States charter also included large sections that were copied from the 1694 charter of the Bank of England. However, one important difference was that the Bank of England charter held shareholders liable for debts while the Bank of the United States charter made the board of directors liable for debts (Kehl, 1941).

DIVIDENDS IN THE NINETEENTH CENTURY

Railroad companies and manufacturing companies grew dramatically in the United States and Britain in the early 1800s, and many corporations paid generous dividends to lure investment capital. Frankfurter and Wood (1997, p. 21) posit that, "by the beginning of the [nineteenth] century, dividends had become symbolic liquidations rather than distributions of net profits." Corporate charters often included provisions that addressed dividend policy. Legislation was passed in the United States and elsewhere to define the nature of dividends and the conditions under which a corporation could or could not pay a dividend. Along with the laws concerning dividends, important developments in the nineteenth century included the repeal of the Bubble Act; acceptance of the concept of limited liability; and innovative methods for raising capital such as preferred stock. Notable trends at the end of the century included the rise of industrial stocks, a greater number of people investing in stocks, and a greater demand for corporate transparency.

Legislation in the Early Nineteenth Century

Although a full survey of the legislative acts during this dynamic period is beyond the scope of this chapter, a discussion of the history of corporate dividend policy requires pointing out that the concept of the corporation developed over time along with dividend policy. This section offers a few examples of important legislative acts in the first half of the nineteenth century that contributed to the development of the modern corporation.

Between the passage of the Bubble Act in 1720 and the early nineteenth century, the corporation as a form of business lost much of its importance because of the restrictions imposed by the Bubble Act. Although businesses often found ways to circumvent the restrictions during the Industrial Revolution in the eighteenth century and Parliament made occasional exceptions, enforcement increased in the beginning of the nineteenth century.

The demand for capital and the eventual boom of 1824 led to the repeal of the Bubble Act. Legislation in the decades that followed increased the liquidity of shares and gave shareholders limited liability, which are basic characteristics of today's corporate framework (Todd, 1932; Hunt, 1936; Harris, 2000). Fay (1948) identified the repeal of the Bubble Act as the first in a series of legal landmarks in this period. According to Fay (p. 272) other landmarks include

> *The Act for better enabling Her Majesty to confer certain powers and immunities on trading and other companies of 1837, the Joint Stock Companies' Registration and Regulation Act of 1844 and the comprehensive consolidating Act of 1862, which established general limited liability—the Magna Carta of English company law, as it has been termed.*

In the United States, where the Bubble Act did not directly apply in the nineteenth century, corporations continued their growth in both size and number. To attract capital, charters of corporations routinely included rules on dividend payments and remedies to creditors in the event that the board of directors paid excessive dividends. The goal was to let equity investors know that they would receive dividends and to allay the fears of lenders concerning overpayment of dividends. The rules varied from charter to charter, but the courts had yet to establish legal precedents.

The American states soon began passing statutes on dividend policies. In 1825, the New York legislature passed a state statute stipulating that corporations could pay dividends only from profits. Five years later, Massachusetts adopted a law that prohibited insolvent firms from declaring a dividend. This law also stipulated that a corporation could not pay a dividend if it would make the corporation insolvent (Kehl, 1941). Other states passed similar laws, which were probably a reaction to the appearance of hundreds of new manufacturing corporations in the first quarter of the nineteenth century. More than half of these new corporations were incorporated in New York and Massachusetts (Davis, 1917).

Another development in the United States was the introduction of a corporate income tax during the Civil War. Although Congress repealed the tax after the war, such legislation started a controversy concerning the possible effect of taxes on dividend policy.

New Industries and Dividends

Many businesses developed in the nineteenth century, including more industrial firms at the end of the century. The competition for capital throughout the century necessitated the payment of dividends, which companies paid in most years except in the case of war and financial crisis. Innovative methods for attracting capital developed including the issuance of preferred stock.

At least ten companies paid a preferential dividend between 1777 and 1829. The first issuers of "preference" shares were canal and railway companies. In 1829, for example, the British Parliament sanctioned the Edinburgh and Dalkeith Railway to issue noncumulative but participating preference shares. By 1850, scores of companies had issued what is now known as preferred stock. Investors usually saw the issuance as a short-term measure. Preferred shares often became ordinary shares when the company achieved a certain level of profitability, for example, a level of profitability sufficient to pay the ordinary shares the same dividend as that paid to the preferential shares (Evans, 1936; Baskin and Miranti, 1997). During the later part of the century in the United States, industrial firms sold preferred shares that had both fixed claims on earnings as well as real assets as collateral (Navin and Sears, 1955).

As for regular dividends paid on common stock, dividend payments usually fluctuated with profits and the fortunes of the economy. For example, cotton manufacturers and textile mills paid generous dividends for most of the early and mid-1800s (Clark, 1929a). During and just after the War of 1812, many mills closed and did not pay dividends. Likewise, the mills failed to pay dividends during the panic of 1837. After each episode, dividend payments resumed and annual dividends were often more than 10 percent of paid-in capital. In contrast to events during the War of 1812, large payouts continued during the Civil War as profits increased. The payouts continued after the Civil War until the Panic of 1874 (Clark, 1929b).

Prosperity returned after 1874, and various changes occurred, including an increase in the number of industrial firms issuing stocks, increased demand for disclosure, and the appearance of many new types of companies, such as oil companies, industrial companies, and large department stores. Some of these companies were initially partnerships that later became corporations. One reason investors readily supplied capital was to receive dividends. For example, Standard Oil paid a large dividend ranging from 5 percent to 30 percent of invested capital (Faulkner, 1924).

The rise of the industrials after the Civil War captured the attention of investors for many reasons. The returns of industrial stocks began to exceed that of railroad stocks, and their dividend payments were substantial. Industrials performed well during the recession that occurred in the years 1893 to 1897. In the years that followed, analysts began recognizing that common stocks provided an inflation hedge and provided sufficient return to compensate for their volatility (Snowden, 1990).

In the last part of the nineteenth century, most new corporations started paying dividends immediately after their inception. The firms often paid dividends out of invested capital, a policy that led to distress and bankruptcy in many instances

(Faulkner, 1924). Such unsavory policies did not begin with the new companies at the end of the century. Railroads had been declaring dividends before they had determined profits and had paid dividends out of accumulated capital in earlier decades (Kindleberger, 1984). A lack of corporate transparency allowed such practices to occur and even promoted them, because, as was the case in previous periods, a high dividend payout increased investor confidence and attracted capital. As Frankfurter and Wood (1997, p. 27) note, "The general lack of publicly available information required investors to value industrial securities using solely their dividend history."

No discussion of corporate practices in this era would be complete without mentioning the trusts. Corporate directors in a given industry, such as oil, whiskey, and sugar refining, deposited their securities with a group of trustees who controlled production to create monopoly profits for the corporations involved. The resulting increase in profits and dividend payments from the creation of such monopolistic entities attracted investors despite the fact that trusts revealed very little information about operations and earnings (Navin and Sears, 1955). This paucity of information was not unique to the trusts. Hawkins (1963, p. 136) notes that before 1880 managers displayed a "predilection toward corporate secrecy" that resulted from vague state laws concerning financial reporting and the fact that the public did not demand information.

An increase in the breadth of ownership of corporate shares beyond the traditional insiders occurred, which led to the demand for greater and better disclosure of information. Corporations were becoming truly public companies. According to Navin and Sears (1955, p. 105), "By the turn of the century the transition was well under way from closely held 'inside' ownership of American business to semipublic, 'outside' hands." Despite U.S. regulations requiring disclosure, firms often did not comply with the laws or exchange requirements.

In Britain, the introduction of limited liability had led to the formation of many speculative and fraudulent corporations. Investors demanded more information about a company's solvency and not just its income from which a dividend would be paid. By 1890, the skill of the Board of Trade had increased to accommodate that demand for information (Todd, 1932). According to Hawkins (1963, p. 145), by 1900 in the United States, "The emergence of big business and the sudden expansion of the number of investors in manufacturing concerns led to a demand for fuller and more reliable corporate financial disclosure." This demand would explain the appearance of the Dow Jones Industrial Average and the publication of *Moody's Industrial Security* around this time.

DIVIDENDS IN THE TWENTIETH AND TWENTY-FIRST CENTURIES

Navin and Sears (1955, p. 105) note, "The turn of the twentieth century, it would appear, saw the introduction of so much that was new in American business as to mark the end of an old system and the beginning of a new." The basic principles of the modern corporation had taken shape. Dividend policies continued to vary over time, with both upward and downward trends in dividend payouts, and researchers have debated the causes of the trends in dividend payouts.

Subsequent chapters of this book posit theories and supporting evidence for the trends and address why firms pay dividends. Thus, this last section of the chapter does not delve deeply into those issues. This final section, following the precedent of Brittain (1966), summarizes the trends by breaking them down into periods. Those periods are 1900–1920, 1921–1929, 1930–1947, and 1948–1962. The final portion of this section discusses some of the dividend policy patterns observed in the most recent half century.

Dividend Trends: 1900–1962

The historical record of a stock index composed by Jones and Wilson (2002) shows that earnings, dividends, and dividend yields all exhibit substantially positive time trends from 1901 to 1920. However, prices did not exhibit such an upward trend. In addition, there was not a significant relationship between stock prices and each of the other variables, namely, earnings, dividends, and dividend yields. Other researchers have also made this observation. For example, Snowden (1990) reports a weak relationship between the stock prices of U.S. corporations and their dividend payments because the prices did not keep pace with the growth of dividend payments. Evidence provided by Jones and Wilson (2002) confirms Baskin's (1988) observation that dividend payouts varied widely during the 1910s and 1920s. Although some dividend smoothing existed during and before this period, such smoothing did not become a common practice until after 1920 (Van Strum, 1925).

The second decade of the twentieth century also provides early evidence of the effect of tax law on investor preferences for stocks that pay dividends. Income tax laws enacted during this time led individuals with high incomes to move some of their investments into corporations that did not pay dividends (McIntyre, 1939). Meanwhile the number of stockholders increased dramatically for various reasons, such as the decline in brokerage commissions for small purchases and the maturation of Liberty Bonds after World War I (Carosso, 1970).

Although there was a large dip in earnings in 1921, which produces some anomalous observations, Jones and Wilson's (2002) data generally show that during the second decade of the twentieth century, dividends doubled, as did earnings, and the payout ratio was fairly constant. This result is congruous with statistics reported by Brittain (1966). Because prices rose more quickly than earnings, the dividend yield fell. The prices of stocks in some speculative new industries, such as airplanes and the media, rose dramatically during this time while paying little, if any, dividends (Carosso, 1970).

The dividend payout varied widely in the years after the 1929 stock market crash. There was a general downward trend through the 1930s and during World War II (Jones and Wilson, 2002). The main reason for the decline from 1930 to 1947 was that dividends did not keep pace with periods of rapid profit increases during those 17 years, but the decline was not a steady trend. For the first eight years, from 1930 to 1937, low and varying profits during the Great Depression produced unusual values for the payout ratio in some years. Also, the undistributed profits tax in 1936 and 1937 influenced dividend policy in those years (Brittain, 1966). As a point of interest, during World War II, some corporations paid dividends in the form of Liberty Bonds in support of the war effort (Lease et al., 2000).

The payout ratios increased by about 6 percent per year from 1948 to 1962, which is comparable to the 8 percent per year increase during the period from 1919 to 1929. The trends were fairly similar across firms and industries. The rapid rise in dividend payments is noteworthy given that the postwar trend in after-tax net profits averaged only about 2 percent per year (Brittain, 1966).

The Developing Research on Dividends

In the years following World War II, researchers began devoting much attention to dividend policy. According to Brav, Graham, Harvey, and Michaely (2005, p. 484), "In 1956, John Lintner laid the foundation of the modern understanding of dividend policy." On the basis of data from a survey of managers from 28 companies, Lintner (1956) posits a target-payout hypothesis, which proposes that dividends are a function of long-term sustainable earnings. The divergence in earnings and dividend growth, as well as the occasional special dividend and paucity of regular dividends, produced skeptics of the target-payout hypothesis such as Michaelsen (1966). The introduction of the dividend-irrelevance theorem by Miller and Modigliani (1961), the increased use of share repurchases in the past 50 years, and the changing tax laws have contributed to the growing research into dividend policy.

Nearly 50 years after Lintner (1956), Brav et al. (2005) summarize survey responses from 384 financial executives. One of their conclusions is that, in general, maintaining a target ratio has declined in importance and is no longer of primary concern. The responses indicate that managers try to maintain a particular dividend level and to avoid dividend cuts. Only about 21 percent of managers reported that the tax rate is an important or very important factor affecting dividend decisions. However, more than 40 percent of managers indicated that taxes play a role in choosing between paying a dividend and repurchasing shares.

The Miller and Modigliani (1961) dividend-irrelevance theorem assumes that the tax rate is zero. Given this and other assumptions, the theorem posits that investors do not consider a firm's dividend policy when choosing whether to invest in that firm. Therefore, efforts by managers to attract investors with a certain dividend policy are pointless. There are two major reasons for this result. First, dividend-averse investors would not shun a dividend-paying stock because they can reinvest unwanted dividends back into the company. Second, investors who prefer dividends can create synthetic, or "homemade," dividends by routinely selling off small amounts of a position in a stock that does not pay dividends.

The reaction of companies to changes in the tax law can give an indication of the importance of taxes to dividend policy. In the case of the Undistributed Profits Tax of 1936–1937, for example, Calomiris and Hubbard (1995) conclude that the vast majority of firms increased dividend payout rates in 1936 to limit their tax liability under the new law, and the high payouts lasted only for the two years that the tax law was in effect. Soon after the implementation of the tax, researchers such as McIntyre (1939) and Guthman (1940) reported similar observations.

Using results from a survey of chief executive officers from 163 large U.S. corporations, Abrutyn and Turner (1990) report that 85 percent of respondents indicated that they did not intend to change dividend policy in response to the Tax Reform Act of 1986. Bolster and Janjigian (1991) do not find statistically significant evidence of a change in dividend payouts after the enactment of the Tax Reform Act of 1986. Papaioannou and Savarese (1994) and Casey, Anderson, Mesak, and Dickens (1999) reported mixed effects, stating that some corporations increased their dividend payouts while others decreased them.

A similar controversy surrounds the more recent Jobs and Growth Tax Relief Reconciliation Act passed in May 2003. Among other provisions, the act lowered the tax rate on dividends received from 2003 to 2008. Within a few months after the tax went into effect, Brav et al. (2005) reported that more than 66 percent of the executives who responded to a survey after the passage of the act said that the tax cut would probably not or definitely not affect their dividend decisions. Only 13 percent of respondents from corporations that did not pay dividends indicated that the tax cut would lead to their firms paying dividends. Between the time the tax cut went into effect and early 2004, only 6 percent of nonpayers had begun paying dividends. This evidence supports the conclusion that taxes play only a secondary role in dividend policy.

Advocates of the 2003 tax law emphasize that it has had an important affect on dividend policy and share prices. Advocates cite how the regular annual dividends paid by corporations in the S&P 500 rose from $146 billion before the law to $172 billion in the first year after the act was passed. According to Moore and Kerpen (2004), 22 non–dividend payers in the S&P 500 became payers. The tax cut on dividends is only temporary and applies only to the years 2003 to 2008. Future changes in the tax law will provide additional evidence to consider.

As already noted, the Brav et al. (2005) survey asked managers whether taxes influenced their choice between repurchasing shares or paying a dividend, and more than 40 percent of managers indicated that taxes played a role in that choice. With respect to this question, the response came before the reduction in the dividend tax rate in 2003 and may reflect the fact that a repurchase has an advantage to shareholders in that it provides a distribution that is subject only to the shareholder's capital gains tax rate.

The wide use of stock repurchases is a fairly recent phenomenon. According to Brav et al. (2005, p. 485), "Repurchases were virtually nonexistent when Lintner (1956) and Miller and Modigliani (1961) wrote their papers." As the use of repurchases has increased, researchers continue to investigate the relationship of share repurchases with dividend policy. Brav et al. report that managers view dividend decisions on par in importance with investment decisions. In addition, they make repurchase decisions after investment decisions and view repurchases as a much more flexible device than dividend payment. Managers tend to increase repurchases when the stock price is low, good investments are scarce, their stock's float is adequate, and stock dilution from stock options might occur. Such other considerations may explain why repurchases tend to be a complement to the payment of dividends and not a substitute. According to Fama and French (2001), companies increasing their repurchases in recent decades are already paying high dividends. DeAngelo et al. (2000) conclude that there is no support for the theory that repurchases are substitutes for special dividends. Subsequent chapters of this text discuss these issues in more depth and detail.

CONCLUSIONS

Dividend policy has evolved and adjusted in response to changing business conditions, market parameters, and regulations. This chapter summarizes some key developments that have led to current dividend practices, which are not homogeneous and are still evolving. Although some important regulations have directly addressed dividend policy, such as restrictions on the amount that companies can pay, many developments reflect the recognition by managers of the relationship between dividend policy and other aspects of the corporation, such as share price. Some of these developments include managers recognizing (1) the tenuous link between dividend payment and share price in the seventeenth and eighteenth centuries, (2) the role of paying dividends in the ability to raise new equity capital in the nineteenth century, (3) the benefits of dividend smoothing, (4) the use of share repurchases to complement dividend policy, and (5) the notion that paying dividends may not even be necessary.

By understanding that dividend policy has evolved and did not just appear in its current form provides important perspectives about why dividend policies vary widely across firms and over time. Although researchers provide additional insights into the various dividend policies, this chapter introduces only a few studies on current dividend policy research. The remaining chapters of this book go into more depth and discuss how this research can aid managers in determining the optimal dividend policy for their firm.

REFERENCES

Abrutyn, Stephanie, and Robert W. Turner. 1990. "Taxes and Firms' Dividend Policies: Survey Results." *National Tax Journal* 43:4, 491–496.

Baskin, Jonathan. 1988. "The Development of Corporate Financial Markets in Britain and the United States, 1600–1914: Overcoming Asymmetric Information." *Business History Review* 62:2, 199–237.

Baskin, Jonathan, and Paul J. Miranti, Jr. 1997. *A History of Corporate Finance*. New York: Cambridge University Press.

Beatty, Jack. 2001. *Colossus: How the Corporation Changed America*. New York: Broadway Books.

Bolster, Paul J., and Vahan Janjigian. 1991. "Dividend Policy and Valuation Effects of the Tax Reform Act of 1986." *National Tax Journal* 44:4, 511–518.

Brav, Alon, John Graham, Campbell Harvey, and Roni Michaely. 2005. "Payout Policy in the 21st Century." *Journal of Financial Economics* 77:3, 483–527.

Brittain, John. 1966. *Corporate Dividend Policy*. Washington, D.C.: Brookings Institution.

Calomiris, Charles, and R. Glenn Hubbard. 1995. "Internal Finance and Investment: Evidence from the Undistributed Profits Tax of 1936–37." *Journal of Business* 68:4, 443–482.

Carosso, Vincent. 1970. *Investment Banking in America: A History*. Cambridge, MA: Harvard University Press.

Casey, Mike, Dwight Anderson, Hani Mesak, and Ross Dickens. 1999. "Examining the Impact of the 1986 Tax Reform Act on Corporate Dividend Policy: A New Methodology." *Financial Review* 34:3, 33–46.

Clark, Victor S. 1929a. *History of Manufacturers in the United States: Volume I, 1607–1860*. New York: McGraw-Hill.

Clark, Victor S. 1929b. *History of Manufacturers in the United States: Volume II, 1860–1893*. New York: McGraw-Hill.

Davis, Joseph. 1917. *Essays in the Earlier History of American Corporations*. Cambridge, MA: Harvard University Press.

DeAngelo, Harry, Linda DeAngelo, and Douglas J. Skinner. 2000. "Special Dividends and the Evolution of Dividend Signaling." *Journal of Financial Economics* 57:3, 309–354.

DeAngelo, Harry, Linda DeAngelo, and Douglas Skinner. 2004. "Are Dividends Disappearing? Dividend Concentration and the Consolidation of Earnings." *Journal of Financial Economics* 72:3, 425–456.

Ehrenburg, Richard. 1963. *Capital and Finance in the Age of the Renaissance*. London: Augustus M. Kelly.

Evans, George. 1936. *British Corporation Finance, 1775–1850*. Baltimore: Johns Hopkins University Press.

Fama, Eugene F., and Kenneth R. French. 2001. "Disappearing Dividends: Changing Firm Characteristics or Lower Propensity to Pay?" *Journal of Financial Economics* 60:1, 3–43.

Faulkner, Harold. 1924. *American Economic History*. New York: Harper and Brothers.

Fay, Clark. 1948. Review of *The Development of the Business Corporation in England, 1800–1867*, by B. C. Hunt. *Economic Journal* 58:230, 271–275.

Frankfurter, George M., and Bob G. Wood, Jr. 1997. "The Evolution of Corporate Dividend Policy." *Journal of Financial Education* 23:1, 16–33.

Frankfurter, George M., and Bob G. Wood, Jr. 2003. *Dividend Policy: Theory and Practice*. San Diego, CA: Academic Press.

Guthman, Harry G. 1940. "The Effect of the Undistributed Profits Tax upon the Distribution of Corporate Earnings: A Note." *Econometrica* 8:4, 354–356.

Harris, Ron. 2000. *Industrializing English Law: Entrepreneurship and Business Organization, 1720–1844*. Cambridge: Cambridge University Press.

Hawkins, David. 1963. "The Development of Modern Financial Reporting Practices among American Manufacturing Corporations." *Business History Review* 37:3, 135–168.

Hunt, Bishop. 1936. *The Development of the Business Corporation in England, 1800–1867*. Cambridge, MA: Harvard University Press.

Jones, Charles, and Jack Wilson. 2002. "An Analysis of the S&P 500 Index and Cowles' Extensions: Price Indexes and Stock Returns: 1870–1999." *Journal of Business* 75:3, 505–533.

Kehl, Donald. 1939. "The Origin and Early Development of American Dividend Law." *Harvard Law Review* 53:1, 36–67.

Kehl, Donald. 1941. *Corporate Dividends*. New York: Ronald Press Company.

Kindleberger, Charles. 1984. *A Financial History of Western Europe*. London: George Allen and Unwin.

Lease, Ronald, Kose John, Avner Kalay, Uri Loewenstein, and Oded Sarig. 2000. *Dividend Policy: Its Impact on Firm Value*. Boston: Harvard Business School Press.

Lintner, John. 1956. "Distribution of Incomes of Corporations among Dividends, Retained Earnings, and Taxes." *American Economic Review* 46:2, 97–113.

Masselman, George. 1963. *The Cradle of Colonialism*. New Haven, CT: Yale University Press.

McIntyre, Francis. 1939. "The Effect of the Undistributed Profits Tax on the Distribution of Corporate Earnings: A Statistical Appraisal." *Econometrica* 7:4, 336–348.

Michaelsen, Jacob. 1966. "The Determinates of Corporate Dividend Policies." *Journal of Financial and Quantitative Analysis* 1:1, 29–29b.

Miller, Merton, and Franco Modigliani. 1961. "Dividend Policy, Growth and the Valuation of Shares." *Journal of Business* 34:4, 411–433.

Moore, Stephen, and Phil Kerpen. 2004. "Show Me the Money! Dividend Payouts after the Bush Tax Cut." Cato Institute Briefing Papers No. 88, October 11.

Navin, Thomas, and Marian V. Sears. 1955. "The Rise of a Market for Industrial Securities, 1887–1902." *Business History Review* 29:2, 105–138.

Papaioannou, George, and Craig Savarese. 1994. "Corporate Dividend Policy Response to the Tax Reform Act of 1986." *Financial Management* 23:1, 56–63.

Patterson, Margaret, and David Reiffen. 1990. "The Effect of the Bubble Act on the Market for Joint Stock Shares." *Journal of Economic History* 50:1, 163–171.

Scott, William. 1912. *The Constitution and Finance of English, Scottish, and Irish Joint Stock Companies to 1720.* Cambridge: Cambridge University Press.

Snowden, Kenneth A. 1990. "Historical Returns and Security Market Development, 1872–1925." *Explorations in Economic History* 27:4, 381–420.

Temin, Peter, and Hans-Joachim Voth. 2004. "Riding the South Sea Bubble." *American Economic Review* 94:5, 1654–1668.

Todd, Geoffrey. 1932. "Some Aspects of Joint Stock Companies, 1844–1900." *Economic History Review* 4:1, 46–71.

Van Loon, Hendrik. 1913. *The Fall of the Dutch Republic.* London: Constable and Co.

Van Strum, Kenneth. 1925. *Investing in Purchasing Power.* New York: Barron's.

Werner, Walter, and Steven Smith. 1991. *Wall Street.* Edinburgh: Edinburgh University Press.

ABOUT THE AUTHOR

Erik Benrud, FRM, CAIA, CFA, received his Ph.D. from the University of Virginia and is an associate clinical professor of finance at LeBow College of Business, Drexel University. In addition to having taught a wide variety of topics in finance around the world, he has published articles on multifarious subjects, including modeling competition in financial markets, using financial forecasts to price options, and teaching finance over the Internet. He has received teaching and research awards at Association to Advance Collegiate School of Business–accredited universities.

CHAPTER 3

Trends in Dividends: Payers and Payouts

CHRISTIAN ANDRES
Assistant Professor of Finance, University of Bonn

ANDRÉ BETZER
Assistant Professor of Finance, University of Bonn

LUIS CORREIA DA SILVA
Managing Director, Oxera

MARC GOERGEN
Professor of Finance, Cardiff Business School

INTRODUCTION

This chapter reviews recent trends in dividends and dividend payers and focuses on the phenomenon of disappearing dividends appearing in the United States during the end of the twentieth century. Fama and French (2001) document this trend in the first study on disappearing dividends. The first section of this chapter reviews the evidence on this phenomenon and discusses possible reasons for the decrease in the propensity to pay dividends. Although researchers have advanced several possible explanations, no universally accepted explanation currently exists for the phenomenon. The second section focuses on the literature questioning the existence of the trend. One strand of the literature argues that no such trend exists, while another strand contends that the break with conventional dividend policy has been only temporary, as the propensity to pay dividends has been on the increase since the new millennium.

DISAPPEARING DIVIDENDS

Background

Although the majority of exchange-listed companies have historically preferred to pay out cash in the form of dividends, academics have long debated what causes companies to pay dividends. According to Miller and Modigliani's (1961) seminal irrelevance propositions, a company's value is determined only by its earnings, which implies that the decision to distribute cash to shareholders is irrelevant. The agency cost-based theories proposed by Easterbrook (1984) and Jensen (1986) provide a theoretical foundation for payouts to shareholders. Both theories argue that paying out funds to the owners of the firm reduces the amount of cash under the management's control and thus the potential basis for value-decreasing agency conflicts. However, the channel through which funds are distributed (cash dividends or share repurchases) does not affect the outcome of either theory.

In the United States, tax regulations have favored capital gains over dividends for decades. Hence, from a tax perspective, corporations should prefer share repurchases over dividends. The relative tax advantage of capital gains implies that if dividends have any effect on a company's value, that impact should be negative. Black (1976) terms the *dividend puzzle* the stylized fact that, despite the tax disadvantage associated with dividends, firms often pay a dividend to their shareholders. However, Fama and French (2001) recently report a general decline in the percentage of dividend-paying companies. This raises the question as to whether there is still a dividend puzzle.

The Evidence

In their empirical study on a large sample of exchange-listed U.S. corporations, Fama and French (2001) document that the proportion of firms that pay cash dividends decreased dramatically during the 1980s and 1990s. Their study fueled a debate on the so-called disappearing dividend phenomenon. Historically, more than 50 percent of U.S. firms were dividend payers. One of the very few exceptions occurred during the Great Depression, when the percentage of dividend-paying firms fell from 66.9 percent in 1930 to 33.6 percent in 1933. Thereafter, the percentage rose steadily, with more than 90 percent of New York Stock Exchange (NYSE)–listed firms paying dividends in 1951 and 1952. With the addition of American Stock Exchange (AMEX) and NASDAQ firms to the data set examined by Fama and French in 1963 and 1973, the proportion of payers drops to just over 50 percent. After reaching a peak of 66.5 percent in 1978, the proportion of firms paying cash dividends declines continuously, reaching 30.3 percent in 1987 and further decreasing to 20.8 percent in 1999. These trends suggest a gradual disappearance of dividends (see Figure 3.1).

In total, there were 2,419 dividend payers in 1978 and only 1,063 in 1999. The sharp decline indicates that, despite the surge in the number of exchange-listed firms during the 1990s, the number of dividend payers decreases. In line with these figures, on average, every year 5 percent of firms stopped paying cash dividends during the period of 1978 to 1999. On the other hand, only 2.5 percent of former payers (i.e., companies that paid dividends at some point in the past) resumed paying dividends in 1999. From 1963 to 1977, the equivalent figure of firms resuming dividend payments was much higher at 11.8 percent.

Baker and Wurgler (2004a) confirm these findings but also show that changes in the propensity to pay dividends are not a new phenomenon. A closer look at the percentage of dividend payers over the past four decades reveals four distinct trends (see Figure 3.2).

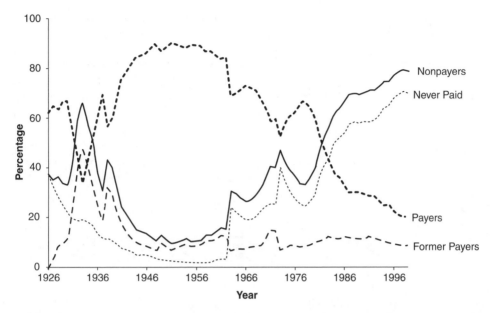

Figure 3.1 Trends in the Proportion of Dividend Payers and Nonpayers

The sample is from CRSP and includes NYSE, AMEX, and NASDAQ securities with share codes of 10 or 11. The sample excludes utilities (SIC codes 4900–4949) and financial firms (SIC codes 6000–6999). A firm is classed as a payer if it pays dividends in year *t* and is classed as a nonpayer if it does not. The subgroup of nonpayers includes all the firms that have never paid a dividend and that of the former payers includes all the firms that do not pay a dividend in year *t* but did pay one in a previous year. *Source:* Fama and French (2001, p. 8).

Although the post-1978 decline is the largest and longest one, the percentage of dividend payers also decreased before, from 1967–1969 through to 1972–1974. In addition, the graph also shows that the propensity to pay increased from 1963 through to 1967–1968, and again from 1973–1974 through to 1977. The evidence provided by Baker and Wurgler (2004a) indicates that even though the post-1978 decline has received the most attention, dividends have disappeared and reappeared before.

As mentioned previously, all three exchanges—NYSE, AMEX, and NASDAQ—experienced a large increase in the number of listed firms during the past 30 years. Based on Compustat data, listings more than doubled from 1,600 during 1968–1972 to 4,831 during 1993–1998. Given that the typical initial public offerings (IPOs) of the 1980s and the 1990s were small companies that tapped into the equity market to finance their growth, a reasonable hypothesis is that the new listings are driving the lower average propensity to pay dividends. Indeed, the population of firms may have shifted away from firms that have historically paid dividends.

Fama and French (2001) examine this issue in detail and identify three important factors in the decision to pay dividends: (1) profitability, (2) investment opportunities, and (3) size. They show that average firm profitability decreased

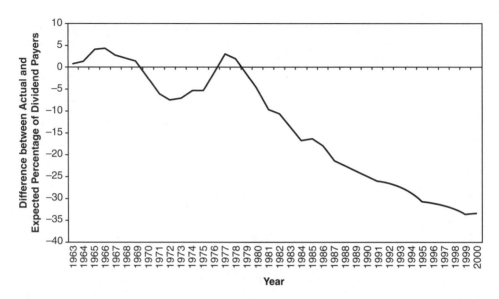

Figure 3.2 Propensity to Pay Dividends
The table shows the propensity to pay dividends, defined as the difference between the actual and expected percentage. The actual percentage is the number of dividend payers divided by the number of firms in the sample that year. The expected percentage is the expected percentage of dividend payers based on prevailing sample characteristics. The expected percentage of payers is estimated with a logit model that includes the NYSE market capitalization percentile, asset growth, and profitability.
Source: Baker and Wurgler (2004a, p. 276).

over time. They attribute their finding to the increasing incidence of unprofitable IPOs after 1978. Until then, more than 90 percent of firms that went public had positive earnings before interest. Associated with the surge in new listings, the profitability of IPOs deteriorated. At the end of their observation period, only about 50 percent of new listings had positive earnings and the percentage of dividend payers among newly listed firms was only 5.2 percent.

In addition, newly listed firms are smaller and have much higher growth opportunities, both of which are characteristics normally associated with low dividends. Fama and French (2001) confirm this pattern by showing that firms that have never paid dividends are smaller and have higher investment outlays. On the basis of these observations, they conclude that the steady decline in the percentage of dividend-paying firms after 1978 can partly be attributed to a tilt of the population of listed companies toward firm characteristics that are typically associated with firms that have never paid dividends.

Fama and French (2001) further show that dividends also become less likely among those firms with the typical characteristics of dividend payers. In 1978, more than 70 percent of profitable firms paid dividends, whereas the percentage is much lower, at 30 percent, in 1998. The authors conclude that, in addition to the changing characteristics of listed firms, a generally lower propensity to pay, even among large and profitable firms, plays a crucial role in the falling proportion of dividend payers. DeAngelo, DeAngelo, and Skinner (2000), who provide evidence that special dividends have also disappeared in recent years, supplement these findings. Typically, firms used to pay special dividends almost as predictably as profitable companies paid regular dividends.

The distinct trend of disappearing dividends during the 1980s and 1990s raises several questions. Because Fama and French (2001) argue that the decline cannot solely be attributed to a higher percentage of unprofitable start-up companies, this suggests that firms with the characteristics typically associated with payers have changed their payout policies. As a reaction to Fama and French's article, researchers have advanced several possible explanations in the academic literature.

Possible Reasons for the Disappearance of Dividends

In addition to investigating changing firm characteristics, several articles analyze the role of share repurchases. This section reviews the relationship among dividends, share repurchases, and the so-called substitution hypothesis.

Following the irrelevance proposition of Miller and Modigliani (1961), share repurchases and dividends are perfect substitutes. Furthermore, most of the theories that explain the existence of dividends as a signaling device (Bhattacharya, 1979) or as a device to mitigate agency problems (Easterbrook, 1984; Jensen, 1986) imply that firms can use share repurchases and cash dividends interchangeably. In contrast, John and Williams (1985) and Allen, Bernardo, and Welch (2000) develop models in which the two types of payout are not substitutes.

Until recently, tax regulation in the United States favored capital gains over dividends. If capital gains are taxed at a more favorable rate than ordinary income and if managers act in the best interest of their shareholders, firms should distribute funds only in the form of share repurchases. In other words, assuming that investors' tax rates on dividends are higher, shareholders lose the tax differential between capital gains and ordinary income for every dollar that firms pay out to them as a cash dividend. Therefore, why share repurchases were rare before the 1980s is perplexing. Bagwell and Shoven (1989) and Grullon and Michaely (2002) report that repurchases emerged as an economically significant alternative to cash dividends in the early 1980s. Between 1983 and 1984, the aggregate expenditure on the repurchase of common and preferred stocks more than tripled from $9.2 billion to $28.6 billion. In 1999 alone, U.S. companies repurchased stock worth more than $200 billion. So how does this pattern fit with the disappearing dividend phenomenon?

Grullon and Michaely (2002) argue not only that share repurchases have become an important form of payout but also that firms finance share repurchases with funds that they otherwise would have distributed as dividends. Figure 3.3 supports this interpretation and shows that a growing repurchase payout ratio during the 1980s and 1990s accompanies the decreasing dividend payout ratio that Fama and French (2001) documented.

Although a decline in the dividend payout ratio accompanies the increase in the repurchase ratio, the total dividend payout ratio remained fairly constant. Grullon and Michaely (2002) use Lintner's (1956) partial adjustment model to investigate whether firms treat dividends and repurchases as alternative payout methods. Using the model, they estimate the expected dividend payout for a firm on the basis of its past dividend policy and compare the actual dividend payment

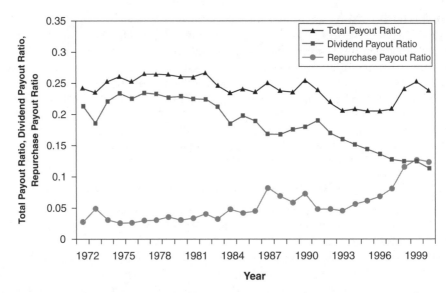

Figure 3.3 Total Payout Ratio, Dividend Payout Ratio, and Repurchase Payout Ratio
The figure shows the equally weighted average total payout ratio, dividend payout ratio, and repurchase payout ratio for a sample of U.S. firms. The data sample consists of all firm-year observations on Compustat for the period 1972 to 2000 with the relevant data. The dividend payout ratio is defined as dividends on common stock over earnings (before extraordinary items). Observations with a total payout ratio greater than one have been dropped.
Source: Grullon and Michaely (2002, p. 1656).

to the predicted one. They then relate the deviation between the two figures to the firms' share repurchase activity. Consistent with the substitution hypothesis, their results indicate a negative relationship between the dividend forecast error (actual minus expected dividend) and the repurchase yield. The evidence implies that a high repurchase yield (i.e., more funds being spent on share repurchases) comes at the expense of an increase in cash dividends. Even after controlling for differences in firm characteristics, the authors find that dividend-paying firms seem to have substituted share repurchases for dividends. Skinner (2008) uses a similar methodology and confirms the results of Grullon and Michaely.

The findings of both articles stand in contrast to those of Fama and French (2001), who argue that share repurchases are rather unimportant in explaining the decline in the percentage of dividend payers. Fama and French compare aggregate repurchases and dividends as a percentage of aggregate earnings and conclude that repurchases primarily increase the already-high cash payouts of dividend payers. The differences in results can be traced to the different measures for share repurchases. The Fama and French measure includes not only stock repurchases but also equity issuances and employee stock options, and thereby it effectively compares gross dividends to net repurchase activity.

Regarding the characteristics of repurchasing companies, Skinner (2008) identifies two groups of payers: firms that consistently both pay dividends and carry out repurchases and firms that only repurchase their stock. For firms with both dividends and repurchases, total payouts track earnings closely. Skinner further shows that earnings are equally well suited for explaining payouts for firms that only repurchase stock, suggesting that these firms use repurchases as a substitute for dividends. Companies that rely exclusively on stock repurchases are, on average, newer firms with no history of paying dividends. In contrast, firms that use both forms of payout tend to be larger and have fewer growth opportunities. The overwhelming majority of these firms already paid dividends in the 1980s, which implies that the firms continuing to pay dividends have a history of dividends and now use share repurchases instead of an increase in the cash dividend. Grullon and Michaely (2002) supplement these findings and report that share repurchases have recently become the preferred form of initiating a cash payout. In summary, the behavior of these two types helps explain the decline in the fraction of dividend payers.

Regarding the hypothesis of changing firm characteristics, Skinner (2008) finds that losses are uncommon among dividend-paying companies. Together with a large increase in the fraction of unprofitable firms (i.e., young start-ups), this pattern is consistent with the findings of Fama and French (2001) and implies that the lower profitability of new listings also serves to explain the lower propensity of companies to pay cash dividends.

Given the decade long tax advantage of share repurchases over dividends, the fact that companies did not start to repurchase stock until the early 1980s seems odd. Why did companies react so late? Grullon and Michaely (2002) present an explanation based on opaque Securities and Exchange Commission (SEC) regulations before 1982. Until 1982, managers were uncertain about the legality of share repurchases as a form of payout policy. Anecdotal evidence shows that the SEC occasionally prosecuted companies for manipulating stock prices during repurchase programs. In 1982, the SEC established guidelines for repurchasing shares on the open market (Rule 10b-18). The rules provided a safe harbor for managers who were until then reluctant to repurchase shares because of the risk of being charged with market manipulation. Grullon and Michaely provide evidence suggesting that SEC regulations constrained share repurchase activity before the adoption of Rule 10b-18.

Grinblatt and Titman (1998) propose another possible explanation. They suggest that the high incidence of cash dividends was a "mistake" made by financial managers. They state the following: "While we can only speculate on why U.S. firms paid out so much in tax-disadvantaged dividends at that time, our best guess is that the decisions of financial managers at that time were simply wrong" (p. 529).

Jagannathan, Stephens, and Weisbach (2000) provide another rationale for the increasing use of share repurchase programs. On the basis of Lintner's (1956) findings, they hypothesize that dividends represent an ongoing commitment to pay out funds to shareholders, while repurchases are primarily used to distribute cash flows that are potentially temporary. Managers' reluctance to cut dividends results from the expectations of market participants and the negative signal that a cut may convey. Several studies document significantly negative stock price reactions surrounding the announcement of dividend cuts (see, e.g., Denis, Denis, and Sarin, 1994).

On the other hand, repurchases do not constitute a long-term commitment. In the past, firms sometimes announced share repurchase programs but ended up not repurchasing any shares. Given the underlying market expectations, share repurchases seem to be an ideal method to pay out temporary hikes in cash flows. Empirical evidence by Jagannathan et al. (2000) confirms this hypothesis and shows that repurchasing firms have more uncertain cash flows. Accordingly, share repurchases are volatile and vary with business cycles.

A survey by Brav, Graham, Harvey, and Michaely (2005) further supplements the finding that managers tend to use repurchases to pay out temporary cash flows. Interviewing a large number of financial executives of public and private firms, the authors report that "many managers now favor repurchases because they are viewed as being more flexible than dividends" (p. 484). In addition, managers seem to use this flexibility to time the market and repurchase stock when they believe their stock price is too low. Interestingly, most executives indicated that tax considerations were not a dominant factor when choosing between repurchases and dividend payments.

Amihud and Li (2006) propose a different explanation for the disappearing dividend phenomenon. Their explanation builds on the dividend-signaling literature (see, e.g., Allen and Michaely, 2003) and suggests that dividends are disappearing because of a decline in the information content of dividend announcements. To obtain a signaling equilibrium, the decision to pay dividends must be costly. Otherwise, low-quality firms would be able to mimic high-quality firms. Paying dividends entails multiple costs. Once a firm pays out these funds, it must raise costly new capital to finance investments. In addition, as mentioned earlier, dividend payments induce higher tax liabilities. The fact that stock prices react positively to dividend announcements (Aharony and Swary, 1980) even with the absence of these costs reflects the positive signal of the firm's quality (and thereby the firm's value) that these announcements convey.

Amihud and Li's (2006) study examines the stock price reaction to dividend announcements and shows that it has been declining over time. Consistent with the documented decline in the propensity of firms to pay dividends, they find that cumulative abnormal returns (CARs) generated by announcements of dividend changes (both increases and decreases) decline toward zero over time. Given that dividend announcements seem to have become less informative, the authors conclude that managers may be reluctant to bear the costs generated by dividends.

Related to the findings presented by Amihud and Li (2006), Grullon and Michaely (2002) assess the effect of share repurchases on the market reaction of firms that announce dividend cuts. They observe that CARs are significantly less negative for nonrepurchasing firms than for firms that repurchased shares over the two years before the dividend-change announcement. Amihud and Li do not report CARs for the two categories separately but find an insignificant influence of share repurchases on CARs in their cross-sectional analysis.

Amihud and Li (2006) attribute the declining informational content of dividends to changes in the shareholder structure. From 1980 until 1990, the average proportion of a firm's equity held by institutional investors increased from 29 percent to 53 percent. A common notion is that institutional investors are better informed than retail investors, as they have the ability to spend more resources on gathering and processing information. Evidence by Healy, Hutton, and Palepu (1999) also shows that more information is available on firms with large institutional holdings. In line with these arguments, Amihud and Li suggest that greater institutional holdings are related to lower informational content of dividends because the stock price already incorporates part of the information that the dividend announcement supposedly conveys. As a result, the larger are the firm's institutional holdings, the smaller is the role of dividends as a means of conveying information. Altogether, the authors suggest that the declining role of dividends is a result of the increase in institutional shareholdings.

Finally, Baker and Wurgler (2004a) examine empirically whether the catering view of dividends as proposed in Baker and Wurgler (2004b) can help explain the declining propensity to pay dividends. In their model, Baker and Wurgler (2004b) argue that managers cater to investor demand for dividends. That is, firms rationally decide to pay dividends when investors put a premium on dividend-paying firms and decide not to pay dividends when investors prefer nonpayers. In their empirical study, they identify four distinct trends in the propensity to pay dividends during 1963–2000 (see the previous subsection "The Evidence") and test whether these trends can be connected to a proxy for catering incentives.

Baker and Wurgler (2004a) find a high correlation between dividend premiums and the annual increase in the propensity to pay dividends. The changes in the dividend premium coincide with the increase in the propensity to pay between 1963 and 1967, the decrease between 1968 and 1970, and the post-1978 disappearance that Fama and French (2001) document. In addition, the authors conduct a review of articles in the *New York Times* to understand time-varying investor demand for dividends. Their results suggest that the dividend premium tends to be negative when investor sentiment for growth stocks (usually nonpayers) is high. Following crashes in growth stocks, investors seem to prefer "safe" stocks that provide regular cash payments rather than promises about future profitability. As a result, the dividend premium rises and dividends appear. This reasoning suggests that after more than 20 years of disappearing dividends, cash dividends seem to be enjoying a renaissance after the burst of the tech bubble.

To conclude, there is no single explanation for the decreasing propensity of firms to pay dividends after 1978, which scholars refer to as the disappearing dividend phenomenon. However, researchers have proposed four major explanations. First, an increasing fraction of newly listed firms that are small and unprofitable has tilted the population of publicly traded firms toward the firm characteristics typically associated with nonpayers of dividends.

Second, share repurchases have become an increasingly important means of paying out funds to shareholders. The empirical evidence indicates that cash that firms would have otherwise paid out in the form of dividends financed the increase in repurchase activity. In addition, young firms without a dividend history seem to use repurchases rather than dividends because of the higher flexibility of the former.

Third, the propensity of public firms to pay dividends may be due to a decline in the informational content of dividend announcements. Because institutional investors, who are supposedly better informed, play a more important role in public companies, the use of dividends as a means to convey information may have become too costly.

Fourth, lower demand for dividends by investors may have caused the decrease in the propensity to pay. Investors seem to have put a premium on nonpayers throughout the 1980s and 1990s. In this sense, the lower proportion of dividend payers may be the result of managers attempting to cater to the implied investor demand.

REAPPEARING DIVIDENDS

Background

Recent evidence from U.S. dividend literature suggests that cash dividends have not completely disappeared and are now experiencing a comeback. There are two different approaches dealing with the phenomenon of reappearing dividends. On the one hand, DeAngelo, DeAngelo, and Skinner (2004) and Skinner (2008) show that dividends never disappeared. They document that, despite a large decrease in dividend-paying companies and a reduced propensity to pay dividends, the total amount of cash dividends paid by U.S. industrial firms has continued to increase. The fact that earnings and dividends are highly concentrated among the most profitable U.S. industrial firms can explain this development.

On the other hand, Julio and Ikenberry (2004), Blouin, Raedy, and Shackelford (2004), Chetty and Saez (2005), and Bank (2006) acknowledge the phenomenon of disappearing dividends but also provide evidence that there has been a reversal in the dividend policy of U.S. firms since 2001. After the disappearing dividend phenomenon at the end of the twentieth century as described by Fama and French (2001), the percentage of dividend-paying companies and the dividend payout ratios (defined as the ratio of total cash dividends paid over total earnings) of U.S. industrial firms have surged.

Little evidence exists that cash dividends disappeared in the rest of the world (see, e.g., Denis and Osobov, 2008). Furthermore, the disappearing dividend phenomenon in countries outside of the United States differs substantially from the U.S. evidence in two ways. First, the decline in the fraction of dividend payers is much less pronounced than in the United States. Second, the decrease in the propensity of dividend-paying firms is economically small, and the decrease has appeared only recently (Ferris, Sen, and Yui, 2006).

In the case of the United States, DeAngelo et al.'s (2004) study is a reaction to the misinterpretation of Fama and French's (2001) work by the popular press, such as the *New York Times* and the *Economist*. Fama and French show that, on average, the likelihood of U.S. firms paying a cash dividend decreases. They document a sharp decline in dividend-paying companies after 1978 until the end of the twentieth century. However, this decline in dividend-paying companies does not necessarily imply, as is commonly assumed, that dividend payments decrease and therefore become less relevant. Indeed, Fama and French provide evidence that cash dividends rose in nominal and real terms over the 1978–2000 period. They show that the increase in real dividends paid by the most profitable U.S. firms more than compensates for the large decline in dividend payers in general. Furthermore, the current nonpayers previously paid a very small, economically insignificant amount of cash dividends.

Julio and Ikenberry (2004) not only find evidence for an increase in aggregate dividend payments but also report an increased propensity to pay cash dividends since the beginning of the twenty-first century in the United States. They identify several factors that caused the resurgence of cash dividends. Using quarterly data for U.S. industrial companies from Compustat and the Center for Research in

Security Prices (CRSP) for the period 1984–2004, Julio and Ikenberry show that the percentage of firms paying cash dividends fell from 32 percent in 1984 to 15 percent in 2001. A reversal in the trend occurred after 2001, when the percentage steadily rose back to roughly 20 percent by 2004. During the same period, an inverse relationship exists between the evolution of dividends and the trend in share repurchases. This led the authors to conclude that dividends and share repurchases are substitutes for each other.

Julio and Ikenberry (2004) also investigate the power of five plausible explanations for the reappearance of cash dividends. First, they investigate the influence of the Jobs and Growth Tax Relief Reconciliation Act of 2003 on the reemergence of dividends. This law reduces the tax rate on dividends from 38.1 percent to 15 percent until December 31, 2008, when the tax rate will be set back to its previous level, assuming that no law extends the tax cut beyond 2008. This study shows that after President George W. Bush's first announcement of the dividend tax cut in the Economic Club of Chicago on January 7, 2003, dividend initiations by previously nonpaying industrial firms increased significantly in the following quarters of 2003. In addition, the authors find support for the tax-cut hypothesis by noting that firms with a comparatively low payout ratio before the tax cut significantly raised their payout ratio afterward. Despite this empirical evidence, Julio and Ikenberry remain cautious about the overall explanatory power of the tax cut regarding the reappearance of dividends. Indeed, the resurgence of dividend increases among dividend payers had already started two years before the first mention of the new tax law.

Second, Julio and Ikenberry (2004) argue that in the aftermath of the Enron scandal in 2002, investors' demand for good corporate governance standards increased. Jensen (1986) was among the first scholars to recognize the corporate governance role of dividends. His free cash flow hypothesis states that dividend payments and high debt ratios reduce the free cash flow of a company. Free cash flow often serves as a proxy for potential agency problems between management and shareholders. Julio and Ikenberry find that companies with comparatively low leverage ratios—debt being a substitute corporate governance mechanism for dividends—increased their dividend payouts significantly at the beginning of the twenty-first century. Their finding indicates that the reappearing dividends are partly due to their increased corporate governance role.

Third, the maturity argument explains a large part of the dividend increase after 2001. According to this argument, high-growth companies should not distribute their cash flows in the early years of their existence. Instead, they should invest their internally generated cash flows into profitable investment opportunities until they reach a level of stable cash flows and their profitable investment opportunities are reduced. Julio and Ikenberry (2004) develop a simple empirical model that predicts a firm's dividend payments as a function of its size, industry, and age. In out-of-sample tests, their model seems to predict quite well the reappearance of dividend payments after 2001. As confirmation of their results, Julio and Ikenberry note "a large number of firms in 2003 (which entered the capital market in the [1990s] as growth companies and hence paid no dividends) had aged to the point where they needed to consider paying some form of dividend" (p. 96).

Fourth, Julio and Ikenberry (2004) examine whether a firm's investment opportunities affect its dividend payouts. Their theory predicts that firms should only pay out dividends if they have no profitable investment opportunities. Both the proxies for growth opportunities (the percentage growth in total assets and the level of a company's cash acquisitions over time) and dividend payments increased in 2003 and 2004. Therefore, the authors reject the investment opportunity hypothesis as a possible explanation for the recent resurgence of dividends.

Finally, Julio and Ikenberry (2004) test the explanatory power of Baker and Wurgler's (2004a) catering theory. The theory states that, without any rational and fundamental reason, investors pay premiums for dividend-paying companies during certain periods. The theory implies that firms tend to increase their dividend payments in those periods. However, Julio and Ikenberry's study finds no compelling evidence for the catering hypothesis, as they do not find a positive correlation between the premiums and dividend payments over the period in question.

Several studies emphasize the role of the 2003 U.S. tax reform in the recent surge in dividend payments. Blouin et al. (2004), Chetty and Saez (2005), and Bank (2006) provide further support that the tax reform is behind the reappearance of dividends in recent years. From 1980 to 2004, Chetty and Saez show that both the amount of dividends paid and the initiations of dividend payments increased as a result of the tax reform in 2003. Furthermore, they find a concentration of dividend increases in companies most heavily affected by the tax reform. Such companies are those that have highly taxable executive stock ownership, highly taxable independent directors' stock ownership, and highly taxable institutional ownership. Conversely, firms with tax-exempt investors, such as pension funds and nonprofit organizations as well as firms with no large block holders, did not respond to the tax cut. Chetty and Saez conclude that the tax preferences of influential shareholders determine firms' dividend policy as a response to tax reforms. They also find that the amount of stock repurchases and hence the total payout has increased after the tax reform, which indicates that dividend increases did not crowd out share repurchases during this period.

Blouin et al.'s (2004) study is consistent with Chetty and Saez's (2005) results. Blouin et al. also find a large increase in regular and special dividends after the tax reform, which is concentrated in companies that exhibit large insider ownership. Similar to Chetty and Saez, Blouin et al. report that the payout policy of individual firms has not changed unless there are influential shareholders who are heavily affected by the tax reform. However, contrary to Chetty and Saez, the authors find support for the substitution hypothesis, as stock repurchases declined in the first two quarters after the dividend tax cut.

Bank (2006) discusses the effects of the Jobs and Growth Tax Relief Reconciliation Act of 2003 on dividend payout policy in the long run. He argues that recent empirical evidence from countries other than the United States (see, e.g., Bank et al. 2006, on the United Kingdom) suggests that the 2003 U.S. tax reform may have no effect on companies' dividend payout policy in the long run. The fact that dividend payers in recent years have been concentrated among very large public companies supports this rationale. These companies do not exhibit the characteristics that, according to Blouin et al. (2004) and Chetty and Saez (2005), are responsible for the adjustment of dividend policy to tax reforms.

Furthermore, Bank et al. (2006, p. 4) contend that the "new" view in finance theory, which suggests that a firm's decision to pay out dividends is independent of tax considerations, supports their reasoning because it assumes that "all profits will eventually be distributed to shareholders in a transaction taxed at the same rate." In contrast to this new view, the old view states that tax policy affects dividend payouts. Under the old view, the optimal dividend-payout ratio is such that the marginal benefit outweighs the marginal cost of the dividend. Following Julio and Ikenberry (2004), Blouin et al. (2004), and Chetty and Saez (2005), Bank et al. conclude that "there are a variety of other possible explanations for the rise in dividends" (p. 3) following the tax reform of 2003. Thus, a need exists for further research in this area, as empirical evidence is far from conclusive.

Did Dividends Ever Disappear in the Rest of the World?

Several empirical studies investigate whether countries other than the United States have experienced the disappearing dividends phenomenon. Given the institutional differences between the United States and other developed financial markets, the rationale for why this phenomenon should have been observed in the rest of the world is unclear. In particular, two institutional differences across countries should have a substantial effect on dividend-payout policy.

First, at the end of the twentieth century, tax codes differed substantially between the United States and countries such as the United Kingdom and Germany (for a detailed discussion, see McDonald, 2001; Renneboog and Trojanowski, 2005). In the United States, corporate income is taxed twice, at both the firm level and the shareholder level. As a consequence, only tax-exempt investors, such as pension funds, should be indifferent between dividend payments and retained earnings. All other investors should prefer that companies retain earnings. In the United Kingdom to date and in Germany until the beginning of 2001, the imputation system has provided a setting where the tax treatment of dividends is more favorable than in the United States. In this system, shareholders are compensated for the corporation's tax payment by receiving a tax credit in addition to the net cash dividend. In contrast to the United States, tax-exempt investors should, therefore, prefer dividends to retained profits. For all other investors, their preference depends on their personal tax rate (except for foreign investors in Germany who did not receive tax credits until the tax reform in 2001 and consequently should have preferred retained earnings before 2001).

Second, France, Germany, and Japan did not allow stock repurchase programs until the late 1990s (Denis and Osobov, 2008). Furthermore, share repurchases were prohibited in the United Kingdom until the early 1980s and were not tax efficient until the mid-1990s (Rau and Vermaelen, 2002). As a consequence, companies could not use share repurchases in these countries as a substitute for dividends in the same way that U.S. companies could (Grullon and Michaely, 2002).

Using firm-level data for the period 1974–1999, Benito and Young (2001) investigate the dividend policy of U.K. firms in the long run. They focus on cash dividend payments as a payout mechanism and consequently ignore share repurchases. Benito and Young detect an increase in the proportion of companies omitting their dividend during the recession periods of 1974–1995. Although economic growth characterizes the period of 1995–1999, the authors observe a significant surge from 14.3 percent to 25.2 percent in the proportion of U.K. companies that abandon their dividend payments. According to the authors, the increase in publicly listed companies that have never paid a dividend largely explains this increase in dividend omissions. Furthermore, Benito and Young find that over the whole sample period, the firm characteristics of cash flow, leverage, size, and growth opportunities are significant drivers for dividend omissions. These characteristics essentially account for the strong incidence of dividend omissions at the end of the twentieth century in the United Kingdom. The authors conclude that, in contrast to the U.S. experience, U.K. companies did not exhibit a lower propensity to pay dividends during the 1974–1999 period.

Renneboog and Trojanowski's (2005) study is the first empirical analysis of U.K. firm data that analyses cash dividends and share repurchases jointly. Their sample covers more than two-thirds of U.K.-listed firms from 1992 to 1998. They document that roughly 85 percent of U.K. firms paid cash dividends over the sample period, in contrast to only 24 percent of U.S. firms over the same period (Fama and French, 2001). In addition, there is an increasing trend in the proportion of U.K. dividend payers from 84 percent in 1992 to 93 percent in 1998. In comparison, the average percentage of firms that repurchase shares during the sample period is rather small, less than 6 percent despite an upward trend in buyback programs as the proportion increases from 5 percent in 1992 to 11 percent in 1998. These trends are consistent with the preferences of tax-exempt investors for cash dividends.

Tax-exempt investors constituted the largest part of U.K. shareholders during the period. During the same period, the proportion of U.S. firms repurchasing stock jumped to more than 80 percent (Grullon and Michaely, 2002). In contrast, in the United Kingdom, not only do dividend payers largely outnumber firms repurchasing shares but also the median dividend paid over the sample period (roughly £1.4 million) is significantly higher than the median repurchase (roughly £800,000). The fact that cash dividends account for more than 90 percent of total payouts over the whole sample period underscores the relatively minor role of share buybacks in the United Kingdom. Finally, the authors provide evidence for stable dividend payout ratios during the 1992–1998 period in the United Kingdom. In summary, Renneboog and Trojanowski (2005, p. 30) confirm Benito and Young's (2001) U.K. results and "find that U.K. firms do not exhibit a decreasing propensity to distribute funds to shareholders."

On the basis of more recent data than those of Benito and Young (2001) and Renneboog and Trojanowski (2005), Ferris et al. (2006) find a decrease in the propensity to pay dividends during 1997–2002 in the United Kingdom. Consistent with Benito and Young, the number of firms paying dividends remains constant until the mid-1990s, when the proportion of nonpaying firms increases substantially. By 2001, only 54 percent of the sample firms pay cash dividends, compared to roughly 76 percent in 1988. A surge in the number of firms that have never paid a dividend causes this development (Benito and Young, 2001; Ferris et al., 2006). Moreover, the proportion of new listings paying dividends decreases from 60 percent in 1988 to 29 percent in 2002. However, an increase in repurchase programs during the period, which is consistent with the findings of Renneboog and Trojanowski, cannot explain the overall decline in dividend-paying firms from 1997 to 2002.

Controlling for the characteristics of nonpaying firms, Ferris et al. (2006) find a decrease in the propensity to pay cash dividends in the United Kingdom despite emphasizing that the disappearing dividend phenomenon in the United Kingdom differs substantially from that in the United States. They offer the following evidence to support this argument. First, the proportion of dividend-paying firms in the United Kingdom only declines to a sample low of 54 percent in 2001 compared to the corresponding U.S. proportion of 21 percent in 1999. Second, and more important, the decline in the propensity to pay cash dividends appears only in the last years of the sample period. By contrast, the U.S. trend of a lower propensity to pay dividends had already started in 1978 (Fama and French, 2001). Therefore, Ferris et al. (p. 1151) conclude that the recent development in the United Kingdom "is not part of a generalized long-term trend as seems to be true in the United States."

Denis and Osobov (2008) investigate the propensity to pay dividends in the United States, United Kingdom, Canada, Germany, France, and Japan over the period 1989–2002. Consistent with DeAngelo et al.'s (2004) results for the United States, the authors find a rise in aggregate real dividends between 1990 and 2002 in all countries except Canada. Furthermore, they observe a concentration of dividend payments among the largest and most profitable firms in all six countries.

Figure 3.4 shows the total number and proportion of dividend payers in the six countries included in the sample. The figure displays a decrease in the fraction of dividend payers in the six countries, but the magnitude of decrease differs across the countries. The decline in the United States and Canada (from 61 percent to 19 percent and from roughly 69 percent to roughly 20 percent, respectively) is more pronounced than in France and Japan (from roughly 81 percent to roughly 61 percent and from about 89 percent to about 84 percent, respectively). From 1989 to 2002, the total number of dividend payers rises in Germany, France, and Japan but remains stable in the United States and Canada. Only the United Kingdom experiences a sharp decline in the number of dividend-paying firms starting in 1997. This pattern is consistent with that of Ferris et al. (2006). Moreover, the authors find that dividend payments are significantly driven by the firms' profitability, their size, and their ratio of retained earnings over total equity in all six countries, which measures the proportion of the firm's equity that is generated within the firm.

Data from all six countries suggest that characteristics of publicly listed companies are shifting toward those of nonpayers. Yet when Denis and Osobov (2008) control for the firms' determinants of dividend payment, they find little evidence of a decline in the propensity to pay dividends over 1994–2002 in all six countries. Indeed, the decline in the propensity to pay dividends is economically small and not always robust to alternative proxies of firm characteristics, such as in France and Germany. According to the authors, this decline can largely be attributed to an increasing number of new listings that do not start dividend payments when they are expected to do so. Denis and Osobov conclude that "the data cannot reject the hypothesis that there has been no meaningful change in corporate dividend policies in the sample countries over the 1989 to 2002 period" (p. 63).

A study by von Eije and Megginson's (2007) covers data from the 15 countries that formed the European Union before May 2004. They examine the trend in dividend policy from 1989 to 2003. Consistent with Denis and Osobov (2008), the authors document a sharp decrease in the proportion of dividend-paying firms from 91 percent to 62 percent and a significant increase in the aggregate real dividend (from €25 billion in 1989 to more than €80 billion per year between 2000 and 2003). Increases are concentrated among the largest and most profitable EU firms. They find that firm size and asset growth significantly influence the likelihood of paying dividends by EU firms. Furthermore, by controlling for profitability, size, and growth opportunities, they support Denis and Osobov's finding of an

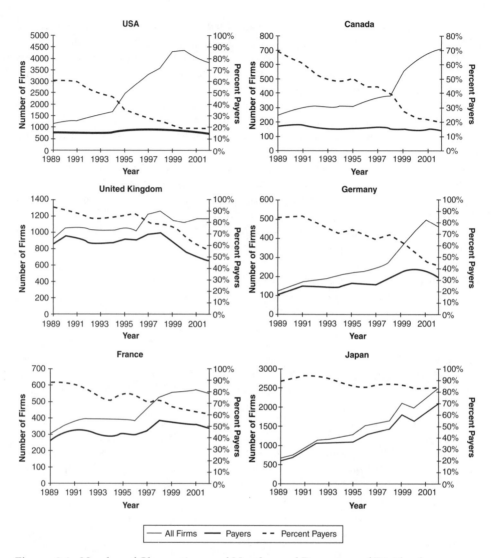

Figure 3.4 Number of Observations and Number and Percentage of Dividend Payers by Country

The sample includes all companies in Canada, France, Germany, Japan, the United Kingdom, and the United States with complete data in the Worldscope database over the 1989–2002 period.
Source: Denis and Osobov (2008, p. 69).

economically small decline in the propensity to pay dividends from 1994 to 2003 in the EU countries, which is mainly driven by new listings.

Moreover, von Eije and Megginson (2007) identify other determinants that affect the likelihood of dividend payments in the European context. Consistent with the maturity hypothesis and La Porta, Lopez-de-Silanes, Shleifer, and Vishny's (2000) findings, firm age and being based in a common law country are both positively related to dividend payments and the propensity to pay dividends. La Porta et al. argue that common law countries provide greater levels of investor protection than civil law countries. Common law is the legal family that covers U.K. and U.S. law as well as the Commonwealth countries. Civil law covers all the other legal families: French, German, and Scandinavian law. Von Eije and Megginson conclude that despite the increasing European economic integration, dividend policies in the EU countries have not yet converged.

In summary, while some dispute the existence of the phenomenon of disappearing dividends, others present empirical evidence that the proportion of companies paying a cash dividend has been on the increase since the beginning of the new millennium. According to Julio and Ikenberry (2004), among others, several factors led to the trend reversal. Moreover, evidence exists that the fraction of dividend-paying firms in the rest of the world also declined at the end of the twentieth century. However, the evidence for a declining propensity to pay dividends in other countries, which Fama and French (2001) observed in the United States, is not compelling because (1) the decline in the fraction of dividend payers is much less pronounced than in the United States and (2) the decrease in the propensity of dividend-paying firms is economically small and has been observed only recently (Ferris et al., 2006).

CONCLUSIONS

This chapter examines the phenomenon of disappearing dividends, which appeared in the United States during the end of the twentieth century, as first observed by Fama and French (2001). Researchers advanced various explanations for the decrease in the propensity to pay dividends. However, no universally accepted explanation for the phenomenon exists to date. While one strand of the literature questions the existence of this phenomenon, another contends that the phenomenon has been only temporary, as the propensity to pay dividends has been on the increase since the new millennium. Finally, although studies on countries other than the United States report a similar decline in the propensity to pay dividends, the magnitude of the phenomenon is much less pronounced and, contrary to the United States where the phenomenon first appeared in 1978, the trend of disappearing dividends in EU countries and Japan is much more recent.

REFERENCES

Aharony, Joseph, and Itzhak Swary. 1980. "Quarterly Dividend and Earnings Announcements and Stockholders Returns: An Empirical Analysis." *Journal of Finance* 35:1, 1–12.

Allen, Franklin, Antonio Bernardo, and Ivo Welch. 2000. "A Theory of Dividends Based on Tax Clientele." *Journal of Finance* 55:6, 2499–2536.

Allen, Franklin, and Roni Michaely. 2003. " Payout Policy." In *Handbook of the Economics of Finance 1A*, ed. George M. Constantinides, Milton Harris, and René Stulz, 337–429. Amsterdam: North-Holland-Elsevier.

Amihud, Yakov, and Kefei Li. 2006. "The Declining Information Content of Dividend Announcements and the Effects of Institutional Holdings." *Journal of Financial and Quantitative Analysis* 41:3, 637–660.

Bagwell, Laurie, and John Shoven. 1989. "Cash Distributions to Shareholders." *Journal of Economic Perspectives* 3:3, 129–149.

Baker, Malcolm, and Jeffrey Wurgler. 2004a. "Appearing and Disappearing Dividends: The Link to Catering Incentives." *Journal of Financial Economics* 73:2, 271–288.

Baker, Malcolm, and Jeffrey Wurgler. 2004b. "A Catering Theory of Dividends." *Journal of Finance* 59:3, 1125–1165.

Bank, Steven A. 2006. "Dividends and Tax Policy in the Long Run." UCLA School of Law, Law-Econ Research Paper No. 06-06, available at http://ssrn.com/abstract=886583.

Bank, Steven A., Brian R. Cheffins, and Marc Goergen. 2006. "Dividends and Politics." Law Working Paper 24/2004, European Corporate Governance Institute, available at http://ssrn.com/abstract=636523 or DOI: 10.2139/ssrn.636523.

Benito, Andrew, and Garry Young. 2001. "Hard Times of Great Expectations? Dividend Omissions and Dividend Cuts by U.K. Firms." Working Paper, Bank of England.

Bhattacharya, Sudipto. 1979. "Imperfect Information, Dividend Policy, and 'The Bird in the Hand' Fallacy." *Bell Journal of Economics* 10:1, 259–270.

Black, Fischer. 1976. "The Dividend Puzzle." *Journal of Portfolio Management* 2:2, 5–8.

Blouin, Jennifer, Jana Raedy, and Douglas Shackelford. 2004. "The Initial Impact of the 2003 Reduction in the Dividend Tax Rate." Working Paper, University of North Carolina at Chapel Hill.

Brav, Alon, John R. Graham, Campbell R. Harvey, and Roni Michaely. 2005. "Payout Policy in the 21st Century." *Journal of Financial Economics* 77:3, 483–527.

Chetty, Ray, and Emmanuel Saez. 2005. "Dividend Taxes and Corporate Behavior: Evidence from the 2003 Dividend Tax Cut." *Quarterly Journal of Economics* 120:3, 791–833.

DeAngelo, Harry, Linda DeAngelo, and Douglas J. Skinner. 2000. "Special Dividends and the Evolution of Dividend Signaling." *Journal of Financial Economics* 57:3, 309–354.

DeAngelo, Harry, Linda DeAngelo, and Douglas J. Skinner. 2004. "Are Dividends Disappearing? Dividend Concentration and the Consolidation of Earnings." *Journal of Financial Economics* 72:3, 425–456.

Denis, David J., and Igor Osobov. 2008. "Why Do Firms Pay Dividends? International Evidence on the Determinants of Dividend Policy." *Journal of Financial Economics* 89:1, 62-82.

Denis, David, Denise Denis, and Atulya Sarin. 1994. "The Information Content of Dividend Changes: Cash Flow Signalling, Overinvestment, and Dividend Clienteles." *Journal of Financial and Quantitative Analysis* 29:4, 567–587.

Easterbrook, Frank H. 1984. "Two Agency-Cost Explanations of Dividends." *American Economic Review* 74:4, 650–659.

Fama, Eugene F., and Kenneth R. French. 2001. "Disappearing Dividends: Changing Firm Characteristics or Lower Propensity to Pay?" *Journal of Financial Economics* 60:1, 3–43.

Ferris, Stephen, Nilanjan Sen, and Ho Pei Yui. 2006. "God Save the Queen and Her Dividends: Corporate Payouts in the United Kingdom." *Journal of Business* 79:3, 1149–1173.

Grinblatt, Mark, and Sheridan Titman. 1998. *Financial Markets and Corporate Strategy*. Boston: Irwin/McGraw-Hill.

Grullon, Gustavo, and Roni Michaely. 2002. "Dividends, Share Repurchases, and the Substitution Hypothesis." *Journal of Finance* 57:4, 1649–1684.

Healy, Paul M., Amy P. Hutton, and Krishna G. Palepu. 1999. "Stock Performance and Intermediation Changes Surrounding Increases in Disclosure." *Contemporary Accounting Research* 16:3, 485–520.

Jagannathan, Murali, Clifford P. Stephens, and Michael S. Weisbach. 2000. "Financial Flexibility and the Choice between Dividends and Stock Repurchases." *Journal of Financial Economics* 57:3, 355–384.

Jensen, Michael C. 1986. "Agency Costs of Free Cash Flow, Corporate Finance and Takeovers." *American Economic Review* 76:2, 323–329.

John, Kose, and John Williams. 1985. "Dividends, Dilution, and Taxes: A Signalling Equilibrium." *Journal of Finance* 40:4, 1053–1070.

Julio, Brandon, and David L. Ikenberry. 2004. "Reappearing Dividends." *Journal of Applied Corporate Finance* 16:4, 89–100.

La Porta, Rafael, Florencio Lopez-de-Silanes, Andrei Shleifer, and Robert W. Vishny. 2000. "Agency Problems and Dividend Policies around the World." *Journal of Finance* 55:1, 1–33.

Lintner, John. 1956. "Distribution of Incomes of Corporations among Dividends, Retained Earnings, and Taxes." *American Economic Review* 46:2, 97–113.

McDonald, Robert L. 2001. "Cross-Border Investing with Tax Arbitrage: The Case of German Dividend Tax Credits." *Review of Financial Studies* 14:3, 617–657.

Miller, Merton H., and Franco Modigliani. 1961. "Dividend Policy, Growth, and the Valuation of Shares." *Journal of Business* 34:4, 411–433.

Rau, Ragahavendra, and Theo Vermaelen. 2002. "Regulation, Taxes and Share Repurchases in the United Kingdom." *Journal of Business* 75:2, 245–282.

Renneboog, Luc, and Grzegorz Trojanowski. 2005. "Patterns in Payout Policy and Payout Channel Choice of U.K. Firms in the 1990s." Working Paper, European Corporate Governance Institute.

Skinner, Douglas J. 2008. "The Evolving Relation between Earnings, Dividends, and Stock Repurchases." *Journal of Financial Economics* 87:3, 582–609.

von Eije, J. Henk, and William Megginson. 2007. "Dividend Policy in the European Union." Working Paper, University of Groningen.

ABOUT THE AUTHORS

Christian Andres is assistant professor of finance at the University of Bonn, Germany. He holds a master's degree and a Ph.D. from the University of Bonn. During his doctoral studies, he spent several months as a visiting scholar at the University of Sheffield, in the United Kingdom, and at the University of Florida. His primary research interests are in the areas of empirical corporate finance and corporate governance.

André Betzer holds a bachelor's degree in economics from the University of Toulouse (France). He earned his master's and Ph.D. degrees in economics from the University of Bonn (Germany). Since June 2006, he has worked as assistant professor of finance at the University of Bonn. His research focuses mainly on issues of corporate finance and corporate governance.

Luis Correia da Silva holds a degree in economics from the Free University of Brussels, an MBA from Solvay Business School (Brussels), and a D.Phil. in economics from the University of Oxford. He is managing director of Oxera, where he heads its Corporate Finance and Regulation practice areas. He is the coauthor of *Dividend Policy and Corporate Governance* (Oxford University Press) and *Asset Management and Investor Protection* (Oxford University Press), and he has published in *Journal of Corporate Finance*, *Utilities Policy*, and others.

Marc Goergen has a degree in economics from the Free University of Brussels, an MBA from Solvay Business School (Brussels), and a D.Phil. from the University of Oxford. He has held appointments at the University of Manchester Institute of Science and Technology, and at the Universities of Manchester, Reading and Sheffield. He holds a chair in finance at Cardiff Business School. His research interests are in international corporate governance, mergers and acquisitions, dividend policy, corporate investment models, insider trading, and initial public offerings. He has widely published in academic journals such as *European Financial Management, Journal of Corporate Finance, Journal of Finance, Journal of Financial Intermediation,* and *Journal of Law, Economics and Organization.* He has also contributed chapters to numerous books and written two books (*Corporate Governance and Financial Performance,* published by Edward Elgar, and *Dividend Policy and Corporate Governance,* published by Oxford University Press). He is a research associate at the European Corporate Governance Institute.

CHAPTER 4

Factors Influencing Dividends

DAVID DENIS
Burton Morgan Chair of Private Enterprise, Krannert School of Management,
Purdue University

GOHAR STEPANYAN
Ph.D. Candidate, Krannert School of Management, Purdue University

INTRODUCTION

What determines the magnitude of dividend payouts? Understanding this issue, which has vexed financial economists for nearly 50 years, is important because corporations distribute a substantial amount of their resources to shareholders every year. As shown in Table 4.1, the past two decades have witnessed a steady increase in the nominal dollar amount paid out as dividends in the United States, reaching nearly $165 billion in 2005. When combined with payouts in the form of share repurchases, aggregate payouts to shareholders totaled nearly $372 billion in 2005.

The seminal work of Miller and Modigliani (1961) (hereafter MM) influenced the early inquiries into the motives and consequences of dividend policy. In their framework, investment policy is fixed and known by investors. Moreover, there are no market imperfections such as taxes, transaction costs, and asymmetric information. The contribution of MM was to show that under these conditions, all feasible dividend policies involve the distribution of the full present value of free cash flows. Consequently, investors would be indifferent among the set of feasible dividend polices. That is, the value of the firm would be independent of the dividend policy adopted by management.

Nonetheless, the fact that managers and security analysts spend much time worrying about dividend policy suggests that it must be relevant in some sense. Financial economists have explored this relevance by relaxing MM's (1961) perfect capital markets assumptions. The adjusted model has led to dividend theories based on tax-based clienteles, alternative tax regimes, agency problems, and information signaling, among others. Each of these classes of theories implies that dividends are relevant in predictable ways. That is, dividends should vary across firms and over time in systematic ways.

This chapter provides a synthesis of the academic evidence on the cross-sectional and time-series determinants of dividends. These factors represent three major categories: (1) firm characteristics, (2) market characteristics, and (3)

Table 4.1   Annual Aggregate Cash Distributions to Shareholders: 1971–2005

Year	Total Cash Payout ($MM)	Dividend Payout ($MM)	Repurchase Payout ($MM)
1971	16,661.18	15,910.02	751.16
1972	17,815.54	16,572.66	1,242.88
1973	21,145.54	18,575.64	2,569.90
1974	22,008.71	20,590.72	1,418.00
1975	22,189.88	21,417.19	772.69
1976	25,925.49	24,684.48	1,241.01
1977	32,012.38	29,126.11	2,886.26
1978	33,998.85	31,568.56	2,430.29
1979	37,449.58	34,798.66	2,650.92
1980	39,551.79	37,219.13	2,332.66
1981	44,560.81	40,639.65	3,921.16
1982	56,019.41	41,083.96	14,935.45
1983	45,063.42	39,727.30	5,336.13
1984	56,603.29	38,789.69	17,813.60
1985	69,259.49	43,532.53	25,726.96
1986	63,536.12	42,627.10	20,909.02
1987	81,388.32	51,465.70	29,922.62
1988	82,928.03	57,622.96	25,305.07
1989	75,762.43	54,246.39	21,516.04
1990	77,948.72	55,741.48	22,207.24
1991	67,147.63	56,109.68	11,037.95
1992	76,920.01	61,040.66	15,879.35
1993	84,006.91	65,453.16	18,553.75
1994	95,497.27	68,722.67	26,774.60
1995	108,193.28	69,119.70	39,073.59
1996	131,764.01	76,609.69	55,154.32
1997	159,335.31	81,239.35	78,095.96
1998	184,898.03	85,006.76	99,891.28
1999	211,668.87	84,605.26	127,063.62
2000	215,949.82	92,362.21	123,587.61
2001	181,767.97	93,999.21	87,768.76
2002	194,378.32	99,180.88	95,197.45
2003	195,653.15	99,518.03	96,135.12
2004	261,553.24	120,651.63	140,901.61
2005	371,636.25	164,723.40	206,912.85

Notes: Annual cash dividends, share repurchases, and total payouts to shareholders between 1971 and 2005 by all nonfinancial nonutility firms from CRSP/COMPUSTAT merged database that are incorporated in the United States; traded on NYSE, AMEX, or NASDAQ; have securities with CRSP share codes equal to 10 or 11 (ordinary common shares) as of the last trading month of each fiscal year in question; and are not missing values for dividends, repurchases, and earnings before extraordinary and special items for a given year. All dollar amounts are expressed in millions.

substitute forms of payout. Next, the chapter provides a discussion of how the set of factors that systematically affects dividend decisions relate to traditional dividend theories. The purpose of this chapter is not to provide an exhaustive survey of the literature but rather to summarize representative studies that highlight the state of knowledge in the field.

FIRM CHARACTERISTICS

Various authors have hypothesized that dividends are associated with characteristics of firm fundamentals such as firm size, profitability, growth opportunities, and maturity. In addition, others have suggested that dividends are related to more discretionary firm characteristics, such as leverage and aspects of the firm's corporate governance structure. In this section, we summarize the evidence on the extent to which various firm characteristics are associated with dividend policy. This evidence, which Table 4.2 presents, comes from cross-sectional tests of the propensity

Table 4.2 Firm Characteristics Associated with Dividends

Characteristic	Representative Studies	Sign of Association
Firm Size	Smith and Watts (1992)	+
	Gaver and Gaver (1993)	+
	Fama and French (2001)	+
	DeAngelo, DeAngelo, and Stulz (2006)	+
	Denis and Osobov (2008)	+
Profitability	Fama and French (2001)	+
	DeAngelo, DeAngelo, and Skinner (2004)	+
	DeAngelo, DeAngelo, and Stulz (2006)	+
	Denis and Osobov (2008)	+
Growth Opportunities	Smith and Watts (1992)	−
	Gaver and Gaver (1993)	−
	Fama and French (2001)	−
	DeAngelo, DeAngelo, and Stulz (2006)	−
	Denis and Osobov (2008)	Mixed
Firm Maturity	Grullon, Michaely, and Swaminathan (2002)	+
	DeAngelo, DeAngelo, and Stulz (2006)	+
	Denis and Osobov (2008)	+
Regulation	Smith and Watts (1992)	+
	Gaver and Gaver (1993)	+
Leverage	Smith and Watts (1992)	+
	Gaver and Gaver (1993)	+
Incentive Compensation	Smith and Watts (1992)	+
	Fenn and Liang (2004)	−
Insider Stock Holdings	Rozeff (1982)	−
Institutional Stock Holdings	Grinstein and Michaely (2005)	+

Notes: This table provides a summary of studies that analyze the relationship between firm characteristics and dividends. For each characteristic, the table lists the individual studies and the sign of the association between dividends and the firm characteristic that they report.

to pay dividends, tests of the magnitude of dividend payout and dividend yield, and tests of aggregate payout.

Firm Fundamentals

Fama and French (2001) estimate logit models in which the dependent variable is equal to one if the firm pays regular common dividends in a given year and zero otherwise. They find that the likelihood of dividend payments is positively associated with firm size and profitability and negatively associated with the firm's market-to-book ratio (a measure of growth opportunities). DeAngelo, DeAngelo, and Stulz (2006) extend the Fama-French analysis to include a measure of firm maturity (or life cycle stage), which is the ratio of retained earnings to the book value of equity (RE/BE). They find that the propensity to pay dividends is positively associated with RE/BE. This firm maturity effect does not subsume the Fama-French characteristics, but the evidence of DeAngelo et al. implies that RE/BE has the greatest economic impact on the propensity to pay dividends. Grullon, Michaely, and Swaminathan (2002) corroborate the link between dividends and firm maturity by reporting that firms increasing dividends exhibit declines in systematic risk and future reductions in profitability. These firms also fail to increase capital expenditures.

Smith and Watts (1992) and Gaver and Gaver (1993) adopt a similar cross-sectional approach, but instead of estimating models that predict whether a firm pays dividends, they estimate models in which dividend yield and dividend payout are the dependent variables. Using industry-level data, Smith and Watts find that dividend yield is positively related to firm size and whether the firm is regulated. Dividend yield is negatively associated with measures of growth options. Using firm-level data, Gaver and Gaver confirm that growth firms have lower payout ratios and lower dividend yield.

The relationship between dividends and firm fundamentals also appears to be robust across countries. Denis and Osobov (2008) analyze dividend policies in six developed financial markets—United States, United Kingdom, Canada, Germany, France, and Japan—and find that firm size, profitability, and firm maturity are associated with the propensity to pay dividends in all six countries. The association between dividends and growth opportunities is less robust. In studies of the determinants of dividends in the United Kingdom, Benito and Young (2001), Renneboog and Trojanowski (2005), and Ferris, Sen, and Yui (2006) all find evidence similar to that of Denis and Osobov, while von Eije and Megginson (2008) report similar findings in a sample of European Union firms.

Finally, DeAngelo, DeAngelo, and Skinner (2004) report that aggregate dividends are heavily concentrated among the largest, most profitable firms in the United States. Denis and Osobov (2008) confirm that this pattern also holds up internationally.

Other Nonfundamental Firm Characteristics

Empirical studies also link dividend polices with other firm characteristics such as capital structure policy, incentive compensation plans, and ownership structure. For example, Smith and Warner (1979) and Kalay (1982) show that covenants contained in bond contracts constrain dividends. Nonetheless, Smith and Watts (1992) find a positive association between dividend yield and leverage and attribute this association to managers' joint determination of dividend and leverage policies based on the firm's growth opportunities.

Smith and Watts (1992) also report a positive association between dividend yield and bonus or stock option plans for top executives. They again argue that the impact of growth options on the joint determination of dividend and compensation policies drives this relationship. However, Fenn and Liang (2001) find that, controlling for free cash flow, dividends are negatively correlated with stock options in more recent years when share repurchases have become more common. They attribute this to managers having greater stock options substituting repurchases for dividends because dividends reduce the value of their option holdings.

A final group of studies empirically examines the association between equity ownership structure and dividend policies. In an early study, Rozeff (1982) finds a negative relationship between dividends and insider stock holdings. More recently, Fenn and Liang (2001) find a positive association between dividend payout and insider stock ownership among low-ownership firms. Their evidence shows no relationship between payout and insider stock ownership for firms with high ownership.

With respect to other equity owners, Grinstein and Michaely (2005), analyze the relationship between institutional shareholdings and dividend policy. They find evidence that institutional ownership is greater in dividend-paying firms than in non-dividend-paying firms. However, they find no evidence that higher dividend payouts attract greater institutional ownership. Thus, they conclude that institutions do not monitor and control managers through corporate payout policy.

Table 4.2 provides a summary of the various firm characteristics associated with dividend policy. Overall, the existing evidence indicates that dividend policy is strongly related to fundamental firm characteristics such as growth opportunities, profitability, firm size, and firm maturity, as well as endogenous corporate policy choices such as leverage and incentive compensation and attributes of the firm's equity ownership structure.

MARKET CHARACTERISTICS

A separate line of research hypothesizes a relationship between dividends and characteristics of the market environment in which companies operate. Examples of these characteristics include taxes, investor protection laws, investor sentiment toward dividend-paying stocks, public versus private status, characteristics of newly listed companies, and product market competition.

Taxes

To the extent that the government taxes dividends differently than capital gains, this can, in theory, affect a company's payout policy. Attempts to empirically analyze whether taxes affect dividend decisions are complicated by the fact that marginal tax rates of investors are difficult to observe. For this reason, much of the research on this question relies on indirect tests. The discussion in this section draws in part from Graham's (2003) survey of this issue.

Evidence on whether taxes affect investor preferences for dividend-paying stocks is mixed. Scholz (1992) analyzes data from the 1983 Survey of Consumer Finances and reports a negative relationship between the dividend yield of investors' stock holdings and the relative taxation of dividends. However, Allen and Michaely (2003) find that the wealthiest and presumably highest-tax-bracket investors receive the bulk of dividends. The latter finding casts doubt on taxes on dividends being a first-order determinant of investor decisions.

Other studies attempt to more directly analyze whether taxes affect corporate payout decisions. Perez-Gonzalez (2003) finds that when tax reforms increase (decrease) the taxation of dividends relative to capital gains, firms with more retail shareholders (taxable investors) decrease (increase) their dividend. Poterba and Summers (1984) report similar findings for aggregate dividends in the United Kingdom. These studies imply that taxes do, in fact, affect corporate payout policy.

Finally, Lie and Lie (1999) find that firms with low dividend payout (presumably high-tax-bracket investors) are more likely to use share repurchases than to increase regular dividends or to pay out cash through special dividends. They conclude that investor taxes affect payout policy.

Investor Protection Laws

At least dating back to Easterbrook (1984), the finance literature has hypothesized that dividends are a function of agency problems between firm insiders and outside investors. More recently, many authors have recognized that one of the principal remedies to agency problems is the existence and enforcement of laws that protect shareholders from expropriation by insiders. Together, these streams of literature imply that dividends should be a function of the legal environment in which firms operate. La Porta, Lopez-de-Silanes, Shleifer, and Vishny (2000) formalize this notion by developing and testing two agency cost models of dividend policy. Under the so-called outcome model, dividends are an outcome of effective legal protections of minority shareholders. That is, legal protections effectively compel insiders and majority shareholders to make payouts to shareholders rather than expropriating the minority owners. Under La Porta et al.'s "substitute" model, dividends are a substitute for legal protection. To be able to raise external funds on attractive terms, firms pay dividends so as to establish a reputation for not expropriating minority shareholders.

To test these agency cost models, La Porta et al. (2000) analyze the dividend policies of more than 4,000 firms from 33 countries around the world. Using indices for the quality of legal protection of minority shareholders as a proxy for lower agency problems, they find consistent support for the outcome agency model of dividends. First, firms operating in countries with better protection of minority shareholders pay higher dividends. Second, in those countries, high-growth companies pay lower dividends than do low-growth companies, consistent with the idea that legally protected shareholders are willing to wait for their dividends when a company has good investment prospects.

Faccio, Lang, and Young (2001) build on La Porta et al.'s (2000) work by testing the relationship between dividend rates in Western Europe and East Asia and the disparity between the controlling shareholder's ownership rights (O) and its control rights (C). Specifically, Faccio et al. use the ratio of ownership to control rights

(O/C) as a measure of the corporation's vulnerability to insider expropriation. For example, this ratio is low if a controlling shareholder controls the corporation via a long chain of intermediate corporations. Under this scenario, in which the controlling shareholder is at the base of a pyramidal ownership structure, the controlling shareholder has greater opportunities for intragroup transactions that expropriate minority shareholders.

Faccio et al. (2001) find that among corporations that are tightly affiliated to a business group, group-affiliated corporations with lower O/C ratios pay higher dividends. By contrast, among corporations that are loosely affiliated with business groups—for example, those with control linkages between 10 percent and 20 percent—dividend rates are lower for firms with lower O/C ratios. The authors interpret the findings as suggesting that investors anticipate expropriation in tightly affiliated firms and demand higher dividends to allay concerns. However, they argue that investors are less alert to such expropriation in loosely affiliated firms. One explanation for this reaction is that the low transparency of such sprawling, loosely affiliated groups increases the difficulty of shareholders' discovering where control resides to identify and oppose unfair intragroup transactions.

Investor Sentiment

Baker and Wurgler (2004a) develop and test the hypothesis that prevailing investor demand for dividend payers drives the decision to pay dividends. That is, as investor sentiment shifts toward dividend-paying firms, the firms trade at a premium relative to nonpayers. Firms cater to this sentiment by adjusting dividend policies in the direction of the dividend premium prevailing in the market at that time. Using time variation in four proxies for the dividend premium, Baker and Wurgler document that nonpayers are more likely to initiate dividends when the dividend premium is high and, conversely, are more likely to omit dividends when the dividend premium is negative.

In another study, Baker and Wurgler (2004b) analyze whether the catering theory of dividends sheds some light on the reduced propensity to pay dividends originally documented by Fama and French (2001). Baker and Wurgler identify four distinct trends in the propensity to pay between 1963 and 2000—two periods of increased propensity and two periods of reduced propensity—and empirically link these trends with changes in the dividend premium. Their findings are generally consistent with investor sentiment influencing the propensity to pay dividends. The only period that appears to be strongly inconsistent with the catering hypothesis is the early 1970s, a period in which Nixon-era wage and price controls influenced dividends.

One of the major limitations of Baker and Wurgler's (2004a) study is that it primarily analyzes why firms initiate or omit dividends as opposed to how firms make decisions about changing the level of existing dividends. To address this limitation, Li and Lie (2006) extend Baker and Wurgler's catering theory to include decreases and increases in existing dividends. They report that the dividend premium is related to both the probability of dividend decreases and increases and the magnitude of dividend changes. Li and Lie also find that the announcement returns for dividend decreases are negatively related to the dividend premium, while the announcement returns for dividend increases are positively related to the dividend premium. They interpret this evidence as indicating that the capital market conditions the market's response to dividend change announcements on the aggregate dividend premium.

Although the preceding findings suggest that investor sentiment is an important determinant of dividend policies in U.S. firms, two recent studies question the robustness of these findings. First, Hoberg and Prabhala (2006) find that once they control for risk, catering incentives are no longer significant in explaining the declining propensity to pay dividends among U.S. firms. Second, in their study of dividend policies in several countries, Denis and Osobov (2008) conclude that their evidence casts considerable doubt on the importance of catering incentives on the propensity to pay dividends in the United States, United Kingdom, Canada, Germany, France, and Japan.

Public versus Private Status

For the most part, the academic literature has scrutinized the corporate payout policies of publicly traded firms because data on these firms are readily available. By contrast, research has largely ignored dividend policies of private firms. This raises the question of whether a firm's listing status (i.e., whether it is public or private) has an impact on its dividend policy. To address this issue, Michaely and Roberts (2007) compare the dividend policies of publicly traded and privately held firms to identify the forces shaping their respective dividend decisions. As documented in the existing literature, Michaely and Roberts report that public firms engage in dividend smoothing. That is, relative to otherwise similar private firms, public firms are averse to omitting, cutting, and initiating dividends. Moreover, public firms appear to be relatively averse to large dividend increases. These findings are consistent with the view that the scrutiny of public equity markets appears to induce managers to follow more conservative dividend policies, that is, relatively small, consistent increases in dividends coupled with a reluctance to reduce dividends.

In addition, the findings of Michaely and Roberts (2007) have implications for the interaction between agency conflicts and governance mechanisms in determining dividend policies. Specifically, their evidence implies that conflicts of interest between controlling and minority shareholders tend to reduce dividend payments in many private firms. In addition, the array of institutional and governance mechanisms present in public markets mitigates these conflicts and leads to substantially higher dividends in public firms. Moreover, the dividends tend to be more responsive to fluctuations in investments in public firms than in private firms.

Characteristics of Newly Listed Public Companies

Although the previously mentioned findings suggest that whether a firm is publicly traded has an impact on its dividend policy, recent research also suggests that the characteristics of publicly traded firms have changed over time in the United States toward those characteristics more typical of non-dividend-paying firms. Specifically, Fama and French (2001) report that since 1978, publicly traded firms in the United States have increasingly exhibited the characteristics of firms that have never paid dividends, such as small size, low earnings, and large investment relative to earnings. The driving forces underlying this change in the population of firms are the huge increase in new listings after 1978 and the changing nature of the new lists. According to Fama and French (2004), the cross-sectional distribution of profitability for newly listed firms over time has become considerably more left skewed, while the distribution of growth opportunities has become considerably more right skewed. As a result, newly listed, dividend-paying firms became increasingly rare throughout the 1980s and 1990s.

Denis and Osobov (2008) extend this research on the propensity to pay dividends to several developed international financial markets such as the United Kingdom, Canada, Germany, France, and Japan. They document that, over the past decade, the composition of the population of publicly traded firms in all countries has changed toward greater representation of firms with characteristics typical of nonpayers, In addition, Denis and Osobov find newly listed firms that fail to initiate dividends appear to drive any observed declines in the propensity to pay dividends, This evidence is consistent with results reported in the United States.

Product Market Competition

Through its effect on agency conflicts, product market competition may be an additional external disciplinary factor that affects the decision to pay out excess cash to shareholders. Grullon and Michaely (2007) analyze whether the link between product market competition and managerial incentives has any implications for corporate payout policy. As do La Porta et al. (2000), Grullon and Michaely distinguish between an outcome and a substitute model of dividends. Under their version of the outcome model, managers in highly competitive markets distribute more cash to their shareholders because the disciplinary forces of competition are more likely to penalize managers if they overinvest. Alternatively, managers in less competitive markets can use dividends as a substitute for competition to establish a good reputation in the capital markets to be able to raise capital on better terms in the future.

Grullon and Michaely (2007) find that firms in more concentrated or less competitive industries have significantly lower payout ratios than do firms in less concentrated industries, which supports the prediction of the outcome model. However, an alternative explanation for this result could be that firms in more concentrated markets pay lower dividends because they need to accumulate cash to prevent predatory behavior from competitors (predation hypothesis). The predatory behavior should be less pronounced among dominant firms because these firms have more resources and market power to prevent any predatory attack. If the predation hypothesis is true, the negative relationship between industry concentration levels and payout ratios should be stronger among the nondominant firms. Yet Grullon and Michaely's empirical findings indicate that the negative relationship between industry concentration levels and corporate payouts is much stronger among dominant firms that are more likely to have high agency costs of free cash flows, thus reinforcing the idea that corporate payouts are the outcome of the disciplinary forces of product market competition.

SUBSTITUTE FORMS OF PAYOUT

Before the mid-1980s, firms used cash dividends as the dominant means to return capital to stockholders. As shown in Table 4.1, however, share repurchases have become increasingly popular in recent years and now account for more than 50 percent of aggregate payouts in the United States. Roughly coincident with this surge in share repurchases has been a decline in the proportion of U.S. dividend-paying firms. Fama and French (2001) show that this proportion drops from 67 percent in 1978 to 21 percent in 1999. These patterns raise the possibility that firms are increasingly using repurchases as a substitute for dividends.

Because share repurchases are, in theory, onetime events or programs, several studies have explored the possibility that firms use repurchases to pay out temporary earnings and use dividends to pay out more permanent earnings. Jagannathan, Stephens, and Weisbach (2000) report that the likelihood of a firm using repurchases rather than dividends increases when a firm's cash flows consist of a higher proportion of nonoperating income relative to operating income, when a firm's earnings volatility before the repurchase is high, and when a firm's future cash flows are expected to decrease. They interpret this evidence as an indication that managers tend to use dividends to pay out permanent cash flows and repurchases to pay out temporary cash flows. Consistent with this view, Guay and Harford (2000) report that cash-flow shocks preceding substantial dividend increases are significantly more permanent than cash-flow shocks preceding repurchases. In addition, postshock cash flows of dividend-increasing firms exhibit less reversion to preshock levels than do repurchasing firms.

The preceding studies imply that dividends and share repurchases are alternative means of distributing cash to shareholders. However, Guay and Harford (2000) do not directly address whether repurchases substitute for dividends. More recent studies provide evidence on this issue. For example, Fama and French (2001) show that their sample firms primarily undertake share repurchases that are already dividend payers. Consequently, their evidence implies that share repurchases during the period 1983–1998 primarily reflect an increase in the desired payout ratios of dividend payers. In other words, the main effect of repurchases is to increase the cash payouts of dividend payers and not to replace dividends as the form of payout.

Of course, repurchases do not have to replace dividends completely as the form of corporate payout. In recent years, repurchases may substitute for what otherwise would have been increases in dividend payouts. Grullon and Michaely (2002) provide some evidence that this might be the case. They conjecture that if firms are substituting repurchases for dividends, there should be a negative correlation between dividend-forecast errors (actual minus expected dividends) and share repurchase activity. Using Lintner's (1956) dividend model to generate expected future dividend payments, they report that dividend forecast errors are indeed negatively correlated with the share repurchase activity. Hence, as firms pay out greater amounts in the form of share buybacks, they are inclined to pay out less-than-expected amounts in the form of dividend payments. Grullon and Michaely also report that the market reaction surrounding the announcement of dividend decreases is significantly less negative for repurchasing firms than for nonrepurchasing firms, further supporting the idea that share repurchases and dividends are close substitutes. Investors seem to penalize a firm less for a dividend reduction when they perceive that a firm is substituting share repurchases for those dividends. On the basis of these findings, Grullon and Michaely conclude that corporations are substituting share repurchases for dividends.

More recently, Dittmar and Dittmar (2004) find that when permanent earnings increase, firms increase dividends only modestly while substantially increasing repurchases. However, when temporary earnings increase, firms use funds only to repurchase stock. Moreover, this pattern of behavior has strengthened over time. They report that the sensitivity of dividends to changes in permanent earnings fell by more than 75 percent after 1977. Apparently, firms are increasingly using repurchases to pay out a set of earnings that they have historically paid out as dividends.

Finally, Skinner (2007) extends the findings of Grullon and Michaely (2002) by analyzing the evolution of the relationship among earnings, dividends, and repurchases at both the aggregate level and the firm level. He documents an increasingly strong relationship between repurchases and earnings, manifested in a faster speed of adjustment of repurchases to earnings. In other words, the link between repurchases and earnings has strengthened over time in a manner suggesting that repurchases are replacing dividends. This result holds for those large, mature, and profitable firms that continue to pay dividends but now also make regular repurchases, as well as for firms that only make repurchases. The former group's dividend policies become increasingly conservative while repurchases increasingly absorb the variation in earnings, indicating that the overall relationship between the firms' earnings and total payout (dividends plus repurchases) is strong. As documented in Figure 4.1, over the period 1971–2005 for firms that both pay dividends and repurchase shares, aggregate dividends increased steadily and were largely independent of the variations in earnings. By contrast, repurchases have become increasingly closely tied with earnings.

Thus, U.S. firms increasingly appear to use share repurchases as a substitute form of payout to shareholders. This behavior is in contrast to much of the rest of the world, where share repurchases are far less common, as Denis and Osobov (2008) note.

CONCLUSIONS

Our discussion highlights numerous empirical determinants of corporate dividend payments. To varying degrees, academic research has documented support for the arguments that dividends are associated with several firm characteristics such as size, profitability, growth opportunities, maturity, leverage, equity ownership, and incentive compensation. There is also an association between dividends and characteristics of the market in which the firm operates, such as tax laws, investor protection, product market competition, investor sentiment, and public or private status, as well as the availability of substitute forms of corporate payout, primarily, share repurchases. These findings have several implications for theories of corporate dividends.

First, the fact that dividends are so strongly associated with firm size, maturity, and profitability casts doubt on information signaling as a first-order determinant of dividends. Presumably, firms most in need of signaling private information

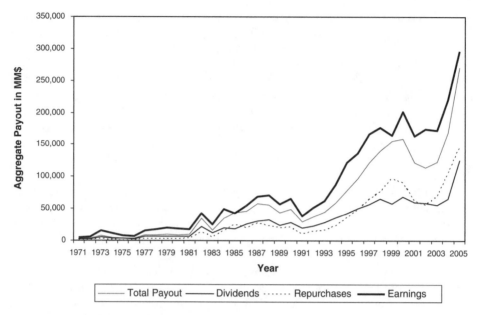

Figure 4.1   The Evolving Relationship between Earnings and Repurchase for Firms that Repurchase and Pay Dividends

This figure reports the dollar magnitude of total payouts, dividends, share repurchases and earnings for firms from the CRSP/Compustat merged database (excluding financials and utilities) that are incorporated in the United States; traded on NYSE, AMEX, or NASDAQ; have securities with CRSP share codes equal to 10 or 11 (ordinary common shares) as of the last trading month of each fiscal year in question; are not missing values for earnings before extraordinary and special items; and have positive values for both dividends and share repurchases for a given year. All dollar amounts are expressed in millions.

would be young, small firms that are less profitable. However, the opposite types of firms (large, mature, and profitable) are the primary dividend payers.

Second, although taxes appear to play some role in corporate payout policies and investment decisions of investors, taxes do not seem to be a first-order determinant of dividend policies in that wealthy taxable investors receive a large proportion of dividends paid in the United States. This would seem to cast doubt on theories of dividend policy that focus on tax-based clienteles.

To this point, the empirical determinants of dividends appear to be most consistent with agency cost–based theories of payout policy in that firms with the largest potential agency costs of free cash flow such as mature, profitable firms are the ones that pay the highest dividends. Explaining why firms might prefer dividends over share repurchases (and vice versa) and why they initiate dividend payout will require more refined versions of these theories.

REFERENCES

Allen, Franklin, and Roni Michaely. 2003. "Payout Policy." In *Handbook of the Economics of Finance*, ed. George Constantinides, Milton Harris, and René M. Stulz, 337–429. Amsterdam: Elsevier-North Holland.

Baker, Malcolm, and Jeffrey Wurgler. 2004a. "A Catering Theory of Dividends." *Journal of Finance* 59:3, 1125–1165.

Baker, Malcolm, and Jeffrey Wurgler. 2004b. "Appearing and Disappearing Dividends: The Link to Catering Incentives." *Journal of Financial Economics* 73:2, 271–288.

Benito, Andrew, and Garry Young. 2001. "Hard Times or Great Expectations? Dividend Omissions and Dividend Cuts by U.K. Firms." Working Paper, Bank of England.

DeAngelo, Harry, Linda DeAngelo, and Douglas J. Skinner. 2004. "Are Dividends Disappearing? Dividend Concentration and the Consolidation of Earnings." *Journal of Financial Economics* 72:3, 425–456.

DeAngelo, Harry, Linda DeAngelo, and René M. Stulz. 2006. "Dividend Policy and the Earned/Contributed Capital Mix: A Test of the Lifecycle Theory." *Journal of Financial Economics* 81:2, 227–254.

Denis, David J., and Igor Osobov. 2008. "Why Do Firms Pay Dividends? International Evidence on the Determinants of Dividend Policy." *Journal of Financial Economics* 89:1, 62–82.

Dittmar, Amy, and Robert Dittmar. 2004. "Stock Repurchase Waves: An Explanation of the Trends in Corporate Payout Policy." Working Paper, University of Michigan.

Easterbrook, Frank H. 1984. "Two Agency-Cost Explanations of Dividends." *American Economic Review* 74:4, 650–659.

Faccio, Mara, Larry H. P. Lang, and Leslie Young. 2001. "Dividends and Expropriation." *American Economic Review* 91:1, 54–78.

Fama, Eugene F., and Kenneth R. French. 2001. "Disappearing Dividends: Changing Firm Characteristics or Lower Propensity to Pay?" *Journal of Financial Economics* 60:1, 3–43.

Fama, Eugene F., and Kenneth R. French. 2004. "New Lists: Fundamentals and Survival Rates." *Journal of Financial Economics* 73:2, 229–269.

Fenn, George W., and Nellie Liang. 2001. "Corporate Payout Policy and Managerial Stock Incentives." *Journal of Financial Economics* 60:1, 45–72.

Ferris, Stephen P., Nilanjan Sen, and Ho P. Yui. 2006. "God Save the Queen and Her Dividends: Corporate Payouts in the United Kingdom." *Journal of Business* 79:3, 1149–1173.

Gaver, Jennifer, and Kenneth Gaver. 1993. "Additional Evidence on the Association between the Investment Opportunity Set and Corporate Financing, Dividend, and Compensation Policies." *Journal of Accounting and Economics* 16:1–3, 125–160.

Graham, John R. 2003. "Taxes and Corporate Finance: A Review." *Review of Financial Studies* 16:4, 1075–1129.

Grinstein, Yaniv, and Roni Michaely. 2005. "Institutional Holdings and Payout Policy." *Journal of Finance* 60:3, 1389–1426.

Grullon, Gustavo, and Roni Michaely. 2002. "Dividends, Share Repurchases, and the Substitution Hypothesis." *Journal of Finance* 57:4, 1649–1684.

Grullon, Gustavo, and Roni Michaely. 2007. "Corporate Payout Policy and Product Market Competition." Working Paper, Cornell University.

Grullon, Gustavo, Roni Michaely, and Bhaskaran Swaminathan. 2002. "Are Dividend Changes a Sign of Firm Maturity?" *Journal of Business* 75:3, 387–424.

Guay, Wayne, and Jarrad Harford. 2000. "The Cash-Flow Permanence and Information Content of Dividends versus Repurchases." *Journal of Financial Economics* 57:3, 385–415.

Hoberg, Gerard, and Nagpurnanand R. Prabhala. 2006. "Dividend Policy, Risk and Catering." Working Paper, University of Maryland.

Jagannathan, Murali, Clifford Stephens, and Michael Weisbach. 2000. "Financial Flexibility and the Choice between Dividends and Stock Repurchases." *Journal of Financial Economics* 57:3, 355–384.

Kalay, Avner. 1982. "Stockholder-Bondholder Conflict and Dividend Constraint." *Journal of Financial Economics* 10:2, 211–233.

La Porta, Rafael, Florencio Lopez-de-Silanes, Andrei Shleifer, and Robert W. Vishny. 2000. "Agency Problems and Dividend Policies around the World." *Journal of Finance* 55:1, 1–33.

Li, Wei, and Erik Lie. 2006. "Dividend Changes and Catering Incentives." *Journal of Financial Economics* 80:2, 293–308.

Lie, Erik, and Heidi J. Lie. 1999. "The Role of Personal Taxes in Corporate Decisions: An Empirical Analysis of Share Repurchases and Dividends." *Journal of Financial and Quantitative Analysis* 34:4, 533–552.

Lintner, John. 1956. "Distribution of Incomes of Corporations among Dividends, Retained Earnings, and Taxes." *American Economic Review* 46:2, 97–118.

Michaely, Roni, and Michael R. Roberts. 2007. "Corporate Dividend Policies: Lessons from Private Firms." Working Paper, University of Pennsylvania.

Miller, Merton H., and Franco Modigliani. 1961. "Dividend Policy, Growth, and the Valuation of Shares." *Journal of Business* 34:4, 411–433.

Perez-Gonzalez, Francisco. 2003. "Large Shareholders and Dividends: Evidence from U.S. Tax Reforms." Working Paper, Columbia University.

Poterba, James, and Lawrence H. Summers. 1984. "New Evidence that Taxes Affect the Valuation of Dividends." *Journal of Finance* 39:5, 1397–1415.

Renneboog, Luc, and Grzegorz Trojanowski. 2005. "Patterns in Payout Policy and Payout Channel Choice of U.K. Firms in the 1990s." Working Paper, European Corporate Governance Institute.

Rozeff, Michael. 1982. "Growth, Beta, and Agency Costs as Determinants of Dividend Payout Ratios." *Journal of Financial Research* 5:3, 249–259.

Scholz, John K. 1992. "A Direct Examination of the Dividend Clientele Hypothesis." *Journal of Public Economics* 49:3, 261–285.

Skinner, Douglas. 2007. "The Evolving Relation between Earnings, Dividends, and Stock Repurchases." *Journal of Financial Economics* 87:3, 582–609.

Smith, Clifford W., and Jerold B. Warner. 1979. "On Financial Contracting: An Analysis of Bond Covenants." *Journal of Financial Economics* 7:2, 117–161.

Smith, Clifford W., and Ross L. Watts. 1992. "The Investment Opportunity Set and Corporate Financing, Dividend, and Compensation Policies." *Journal of Financial Economics* 32:3, 263–292.

von Eije, J. Henk, and William L. Megginson. 2008. "Dividends and Share Repurchases in the European Union." *Journal of Financial Economics* 89:2, 347–374.

ABOUT THE AUTHORS

David Denis is the Burton Morgan Chair of Private Enterprise at the Krannert School of Management, Purdue University. He earned a BS in finance and managerial statistics from Syracuse University in 1982, an MBA from the University of Michigan in 1984, and a Ph.D. in finance from the University of Michigan in 1988. He is the author of more than 40 published articles in leading peer-reviewed journals on topics related to corporate governance, corporate financial policies, corporate organizational structure, corporate valuation, and entrepreneurial finance. Denis has also coedited a book on corporate restructuring. He currently serves as coeditor of *Journal of Corporate Finance* and as Associate Editor of *Journal of Financial Research, Financial Review, Annals of Finance,* and *Journal of Applied Finance.* Denis served as Associate Editor of *Journal of Finance* from 2001 to 2003 and is currently a member of the board of directors of Financial Management Association International.

Gohar Stepanyan is a Ph.D. candidate in finance, currently holding the Bilsland Dissertation Fellowship from Purdue University Graduate School. She graduated with distinction from the Yerevan Institute of Architecture and Construction, Armenia, and received an MBA from the David Eccles School of Business at the University of Utah. While studying in Utah, she was a recipient of a prestigious Edmund S. Muskie Graduate Fellowship, a program of the Bureau of Educational and Cultural Affairs of the U.S. Department of State, established by the U.S. Congress in 1992 for students from Eurasia. In Armenia, Stepanyan worked for the Ministry of Finance and Economy, in the private sector, and in a nonprofit international organization. In the United States, as a master's student, she had a summer internship with American Express. Since 2006, Stepanyan has been an active member of the Financial Management Association, serving on the Program Committee, discussing and presenting papers, and chairing sessions.

CHAPTER 5

Cross-Country Determinants of Payout Policy: European Firms

FRANCK BANCEL
Professor of Finance, ESCP-EAP, Paris

NALINAKSHA BHATTACHARYYA
Associate Professor, University of Alaska, Anchorage

USHA R. MITTOO
Bank of Montreal Professor of Finance, University of Manitoba

INTRODUCTION

Dividend policy has been an enigma for finance researchers. More than three decades ago, Black (1976, p. 5) wrote, "The harder we look at the dividend picture, the more it seems like a puzzle, with pieces that just don't fit together." Twenty years later Allen and Michaely (1995, p. 833) drew the following conclusion: "Much more empirical and theoretical research on the subject of dividends is required before a consensus can be reached." In the twenty-first century, Brealey and Myers (2002) echo this conclusion when they include the dividend puzzle as one of the top ten puzzles in finance. Academic endeavors addressing the dividend puzzle follow one of two paths—theoretical and empirical.

The development of the theory underlying dividend policy started with Miller and Modigliani (1961) (hereafter MM) when they posited their famous dividend irrelevance theorem. The MM theorem states that in a perfect capital market with a given investment program, dividend policy is irrelevant in determining the value of the firm. Theoretical researchers since MM have examined market imperfections and developed different paradigms for dividend policy. The different explanations of dividend policy include, but are not limited to, the following:

- Clientele hypothesis (Miller and Modigliani, 1961; Allen, Bernardo, and Welch, 2000)
- Signaling theory (Heinkel, 1978; Bhattacharya, 1979; John and Williams, 1985; Miller and Rock, 1985; Ambarish, John, and Williams, 1987; Williams, 1988)
- Free cash flow hypothesis (Easterbrook, 1984; Jensen, 1986)
- Catering theory of dividends (Baker and Wurgler, 2004)
- Screening model of dividends (Bhattacharyya, 2007)

Empirical modeling of dividend policy started with Lintner (1956), who proposed a dividend adjustment model based on a survey. Since then, empirical researchers have relied on either archival data (e.g., DeAngelo, DeAngelo, and Skinner, 1992; Denis, Denis, and Sarin, 1994; Bar-Yosef, Callen, and Livnat, 1996; DeAngelo and DeAngelo, 2000; Bernhardt, Douglas, and Robertson, 2005) or survey data (e.g., Baker and Powell, 1999, 2000; Brav, Graham, Harvey, and Michaely, 2005; Bancel, Bhattacharyya, and Mittoo, 2006). Other chapters in this book deal with different aspects of the dividend puzzle in detail.

Most research in dividend policy involves the North American financial markets and their associated regulatory environment. By contrast, this chapter focuses on dividend policies of European firms and other legal and regulatory regimes. As such, this chapter provides better insights into the economic motivations underlying dividends and a more holistic understanding of the dividend puzzle.

The chapter begins by examining the evolution of dividend policy to determine whether the key trends identified in the United States, such as the declining fraction of dividend payers and the concentration of dividends among large firms, also occur in Europe. Next, the chapter examines the major determinants of European payout policy, drawing largely from Bancel et al. (2006).

DIVIDEND POLICIES OF EUROPEAN FIRMS

Distinctive Features of European Corporate Governance

The first major study examining dividend policies of countries around the world is by La Porta, Lopez-de-Silanes, Shleifer, and Vishny (2000). According to their agency theory model, dividends exist to overcome agency problems because investors in countries with good legal protection use their legal standing to extract dividends from firms, especially when reinvestment opportunities are poor. They find that dividend payouts are economically and statistically significantly higher in common law countries, where investor protection is typically better than in civil law countries.

Several authors also show that corporate governance issues are key determinants of firms' dividend policies. European corporate governance has several features that are distinctive from the practices in North America and may affect the dividend policies of European companies. First, shareholder concentration is much higher in Europe than in the United States. Becht and Roell (1999, p. 1051) report, "The most striking fact about block holdings in Europe is that they are so much higher than in the [United States]." The relatively large block holdings in Europe imply that, in addition to other issues of corporate governance, European firms might have a different source of agency conflict, namely, between large block holders and small block holders (Gugler and Yurtoglu, 2003). Second, European workers and European banks have a much greater voice in corporate governance than do their American counterparts (Cunningham, 1999). Third, some European countries, such as Greece, have a mandatory dividend requirement (La Porta et al. 2000).

These environmental differences mean that conclusions drawn from studies of dividend policies of North American companies may not capture the European reality. For example, Goergen, Renneboog, and Correia da Silva (2005) find that German firms have a more flexible dividend policy than do their American counterparts. They also report that firms controlled by banks are more willing to omit dividends than are firms controlled by other shareholders. Similarly, Gugler (2003) finds a relation between dividend policy and corporate governance. The differences in institutional structure of corporate governance motivate the need for a separate study of dividend policies of European firms.

Trends in European Dividend Policy

This section examines the evolution of European dividend policies from 1994 to 2006 and compares the payout patterns across different countries and industries. This investigation also examines whether the key trends identified in recent U.S. studies, including a declining fraction of dividend payers (Fama and French, 2001), concentration of dividends among few firms (DeAngelo, DeAngelo, and Skinner, 2004), and a return of dividends in recent years (Julio and Ikenberry, 2005), occur in Europe.

The dividend policies examined represent European firms belonging to the European large index in Datastream over the period 1994–2006. This sample permits cross-country comparisons by minimizing firm-specific differences, such as firm size and liquidity, which influence dividend policies. The sample also includes utility and financial firms because the U.S. evidence shows that these sectors, unlike industrial firms, exhibit increasing propensity to pay dividends (DeAngelo et al., 2004).

A total of 2,036 listed companies from 22 European countries constitute the European large index of Datastream in 2006. The number of sample firms increases steadily over time, reflecting the rising number of new European listings. The number of sample firms rises from 1,106 in 1994 to 1,464 in 1997, 1,754 in 2000, and 1,923 in 2003. Other information collected from Datastream includes the number of firms paying dividends, payout ratios, sectors, market value of equity, and country of origin.

Table 5.1 shows the geographical distribution of the sample firms in 2006. The United Kingdom represents the greatest proportion of firms (21.6 percent), followed by Germany (11.8 percent), France (8.2 percent), Italy (7.8 percent), Switzerland (7.2 percent), and the Netherlands (5.7 percent). Another five civil law countries (Belgium, Spain, Greece, Portugal, and Turkey) represent about 17 percent of the sample. The Scandinavian countries (Denmark, Finland, Norway, and Sweden) account for 10 percent of the sample. The four Eastern European countries (Czech Republic, Hungary, Poland, and Russian Federation) account for about 6 percent of the sample. The three other countries (Austria, Luxembourg, and Ireland) account for about 5 percent of the sample.

FRACTION OF DIVIDEND-PAYING FIRMS

Table 5.2 reports the percentage of sample firms that pay dividends and shows a steady decline in the fraction of dividend-paying firms over time. The fraction of dividend payers falls from 85.5 percent in 1994 to 73.0 percent in 2003, and then rises to 77.4 percent in 2006. The number of dividend-paying firms increases from 2003 to 2006. This return of dividend pattern is similar to that which Julio and Ikenberry (2005) document. They show that the fraction of U.S. industrial firms paying dividends increased by 5 percent since 2001. However, the increase in Europe may be linked to the strong economic conditions and higher average profitability

Table 5.1   Firms by Country of Origin (Year 2006)

Country	Number of Firms	Percentage
Austria	43	2.1
Belgium	83	4.1
Czech Republic	16	0.8
Denmark	46	2.3
Finland	49	2.4
France	167	8.2
Germany	241	11.8
Greece	50	2.5
Hungary	24	1.2
Ireland	39	1.9
Italy	158	7.8
Luxembourg	28	1.4
Netherlands	116	5.7
Norway	41	2.0
Poland	47	2.3
Portugal	48	2.4
Russian Federation	30	1.5
Spain	112	5.5
Sweden	68	3.3
Switzerland	147	7.2
Turkey	44	2.2
United Kingdom	439	21.6
Total	2,036	100.0

Notes: Table 5.1 presents the geographical distribution of the sample firms in 2006 used to examine the evolution of the European dividend firm policies from 1994 to 2006.

of European firms in 2005 and 2006. Thus, whether this reappearance of dividends translates into a new dividend trend or is only a temporary effect is unclear.

Figure 5.1 presents the fraction of dividend payers for the six largest countries in the sample (United Kingdom, Germany, France, Italy, Switzerland, and the Netherlands). Each of the six countries exhibits a declining fraction of dividend payers, although some differences exist across countries. The United Kingdom shows a continuously declining trend during this period, from 91.4 percent in 1994 to 72.7 percent in 2006. The Netherlands has the sharpest decline, from 91.1 percent in 1994 to 70.6 percent in 2003, but that increases to 75.4 percent in 2006. Italy reveals a rising trend in dividends from 1994 (71.3 percent) to 2006 (86.1 percent), except for a dip to 70.9 percent in 2003.

Table 5.2   Dividend-Paying Firms in Europe (%)

Type of Firm	1994	1997	2000	2003	2006
Nonpaying	14.5	16.1	21.3	27.0	22.6
Paying	85.5	83.9	78.7	73.0	77.4

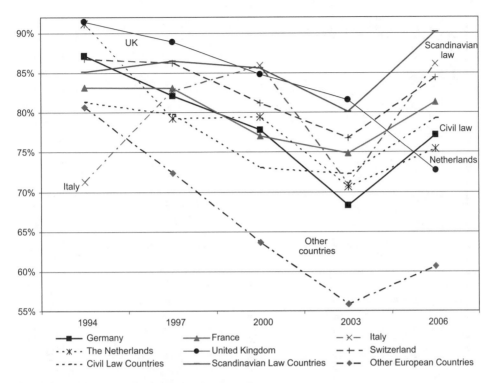

Figure 5.1   Percentage of Dividend-Paying Firms

Figure 5.1 presents the fraction of dividend payers for the six largest countries in the sample (the United Kingdom, Germany, France, Italy, Switzerland, and the Netherlands), for other civil law countries, for Scandinavian law countries, and for other European countries.

Figure 5.1 also compares the propensity to pay for the remaining countries, which are divided into three broad groups. The other civil law countries (Belgium, Spain, Greece, Portugal, and Turkey) reveal a similar trend: a decline in the dividend-paying firms from more than 81.3 percent in 1994 to 72.2 percent in 2003, and a rise to 79.2 percent in 2006. The Scandinavian countries (Denmark, Finland, Norway, and Sweden) show a slightly rising trend in dividend-paying firms, from 85.2 percent in 1994 to 90.1 percent in 2006, except for a dip to 80.1 percent in 2003. The remaining seven countries grouped together as "other" European countries (Ireland, Luxembourg, Austria, Czech Republic, Hungary, Poland, and Russian Federation) experience the steepest decline, from 80.6 percent to 55.9 percent in 2003. The newly listed firms in the Eastern European countries could explain this decline because they form more than half of this subsample. Overall, the European evidence is consistent with the U.S. evidence in Fama and French (2001) that the fraction of dividend-paying firms has declined through time.

Payout Ratios by Country

Table 5.3 presents average dividend payouts for each country in 1994, 1997, 2000, 2003, and 2006 for all sample firms and dividend payers. Average payouts for both groups remain relatively stable between 1994 and 2006 (35.1 percent and

Table 5.3 Average Dividend Payouts by Country (%)

Country	1994 All Firms	1994 Paying Firms	1997 All Firms	1997 Paying Firms	2000 All Firms	2000 Paying Firms	2003 All Firms	2003 Paying Firms	2006 All Firms	2006 Paying Firms	1994–2006 All Firms	1994–2006 Paying Firms
Czech Republic	—	—	17.8	53.3	16.7	38.3	35.7	81.5	34.5	78.8	26.2	63.0
Finland	26.3	30.0	34.2	38.0	49.5	49.5	59.1	64.7	57.1	57.1	45.2	47.8
Greece	51.5	51.5	41.7	46.2	36.7	41.3	41.3	48.4	39.3	45.7	42.1	46.6
Netherlands	40.7	44.6	35.4	44.4	33.2	41.7	38.8	54.5	34.7	45.7	36.6	46.2
Italy	33.3	46.8	36.1	43.6	39.2	45.6	36.2	51.1	37.7	43.8	36.5	46.2
Luxembourg	40.9	51.1	33.9	42.9	35.5	48.0	28.3	46.6	28.1	39.3	33.3	45.6
Turkey	42.8	45.5	42.3	50.7	32.3	58.2	16.9	28.4	32.4	39.4	33.3	44.4
Germany	41.8	47.9	36.6	44.6	34.6	44.4	30.9	45.3	30.6	39.6	34.9	44.4
Portugal	29.9	38.9	38.7	50.6	27.7	48.7	20.3	41.4	21.8	38.8	27.7	43.7
Belgium	46.7	50.7	29.6	36.4	32.9	38.9	40.1	48.2	35.5	41.5	37.0	43.1
Hungary	25.9	64.8	18.6	27.9	21.3	37.7	15.6	37.4	19.3	42.0	20.1	42.0
Austria	51.5	60.6	33.6	40.9	27.8	33.9	27.9	39.8	22.0	32.7	32.6	41.6
Sweden	33.1	36.5	33.7	37.6	32.5	37.2	45.7	52.8	40.0	41.9	37.0	41.2
Spain	32.8	48.5	29.3	39.1	27.2	38.2	27.1	36.9	30.3	37.3	29.3	40.0
United Kingdom	35.2	38.5	32.5	36.5	33.4	39.4	34.0	41.7	31.5	43.4	33.3	39.9
France	32.0	38.5	29.6	35.6	25.6	33.5	30.3	41.1	29.6	36.9	29.4	37.1
Poland	21.5	21.5	13.9	21.9	10.7	26.7	16.8	50.3	28.3	55.5	18.2	35.2
Norway	20.5	26.9	19.0	27.0	23.4	35.6	25.9	47.0	28.3	38.6	23.4	35.0
Switzerland	30.1	34.7	26.9	31.2	23.5	28.9	28.3	36.9	30.0	35.6	27.8	33.5
Ireland	25.3	30.6	20.2	26.6	21.1	30.8	19.6	32.7	18.5	32.8	20.9	30.7
Denmark	19.1	23.6	20.2	22.6	24.6	30.2	21.6	27.6	26.2	31.7	22.3	27.1
Russian Federation	—	—	14.6	16.7	7.4	9.6	23.0	27.4	22.5	25.9	16.9	19.9
Total	35.1	41.1	31.8	38.2	30.8	39.1	32.0	43.9	31.8	41.0	30.2	40.1

Notes: Table 5.3 presents the dividend payouts for all sample firms and dividend-paying firms by country from 1994 to 2006. The right-most column presents the average payout ratios for all firms and dividend-paying firms. The listing of the countries is from the highest to the lowest dividend-paying firms over the period from 1994 to 2006.

31.8 percent for all firms, and 41.1 percent and 41.0 percent for dividend-paying firms, respectively). The average payouts for dividend-paying firms tend to be similar across large European countries varying between 37.1 percent and 46.2 percent. However, the payouts differ substantially across other countries from a low of 16.9 percent (Russia) to a high of 45.2 percent (Finland) for all firms. Among dividend payers, the Czech Republic and Finland have higher average payouts (63.0 percent and 47.8 percent, respectively), whereas Russian firms have the lowest average payout (19.9 percent for 1997 to 2006). The trends in dividend payouts also vary substantially across countries. For example, Germany shows a continuous decline in payouts (all firms), from 41.8 percent in 1994 to 30.6 percent in 2006, whereas Finland exhibits a steep rising trend, from less than 26.3 percent in 1994 to 59.1 percent in 2003, retreating to 57.1 percent in 2006.

Figure 5.2 compares the average payout ratios for the dividend payers across the six largest countries in the sample. The U.K. firms show a slightly upward trend in payout ratios over time, from 38.5 percent in 1994 to 43.4 percent in 2006, despite the declining fractions of dividend payers noted in Figure 5.1. The German firms, on the other hand, show continuously declining payout ratios, from 47.9 percent in 1994 to 39.6 percent in 2006. Switzerland has the lowest average payout ratio among the six countries (33.5 percent), with little variation through time. The other civil law countries and European countries also exhibit a declining

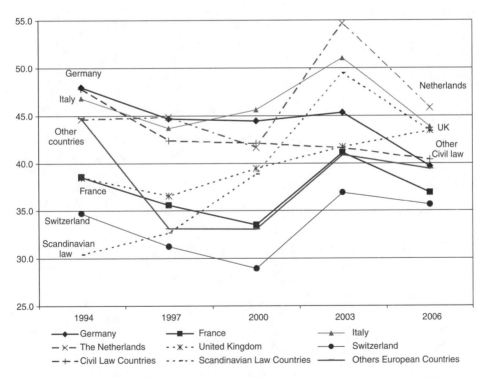

Figure 5.2 Average Dividend Payouts for Dividend-Paying Firms by Country (%)
Figure 5.2 compares the average payouts for the dividend payers across the six largest countries in the sample (United Kingdom, Germany, France, Italy, Switzerland, and the Netherlands), for other civil law countries, for Scandinavian law countries, and for other European countries.

trend of payout ratios, whereas the Scandinavian countries show an increasing trend, from 30.4 percent in 1994 to 43.3 percent in 2006.

Several factors could explain these differences between European countries, such as shareholding structures or firms' sector specializations, which may vary across countries, or some bias linked to the country size. Payout ratios are also cyclical and change according to economic conditions. For example, payout ratios for dividend-paying firms peaked in 2003 (43.9 percent) rather than in 2000 (39.1 percent) or 2006 (41.0 percent), reflecting the natural rise of payout ratios in recessionary periods (2001 and 2002) and fall in periods of strong economic conditions (2004 and 2005).

Payout Ratios by Industry

Table 5.4 presents the dividend payouts for all sample firms by sectors. As expected, the payouts differ substantially across sectors, varying from a low of 4.0 percent (equity investment instruments) to a high of 54.4 percent (tobacco) in 2006. Tobacco (average payout of 60.5 percent between 1994 and 2006) and utility firms (electricity and gas, water, and multiple utilities' average payout was 47.5 percent and 45.7 percent, respectively) have the highest dividend payouts. These firms generate considerable cash flows and do not need to reinvest in their business relative to other industrial companies. On the opposite extreme, high-tech firms such as software and computer services firms (16.1 percent), technology and hardware equipment firms (16.5 percent), and pharmaceutical and biotechnology firms (20.0 percent) have the lowest payouts. These firms invest a large part of their cash flows in research and development or other assets. Many of these firms are also initial-public-offering firms that do not pay dividends (DeAngelo, DeAngelo, and Stulz, 2006). As Correia da Silva, Goergen, and Renneboog (2004) note, some evidence indicates that firms in cyclical industries have lower average payouts, such as the automobile (28.6 percent) or oil equipment and service (25.4 percent) sectors.

Figure 5.3 presents the payout patterns for dividend-paying firms across industries from 1994 to 2006. This figure indicates the influence of economic and market conditions as well as changing characteristics of listed firms on dividend payouts. Most sectors show a decline in payouts from 1994 to 2000, a sharp increase in 2003, and a decline in 2006. The dividend ratios for most sectors peak in 2003, which is similar to the trend observed for country payout ratios, indicating the effect of the recessionary period in 2001 and 2002. The utility firms show a steady payout ratio of 48 percent with little variation over time. The telecommunications and oil and gas sectors, on the other hand, exhibit much higher volatility in payouts. For example, dividend payouts for telecommunications declined from 50.7 percent in 1994 to 33.1 percent in 2000 at the height of the dot-com bubble, and then rose to 40.8 percent and 56.9 percent in 2003 and 2006, respectively. The payouts for technology firms also remained at about 30 percent until 2000, and then increased to about 41 percent in 2003 and 2006.

Payout Ratios by Firm Size

Large firms generally have easy access to capital markets and should be less concerned about retained earnings to finance investments. Moreover, large firms also

Table 5.4   Average Dividend Payouts by Industry for All Sample Firms

Sectors	Average Dividend Payouts (%)					
	1994	1997	2000	2003	2006	1994–2006
Tobacco	61.0	71.3	51.1	64.8	54.4	60.5
Electricity	53.9	45.2	50.4	45.1	42.8	47.5
Gas, water, and multiple utilities	43.0	39.2	40.0	53.7	52.4	45.7
Life insurance	47.3	38.0	50.1	47.3	45.3	45.6
Real estate	49.6	44.9	42.5	42.6	28.2	41.6
General retailers	44.7	36.3	41.2	41.4	42.8	41.3
Food and drug retailers	39.6	40.8	38.7	40.4	44.7	40.8
Banks	43.4	36.8	33.4	37.4	36.2	37.4
General financial	41.6	32.3	33.2	43.2	35.7	37.2
Non–life insurance	36.8	37.5	41.9	33.4	36.0	37.1
Media	37.7	33.8	35.4	33.9	42.3	36.6
Aerospace and defense	44.0	31.8	31.5	40.2	34.9	36.5
Industrial transportation	32.8	34.2	35.2	39.4	40.7	36.5
Support services	38.6	38.0	30.8	40.5	34.0	36.4
Beverages	38.2	40.4	32.9	31.5	34.7	35.5
General industrials	32.8	28.6	41.6	40.6	31.7	35.0
Construction and materials	33.5	35.3	33.4	33.7	32.9	33.8
Industrial engineering	33.2	32.4	34.9	34.2	32.6	33.5
Chemicals	39.8	34.2	29.0	30.4	31.4	33.0
Food producers	34.9	29.3	31.4	32.5	34.1	32.4
Mobile telecommunications	42.8	31.5	19.0	28.2	38.0	31.9
Personal goods	30.9	32.4	34.4	28.9	32.0	31.7
Household goods	40.6	32.5	29.3	23.8	31.1	31.5
Electronics and electrical equipment	33.7	32.2	30.1	28.4	32.6	31.4
Industrial metals	28.6	27.7	31.8	35.4	32.6	31.2
Forestry and paper	21.4	30.8	27.9	36.4	37.6	30.8
Fixed-line telecommunications	39.0	31.9	17.0	19.8	39.7	29.5
Travel and leisure	30.9	26.4	30.1	29.0	26.5	28.6
Automobiles and parts	33.1	29.3	31.5	22.1	26.7	28.6
Mining	27.3	24.4	30.5	29.8	21.3	26.7
Oil and gas producers	30.9	35.2	18.1	19.7	23.8	25.6
Oil equipment and services	27.2	18.8	21.8	31.0	28.1	25.4
Health-care equipment and services	32.8	30.7	16.3	26.1	20.4	25.3
Leisure goods	14.8	20.9	24.9	29.6	31.6	24.4
Pharmaceuticals and biotechnology	24.4	17.2	17.9	18.8	21.7	20.0
Technology hardware and equipment	20.5	19.0	12.8	14.1	15.9	16.5
Software and computer services	15.4	15.5	12.0	14.6	23.0	16.1
Equity investment instruments	4.9	4.3	5.8	4.8	4.0	4.8
Total	35.1	31.8	30.8	32.2	31.8	32.4

Note: Table 5.4 presents the dividend payout ratios for all sample firms by sectors from 1994 to 2006. The right-most column presents the average payouts arranged from highest to lowest.

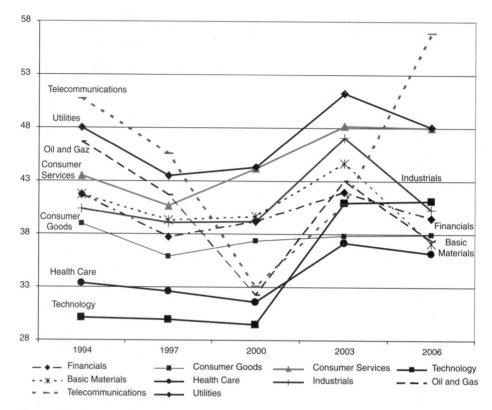

Figure 5.3 Average Dividend Payouts for Dividend-Paying Firms by Industry (%)
Figure 5.3 presents the payout patterns for dividend-paying firms across industries for the six largest countries from 1994 to 2006.

have institutional investors that may pressure management to pay dividends. Consequently, large firms should pay higher dividends. As shown in Table 5.5, the payout ratio is an increasing function of the firm size measured by its market capitalization. The sample firms with the largest market capitalization (10 billion euros and greater) have the highest average dividend payouts (39.7 percent), whereas firms with market capitalization of less than 250 million euros have the lowest

Table 5.5 Average Dividend Payouts by Firm Size (%)

Market Value 12/31/2006	Dividend Payouts in 2006 (%)
Greater than 10 billion euros	39.7
Between 1 billion euros and less than 10 billion euros	35.0
Between 250 million euros and less than 1 billion euros	28.6
Less than 250 million euros	22.1

Note: Table 5.5 presents the 2006 average payout ratios for all sample firms according to their size as estimated by the market value of equity.

dividend payouts (22.1 percent). This result is consistent with Correia da Silva et al. (2004) and von Eije and Megginson (2008) for Europe, who show that dividends are concentrated among a few profitable European companies. The evidence is also similar to U.S. data presented by DeAngelo et al. (2004).

Dividend Trends: Comparison of Europe and the United States

Von Eije and Megginson (2008) examine dividend policies between 1989 and 2003 of industrial firms from 15 European countries that were members of the European Union on May 2004. They also document a steady decrease in the fraction of European-listed companies paying dividends, from 91 percent in 1989 and 1990 to 62 percent in 2003. Furthermore, they show that the decline in dividend-paying firms started much later in Europe than in the United States (1990 versus 1952) but was more rapid once the trend started. Other evidence shows that dividends and earnings are concentrating as sharply among European as among American companies. In addition, firm characteristics such as size and asset growth, which explain the propensity to pay dividends in the United States, also influence both the propensity to pay and payouts in Europe.

According to von Eije and Megginson (2008), total nominal (real) dividends paid by EU-15 listed companies roughly tripled between 1994 and 1999, and then stabilized at between 82 billion and 100 billion euros per year between 2000 and 2003, largely due to the recession and stock market collapse after March 2000. They mainly attribute the sharp rise in dividends during the late 1990s to increased dividends paid by the original 974 dividend payers of 1989. Their rationale is consistent with that of DeAngelo et al. (2004), who find an increasing concentration of dividends among U.S. payers. Yet von Eije and Megginson do not find a significant correlation between the fraction of retained earnings in a European firm's total equity and dividend payout. This finding contrasts sharply with U.S. evidence documented by DeAngelo et al. (2006). Although their evidence suggests that companies with headquarters in a common law country are more likely to pay dividends, von Eije and Megginson find neither systematic dividend-catering effects in Europe nor conclusive evidence of a continent-wide convergence in dividend policy.

Denis and Osobov (2008) compare the payout policies of companies in six major countries (United States, United Kingdom, Canada, France, Germany, and Japan) using data from 1989 to 2002. They test the life cycle, signaling, clientele, and catering explanations by analyzing the concentration of dividend payments as well as the association between dividend premium and the propensity to pay dividends. Their findings cast doubt on signaling, clientele, and catering explanations for dividends but support agency cost-based life cycle theories.

EUROPEAN DIVIDEND POLICY: SURVEY OF MANAGERS

Surveys of managers provide a useful way to examine the theory and practice of dividend policy. The survey method complements other types of empirical studies because it allows researchers to directly ask questions about the implications and assumptions of different theories and to gather publicly unavailable data. In a seminal paper, Lintner (1956) developed a model based on a survey of U.S. managers. His model suggests that managers (1) are reluctant to cut dividends, (2) smooth dividends over time, and (3) tie dividend increases to the firm's long-term sustainable earnings. Since then, researchers have used managerial surveys to understand the determinants of firms' dividend decisions (e.g., Baker, Farrelly, and Edelman, 1985; Baker and Powell, 1999, 2000; Baker, Powell, and Veit, 2001, 2002). More recently, Brav et al. (2005) conducted a comprehensive survey of 384 U.S. chief financial officers (CFOs) to determine the key factors that drive dividend and share repurchase policies, and to examine different theories.

Bancel et al. (2006) survey managers from 16 European countries to examine cross-country determinants of payout policy. Their study draws largely from the Brav et al. (2005) survey but also includes several questions that may be relevant in the European context, such as questions about the firm's ownership concentration. Their initial sample consists of firms with daily trading information reported in the *Financial Time European Stock Exchange*. These firms represent different sectors and are typically part of a national stock market index or a European market index. The survey yielded 93 responses, representing an 8.2 percent response rate, which is comparable to other cross-country surveys. Using a five-point importance scale, Bancel et al. asked CFOs to rank the importance of different factors that might influence their firm's payout policy.

Tables 5.6 through 5.8 summarize the CFOs' responses on different questions. Column 1 reports the percentage of respondents considering a factor as important or very important. Column 2 provides the mean rating. Column 3 shows whether the mean rating is significantly different from zero on the basis of a t-test. For ease of comparison, Columns 4 and 5 provide the views of U.S. CFOs on these factors from Brav et al. (2005).

Dividend Policy

European managers strongly agree with the major implications of the Lintner (1956) model. As Panel A of Table 5.6 shows, an overwhelming majority of respondents (89.0 percent) consider stability and level of future earnings to be an important factor in dividend decisions (A2). In addition, 77.8 percent of the respondents consider a sustainable change in earnings as important (A1). This evidence is consistent with the results of Healy and Palepu (1988), who find that earnings increases (decreases) precede dividend initiations (omissions). About 68 percent of the managers surveyed express a desire to payout a given fraction in the long run (A3). As Panel C of Table 5.6 shows, maintaining consistency with the company's historical dividend policy is important to about 67 percent of the respondents (C16).

As Panel A of Table 5.7 indicates, most CFOs agree that their firms try to avoid reducing dividends (A2, 82.8 percent) and try to maintain a smooth dividend stream from year to year (A13, 77.4 percent). Respondents also agree with the statement that an optimal dividend policy would strike a balance between current dividends and future growth (A7, 78.2 percent). However, only 54.3 percent of CFOs agree with Lintner (1956) that firms have a target dividend payout ratio and work toward achieving that target (A14). While about 90 percent of the CFOs agree that their firms have some dividend target in mind, they use different dividend

Table 5.6 Managerial Views of Factors Influencing Dividend Policy Decisions

	Europe			U.S.	
	Important or Very Important (%)	Mean	H_0: Average Rating = 0	Important or Very Important (%)	Mean
Panel A. Capital structure and financing issues					
Stability and level of future earnings (A2).	89.0	1.36	***	70.7	0.90
A sustainable change in earnings (A1).	77.8	1.08	***	66.7	0.80
Desire to pay out a given fraction of earnings in the long run (A3).	68.5	0.85	***	59.4	0.09
Current degree of financial leverage (A6)	51.1	0.53	***	40.6	−0.58
Market price of our stock (if our stock is a good investment relative to its true value (A4).	36.3	0.24	***	35.1	0.00
Having extra cash/liquid assets relative to our desired cash holdings (A5).	28.1	0.19	**	30.2	−0.20
Panel B. Relation with shareholders					
The influence of our institutional shareholders (B8).	58.1	0.56	***	53.2	0.40
Attracting institutional investors because they monitor management decisions (B9).	50.5	0.49	***	32.9	−0.10
Need to keep minority shareholders happy (B10).	29.4	0.08			
Personal taxes our stockholders pay when receiving dividends (B7).	20.7	−0.08		21.4	−0.50
Panel C. Other					
Maintaining consistency with our historic dividend policy (C16).	67.4	0.83	***	84.8	1.20
The availability of good investment opportunities for our firm to pursue (C11).	59.8	0.71	***	47.4	0.20
The dividend policies of competitors or other companies in our industry (C13).	34.4	0.14		38.5	−0.20

(Continued)

Table 5.6   *(Continued)*

	Europe			U.S.	
	Important or Very Important (%)	Mean	H_0: Average Rating = 0	Important or Very Important (%)	Mean
Paying out to reduce cash, disciplining our firm to make efficient decisions (C14).	21.7	−0.05		12.6	−0.90
To pay dividends indicates to investors that we are running low on profitable investments (C12).	13.3	−0.18	**	18.2	−0.90
Contractual constraints such as dividend restrictions in debt contracts (C15).	7.9	−0.16	**	42.3	−0.26
Justify pay increases/decreases for workers (C17).	4.4	−0.24	***		
Our senior executives' compensation (C18).	3.3	−0.23	***		

Notes: Table 5.6 presents responses from managers about factors influencing dividend policy decisions using a five-point scale from 0 (not important) to 4 (very important). The table contains the overall mean as well as the percentage of respondents answering 3 and 4 (important and very important, respectively). $^*p < .10$, $^{**}p < .05$, and $^{***}p < .01$. U.S. data are from Brav et al. (2005).

targets, such as dividend per share (35 percent), growth in dividends per share (23 percent), and dividend yield (11 percent), which are not tabulated. Finally, most respondents from European firms do not agree with the prediction of the Lintner model that dividend changes follow a partial adjustment factor and lag behind earnings. As Panel A of Table 5.7 shows, 34.8 percent of the CFOs agree with the statement that "dividend changes generally lag behind earnings changes" represents their company's dividend decisions (A6).

Some support exists for the clientele effect suggested in several dividend models. Panel B of Table 5.6 shows that the majority of respondents agree that the influence of institutional investors is an important determinant of their dividend policy and that attracting institutional investors is important in their company's decision to pay dividends. This evidence is consistent with the variant of clientele paradigm suggested by Allen et al. (2000).

Tax issues do not seem to play a key role in the dividend policy for European managers. As Panel B of Table 5.6 shows, only 20.6 percent of the respondents consider that personal taxes of stockholders have a major influence on dividend policy (B7); 11.8 percent of respondents consider that the firm has to retain funds over paying dividends because of the way capital gains are taxed (Table 5.7, B20). As Panel A of Table 5.7 indicates, little support exists for signaling models, as few respondents (18.5 percent) agree with a signaling proposition that their firms pay dividends to show that they are strong enough to pass up some profitable

Table 5.7 Managerial Views on Issues Involving Dividend Policy

	Europe			U.S.	
	Important or Very Important (%)	Mean	H_0: Average Rating = 0	Important or Very Important (%)	Mean
Panel A. Dividend policy practices					
We try to avoid reducing dividends per share (A2).	82.8	1.22	***	94.0	1.60
An optimal dividend policy strikes a balance between current dividends and future growth that maximizes stock price (A7).	78.3	0.97	***	92.5	1.30
We try to maintain a smooth dividend stream from year-to-year (A13).	77.4	1.09	***	90.1	1.30
A firm should set a target dividend payout ratio and adjust its current payout toward the target (A14).	54.4	0.48	***	60.5	0.48
Dividends are as important now to the valuation of common stocks as they were 15 years ago (A3).	53.3	0.57	***	41.0	0.00
We make dividend decisions after our investment plans are determined (A1).	44.6	0.38	***	33.5	−0.20
Paying dividends is a priority (many financial decisions are secondary compared with dividends (A5).	44.1	0.25	**		
A firm's dividend policy generally affects its cost of capital (A8).	37.0	0.25	***	51.1	0.32
Dividend changes generally lag behind earnings changes (A6).	34.8	0.20	**	76.5	0.80
A firm should view cash dividends as a residual after financing desired investments from earnings (A9).	31.9	0.10		47.1	0.21
We pay dividends to show that our firm is strong enough to pass up some profitable investments (A12).	18.5	−0.05		4.2	−1.20
We use our dividend as a tool to attain a desired credit rating (A4).	7.7	−0.24	***	24.7	−0.40

(Continued)

Table 5.7   (*Continued*)

	Europe			U.S.	
	Important or Very Important (%)	Mean	H_0: Average Rating = 0	Important or Very Important (%)	Mean
Investment banks help us to determine our dividend policy (A10).	6.5	−0.14	**		
Dividend changes will have an impact on executive compensation (A11).	1.1	−0.28	***		
Panel B. Relation with investors					
Paying dividends makes a firm's stock less risky for shareholders (vs. retaining earnings) (B15).	60.2	0.56	***	36.5	0.00
Investors generally prefer cash dividends today to uncertain future price appreciation (B19).	53.8	0.49	***	17.2	−0.47
Investors invest in firms whose dividend policies complement their particular tax circumstances (B18).	26.9	0.10		40.1	0.23
We pay dividends so that minority shareholders may not feel aggrieved (B21).	15.2	−0.15	**		
We pay dividends to show that our stock is valuable enough that investors buy it even though we have to pay relatively costly dividend taxes (B20).	11.8	−0.16	**	17.1	−0.60
Investors prefer that a firm retain funds over paying dividends because of the way capital gains are taxed as compared with dividends (B17).	10.9	−0.17	**	24.1	−0.07
We simultaneously decide to increase dividends for shareholders and pay for workers (B16).	2.2	−0.25	***		

Notes: Managers are asked to give their opinions about issues involving dividend policy using a five-point scale from 0 (not important) to 4 (very important). The table contains the overall mean as well as the percentage of respondents who answered 3 and 4 (important and very important, respectively). $^*p < .10$, $^{**}p < .05$, and $^{***}p < .01$. U.S. data are from Brav et al. (2005).

investments (A12). Panel C of Table 5.6 also indicates that only 21.8 percent of respondents agree with the idea that that the purpose of dividends is to discipline the company and make efficient decisions (C14).

Share Repurchase Policy

Table 5.8 provides the CFOs' responses to questions about the factors influencing share repurchases. Most executives view repurchases as a tool for flexibility rather than as an alternative to dividends. About 90 percent of the respondents agree or strongly agree that the market price of the stock is the major factor in the repurchase decision (Q1). This evidence is consistent with the ability of managers to time the repurchases to take advantage of lower market prices as reported in Brockman and Chung (2001) and Ginglinger and Hamon (2003). In contrast, as Panel A of Table 5.6 indicates, only 36.3 percent of respondents view the market price of the stock as important in dividend policy (A4).

The next most important factor is the availability of investment opportunities for firms to pursue (Q2, 77.8 percent). About 64 percent of CFOs consider both merger and acquisitions strategy and having extra cash or liquid assets as factors influencing repurchase decisions (Q3 and Q6, respectively). Slightly more than half (52 percent) of the CFOs agree that increasing earnings per share is an important factor in repurchases (Q9). This corroborates earlier findings (Vafeas, Vlittis, Katranis, and Ockree, 2003; Hribar, Jenkins, and Johnson, 2004) that the desire to manage earnings often motivates share repurchase. Respondents view the stability of future earnings and sustainable change in earnings as major determinants of cash dividends as relatively less important for repurchases (Q4). Few managers consider that statements involving the influence of institutional shareholders, offsetting the dilutive effect of stock option plans, the personal tax of shareholders, reinforcing the control of major shareholders, and reducing cash have a major influence on the repurchase decisions (Q7, Q10, Q14, Q11, and Q8, respectively).

Comparison of European and U.S. Managers' Views

Tables 5.6 through 5.8 (Columns 1–5) provide a comparison of European and U.S. managers' views about the major determinants of payout policy. A major finding of Brav et al. (2005) is that firms spend much time on repurchases. They also document a decline in the number of firms that pay dividends, indicating that corporate payout policies have changed over the past 50 years.

Both European and U.S. CFOs identify stability and level of future earnings and reluctance to cut dividends as the most important determinants of dividend policy (Table 5.6, A2, and Table 5.7, A2). Although European firms engage in fewer repurchases than their U.S. counterparts (LaPorta et al., 2000; Rau and Vermaelen, 2002), the important factors governing share repurchase policy appear to be similar between the two groups, as shown in Table 5.8. European managers identify market price of stock and availability of good investment opportunities as the major determinants of their repurchase policy, which is similar to their U.S. peers (Table 5.8, Q1 and Q2). The tests for the equality of the paired relative rankings of all factors across the two groups show no significant difference, which supports the

Table 5.8   Managerial Views of Factors Influencing Repurchase Decisions

	Europe			U.S.	
	Important or Very Important (%)	Mean	H_0: Average Rating = 0	Important or Very Important (%)	Mean
Market price of our stock (if our stock is a good investment relative to its true value (Q1).	90.1	1.38	***	86.6	1.30
The availability of good investment opportunities for our firm to pursue (Q2).	77.8	1.14	***	79.6	1.10
Merger and acquisition strategy (external stocks for growth transactions) (Q3).	64.4	0.80	***	72.7	0.90
Having extra cash/liquid assets relative to our desired cash holdings (Q6).	64.0	0.75	***	60.6	0.60
Increasing earnings per share (Q9).	51.7	0.57	***	75.0	0.90
Stability of future earnings (Q4).	50.6	0.46	***	65.9	0.70
A sustainable change in earnings (Q5).	46.7	0.39	***	65.5	0.70
The influence of our institutional shareholders (Q7).	30.0	0.08		51.5	0.40
Offsetting the dilutionary effect of stock option plans or other stock programs (Q10).	29.2	0.19	**	67.1	0.80
Repurchasing shares to reduce cash, thereby disciplining our firm to make efficient decisions (Q8).	27.8	0.08		20.2	−0.60
The company wants to cancel share (Q15).	20.0	−0.02			
Repurchase shares is a better alternative than dividends to give cash to investors (Q13).	18.9	0.09			
Personal taxes of our stockholders (Q14).	14.4	−0.10		28.6	−0.30
A temporary change in earnings (Q12).	12.2	−0.18	**	34.7	−0.10
To reinforce the control of major shareholders (Q11).	8.9	−0.13	**		

Notes: Managers are asked to give their opinions about factors influencing repurchase decisions on a five-point scale from 0 (not important) to 4 (very important). This table contains the overall mean as well as the percentage of respondents that who 3 and 4 (important and very important, respectively). $^*p < .10$, $^{**}p < .05$, and $^{***}p < .01$. U.S. data are from Brav et al. (2005).

notion that European and U.S. managers use similar factors in determining their payout policy. The European managers' views provide some support for agency and clientele theories but less support for signaling theory similar to that in Brav et al. (2005).

European managers largely agree with the U.S. managers about the inertia and conservatism of dividend policy, as documented by Lintner (1956). Both groups agree that they try to maintain a smooth dividend stream from year to year and use a number of dividend targets (Table 5.7, A13 and A14). As Panel A of Table 5.7 shows, however, only 34.8 percent of the European managers agree that dividends changes lag behind earnings changes compared to 76.5 percent of the U.S. managers (A6).

European and U.S. managers also have different views on several other factors. European managers believe that dividends are a key element in the stock risk perception and that investors have a clear preference for immediate liquidity (60 percent and 54 percent, respectively, for Europe, versus 36 percent and 17 percent, respectively, for the United States; Table 5.7, B15 and B19). Moreover, contractual constraints, such as dividend restrictions in debt contracts, are an important factor for 42 percent of U.S. managers but for only 8 percent of European managers (Table 5.6, C15). European CFOs also differ with their U.S. peers about the importance of other determinants of repurchase policy. For instance, European CFOs view the usage of share repurchase programs for increasing earnings per share and overcoming the dilutive impact of stock option plans as relatively less important than do U.S. CFOs (75 percent and 67 percent, respectively, for U.S. managers, compared to 52 percent and 29 percent, respectively, for European managers; Table 5.8, Q9 and Q10). One potential explanation for this difference is that U.S. firms systematically cancel repurchase shares, but such cancellations do not typically occur for most European countries.

Bancel et al. (2006) document several cross-country variations in dividend policy that differences in legal systems cannot easily explain. For example, the managers in German-system countries express significantly less concern with cutting dividends than do their peers in civil law countries, despite having similar views on other implications of the Lintner (1956) model. This higher downward flexibility of German dividend policy is consistent with Goergen et al. (2005), who document that the occurrence of loss is a key determinant of German dividend policy and that the majority of dividend cuts and omissions by German firms are temporary. Differences in ownership structure could be the driving force. Because banks have a strong influence on corporate governance in Germany, German banks may use their influence over German companies to protect their creditor claims. Close monitoring of firms by banks in the German system reduces the usefulness of dividend policy as a bonding mechanism, thereby leading to more flexible dividends (Amihud and Murgia, 1997; Goergen et al., 2005).

Gugler (2003) investigates the relationship between different types of shareholders and dividend policies for Austrian firms. He finds that the flexibility of dividend policy varies with different types of shareholders. That is, state-controlled firms have the highest dividend payout and practice more dividend smoothing, whereas family-controlled firms do not smooth dividends.

Bancel et al. (2006) also show that Scandinavian managers are more concerned about the current degree of financial leverage than are their civil law peers. This evidence is consistent with Baker, Mukherjee, and Paskelian (2006), who report that, in addition to the Lintner (1956) factors, the current degree of financial leverage and liquidity constraints are important determinants of Norwegian dividend policy. As Tables 5.6 and 5.7 show, some differences exist between the European English-system CFOs and U.S. managers. For example, European managers rank factors such as current level of financial leverage and importance of dividends for stock valuation much higher than do their U.S. peers.

In summary, the survey evidence supports the notion that European and U.S. managers use similar factors in their dividend decisions. In addition, survey results document some cross-country differences that could be driven by differences in firm characteristics, such as firm size and ownership structure, and other country-specific institutional and regulatory environmental factors.

CONCLUSIONS

This chapter examines the evolution of European dividend policies and the cross-country determinants of these policies. The results reveal both common and distinct factors that explain dividend policies across countries. European firms exhibit a declining propensity to pay dividends and an increasing concentration of dividends in a few large firms in recent years, which are similar to those trends observed in the United States. The evidence also supports the conclusions of Fama and French (2001) in the United States that the decline is due to changing firm characteristics and a declining propensity to pay with changing characteristics of the listed companies.

Some cross-country differences also exist, such as an increasing trend in dividend-paying firms and payout ratios for Scandinavian firms and a steeper decline for German firms. Von Eije and Megginson (2008) find that dividend policies of European companies are similar in many ways to those of U.S. firms, but they do not find conclusive evidence of continent-wide convergence in dividend policy for 15 countries that are part of the European Union. They also find no significant correlation between the fraction of retained earnings in a European firm's total equity and dividend payout. This result contrasts sharply with U.S. evidence documented in DeAngelo et al. (2006). Von Eije and Megginson find no systematic effects of catering by EU companies, which also contradicts some U.S. evidence.

Bancel et al. (2006) find the factors driving European managers' views on dividend policy are similar to their U.S. peers as reported in Brav et al. (2005). European managers strongly agree with findings by Lintner (1956) that they smooth dividends and find them difficult to cut. The determinants of repurchase policy are also similar between European and U.S. managers. Some cross-country differences in managers' views are difficult to explain by legal systems and may reflect the influence of country or firm-specific factors. For example, the German managers are less concerned about cutting dividends than are their other civil law peers, which could reflect the strong influence of banks on corporate governance in Germany.

In summary, the European studies provide some reassuring evidence that the major factors influencing dividend policy are similar across countries. However, some country-specific differences exist, indicating that dividend policy is a complex interaction of the country's legal and institutional structure as well as firm characteristics such as ownership structure. Researchers need to conduct additional studies to better understand the cross-country determinants of dividend policy.

REFERENCES

Allen, Frank, Antonio E. Bernardo, and Ivo Welch. 2000. "A Theory of Dividends Based on Tax Clienteles." *Journal of Finance* 55:6, 2499–2536.

Allen, Frank, and Roni Michaely. 1995. "Dividend Policy." In *Handbooks in Operations Research and Management Science*, ed. Robert A. Jarrow, Vojislav Maksimovic, and William T. Ziemba, 793–837. Amsterdam: Elsevier.

Ambarish, Ramasastry, Kose John, and Joseph Williams. 1987. "Efficient Signalling with Dividends and Investments." *Journal of Finance* 42:2, 321–343.

Amihud, Yakov, and Maurizio Murgia. 1997. "Dividends, Taxes, and Signaling: Evidence from Germany." *Journal of Finance* 52:1, 397–408.

Baker, H. Kent, Gail E. Farrelly, and Richard B. Edelman. 1985. "A Survey of Management Views on Dividend Policy." *Financial Management* 14:3, 78–84.

Baker, H. Kent, Tarun K. Mukherjee, and Ohannes George Paskelian. 2006. "How Norwegian Managers View Dividend Policy." *Global Finance Journal* 17:1, 155–176.

Baker, H. Kent, and Gary E. Powell. 1999. "How Corporate Managers View Dividend Policy." *Quarterly Journal of Business and Economics* 38:2, 17–35.

Baker, H. Kent, and Gary E. Powell. 2000. "Determinants of Corporate Dividend Policy: A Survey of NYSE Firms." *Financial Practice and Education* 10:1, 29–40.

Baker, H. Kent, Gary E. Powell, and E. Theodore Veit. 2001. "Factors Influencing Dividend Policy Decisions of Nasdaq Firms." *Financial Review* 36:3, 19–38.

Baker, H. Kent, Gary E. Powell, and E. Theodore Veit. 2002. "Revisiting Managerial Perspectives on Dividend Policy." *Journal of Economics and Finance* 26:3, 267–283.

Baker, Malcolm, and Jeffrey Wurgler. 2004. "A Catering Theory of Dividends." *Journal of Finance* 59:3, 1125–1165.

Bancel, Franck, Nalinaksha Bhattacharyya, and Usha Mittoo. 2006. "Do Agency Problems Explain Cross-Country Variations in Payout Policy? European Evidence." Working Paper, University of Manitoba and ESCP-EAP.

Bar-Yosef, Sasson, Jeffrey Callen, and Joshua Livnat. 1996. "Modeling Dividends, Earnings, and Book Value Equity: An Empirical Investigation of the Ohlson Valuation Dynamics." *Review of Accounting Studies* 1:3, 207–224.

Becht, Marco, and Ailsa Roell. 1999. "Blockholdings in Europe: An International Comparison." *European Economic Review* 43:4–6, 1049–1056.

Bernhardt, Dan, Alan Douglas, and Fiona Robertson. 2005. "Testing Dividend Signaling Models." *Journal of Empirical Finance* 12:1, 77–98.

Bhattacharya, Sudipto. 1979. "Imperfect Information, Dividend Policy, and 'The Bird in the Hand' Fallacy." *Bell Journal of Economics* 10:1, 259–270.

Bhattacharyya, Nalinaksha. 2007. "Good Managers Invest More and Pay Less Dividends: A Model of Dividend Policy." *Advances in Financial Economics* 12, 91–117.

Black, Fischer. 1976. "The Dividend Puzzle." *Journal of Portfolio Management* 2:2, 5–8.

Brav, Alan, John Graham, Campbell R. Harvey, and Roni Michaely. 2005. "Payout Policy in the 21st Century." *Journal of Financial Economics* 77:3, 483–527.

Brealey, Richard A., and Stewart C. Myers. 2002. *Principles of Corporate Finance.* Boston: Irwin/McGraw-Hill.

Brockman, Paul, and Dennis Chung. 2001. "Managerial Timing and Corporate Liquidity: Evidence from Actual Share Repurchases." *Journal of Financial Economics* 61:3, 417–448.

Correia da Silva, Luis, Marc Goergen, and Luc Renneboog. 2004. *Dividend Policy and Corporate Governance.* Oxford: Oxford University Press.

Cunningham, Lawrence A. 1999. "Commonalities and Prescriptions in the Vertical Dimension of Global Corporate Governance." *Cornell Law Review* 84:5, 1133–1194.

DeAngelo, Harry, and Linda DeAngelo. 2000. "Controlling Stockholders and the Disciplinary Role of Corporate Payout Policy: A Study of the Times Mirror Company." *Journal of Financial Economics* 56:2, 153–207.

DeAngelo, Harry, Linda DeAngelo, and Douglas J. Skinner. 1992. "Dividends and Losses." *Journal of Finance* 47:5, 1837–1863.

DeAngelo, Harry, Linda DeAngelo, and Douglas J. Skinner. 2004. "Are Dividends Disappearing? Dividend Concentration and the Consolidation of Earnings." *Journal of Financial Economics* 72:3, 425–456.

DeAngelo, Harry, Linda DeAngelo, and René M. Stulz. 2006. "Dividend Policy and the Earned/Contributed Capital Mix: A Test of the Lifecycle Theory." *Journal of Financial Economics* 81:2, 227–254.

Denis, David J., Diane K. Denis, and Atulya Sarin. 1994. "The Information Content of Dividend Changes: Cash Flow Signaling, Overinvestment, and Dividend Clienteles." *Journal of Financial and Quantitative Analysis* 29:4, 567–587.

Denis, David J., and Igor Osobov. 2008. "Why Do Firms Pay Dividends? International Evidence on the Determinants of Dividend Policy." *Journal of Financial Economics* 89:1, 62–82.

Easterbrook, Frank H. 1984. "Two Agency-Cost Explanations of Dividends." *American Economic Review* 74:4, 650–659.

Fama, Eugene, and Kenneth R. French. 2001. "Disappearing Dividends: Changing Firm Characteristics or Lower Propensity to Pay?" *Journal of Financial Economics* 60:1, 3–43.

Ginglinger, Edith, and Jacques Hamon. 2003. "Actual Share Repurchase and Corporate Liquidity." Paper presented at the 2004 meeting of the European Financial Management Association, Basel, available at http://ssrn.com/abstract=49916.

Goergen, Marc, Luc Renneboog, and Luis Correia Da Silva. 2005. "When Do German Firms Change Their Dividends?" *Journal of Corporate Finance* 11:1–2, 375–399.

Gugler, Klaus, 2003. "Corporate Governance, Dividend Payout Policy, and the Interrelation between Dividends, R&D, and Capital Investment." *Journal of Banking and Finance* 27:7, 1297–1321.

Gugler, Klaus, and B. Burcin Yurtoglu. 2003. "Corporate Governance and Dividend Pay-out Policy in Germany." *European Economic Review* 47:4, 731–758.

Healy, Paul M., and Krishna G. Palepu. 1988. "Earnings Information Conveyed by Dividend Initiations and Omissions." *Journal of Financial Economics* 21:2, 149–175.

Heinkel, Robert Lee. 1978. *Essays on Financial Markets with Asymmetric Information*, Ph.D. dissertation, University of California, Berkeley.

Hribar, Paul, Nicole Thorne Jenkins, and W. Bruce Johnson. 2004. "Stock Repurchases as an Earnings Management Device." Working Paper, http://ssrn.com/abstract=524062.

Jensen, Michael C. 1986. "Agency Costs of Free Cash Flow, Corporate Finance, and Takeovers." *American Economic Review* 76:2, 323–329.

John, Kose, and Joseph Williams. 1985. "Dividends, Dilution and Taxes: A Signalling Equilibrium." *Journal of Finance* 40:4, 1053–1070.

Julio, Brandon, and David L. Ikenberry. 2005. "Reappearing Dividends." *Journal of Applied Corporate Finance* 16:4, 89–100.

La Porta, Rafael, Florencio Lopez-De-Silanes, Andrei Shleifer, and Robert W. Vishny. 2000. "Agency Problems and Dividend Policies around the World." *Journal of Finance* 55:1, 1–33.

Lintner, John. 1956. "Distribution of Incomes of Corporations among Dividends, Retained Earnings, and Taxes." *American Economic Review Papers and Proceedings of the Sixty-eighth Annual Meeting of the American Economic Association* 46:2, 97–113.

Miller, Merton H., and Franco Modigliani. 1961. "Dividend Policy, Growth and the Valuation of Shares." *Journal of Business* 34:4, 411–433.

Miller, Merton H., and Kevin Rock. 1985. "Dividend Policy under Asymmetric Information." *Journal of Finance* 40:4, 1031–1051.

Rau, P. Raghavendra, and Theo Vermaelen. 2002. "Regulation, Taxes, and Share Repurchases in the United Kingdom." *Journal of Business* 75:2, 245–282.

Vafeas, Nikos, Adamos Vlittis, Philippos Katranis, and Kanalis Ockree. 2003. "Earnings Management around Share Repurchases: A Note." *Abacus* 39:2, 262–272.

von Eije, J. Henk, and William L. Megginson. 2008. "Dividend Policy and Share Repurchases in the European Union." *Journal of Financial Economics* 89:2, 347–374.

Williams, Joseph. 1988. "Efficient Signalling with Dividends, Investment and Stock Repurchases." *Journal of Finance* 43:3, 737–747.

ABOUT THE AUTHORS

Franck Bancel is Professor of Finance at ESCP-EAP. He received his Ph.D. from University of Grenoble II and his "Habilitation à Diriger des Recherches (HDR)" from Paris IX Dauphine. Franck Bancel has published many articles in academic journals, such as *Financial Management, European Financial Management*, and *Revue d'Economie Financière* as well as several books, including *Fusions d'entreprises* (Eyrolles, 2008). He served as associate dean for research from 2002 to 2006 and as director of the ESCP-EAP Ph.D. program of the Paris campus from 2003 to 2006.

Nalinaksha Bhattacharyya is an associate professor at the University of Alaska, Anchorage. He obtained his Ph.D. in finance from the University of British Columbia and his Ph.D in Business Management from the University of Calcutta. He has had both industrial and academic experience. Bhattacharyya has held faculty positions in the United States, Canada, and India. His research interests are eclectic and interdisciplinary. In finance, he has worked in the areas of dividend policy, executive compensation, preference representation, and corporate finance. He has published in academic journals including *Accounting and Finance, Advances in Financial Economics, Managerial Finance, European Journal of Operational Research, International Journal of Bank Marketing*, and *Journal of Academic Ethics*. Bhattacharyya has also guest edited an issue of *Managerial Finance* and was the division chair and academic reviewer for the Finance Division of the Administrative Sciences Association of Canada's Annual Meeting.

Usha R. Mittoo is Bank of Montreal Professor of Finance at the University of Manitoba. She received her Ph.D. in finance from the University of British Columbia. Her main research is in international capital markets and corporate finance areas. She has published in several top finance journals, including *Journal of Finance, Journal of Corporate Finance, Journal of Banking and Finance, Financial Management*, and *European Financial Management*. She has also published in practitioner-oriented journals including *Journal of Applied Corporate Finance*. Mittoo is currently on the editorial boards of several journals, including the *Canadian Journal of Administrative Sciences*.

PART II

Cash Dividends: Theoretical and Empirical Evidence

CHAPTER 6

Dividend Irrelevance Theory

JAMES S. ANG
Bank of America Eminent Scholar and Professor of Finance, Florida State University

STEPHEN J. CICCONE
Associate Professor of Finance, University of New Hampshire

INTRODUCTION

In the relatively brief history of analytical finance, two of the most influential researchers are Merton Miller and Franco Modigliani (hereafter MM). Their impact on the field is indisputable. Today, their work appears in virtually all corporate finance textbooks, and writers in the field of analytical finance frequently cite their work. Years after their major achievements, they received the Nobel Prize, perhaps the most notable distinction in economics. Modigliani won the prize in 1985, and Miller shared the prize with two others in 1990.

One of the core issues in their work is firm valuation. In Modigliani and Miller (1958), perhaps their most influential paper, they show that under certain assumptions the mixture of debt and equity that a firm holds does not affect overall firm value. A few years later, MM (1961) reported a similar result for dividend payout policy. Thus, in perfect capital markets, value results from investment decisions, while financing decisions are irrelevant. Given a choice between financing new projects with retained earnings or with new equity, firm managers should be indifferent.

This chapter briefly explores the origins of dividend irrelevance and proceeds with a theoretical proof and an intuitive explanation of the crucial MM work. The chapter then discusses challenges to dividend irrelevancy and focuses on the market imperfections noted by researchers as affecting the irrelevancy result. While today irrelevance theory is clearly under attack, there is no question about its importance in the history of financial theory.

THEORIES BEFORE IRRELEVANCE

Although virtually all papers exploring dividend irrelevancy cite MM (1961) as the inspiration, the authors had an important predecessor. In his pioneering but often overlooked work, Williams (1938) lays out a theory of capital structure irrelevance that would prove pivotal to MM's later work. He also devises a stock valuation formula nearly identical to that of Gordon (1959). Williams discusses the theory of homemade leverage in which the cost of equity is an increasing function of the leverage ratio (similar to MM's 1958 Proposition II) and the trade-off between dividends and invested assets. To quote Williams:

> *Clearly, if a single individual or a single institutional investor owned all of the bonds, stocks and warrants issued by the corporation, it would not matter to this investor what the company's capitalization was (except for details concerning the income tax). Any earnings collected as interest could not be collected as dividends. To such an individual it would be perfectly obvious that total interest- and dividend-paying power was in no way dependent on the kind of securities issued to the company's owner. Furthermore no change in the investment value of the enterprise as a whole would result from a change in the capitalization. . . . It leads us to speak of the Law of the Conservation of Investment Value, just as physicists speak of the Law of Conservation of Matter, or the Law of the Conservation of Energy. (pp. 72–73)*

Unfortunately for Williams, academics soon forgot about his arguments about capital structure. Instead, researchers started attaching primary importance to dividends in firm valuation models. Graham and Dodd (1951) advocate for high dividend payouts, believing that stock prices reflect an intrinsic value related to dividends and earnings. As Gordon notes (1959), Graham and Dodd unfortunately neither specify a valuation model nor provide any empirical support for their beliefs. Gordon corroborates Graham and Dodd's insights but also formulates a valuation model in which dividends and the discount rate are the only relevant variables. Here is Gordon's famous model:

$$V_0 = \sum_{t=1}^{\infty} \frac{D_t}{(1 + r_t)^t} \tag{6.1}$$

In Equation 6.1, V_0 is the value of the firm, D_t is the dividend paid at time t, and r_t is the appropriate discount rate of rate of profit, according to Gordon. The model demonstrates that increasing dividends directly increases the share price. Paying dividends leads to less cash for investing, which in turn leads to a lower growth rate of dividends. However, Gordon (1959, p. 103) believes that lower dividends lead to a higher discount rate, r_t, stating, "The rate of profit required on a share increases with the fraction of income retained." The increase in price due to a lower cost of capital can compensate investors for the decrease in price due to lower growth.

Lintner (1956) surveys the dividend policies of a sample of firms and finds that companies prefer to maintain dividends. According to Lintner (p. 99), managers try to smooth dividends over time, stating that "most management sought to avoid making changes in their dividend rates that might have to be reversed within a year or so." Lintner (p. 100) continues, "Any reason which would lead management to decide to change an existing rate ... had to seem prudent." Lintner clearly understands that dividend policy is a major decision made by firm management. Savings and retained earnings decisions are based on dividend actions. He also recognizes the informational component of dividends, although formal dividend-signaling theories would not be proposed for another 20 years (Bhattacharya, 1979).

In summary, the prevailing opinion just before MM's breakthrough research was that dividends were highly relevant to shareholder wealth and high-dividend-paying firms sold at a premium over low-dividend-paying firms. Consequently,

MM not only are among the first to apply analytically rigorous methods to a finance problem but also are revolutionaries who rebelled against the popular sentiment of the times.

MM'S DIVIDEND IRRELEVANCE

The most important precursor to MM (1961) was another paper they authored about debt versus equity financing. In this paper, MM (1958) prove that under certain assumptions, a firm's total value does not depend on the mixture of debt and equity, demonstrating capital structure irrelevancy. Capital structure and dividend policy are closely related. Cash paid as dividends leaves the firm with less equity and potentially a greater need to raise additional stock or debt in the future. Consequently, MM's capital structure result is so crucial to dividend irrelevance that their proof is presented here.

MM (1958) rely on arbitrage arguments and assume perfect capital markets, which includes zero taxes, one marketwide constant interest rate, and unlimited borrowing. Their use of arbitrage arguments for prices would later prove to be as important to financial theory as their irrelevancy result. For example, Ross (1976) also relies on arbitrage arguments in his famous arbitrage pricing model. Stiglitz (1969, 1974) argues that borrowing and lending must occur at the risk-free rate, although this argument is controversial (see, for example, Fama, 1978).

Implicit in MM's framework is the assumption that both companies have the same assets, an assumption that holds the investment decision neutral. This assumption is crucial because it allows them to claim that if two firms have the same assets, the simple balance sheet equation (assets equal liabilities plus equity) must hold regardless of the mix of debt and equity.

Formally, MM (1958) consider two firms, company 1 and company 2, differing only in capital structure. Company 1 is entirely stock financed and has a total value of V_1, while company 2 has some debt and a total value (stocks plus bonds) of V_2. An investor in company 2 buys s_2 dollars out of S_2 dollars of total outstanding stock, thereby holding a proportion of shares denoted α. This investor receives a return, Y_2, equal to the following:

$$Y_2 = \frac{s_2}{S_2}(X - rD_2) = \alpha(X - rD_2) = \alpha X - \alpha rD_2, \qquad (6.2)$$

where X is the income distributed to shareholders, D_2 is the debt outstanding of company 2, and r is the debt interest rate. If this investor sells his holdings of company 2, he can invest s_1 equal to $\alpha(S_2 + D_2)$ dollars in company 1. To do this, this investor uses the αS_2 sale realization and borrows an additional αD_2. The new proportion of earnings is equal to the following:

$$\frac{s_1}{S_1} = \frac{\alpha(S_2 + D_2)}{S_1}. \qquad (6.3)$$

The investor's return on company 1, Y_1, equals

$$Y_1 = \frac{\alpha(S_2 + D_2)}{S_1}X - r\alpha D_2 = \alpha\frac{V_2}{V_1}X - r\alpha D_2. \qquad (6.4)$$

From Equation 6.4, if V_2 is greater than V_1 then the return on company 1, Y_1, is greater than the return of company 2, Y_2. Owners of company 2 will sell their shares, depressing the company 2 price, and buy shares of company 1, increasing its price. Eventually, through arbitrage, investors will make the two prices equivalent.

If V_1 is greater than V_2, then shareholders holding company 1 receive the return here:

$$Y_1 = \frac{s_1}{S_1} X = \alpha X. \tag{6.5}$$

Instead of holding only company 1 stock, the investor can exchange ownership to company 2 consisting of s_2 dollars of stock and d dollars of debt. If the investor holds the same proportion of stock and bond ownership as the company 2 proportion, the dollar amount of the investor's investments in stocks (s_2) and bonds (d) is as follows:

$$s_2 = \frac{S_2}{V_2} s_1, \text{ and} \tag{6.6}$$

$$d = \frac{D_2}{V_2} s_1. \tag{6.7}$$

Note that $S_2 + D_2 = V_2$. The total return is now equal to the return from stocks plus the returns from bonds (rd) as specified here:

$$Y_2 = \frac{s_2}{S_2}(X - rD_2) + rd = \frac{s_1}{V_2}(X - rD_2) + r\frac{D_2}{V_2}s_1 = \frac{s_1}{V_2} X = \alpha \frac{S_1}{V_2} X. \tag{6.8}$$

If V_1 is greater than V_2, then Y_2 is greater than Y_1. Investors will sell a portion of their company 1 shares and replace them with some company 2 shares. MM (1958) thus provide the insight that individuals forming mixed portfolios effectively undo the leverage decisions of a firm. This insight, that investors can replicate the capital structure decisions of firms, is critical to the MM proof and is often referred to as "homemade leverage."

Ang and Hunsader (1996) note practical issues with homemade leverage. Implementing a homemade dividend policy often requires that individuals sell shares in order to receive cash and buy shares in order to disperse excess cash. If a volatile stock pays greater dividends when share prices are high (after good performance) and less dividends when share prices are low (after poor performance), investors may end up buying shares due to excess dividends at the high prices and selling shares due to dividend shortfalls at the low prices.

This relatively simple proof (by today's standards, at least) proves capital structure irrelevancy under certain assumptions and establishes one of the cornerstones of financial theory. MM refer to their conclusion as Proposition I. Their proposition is now popularly referred to as MM Proposition I or simply MM I.

An intuitive example helps to explain the MM I logic. Investors can invest in either the stocks or the bonds of a firm. Stockholders are entitled to a portion of earnings, while bondholders receive interest. If firm A has only equity, a 10% required rate of return, and $1,000 of annual profits in perpetuity, its stockholders hold $10,000 ($1,000/0.10) of firm value.

If another firm, firm B, is exactly the same except for $500 of 10% debt it holds, it will pay out $50 of interest each year, leaving only $950 for stockholders. The total stock value is therefore $9,500 ($950/0.10). However, the total bond value in perpetuity is $500 ($50/0.10). Summing the stock and bond values together equals the same $10,000 total value as firm A. On the basis of this logic, the financing of long-term debt, short-term debt, or equity investments is irrelevant.

The paper was instantly controversial, and researchers soon questioned the findings in subsequent work. For example, Durand (1959) contends that the perfect capital market assumptions limit the applicability of the MM I result. Despite the criticism, the capital structure irrelevance arguments, MM's analytical, arbitrage-based proof, and the importance of market frictions became well accepted in the finance literature.

Soon after tackling the capital structure issue, MM applied similar principles to dividends. The dividend decision is related to the capital structure question because dividend policy represents a financing choice. The payment of dividends leaves fewer internal funds for investment requiring greater amounts of external financing. Often neglected in the finance literature is the strong interrelationship between capital structure and dividend irrelevancy in explaining the asset side of the balance sheet. Capital structure irrelevancy contends that the decision does not matter in determining firm assets. Dividend policy irrelevancy contends that internal versus external funding of investments also does not matter in determining firm assets.

MM (1961) make three explicit assumptions: perfect capital markets, rational behavior, and perfect certainty. They further define each assumption. Perfect capital markets imply price-taking behavior, costless pricing information, zero transaction costs (including zero taxes and issuance costs), and no tax differentials between dividends and capital gains. Rational behavior indicates that investors prefer more to less wealth and are indifferent between dividends and capital gains. Perfect certainty implies that no information asymmetry exists between firm management and outside investors, as investors know all relevant future cash flows and profits.

Under these assumptions, MM (1961) define the rate of return, r_e, for any firm as the sum of dividends, d_t, and capital gains divided by the current price, p_t. They hold r_e constant over their time period:

$$r_e = \frac{d_t + p_{t+1} - p_t}{p_t}.$$ (6.9)

Solving for p_t gives the following result:

$$p_t = \frac{d_t + p_{t+1}}{1 + r_e}.$$ (6.10)

Equation 6.10 states that the per-share price today is equal to the dividends per share to be paid in time t plus the price at time t_{+1} all discounted to the present. They then restate Equation 6.10 in terms of firm value as opposed to price per share as

$$V_t = \frac{D_t + n_t p_{t+1}}{1 + r_e},$$ (6.11)

where V_t equals total firm value at time t, n_t equals the number of shares outstanding, and D_t equals the total dividends paid during time period t. MM restate value as a function of the total dividends paid and the firm value at time t_{+1} less any new shares issued, m_{t+1}, times their ex-dividend price, p_{t+1}.

$$V_t = \frac{D_t + V_{t+1} - m_{t+1}p_{t+1}}{1 + r_e}. \tag{6.12}$$

Aside from the discount rate (r_e), in Equation 6.12, three variables can affect the value of the firm: current dividends, the total firm value at the future period, and the value of any new shares issued. MM recognize that any increase in dividends (D_t) necessarily increases the dollar amount of new shares issued ($m_{t+1}p_{t+1}$). They prove this by expressing $m_{t+1}p_{t+1}$ in terms of D_t. Defining I_t as the level of investment and X_t as the total net profit, they describe the amount of new capital needed:

$$m_{t+1}p_{t+1} = I_t - (X_t - D_t). \tag{6.13}$$

Finally, MM substitute Equation 6.13 into Equation 6.12 to get the result here:

$$V_t = \frac{D_t + V_{t+1} - I_t + X_t - D_t}{1 + r_e} = \frac{V_{t+1} - I_t + X_t}{1 + r_e}. \tag{6.14}$$

Equation 6.14 establishes dividend irrelevance, as the value of the firm does not depend on dividends (D_t). Instead, value is dependent upon the level of investment and future profits.

Predecessors and contemporaries of MM (1961) often cite what MM call "bird in hand" fallacies to explain investor preference for dividends. These fallacies claim that investors prefer dividends because their receipt represents guaranteed cash (see, for example, Gordon, 1962). These cash receipts are more valuable because they are not affected by uncertainty, including possible poor future firm performance. MM, however, explain away the value of receiving dividends in hand. In essence, cash-strapped investors can simply sell a proportion of shares to mimic dividend receipts. If investors reinvest these dividends, their total return, whether from capital gains or dividends, is the same.

As an example, MM (1961) review a special case mentioned by Gordon (1962). In this case, all financing is internal, and the firm's dividend growth rate is equal to the cost of equity times the earnings retention ratio. Gordon argues that lower dividend payouts and higher earnings retention ratios lead to higher costs of equity because of the increased risk of the future cash flows. A higher cost of equity leads to lower prices in Gordon's valuation model (Equation 6.1 herein).

MM counter that a change in dividend policy may change the distribution of the total return between dividends and capital gains but does not change the total return itself. Furthermore, if Gordon (1962) is right, low-payout firms would have consistently higher realized returns because of higher costs of equity, a position MM believe that Gordon would staunchly oppose.

As with capital structure irrelevancy, an example helps to illustrate the MM dividend irrelevance result. Suppose ABC Corporation has $200 cash and $800 of

Table 6.1 Market Value of ABC Corporation

Cash	$200	Debt	$0
Noncash assets	800		
Total assets	$1,000	Total equity	$1,000

noncash assets on its balance sheet, stated at market value. It also has no debt, leaving equity equaling assets at $1,000. If there are 100 shares outstanding, each share is worth $10 ($1,000/100). The balance sheet is shown in Table 6.1.

The firm needs the $200 cash to fund its investments, but it also wants to reward its shareholders with a $200 cash dividend. Therefore, the firm decides to pay the $200 dividend while subsequently issuing $200 of new equity.

If the firm issues new equity, the new shares will dilute the value of the old shares. However, the old shareholders will receive the dividend to compensate for the diluted value. In this case, if the firm declares a $2 dividend per share, it will distribute the cash leaving a total stock value of $8 per share [($1,000 − $200)/100]. Investors holding or buying shares before the ex-dividend date will therefore gain the $2 future dividend plus the $8 of stock value. Their shares are worth $10 as before. On the ex-dividend date, investors will no longer receive the dividend, and the price will correspondingly drop by $2 to $8. The $8 price is equal to the new total market value of assets divided by the number of shares ($800/100).

The new equity issued must recoup the $200 cash paid out as a dividend. As the shares sell for $8, the number of new shares issued is 25 ($200/$8). After the firm issues the new shares, the balance sheet looks the same as before, only there are now 125 shares, and each share is worth $8 ($1,000/125). This simple illustration serves to show that investors are indifferent to dividend policy under the MM assumptions such as no taxes, no transaction costs, and no information asymmetry.

Reaction to MM (1961) was swift. Indeed, their boldness did not escape the notice of Gordon (1963, p. 264), who writes the following:

> *In two papers and in a recent book I have presented theory and evidence which lead to the conclusion that a corporation's share price (or its cost of capital) is not independent of the dividend rate. As you know, MM (Modigliani and Miller) have the opposite view, and they argued their position at some length in a recent paper. Moreover, the tone of their paper made it clear that they saw no reasonable basis on which their conclusion could be questioned. Since they were so sure of their conclusion, it would seem advisable for me to review carefully my thinking on the subject.*

Gordon (1963) defends his earlier work (for example, Gordon, 1962) and challenges the MM (1961) assumptions regarding a constant discount rate. He states (1963, p. 267) the following: "The issue, therefore, is whether the behavior of investors under uncertainty is correctly represented by a model in which the discount rate that equates a dividend expectation with its price is a function of the dividend rate."

He argues that dividend decisions may change the level of investor risk aversion or the uncertainty of future dividends, thus changing the discount rate. He then constructs a model indicating that stock prices are not independent of financing decisions. While not explicitly mentioning information asymmetry, his arguments may be considered an anticipation of that view.

Brennan (1971) examines the two prevailing arguments: the Gordon (1959, 1963) contention that increasing dividends increases share price and reduces the discount rate and the MM (1961) contention that dividends are irrelevant. Brennan (p. 1119) upholds the MM view and believes that Gordon's (1963) proof of relevancy relies on a "confounding of investment and dividend policy effects."

Rubinstein (1976) separates and categorizes two approaches to proving irrelevancy: (1) substitute financing and (2) neutral reinvestment. Miller and Modigliani (1961) adopt the first approach, while Gordon (1963) and Brennan (1971) adopt the second approach. The substitute financing approach assumes that the firm pays all free cash flows as dividends. The neutral financing approach assumes that the firm reinvests any retained free cash flows at the cost of equity. Rubinstein then formally values the cash flow stream assumed by the neutral financing approach and shows that it equals that of the substitute financing approach, a finding that should mitigate the conflict between Gordon (1963) and MM (1961).

In summary, this section shows the proofs behind both capital structure and dividend irrelevancy. While capital structure decisions determine the debt versus equity mix, the dividend decision ultimately determines whether the firm finances projects internally or externally. The conditions and assumptions required to make dividends irrelevant are also the ones that make internal financing equivalent to external financing.

THE IMPACT OF MARKET IMPERFECTIONS

As MM (1961) assumed perfect capital markets, most arguments against irrelevance focus on market imperfections. Some authors, such as Lease, John, Kalay, Loewenstein, and Sarig (2000) and Baker, Powell, and Veit (2002) sort imperfections into two groups: the big three and the little three. The big three are taxes, information asymmetry, and agency costs. The little three are transaction costs, flotation expenses, and behavioral considerations. Interestingly, MM believed at the time of their publication that dividend policy was truly irrelevant, even allowing for imperfections. Other researchers, however, viewed the imperfections as more important. As the lack of imperfections is critical for establishing irrelevancy, this section provides an overview of how the major imperfections might affect the MM results.

Taxes

Taxes are among the first of the imperfections to be researched. MM (1961, p. 432) mention this source in their seminal work as being "undoubtedly the major systematic imperfection in the market." As dividends are traditionally taxed at higher rates than capital gains, firms making smaller dividend payments should trade at a premium. However, MM dismiss this imperfection by virtue of immaterial differences in the tax rates, a sharp increase in shares held by investors with no tax differential (for example, by charities, foundations, and low-income retirees), and the fact that most previous researchers believed that high-dividend-paying firms should trade at a premium rather than a discount.

Soon thereafter, MM (1963) reverse their position regarding taxation on capital structure irrelevancy by arguing that, with corporate income taxes, firms should prefer capital structures that are 100 percent debt. However, as noted by Farrar and Selwyn (1967) and Brennan (1970), different corporate and personal tax treatments change the MM conclusion. Farrar and Selwyn argue that with higher taxes on personal income than on capital gains, an optimal dividend policy exists: all firms should maintain a zero dividend policy. Brennan arrives at the same conclusion and implicitly argues for greater share repurchases. In his statement here, Brennan (p. 424) attempts to reconcile the optimal policy of zero dividends with the observation that most corporations do in fact pay regular dividends: "Such behavior must be rationalized by the assumption that such corporations are behaving under an actual or perceived constraint on systematic share re-purchase as an alternative to dividend payment."

The arguments for zero dividends due to tax considerations are compelling. In a famous article, the renowned economist Fischer Black goes so far as to claim the payments of dividends represent a puzzle. In this article, Black (1976) contends that managerial or investor incentives simply cannot explain observed dividend behavior of positive payments. Notably, Black predates Easterbrook's (1984) work on dividend-related agency costs. DeAngelo and DeAngelo (2006), however, challenge Black's view.

Several studies test the empirical implications of Farrar and Selwyn (1967) as well as Brennan (1970) by simultaneously exploring dividends, taxes, and stock returns. Black and Scholes (1974) find no significant relationship between the dividends and stock prices, thus providing support for irrelevance. According to Miller and Scholes (1978), this finding does not support either the conventional view that the market prefers dividends or the contrary view that dividend-paying stocks should command a return premium to compensate for tax penalties on dividend income. Miller and Scholes believe the ability of investors to offset dividend income by interest deductions and to invest dividend proceeds in tax-sheltered vehicles such as life insurance and pension funds mitigates the tax disadvantage to dividends.

Litzenberger and Ramaswamy (1979) use a tax version of the capital asset pricing model (CAPM) and find a relationship between dividend yields and stock returns. However, Miller and Scholes (1982) argue that short-term dividend yield measures bias studies that attempt to associate higher dividend yields with higher risk-adjusted rates of return. Suffering from such a bias, Litzenberger and Ramaswamy are in essence finding information effects, not tax effects. Kalay and Michaely (2000) also cite issues with the Litzenberger and Ramaswamy study and believe that tax hypotheses of dividend policy are problematic. Peterson, Peterson, and Ang (1985) show that investors do not attempt to minimize dividend-related taxes, suggesting that investors consider tax effects a trivial component of their dividend-related decisions.

Information Asymmetry

Although taken together the research into tax-related frictions does not dismiss dividend irrelevance, other market frictions represent potentially tougher challenges. The second major imperfection is information asymmetry. Like taxes, MM (1961) directly address this challenge. They state the following:

> We might take note briefly of a common confusion about the meaning of the irrelevance proposition occasioned by the fact that in the real world a change in the dividend rate is often followed by a change in the market price (sometimes spectacularly so). Such a phenomenon would not be incompatible with irrelevance to the extent that it was merely a reflection of what might be called the "information content" of dividends, an attribute of particular dividend payments hitherto excluded by assumption from the discussion and proofs. That is, where the firm has adopted a policy of dividend stabilization with a long-established and generally appreciated "target payout ratio," investors are likely to . . . interpret a change in the dividend rate as a change in management's views of future profit prospects for the firm. The dividend change, in other words, provides the occasion for the price change though not its cause, the price still being solely a reflection of future earnings and growth opportunities. (p. 430)

Researching before the popularization of market efficiency theories, MM (1961, p. 430) go so far as to claim that investors' reaction to dividend changes is "mistaken" and that the irrelevance proposition holds unless "the price changes in such cases were not reversed when the unfolding of events had made clear the true nature of the situation."

Unfortunately, their latter argument holds little merit today given the fairly wide acceptance that dividend change announcements result in permanent stock price changes (see, for example, Asquith and Mullins, 1983). The MM argument also shows that they do not believe that a relationship exists between dividends and share prices. This sharply contrasts with the modern belief that the dividend valuation model of Gordon (1959) is theoretically accurate.

Rigorous theoretical treatments begin with Bhattacharya (1979), who proposes an environment in which outside investors have imperfect information about future cash flows and the government taxes dividends disadvantageously. In this framework, paying dividends is costly and can therefore function as a signal of expected cash flows. Miller himself, in Miller and Rock (1985, p. 1040), allows for information asymmetry, admitting that the assumptions under which information asymmetry do not matter "have little survival value and hence hold little interest for economists." Furthermore, Myers and Majluf (1984), in their famous paper on corporate financing behavior, posit that dividends can help convey managers' superior information to the market.

John and Williams (1985) present the crux of signaling arguments. In their framework, the government taxes dividends disadvantageously, and outsiders costlessly observe firm financial information by examining audited financial statements. These financial statements cannot provide complete information on production technology. Insiders can fully communicate the information only through dividends or new shares issuances. When prospects are favorable, stockholders who want to avoid dilution of their fractional ownership stakes prefer dividends. Outsiders recognize the signaling power of dividends and bid share prices upward. The increase in share prices compensates stockholders for the tax disadvantage of dividends while preserving the proportion of ownership.

Asymmetric information can also affect the internal versus external financing decision. If firms are undervalued, external equity is costlier than internal equity.

Firms paying dividends reduce internal equity, resulting in a considerable commitment to use external financing.

A major issue with signaling arguments is figuring out exactly what the signal is. Most signaling-related studies assume that dividend increases or initiations serve as harbingers of future earnings increases. Indeed, Asquith and Mullins (1983) find that stocks increase by an average of about 3 percent after the announcement of a dividend initiation. Unfortunately, the evidence supporting signaling is mixed. Although several studies, such as Brickley (1983), support dividend signaling, the preponderance of evidence seems to oppose dividend signaling. For example, studies that do not support signaling include Watts (1973), DeAngelo, DeAngelo, and Skinner (1996), and Grullon and colleagues (2005). Chen, Firth, and Gao (2002) show a lack of support for signaling using a sample of Chinese firms. Consequently, the positive announcement effect of a dividend increase is likely attributable to reasons other than the dividend being a signal of future increases in cash flows or profits.

While empirical evidence in support of signaling is weak, Ang (1987) questions signaling on a theoretical level. One of Ang's contentions is that dividends are too costly given the strength of their signal. Firms can use cheaper signals just as effectively. Ang (p. 40) also contends that signaling represents an "assignment problem." Managers should bear the cost of false signaling, but unfortunately, shareholders often bear the cost.

Agency Costs

Although the first two of the big three cannot dismiss dividend irrelevancy, perhaps the biggest threat is the last: the existence of agency costs. Cash-related agency problems may occur when managers in high-performing firms hold too much cash. They may spend this cash unwisely, resulting in the free cash flow problem articulated by Jensen (1986).

Easterbrook (1984) first formally postulated using dividends to reduce free cash flow. According to Easterbrook (p. 652), "Dividends exist because they influence the firms' financing policies, because they dissipate cash and induce firms to float new securities." Agency costs arise from two situations. The first cost arises because managers need to be monitored. The second cost relates to management's preference for low-risk, low-return investments, due to their concern over job security or any personal wealth tied to the corporation. Shareholders, in contrast, demand riskier, higher-returning investment projects to maximize their return.

Easterbrook (1984) believes market forces associated with new security issuances serve to alleviate these concerns. He states the following:

> Both the monitoring and the risk-aversion problem are less serious if the firm is constantly in the market for new capital. When it issues new securities, the firm's affairs will be reviewed by an investment banker or some similar intermediary acting as a monitor for the collective interest of the shareholders, and by the purchasers of the new instruments. The same occurs when the firm issues new debt. ... Managers who need to raise money consistently are more likely to act in investor's interests than managers who are immune from this kind of scrutiny. (p. 654)

In this framework, Easterbrook (1984, p. 655) notes that consistent dividends "compel firms to raise new money in order to carry out their activities." Thus, the investment bankers and others involved in raising capital serve to reduce agency costs, as they are important monitors of firm management. In turn, management can maximize shareholder value and issue new securities at the highest possible price.

Agency explanations have received great favor of late. For example, La Porta, Lopez-de-Silanes, Shleifer, and Vishny (2000) examine dividend policies in a sample of 33 countries and find evidence consistent with an outcome model in which firms pay dividends because minority shareholders pressure insiders to disperse excess cash. DeAngelo, DeAngelo, and Stulz (2006) shift the focus from dividends serving to reduce excess free cash flows toward dividends marking the stages in the financial life cycle. More mature firms have higher cash to equity or assets and therefore tend to pay greater dividends.

Agency problems also reduce the perceived value of internal equity, which causes the external equity stakeholders to demand a higher return and a consequently lower price. Thus, when considering the source of funding, irrelevancy does not hold because the costs of internal and external funds are unequal.

Clientele Effects

Of the lesser imperfections, the clientele effects are perhaps the most notable. In this framework, certain investors demand dividends and firms will adjust their dividend policy to cater to certain types of investors.

MM (1961) recognize the possibility of clientele effects. They state (p. 431), "Each corporation would tend to attract to itself a 'clientele' consisting of those preferring its payout ratio." MM discount the importance of such effects, however, by claiming that valuation does not change despite different clienteles.

Regardless of the beliefs of MM, clientele effects may affect investor demand for dividends in several ways. As Shefrin and Statman (1984) note, investors may prefer cash dividends for psychological reasons. Moreover, Allen, Bernardo, and Welch (2000) report that tax-related clienteles may exist.

Tax-based clienteles are related to signaling. For example, the signaling framework of John and Williams (1985) allows for different investor cash preferences. John and Williams (p. 1065) support their argument regarding the ability of dividends to satisfy different clienteles by stating: "Also, other things equal, dividend-paying firms have clienteles of stockholders who demand cash – such as widows, senior citizens, and financial institutions." This is a particularly important conclusion because in the framework of John and Williams share repurchases do not appear to replace dividends. This is in contrast to the Miller and Rock (1985) framework, which does not consider the demand for cash. Additionally, dividends are a costly, and hence a more credible, signal because of the tax expense.

Baker and Wurgler (2004) take the Shefrin and Statman (1984) behavioral theories a step further. They propose a catering theory of dividend payments in which managers pay higher dividends when they believe that investors place a stock price premium on high-dividend-paying firms. Baker and Wurgler (p. 1126) conclude, "The results suggest that dividends are highly relevant to share price, but in different directions at different times." As with most behavioral frameworks, their conclusions are controversial because they relax the standard market efficiency assumptions.

Clientele effects do not necessarily refute irrelevance theory. In at least two scenarios, dividend irrelevance may still hold. In the first scenario, the aggregate number of investors preferring a certain dividend policy is constant. Once an equilibrium distribution of firms and clienteles is reached, a firm altering its dividend policy will not change the distribution or pricing. In the second scenario, a shock, such as a tax law change, occurs. This shock will increase the demand for one clientele type bidding up the demand for firms with the preferred policy. Other firms will observe the increased demand and respond by appropriately increasing their dividends. These adjustments restore the price equilibrium.

Taken together, the studies cited in this section, representing but a small portion of the total volume of work into imperfections, clearly demonstrate the importance that researchers have given MM irrelevance theory. Irrelevance theory is clearly the benchmark to beat—the null hypothesis, so to speak. Researchers have responded by identifying several areas that may generate dividend relevance. However, a recent reevaluation of the underpinnings of irrelevance theory calls into question the validity of the relevance research. The next section provides a discussion of this new challenge.

RECENT CHALLENGES TO IRRELEVANCE

DeAngelo and DeAngelo (2006) provide a scathing attack on the MM propositions. DeAngelo and DeAngelo (p. 295) condemn MM irrelevance in plain terms:

> For corporate finance research, a more troubling consequence of the MM irrelevance theorem is that its central lesson—that investment policy alone determines value—has both limited our vision about the importance of payout policy and sent researchers off searching for frictions that would make payout policy matter, while it has mattered all along even in the standard (frictionless) Fisherian model.

Later, DeAngelo and DeAngelo (p. 296) boldly proclaim that the MM irrelevance theorem is of "trivial import."

In contrast to previous criticisms that focus on market frictions, DeAngelo and DeAngelo's (2006) arguments focus on the proof of the irrelevance theorem itself, specifically targeting free cash flows. They maintain that MM's payout policy irrelevance requires firms to pay out 100 percent of the free cash flow each period. This criticism stems from MM's assumptions surrounding Equation 6.13: $m_{t+1}p_{t+1} = I_t - (X_t - D_t)$. Letting S_t equal $m_{t+1}p_{t+1}$ and FCF_t denote free cash flows, DeAngelo and DeAngelo rearrange Equation 6.13 to define the dividend level:

$$D_t = X_t - I_t + S_t = FCF_t + S_t. \tag{6.15}$$

Equation 6.15 specifies that with a fixed investment policy, dividends are equal to free cash flows plus stock issuances. According to DeAngelo and DeAngelo

(2006, p. 306), the implicit yet dubious assumption is therefore the full payout of free cash flows, rendering the MM proof a "meaningless tautology." DeAngelo and DeAngelo reestablish dividend policy relevance by maintaining that once managers are allowed to retain a portion of earnings, they can also choose to invest in negative net present value projects.

In a related paper, DeAngelo and DeAngelo (2007) maintain that pedagogy should focus on the optimal full payout strategy (i.e., proper investment policies) as opposed to dividend irrelevance. They lament the fact that so much research has been devoted to signaling imperfections when Black's (1976) dividend puzzle is easily solved: The optimal corporate policy decision is to simply deliver the full present value of free cash flows to investors.

When the scale of investments is allowed to change, which relaxes the MM (1961) assumptions and is more general than the DeAngelo and DeAngelo (2006) framework, firms without profitable investment opportunities must distribute all free cash flows to make the cost of internal and external equity equal. If firms do not distribute all free cash flows, then internal equity is cheaper than external equity. An unresolved issue is what happens when investment policy is optimal, indicating that there are no free cash flows but that firms want to expand. In this situation, MM (1961) irrelevancy can be established only if firms are indifferent between a zero-dividend/internal-financing policy and a non-zero-dividend/external-financing policy. This issue is not well analyzed or understood.

The DeAngelo and DeAngelo (2006) findings are controversial. They even directly provide rejoinders to criticisms raised by readers of previous working drafts. Berlingeri (2006) agrees on the inadequacy of the MM dividend irrelevance proof but refutes DeAngelo and DeAngelo's conclusion using an arbitrage-based argument. Even after this analysis, debate will probably continue in this area.

CONCLUSIONS

Despite the flaws, the influence of MM's irrelevance theorems on financial theory cannot be understated. Some such as Brennan (1971) consider MM the founders of analytical finance. Undoubtedly, their dividend policy research suffers from limitations. Aside from the issues with the irrelevance proof, their conclusion has little practical value. Dividends clearly do matter. Given dividend relevance, future researchers will likely view MM as Aristotles of finance. While he laid the foundation for the modern scientific method, Aristotle's findings have not proved the test of time. Yet, in his defense, Aristotle made astronomical theories about the sun revolving around the earth without the aid of a telescope. Likewise, MM researched dividends without the aid of modern analytical techniques, data, and computing power. Thus, their reasoning and conclusions appear naive by today's standards. Luckily, researchers only took 40 years or so to seriously question MM's suspect reasoning. Aristotle's views on cosmology endured for more than 1,000 years. Furthermore, despite the volume of research devoted to their relevance and even existence, dividends continue to remain mysterious. Whether the DeAngelo and DeAngelo (2007, 2000b) arguments become widely accepted remains to be seen, but hopefully, researchers will solve this mystery in the near future.

REFERENCES

Allen, Franklin, Antonio E. Bernardo, and Ivo Welch. 2000. "A Theory of Dividends Based on Tax Clienteles. *Journal of Finance* 55:6, 2499–2536.

Ang, James S. 1987. "Do Dividends Matter? A Review of Corporate Dividend Theories and Evidence." *Monograph Series in Finance and Economics*. New York: Salomon Brothers Center for the Study of Financial Institutions and the Graduate School of Business Administration, New York University.

Ang, James S., and Kenneth J. Hunsader. 1996. "The Lifetime Consumption, Dividends, and Leverage Problem: An Application of Spreadsheet with Real Data." *Financial Practice and Education* 6:2, 30–40.

Asquith, Paul, and David W. Mullins. 1983. "The Impact of Initiating Dividend Payments on Shareholders' Wealth." *Journal of Business* 56:1, 77–96.

Baker, H. Kent, Gary E. Powell, and E. Theodore Veit. 2002. "Revisiting the Dividend Puzzle: Do All of the Pieces Now Fit?" *Review of Financial Economics* 11:4, 241–261.

Baker, Malcolm, and Jeffrey Wurgler. 2004. "A Catering Theory of Dividends." *Journal of Finance* 59:3, 1125–1165.

Berlingeri, Hugo Oscar. 2006. "Yes, after All, in an MM World, Dividends Are Irrelevant." Working Paper, Pontificia Universidad Católica Argentina.

Bhattacharya, Sudipto. 1979. "Imperfect Information, Dividend Policy, and 'The Bird in the Hand' Fallacy." *Bell Journal of Economics* 10:1, 259–270.

Black, Fischer. 1976. "The Dividend Puzzle." *Journal of Portfolio Management* 2:2, 5–8.

Black, Fischer, and Myron Scholes. 1974. "The Effects of Dividend Yield and Dividend Policy on Common Stock Prices and Returns." *Journal of Financial Economics* 1:1, 1–22.

Brennan, Michael. J. 1970. "Taxes, Market Valuation and Corporate Financial Policy." *National Tax Journal* 23:4, 407–416.

Brennan, Michael. J. 1971. "A Note on Dividend Irrelevance and the Gordon Valuation Model." *Journal of Finance* 26:5, 1115–1121.

Brickley, James. 1983. "Shareholders Wealth, Information Signaling, and the Specially Designated Dividend: An Empirical Study." *Journal of Financial Economics* 12:2, 187–209.

Chen, Gongmeng, Michael Firth, and Ning Daniel Gao. 2002. "The Information Content of Concurrently Announced Earnings, Cash Dividends, and Stock Dividends: An Investigation of the Chinese Stock Market." *Journal of International Financial Management and Accounting* 13:2, 101–124.

DeAngelo, Harry, and Linda DeAngelo. 2007. "Payout Policy Pedagogy: What Matters and Why?" *European Financial Management* 13:1, 11–27.

DeAngelo, Harry, and Linda DeAngelo. 2006. "The Irrelevance of the MM Dividend Irrelevance Theorem." *Journal of Financial Economics* 79:2, 293–315.

DeAngelo, Harry, Linda DeAngelo, and Douglas J. Skinner. 1996. "Reversal of Fortune: Dividend Signaling and the Disappearance of Sustained Earnings Growth." *Journal of Financial Economics* 40:3, 341–371.

DeAngelo, Harry, Linda DeAngelo, and René M. Stulz. 2006. "Dividend Policy and the Earned/Contributed Capital Mix: A Test of the Life-Cycle Theory." *Journal of Financial Economics* 81:2, 227–254.

Durand, D. 1959. "The Cost of Capital, Corporation Finance, and the Theory of Investment: A Comment." *American Economics Review* 49:4, 639–654.

Easterbrook, Frank H. 1984. "Two Agency Cost Explanations of Dividends." *American Economic Review* 74:4, 650–659.

Fama, Eugene F. 1978. "The Effects of a Firm's Investment and Financing Decisions on the Welfare of Its Security Holders." *American Economic Review* 68:3, 272–284.

Farrar, Donald E., and Lee L. Selwyn. 1967. "Taxes, Corporation Financial Policy and Return to Investors." *National Tax Journal* 20:4, 444–454.

Gordon, Myron J. 1959. "Dividends, Earnings and Stock Prices." *Review of Economics and Statistics* 41:2 (part 1), 99–105.

Gordon, Myron J. 1962. "The Savings, Investment, and Valuation of a Corporation." *Review of Economics and Statistics* 44:1, 37–51.

Gordon, Myron J. 1963. "Optimal Investment and Financing Policy." *Journal of Finance* 18:2, 264–272.

Graham, Benjamin, and David Dodd. 1951. *Security Analysis.* New York: McGraw-Hill Companies.

Grullon, Gustavo, Roni Michaely, Shlomo Benartzi, and Richard H. Thaler. 2005. "Dividend Changes Do Not Signal Changes in Future Profitability." *Journal of Business* 78:5, 1659–1682.

Jensen, Michael C. 1986. "Agency Costs of Free Cash Flow, Corporate Finance, and Takeovers." *American Economic Review* 76:2, 323–329.

John, Kose, and Joseph Williams. 1985. "Dividends, Dilution, and Taxes: A Signaling Equilibrium." *Journal of Finance* 40:4, 1053–1070.

Kalay, Avner, and Roni Michaely. 2000. "Dividends and Taxes: A Re-examination." *Financial Management* 29:2, 55–75.

La Porta, Rafael, Florencio Lopez-de-Silanes, Andrei Shleifer, and Robert W. Vishny. 2000. "Agency Problems and Dividend Policies around the World." *Journal of Finance* 55:1, 1–33.

Lease, Ronald, Kose John, Avner Kalay, Uri Lowenstein, and Oded Sarig. 2000. *Dividend Policy: Its Impact on Firm Value.* Oxford: Oxford University Press.

Lintner, John. 1956. "Distribution of Incomes of Corporations among Dividends, Retained Earnings, and Taxes." *American Economic Review* 46:2, 97–113.

Litzenberger, Robert H., and Krishna Ramaswamy. 1979. "The Effects of Personal Taxes and Dividends on Capital Asset Prices: Theory and Empirical Evidence." *Journal of Financial Economics* 7:2, 163–195.

Miller, Merton H., and Franco Modigliani. 1961. "Dividend Policy, Growth, and the Valuation of Shares." *Journal of Business* 34:4, 411–433.

Miller, Merton H., and Kevin Rock. 1985. "Dividend Policy under Asymmetric Information." *Journal of Finance* 40:4, 1031–1051.

Miller, Merton, and Myron Scholes. 1978. "Dividends and Taxes." *Journal of Financial Economics* 6:4, 333–364.

Miller, Merton, and Myron Scholes. 1982. "Dividends and Taxes: Some Empirical Evidence." *Journal of Political Economy* 90:6, 1118–1141.

Modigliani, Franco, and Merton Miller. 1958. "The Cost of Capital, Corporation Finance, and the Theory of Investment." *American Economic Review* 48:3, 261–297.

Modigliani, Franco, and Merton H. Miller. 1963. "Corporate Income Taxes and the Cost of Capital: A Correction." *American Economic Review* 53:3, 433–443.

Myers, Stewart, and Nicholas Majluf. 1984. "Corporate Financing and Investment Decisions When Firms Have Information That Investors Do Not Have." *Journal of Financial Economics* 13:2, 187–221.

Peterson, Pamela P., David R. Peterson, and James S. Ang. 1985. "Direct Evidence on the Marginal Rate of Taxation on Dividend Income." *Journal of Financial Economics* 14:2, 267–282.

Ross, Stephen A. 1976. "The Arbitrage Theory of Capital Asset Pricing." *Journal of Economic Theory* 13:3, 341–360.

Rubinstein, Mark. 1976. "The Irrelevancy of Dividend Policy in an Arrow-Debreu Economy." *Journal of Finance* 31:4, 1229–1230.

Shefrin, Hersh M., and Meir Statman. 1984. "Explaining Investor Preference for Cash Dividends." *Journal of Financial Economics* 13:2, 253–282.

Stiglitz, Joseph E. 1969. "A Re-examination of the Modigliani-Miller Theorem." *American Economic Review* 59:5, 784–793.

Stiglitz, Joseph E. 1974. "On the Irrelevance of Corporate Financial Policy." *American Economic Review* 64:5, 851–866.

Watts, Ross. 1973. "The Information Content of Dividends." *Journal of Business* 46:2, 191–211.

Williams, John Burr. 1938. *The Theory of Investment Value*. Cambridge, MA: Harvard University Press.

ABOUT THE AUTHORS

James S. Ang is the Bank of America Eminent Scholar and a Professor of Finance at Florida State University. He received his Ph.D. from Purdue University. His academic experience includes Oklahoma State University, Concordia University, and the London Business School. Ang is a past editor of *Financial Management* and a former president of the Financial Management Association. He has published more than 150 journal articles in virtually every major area of finance.

Stephen J. Ciccone is an Associate Professor of Finance at the University of New Hampshire. He received his Ph.D. in finance from Florida State University, graduating in 2000. Before entering academia, he worked as an auditor at Arthur Andersen in Fort Lauderdale. His research interests include dividend policy, analyst forecast properties, and stock market anomalies. He has presented papers at numerous finance conferences around the world, and his work has appeared in several finance and accounting journals.

CHAPTER 7

Residual Dividend Policy

DAVID M. SMITH
Associate Professor of Finance, University at Albany

INTRODUCTION

This chapter examines the motivation for and evidence pertaining to a residual dividend policy. Underlying a residual dividend policy is the tenet that a firm's investment, financing, and dividend policies should be interrelated, even in the short run. With such a policy, the cash flows remaining after the firm makes its new investments determine the dividend size.

In theory, value-maximizing managers will invest only to the degree that positive net present value (NPV) investments are available. When managers exhaust all such opportunities, the firm pays the residual cash flow as the dividend. At times a firm may experience capital constraints and have greater investment opportunities than it has cash flow. In this case, the dividend will be zero. A residual dividend policy can be viewed as one in which the default is to pay no dividend, yet the firm pays a special dividend whenever it meets certain conditions. These conditions include smaller investment opportunities than cash flow and no plans to retire debt or stock. Firms may regularly meet these conditions, even creating the impression of a smoothed dividend policy.

Preinreich (1932) and Sage (1937) provide what is probably the first description in the academic literature of a residual dividend policy. Both develop elements of the idea, but neither labels it as a residual policy. Preinreich (p. 284) notes, "In general it may be said that from the stockholder's point of view the ideal corporate dividend policy would be one which would distribute his entire increase of wealth at regular intervals by . . . paying cash dividends with that portion of corporate earnings which can not be reinvested." According to Sage (pp. 245–246), "'middle-of-the-roaders' [are] those managements that [follow a] policy that best avoids the extremes of 'plowing back' and of 'paying out' all earnings and adopt a 'middle course' in combining the better elements of each."

In their classic article demonstrating dividend policy irrelevance, Miller and Modigliani (1961) (hereafter MM) set forth a framework indicating that firms pay out as dividends all cash flows after profitable investments, namely, a residual dividend policy. DeAngelo and DeAngelo (2006) note that this assumption is the key to MM's dividend irrelevance result.

The remainder of this chapter contains a discussion of the conceptual basis for a residual dividend policy, a stylized example, and empirical evidence surrounding the concept. The empirical evidence takes three forms: macro analysis of dividend payment behavior, accounting and market analysis, and survey analysis.

CONCEPTUAL BASIS

The minimum cash dividend size is zero, while the firm's free cash flows dictate the maximum dividend size in the long run. According to Smith and Warner (1979), leveraged firms often face constraints on dividend payments due to debt covenants even in the short run. Bradley and Roberts (2004) report that 85 percent of the private debt issues they examine have dividend restriction covenants. The constraints typically take the form of limiting cash dividend payments to no more than the firm's cumulative net earnings plus the proceeds from equity shares issued, less cumulative dividends paid. A question for dividend-paying firms is which dividend amount is appropriate. Smith and Warner predict that dividend policy restrictiveness creates less of an incentive for firms to underinvest in profitable projects and creates greater benefits for firms with longer debt maturity. Myers (1977) describes causes of the underinvestment problem.

Drawing on agency theory as formalized by Jensen and Meckling (1976), Jensen (1986) offers a strong justification for following a residual dividend policy. He notes that when managers fail to pay out the cash remaining after making all profitable investments, they are prone to use those resources in ways that are destructive to shareholder wealth. These suboptimal uses include investing in negative NPV projects and consuming excessive perquisites. Following Jensen's prescription to its extreme, firms should pay out all residual cash flow, removing a major source of temptation from managers to overinvest and consume excessive perquisites and avoiding the consequent value destruction.

Easterbrook (1984) suggests that paying dividends frequently creates conditions that require external financing. External financing brings skillful monitoring by market participants such as underwriters, rating agencies, and the security holders themselves. Easterbrook's analysis considers dividends as partially driving the firm's capital acquisition strategy rather than financing needs driving the dividend decision. Keeping with his framework, a value-maximizing firm would follow a modified residual dividend policy in which the firm consistently pays out cash flows in excess of those remaining after investment, necessitating external financing. Easterbrook points out that share repurchases could serve the same purpose as dividends in reducing agency costs.

Similarly, Jensen (1986) notes that debt issues may serve the same purpose as dividends, taking excess cash flows out of the hands of managers and reducing agency problems. By pledging to pay out future cash flows to security holders, albeit to bondholders rather than stockholders, managers avoid wasting the firm's cash flows on projects such as ill-advised takeovers. In support of his argument, Jensen cites empirical studies that uniformly report positive average stock price reactions to leverage-increasing corporate actions. A counterargument against public debt is that the firm is likely to disclose to various parties some of its proprietary information in the issuance process. Thus, by retaining more internally generated funds than are necessary for current investment, the firm helps ensure that its competitive secrets remain safe.

The circumstances surrounding corporate cash holdings relate to the question of whether a residual dividend policy is necessary or desirable. Blanchard, Lopez-de-Silanes, and Shleifer (1994) find evidence supporting the primacy of managerial self interest in the use of cash. Blanchard et al. (p. 337) observe that for firms receiving cash windfalls, "the evidence supports the agency model of managerial behavior, in which managers try to ensure the long-run survival and independence of the firms with themselves at the helm."

Recent research by Foley, Hartzell, Titman, and Twite (2007) links high cash balances to the sometimes-severe tax treatment for multinationals repatriating cash to their home countries. Apart from such special cases, financial economists often view high cash holdings with a jaundiced eye because of the suspicion that managers are likely to use the funds suboptimally. Mikkelson and Partch (2003) study 89 firms that, between 1986 and 1991, followed an extreme policy of holding more than 25 percent of their assets in cash. Contrary to the predictions of agency theory, they find that the firms following this high-liquidity policy invest more in new assets and grow faster. Moreover, their management and governance characteristics do not suggest inferior agency incentives relative to matched firms.

Harford, Mansi, and Maxwell (2008) also report counterintuitive findings, noting that between 1993 and 2004, firms scoring low on governance metrics actually held low cash balances. Such managers were quick to disgorge excess cash to fund items such as share repurchases and acquisitions. Weak-governance managers were disinclined to use their cash for dividend initiations or increases. Harford et al. argue that weak-governance managers with high cash balances fear the attention that high cash draws to their poor governance situations. The managers may also recognize that in some instances others could use the large cash hoard to self-finance corporate control actions against them.

Under a residual dividend policy, managers can plan the payout level only to the extent that they accurately forecast cash flows and investment opportunities. Forecasting either of these is challenging, and forecasting both may be virtually impossible. Researchers such as Penman (1980) report relatively large errors in management forecasts of their firms' net earnings. Thus, the dividend level under a residual policy is unplanned and falls at the far end of a policy continuum relative to a fully managed dividend policy.

Some investors prefer stable dividends. If dividend clienteles exist among shareholders, one shareholder group may prefer high, stable dividends while another may prefer that all returns be capital gains. Different shareholder preferences could arise as a result of diverse portfolio objectives and constraints, including cash flow timing needs, regulatory and fiduciary requirements, and the tax situation of shareholders. For example, certain U.S. pension funds, subject to the Employee Retirement Income Security Act, restrict their investment universe to dividend-paying stocks. In this case, dividend payments are a necessity rather than a mere preference. Imagining a distinct clientele to which a pure residual policy would appeal is difficult.

A residual policy may produce signals that shareholders interpret unconventionally. Investors in a firm following a residual policy are likely to regard dividend changes as a signal of the firm's investment opportunities. For example, they may interpret increased dividends as indicating a paucity of opportunities, which would represent a negative signal. Rational managers whose compensation

Table 7.1 Example of a Residual versus a Managed Dividend Policy

	Time				
	Year 1	Year 2	Year 3	Year 4	Year 5
Internal cash flows	$100	$95	$120	$115	$135
Desirable investment opportunities	85	105	95	120	100
Excess free cash flow	15	0	25	0	35
Dividend under a residual policy	15	0	25	0	35
Dividend under a managed policy	5	10	15	20	25
Managed dividend minus residual dividend	−10	10	−10	20	−10

This table provides a stylized depiction of the contrast between dividends under a residual dividend policy versus a managed dividend policy.
Source: Adapted from Lease et al. (2000, p. 30).

levels are linked to stock returns naturally want to avoid sending a negative sig-nal. Although this is not necessarily a disadvantage of following a residual policy, managers should understand that it is a likely implication.

Lease, John, Kalay, Loewenstein, and Sarig (2000) provide a useful stylized depiction of various dividend policies and, in particular, the contrast between residual versus managed dividend policies. As Table 7.1 shows, the first policy illustrates a pure residual policy, determined by subtracting the cost of desirable investment opportunities from the firm's internal cash flow in each year. The firm pays the remaining cash flow as a dividend. A pure residual policy can produce a highly unstable dividend, which investors would likely regard as unreliable. A managed policy produces a smoother dividend series that investors would likely view as more predictable.

Managed dividend payouts start low and grow by a constant amount yearly. In year 2 and thereafter, the managed dividend policy results in a steadily increas-ing dividend. Under a managed policy, the size of the dividend bears a looser relationship to a firm's excess free cash flow. In the stylized example, the dividend amounts total $75 under either dividend policy, but the timings differ sharply. In year 4, the managed policy would require external financing of $10, because only $10 in cumulative excess cash flow is available to pay the dividend.

Proponents of a managed policy would laud its consistency and predictability, while proponents of a residual policy are likely to contend that the managed policy would produce lower total dividends over the long run. That is, the excess cash of $10 retained in year 1 under a managed policy would tempt managers to make unwise investments, resulting in incremental future dividends that have a present value below $10. Moreover, the cost of financing the additional $10 in year 4 would reduce profitability and cause subsequent dividends to be lower.

The residual dividend policy as described here assumes that the firm will use only internally generated funds for new investment. Another assumption is that the firm has no debt outstanding or that management will allow the current leveraged capital structure to change. Now reconsider the residual dividend policy under the assumption that the firm raises new debt capital each year to partially finance new

Table 7.2 Example of a Residual Dividend Policy for Unlevered versus Levered Firms

	Time				
	Year 1	Year 2	Year 3	Year 4	Year 5
Internal cash flows	$100	$95	$120	$115	$135
Desirable investment opportunities	85	105	95	120	100
Dividend under residual policy					
Unlevered	15	0	25	0	35
20% debt	32*	11	44	19	55
60% debt	66	53	82	67	95

Notes: The residual policy dividend is calculated as internal cash flow less the equity-funded cost of the desirable investment opportunities. In this cell, the dividend is $100 − (1 − 0.20) × $85 = $32. This table provides a stylized depiction of the contrast among residual dividend policy payment amounts for firms with differing capital structures.

investments. Table 7.2 presents three choices: a base case of an unlevered capital structure, along with capital structures of 20 percent debt and 60 percent debt.

As Table 7.2 shows, the use of financial leverage to partially fund new investment projects places lower demands on the firm's internal cash flow. This dramatically reduces the likelihood of a zero dividend. In practice, the internal cash flows should reflect the fact that debt is costly.

As discussed in the subsequent section, empirical evidence strongly indicates that although firms keep investment policy in mind when setting dividend policy, they almost never follow a pure residual dividend policy. The evidence comes in three main forms: macro analysis of dividend behavior, inferences from analyzing accounting data, and surveys of managers.

MACRO ANALYSIS OF DIVIDEND BEHAVIOR

Fama and French (2001) show that the incidence of dividend payment by U.S. firms decreased markedly between the 1970s and 1990s. They also note that the population of firms has changed in favor of smaller, less profitable, higher-sales-growth companies that do not pay dividends. This change in the universe of firms partially explains the decline in divided initiation events and the aggregate payout ratio. The global economy presents numerous and diverse investment opportunities for firms, which argues in favor of aggressive earnings retention. Fama and French find a declining payout ratio for preexisting dividend payers, but this cannot be fully attributed to growth opportunities. Regardless of firm characteristics—size, earnings trend, previous dividend history, and growth opportunities—the propensity of firms to pay dividends has decreased substantially since the 1970s. Thus, managers' use of regular dividends to produce anything resembling a residual dividend policy has decreased.

Arnott and Asness (2003) show that at the macro level, subsequent earnings growth tends to be positively related to the current dividend payout ratio. Unlike most studies designed to test residual theory, their analysis for the period from 1871 to 2001 relates dividend payout policy to lagged earnings. They find that the dividend payout ratio explains more than 24 percent of the variability in five-year earnings growth since 1871 and more than 53 percent since 1946. According to Shiller's (2008) web site, since 1946, payout ratios exceeded 70 percent in 1946 and 1992, and they were below 35 percent in 1974, 1979, and for most of 1995–2001. Although the precise reasons for the positive payout growth remain unclear, Arnott and Asness conclude that aggressive retention and reinvestment of current earnings do not produce high future earnings growth. As a robustness check, they split the sample period into pre-1980 and 1980-forward and recognize 1980 as the beginning of the intensive stock-repurchasing era. The results are largely invariant to subperiod, suggesting that stock repurchases have not altered the fundamental relation between payout and growth.

INFERENCES FROM ACCOUNTING DATA AND MARKET REACTIONS

Although most firms do not follow a payout policy resembling a residual policy, evidence suggests that the market reacts to dividend declarations in the context of the firm's investment opportunity set. Lang and Litzenberger (1989) provide some of the most compelling evidence. They examine the stock market's reaction to corporate dividend changes for a sample of firms with Tobin's Q ratios greater than and less than 1.0. A Q ratio greater than 1.0 reflects the market's assessment that the firm's assets in place have a positive NPV. Tobin's Q ratios less than 1.0 suggest that the firm has overinvested in unprofitable assets. For firms in Lang and Litzenberger's sample, the market's reaction to dividend declarations is greater for firms having Tobin's Q ratios less than 1.0 than for those with Tobin's Q ratios greater than 1.0. This suggests that the market particularly welcomes cash payouts by firms appearing to have no attractive investment opportunities. Moreover, Lang and Litzenberger interpret their results to be evidence against dividends as a signaling mechanism.

The interaction between investment policy and dividend policy extends to dividend cuts as well, but the empirical record is far less rich. The stock market generally interprets dividend cuts as bad news. Woolridge and Ghosh (1985) examine a small sample of firms that cut dividends for the stated reason of increasing investment in profitable projects. While Woolridge and Ghosh confirm that the market reaction is negative for their sample as well, they show that the firm's value in the stock market is largely restored if it follows through on the stated plans to increase investment. Lonie, Abeyratna, Power, and Sinclair (1996) obtain similar results for the U.K. market.

Denis, Denis, and Sarin (1994) examine dividend changes between 1962 and 1988. In contrast to the predictions of the overinvestment hypothesis, they find that dividend-increasing (decreasing) firms that have Tobin's Q ratios less than 1.0 actually increase (decrease) their subsequent capital expenditures. Although they do not reach a definitive conclusion about the use of dividends specifically to address agency problems, Denis et al. (p. 586) state that their results are "consistent with the argument made by Jensen (1986) and others that regular dividend payments are likely to be weak substitutes for debt payments in controlling free cash flow problems." As noted later, Fama and French (2002) reach comparable conclusions about the substitutability of dividends and short-term borrowing.

In a similar analysis, Yoon and Starks (1995) find a positive relation between the magnitude of dividend changes and subsequent capital investments during the 1969–1988 period. Their results hold for both high and low Tobin's-Q firms. This evidence conflicts with Lang and Litzenberger's (1989) predictions that dividend increases signal managers' inclination to cut back on investments that may be value decreasing. Under the Lang and Litzenberger free cash flow/overinvestment framework, decreases in capital investments should follow dividend increases.

The findings of other studies on the relation between dividends and investments suggest that the issue remains unresolved. For example, Elston (1996) offers evidence that the relation between dividend and investment policy was relatively weak for large U.S. firms from 1975 to 1988. Slater and Zwirlein (1996), in contrast, show a negative relation between dividend payout and investment for S&P 400 Industrial Index firms between 1986 and 1989.

With a residual policy, the dividend is essentially the "plug" figure in setting the free cash flow equal to zero. If a residual policy were common, dividend payouts would change when investment activity changed. Fama and French (2002) show that dividends generally do not change in response to changes in a firm's short-term investment opportunities. Rather, firms keep their dividends relatively stable and adjust for cash flow needs using short-term borrowing. Fama and French conclude:

> Our tests produce a clear story about short-term financing decisions in response to earnings and investment. For dividend payers, it is a pecking order story. The pecking order model posits that dividends are sticky, leaving variation in earnings and investment to be absorbed largely by debt. The dividend regressions … say that long-term dividend policy conforms to the Lintner model, and there is little evidence that dividends vary to accommodate short-term variation in investment. (p. 30)

Notwithstanding Fama and French's (2002) conclusion that debt rather than cash is the true residual account for firms in general, some researchers have observed a residual-type dividend policy for a subset of firms. Using regression on factors extracted from a factor analysis, Alli, Khan, and Ramírez (1993) find evidence consistent with a negative relation between firm capital expenditures and dividends. They interpret this finding as support for a residual policy. Aivazian, Booth, and Cleary (2006) find a strong relation between the nature of U.S. firms' dividend policies from 1985 to 1999 and whether those firms had a bond rating. They contend that firms accessing the public debt markets tend to be large, profitable enterprises with high levels of tangible assets. Such firms generally engage the rating agencies to provide a bond rating. These are also common characteristics of dividend-paying firms. Aivazian et al. show that firms with bond ratings tend to smooth their dividends, much as Lintner (1956) observed in his sample of large firms.

According to Aivazian et al. (2006), smaller, less profitable firms with low levels of tangible assets tend to use private bank debt. Relative to public bondholders, bank lenders are informed investors. Informed bank borrowers do not need for the firm to use dividend policy to help solve adverse selection problems. Such firms are free to pay out their excess earnings as dividends, and consequently, the dividends are frequently volatile. In summary, Aivazian et al. show that firms with a bond rating follow a managed dividend policy, while those without a bond rating tend to follow a residual policy.

An empirical question that arises when considering whether a firm follows a residual policy is the timing of the earnings out of which dividends are netted. Grullon, Michaely, and Swaminathan (2002) examine whether dividends indicate the paying firm's stage of maturity. They demonstrate that firms increasing their dividends experience a decrease in systematic risk, which is one of the chief drivers of higher announcement-period stock returns for the firms. Dividend-increasing firms also suffer drops in profitability and do not change their capital expenditures. In short, dividend increases appear in some cases to come before the revelation that capital expenditures remained flat, in this instance leading when market participants may normally think of dividends as lagging.

SURVEY EVIDENCE

The survey studies of dividend policy show that companies generally do not profess to intentionally follow a residual policy. Yet the residual dividend approach has long had some adherents among corporate managers.

Baker, Farrelly, and Edelman (1985) analyze survey responses of 318 firms from three industry types: manufacturing firms, wholesalers and retailers, and utilities. Across all three industry types, managers express little support for the notion that investment and dividend policies are linked, and even less support for a connection between financing and dividend policies. Specifically, the statement that "dividend distributions should be viewed as a residual after financing desired investments from available earnings" received slight to strong agreement from only 35 percent of the manufacturing firm and wholesale or retail firm managers, and from only 10.6 percent of the utility firm managers.

Since the time of Baker et al.'s (1985) paper, the popularity of a residual policy has ebbed. Brav, Graham, Harvey, and Michaely (2005) examine dividend policy survey responses of 384 corporate financial managers. Their chief evidence pertaining to residual policy is that about two-thirds of managers from responding firms maintain a target dividend per share or growth rate per share. If managers were to follow a residual policy, they would maintain a target residual cash amount or ratio.

A pure residual policy would necessitate occasional dividend cuts. More than 50 years of evidence, starting with Lintner (1956) and including Baker et al. (1985) and Brav et al. (2005), reveals a strong managerial aversion to dividend cuts. Baker et al. find that manufacturing firms, wholesalers and retailers, and utilities all express dividend-cut aversion as their most strongly held view on dividend policy. Brav et al. also report that managers are extremely reluctant to cut dividends, and that they will go to great lengths, including selling assets and laying off workers, to avoid taking such a step. In fact, managers in their sample who initiated dividend payments report having second thoughts about initiating dividends as large as they did.

Baker and Smith (2006) survey 618 firms about their dividend policy. Of these, half are firms that maintained consistently low levels of annual cash flow after dividends throughout the 1990s. The authors interpret this persistent pattern as a reflection of residual dividend policy behavior. The other half of the sample contains dividend-paying firms with high cash flow after dividends, highly variable cash flows, or both. As Table 7.3 shows, irrespective of which subsample of

Table 7.3 Corporate Manager Survey Responses to Statements about Residual Dividend Policy

Statement	n	Level of Agreement					Mean	χ^2	Group
		Strongly Disagree −2	Disagree −1	No Opinion 0	Agree +1	Strongly Agree +2			
My firm views its investment, financing, and dividend decisions as interrelated.	65	3.1%	4.6%	13.9%	36.9%	41.5%	1.09	0.46	Residual
	47	4.3	8.4	4.3	36.2	46.8	1.13		Matched
My firm views cash dividends as a residual after funding desired investments from earnings.	65	23.1	36.9	24.6	9.2	6.2	−0.62	2.38	Residual
	46	26.1	34.8	15.2	13.0	10.8	−0.52		Matched
My firm's expenditures on new capital investments typically affect its dividend payments.	65	30.8	30.8	21.5	12.3	4.6	−0.71	0.92	Residual
	47	34.0	23.4	21.3	14.9	6.4	−0.64		Matched
My firm often needs additional external financing as a result of paying cash dividends.	65	56.9	15.4	10.8	12.3	4.6	−1.08	1.80	Residual
	47	63.8	10.6	14.9	8.5	2.1	−1.26		Matched

This table contains statements pertaining to a residual dividend policy and the percentage of respondents expressing agreement or disagreement with each statement. The responses are ranked in order of level of agreement from highest to lowest according to the means of the residual group. The chi-square tests show whether the distribution of responses between the residual and matched groups differs significantly. None of the mean responses between the residual and matched groups differs significantly at normal levels.
Source: Adapted from Baker and Smith (2006, Table 6).

managers was questioned, less than one-quarter of managers agree with either of the following statements: "My firm views cash dividends as a residual after funding desired investments from earnings" and "My firm's expenditures on new capital investments typically affect its dividend payments." If firms followed a residual dividend policy, respondents should express agreement with these statements. Surprisingly, the subsample of firms behaving as though they follow a residual policy is less likely than control firms to express agreement with either statement. In a separate analysis, only 6 of 202 respondents gave, "Availability of profitable investment opportunities" as one of the two most important factors in determining their dividend policy. In summary, the evidence suggests that few firms in the present era profess to follow a residual dividend policy.

In a sample of 164 British firms, Dhanani (2005) obtains similar results. Two-thirds of respondents indicate explicit disagreement with the following statement: "Dividends are a cash residue returned to investors after investment decisions have been made." Parsing the results, Dhanani notes that firms with higher growth opportunities are somewhat more likely to express agreement.

CONCLUSIONS

Strong arguments exist in favor of a residual cash dividend policy as a means to optimize the efficiency of corporate resource use. Yet most firms do not follow a residual dividend policy. For various reasons, managers generally follow a managed payout policy that involves dividend smoothing. This managed policy also involves the retention of cash beyond investment needs in some periods and short-term borrowing to meet temporary cash flow shortages during other periods. From a managerial perspective, maintaining a predictable dividend series, with no cuts or omissions, is far more important than returning unused cash to shareholders in the short run.

Certain elements of the corporate population show a higher proclivity to follow a residual policy, particularly those firms that use private bank debt rather than publicly issued bonds. Still, on the continuum between a pure residual policy and a pure managed policy, accounting data show that most dividend-paying firms are firmly on the managed end. The CFO survey evidence over several decades provides definitive confirmation of firms' intent to be in that position.

REFERENCES

Aivazian, Varouj A., Laurence Booth, and Sean Cleary. 2006. "Dividend Smoothing and Debt Ratings." *Journal of Financial and Quantitative Analysis* 41: 2, 439–453.

Alli, Kasim L., A. Qayyum Khan, and Gabriel G. Ramírez. 1993. "Determinants of Corporate Dividend Policy: A Factorial Analysis." *Financial Review* 28: 4, 523–547.

Arnott, Robert D., and Clifford S. Asness. 2003. "Surprise! Higher Dividends = Higher Earnings Growth." *Financial Analysts Journal* 59: 1, 70–87.

Baker, H. Kent, Gail Farrelly, and Richard Edelman. 1985. "A Survey of Management Views on Dividend Policy." *Financial Management* 14: 3, 78–84.

Baker, H. Kent, and David M. Smith. 2006. "In Search of a Residual Dividend Policy." *Review of Financial Economics* 15: 1, 1–18.

Blanchard, Olivier Jean, Florencio Lopez-de-Silanes, and Andrei Shleifer. 1994. "What Do Firms Do with Cash Windfalls?" *Journal of Financial Economics* 36: 3, 337–360.

Bradley, Michael, and Michael R. Roberts. 2004. "The Structure and Pricing of Corporate Debt Covenants." Working Paper, Duke University.

Brav, Alon, John R. Graham, Campbell R. Harvey, and Roni Michaely. 2005. "Payout Policy in the 21st Century." *Journal of Financial Economics* 77: 3, 483–527.

DeAngelo, Harry, and Linda DeAngelo. 2006. "The Irrelevance of the MM Dividend Irrelevance Theorem." *Journal of Financial Economics* 79: 2, 293–315.

Denis, David J., Diane K. Denis, and Atulya Sarin. 1994. "The Information Content of Dividend Changes: Cash Flow Signaling, Overinvestment, and Dividend Clienteles." *Journal of Financial and Quantitative Analysis* 29: 4, 567–587.

Dhanani, Alpa. 2005. "Corporate Dividend Policy: The Views of British Financial Managers." *Journal of Business Finance and Accounting* 32: 7/8, 1625–1672.

Easterbrook, Frank H. 1984. "Two Agency-Cost Explanations of Dividends." *American Economic Review* 74: 4, 650–659.

Elston, Julie Ann. 1996. "Dividend Policy and Investment: Theory and Evidence from U.S. Panel Data." *Managerial and Decision Economics* 17: 3, 267–75.

Fama, Eugene F., and Kenneth R. French. 2001. "Disappearing Dividends: Changing Firm Characteristics or Lower Propensity to Pay?" *Journal of Financial Economics* 60: 1, 3–43.

Fama, Eugene F., and Kenneth R. French. 2002. "Testing Trade-Off and Pecking Order Predictions about Dividends and Debt." *Review of Financial Studies* 15: 1, 1–33.

Foley, Fritz C., Jay C. Hartzell, Sheridan Titman, and Garry Twite. 2007. "Why Do Firms Hold So Much Cash? A Tax-Based Explanation." *Journal of Financial Economics* 86: 3, 579–607.

Grullon, Gustavo, Roni Michaely, and Bhaskaran Swaminathan. 2002. "Are Dividend Changes a Sign of Firm Maturity?" *Journal of Business* 75: 3, 387–424.

Harford, Jarrad, Sattar A. Mansi, and William F. Maxwell. 2008. "Corporate Governance and Firm Cash Holdings in the U.S." *Journal of Financial Economics* 87: 3, 535–555.

Jensen, Michael C. 1986. "Agency Costs of Free Cash Flow, Corporate Finance, and Takeovers." *American Economic Review* 76: 2, 323–329.

Jensen, Michael C., and William H. Meckling. 1976. "Theory of the Firm: Managerial Behavior, Agency Costs and Ownership Structure." *Journal of Financial Economics* 3: 4, 305–360.

Lang, Larry H. P., and Robert Litzenberger. 1989. "Dividend Announcements: Cash Flow Signaling vs. Free Cash Flow Hypothesis." *Journal of Financial Economics* 24: 1, 137–154.

Lease, Ronald, Kose John, Avner Kalay, Uri Loewenstein, and Oded Sarig. 2000. *Dividend Policy: Its Impact of Firm Value.* Boston: Harvard Business School Press.

Lintner, John. 1956. "Distribution of Incomes of Corporations among Dividends, Retained Earnings, and Taxes." *American Economic Review* 46: 2, 97–113.

Lonie, Alisdair A., Gunasekarage Abeyratna, David M. Power, and C. Donald Sinclair. 1996. "The Stock Market Reaction to Dividend Announcements." *Journal of Economic Studies* 23: 1, 32–52.

Mikkelson, Wayne H., and M. Megan Partch. 2003. "Do Persistent Large Cash Reserves Hinder Performance?" *Journal of Financial and Quantitative Analysis* 38: 2, 275–294.

Miller, Merton H., and Franco Modigliani. 1961. "Dividend Policy, Growth, and the Valuation of Shares." *Journal of Business* 34: 4, 411–433.

Myers, Stewart C. 1977. "Determinants of Corporate Borrowing." *Journal of Financial Economics* 5: 2, 147–175.

Penman, Stephen B. 1980. "An Empirical Investigation of the Voluntary Disclosure of Corporate Earnings Forecasts." *Journal of Accounting Research* 18: 1, 132–160.

Preinreich, Gabriel A. D. 1932. "Stock Yields, Stock Dividends and Inflation." *Accounting Review* 7: 4, 273–289.

Sage, George H. 1937. "Dividend Policy and Business Contingencies." *Harvard Business Review* 15: 2, 245–252.

Shiller, Robert. 2008. Availiable at http://www.econ.yale.edu/~shiller/data.htm.

Slater, Stanley F., and Thomas J. Zwirlein. 1996. "The Structure of Financial Strategy: Patterns in Financial Decision Making." *Managerial and Decision Economics* 17: 3, 253–266.

Smith, Clifford W., Jr., and Jerold B. Warner. 1979. "On Financial Contracting: An Analysis of Bond Covenants." *Journal of Financial Economics* 7: 2, 117–161.

Woolridge, J. Randall, and Chinmoy Ghosh. 1985. "Dividend Cuts: Do They Always Signal Bad News?" *Midland Corporate Finance Journal* 3: 2, 20–32.

Yoon, Pyung Sig, and Laura T. Starks. 1995. "Signaling, Investment Opportunities, and Dividend Announcements." *Review of Financial Studies* 8: 4, 995–1018.

ABOUT THE AUTHOR

David M. Smith is an Associate Professor of Finance and Director of the Center for Institutional Investment Management at the University at Albany. He earned his bachelor's and doctoral degrees in finance from Virginia Tech and holds the CFA, CMA, and CFM designations. He has published more than 20 peer-reviewed articles on corporate finance and investment topics. Smith is also the recipient of several teaching and research recognitions, including the State University of New York Chancellor's Award for Teaching Excellence and the Financial Planning Association's Financial Frontiers Award for research. He has served on numerous boards, including the Board of Regents for the Institute of Certified Management Accountants and the Council of Examiners for CFA Institute.

CHAPTER 8

Taxes and Clientele Effects

SAMIR SAADI
Ph.D. candidate, Queen's School of Business, Queen's University

SHANTANU DUTTA
Assistant Professor of Finance, University of Ontario Institute of Technology

INTRODUCTION

In their seminal paper, Miller and Modigliani (1961) (hereafter MM) show that in an ideal world, dividend policy is irrelevant. Consequently, in a world without corporate and personal taxes, shareholders should be indifferent between receiving dividends and receiving capital gains. Yet when the tax rate on capital gains is less than the personal tax rate on ordinary income, shareholders as rational investors should prefer to receive income in the form of capital gains rather than dividends. On the other hand, if the tax rate on capital gains is greater than the personal tax rate, shareholders should prefer to receive income in the form of dividends rather than capital gains.

Because individual investors usually have a higher personal tax rate on ordinary income than on capital gains, firms theoretically should not pay dividends if they want to maximize shareholder wealth. Instead, companies should use share repurchases to distribute corporate earnings, which would allow their shareholders to avoid paying higher income-tax rates on dividends. Thus, a logical question is, Why do firms keep paying cash dividends if their shareholders have a higher after-tax payoff through share repurchase? This question continues to puzzle financial economists and makes dividend payout one of the greatest enigmas of modern finance.

Over the past several decades, a large volume of literature has emerged searching for the missing pieces of what Black (1976) called the dividend puzzle. Financial economists have developed various theories to help explain this puzzle, including tax preference and dividend clienteles. According to the tax preference explanation, investors should prefer that firms retain cash instead of pay dividends because the tax rate on dividends is typically higher than on long-term capital gains. Firms should keep dividend payments low if they want to maximize share price. Yet early studies that examine the effect of taxes on dividend policy provide mixed evidence. Consistent with the clientele effect, Pettit (1977) finds that younger individual investors, investors in low tax brackets, and investors with substantial differences between their ordinary income tax and capital gains tax rates prefer to hold stocks with a high dividend yield. By contrast, Lewellen, Stanley, Lease, and Schlarbaum (1978) use the same database as Pettit but report only a weak relationship between dividend yields of investors' portfolios and their marginal tax rates.

Other studies investigate the dividend and tax relationship by examining major changes in tax regimes such as the 1986 and 2003 Tax Reform Act in the United States (Bloster and Janjigian, 1991; Means, Charoenwong, and Kang, 1992; Papaioannou and Savarese, 1994, Casey and Dickens, 2000). Such changes provide natural experiments to analyze the association between taxes and dividend policy. Despite extensive research, researchers still dispute the effects of dividend taxation on dividend policies largely because of the lack of compelling tax variations and fully convincing research designs. The purpose of this chapter is to discuss the relationship between taxation and dividend policy including an overview of the evolving literature over the past five decades.

DIVIDEND POLICY IN A WORLD WITHOUT TAXES

In an influential study, MM (1961) show that in an ideal world characterized by perfect capital markets, rational behavior, and perfect certainty, firms should be indifferent between distributing earnings to shareholders through dividends or through share repurchases. MM define this concept as dividend irrelevance. An implication of MM's findings is that dividend policy does not affect either firm value or shareholder wealth.

Although the following proof of dividend irrelevance theory is straightforward, understanding the assumptions needed for this theory to hold is important. First, under the assumption of perfect capital markets, no trader (buyer or seller) of securities is large enough to substantially influence the market price; information is free and equally accessible to all traders; there are no transaction costs or brokerage fees; and no tax differentials exist between distributed and undistributed profits or between dividends and capital gains. Second, if rational behavior holds, investors prefer more wealth to less and are indifferent about whether increases in their wealth take the form of cash payments or capital gains. Third, under perfect certainty, each investor has full assurance with respect to both the future investment program and profits of every corporation.

Under these assumptions, the price of a share is such that its rate of return for a given period is equal to:

$$r_t = \frac{p_{t+1} - p_t + d_t}{p_t}, \tag{8.1}$$

where p_{t+1} is the price of the share at the beginning of period $t + 1$; p_t is the price of the share at the beginning of period t; and d_t is the total dividend per share paid over the period t. A common way to define the rate of return is as the sum of capital gains $[(p_{t+1} - p_t)/p_t]$ and dividend yields (d_t/p_t).

The concept of dividend irrelevance is better shown when using the value of the firm as a whole instead of the value per share. Let n_t be the number of shares outstanding at beginning of period t. Hence, the value of the firm at the beginning of period t is $V_t = n_t \times p_t$ and the total dividends paid over the period t

is $D_t = n_t \times d_t$. The value of the firm can be written as a function of total dividends paid by multiplying the numerator and the denominator of Equation 8.1 by n_t, replace $n_t \times p_t$ and $n_t \times d_t$ by V_t and D_t, respectively, and solving for V_t:

$$V_t = \frac{n_t \times p_{t+1} + D_t}{1 + r_t}. \tag{8.2}$$

Assuming a firm issues no new shares over the period t, $n_t \times d_{t+1}$ is simply the value of the firm at the beginning of period $t + 1$, which is denoted as V_{t+1}. But if the firm issues say m_t new shares, its value at the beginning of period $t + 1$ becomes $V_{t+1} = n_{t+1} \times P_{t+1}$ with $n_{t+1} = n_f + m_f$, and Equation 8.2 can be restated as follows:

$$V_t = \frac{V_{t+1} - m_t \times p_{t+1} + D_t}{1 + r_t}. \tag{8.3}$$

Now, let I_t be the level of investment or increase in the firm's holding of tangible assets in period t, and let X_t be the firm's total net profits for the period. The firm finances the amount of capital required to undertake investments (I_t) and to distribute dividends (D_t) through net profits (X_t) and sale of new shares ($m_t \times P_{t+1}$). Thus, the use of capital should equate to the source of capital:

$$I_t + D_t = X_t + m_t \times p_{t+1}. \tag{8.4}$$

Equation 8.4 is the key to proving dividend irrelevance theory by substituting the expression of either D_t or ($m_t \times P_{t+1}$) into Equation 8.3. From Equation 8.4, D_t becomes:

$$D_t = X_t + m_t \times p_{t+1} - I_t. \tag{8.5}$$

Substituting Expression 8.5 into Equation 8.4 results in:

$$V_t = \frac{V_{t+1} + X_t - I_t}{1 + r_t}. \tag{8.6}$$

Notice that the amount of current dividends, D_t, does not appear directly in Equation 8.6. Because V_{t+1}, X_t, I_f, and r_t are all independent of D_t; a firm's current dividend policy does not affect its value. Future dividend policy also does not affect V_t because V_{t+1} is independent of D_{t+1}. In other words, in an ideal world, the value of a firm should depend on its profitability and investment policy and not on how the firm distributes net profits to shareholders. Moreover, dividend policy is irrelevant not only to firm value but also to shareholder wealth, because in a world without taxes, shareholders should be indifferent between receiving cash payments or capital gains by allowing the firm to retain its earnings and to use them to repurchase shares.

DIVIDEND POLICY IN A WORLD WITH TAXES

As just shown in MM's ideal world, dividend policy is irrelevant to both firm value and shareholder wealth. Let's see whether the dividend irrelevance theory still holds after introducing corporate and personal taxes. One important issue is to determine whether shareholders are indifferent between dividends and share repurchases. Farrar and Selwyn (1967) answer this question using a partial equilibrium model in which they assume that shareholders maximize after-tax income, as denoted by Z_t.

Assume that t_c is the corporate tax rate; t_{pi} is the personal tax rate on the income of the ith shareholder; t_{gi} is the tax rate on capital gains; D_c is the corporate debt; D_{pi} is the personal debt; and k is the interest rate on debt assumed to be the same for corporate and personal debt. To determine under which alternative the ith shareholder is better off requires computing shareholder's after-tax income under each alternative and then choosing the alternative that provides the most after-tax income. If the firm decides to disburse all its profits as dividends, the ith shareholder will have the following after-tax income:

$$Z_i^d = [(X_t - kD_c)(1 - t_c) - kD_{pi}](1 - t_{pi}). \tag{8.7}$$

If the firm decides to retain and use all its profits to repurchase shares, shareholders will receive the following after-tax income, which is taxed as capital gains:

$$Z_i^g = (X_t - kD_c)(1 - t_c)(1 - t_{gi}) - kD_{pi}(1 - t_{pi}). \tag{8.8}$$

For ease of comparison with Equation 8.7, Equation 8.8 can be written as follows:

$$Z_i^g = [(X_t - kD_c)(1 - t_c) - kD_{pi}](1 - t_{gi}) + kD_{pi}(t_{pi} - t_{gi}). \tag{8.9}$$

Thus, when the government taxes ordinary income at a lower rate than capital gains ($t_{pi} < t_{gi}$), the ith shareholder as a rational investor should prefer to receive income in the form of dividends rather than capital gains, because $Z_i^p > Z_i^g$. If $t_{pi} = t_{gi}$, as is currently the case in the United States, then $Z_i^p = Z_i^g$ and the ith shareholder should be indifferent between receiving dividends or capital gains. However, when the government taxes ordinary income more heavily than capital gains ($t_{pi} > t_{gi}$), shareholders should prefer to receive income in the form of capital gains rather than dividends, because $Z_i^p < Z_i^g$. Therefore, to distribute corporate earnings, firms should not pay dividends but should use share repurchases. Ironically, several studies document large payouts of cash dividends when the tax rate on capital gains is greater than the personal tax rate on dividends (Feenberg, 1981; Peterson, Peterson, and Ang, 1985; Saadi and Chkir, 2008).

Miller and Scholes (1978) attempt to explain this puzzle by claiming that individual investors should be indifferent between the two forms of payment by avoiding the dividend tax. They contend that shareholders can avoid the tax on dividends by borrowing money and investing the funds in tax-deferred insurance annuities. To illustrate, suppose that ith shareholder has $6,000 in dividend income. To defer the taxes on this dividend, the shareholder would borrow $100,000 at

6 percent and invest the proceeds in a tax-deferred insurance annuity that pays an interest rate of 6 percent. The $6,000 of interest on the loan offsets the $6,000 of taxable dividend income, which permits the shareholder to defer the tax on the dividend income until after withdrawing the money from the insurance annuity. In practice, shareholders rarely follow the dividend tax-avoidance scheme of Miller and Scholes. In fact, studies by Feenberg (1981) and Peterson et al. (1985) show that investors still pay large amounts of tax on dividend income.

For instance, until 1982 the U.S. tax rate on dividend income was as high as 70 percent, which was considerably higher than the tax rate on capital gains. Yet companies often had large dividend payouts. What caused corporations to pay dividends, despite the tax disadvantages, instead of using share repurchases? One potential explanation is that managers did not fully understand the association between dividend policy and share repurchase. In fact, share repurchases did not begin to gain popularity until the Securities and Exchange Commission (SEC) adopted Rule 10b-18, which provides clarifications on share repurchase. According to Grullon and Michaely (2002), share repurchases in the United States increased from about $6.6 billion in 1980 to $202.8 billion in 1999. By contrast, U.S. corporations paid out $197.8 billion as dividends in 1999, marking the first time that share repurchases exceeded cash dividends. Studies by Denis and Osobov (2008) and von Eije and Megginson (2008) document the increase in share repurchases in both Canada and Europe. The simultaneous decline in the propensity to pay dividends, first documented by Fama and French (2001), led some managers to consider share repurchase as a substitute for paying dividends after the adoption of SEC Rule 10b-18.

The tax disadvantage of dividend income does not apply to all investors. Although taxable investors should have a greater preference for capital gains than dividends, tax-exempt investors such as pension funds should prefer comparable corporations that pay dividends over those that do not. Thus, firms with low dividend payouts should attract investors in low tax brackets and/or tax-exempt investors, while firms with high dividend payouts should attract investors in high tax brackets. Researchers refer to this situation as dividend clienteles or clientele effects.

DIVIDEND CLIENTELES

Ogden, Jen, and O'Connor (2003, p. 479) define clientele effects as "a set of investors who are attracted to the stocks of firms that have the dividend policy they prefer, based on their tax or liquidity circumstances." The authors argue that managers can enhance the share price via the clientele effect by adopting a dividend policy that appeals to investors whose preferences are not met by other firms currently in the stock market. Recent studies by Chetty and Saez (2005) and Brav, Graham, Harvey, and Michaely (2008) link dividends to corporate governance and suggest that the preferences of controlling shareholders may influence a firm's response to tax changes.

MM (1961, p. 431) mention the clientele effect as follows:

If for example the frequency distribution of corporate payout ratios happened to correspond exactly with the distribution of investor preferences for payout ratios, then the existence of these preferences would clearly lead ultimately to a situation whose implications were different, in no fundamental respect, from the perfect market case. Each corporation would tend to attract to itself a clientele consisting of those preferring its particular payout ratio, but one clientele would be as good as another in terms of the valuation it would imply for firms.

Although many studies examine the issue of dividend clientele, no consensus exists about the findings. While some empirical studies support this prediction, others provide contradictory evidence. Researchers use two major methodologies to examine tax-induced dividend clienteles. The first approach uses a variant of the capital asset pricing model (CAPM), and the second examines the behavior of the stock price on the ex-dividend day.

An example of the first method is the study by Pettit (1977), which uses a multiple regression model to analyze the portfolio position of individual accounts handled by large retail brokerage houses. Consistent with the clientele effect, Pettit finds that younger individual investors in low tax brackets and investors with substantial differences between their ordinary income tax and capital-gains tax rates prefer to hold stocks with a high dividend yield. Using the same database as Pettit, Lewellen et al. (1978) find a weak association between dividend yields of investors' portfolios and their marginal tax rates. They fail to find evidence of companies adjusting their dividend policy in order to satisfy the preferences of investors who are in different tax brackets. By contrast, Lewellen et al. report that dividend payouts appear stable over time.

Ex-Dividend Day Studies

Using the second approach to measure clientele effects, Elton and Gruber (1970) examine price movements around the ex-dividend dates of stocks listed in the U.S. stock market from April 1966 through March 1967. Assuming that shareholders prefer to maximize after-tax wealth, Elton and Gruber derive an expression relating the stock prices on the ex-dividend day and the marginal tax rate of shareholders. Consider an investor holding a known number of dividend-paying shares bought at unit price P_p. Let P_c be the price at which an investor can sell shares on the with-dividend day and t_g be the capital gains tax rate. If $P_c > P_p$, and the seller has held the stock long enough for the sale to be classified as a capital gain, the investor's after-tax cash flow from selling with dividends, ignoring time value of money and assuming risk neutrality equals $P_c - (P_c - P_p)(t_g)$. On the other hand, if the seller waits until the ex-dividend day to sell, the price that the investor receives is P_x. Ceteris paribus, the after-tax valuation of the cash flows now equals $P_x - (P_x - P_p)(t_g) + D(1 - t_p)$, where t_p represents the tax rate on personal income.

According to Elton and Gruber (1970), the equilibrium around the ex-dividend day is such that marginal stockholders are indifferent between selling the shares with or without dividends. Thus, the following relationship should hold:

$$P_c - (P_c - P_p)(t_g) = P_x - (P_x - P_p)(t_g) + D(1 - t_p). \qquad (8.10)$$

Simplifying Equation 8.10, the ratio of price drop to dividends equals:

$$\frac{P_c - P_x}{D} = \frac{1 - t_p}{1 - t_g}. \qquad (8.11)$$

In a world without taxes, ignoring the time value of the money in the short period between the ex-dividend date and the dividend payment date, the stock price should drop by the value of the dividend on a stock's ex-dividend day to prevent arbitrage. Yet in one the earliest published studies on ex-dividend day pricing, Campbell and Beranek (1955) observe that the average ex-dividend day stock price drop is slightly less than the dividend.

Elton and Gruber (1970) provide a tax-based argument and state that ex-dividend day share prices are set in such a way that marginal long-term investors are indifferent between buying and/or selling before and after the ex-dividend day. Consequently, the ex-dividend day drop in stock price relative to dividends should reflect the differential taxation of dividends and capital gains of the long-term investors. This magnitude could indicate the identity and the tax status of the long-term investor. Because the tax rate on dividends generally exceeds the rate on long-term capital gains, the stock price does not need to drop by the full amount of the dividend on the ex-dividend day. Studies by Elton and Gruber (1970) and Elton, Gruber, and Rentzeler (1984) find evidence leading to the conclusion that investors in high tax brackets prefer stocks with low dividend yields, while investors in low brackets prefer stocks with high dividend yields. This evidence supports the dividend clientele idea of MM (1961).

Because the MM hypothesis is a key tenet of modern finance in terms of dividend relevance and dividend clientele effects, many researchers have investigated the Elton and Gruber (1970) results. Studies that reexamine the U.S. market include Poterba (1986), Lamdin and Hiemstra (1993), Bhardwaj and Brooks (1999), Koski (1996), McDonald (2001), Bell and Jenkinson (2002), Graham, Michaely, and Roberts (2003), and Green (1980). Non-U.S. studies include those in the following countries: Canada (Athanassakos, 1996; Booth and Johnson, 1984; Bauer, Beveridge, and Sivakumar, 2002); China (Milonas, Travlos, and Xiao, 2002); the Netherlands (Florentsen and Rydqvist, 2002); Germany (McDonald, 2001); Greece (Milonas and Travlos, 2001); Hong Kong (Kadapakkam, 2000); Italy (Michaely and Murgia, 1995); Japan (Kato and Loewenstein, 1995); New Zealand (Bartholdy and Briown, 2002); Spain (Gardecazabal and Regulez, 2002); Sweden (Daunfeldt, 2002; Green and Rydqvist, 1999), and the United Kingdom (Ang, Blackwell, and Megginson, 1991; Poterba and Summers, 1984, 1985).

More specifically, studies by Bali and Hite (1998) and Frank and Jagannathan (1998) relate the ex-dividend day premium to market microstructure effects and suggest that the ex-dividend day premium may deviate from one even in the absence of taxes to reflect tick size and bid-ask bounce. In addition, Frank and Jagannathan find that price discreteness has a similar effect on observed price behavior, as would be the case if long-term traders determined prices. These studies suggest that the behavior of share prices on the ex-dividend date may be unrelated to taxes but can better be explained by market microstructure.

Similarly, some earlier studies question Elton and Gruber's (1970) conjecture that long-term investors set ex-dividend day share prices. For example, Kalay (1982) cannot explain why the imputed tax rates vary with the dividend yield. Miller and Scholes (1982) extend Kalay's argument and caution researchers against interpreting any estimated association between short-run dividend yields and returns as evidence of tax-clienteles effects. Heath and Jarrow (1988) relax Kalay's assumption of risk neutrality and show that no category of investors is likely to set ex-dividend day share prices. On the other hand, Koski and Scruggs (1998) analyze the identity of traders around ex-dividend days and find strong evidence of dividend capture trading by security dealers, some evidence of corporate dividend capture trading, but little evidence of tax clientele trading.

In a study analyzing ex-dividend day pricing under different tax regimes of two mutual funds, Elton, Gruber, and Blake (2005, p. 585) conclude that the microstructure explanation for the price drop is wrong and provide new evidence of the tax explanation of ex-dividend day behavior:

> *The microstructure arguments presented in the literature of financial economics state that the fall in stock price should be less than the dividend. By testing ex-dividend effects on a sample of funds where dividends are tax-advantaged, we find that taxes should and do cause the fund price to fall by more than the amount of the dividend. This is consistent with a tax argument and inconsistent with a microstructure argument. Examining the sample of tax-free dividends, we find that the E&G measure change across the two regimes exactly as the theory suggests they should if taxes mattered.*

Graham et al. (2003) also examine the microstructure argument by comparing ex-dividend day returns before and after decimalization in the United States. Their results are inconsistent with the price discreetness or transaction costs effects. They show that reducing the capital gains tax rate in 1997 affects ex-dividend day prices, as postulated by Elton and Gruber (1970).

In a Canadian study, Bauer et al. (2002, p. 21) conclude that neither the tax differential nor the tick size explain the price drop and ask, "While short term trading may be a factor in the market and this effect is not directly examined, it would still leave the main question unanswered: why don't ex-dividend day prices fully adjust to start with?" Given the strong evidence of Elton et al. (2005), refuting that taxes do not influence ex-dividend day price is difficult. On the other hand, the high presence of dividend-capturing traders or arbitragers around the ex-dividend day, as observed by Koski and Scruggs (1998), indicates the influence of short-term trading activity in determining the price-drop-to-dividend ratio. However, the short-term trading theory alone fails to completely explain this ratio. A recent study by Dutta, Jog, and Saadi (2005) shows that the tax effect and short-term trading arguments both explain the behavior of stock prices on the ex-dividend day in the Canadian market.

TAX RATE CHANGES AND DIVIDEND POLICY

As discussed in the previous section, studies examining the effect of taxes on the valuation of corporate equity are inconclusive. Some studies such as Elton and Gruber (1970) provide evidence of a tax-induced dividend clientele. Others such as that of Kalay (1982) argue that market microstructure and short-term trading by tax-exempt investors render making inferences impossible about investors' relative effective tax rate on the basis of stock price adjustments on the ex-dividend day.

The existence of tax-induced dividend clienteles can influence dividend policy in several ways. For example, if the tax differential between capital gains and dividends affects the stock price, this could lead to altering dividend policy. Levying income taxes on investors who receive dividend payments is likely to reduce the demand for dividends and thus prompt corporations to retain a larger share of their profits. On the other hand, an increase in the tax on capital gains relative to the tax on dividends should enhance the demand for dividends and prompt corporations to increase their dividend payout. Alternatively, the existence of clientele effects could give a firm the opportunity to increase its market value by adopting a dividend policy that appeals to investors whose preferences are not satisfied by other firms.

The Tax Reform Act of 1986

Several studies investigate the relationship between taxes and dividends by examining substantial changes in the tax regime. Each tax reform represents an opportunity to examine the influence, if any, of taxes on dividend policy. For instance, earlier studies use the 1986 Tax Reform Act (TRA) as a natural experiment to analyze the connection between changes in U.S. taxes and dividend policy. Before the TRA, tax rates favored long-term capital gains taxed at a maximum marginal rate of 20 percent compared to the maximum rate of 50 percent for dividends. After the TRA, the tax rate on both dividends and capital gains was 28 percent. Thus, the TRA substantially reduced the tax preference for long-term capital gains. Studies dealing with this event typically focus on the impact of taxes on stock price not on its effect on dividend policy.

Two studies focus on the anticipated dividend policy response of firms to the passage of the TRA of 1986. Ben-Horim, Hochman, and Palmon (1987) find that the TRA affects security holders and firms differently depending on whether their marginal tax rates increased or decreased. The authors predict that firms should increase their payout ratios in response to the TRA.

Abrutyn and Turner (1990) use a survey to forecast the effects of the TRA on dividend policy. They survey 550 chief executive officers (CEOs) of the largest 1,000 corporations in the United States. Abrutyn and Turner indicate that 85 percent of CEOs surveyed expect no change and only 11 percent anticipate an increase in dividend payout ratios as a result of the TRA. Their study also reveals surprising results about the importance of shareholders' tax rates in determining dividend policy. Specifically, Abrutyn and Turner (p. 495) report, "Only 18 percent of the firms included any explanation based on shareholders' tax rates in their top two explanations; a full 58 percent of the respondents claimed not to know the tax status of their shareholders. Thus the tax clientele hypothesis received the weakest support."

Bloster and Janjigian (1991) are the first to explicitly examine the effect of the TRA on dividend policy. Using a sample of 883 nonfinancial firms, they report that the mean payout ratio for the pre-TRA years is virtually identical to the comparable value for the post-TRA years. This evidence means that the tax reform did not affect dividend policy. Means et al. (1992) find that dividend yields trend downward over the period 1984–1986 but start trending upward after the TRA's passage. They conclude that firms change their dividend policy in response to tax changes. Unfortunately, the method used by Means et al. suffers a major shortcoming, namely, dividend yields with an upward trend could cause a stable dividend despite decreasing prices.

Papaioannou and Savarese (1994) use a sample of 283 firms drawn from the Fortune 500 and Fortune 50 to test for differences between dividend payout ratios for the pre- and post-TRA periods. Applying one-tailed matched-pairs t-tests to the sample of 243 industrial firms and the 40 utility firms, the authors find no statistically significant difference between the post- and pre-TRA dividend payout ratios. When applying the same test on the 243 industrial firms classified into five quintiles according to their pre-TRA average dividend payout ratios, Papaioannou and Savarese report evidence of significant changes in dividend payout ratios after passage of the TRA. More recently, Casey, Anderson, and Dickens (1999) use a modified version of Rozeff's (1982) model to examine the impact of the TRA on dividend policy and find that the TRA has no significant impact on the aggregate level of dividends.

The Jobs and Growth Tax Relief Reconciliation Act of 2003

The Jobs and Growth Tax Relief Reconciliation Act (JGTRRA) of 2003 reduced the tax on dividends to 15 percent from the top ordinary income tax rate of 38.6 percent. This dividend tax reform, which eliminates the tax differential between dividend income and capital gains, represents the lowest federal tax rate on dividends in almost 90 years. The JGTRRA presents a new opportunity for researchers to examine how dividend policy responds to shareholders' tax characteristics.

Chetty and Saez (2005) show a link between the dividend tax cut of JGTRRA and an increased number of dividend initiations by nonfinancial and nonutility firms. Julio and Ikenberry (2004) argue, however, that taxes cannot be the main factor leading to the "reappearance of dividends," as this trend started in late 2000, which was before discussion of the 2003 tax reform. Chetty and Saez (2006) contend that Julio and Ikenberry's conclusion suffers from sample selection bias. Extending the analysis of their 2005 study, Chetty and Saez show that the dividends-trend reversal starts during the first quarter of 2003 just before the introduction of the tax reform, not in 2001, and then accelerates after enactment of the reform. Recently, Brav et al. (2008) use a survey to examine managerial response to the effects of JGTRRA on dividend payout decisions and find that the tax cut has a second-order influence on firms to initiate or increase dividends.

Because the 2003 tax reform introduced tax cuts for direct retail investors and institutions investing funds for retail investors such as mutual funds, a likely expectation would be for firms with relatively large holdings of retail investors to initiate or increase dividends. Yet the overall results suggest that U.S. public firms set dividend payouts that best fit their major shareholders' interests (Chetty and Saez, 2005; Brav et al., 2008). Even in the United States, where public firms are widely held and the legal environment offers strong legal protection to minority shareholders, several empirical studies report evidence of managers and large shareholders undermining minority shareholders' interests. For instance, Chetty and Saez show that firms controlled by institutions unaffected by the tax-rate reduction do not respond to the tax reform, but firms with large shareholding independent directors and high taxable institutional ownership do respond to the reform by initiating or increasing their dividend payout.

Similarly, Brown, Liang, and Weisbenner (2007) find that firms with large executive stock ownership initiated or increased dividends in response to the 2003 dividend tax cut, while firms with large executive stock options holdings did not do so because stock options are not dividend protected. According to Brav et al. (2008), managers of U.S. public firms gave little importance to changes in retail investors' tax characteristics after the 2003 tax reform.

Canadian Tax Reform

Studies using important tax changes as an opportunity to examine the interaction between taxation and dividend policy extend beyond the U.S. market. In Canada, for instance, Khoury and Smith (1977) use Lintner's (1956) model to test the effect of the Canadian Tax Reform of 1972 (TR72) on dividend payout. According to Khoury and Smith, the introduction of the capital-gains tax in 1972 induced an increase in dividend payout of Canadian firms. Yet tempering their findings is appropriate because of the asymmetry between the length of the pre-TR and post-TR periods. Because of lack of data, Khoury and Smith use two years for the pre-TR72 period (1972 and 1973) but ten years for the post-TR72 period (1962 to 1971).

Adjaoud and Zeghal (1993) follow the same methodology as of Papaioannou and Savarese (1994) to examine the impact of introducing the $500,000 capital-gains exemption in 1985 on Canadian dividend policy. Adjaoud and Zeghal find that introducing the 1985 capital-gains exemption influenced Canadian firms to lower their dividend payouts. Unfortunately, their study suffers from shortcomings in sample selection. In fact, on the basis of the expectation that dividend payouts would decrease after TR72, the authors eliminate all the companies that did not pay dividends during the 1982–1984 period. This could bias the results because the absence of dividends might be due to negative earnings during the three-year pre-TR period. These firms might have distributed dividends once they realize profits.

Recently, Saadi and Chkir (2008) examine the effect of two important changes in the taxation of capital gains to determine the interaction between taxation and dividend policy (TR 1987 and TR 1994). Their results generally show no increase by Canadian firms in their dividend payouts after reducing the capital gains exemption in 1987 but indicate an increase after eliminating the remaining $100,000 capital gains exemption in 1994.

DIVIDEND TAXATION AND CORPORATE GOVERNANCE

Researchers face a great challenge in developing a single dividend theory that is capable of explaining all dividend patterns reported in empirical studies. Nonetheless, the emergence of corporate governance as a response to recent corporate misbehavior sheds new light on agency theory as a plausible economic model for explaining why firms pay dividends despite their tax disadvantages. Under the agency model framework, firms pay dividends to mitigate agency problems between managers and owners. The payout level and the extent to which a firm is responsive to its shareholders' interest depend on many factors including ownership structure (dispersed or highly concentrated, the level of separation between ownership and control, and the identity of block holders) and the level of share-holders' protection.

A high propensity to pay dividends by firms in which managers own a considerable portion of the shares may reflect managers' preferences and not necessarily those of other shareholders. When holding a high portion of ownership rights or voting rights, managers are more likely to expropriate wealth from outside shareholders. For instance, high managerial ownership can prevent hostile takeovers that often occur when outside bidders target poorly performing firms and replace their inefficient managers with rival management teams.

Using a sample of 308 firms traded on the Toronto Stock Exchange, Eckbo and Verma (1994) find that cash dividends decrease as the voting power of owner-managers increases and are typically zero in manager-controlled firms. Farinha (2003) reports evidence of a strong U-shaped relationship between dividend payouts and insider ownership. Specifically, Farinha documents that after a critical entrenchment level estimated in the region of 30 percent, the coefficient of insider ownership changes from negative to positive, a result interpreted by the author as evidence of managerial entrenchment.

The Role of Dominant Shareholders

The widely supported evidence of ownership concentration around the world has shifted the attention from the classic agency conflict between shareholders and managers to agency conflicts between minority shareholders and large controlling shareholders. These dominant shareholders usually exert full control over managers and frequently hold control power in excess of their cash flow rights, providing them with strong incentives to extract private benefits at the expense of minority shareholders.

The nature or sign of the influence that a large controlling shareholder may have on dividend policy depends on its identity. When a large shareholder is a family or corporation, this shareholder may use a controlling position in the firm to pursue private goals that undermine minority shareholders' interests such as distributing no or low dividends (Shleifer and Vishny, 1986; Burkart, Gromb, and Panunzi, 1997). By contrast, large controlling shareholders may play a monitoring role that benefits minority shareholders and positively influences dividend payout. As Shleifer and Vishny (p. 754) note, "Large shareholders thus address the agency problem in that they have both a general interest in profit maximization, and enough control over the assets of the firms to have their interest respected."

Several theoretical and empirical studies focus on the role of large shareholders, such as institutional investors, in controlling managerial misconduct and in reducing agency problems within a firm. Institutional investors may prefer a high level of dividends for two major reasons. Earlier studies such as that of Bond, Chennells, and Devereux (1996) posit that the high level of dividends paid could reflect the short-term attitudes held by institutions and the tax exemption on dividends that institutional investors such as mutual funds enjoy in most developed country. Examining the U.K. context, Bond et al. (1996, p. 17) state, "To the extent that tax-exempt shareholders such as pension funds are now the most influential investors in many U.K. companies, their tax preference for dividend income is likely to result in significantly higher dividend payout ratios than would be chosen by companies in the absence of this tax bias."

More recent studies such as those of Chetty and Saez (2005) and Brav et al. (2008) support these observations. Perez-Gonzales (2003) and Holmen, Knopf, and Peterson (2008) show empirically that after tax changes, firms with large shareholders adjust their dividends payouts in a way that reduces the tax burden for such shareholders. Hence, controlling shareholders' preferences may explain the inconsistency within the extant empirical results with respect to the effect of taxation on dividend policy. These preferences are likely to influence a firm's response to a tax change.

Although the taxation of dividends seems to have a second-order influence on firms' dividend policy (Julio and Ikenberry, 2004; Brav et al., 2008), it has a major impact on the shape of corporate ownership structure around the world. According to Morck (2004), a major obstacle to forming pyramidal groups is intercorporate dividend taxation. He cites the example of the United States being the only country among a sample of 33 countries to introduce such tax reforms.

In a related paper, Morck, Wolfenzon, and Yeung (2004) examine the evolution of corporate ownership in Canada during the twentieth century. They report that the emergence of family-controlled pyramidal groups is the outcome of government policies that limit competition and introduce generous tax reforms favoring wealthy families. The authors show that the absence of intercorporate dividend taxation coupled with the abolition of inheritance taxes in the early 1970s has led to the reemergence of family pyramids in Canada.

CONCLUSIONS

Dividend policy is a topic of ongoing debate among financial economists. Despite several decades of research resulting in the emergence of many conflicting theoretical models and empirical findings, questions still remain unanswered. One of these critical questions involves the nature of the relationship between taxation and dividend policy. The extant theoretical and empirical evidence provide contradictory results involving the impact of taxation on both stock price and dividend policy. While many studies investigate the impact of taxation on share price, only a few look at its impact on dividend policy.

In recent years, solving the dividend puzzle has become more challenging with the inclusion of additional factors such as corporate governance structure. Within the agency model framework, such factors provide plausible reasons for the existence of large dividend payments despite their tax disadvantage. In fact, recent studies show that the way firms respond to tax changes depends on the preferences of controlling shareholders. Firms controlled by tax-exempt institutions such as pension funds are unaffected by the tax rate changes, but firms with large shareholdings, independent directors and high taxable institutional ownership respond to tax reform.

In the future, researchers should conduct studies to further explore the nature of the relationship between taxation and dividend behavior. They need to pay particular attention to both the influence of the ultimate ownership structure and the identity of the ultimate owners. In fact, recent studies reveal that large shareholders tend to use different mechanisms such as pyramidal ownership structures, cross-holdings, and multiple-class shares to enhance the separation between ownership and control rights (Claessens, Djankov, and Lang, 2000; Faccio and Lang, 2002). These control-enhancing mechanisms enable the ultimate owners to increase a firm's opacity and hide its expropriation behavior to secure the implementation of self-enriching plans. A growing number of studies shows that the type of the ultimate owner is not neutral in determining dividend policy (DeAngelo, DeAngelo, and Skinner, 2000; Faccio, Lang, and Young, 2001; Gugler, 2003). For instance, Faccio et al. (2001) suggest that ultimate owners prefer distributing higher dividends for affiliated firms with large separation between ownership and control to dissipate the dilution concerns of minority shareholders. Hence, a worthwhile venue of research would be to examine the effect of ultimate ownership structure on the relationship between taxation and dividend policy.

REFERENCES

Abrutyn, Stephanie, and Robert W. Turner. 1990. "Taxes and Firms' Dividend Policies: Survey Results." *National Tax Journal* 43:4, 491–497.

Adjaoud, Fodil, and Daniel Zeghal. 1993. "Fiscalité et Politique de Dividende au Canada: Nouveau Résultats." *Fineco* 3:1, 143–151.

Ang, James S., David W. Blackwell, and William L. Megginson. 1991. "The Effect of Taxes on the Relative Valuation of Dividends and Capital Gains: Evidence from Dual-class British Investments Trusts." *Journal of Finance* 46:1, 383–400.

Athanassakos, George. 1996. "Tax Induced Trading Volume around Ex-Dividend Days under Different Tax Regimes: The Canadian Experience 1970–1984." *Journal of Business and Accounting* 23:3, 557–584.

Bali, Rakesh, and Gailen L. Hite. 1998. "Ex-Dividend Day Stock Price Behavior: Discreteness or Tax-Induced Clienteles?" *Journal of Financial Economics* 47:2, 127–159.

Bartholdy, Jan, and Kate Briown. 2002. "Testing for Multiple Types of Marginal Investors in Ex-Day Pricing." Working Paper No. 02-12, Aarhus School of Business, Denmark.

Bauer, Larry, Steve Beveridge, and Ranjini Sivakumar. 2002. "The Influence of Taxes and Tick Size on Ex-Dividend Day Prices." Working Paper, School of Accountancy, University of Waterloo.

Bell, Leonie, and Tim Jenkinson. 2002. "New Evidence on the Impact of Dividend Taxation and on the Identity of the Marginal Investor." *Journal of Finance* 57:3, 1321–1346.

Ben-Horim, Moshe, Shalom Hochman, and Oded Palmon. 1987. "The Impact of the 1986 Tax Reform Act on Corporate Financial Policy." *Financial Management* 16:3, 29–35.

Bhardwaj, Ravinder, and LeRoy D. Brooks. 1999. "Further Evidence on Dividend Yields and the Ex-Dividend Day Stock Price Effect." *Journal of Financial Research* 22:4, 503–514.

Black, Fisher. 1976. "The Dividend Puzzle." *Journal of Portfolio Management* 2:2, 5–8.

Bloster, Paul J., and Vahan Janjigian. 1991. "Dividend Policy and Valuation Effects of the Tax Reform Act of 1986." *National Tax Journal* 44:4, 511–518.

Bond, Stephen, Lucy Chennells, and Michael Devereux, 1996. "Company Dividends and Taxes in the U.K." *Fiscal Studies* 16:3, 1–18.

Booth, Laurence D., and David J. Johnson. 1984. "The Ex-Dividend Day Behavior of Canadian Stock Price: Tax Changes and Clientele Effects." *Journal of Finance* 39:2, 457–476.

Brav, Alon, John Graham, Campbell Harvey, and Roni Michaely. 2008. "Managerial Response to the May 2003 Dividend Tax Cut." *Financial Management*, 37:4, 611–624.

Brown, Jeffrey R., Nellie Liang, and Scott Weisbenner. 2007. "Executive Financial Incentives and Payout Policy: Firm Responses to the 2003 Dividend Tax Cut." *Journal of Finance* 62:4, 1935–1965.

Burkart, Mike, Denis Gromb, and Fausto Panunzi. 1997. "Large Shareholders, Monitoring and the Value of the Firm." *Quarterly Journal of Economics* 112:3, 693–728.

Campbell, James A., and William Beranek. 1955. "Stock Price Behavior on Ex-Dividend Dates." *Journal of Finance* 10:4, 125–429.

Casey, K. Michael, David C. Anderson, and Ross N. Dickens. 1999. "Examining the Impact of the 1986 Tax Reform Act on Corporate Dividend Policy: A New Methodology." *Financial Review* 34:3, 33–46.

Casey, K. Michael, and Ross N. Dickens. 2000. "The Effect of Tax and Regulatory Changes on Commercial Bank Dividend Policy." *Quarterly Review of Economics and Finance* 40:4, 279–293.

Chetty, Raj, and Emmanuel Saez. 2005. "Dividend Taxes and Corporate Behavior: Evidence from the 2003 Dividend Tax Cut." *Quarterly Journal of Economics* 120:3, 791–833.

Chetty, Raj, and Emmanuel Saez. 2006. "The Effects of the 2003 Dividend Tax Cut on Corporate Behavior: Interpreting the Evidence." *American Economic Review* 96:2, 124–129.

Claessens, Stign, Simeon Djankov, and Larry H. P. Lang. 2000. "The Separation of Ownership and Control in East Asian Corporations." *Journal of Financial Economics* 58:1–2, 81–112.

Daunfeldt, Sven-Olov. 2002. "Tax Policy Changes and Ex-Dividend Behavior: The Case of Sweden." Working Paper No. 0585, University of Umea.

DeAngelo, Harry Linda DeAngelo, and Douglas J. Skinner. 2000. "Special Dividends and the Evolution of Dividend Signaling." *Journal of Financial Economics* 57:3, 309–354.

Denis, David J., and Igor Osobov. 2008. "Why do Firms Pay Dividends?: International Evidence on the Determinants of Dividend Policy." *Journal of Financial Economics* 89:1, 62–82.

Dutta, Shantanu, Vijay Jog, and Samir Saadi. 2005. "Re-Examination of the Ex-Dividend Day Behavior of Canadian Stock Prices." Working Paper, Carleton University.

Eckbo, B. Espen, and Savita Verma. 1994. "Managerial Shareownership, Voting Power, and Cash Dividend Policy." *Journal of Corporate Finance* 1:1, 33–62.

Elton, Edwin J., and Martin J. Gruber. 1970. "Marginal Stockholder Tax Rates and the Clientele Effect." *Review of Economics and Statistics* 52:1, 68–74

Elton, Edwin J., Martin J. Gruber, and Christopher R. Blake. 2005. "Marginal Stockholder Tax Effects and Ex-Dividend Day Behavior Thirty-Two Years Later." *Review of Economics and Statistics* 87:3, 579–586.

Elton, Edwin J., Martin J. Gruber, and Joel Rentzler. 1984. "The Ex-Dividend Day Behavior of Stock Prices: A Re-examination of the Clientele Effect: A Comment." *Journal of Finance* 39:2, 551–556.

Faccio, Mara, and Larry H. P. Lang. 2002. "The Ultimate Ownership of Western European Corporations." *Journal of Financial Economics* 65:3, 365–395.

Faccio, Mara, Larry H. P. Lang, and Leslie Young. 2001. "Dividends and Expropriation." *American Economic Review* 91:1, 54–78.

Fama, Eugene F., and Kenneth R. French. 2001. "Disappearing Dividends: Changing Firm Characteristics or Lower Propensity to Pay?" *Journal of Financial Economics* 60:1, 3–43.

Farinha, Jorge. 2003. "Dividend Policy, Corporate Governance and the Managerial Entrenchment Hypothesis: An Empirical Analysis." *Journal of Business Finance and Accounting* 30:9–10, 1173–1209.

Farrar, Donald E., and Lee L. Selwyn. 1967. "Taxes, Corporate Financial Policy and Return to Investors." *National Tax Journal* 20:4, 444–454.

Feenberg, Daniel. 1981. "Does the Investment Interest Limitation Explain the Existence of Dividends?" *Journal of Financial Economics* 9:3, 265–269.

Florentsen, Bjarne, and Kristian Rydqvist. 2002. "Ex-Day Behavior When Investors and Professional Traders Assume Reverse Roles: The Case of Danish Lottery Bonds." *Journal of Financial Intermediation* 11:2, 152–175.

Frank, Murray, and Ravi Jagannathan. 1998. "Why Do Stock Prices Drop by Less than the Value of the Dividend? Evidence from a Country without Taxes." *Journal of Financial Economics* 47:2, 161–188.

Gardecazabal, Javier, and Matias Regulez. 2002. "The Weekend-Dividend Effect in the Spanish Market." Working Paper, University of the Basque Country.

Graham, John R., Roni Michaely, and Michael R. Roberts. 2003. "Do Price Discreteness and Transactions Costs Affect Stock Returns?" *Journal of Finance* 58:6, 2611–2635.

Green, Jerry R. 1980. "Taxation and the Ex-Dividend Day Behavior of Common Stock Prices." Working Paper No. 0496, National Bureau of Economic Research.

Green, Richard C., and Kristian Rydqvist. 1999. "Ex-Day Behavior with Dividend Preference and Limitations to Short-Term Arbitrage: The Case of Swedish Lottery Bonds." *Journal of Financial Economics* 53:2, 145–187.

Grullon, Gustavo, and Roni Michaely. 2002. "Dividends, Share Repurchases, and the Substitution Hypothesis." *Journal of Finance* 57:4, 1649–1684.

Gugler, Klaus. 2003. "Corporate Governance, Dividend Payout Policy, and the Interrelation between Dividends and Capital Investment." *Journal of Banking and Finance* 27:7, 1297–1321.

Heath, David C., and Robert A. Jarrow. 1988. "Ex-Dividend Stock Price Behavior and Arbitrage Opportunities." *Journal of Business* 61:1, 95–108.

Holmen, Martin, John D. Knopf, and Peterson Stefan. 2008. "Inside Shareholders' Effective Tax Rates and Dividends." *Journal of Banking and Finance* 32:9, 1860–1869..

Julio, Brandon, and David L. Ikenberry. 2004. "Reappearing Dividends." *Journal of Applied Corporate Finance* 16:4, 89–100.

Kadapakkam, Palani-Rajan. 2000. "Reduction of Constraints on Arbitrage Trading and Market Efficiency: An Examination of Ex-Day Returns in Hong Kong after Introduction of Electronic Settlement." *Journal of Finance* 55:6, 2841–2861.

Kalay, Avner. 1982. "The Ex-Dividend Day Behavior of Stock Prices: A Re-examination of the Clientele Effect." *Journal of Finance* 37:4, 1059–1070.

Kato, Kiyoshi, and Uri Loewenstein. 1995. "The Ex-Dividend Day Behavior of Stock Prices: The Case of Japan." *Review of Financial Studies* 8:3, 817–847.

Khoury, Nabil, and Kevin V. Smith. 1977. "Dividend Policy and the Capital Gain Tax in Canada." *Journal of Business Administration* 8:2, 19–37.

Koski, Jennifer Lynch. 1996. "A Microstructure Analysis of Ex-Dividend Stock Price Behavior before and after the 1984 and 1986 Tax Reform Acts." *Journal of Business* 69:3, 313–338.

Koski, Jennifer Lynch, and John T. Scruggs. 1998. "Who Trades Around the Ex-Dividend Day? Evidence from NYSE Audit File Data." *Financial Management* 27:3, 58–72.

Lamdin, Douglas, and Craig Hiemstra. 1993. "Ex-Dividend Day Share Price Behavior: Effects of the Tax Reform Act of 1986." *Review of Economics and Statistics* 75:4, 778–783.

Lewellen, Wilbur G., Kenneth L. Stanley, Ronald C. Lease, and Gary G. Schlarbaum. 1978. "Some Direct Evidence on the Dividend Clientele Phenomenon." *Journal of Finance* 33:5, 1385–1399.

Lintner, John. 1956. "Distribution of Incomes of Corporations among Dividends, Retained Earnings and Taxes." *American Economics Review* 46:2, 97–113.

McDonald, Robert L. 2001. "Cross-Border Investing with Tax Arbitrage: The Case of German Dividend Tax Credits." *Review of Financial Studies* 14:3, 617–657.

Means, Dwight B., Charlie Charoenwong, and Young-Kwon Kang. 1992. "Changing Dividend Policies Caused by the Tax Reform Act of 1986: An Empirical Analysis." *Journal of Economics and Finance* 16:3, 153–160.

Michaely, Roni, and Maurizio Murgia. 1995. "The Effect of Tax Heterogeneity on Prices and Volume around the Ex-Dividend Day: Evidence from the Milan Stock Exchange." *Review of Financial Studies* 8:2, 369–399.

Miller, Merton H., and Franco Modigliani. 1961. "Dividend Policy, Growth, and the Valuation of Shares." *Journal of Business* 34:4, 411–433.

Miller, Merton H., and Myron S. Scholes. 1978. "Dividends and Taxes." *Journal of Financial Economics* 6:4, 333–364.

Miller, Merton H., and Myron S. Scholes. 1982. "Dividends and Taxes: Some Empirical Evidence." *Journal of Political Economy* 90:6, 1118–1141.

Milonas, Nikolaos, and Nikolaos G. Travlos. 2001. "The Ex-Dividend Day Stock Price Behavior in the Athens Stock Exchange." Working Paper No. 01-12, Cardiff University Business School.

Milonas, Nikolaos, Nikolaos G. Travlos, and Jin Xiao. 2002. "The Ex-Dividend Day Stock Price Behavior in the Chinese Stock Market." Working Paper No. 02-18, Cardiff University Business School.

Morck, Randall. 2004. "How to Eliminate Pyramidal Business Groups: The Double Taxation of Inter-Corporate Dividends and Other Incentive Uses of Tax Policy." Working Paper No. 10944, National Bureau of Economic Research.

Morck, Randall, Daniel Wolfenzon, and Bernard Yeung. 2004. "Corporate Governance, Economic Entrenchment, and Growth." Working Paper No. 10692, National Bureau of Economic Research.

Ogden, Joseph P., Frank C. Jen, and Philip F. O'Connor. 2003. *Advanced Corporate Finance: Policies and Strategies.* Upper Saddle River, NJ: Prentice Hall.

Papaioannou, George J., and Craig M. Savarese. 1994. "Corporate Dividend Policy Response to the Tax Reform Act of 1986." *Financial Management* 23:1, 56–63.

Perez-Gonzales, Francisco. 2003. "Large Shareholders and Dividends: Evidence from U.S. Tax Reforms." Working Paper, University of Columbia.

Peterson, Pamela P., David R. Peterson, and James S. Ang. 1985. "Direct Evidence on the Marginal Rate Taxation on Dividend Income." *Journal of Financial Economics* 14:2, 267–282.

Pettit, Richardson R. 1977. "Taxes, Transaction Cost and the Clientele Effect of Dividends." *Journal of Financial Economics* 5:3, 419–436.

Poterba, James M. 1986. "Interpreting Ex-Dividend Evidence: The Citizens Utilities Case Reconsidered." Working Paper No. W1131, National Bureau of Economic Research.

Poterba, James M., and Lawrence H. Summers. 1984. "New Evidence That Taxes Affect the Valuation of Dividends." *Journal of Finance* 39:5, 1397–1415.

Poterba, James M., and Lawrence H. Summers. 1985. "The Economic Effects of Dividend Taxation." In *Recent Advances in Corporate Finance*, ed. Edward I. Altman and Marti G. Subrahmanyam, 227–284. Homewood, IL: Richard D. Irwin Publishers.

Rozeff, Michael S. 1982. "Growth, Beta and Agency Costs as Determinants of Dividend Payout Ratios." *Journal of Financial Research* 5:3, 249–259.

Saadi, Samir, and Imed Chkir. 2008. "Taxation and Dividend Policy: New Empirical Evidence." *Journal of Corporate Ownership and Control* 5:4, 266–273.

Shleifer, Andrei, and Robert W. Vishny. 1986. "Large Shareholders and Corporate Control." *Journal of Political Economy* 94:3, 461–488.

von Eije, Henk, and William L. Megginson. 2008. "Dividends and Share Repurchase in the European Union." *Journal of Financial Economics* 89:2, 347–374.

ABOUT THE AUTHORS

Samir Saadi is a finance Ph.D. candidate at Queen's School of Business. He is also a Research Associate and part-time Instructor of Finance at the Telfer School of Management, University of Ottawa. His research interests include dividend policy, executive compensation, and international finance. Saadi is a recipient of several best-paper awards at national and international conferences. He has published in finance and applied economics journals including *Journal of Multinational Financial Management*, *Journal of International Financial Markets, Institutions and Money*, *Global Finance Journal*, *Journal of Theoretical and Applied Finance*, *Review of Financial Economics*, and *International Journal of Managerial Finance*.

Shantanu Dutta is an Assistant Professor of Finance at University of Ontario Institute of Technology. He previously taught at St. Francis Xavier University (Nova Scotia) and Assumption University (Bangkok) as a full-time faculty member. Before his career in academe, he was a finance manager and project controller at Lafarge, a world leader in construction materials. Dutta's research focuses on corporate governance, mergers and acquisitions, market efficiency, dividend policy, and technology management. He has published in *Journal of Banking and Finance*, *Global Finance Journal*, *Canadian Investment Review*, *International Journal of Theoretical and Applied Finance*, *International Journal of Managerial Finance*, *International Journal of Technology Transfer*, and *International Journal of Global Energy Issues*. He has also participated and presented papers in many scholarly conferences. Dutta is a recipient of the Barclay Global Investor Canada Research Award.

CHAPTER 9

Agency Costs and the Free Cash Flow Hypothesis

TARUN MUKHERJEE
Professor of Finance and Moffett Chair in Financial Economics,
University of New Orleans

INTRODUCTION

Does dividend policy affect firm value? According to Miller and Modigliani (1961), under certain assumptions, dividend policy is irrelevant to firm value. However, most studies present similar results indicating that the stock market reacts positively to cash disbursements via dividend initiations and increases, specially designated dividends, or self-tender offers but negatively to dividend decreases or eliminations (see, e.g., Pettit, 1972; Aharony and Swary, 1980; Dann, 1981; Vermaelen, 1981; Asquith and Mullins, 1983; Brickley, 1983, Howe, He, and Kao, 1992; Denis, Denis, and Sarin, 1994; Lie, 2000). In other words, dividend policy seems to contribute to firm value. Although various arguments have emerged to explain why the stock reacts the way it does, two popular theories are cash flow signaling and free cash flow models.

The basis of the dividend signaling model is information asymmetry that exists between managers and stockholders. The proponents of this model argue that dividends reduce information asymmetry by acting as a credible signal from corporate insiders to the firm's shareholders (Bhattacharya, 1979; Miller and Rock, 1985; John and Williams, 1985). Simply stated, dividend initiations or increases convey good news, while dividend reductions or omissions convey bad news. Several studies provide support for this hypothesis, including those of Healy and Palepu (1988), Brickley (1983), and Aharony and Dotan (1994). Similarly, Ofer and Siegel (1987), among others, report that analysts significantly revise their forecasts following dividend changes.

On the other hand, the free cash flow model traces its roots to the agency problem (Jensen and Meckling, 1976) between corporate insiders and external investors. A characteristic of a publicly held firm is the divergence of interests between managers and investors. In this environment, managers, confronted with a low investment opportunity set, have the incentive to hoard excess cash to benefit themselves at the expense of investors. Because managers are reluctant to cut dividends, a dividend initiation or increase means reducing excess cash at the disposal of managers, thereby reducing their ability to misuse these funds (Jensen, 1986). Thus, the market reacts positively to the prospect of the reduced agency cost.

FREE CASH FLOW THEORY

A precursor of the modern free cash flow theory is the traditional residual theory of dividends, which suggests that the amount of dividends is simply the residual of a firm's investment decision. In other words, the firm should pay as dividends any excess cash that remains after funding all positive net present value (NPV) projects. An implication of this theory is that the payout, which is linked to a firm's investment needs, might fluctuate from one year to the next, but in practice, many firms attempt to maintain a stable dividend policy. According to residual theory, the stock price should fall with an increased dividend as this situation implies limited investment opportunities and should rise when the firm decreases its dividend, indicating increased availability of profitable investment opportunities. These empirical predictions are typically the opposite of what occurs in practice.

A more modern version of the free cash flow model assumes that firms pay dividends to overcome the agency problem stemming from the separation of ownership and control in a large company with diffused ownership. In such a corporation, most investors lack the ability or incentive to monitor and control all managerial activities. In the absence of a complete and fully enforceable contract, managers have incentives to engage in activities that may not be in the best interest of the investors.

One manifestation of this is when the managers have large amounts of cash flow but limited investment opportunities for these funds. Richardson (2006) shows that overinvestment typically occurs in firms with the highest level of free cash flow. Self-interested managers will have incentives to invest the excess cash in activities that might decrease firm value. These activities span from unnecessary perks to unwarranted acquisitions and expansions. Therefore, researchers often call this scenario the overinvestment problem. A possible solution to this problem is to reduce discretionary cash available to managers. As the principal proponent of the free cash flow theory, Jensen (1986) suggests that dividend payout is one way to accomplish this goal. Grossman and Hart (1980) and Easterbrook (1984) make similar arguments.

Jensen (1986) argues that managers have incentives to expand the firm beyond its optimal size because the bigger size entails increased resources under their control and higher compensation. This self-serving motive would induce managers to invest in value-reducing or negative NPV projects. Because managers are reluctant to seek external financing to fund these negative NPV projects to avoid further market scrutiny, they rely on internal funds. The presence of substantial free cash flows allows managers to overinvest. Investors are aware of this agency problem and react positively to the news of increased dividends as the overinvestment potential is lessened. The most important implication of the free cash flow theory is that incremental cash disbursements (e.g., dividend initiations or increases) should increase firm value by reducing the potential overinvestment problem. Similarly, a dividend decrease should elicit a negative market reaction.

EMPIRICAL TESTS OF FREE CASH FLOW HYPOTHESES

Price Reaction to Overinvestment Potential

A testable implication of the free cash flow hypothesis is that overinvestment problems are likely to be more pronounced in firms experiencing dwindling investment opportunities, and, therefore, higher prices will accompany a dividend-increase announcement by such firms. Lang and Litzenberger (1989) are the first to test this implication. They hypothesize that the market return in response to dividend changes is larger for firms that are likely to overinvest than firms that are likely to maximize the firm value. They define a firm with a Tobin's Q of less than 1 as an overinvestor and a Q of greater than 1 as a maximizer.

Lang and Litzenberger (1989) use a sample of 429 dividend change (greater than 10 percent in absolute value) announcements from 1979 to 1984 to test this hypothesis. Results in support of this hypothesis will favor the free cash flow model over the signaling model, as the latter makes no such predictions. Using daily returns, the authors find that the average returns (average of positive returns associated with dividend increases and negative returns associated with dividend decreases) for the Q < 1 firms are significantly higher than that of the Q > 1 firms. Using intraday data (over the period one hour before to two hours after) for a reduced sample, they report that dividend change announcements have a significant impact on stock prices of the Q < 1 firms but no impact on the Q > 1 firms.

To ascertain that the composition of sample (number of dividend-increasing versus dividend-decreasing firms) of the Q < 1 and Q > 1 groups do not influence the preceding results, Lang and Litzenberger (1989) perform further investigations. First, they test the following refined predictions of the two competing hypotheses:

1. The market anticipates dividend increases but not dividend decreases for Q > 1 firms. Consequently, only dividend decreases should have a significantly negative impact on the price. Thus, the signaling hypothesis predicts that abnormal returns for Q > 1 are greater in absolute value for dividend decreases than for increases, while the overinvestment hypothesis predicts a symmetrical impact on abnormal returns.
2. For the Q < 1 firms, both the signaling and overinvestment hypotheses predict a significant price impact for both dividend increases and decreases.

Their results do not support the implication of the signaling hypothesis because the abnormal returns for the Q > 1 firms are significant for dividend increases but insignificant for dividend decreases. In addition, the price impact (positive for increases and negative for decreases in dividends) is significantly greater for the Q < 1 firms than for the Q > 1 firms.

Second, Lang and Litzenberger (1989) examine analysts' revision of earnings forecasts surrounding dividend-change announcements. In so doing, they formulate the following predictions of the signaling hypothesis:

- For the $Q < 1$ firms, analysts revise their forecast in the same direction as the dividend changes.
- For the $Q > 1$ firms, analysts respond only to dividend decreases (downward revision).

They show that the effect of dividend announcements on earnings expectations is not statistically significant for either increases or decreases and contend that this evidence is inconsistent with the prediction of the signaling hypothesis. As the overinvestment hypothesis does not make any prediction about changes in cash flow expectations resulting from dividend changes, this finding further supports the overinvestment hypothesis.

Lang and Litzenberger (1989) conclude that their cumulative evidence favors the overinvestment hypothesis over the signaling hypothesis. However, Howe et al. (1992) question the applicability of this conclusion to onetime cash disbursements, while Denis et al. (1994) and Yoon and Starks (1995) question the interpretation of the findings reported by Lang and Litzenberger.

Howe et al. (1992) investigate whether the findings of the Lang and Litzenberger (1989) study hold for a broader set of cash disbursements that are infrequent in nature, namely, tender-offer share repurchases and specially designated dividends (SDDs). Their sample consists of 55 share repurchases and 60 SDDs announcements between January 1979 and December 1989. Following Lang and Litzenberger, Howe et al. divide their sample into $Q < 1$ and $Q > 1$ groups. Unlike Lang and Litzenberger, Howe et al. find no statistically significant difference in announcement effects between the low-Q and high-Q firms for either the repurchase or SDD sample.

Howe et al. (1992) also test whether the low-Q firms with greater free cash flows have higher abnormal returns surrounding repurchase and SDD announcements. They define cash flows as operating income before depreciation minus interest expenses, taxes, and preferred and common dividends, and they normalize this measure by dividing by total assets. The coefficient of the cash flow variable is insignificant at the 5 percent level in all equations. Howe et al. (p. 1963) comment: "We thus have an empirical puzzle: If Jensen's free cash-flow theory applies to dividend changes, it is difficult to see why it does not also apply to the analogous events examined here." They offer the entrenchment hypothesis as a partial solution to this puzzle. Referring to the findings of Morck, Shleifer, and Vishny (1988) and Wruck (1989), Howe et al. argue that, because of the entrenchment motive, a repurchase announcement by low-Q managers sends a mixed signal, possibly muting the effect of lessened overinvestment potential.

Denis et al. (1994) assert that low-Q firms are generally high-dividend-yield firms, while high-Q firms are usually low-yield firms. Consequently, for an equivalent percentage change in dividends, a low-Q firm will exhibit a greater market reaction than a high-Q firm. Thus, Denis et al. contend that the observed negative relationship between Q and the stock price reaction to dividend changes found by Lang and Litzenberger (1989) may be a by-product of a negative relationship between dividend yield and Q. Using a sample of 6,777 large dividend changes over the 1962–1988 period, Denis et al. demonstrate that a negative correlation exists between Q and dividend yield.

Denis et al. (1994) test the ability of three models to explain the positive association between dividend change announcements and stock price changes. In addition to signaling and overinvestment models, they also examine the clientele model espoused by Bajaj and Vijh (1990), because an implication of this model is that investors in low-yield (high-Q) firms, who have a relatively high aversion to dividends, will view an increase in dividends negatively. A summary of the findings of Denis et al. follows:

1. Two-day excess returns are positively related to the standardized size of the dividend change (dividend change divided by the firm's stock price two days before the dividend announcement) and to the level of the dividend yield, but they are unrelated to Q.
2. Analysts update their forecasts of future earnings on the basis of observed dividend change. Consistent with the negative relationship between the magnitude of the dividend change and Q, these earnings revisions are greater for Q < 1 firms than for Q > 1 firms.
3. Firms with Q < 1 increase (decrease) their level of investment (capital expenditures) after dividend increases (decreases).

The authors conclude that their results provide support for the cash flow signaling and dividend clientele hypotheses but little support for the overinvestment hypothesis.

A study by Yoon and Starks (1995) is similar to that of Denis et al. (1994). Yoon and Starks contend that under the signaling hypothesis, the dividend change provides information about current and/or future cash flows, while under the free cash flow hypothesis, the dividend change provides information about changes in the managers' misuse of cash flows. Hence, the major focus of their study is to analyze the relationship between dividend changes and the firm's investment opportunity set and the relationship between wealth effects from the dividend-change announcements and the overinvestment or cash flow signaling hypotheses.

Yoon and Starks's (1995) sample consists of 3,748 dividend-increase and 431 dividend-decrease announcements over the 1969–1988 period. They examine the change in dividends rather than the level of dividend payments. In addition to Tobin's Q, they also use the direction of insider trading as an alternative proxy for investment opportunities. Yoon and Starks do not report the results using the alternate proxy because the results are essentially the same as when using Q. After controlling for the size of the dividend change, the anticipated dividend yield, and the market value of the firm, they do not find differences in the magnitude of stock price reactions to dividend announcements between low-Q and high-Q firms. This result is in contrast with that of Lang and Litzenberger (1989), who find that the absolute value of the announcement return is larger for Q < 1 firms than for Q > 1 firms.

Yoon and Starks (1995) admit that the preceding finding alone may not be definitive evidence against the free cash flow hypothesis, as the control variables (e.g., the magnitude of the change, the dividend yield, and the market value of the firm) used in their study are also related to the firm's investment opportunities.

They suggest that a more appropriate test is to analyze the sources of the wealth effects that the two competing hypotheses suggest. In so doing, Yoon and Starks investigate the relationship between dividend changes and subsequent changes in wasteful investments (as predicted by free cash flow hypothesis) and the association between dividend changes and changes in cash flow expectations (as predicted by the cash flow signaling hypothesis).

If dividend changes reflect modification in management's policy toward overinvestment, overinvesting firms should reduce their capital expenditures after dividend increases. To the contrary, Yoon and Starks (1995) find that firms, regardless of their investment opportunities, significantly increase (decrease) their capital expenditures after dividend increases (decreases) over the three years after the dividend changes. In terms of changes in cash flow expectations, they find that announcements of dividend increases and decreases cause analysts to revise their current earnings forecasts to be consistent with the signaling hypothesis. They also report that analysts tend to lower their long-term earnings growth forecasts following decrease announcements but not after dividend increase announcements. The authors claim that this result potentially explains why dividend decreases cause a greater stock price reaction than do dividend increases. Overall, their evidence favors the cash flow signaling hypothesis over the free cash flow hypothesis.

Lie (2000) questions the approach taken by Howe et al. (1992), Denis et al. (1994), and Yoon and Starks (1995). He asserts that the mixed evidence provided by Lang and Litzenberger (1989) versus Denis et al. and Yoon and Starks on the excess funds hypothesis in the context of regular dividend changes could be attributable to the confounding effects of dividend change expectations and investment opportunities. In contrast, there is no obvious link between Tobin's Q and expectations about SDDs or share repurchases. Therefore, studies of special dividends and share repurchases may offer cleaner tests of the excess funds hypothesis. Lie argues that Howe et al. find no support for the free cash flow hypothesis in a study of special dividends and self-tender offers because they (as well as Denis et al.) use recurring cash flows as the only measure of free cash flow.

According to Lie (2000), excess funds have two dimensions—recurring and nonrecurring. A firm derives recurring excess funds (operating income before depreciation minus interest expenses, taxes, preferred and common dividends) from its normal operation, while a nonrecurring free cash flow (e.g., due to asset sales) is onetime or infrequent in nature. Lie suggests that firms with a nonrecurring accumulation of excess cash should pay out this excess cash through a special dividend or repurchase rather than through an increase in the regular dividend. His rationale is that the latter would also commit the firm to paying higher future dividends, while firms generating recurring excess cash from normal operations should cut current and future overinvestment by increasing the regular dividend.

Lie's (2000) sample consists of 570 SDDs, 7,417 regular dividend increases, and 207 repurchases during the 1978–1993 period. Consistent with prior studies, he finds a significant positive announcement returns for the three types of incremental disbursements, with the mean abnormal returns being 3.5 percent, 1.3 percent, and 8.0 percent, respectively. Lie demonstrates that all disbursing firms tend to have funds in excess of their industry norms. However, firms using onetime cash disbursements have accumulated more (industry-adjusted) cash before the event than have firms that increase regular dividends. The former group typically generates less cash flow both before and after the event. Consistent with this finding, the source of funds for SDDs and repurchases is nonrecurring, while that of regular dividend increases is recurring. Lie performs cross-sectional regressions of the announcement returns with three control variables—dividends as a fraction of market value of equity, index-adjusted market value of equity, and dividend yield. The following summarizes his results:

1. Abnormal returns surrounding the announcements of SDDs are unrelated to cash flows, which is consistent with Howe et al. (1992), but are positively related to cash levels, and this relationship is stronger for firms with poor investment opportunities. Yet this relationship is statistically significant only for large special dividends (dividends scaled by the market value of equity that exceed the sample median).
2. The announcement-period returns around regular dividend increases, which are much smaller than for SDDs, are unrelated to either cash flow or cash levels. This result is attributable to comparatively low cash levels associated with dividend increasing firms or small incremental disbursements.
3. Announcement returns for repurchases are unrelated to cash flows but are related to cash levels, with a more significantly positively relationship attached to the low-Q firms.

Lie's (2000) findings suggest that the stock market perceives large SDDs and repurchases as a remedy to the free cash flow problem. The market reacts most favorably when these firms have large cash levels coupled with poor investment opportunities. Nevertheless, the market does not appear to perceive regular dividend increases as a tool to remedy this agency problem.

Lie (2000) divides the sample into small and large cash disbursements for all three types. For the SDDs, he reports that the coefficients on the cash level and the interaction variable between cash level and low Q are positive and statistically significant only for the large special dividends. For the regular dividend-increase cases, Lie reports that the coefficient on dividend yield and dividend change are insignificant for the small sample but highly significant for the large dividend change sample. This finding prompts him to question the clientele hypothesis of Bajaj and Vijh (1990), as the dividend clientele hypothesis does not explain why the positive relationship should exist for only large dividend changes. For the self-tender offers, both large and small subsamples indicate that the coefficient of the interaction variable between cash flow and low Q is positive and highly significant.

Lie's (2000) next step involves testing the effect of alternative agency control mechanisms. In so doing, he tests the following idea: if efficient control mechanisms prevent managers from wasting excess funds on poor projects, the relationship between announcement returns and the interaction variable between cash levels and the low-Q firms should be stronger for firms with poor control mechanisms. He tests this idea on the repurchases and large-special-dividends subsamples. He uses four indicators of poor control mechanisms—insider holdings less than 5 percent and more than 20 percent, outsiders on the board less than 50 percent, and no outside block holders. He finds no evidence showing that the market is less concerned about excess cash levels if the firm has effective control mechanisms in place.

Lie (2000) suggests two major implications of his study. First, the free cash flow hypothesis predicts a positive relationship between the stock-price reaction and cash levels for low-Q firms (and no relationship for high-Q firms), while the signaling hypothesis offers no clear prediction about the relation between the stock price reaction and cash levels. The results demonstrate that incremental disbursements of funds can enhance shareholder value by curbing potential overinvestment (low-Q firms) by managers and therefore are more consistent with the free cash flow hypothesis. Second, no evidence suggests that small special dividends and regular dividend increases mitigate the overinvestment problem. Referring to Grinblatt, Masulis, and Titman's (1984) argument in the context of stock splits and stock dividends, Lie (p. 245) comments: "It is possible that small dividends, regardless of their label, are used for reasons unrelated to agency issues, for example to call attention to the firm."

Researchers have more directly tested investors' concern about managers' potential misuse of free cash flows. For example, Christie and Nanda (1994) provide perhaps the most convincing proof of this concern. They document a positive share-price reaction to President Roosevelt's unexpected announcement in 1936 that taxes would be imposed on undistributed corporate profits. They also find that firms more prone to suffer from free cash flow problems have a more positive reaction. Their results demonstrate that shareholders' concern for potential misuse of excess cash outweighs their concern over the direct cost resulting from the new tax. DeAngelo and DeAngelo (2000) document an initial negative market reaction to the news of potentially poor reinvestments by Times Mirror from the sale of its cable division and a subsequent positive reaction to the news of dividend distribution of this cash flow instead.

Dividend Changes: Leading or Lagging Indicator of Profitability?

According to the signaling hypothesis, a dividend increase bodes well, and a dividend decrease conveys bad news about the firm's future. Thus, a major implication of the signaling hypothesis is that dividend changes should be followed by changes in profitability (earnings growth rates or return on assets) in the same direction. Allen and Michaely (2003) suggest that without the empirical support of this crucial requirement dividend loses information content and, therefore, signaling capability. The free cash flow hypothesis implies that the positive market reaction to a dividend increase occurs because it reduces the overinvestment potential for firms with a limited opportunity set. In other words, the free cash flow hypothesis does not require a positive association between changes in dividends and changes in future earnings.

Several studies examine the relationship between changes in dividends and postannouncement changes in earnings. For a sample of 35 firms that increased their dividends by more than 20 percent, Brickley (1983) finds a significant earnings increase in the year of and the year after the dividend increase. Healy and Palepu (1988), using a sample of 131 dividend-initiating firms, find that earnings increase rapidly in the preannouncement period and continue to increase in the postannouncement years. However, they also find that earnings of dividend-omitting firms improve significantly in the several years after the announcement, which contradicts the predictions of the cash flow signaling model. DeAngelo, DeAngelo, and Skinner (1992) report that dividend-reducing firms experience declining current and future earnings. Aharony and Dotan (1994) find that earnings continue to increase for at least four quarters after the dividend increase. More recently, Nissim and Ziv (2001) document a positive relationship between dividend and earnings changes. The findings of these studies are generally consistent with the cash flow signaling hypothesis.

On the other hand, several studies find either no relationship or a weak relationship between dividend changes and subsequent earnings changes. Both Watts (1973) and Gonedes (1978) report only a weak relationship between dividend and earnings changes. Penman (1983) reports that, after controlling for management's future earnings forecast, dividends do not contribute additional information. DeAngelo, DeAngelo, and Skinner (1996) study the signaling content of dividends paid by 145 NYSE firms facing a decline in earnings after at least nine consecutive years of growth. They find no evidence that dividend increases help identify firms with superior future earnings.

Benartzi, Michaely, and Thaler (1997) use a sample of 1,025 firms (7,186 firm-year observations) over the 1979–1991 period. After controlling for several factors that can create a spurious relationship between dividend and subsequent earnings changes, they find a very strong lagged and contemporaneous correlation between dividend changes and earnings but little evidence of a positive relationship between dividend changes and future earnings changes. These authors discover that earnings actually increase in the two years after dividend cuts, which contradicts the prediction of the signaling hypothesis.

According to Fama and French (2001), the fraction of U.S. industrial firms paying cash dividends declined steadily from the 1950s to the 1990s. They suggest that one explanation for the decline is the changing characteristics of publicly held companies. For example, firms listed more recently tend to have high-growth opportunities. This finding of a negative relationship between dividend changes and growth opportunities runs counter to the prediction of the cash flow signaling model.

On the basis of a sample of 7,642 dividend changes announced between 1967 and 1993, Grullon, Michaely, and Swaminathan (2002) report that a firm's growth rate subsides when it reaches the maturity stage of its life cycle. A reduced growth rate results in increased free cash flows, which the firms then disburse in the form of dividends or stock repurchases. This proposition, which they term *maturity hypothesis*, predicts a shrinking investment opportunity set, declining systematic risk, and waning profitability.

Using a sample consisting of 6,284 dividend increases and 1,358 dividend decreases from 1967 to 1993, Grullon et al. (2002) report that return on assets, cash levels, and capital expenditures all decrease significantly in the years after large dividend increases. These findings, with the exception of reduced risk (for which neither hypothesis has an explicit prediction), are consistent with the predictions of the free cash flow hypothesis but inconsistent with the cash flow signaling hypothesis. According to Grullon et al. (p. 423), "An increase in dividends may not only convey information about changes in the firm's fundamentals but also about the management's commitment not to overinvest. Thus, the free cash flow hypothesis becomes a significant element of the maturity hypothesis."

Grullon, Michaely, Benartzi, and Thaler (2005) challenge Nissim and Ziv's (2001) assumption of linear mean reversion in earnings, and their findings show a positive relationship between changes in dividend and subsequent earnings. Their sample consists of 2,778 firms announcing dividends (increase, decrease, and no change) between 1963 and 1997. After controlling for the nonlinear patterns in earnings behavior, Grullon et al. report a negative correlation between dividend changes and changes in future profitability, a finding that is inconsistent with the cash flow signaling hypothesis.

According to DeAngelo, DeAngelo, and Stulz (2006), rapidly growing young companies that recently have become public pay little or no dividends, while mature public companies pay the bulk of their retained earnings in dividends. Bulan, Subramanian, and Tanlu (2007) report similar findings. Bulan et al. follow a sample of 2,333 firms from initial public offering to dividend initiation. They report that when compared to noninitiators at the same stage of their life cycles, dividend initiators are larger as well as more mature and more profitable firms with greater cash reserves and fewer growth opportunities. Bulan et al. report no significant improvement in profitability or growth occurring in the immediate postinitiation years.

Dividends and Severity of Agency Problems

Jensen (1986) argues that debt is a more effective mechanism than dividends for reducing the agency costs of free cash flows because the precommitment associated with debt is legally binding. That is, bondholders have the right to take the firm to the bankruptcy court if the company does not deliver on its obligations. This argument, when combined with the arguments set forth in Jensen and Meckling (1976), implies that agency costs associated with free cash flows are negatively related to a firm's debt, managers' equity ownership, monitoring intensity, and depth of a firm's governance structure. Similarly, Barclay, Smith, and Watts (1995) suggest that a major determinant of the magnitude of overinvestment problems is the firm's ownership and governance structure.

Several studies examine the overinvestment problem in the presence of dividends as well as other mechanisms for reducing agency costs of free cash flows. For example, Agrawal and Jayaraman (1994) find that dividend payout ratios of a sample of all-equity firms are significantly higher than those of a control group of levered firms. Further, within the group of all-equity firms, those with lower managerial holdings have higher payout ratios. These results hold after controlling for free cash flows and growth rates. Agrawal and Jayaraman conclude that dividends and managerial ownership are substitute mechanisms for reducing agency costs in all-equity firms.

John and Knyazeva (2006) argue that the market favors precommitment to dividend payments over repurchases to mitigate the agency conflict stemming from poor governance. The basis for this argument is that managers who deviate from a chosen dividend policy incur a cost due to a strong negative market reaction. Yet the market treats share repurchases as more flexible because repurchases are irregular payouts made at the manager's discretion. John and Knyazeva find that firms with weak governance are significantly less likely to use stand-alone repurchases. They also observe that firms with weak corporate governance, on average, pay higher dividends. John and Knyazeva conclude that the type of monitoring mechanisms is relevant for discretionary payouts.

Varying Role of Dividends across the World

Using a sample of 200 German firms covering the 1988–1992 period, Amihud and Murgia (1997) test the premise of tax-based signaling models that the higher tax on dividends is a necessary condition to make investors informed about a company's values. In Germany, dividends are not tax advantaged and are taxed at a lower rate for most investor classes. As such, signaling models predict that dividends are not informative. However, Amihud and Murgia find that the stock-price reaction to dividend news in Germany is similar to that found in the United States. The authors conclude that reasons other than signaling are at work in Germany.

Dewenter and Warther (1998) compare dividend policies of U.S. and Japanese firms, partitioning the Japanese data into *keiretsu*, independent, and hybrid firms. By examining the correlation between dividend changes and stock returns, and the reluctance to change dividends, their results show that Japanese firms, particularly *keiretsu*-member firms, face less information asymmetry and fewer agency conflicts than do U.S. firms. Thus, Japanese firms experience lesser stock price reactions to dividend omissions and initiations and are less reluctant to omit and cut dividends. In addition, the dividends of Japanese firms are more responsive to earnings changes.

Do firms pay a dividend because minority shareholders have the power to prevent insiders from disgorging cash or do firms pay dividends to establish a reputation for being nice to minority shareholders? La Porta, Lopez-De-Silanes, Shleifer, and Vishny (2000) analyze 4,000 companies from 33 countries in 1995 to find an answer to this question. Their major finding is that insiders pay dividends when the law protects the rights of minority shareholders. This finding supports what La Porta et al. describe as the outcome model version of the agency theory of dividends. Specifically, La Porta et al. report that firms in common law countries, where minority shareholders have better investor protection, make higher dividend payouts than do firms in civil law countries with lower investor protection. Also, high-growth firms have lower payouts in common law countries. They find no evidence that in countries with low investor protection, management voluntarily commits itself to pay higher dividends and to more frequent monitoring by the market. La Porta et al. (p. 27) conclude: "Despite the possible relevance of alternative theories, firms appear to pay out cash to investors because the opportunities to steal or misinvest it are in part limited by law, and because minority shareholders have enough power to extract it."

Using a sample of 181 cash dividend announcements over the 1985–1995 period, Travlos, Trigeorgis, and Vafeas (2001) examine their contention that special characteristics of the Cyprus stock market delimit applicability of most traditional explanations for cash and stock dividends in favor of an information-signaling explanation. The empirical results, however, are generally inconsistent with this view. In demonstrating that the ownership and control structure of the firm is a significant determinant of its dividend policy, Gugler (2003) uses a sample of

214 nonfinancial firms over the 1991–1999 period drawn from the 600 largest nonfinancial firms in Austria. He documents that family-controlled, as opposed to state-controlled, firms in Austria, when faced with good investment opportunities, are less reluctant to cut dividends when needed, while firms with low-growth opportunities optimally disgorge cash irrespective of who controls the firm. Gugler concludes that his results are consistent with La Porta et al.'s (2000) outcome model.

Pawlina and Renneboog (2005) investigate the investment cash flow sensitivity of firms in the United Kingdom. They find that investment in the United Kingdom is strongly sensitive to cash flow. This sensitivity stems primarily from the agency costs of free cash flow and not from information asymmetry. Pawlina and Renneboog also conclude that outside block holders, such as the government, financial institutions, and industrial firms (only at high-control levels), reduce the cash flow sensitivity of investment via effective monitoring.

Li, Yin-feng, Song, and Man-shu (2006) perform a structural analysis on the data obtained via a survey of Chinese firms covering the 2003–2006 period. A major finding of this study is that dividend policy of non-state-owned, listed companies in China follows the agency theory. They report that shareholders play a greater role in influencing dividend policy than managers of non-state-owned firms.

Pinkowitz, Stulz, and Williamson (2006) test an agency theory prediction that the value of corporate cash holdings is less in countries with poor investor protection because insiders are better able to extract private benefits in these countries. Consistent with agency theory, they find that the relationship between cash holdings and firm value is weaker in countries with poor protection and that the relationship between dividends and firm value is weaker in countries with stronger investor protection.

Denis and Osobov (2008) use the data from 1989 to 2002 to examine the dividend policies of firms in six major countries, namely, the United States, United Kingdom, Canada, France, Germany, and Japan. They find that the correlation between growth opportunities and the likelihood of dividend payment is negative in common law countries but positive in civil law countries. This evidence supports the agency cost model.

Renneboog and Szilagyi (2007) test the implication that in the presence of a large controlling shareholder, dividends need not function as an agency control device. They examine the dividend policy in the Netherlands, where laws exist to protect stakeholders. Their sample consists of 150 Dutch firms over the 1996–2004 period. They find that firms controlled by corporate insiders, along with institutional investors with superior monitoring skills and incentives, pay the highest dividends. Renneboog and Szilagyi conclude that dividends and shareholder control are complementary rather than substitute mechanisms in mitigating agency concerns in the Netherlands.

Von Eije and Megginson (2008) examine dividend policies of firms in the European Union. Their sample consists of more than 4,100 listed industrial companies announcing cash dividends and share repurchases during the 1989–2005 period in the 15 EU member countries before May 2004. They find that average financial reporting by EU companies steadily increases during the study period from 1.2 to 2.4 times per year, and this increased frequency is associated with a higher amount of cash dividends and shares repurchased. They also report that older firms are more likely to pay cash dividends (as well as higher dividends) than younger firms. In addition, firms in common law countries are more likely to pay cash dividends but are not more likely to repurchase shares than are firms in civil law countries. Von Eije and Megginson find a negative relationship between leverage and cash dividends.

CONCLUSIONS

Researchers consistently report that abnormal return of a dividend-change announcement is of the same sign as the sign of the dividend change. Although researchers have advanced several hypotheses to explain this phenomenon, two highly researched and competing hypotheses are the cash flow signaling hypothesis and the free cash flow hypothesis. According to the cash flow signaling hypothesis, the stock price moves in the same direction as the dividend because dividend changes convey information about the firm's future growth opportunities. The free cash flow hypothesis suggests that price reacts favorably to the announcement of a dividend increase because this increase reduces the agency cost of free cash flow (i.e., the overinvestment potential). Similarly, the stock price reacts negatively to an announcement of reduced dividends because the potential for overinvestment increases. Studies examine the explanatory power of the two competing hypotheses by empirically testing their implications.

An implication of the signaling hypothesis is that a positive relationship should exist between dividend changes and subsequent changes in profitability. Allen and Michaely (2003) describe this implication as the crucial requirement for the signaling hypothesis to hold. The empirical results are mixed. Some studies find a positive relationship between dividend and future earnings changes, while others report a very weak positive relationship, no relationship, or a negative relationship. On the basis of the body of the empirical research, Miller (1987) describes dividends as a lagging rather than a leading indicator of earnings.

Megginson (1996) proposes additional shortcomings of the signaling hypothesis. For example, the signaling hypothesis does not adequately explain the cross-sectional variability of dividend payments across industries, countries, or ownership structures. This hypothesis also does not explain the lack of development of less costly but equally effective methods of conveying information to shareholders. Finally, the signaling hypothesis fails to explain why dividend payments have remained relatively unchanged despite dramatic changes in information-processing technology.

Empirical evidence on the ability of the cash flow signaling hypothesis to explain the market reaction to dividend changes is poor. Survey results by Brav, Graham, Harvey, and Michaely (2005) exacerbate the doubts about the efficacy of the cash flow signaling hypothesis. On the basis of their interviews of top executives, Brav et al. report (p. 505), "Not a single interviewed executive told us that their firm had ever thought of increasing payout as a costly means of separating themselves from the competitors."

Turning to the free cash flow hypothesis, a testable implication, as suggested by Lang and Litzenberger (1989), is that market reactions to dividend changes will be greater of magnitude for low-Q versus high-Q firms. Their empirical evidence supports this supposition. Several authors such as Howe et al. (1992), Denis et al.

(1994), and Yoon and Starks (1995) raise issues with Lang and Litzenberger's findings. Lie (2000) provides convincing arguments and strong empirical support for
an important prediction of the free cash flow hypothesis; namely, the relationship
between the stock-price reaction and cash disbursements based on free cash flow
level is positive for low-Q firms.

Another indirect implication of the free cash flow hypothesis is that the role
of dividends in reducing the agency cost of free cash flows varies depending on
the severity of the agency problem existing in a firm. Agrawal and Jayaraman
(1994) find that all-equity firms pay a significantly higher dividend payout ratio
than a control group of levered firms and firms with lower managerial holdings
have higher payout ratios. John and Knyazeva (2006) observe that firms with
weak corporate governance, on average, pay higher dividends. Also, the free cash
flow hypothesis seems to better explain the variations in dividend policies across
the world than the signaling hypothesis. Christie and Nanda (1994) and DeAngelo and DeAngelo (2000) provide support for investors' concern about potential
overinvestment.

In summary, empirical evidence to date provides stronger support for the
free cash flow hypothesis than cash flow signaling hypothesis in explaining the
market reaction to dividend change announcements. On the basis of the review of
the pertinent literature, Allen and Michaely (2003) conclude that the reason firms
issue dividends and repurchase stock is to reduce overinvestment potential by
management, not to signal the firm value. Megginson (1996, p. 377) suggests that
"the agency cost model is currently the leading mainstream economic model for
explaining observed dividend payouts." The cumulative evidence reported herein
appears to support Megginson's assessment.

REFERENCES

Agrawal, Anup, and Narayanan Jayaraman. 1994. "The Dividend Policies of All-Equity
Firms: A Direct Test of the Free Cash Flow Theory." *Managerial and Decision Economics*
15:2, 139–148.

Aharony, Joseph, and Itzhak Swary. 1980. "Quarterly Dividend and Earnings Announcements and Stockholders' Returns: An Empirical Analysis." *Journal of Finance* 35:1, 1–12.

Aharony, Josef, and Amihud Dotan. 1994. "Regular Dividend Announcements and Future
Unexpected Earnings: An Empirical Analysis." *Financial Review* 29:1, 125–151.

Allen, Franklin, and Roni Michaely. 2003. "Payout Policy." In *Handbook of the Economics of
Finance*, ed. George M. Constantinides, Milton Harris and René M. Stulz, 1A, 337–429.
Amsterdam: Elsevier/North-Holland.

Amihud, Yakov, and Maurizio Murgia. 1997. "Dividends, Taxes, and Signaling: Evidence
from Germany." *Journal of Finance* 52:1, 397–408.

Asquith, Paul, and David W. Mullins, Jr. 1983. "The Impact of Initiating Dividend Payments
on Shareholders' Wealth." *Journal of Business* 56:1, 77–96.

Bajaj, Mukesh B., and Anand M. Vijh. 1990. "Dividend Clienteles and the Information
Content of Dividend Changes." *Journal of Financial Economics* 26:2, 193–219.

Barclay, Michael J., Clifford W. Smith, and Ross L. Watts. 1995. "The Determinants of
Corporate Leverage and Dividend Policies." *Journal of Applied Corporate Finance* 7:5,
4–19.

Benartzi, Shlomo, Roni Michaely, and Richard H. Thaler. 1997. "Do Changes in Dividends
Signal the Future or the Past?" *Journal of Finance* 52:3, 1007–1034.

Bhattacharya, Sudipto. 1979. "Imperfect Information, Dividend Policy, and 'The Bird in the Hand' Fallacy." *Bell Journal of Economics* 10:1, 259–270.

Brav, Alan, John R. Graham, Campbell R. Harvey, and Roni Michaely. 2005. "Payout Policy in the 21st Century." *Journal of Financial Economics* 77:3, 483–527.

Brickley, James A. 1983. "Shareholder Wealth, Information Signaling and the Specially Designated Dividend: An Empirical Study." *Journal of Financial Economics* 12:2, 187–209.

Bulan, Laarni, Narayanan Subramanian, and Lloyd D. Tanlu. 2007. "On the Timing of Dividend Initiations." *Financial Management* 36:4, 31–65.

Christie, William G., and Vikram Nanda. 1994. "Free Cash Flow, Shareholder Value, and the Undistributed Profits Tax of 1936 and 1937." *Journal of Finance* 49:5, 1727–1754.

Dann, Larry. 1981. "Common Stock Repurchases: An Analysis of Returns to Bondholders and Shareholders." *Journal of Financial Economics* 9:2, 113–138.

DeAngelo, Harry, and Linda DeAngelo. 2000. "Controlling Stockholders and the Disciplinary Role of Corporate Payout Policy: A Study of the Times Mirror Company." *Journal of Financial Economics* 56:2, 153–207.

DeAngelo, Harry, Linda DeAngelo, and Douglas J. Skinner. 1992. "Dividends and Losses." *Journal of Finance* 47:5, 1837–1863.

DeAngelo, Harry, Linda DeAngelo, and Douglas J. Skinner. 1996. "Reversal of Fortune: Dividend Signaling and the Disappearance of Sustained Earnings Growth." *Journal of Financial Economics* 40:3, 341–371.

DeAngelo, Harry, Linda DeAngelo, and René M. Stulz. 2006. "Dividend Policy and the Earned/Contributed Capital Mix: A Test of the Life-Cycle Theory." *Journal of Financial Economics* 81:2, 227–254.

Denis, David J., Diane K. Denis, and Atulya Sarin. 1994. "The Information Content of Dividend Changes: Cash Flow Signaling, Overinvestment, and Dividend Clienteles." *Journal of Financial and Quantitative Analysis* 29:4, 567–587.

Denis, David J., and Igor Osobov. 2008. "Why do Firms Pay Dividends? International Evidence on the Determinants of Dividend Policy." *Journal of Financial Economics* 89:1, 62–82.

Dewenter, Kathryn L., and Vincent A. Warther. 1998. "Dividends, Asymmetric Information, and Agency Conflicts: Evidence from a Comparison of the Dividend Policies of Japanese and U.S. Firms." *Journal of Finance* 53:3, 879–904.

Easterbrook, Frank H. 1984. "Two Agency Costs Explanations of Dividends." *American Economic Review* 74:4, 650–659.

Fama, Eugene F., and Kenneth R. French. 2001. "Disappearing Dividends: Changing Firm Characteristics or Lower Propensity to Pay?" *Journal of Financial Economics* 60:1, 3–43.

Gonedes, Nicholas J. 1978. "Corporate Signaling, External Accounting, and Capital Market Equilibrium: Evidence on Dividends, Income, and Extraordinary Items." *Journal of Accounting Research* 16:1, 26–79.

Grinblatt, Mark, Ronald. W. Masulis, and Sheridan Titman. 1984. "The Valuations Effect of Stock Splits and Stock Dividends." *Journal of Financial Economics* 13:4, 461–490.

Grossman, Sanford J., and Oliver D. Hart. 1980. "Takeover Bids, the Free-Rider Problem, and the Theory of the Corporation." *Bell Journal of Economics* 11:1, 42–54.

Grullon, Gustavo, Roni Michaely, and Bhaskaran Swaminathan. 2002. "Are Dividend Changes a Sign of Firm Maturity?" *Journal of Business* 75:3, 387–424.

Grullon, Gustavo, Roni Michaely, Shlomo Benartzi, and Richard H. Thaler. 2005. "Dividend Changes Do Not Signal Changes in Future Profitability." *Journal of Business* 78:5, 1659–1682.

Gugler, Klaus. 2003. "Corporate Governance, Dividend Smoothing, and the Interrelation between Dividends, R&D, and Capital Investment." *Journal of Banking and Finance* 27:7, 1297–1321.

Healy, Paul M., and Krishna G. Palepu. 1988. "Earnings Information Conveyed by Dividend Initiations and Omissions." *Journal of Financial Economics* 21:2, 149–176.

Howe, Keith, M., Jia He, and G. Wenchi Kao. 1992. "One-Time Cash Flow Announcements and Free Cash-Flow Theory: Share Repurchases and Special Dividends." *Journal of Finance* 47:5, 1963–1975.

Jensen, Michael C. 1986. "Agency Costs of Free Cash Flow, Corporate Finance, and Takeovers." *American Economic Review* 76:2, 323–329.

Jensen, Michael C., and William H. Meckling. 1976. "Theory of the Firm: Managerial Behavior, Agency Costs and Ownership Structure." *Journal of Financial Economics* 3:4, 305–360.

John, Kose, and Anzhela Knyazeva. 2006 "Payout Policy, Agency Conflicts, and Corporate Governance." Working Paper, New York University.

John, Kose, and Joseph Williams. 1985. "Dividends, Dilution and Taxes: A Signaling Equilibrium." *Journal of Finance* 40:4, 1053–1070.

Lang, Larry H. P., and Robert H. Litzenberger. 1989. "Dividend Announcements: Cash Flow Signaling vs. Free Cash Flow Hypothesis." *Journal of Financial Economics* 24:1, 181–191.

La Porta, Rafael, Florenico Lopez-De-Silanes, Andrei Shleifer, and Robert W. Vishny. 2000. "Agency Problems and Dividend Policies around the World." *Journal of Finance* 55:1, 1–33.

Li, Li, Qi Yin-feng, Liu Song, and Wang Man-shu. 2006. "Who Makes the Dividend Policy Decision and Their Motives for Doing So: An Analysis Based on a Questionnaire Survey of Non-State-Owned Listed Companies in China." Working Paper, Business School, NanKai University.

Lie, Eric. 2000. "Excess Funds and Agency Problems: An Empirical Study of Incremental Disbursements." *Review of Financial Studies* 13:1, 219–247.

Megginson, William. 1996. *Corporate Finance Theory*. Reading, MA: Addison-Wesley.

Miller, Merton. 1987. "The Information Content of Dividends." In *Macroeconomics: Essays in Honor of Franco Modigliani*, ed. John Bossons, Rudiger Dornbusch, and Stanley Fischer, 37–61. Cambridge, MA: MIT Press.

Miller, Merton H., and Franco Modigliani. 1961. "Dividend Policy, Growth and the Valuation of Shares." *Journal of Business* 34:4, 411–433.

Miller, Merton H., and Kevin Rock. 1985. "Dividend Policy under Asymmetric Information." *Journal of Finance* 40:4, 1021–1051.

Morck, Randall, Andrei Shleifer, and Robert W. Vishny. 1988. "Management Ownership and Market Valuation: An Empirical Analysis." *Journal of Financial Economics* 20:1, 293–315.

Nissim, Doron, and Amir Ziv. 2001. "Dividend Changes and Future Profitability." *Journal of Finance* 56:6, 2111–2133.

Ofer, Aharon R., and Daniel R. Siegel. 1987. "Corporate Financial Policy, Information, and Market Expectations: An Empirical Investigation of Dividends." *Journal of Finance* 42:4, 889–911.

Pawlina, Grzegorz, and Luc Renneboog. 2005. "Is Investment-Cash Flow Sensitivity Caused by Agency Costs or Asymmetric Information? Evidence from the U.K." *European Financial Management* 11:4, 483–513.

Penman, Stephen H. 1983. "The Predictive Content of Earnings Forecasts and Dividends." *Journal of Finance* 38:4, 1181–1199.

Pettit, Richardson. 1972. "Dividend Announcements, Security Performance, and Capital Market Efficiency." *Journal of Finance* 27:5, 993–1007.

Pinkowitz, Lee, René Stulz, and Rohan Williamson. 2006. "Does the Contribution of Corporate Cash Holdings and Dividends to Firm Value Depend on Governance? A Cross-Country Analysis." *Journal of Finance* 61:6, 2725–2751.

Renneboog, Luc, and Peter G. Szilagyi. 2007. "How Relevant Is Dividend Policy under Low Shareholder Protection?" Finance Working Paper No. 128/2006, European Corporate Governance Institute.

Richardson, Scott. 2006. "Over-investment of Free Cash Flow." *Review of Accounting Studies.* 11:2–3, 159–189.

Travlos, Nickolaos, Leons Trigeorgis, and Nikos Vafeas. 2001. "Shareholder Wealth Effects of Dividend Policy Changes in an Emerging Stock Market: The Case of Cyprus." *Multinational Finance Journal* 5:2, 87–112.

Vermaelen, Theo. 1981. "Common Stock Repurchases and Market Signaling." *Journal of Financial Economics* 9:2, 139–183.

von Eije, Henk, and William Megginson. 2008. "Dividend and Share Repurchases in the European Union." *Journal of Financial Economics* 89:2, 347–374.

Watts, Ross L. 1973. "The Information Content of Dividends." *Journal of Business* 46:2, 191–211.

Wruck, Karen. 1989. "Equity Ownership Concentration and Firm Value: Evidence from Private Equity Financing." *Journal of Financial Economics* 23:1, 3–28.

Yoon, Pyung Sig, and Laura T. Starks. 1995. "Signaling, Investment Opportunities, and Dividend Announcements." *Review of Financial Studies* 8:4, 995–1018.

ABOUT THE AUTHOR

Tarun Mukherjee is a Professor of Finance and Moffett Chair in Financial Economics at the University of New Orleans. He has served as coeditor of the *Review of Financial Economics* since 1999. His publications have appeared in many academic and practitioner journals including *Financial Management, Financial Review, Journal of Financial Research,* and *Journal of Business Finance and Accounting.* He has a doctoral degree in finance from Texas Tech University.

CHAPTER 10

Asymmetric Information and Signaling Theory

GREG FILBECK
Professor of Finance, Black Family Endowed Professorship of Insurance and Risk
Management, Behrend College, Penn State University–Erie

INTRODUCTION

The concept of signaling theory find its roots in the work of Lintner (1956), who
demonstrated how market prices often react to changes in dividend rates. This
chapter examines whether dividend policy changes serve as a signaling device.
Miller and Modigliani (1961) (hereafter MM) consider the possibility of a signaling
effect. They state that although the dividend policy chosen by a firm has no effect
on its value (only the sum of the present value of the cash flows does), the market's
perception of a dividend policy change may affect share price. Specifically, in their
discussion of the possibility of "the information content of dividends," MM state:

> *To conclude our discussion of dividend policy under uncertainty, we might take note briefly
> of a common confusion about the meaning of the irrelevance proposition occasioned by the
> fact that in the real world a change in the dividend rate is often followed by a change in
> the market price (sometimes spectacularly so). Such a phenomenon would not be incom-
> patible with irrelevance to the extent that it was merely a reflection of what might be called
> the "information content" of dividends, an attribute of a particular dividend payments
> [sic] hitherto excluded by assumption from the discussion and proofs. That is, where a
> firm has adopted a policy of dividend stabilization with a long-established and generally
> appreciated "target payout ratio," investors are likely to (and have good reason to) interpret
> a change in the dividend rate as a change in management's views of future profit prospects
> for the firm. The dividend change, in other words, provides the occasion for the price change
> though not its cause, the price still being solely a reflection of future earnings and growth
> opportunities. (p. 430)*

Their analysis suggests that "systematic irrationality on the part of the investing public" is a possible reason for the fact that many previous studies report
low-payout companies selling at a discount. Because of this possibility, MM (1961)
conclude that dividend irrelevancy can hold, and at the same time, signaling theory finds a home in financial theory. The market may reevaluate share value on
the basis of a change in dividend payout policy because dividends signal future

163

increases in cash flows. Researchers often cite the arguments of MM as the basis for developing the signaling argument.

SIGNALING MODELS

Ross (1977) was the first to exploit the signaling argument with a formal model motivated by the MM (1961) passage, stating that investors value the perceived stream of future cash flows of the firm. The Ross one-period incentive-signaling model is geared toward changes in capital structure. By using debt, management signals an increased capacity to cover the debt service obligations through increased cash flows. Kalay (1980) shows that the Ross model may be extended for announcements related to dividend policy, in addition to capital structure. Kalay applies the Ross signaling model to dividend decisions, showing that the reluctance of managers to reduce dividends is a necessary condition for the fact that dividends convey information. Ross develops this argument by classifying firms as either Type A or Type B firms. Type A firms, whose returns are equal to a, and Type B firms, whose returns are equal to b, cannot be distinguished from the marketplace at time zero even though the quantity a exceeds the quantity b.

Type A firms are capable of supporting an increased level of dividend activity without increasing the likelihood of bankruptcy but Type B firms are not. In the Ross (1977) model, managers' compensation is positively linked to the market value of the firm, and managers are penalized if the firm becomes bankrupt. Ross assumes that managers have inside information about the firm's future cash flows and may use leverage as a signaling device to outsiders. Type B managers are aware, by assumption, of their situation, and any increase in dividend activity would send a false signal and result in possible bankruptcy proceedings at the end of the period. Type B managers consequently have an incentive not to send a false signal. As a result, when establishing the firm's dividend policy, managers have a wealth incentive to correctly signal firm value. Investors realizing this possibility view an increase in dividend payout as coming from a Type A firm, noting that this firm is worthy of higher valuation. Investors will discover false signals in the upcoming period when a Type B firm cannot sustain a dividend increase. Myers and Majluf (1984) argue that false signals must be costly to the firm in order to serve as a disincentive for firms to mislead investors.

Bhattacharya (1979) develops and extends a model closely related to the Ross (1977) model, which in part helps to explain why firms would choose to pay dividends even though there are tax disadvantages. Current shareholders of a firm are concerned about what outsiders assign as the market value of the firm. This is because many outsiders' planning horizons for realizing wealth are shorter than the payoff period of a firm's investment opportunities. Bhattacharya assumes that sources of information, such as accounting data, are not completely reliable, in that investors cannot fully use such data in determining a firm's profitability. Assuming that outsider investors have imperfect information about firms' profitability and that the tax rate is higher on cash dividends than capital gains, Bhattacharya shows that the favorable signal received from firms increasing their dividends offsets the higher marginal cost of receiving taxable income. He accomplishes this by showing that dividends are a signaling device for current shareholders' objective functions. In other words, investors are willing to pay a higher tax rate (a cost) in exchange for a signal (a benefit) that firms contained in their portfolio have greater value.

A variation of Bhattacharya's (1979) model is the work of Talmor (1981). Using a multivariate model, Talmor argues that dividend policy is only one of the financially related decisions that a firm's manager must make. Each of these decisions potentially serves as a signaling device.

Ofer and Thakor (1987) compare the signaling impact of share repurchases to cash dividends. They argue that stock repurchases are more likely to signal significant underpricing for stocks because of the higher financing costs and managerial risk associated with their usage. They conclude that firms can use both dividends and stock repurchases as a signaling device for the undervaluation of stock price. Yet cash dividends are the more appropriate vehicle for small variations from actual firm value, while stock repurchases are the better method for larger variations from actual firm value.

Hakansson (1982), using a two-period model, looks at signaling theory as a partial explanation for dividend policies in the market. He states that, in addition to being informative, at least one of three necessary conditions must be met in the signaling framework: (1) heterogeneous beliefs, (2) nonadditive utility, and (3) incomplete financial markets. If at least one of these conditions holds, dividends are capable of improving efficiency when they are informative in nature. Hakansson further states that dividend announcements may, under certain circumstances, bring an incomplete market to, or even beyond, the level of efficiency that would be attained if the market were complete.

Asquith and Mullins (1983) focus on what constitutes an unanticipated dividend change in assessing the signaling argument. They believe that investors capitalize the present value of changes in dividend policy on the date the firm makes the announcement, and that the response for dividend initiations is greater than that for subsequent dividend increases. They state that one of the major sources of conflicting results in previous studies has been isolating and controlling for investors' expectations. As a result, they believe that dividend initiations would more likely be unexpected because the naive model (a previous change in the most recent period is an anticipated change for the upcoming period) accurately reflects investors' expectations for initial dividends. That is, investors do not expect the entire initially declared dividend. They argue that subsequent increases only provide marginally new information about the firm, as investors are likely to anticipate some component of the change.

Miller and Rock (1985) develop a model with the assumption that the firm's managers know more than outside investors do about the nature of the firm's current earnings. In addition, the model permits trading shares. This assumption allows the market to react to the firm's announcements, such as dividend policy changes. If these conditions exist, managers should not adhere to the Fisherian criterion (invest in real assets until the marginal internal rate of return equals the security's risk-adjusted rate of return). Instead, managers are encouraged to increase dividends (or to reduce outside financing) for the purpose of increasing the price of common stock. Wasting such profitable investments, however, results in dead-weight costs.

Miller and Rock (1985) suggest that managers might try to eliminate the asymmetries that exist, which would reduce the need to send signals to shareholders. Yet this alternative also involves dead-weight costs. Miller and Rock tie the question of dividend payout and external financing to the concept of net dividends. That is, a financing announcement is actually a negative dividend announcement. This concept views equity issues as akin to a negative dividend payment. They show that both dividends and financing are opposing sides of the same topic. Positive values of net dividends may be viewed as dividends, while negative values of net dividends may be viewed as financing. Miller and Rock state that an unexpected change in earnings has the same impact on firm returns as an unexpected change in dividend payout. They conclude that earnings, dividend, and financing announcements are closely related and that financing announcements are clearly related. In addition, current dividend payment trends, rather than the dividend itself, are the basis on which the market projects future earnings.

Myers (1987) argues that dividend policy serves as a basis to signal future expected earnings. His argument stems from the fact that dividend policy is discretionary, while earnings announcements are not. Investors realize that companies are reluctant to reduce dividends. Accordingly, investors may view a dividend increase as an endorsement by managers that the firm's future earnings prospects must be positive (also see Kalay, 1980).

EMPIRICAL EVIDENCE

The role of dividends in the process of firm valuation is a popular topic in the finance literature. Strong support exists for the view that dividends are important in firm valuation. The early arguments following the MM (1961) conclusion of dividend irrelevance focused primarily on relaxing a rigid set of assumptions in the MM model. Others attempted to correct or improve measurement techniques involving dividend payout procedures.

Friend and Puckett (1964) exemplify the latter of these two arguments when they attempt to correct measurement error in what is known as the multiplier effect. The belief at the time of their study was that dividends have a much larger impact than retained earnings on the value of the firm. Previous studies tied stock prices to current dividends and retained earnings. These studies report an association between high dividend payouts and high price-to-earnings ratios. Drawing from random samples of about 20 firms each from five different industries, Friend and Puckett show that previous empirical findings are biased because of the subjective nature of earnings measurement. Their study looks at these biases, which might include omitted variables, outlier influence on regression coefficients random variations in income, income measurement errors, and least squares bias (resulting from the assumption that dividend payout differences are the result rather than the cause of differences in price-to-earnings ratios). When Friend and Puckett attempt to correct for each of these problems, they find that only in cases with "unusual growth stocks" do dividends have a significantly larger impact than retained earnings on firm value.

One of the bases for MM's conclusions of dividend irrelevancy is that a firm could offset without cost any dividends paid by issuing new equity. Investigating the combined effect of both dividend policy and new equity financing decisions on the market value of the firm's common stock, VanHorne and McDonald (1971) use a share-price model to test two separate effects. First, they relax MM's assumption that firms can issue equity at no cost. The second test is that of the residual theory of dividends. They investigate the decision to pay dividends in excess of available earnings. Relaxing MM's assumption of perfect capital markets, Van Horne and McDonald argue that dividend policy can affect firm value if investors have preferences for dividends versus capital gains (or visa versa) or if costs associated with the sale of new issues of equity securities make these issues a more costly course of equity financing than retained earnings.

The Van Horne and McDonald (1971) study examines the valuation of firms within an industry that both pay dividends and engage in new equity financing. While their findings are inclusive, using data from the utility and electric components industries, they are consistent with the existence of investor preferences for current dividends rather than capital gains (assuming that firms finance additional dividends with new equity issues). Although the conclusions of the study are not particularly notable, the fact that relaxing MM's no-transaction-costs assumption is important for its contribution to forthcoming signaling theory arguments.

Early Works

Pettit (1972) and Watts (1973) both look at the signaling effect and arrive at different conclusions. Pettit considers the possibility of a signaling effect in terms of the speed with which the market reacts to dividend changes (an efficient market test). This, in turn, provides evidence as to how changes in dividend levels convey information to the market. Using a market model, he finds that stock prices fully reflect both positive and negative dividend announcements on the announcement date or the following day. Pettit also finds that the market uses the information conveyed in announcements to determine the value for a security.

Using a different model than Pettit (1972), Watts (1973) tests the hypothesis that dividends contain information about future earnings of the firm. He concludes that the information (signaling) content of dividends can only be trivial. Watts finds a relationship between current unexpected dividend changes and future earnings changes. This relationship is unimportant in a signaling framework because traders cannot earn significant abnormal returns on such information when also considering transactions costs.

Kwan (1981) attempts to reconcile differences in the Pettit (1972) and Watts (1973) studies. Critics often question Pettit's results because of his use of observed dividend changes rather than unexpected dividend changes. Kwan uses a naive model to determine what constitutes an unanticipated change. His model for determining unexpected dividend changes incorporates terms for both moving annualized dividends and earnings. Kwan addresses three methodological issues in an attempt to settle the differences in results obtained in previous studies. He discusses the suitability of models used for handling announcement-day returns, the misclassification of information due to noise, and the confounding event effects. His findings echo Pettit's with respect to the fact that an information effect exists.

Charest (1978) uses a two-factor model to test market efficiency, and his model involves three-month dividend cycles. He also investigates risk and return relationships associated with dividend changes as well as the stability of his results. Charest concludes that the market is slow in adjusting fully to news of dividend changes, especially those dividend decreases for which the effects seem to continue even beyond the quarter in which the news occurred. However, the market is not necessarily inefficient because the results could reflect the failure of the two-factor model.

Dividend Reductions

As a source for a follow-up study, Kalay (1980) uses Pettit's (1972) observation that management should be reluctant to reduce or omit dividend payments. Building on the Ross (1977) model, Kalay argues that a dividend reduction, which occurs because of restrictive covenants contained in debt contracts, should not contain information about future cash flows of the firm. These restrictive covenants exist to prevent wealth transfers from the bondholders to shareholders, as noted by Smith and Warner (1979). Finding a large percentage of forced reductions would argue against information content contained in dividend reductions. Kalay finds little support for his hypothesis that dividend reductions contain no new information, hence arguing for a signaling effect in dividend reductions.

Expropriation Effects

Woolridge (1983) and Handjinicolaou and Kalay (1984) also investigate the information effect of dividend changes from the standpoint of expropriation effects versus announcement effects. Woolridge studies dividend announcement effects on nonconvertible bonds and nonconvertible preferred stock. His results argue in favor of a signaling aspect to dividend changes, as well as support the wealth-transfer hypothesis. That is, increasing the amount of dividends that a company pays out will result in a transfer of wealth from preferred shareholders and bond-holders to common shareholders.

Woolridge (1983) argues for two possible outcomes. His model supposes that investors view dividend payouts as payments coming from collaterizable assets and debt covenants are imperfect protections. Under these circumstances, debt holders, preferred stockholders, and other senior claimants on the firm should view any dividend increase negatively, which would argue for an expropriation effect (wealth transfer). If investors interpret dividend increases as signals of higher future cash flows, however, a positive return should be observed to preferred shareholders and bondholders, which would tend to confirm an information effect. Woolridge provides empirical confirmation of the information effect. Positive abnormal returns occur with dividend-increasing announcements and negative abnormal returns with dividend-decreasing announcements for common stock, preferred stock, and bonds. As a result, Woolridge concludes that the signaling hypothesis dominates the expropriation hypothesis.

Handjinicolaou and Kalay (1984) find that dividend increases do not affect returns but that dividend decreases negatively affect returns. They base their results on an investigation of bond price behavior around dividend announcements. The authors also find that shareholders receive gains associated with positive information. Bondholders, however, share losses associated with negative information. They conclude that this evidence is consistent with the information-content hypothesis.

In a more recent study, Dhillon and Johnson (1994) argue against signaling theory on the basis of negative bondholder returns associated with dividend increases. Because of this wealth expropriation, they conclude that signaling theory may play a less important role in discerning information content than it had previously.

Overinvestment Hypothesis

Other studies challenge the validity of signaling theory. Lang and Litzenberger (1989) argue that the overinvestment hypothesis provides a better explanation for paying dividends. The overinvestment hypothesis states that the marketplace rewards firms that choose to pay (or increase) dividends on the basis of curbing their tendency to overinvest in less profitable projects. They identify overinvesting firms as those having a low Tobin's Q ratio.

Denis, Denis, and Sarin (1994) and Yoon and Starks (1995) refute findings by Lang and Litzenberger (1989) when they take the magnitude of the dividend into consideration. Both studies investigate the relationship between analysts' earnings forecast revisions and changes in the capital expenditure of dividend-paying firms. After simultaneously controlling for the standardized dividend change, dividend yield, and Tobin's Q, both studies find a positive relationship between announcement period excess returns and both the magnitude of the standardized dividend change and dividend yield, but no relation to Tobin's Q.

Viswanath, Kim, and Pandit (2002) find that with the increasing presence of institutional investors with longer horizons, signaling theory no longer explains the market reaction to dividend surprises. Their tests of signaling theory focus on the role of liquidity. In particular, they explore the market reaction to dividend changes as a function of the liquidity level and the correlation between dividend policy and liquidity. Their results support the overinvestment and wealth-transfer hypotheses.

Dividends versus Earnings

Aharony and Swary (1980) and Kane, Lee, and Marcus (1984) support the conclusion that there is information content in dividend announcements. Aharony and Swary examine quarterly dividend and earnings announcements made on different dates within a quarter. They use the market model and a naive model for dividend forecasting. Their findings support the conclusion that changes in quarterly cash dividends provide information in addition to that contained in a quarterly earnings report. They also find that the price adjustment occurs quickly, supporting the semistrong form of the efficient market hypothesis. Kane et al. test for interaction effects between dividend and earnings announcements. They restrict their search to firms that make quarterly dividend and earnings announcements at least ten days apart. The authors develop a dividend and earnings expectation model based on a percentage change formula for determining what constitutes an unanticipated change in dividends or earnings. Kane et al. conclude that both dividend and earnings announcements, individually, have a significant effect on stock price. In addition, a significant interaction effect exists between the two on stock prices.

Another line of research focuses on whether a relationship exists between unexpected dividend changes and investor expectations about future earnings. Ofer and Siegel (1987) find that analysts revise their earnings projections on the basis of unexpected changes in dividend policy. Their evidence shows a high correlation between the size of the earnings revision and the size of the unexpected portion of a dividend increase. Unexpected dividend changes affect not only earnings expectations but also the riskiness of earnings. Dyl and Weigand (1988) show that the riskiness of a firm's earnings and cash flows, stock-price variation, and levels of systematic risk all drop significantly with the initiation of a cash dividend.

Other researchers attempt to separate the signaling impact of dividend changes from that of earnings changes. Healy and Palepu (1988) find a relationship between dividend initiations and positive earnings. In particular, firms initiating dividends also have positive earnings in the year before, the year of, and two years after the dividend initiation. This finding, which is consistent with the work of Lintner (1956), suggests that dividend initiations appear to provide evidence of future earnings growth while also reflecting growth already in place at the time of the initiation. Conversely, Healy and Palepu find that a dividend omission is preceded by two years of earnings declines that continue during the year of the omission and the subsequent year.

Benartzi, Michaely, and Thaler (1997) find that the role of dividends as a signaling device is limited to concurrent unexpected changes in earnings but not to future earnings changes. In addition, they find that firms that increase dividends are less likely to report earnings declines than are firms with similar earnings growth, which do not choose to increase their dividends. Benartzi et al. establish a matched-sample approach in their analysis. In particular, they match dividend-paying stocks with non-dividend-paying stocks on the basis of market capitalization, industry, and past earnings performance with the goal of controlling for earnings patterns and mean reversion.

Nissim and Ziv (2001), assuming linear mean reversion in earnings, use regression analysis in an attempt to uncover the relationship between dividends and future earnings. They find a positive relationship between dividend changes and future earnings changes. Grullon, Michaely, Benartzi, and Thaler (2005) argue that Nissim and Ziv's assumption of linear mean reversion in earnings is inappropriate. On the basis of earlier work by others such as Fama and French (2000), who that find the earnings reversion process is highly nonlinear, Grullon et al. revise Nissim and Ziv's model accordingly and find that a relationship no longer exists between dividend changes and future earnings. Grullon, Michaely, and Swaminathan (2002) find a relationship between dividend changes and shifts in systematic risk. While contending that dividends may have signaling properties, they conclude that dividend changes are not useful in signaling future earnings.

Mougoué and Rao (2003) find that the ability for dividends to be a useful signaling device regarding future earnings announcements applies to smaller firms that are likely to suffer from larger gaps regarding information asymmetry. Likewise, DeAngelo, DeAngelo, and Skinner (1996) argue that errors in earnings estimation models used by managers limit the usefulness of dividend changes as a signaling device of future earnings.

Lipson, Maquieira, and Megginson (1998) examine the performance of newly public firms and compare those firms that initiated dividends with those that did not. They find that earnings increases are greater for recent initial public offerings that initiated a dividend than for those firms that did not. Brook, Carlton, and Hendershott (1998) find that dividend increases tend to result in higher cash flows for firms that have had a sustained period of staple cash flows. Thus, they conclude that a positive relationship exists between dividend changes and future earnings growth.

Proxies for Information Asymmetry

Other researchers have empirically attempted to locate an appropriate proxy for information asymmetry. Khang and King (2006) use returns from insider trades as a measure of information asymmetry. They find an inverse relationship between dividends and insider trade returns. Accordingly, they argue that their results contradict dividend signaling models in which higher dividend payouts result from firms that have higher levels of information asymmetry.

Using a sample of all U.K.-listed industrial companies, Tse (2005) finds that signaling theory does not apply universally to firms. In particular, he confirms that some firms do not appear to use dividends as a signaling device. He finds that the percentage of insiders' share holdings, market capitalization, and asset book values are determinants as to whether firms use dividends as a signaling device.

Gunasekarage and Power (2006) confirm that there does not appear to be a consistent relationship between dividends and signaling. They find that the long-term share price performance in the U.K. stock market is attributable to earnings news rather than dividend policy changes.

Dividends Signaling Future Earnings

Other studies (Healy and Palepu, 1988; DeAngelo, DeAngelo, and Skinner, 1992; Jensen and Johnson, 1995; Benartzi et al., 1997) report what appears to be contradictory evidence about the ability of dividends to signal the direction of future earnings. In particular, all four studies find that within one to two years after a dividend reduction, the direction of earnings growth reverses from negative to positive. These studies conclude that the dividend-decreasing firms have bottomed out in terms of earnings performance at the time of the reduction. So, while shareholders perceive a dividend reduction as a signal of future earnings declines, the reduction is at best short term in nature.

John, Lang, and Netter (1992) and Iqbal and Rahman (2003) explain this anomaly by noting that a dividend reduction is only one of many tools that firms use to get back on track during periods of declining earnings. In particular, the authors find that dividend cuts associated with other operational improvements, such as asset restructuring and layoffs, enable firms to conserve cash and improve future earnings prospects. In contrast, in the absence of operational improvements, such firms do not show earnings improvements in subsequent periods. Iqbal and Rahman conclude that a dividend cut is a reliable signal of poor future earnings only for firms that are profitable at the time of the dividend reduction and do not engage in simultaneous operational improvements.

Special Dividends

Brickley (1983) investigates the announcement effect on specially designated dividends (SDDs), which include those labeled "extra," "special," or "year-end." He compares their returns with those of regular dividend increases. Because of their special nature, the expectation is that SDDs would not contain information about future cash flows. Although Brickley finds the opposite to be true, he determines that regular dividend increases convey more information than SDDs. His finding that payouts following regular dividend increases are significantly greater than those following a SDD reinforces this notion.

DeAngelo, DeAngelo, and Skinner (2000) affirm Brickley's (1983) results while pointing out that the signaling content is typically small. Special dividends have decreased dramatically in recent years as stock repurchases increased. However, the authors point out that these trends are not necessarily related as the number of "very large" specials has actually increased recently. DeAngelo et al. argue that smaller specials are disappearing because the market not only can predict such specials and but also considers them a substitute for a regular dividend signal.

Dividends versus Stock Repurchase

John and Williams (1985) investigate why firms choose to pay a cash dividend, which has adverse tax consequences, instead of initiating a stock repurchase, which does not have adverse tax consequences. They find that the optimal dividend payout is higher when there is a small tax disadvantage of dividends relative to capital gains.

Brennan and Thakor (1990) argue that the basis for the decision to pay dividends versus to initiate a stock repurchase is adverse selection. In other words, investors with more information are more likely to act in a way to disadvantage those investors with less information. In the context of the decision of cash dividend versus stock repurchase, Brennan and Thakor argue that uninformed investors prefer cash dividends. Firms are more likely to react accordingly when the tax cost of such a distribution is not too large and when the cost of investors becoming more informed becomes too large.

Initiations and Omissions of Dividends

Asquith and Mullins (1983) were among the first to investigate the information effect in a several studies dealing with dividend initiations and omission. They concentrate on returns associated with dividend initiations because the market is less likely to anticipate a dividend initiation than a dividend increase. To be included in their study, a firm must not have paid dividends in the previous 10 years before the time of initiation. They form 10 portfolios based on beta estimates.

The results show large abnormal returns, with an increase of 3.7 percent in stockholder wealth. Subsequent increases also produce abnormal returns but not of the same level as dividend initiations. Asquith and Mullins (1983) believe that several factors may have clouded previous studies, including confounding announcements, investor expectations of dividend changes, and a relationship between wealth and the size of dividend changes. When considering the effects of magnitudes of dividends and investor expectations, they find that subsequent dividends have at least as large an impact as the effects of initiations. Tax effects and/or financing costs may account for the difference. Asquith and Mullins conclude that dividends convey valuable information to investors.

Signaling versus the Clientele Effect

In a related study, Richardson, Sefcik, and Thompson (1986) investigate trading volume around the announcement date and between the announcement and ex-dates to consider the possibility of a clientele shift when a dividend change occurs. A clientele shift would be possible because an increase in dividend payout might cause higher-income individuals to sell and lower-income individuals to buy so as to take advantage of their specific tax situation. Their study attempts to distinguish between a volume response to a dividend announcement and a clientele adjustment related to a shift in dividend policy. An increase in volume immediately after a dividend change would argue for an information effect. If it persists until the ex-dividend date, however, the volume changes would argue in favor of a clientele effect. The continued volume increase would imply investors are rebalancing their portfolios from the standpoint of taxes.

Richardson et al. (1986) find abnormal volume increases associated with a change in dividend payout during the announcement week. They claim this is related to the information content of dividends. Their study finds abnormal returns of about 4 percent. A highly significant increase in volume occurs during the week of the initiation of a dividend with only marginally significant increases in volume occurring after the announcement week until the ex-dividend week. This implies that investors do not rebalance their portfolios with a dividend policy change, which is contrary to a clientele effect. Their results provide only weak evidence for a clientele effect as opposed to the stronger evidence of an information effect.

Significance of the Magnitude of Dividend Changes

Dielman and Oppenheimer (1984) conduct a study involving dividend increases and decreases of 25 percent or more. They form three portfolios of stocks in the omission group based on stability and consistency of past dividend payments. The results show that all four groups experience significant abnormal returns on the day of the announcement. The returns persist in all groups, except omission, for about one month. Dielman and Oppenheimer find that the more stable the firm's dividend policy, the greater the decline in stock value when a dividend omission takes place. They argue that their results provide evidence for information content in dividends, with the strongest evidence coming from the omissions group. This is one of the few studies that focuses on dividend omission and explores the relation between dividend changes and stability of a firm's dividend payout.

In a related study, Kalay and Loewenstein (1986) use a mean-adjusted returns model and find that the market expects firms to make dividend announcements according to a timetable consistent with previous announcements. They also investigate delays concerning dividend announcements and find evidence that the market expects firms to deliver bad news late. They report that the market adjusts to potentially bad news around the date on which the dividend announcement was to be made. The adjustment involving an anticipated late announcement of bad news is less than that of an announcement of bad news that the firm actually makes on the expected date. The market continues to gradually adjust until it receives the anticipated bad news. Thus, managers who choose to delay such an announcement can spread out the effect of bad news. Because there are more dividend decreases announced late than at the predicted time, Kalay and Loewenstein state that managers convey information through the timing of announcements in addition to the announcements themselves.

Benesh, Keown, and Pinkerton (1984) provide additional evidence for an information content effect by examining the market reactions to changes in dividend policies. Their results are consistent with an information content associated with dividends. They note significant abnormal returns of 4.3 percent for dividend initiations and resumptions and 1.4 percent abnormal returns with large dividend increases. Dividend omissions produce abnormal negative returns of 7.7 percent, while dividend reductions produce negative abnormal returns of 9.6 percent. They find strong support for the information-content argument and conclude that the market reaction is greater in magnitude for unfavorable versus favorable announcements.

FUTURE DIRECTIONS OF RESEARCH

Although voluminous empirical evidence exists on the information content of dividends, opportunities for future research on this topic remain. Given the shifting trend involving cash dividends versus stock repurchases, fertile ground exists to explore further the signaling impact of repurchases. With fewer firms paying dividends, researchers may focus on whether changes in dividend policy indicate future prospects for the firm or simply a change in corporate policy in keeping with market trends.

CONCLUSIONS

Overall, most empirical evidence tends to support theoretical models regarding the ability of dividend changes to affect share price. Unexpected dividend increases (decreases) are associated with significant share-price increases (decreases). One possible reason for this market reaction is that dividend changes signal future prospects of the firm, which may include future earnings. The premise of signaling theory is that because of information asymmetries existing between firm managers and the market, dividend changes have the ability to reduce these informational differences. In response, the market reappraises the stock value, knowing that the cost of a firm for sending a false signal about future prospects is substantial. While signaling theory alone cannot explain the existence of firm dividend policy and subsequent changes in policy for dividend-paying stocks, it does offer some reasons why firms should carefully consider changes in dividend policy in terms of the market reaction to such changes.

REFERENCES

Aharony, Joseph, and Itzhak Swary. 1980. "Quarterly Dividend and Earnings Announcements and Stockholders' Returns: An Empirical Analysis." *Journal of Finance* 35:1, 1–12.

Asquith, Paul, and David W. Mullins, Jr. 1983. "The Impact of Initiating Dividend Payments on Shareholder Wealth." *Journal of Finance* 56:1, 77–95.

Benartzi, Shlomo, Roni Michaely, and Richard Thaler. 1997. "Do Changes in Dividends Signal the Future or the Past?" *Journal of Finance* 52:3, 1007–1034.

Benesh, Gary A., Arthur J. Keown, and John M. Pinkerton. 1984. "An Examination of Market Reaction to Substantial Shifts in Dividend Policy." *Journal of Financial Research* 7:2, 131–140.

Bhattacharya, Sudipto. 1979. "Imperfect Information, Dividend Policy, and 'The Bird in the Hand' Fallacy." *Bell Journal of Economics* 10:1, 259–270.

Brennan, Michael J., and Anjan V. Thakor. 1990. "Shareholder Preference and Dividend Policy." *Journal of Finance* 45:4, 993–1019.

Brickley, James. 1983. "Shareholder Wealth, Information, Signaling and the Specially Designated Dividend: An Empirical Study." *Journal of Financial Economics* 12:2, 187–210.

Brook, Yaron, William T. Charlton, Jr., and Robert J. Hendershott. 1998. "Do Firms Use Dividends to Signal Large Future Cash Flow Increases?" *Financial Management* 27:3, 46–57.

Charest, Guy. 1978. "Dividend Information, Stock Returns, and Market Efficiency—II." *Journal of Financial Economics* 6:2/3, 297–330.

DeAngelo, Harry, Linda DeAngelo, and Douglas J. Skinner. 1992. "Dividends and Losses." *Journal of Finance* 47:5, 1837–1864.

DeAngelo, Harry, Linda DeAngelo, and Douglas J. Skinner. 1996. "Reversal of Fortune: Dividend Signaling and the Disappearance of Sustained Earnings Growth." *Journal of Financial Economics* 40:3, 341–371.

DeAngelo, Harry, Linda DeAngelo, and Douglas J. Skinner. 2000. "Special Dividends and the Evolution of Dividend Signaling." *Journal of Financial Economics* 57:3, 309–354.

Denis, David J., Diane K. Denis, and Atulya Sarin. 1994. "The Information Content of Dividend Changes: Cash Flow Signaling, Overinvestment, and Dividend Clienteles." *Journal of Financial and Quantitative Analysis* 29:4, 567–588.

Dhillon, Upinder S., and Herb Johnson. 1994. "The Effect of Dividend Changes on Stock and Bond Prices." *Journal of Finance* 49:1, 281–289.

Dielman, Terry E., and Henry R. Oppenheimer. 1984. "An Examination of Investor Behavior during Periods of Large Dividend Changes." *Journal of Financial and Quantitative Analysis* 19:2, 197–216.

Dyl, Edward A., and Robert A. Weigand. 1988. "The Information Content of Dividend Initiations: Additional Evidence." *Financial Management* 27:3, 27–35.

Fama, Eugene F., and Kenneth R. French. 2000. "Forecasting Profitability and Earnings." *Journal of Business* 73:2, 161–175.

Friend, Irwin, and Marshall Puckett. 1964. "Dividends and Stock Prices." *American Economic Review* 54:5, 656–682.

Grullon, Gustavo, Roni Michaely, and Bhaskaran Swaminathan. 2002. "Are Dividend Changes a Sign of Firm Maturity?" *Journal of Business* 75:3, 387–424.

Grullon, Gustavo, Roni Michaely, Shlomo Benartzi, and Richard Thaler. 2005. "Dividend Changes Do Not Signal Changes in Future Profitability." *Journal of Business* 78:5, 1659–1682.

Gunasekarage, Abeyratna, and David M. Power. 2006, "Anomalous Evidence in Dividend Announcement Effect." *Managerial Finance* 32:3, 209–226.

Hakansson, Nils H. 1982. "To Pay or Not to Pay Dividends." *Journal of Finance* 37:2, 415–428.

Handjinicolaou, George, and Avner Kalay. 1984. "Wealth Redistributions or Changes in Firm Value: An Analysis around Dividend Announcements." *Journal of Financial Economics* 13:1, 35–63.

Healy, Paul M., and Krishna G. Palepu. 1988. "Earnings Information Conveyed by Dividend Initiations and Omissions." *Journal of Financial Economics* 21:2, 149–175.

Iqbal, Zahid, and Mohammad Rahman. 2003. "Operational Actions and the Reliability of the Signaling Theory of Dividends: An Investigation of Earnings Anomaly following Dividend Cuts and Omissions." *Quarterly Journal of Business and Economics* 41:1/2, 13–25.

Jensen, Gerald R., and James M. Johnson. 1995. "The Dynamics of Corporate Dividend Reductions." *Financial Management* 24:4, 31–51.

John, Kose, and Joseph Williams. 1985. "Dividends, Dilution, and Taxes: A Signalling Equilibrium." *Journal of Finance* 40:4, 1053–1070.

John, Kose, Larry H. P. Lang, and Jeffry Netter. 1992. "The Voluntary Restructuring of Large Firms in Response to Performance Decline." *Journal of Finance* 47:3, 891–917.

Kalay, Avner. 1980. "Signaling, Information Content, and the Reluctance to Cut Dividends." *Journal of Financial and Quantitative Analysis* 15:4, 855–869.

Kalay, Avner, and Uri Loewenstein. 1986. "The Information Content of the Timing of Dividend Announcements." *Journal of Financial Economics* 16:3, 373–388.

Kane, Alex, Young Ki Lee, and Alan Marcus. 1984. "Earnings and Dividend Announcements: Is There a Corroboration Effect?" *Journal of Finance* 39:4, 1091–1099.

Khang, Kenneth, and Tao-Hsien Dolly King. 2006. "Does Dividend Policy Relate to Cross-sectional Variation in Information Asymmetry? Evidence from Returns to Insider Trades." *Financial Management* 35:4, 71–94.

Kwan, Clarence C. Y. 1981. "Efficient Market Tests of the Informational Content of Dividend Announcements: Critique and Extension." *Journal of Financial and Quantitative Analysis* 16:2, 193–206.

Lang, Larry H. P., and Robert H. Litzenberger. 1989. "Dividend Announcements: Cash Flow Signalling vs. Free Cash Flow Hypothesis?" *Journal of Financial Economics* 24:1, 181–191.

Lintner, John. 1956. "Distribution of Incomes of Corporations among Dividends, Retained Earnings, and Taxes." *American Economic Review* 46:2, 97–113.

Lipson, Marc L., Carlos P. Maquieira, and William Megginson. 1998. "Dividend Initiations and Earnings Surprises." *Financial Management* 27:3, 36–45.

Miller, Merton H., and Franco Modigliani. 1961. "Dividend Policy, Growth, and the Valuation of Shares." *Journal of Business* 34:4, 411–433.

Miller, Merton H., and Kevin Rock. 1985. "Dividend Policy under Asymmetric Information." *Journal of Finance* 40:4, 1031–1051.

Mougoué, Mbodja, and Ramesh P. Rao. 2003. "The Information Signaling Hypothesis of Dividends: Evidence from Cointegration and Causality Tests." *Journal of Business, Finance, and Accounting* 30:3/4, 441–478.

Myers, Stewart C. 1987. "Comments on 'The Informational Content of Dividends.'" In *Macroeconomics: Essays in Honor of Franco Modigliani*, ed. John Bosons, Rudiger Dronbusch, and Stanley Fischer. Cambridge, MA: MIT Press.

Myers, Stewart C., and Nicholas S. Majluf. 1984. "Corporate Financing and Investment Decisions When Firms Have Information that Investors Do Not Have." *Journal of Financial Economics* 13:2, 187–221.

Nissim, Doron, and Amir Ziv. 2001. "Dividend Changes and Future Profitability." *Journal of Finance* 56:6, 2111–2133.

Ofer, Aharon R., and Daniel R. Siegel. 1987. "Corporate Financial Policy, Information, and Market Expectations: An Empirical Investigation of Dividends." *Journal of Finance* 42:4, 889–911.

Ofer, Aharon R., and Anjan V. Thakor. 1987. "A Theory of Stock Price Responses to Alternative Corporate Cash Disbursement Methods: Stock Repurchases and Dividends." *Journal of Finance* 42:2, 365–394.

Pettit, R. Richardson. 1972. "Dividend Announcements, Security Performance, and Capital Market Efficiency." *Journal of Finance* 27:5, 993–1007.

Richardson, Gordon, Stephen Sefcik, and Rex Thompson. 1986. "A Test of Dividend Irrelevance Using Volume Reactions to a Change in Dividend Policy." *Journal of Financial Economics* 17:2, 313–334.

Ross, Stephen A. 1977. "The Determination of Financial Structure: The Incentive-Signaling Approach." *Bell Journal of Economics* 8:1, 23–40.

Smith, Clifford W., Jr., and Jerold B. Warner. 1979. "On Financial Contracting: An Analysis of Bond Covenants." *Journal of Financial Economics* 7:2, 117–161.

Talmor, Eli. 1981. "Asymmetric Information, Signaling, and Optimal Corporate Financial Decisions." *Journal of Financial and Quantitative Analysis* 16:4, 413–435.

Tse, Chin-Bun. 2005. "Use Dividends to Signal or Not: An Examination of the UK Dividend Payout Patterns." *Managerial Finance* 31:4, 12–33.

VanHorne, James, and John G. McDonald. 1971. "Dividend Policy and New Equity Financing." *Journal of Finance* 26:2, 507–520.

Viswanath, P. V., Yu Kyung Kim, and Jayant Pandit. 2002. "Dilution, Dividend Commitments and Liquidity: Do Dividend Changes Reflect Information Signaling?" *Review of Quantitative Finance and Accounting* 18:4, 359–379.

Watts, Ross. 1973. "The Information Content of Dividends." *Journal of Business* 46:2, 191–211.

Woolridge, J. Randall. 1983. "Dividend Changes and Security Prices." *Journal of Finance* 38:5, 1607–1615.

Yoon, Pyung Sig, and Laura T. Starks. 1995. "Signaling, Investing Opportunities, and Dividend Announcements." *Review of Financial Studies* 8:4, 995–1018.

ABOUT THE AUTHOR

Greg Filbeck, CFA, FRM, CAIA, PRM, joined the faculty at the Behrend College, Penn State University–Erie in 2006. He is a professor of finance and holds the Black Family Endowed Professorship of Insurance and Risk Management. In addition to ten years of previous academic experience at Miami University and the University of Toledo, he was senior vice president of Schweser, a division of Kaplan Inc., where he headed the content and curriculum areas and started and led marketing and sales areas. Filbeck trains candidates for the CFA, CAIA, and FRM designations on a worldwide basis and has published more than 50 articles in refereed journals. He is coauthor of the book *Derivatives and Risk Management*. He obtained his doctorate in finance from the University of Kentucky in 1990.

CHAPTER 11

Behavioral Explanations of Dividends

HERSH SHEFRIN
Mario L. Belotti Professor of Finance, Santa Clara University

INTRODUCTION

In neoclassical theory, individual investors realize that dividend policy is irrelevant in a world with zero taxes, zero transaction costs, and symmetric information. This is because of the Modigliani-Miller (hereafter MM) principle stating that investors are immune to cash flow framing effects (Miller, 1988). Therefore, neoclassical theories of dividend payouts tend to focus on the roles of taxes, transaction costs, and asymmetric information.

Consider the following questions: When it comes to dividends, does neoclassical theory explain what individual investors think, say, and do? Do taxes, transactions costs, and asymmetric information play central roles? How about financial advisers and financial journalists? Do taxes, transactions costs, and asymmetric information underlie their perspectives on dividends?

Some casual evidence comes for various media articles about dividends. In the *New York Times* feature "Sunday Investing," De Aenlle (2006) quotes Barbara Walchli, manager of the Aquila Rocky Mountain Equity fund, as predicting that there will be "huge interest in dividend-paying stocks" by retiring baby boomers "looking for income." In line with Walchli's comments, Jonathan Golub, a strategist at J. P. Morgan Asset Management, remarks that retirees view dividends as preferable "because they don't have to touch the principal." James H. Huguet, president of Great Companies Funds in Clearwater, Florida, predicts that investors will shift their portfolios in the direction of "large-capitalization stocks with high dividend payments as a security measure." These comments make no reference to taxes, transaction costs, or asymmetric information because they are not central issues in planning retirement, leaving principal intact, seeking income, and achieving security.

Many articles about dividends mention the phrase "bird in the hand." This phrase comes from one of Aesop's fable about risk, with a bird in the hand being better than two in the bush. An article on dividends appearing in the March 29, 2002, issue of *Barron's* begins by stating, "Investors are beginning to appreciate the value of the proverbial bird in the hand represented by dividends." Similar statements appear in the *Wall Street Journal* column "Getting Going," in which

Clements (2000) writes, "A bird in the hand: While share-price gains are always iffy, collecting dividends is a much surer bet." In a more recent article, Clements (2007) echoes his past comment, asserting "People value the bird in the hand." Taxes, transaction costs, and asymmetric information are not central to the notion of a bird in the hand.

Clement (2007) provides a discussion of dividends in the context of retirement planning. He points out that although 70 percent of Americans are confident that they will save adequately to finance a comfortable retirement, about half of Americans saving for retirement have less than $25,000 in savings. Thus, taxes, transaction costs, and asymmetric information are not central to the issue of savings adequacy.

Jones (2005), a journalist for the *Independent*, writes, "A dividend is a bird in the hand" and then goes on to say: "Even if you do not require income, cash received by way of a dividend ... relieves the strain of waiting for capital appreciation." This perspective is part of financial culture. A *Washington Post* article by Crenshaw (1994) quotes individual investor Susan Strange as stating, "All those sayings, 'a bird in the hand is worth two in the bush,' 'don't count your chickens until the eggs are hatched'—they're all true."

The previously highlighted issues—retirement, inadequate savings, reluctance to touch principal, and perception of cash dividends as a bird in the hand—are all psychological in nature. As such, they do not play a major role in neoclassical dividend theory, if they are even addressed. However, they are central to behavioral dividend theory, which is the subject of the current chapter.

This chapter begins by describing a series of psychological reasons that explain why framing effects lead individual investors to find dividends attractive. The underlying psychology has three components: (1) the behavioral life cycle hypothesis, which focuses on self-control and mental accounting; (2) hedonic editing; and (3) regret.

Next, the chapter provides the empirical evidence. Shefrin and Statman (1984) propose a number of testable behavioral hypotheses about dividends. The hypotheses relate to the impact of age, income, and retirement status on two relationships involving the preference for dividends: (1) between consumer expenditures and the preference for dividends and (2) between tolerance for risk and the preference for dividends. At the heart of these relationships are the issues highlighted previously, namely, retirement, inadequate savings, reluctance to touch principal, and perception of cash dividends as a bird in the hand.

The last part of the chapter provides a discussion of some recent empirical evidence that tests these hypotheses and offers insights into the empirical evidence for the behavioral explanation of dividends. The work of Dong, Robinson, and Veld (2005), Graham and Kumar (2006), Baker, Nagel, and Wurgler (2007), and Rantapuska and Kaustia (2007) strongly supports the behavioral hypotheses advanced by Shefrin and Statman (1984).

Behavioral dividend theory is not after-the-fact rationalization. In fact, researchers developed behavioral dividend theory long before formally testing its hypotheses, as opposed to after the fact, when the empirical relationships came to be documented. Even the press quotations provided previously appeared more than a decade after Shefrin and Statman (1984).

THEORETICAL FRAMEWORK

This section contains a formal behavioral model to explain the role that dividends play in households' dynamic decisions about consumption and portfolio selection. The model generates various predictions about the impact of investor age, retirement status, and income on the holdings of dividend-paying stocks.

For two reasons, the development of the theory proceeds in stages, beginning with a neoclassical model and then modifying the model to accommodate behavioral features. The first reason is to make clear exactly where the behavioral treatment parts company with its neoclassical counterpart. The second reason is to highlight the features that give rise to distinctively behavioral predictions.

The purpose of the first three stages is (1) to develop a neoclassical life cycle model of household consumption as a budget constrained expected utility maximization, (2) to introduce a labor-leisure component, and (3) to add taxes and transaction costs. The next two stages then modify the neoclassical framework to accommodate the three behavioral features described in the introduction.

Neoclassical Structure

Stage 1. Joint Consumption-Portfolio Choice
In neoclassical life cycle theory, a household formulates a lifetime consumption plan by maximizing expected utility subject to a budget constraint. To describe this maximization formally, consider an uncertainty tree with a typical node at date t being denoted by n_t and having associated probability $\Pi(n_t)$. Here time is discrete, with $t = 0, 1, \ldots, T$. Let $c(n_t)$ be the amount the household consumes in the event n_t occurs.

W denotes the household's lifetime portfolio wealth. Consider a set of securities $\{S_j\}$ that is available for trade over time. $D_j(n_t)$ denotes the number of units of physical consumption, which a single unit of security j pays at node n_t. At date t, security S_j pays $D_j(n_t)$, and its ex-dividend price on the n_t-market is given by $Q_j(n_t)$. $D_j(n_t)$ corresponds to interest income in the case of bonds and cash dividends in the case of stocks.

Suppose that a household holds $x_j(n_{t-1})$ units of security j at the end of date $t - 1$ through the beginning of date t. The value of the associated portfolio $\{x_j\}$ and its associated dividends will fund both the household's consumption in event n_t and portfolio choices $\{x_j(n_t)\}$. That is, the household faces the following budget constraint:

$$c(n_t) + \sum_j Q_j(n_t)x_j(n_t) \leq \sum_j [Q_j(n_t) + D_j(n_t)]x_j(n_{t-1}). \tag{11.1}$$

A household uses security j to borrow during n_t by choosing $x_j(n_t) < 0$. By imposing the terminal condition that $x_j(n_T) = 0$ at the terminal date T for all j and requiring that consumption $c(n_t) \geq 0$ always, the household will be forced to pay off all of its debt obligations. In this respect, default is captured through the structure of security payoffs.

Stage 2. Human Capital
The previous model can be extended to accommodate income from human capital. In this case, there are two consumption goods, physical consumption (c) and leisure, where leisure is measured in units of physical consumption. The household has maximum $L(n_t) \geq 0$ units of leisure available and can offer an amount $l(n_t)$ of labor time, where $0 \leq l(n_t) \leq L(n_t)$. If the household works at level $l(n_t)$, then its budget constraint on the n_t-market will be

$$c(n_t) + \sum_{j} Q_j(n_t) x_j(n_t) \leq \sum_{j} [Q_j(n_t) + D_j(n_t)] x_j(n_{t-1}) + w[l(n_t)], \qquad (11.2)$$

where $w[l(n_t)]$ denotes labor income. Correspondingly, the household's utility will be a function of both physical consumption c and consumed leisure $L - l$.

Inequality (Equation 11.2) generalizes inequality (Equation 11.1) in the sense that when the labor-leisure choice is omitted from the problem, $l(n_t) = 0$, in which case Equation 11.2 collapses to Equation 11.1. The generalization enables a household to use labor income to fund additional consumption, if it so chooses. Additional consumption and labor income can be contemporaneous. However, inequality (Equation 11.2) also permits a household to use labor income to increase the value of its portfolio or to borrow against its human capital. If a household borrows against its human capital, by, say, taking out a student loan, then it repays the loan in the future either by consuming less physical goods or leisure than it otherwise would. As with inequality (Equation 11.1), households limit their borrowing because of the need to liquidate their portfolios at the terminal date without experiencing negative consumption or leisure. Households can also invest in education by sacrificing leisure at n_t for additional wage income at n_τ where $\tau > t$. For the purpose of this discussion, it is sufficient to put this issue aside.

Neoclassical Dividend Irrelevance

In this model, the dividend structure of security payoffs is irrelevant to the underlying optimization problem. In this respect, a household can achieve its optimal consumption-leisure choice by using a collection securities indexed by k whose dividend payouts are zero at every date $t < T$. All that is required is that the household be able to choose an $\{x_k\}$-portfolio to satisfy:

$$\sum_{k} Q_k(n_t)[x_k(n_t) - x_k(n_{t-1})] = \sum_{j} Q_j(n_t)[x_j(n_t) - x_j(n_{t-1})] + D_j(n_t))x_j(n_{t-1}).$$

$$(11.3)$$

Equation 11.3 pertains to the manner in which a household adjusts its portfolio holdings, for the purpose of portfolio rebalancing and saving or dissaving. As in the traditional MM framework, Equation 11.3 stipulates that a household can always create homemade dividends to fund consumer expenses by selling a portion of its stock holdings. It does not need dividends to do the job.

Notably, a premise underlying the previous statement is the absence of taxes and transaction costs. If dividends are taxed or portfolio adjustments are costly, then the right-hand sides of inequalities Equation 11.1 and Equation 11.2 will contain an additional term $TT \geq 0$ to reflect taxes and transaction costs that further bind the value of the household's choices for consumption, leisure, and portfolio holdings at each node. In this case, the budget constraint becomes

$$c(n_t) + \sum_j Q_j(n_t)x_j(n_t) \leq \sum_j [Q_j(n_t) + D_j(n_t)]x_j(n_{t-1}) + w[l(n_t)] - TT(n_t),$$

(11.4)

so that inequality Equation 11.4 generalizes inequality Equation 11.2. With inequality 11.4, the household will have to choose its portfolio to balance the tax penalty on dividends against the transaction costs of making portfolio adjustments.

Stage 3. Self-control and Behavioral Life Cycle Hypothesis

In the traditional MM argument, investors can always create homemade dividends to fund consumer expenses by selling a portion of their stock holdings. In practice, older retired investors are reluctant to do so. The behavioral explanation for this reluctance is known as the behavioral life cycle hypothesis.

In the neoclassical framework, the household experiences no difficulty choosing its preferred budget feasible consumption-leisure combination $(c, L - l)$. Here, preferred combination means one that maximizes the expected utility function $E(U(c, L - l))$. In this respect, neoclassical theory imposes a single preference system to rank order alternatives by desirability. There is no conflict internal to the individual.

The behavioral approach introduces the possibility of internal conflict, whereby some households lack the self-control to implement what they assert is in their best long-term interests. Thaler and Shefrin (1981) present a model of such a conflict using dual preferences and apply the framework to explain savings inadequacy. Shefrin and Thaler (1988) suggest that the presence of conflicting dual preferences stems from the human brain being organized into different subsystems and describes their framework as a behavioral life cycle model (BLC).

Shefrin and Thaler (1988) suggest a conflict between long-term preferences associated with a planning subcomponent housed in the brain's prefrontal cortex and an action component housed within the brain's limbic system. These two systems are the planner and the doer, respectively. Notably, McClure, Laibson, Loewenstein, and Cohen (2004) report neurological evidence supporting this general approach. Their study identifies regions of the lateral prefrontal cortex and posterior parietal cortex, which they find are engaged when making intertemporal choices irrespective of delay. However, parts of the limbic system associated with the midbrain dopamine system, including the paralimbic cortex, turn out to be preferentially activated by decisions involving immediately available rewards.

The BLC postulates that if n_t occurs, a household experiences utility $u(n_t)$, whose level depends on the following three variables: consumption $c(n_t)$, leisure $L(n_t - l(n_t))$, and the amount of willpower the household must exercise to implement $(c(n_t), L(n_t) - l(n_t))$. Willpower is assumed to be costly in that exercising willpower reduces utility $u(n_t)$, with successive increases in willpower becoming ever more costly at the margin.

Self-control is more difficult when the cookie jar is full than when it is almost empty. In the BLC, marginal willpower is necessary when households face temptation as they attempt to delay gratification by consuming less or working more. The size of the opportunity sets determines the amount of the temptation at n_t. Achieving a particular consumption-leisure choice $(c(n_t), L(n_t) - l(n_t))$ requires more willpower when the opportunity set is large than when the opportunity set is small.

Shefrin and Thaler (1988) suggest that households attempt to control the amount of temptation they face by relying on a psychological construct known as mental accounting. Mental accounts are natural categories for compartmentalizing information and decision tasks. For example, when households purchase various types of insurance, such as automobile insurance and homeowners insurance, they tend to ignore their full risk profile. Instead they focus on each type of insurance separately, each in individual mental accounts. For example, when contemplating automobile insurance, households tend to focus only on risks directly related to automobiles, not the joint risks associated with automobile accidents and, say, house-related damage. As a result, they fail to take account of diversification opportunities that arise from exposure to multiple risks. The tendency to focus on risks in isolation is known as narrow framing. Given the complexity of dealing with multiple risks, the benefits from using mental accounts might well outweigh the costs.

Shefrin and Thaler (1988) posit that households make positive use of mental accounts to address self-control issues associated with savings and investment. In this respect, households divide their wealth into mental accounts and use mental-accounting-based rules of thumb, or heuristics, when making choices about consumption, leisure, and portfolio composition.

The BLC framework identifies four types of mental accounts: those associated with current income (denoted I), liquid assets (A), home equity (E), and future income (F). At each n_t, the household mentally divides the components of its wealth into four groups, placing each in its own mental account. Households place labor income and dividend income during n_t into the n_t-current income account and securities into the liquid asset account. Home equity is not explicitly modeled here but is formally similar to human capital. Finally, households place future cash flows from income stemming from labor, pensions, 401(k) plans, investment retirement accounts, or Social Security into the future income mental account.

A BLC heuristic features a pecking order, with the order being current income, liquid wealth, home equity, and future income. A BLC rule stipulates that in normal circumstances, the household can fund consumption only from the current income account. In exceptional circumstances, when the value of the current income account is too low to meet consumption needs, the household can access other mental accounts. If it does so, it should first access the liquid asset account and only access other accounts if the value of the liquid asset account is too small. Similar statements apply to the accounts that are further down the pecking order.

Formally, at the beginning of n_t the balance in I account is

$$\sum_j x_j(n_{t-1}) D_j(n_t) + w(l(n_t)) - TT(n_t), \qquad (11.5)$$

and the balance in the A account is

$$\sum_i x_i(n_{t-1}) Q_i(n_t), \qquad (11.6)$$

where the summation index in Equation 11.6 is i (not j) to indicate that only some securities might be deemed admissible for inclusion in A. The F account balance has the form

$$\sum_k x_i(n_{t-1})Q_k(n_t) + \sum_{t>t} w(l(n_\tau))DF(n_\tau), \tag{11.7}$$

where the summation in the left term in Equation 11.7 is for securities not included in Equation 11.6. The right term in Equation 11.7 is the present value of future labor income, the product of wages $w(l(n_\tau))$, and a stochastic discount factor $DF(n_\tau)$.

The BLC heuristic stipulates that in normal circumstances, consumption $c(n_t)$ not exceed the value of Equation 11.5. In this case, the amount of temptation faced is given by Equation 11.5. Holding the value of Equation 11.5 constant, every marginal reduction in consumption $c(n_t)$ reduces utility $u(n_t)$ for two reasons. The first reason is that the household consumes less. The second reason is that the household must exercise willpower to reduce consumption, and willpower is inherently unpleasant. Taken together, the two effects produce $\partial u(n_t)/\partial c(n_t)$, to be used when choosing a maximizing value for $c(n_t)$.

In some circumstances, households will find identifying exceptions and fund consumption from the A account worthwhile. In the BLC model, there is a utility penalty to pay for funding consumption from any account other than the I account. This penalty is a discrete utility cost representing the idea that a household experiences psychological pain if it has to break its rule about only funding consumption from the I account. Therefore, a household always determines whether the benefit of breaking the rule will justify the cost. A highly disciplined household sets a very high penalty, whereas a household lacking discipline sets a low penalty.

Figure 11.1 displays the relationship between consumption and utility, holding leisure and the account balances constant. For sake of illustration, wealth consists of three accounts, I, A, and F, with the balance in each being \$1. In view of the pecking order, a consumption level less than \$1 is funded from the I account and only the I account.

Keep in mind that marginal utility reflects both a direct effect (from consuming less) and an indirect effect (from having to exert the willpower to consume less). The high level of marginal utility near zero consumption reflects the high degree of willpower that the household must exert to reduce consumption at the margin, when consumption is low.

Figure 11.1 displays two points of discontinuity. These reflect the penalties associated with funding consumption from either the A account or F account. The penalties displayed are high. A household would not choose to access either account to finance a small increment in consumption. Indeed for the case depicted in Figure 11.1, the household would derive no net benefit by accessing the F account at all.

The temptation a household faces is given by the balance of all the accounts accessed in the pecking order. Of course, the temptation operating at the margin is the balance of the highest account in the pecking order whose funds are accessed to fund consumption.

Households with potential self-control problems face two main challenges. The first challenge is how to defer consumption to accumulate savings. The second

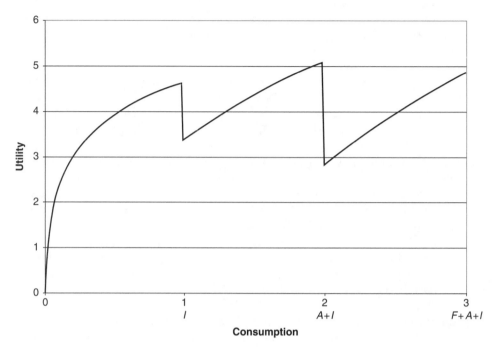

Figure 11.1 Utility of Consumption

This figure displays a household's utility function of consumption. Here the household maintains three mental accounts (I, A, and F). For the purpose of illustration, each account balance is $1. The household follows a pecking order, financing consumption first from the I account, and if necessary then from the A account, and if necessary then from the F account. Points of discontinuity reflect psychic penalties for accessing accounts. Marginal utility reflects a combination of satiation and the cost of exercising willpower to reduce consumption from an account, once accessed.

challenge is how to protect a nest egg from being consumed too quickly. In the BLC framework, utility-maximizing households put decision heuristics in place and make choices in respect to their consumption, work, and portfolios to exploit the structure of those heuristics. These choices are made in the recognition that temptation varies in respect to time and circumstances.

The BLC heuristic addresses the second challenge, protecting a nest egg, by limiting consumption to the I account balance. The first challenge is another matter, for the act of saving appears to take place in connection with the I account. Such saving requires that the household face temptation and exercise the willpower to save, a difficult task. To avoid the challenges of having to exercise the associated willpower, households seek ways to structure their wealth so that the I account balances are not unnecessarily large, instead containing just enough funds to cover prudent consumption expenditures. Households accomplish the act of saving by structuring wealth earmarked for saving to the A and F accounts.

Real-world households undertake various actions to help themselves accumulate savings. One of the most common techniques is to take too few income tax exemptions to receive a large tax refund. In theory, a large tax refund arrives through the I account. Although the refund increases the amount of temptation the household faces at the time, diminishing marginal utility is strong enough to induce the household to save a substantial portion of the refund, even though current consumption might be considerably higher than normal during the period that the household receives its tax refund.

In fiscal 2003, individual income tax refunds amounted to $223 billion. As a share of gross domestic product, income tax refunds in 2003 amounted to 2.1 percent, almost double the 1.1 percent figure that prevailed in 1993. In 2003, the ratio of refunds to income tax receipts was 28 percent, compared to the 15 percent figure that prevailed during the mid-1990s. Income tax refunds are common. Internal Revenue Service data indicate that more than three-quarters of filers receive an income tax refund.

Households also accumulate savings by participating in formal programs such as 401(k) plans and pension plans featuring automatic deductions, as well as voluntary programs such as individual retirement accounts (IRAs). These programs effectively shift wealth from after-tax labor income, which flows through the I account to assets associated with the F account. This combination addresses both challenges for households with potential self-control problems. The deductions address the need to save, and the allocation to the F account, in combination with the BLC pecking-order heuristic, addresses the need to protect the nest egg.

The BLC framework emphasizes that temptation issues need to be addressed in connection with strategic decisions such as choosing the number of income tax exemptions and joining a savings plan. As Thaler and Benartzi (2004) note, these decisions are best made when households are relatively dispassionate and temptation is weak.

Stage 4. Self-control and Dividends
The behavioral theory of dividends developed by Shefrin and Statman (1984) builds on the BLC framework. Consider a household that faces a potential self-control problem and chooses to follow a BLC rule. How does such a rule affect the household's choice of portfolio?

Shefrin and Statman (1984) answer this question by pointing out that the BLC feature, which prohibits access to the A account, is commonly referred to as "don't dip into capital." However, the BLC heuristic places dividend income into the I account, not the A account, and therefore, households can use dividend income to finance consumption.

The *Wall Street Journal* column "Getting Going" from June 20, 2007, discussed in the introduction, specifically describes such behavior. The article quotes John Ameriks, a Vanguard Group economist. Ameriks states that people are "interested in spending from their portfolios" not in "spending down their assets." He goes on to say: "They spend their dividends and interest. They don't regularly spend down their principal."

At the margin, how valuable is dividend income to a household that uses a BLC heuristic? The answer depends on the shadow price of consumption. A household for which $c(n_t)$ is strictly less than Equation 11.5 manages to save out of discretionary income. For such a household, a marginal dollar of dividend income only serves to increase temptation. In this case, dividend income is costly not beneficial. Its shadow price is negative. On the other hand, a household operating at the boundary, meaning that $c(n_t)$ is equal to Equation 11.5, will consider accessing funds from the A account. Indeed it might do so, thereby incurring an entry fee. To the extent that dividend income serves to shift wealth from the A account to the I account, dividend income has a positive shadow price and is valuable.

Households typically save in the early phase of the life cycle by either investing in home equity or accumulating a retirement nest egg. Unless households are participating in programs leading them to save excessively, they will typically prefer that a dollar of wealth be channeled through the A account instead of the I account. Therefore, ceteris paribus, at this stage of the life cycle, they would prefer to receive wealth in the form of capital gains rather than in the form of dividends. The shadow price of dividends (allocated to the I account) will usually be negative for such households.

Later in the life cycle, especially once they reach retirement, households begin to dissave. Households that reach retirement lose labor income. However, they still continue to follow a BLC heuristic in which they are reluctant to dip into capital, to avoid consuming their nest egg too quickly, thereby outliving their assets. Therefore, the shadow price of dividend income, allocated to the I account, will tend to be positive for such households.

The previous discussion gives rise to a series of testable hypotheses. The marginal propensity to finance consumption from wealth directly related to current income, including dividend income, is at least as great as the marginal propensity to consume from other sources of wealth. Notably, the marginal propensity depends on age, retirement status, and current income. For older, retired households, consumption is positively correlated with dividend income. However, the strength of this correlation is weaker for younger households that have not reached retirement. For all ages, the correlation between dividend income and consumption declines with income. For younger households with high incomes, consumption and dividend income are uncorrelated.

Stage 5. Dividends and Risk

The introduction contains a quote from the May 7, 2005, issue of the *Independent* that points out: "Even if you do not require income, cash received by way of a dividend ... relieves the strain of waiting for capital appreciation." In this regard, the behavioral life cycle hypothesis explains why older, retired households often find dividends attractive. Younger, employed households are another matter. They are still receiving wages and salaries. Although younger, employed households might use mental-accounting-based spending rules, dividends are not likely to play an important role in so far as funding consumption. This section describes the implications of prospect theory, hedonic editing, and regret theory for the role that dividends play in investors' tolerance for bearing equity risk.

Thaler and Johnson (1991) develop a theory of hedonic editing, based on prospect theory developed by Kahneman and Tversky (1979). Prospect theory, which is a psychologically based theory constructed to explain the manner in which people make choices in the face of risk and uncertainty, is characterized by three distinct features. The first feature is that people frame the outcomes of their choices in terms of gains and losses relative to a reference point, not in terms of final asset position. In this respect, people tend to be more sensitive to losses than to gains of comparable magnitude, with the utility function being concave in gains and convex in losses. The shape of the utility function, which Kahneman and Tversky (1979) call a value function, reflects the notion of psychophysics: diminishing sensitivity to successive increases in a stimulus. In the case of the value function, the stimulus is the absolute value of the gain or loss.

Prospect theory's second feature is that psychophysics applies to probability weighting. Specifically, sensitivity to probability diminishes with the distance relative to the closer of 0 or 1, the two extreme values that probability values assume. In addition, the probability weights associated with a risky choice need not sum to unity. Kahneman and Tversky (1979) call this property subcertainty. Subcertainty contributes to the preference for risk-free choices over risky choices.

Prospect theory's third feature is the tendency for households to frame choices by using editing procedures that involve mental accounts. Thaler and Johnson (1991) extend Kahneman and Tversky's (1979) framework to capture the idea of hedonic editing. Hedonic editing is the notion of choosing among alternative framing structures on the basis of which one is most pleasing to the decision maker.

In Thaler and Johnson's (1991) hedonic editing model, a decision maker faces a situation when he or she receives information about having incurred outcomes from two related risks. At issue is whether the decision maker would prefer to frame the two outcomes separately or combined. If separately, the decision maker segregates the outcomes; if combined, the decision maker integrates the outcomes.

The intuition underlying the question of whether to integrate or to segregate is that people experience gains and losses separately. To explain the main patterns, consider a series of four cases. In analyzing these cases, assume that utility is additive across segregated outcomes.

1. Given concave utility in the domain of gains, the principle of diminishing marginal utility implies that a decision maker who receives two gains would rather experience the two gains separately rather than combined. In other words, the decision maker would prefer to segregate outcomes rather than integrate outcomes.

2. If the outcomes are mixed and the decision maker incurs a large gain together with a small loss, then the decision maker would prefer to mask the loss through integration. This is because the utility loss from a marginally smaller large gain is less than the large marginal utility, which prospect theory attaches to a small loss.

3. If the outcomes are mixed and the decision maker incurs a large loss together with a small gain, then the decision maker would prefer to segregate the two outcomes. This is because convex utility in the domain of losses implies that the marginal utility of a large loss is small, whereas the marginal utility of a small gain is large.

4. If the decision maker incurs two losses, then convex utility in the domain of losses implies a preference for combining the two losses through integration.

Two features of prospect theory are especially germane to dividends. The first is editing, especially hedonic editing. Editing applies when investors segregate total return into its two natural components, dividends and capital gains. The second feature of prospect theory is subcertainty. If cash dividends are treated as stable and low risk, then those dividends might receive higher weights than capital gains or total return.

In formally applying prospect theory to the preference for dividends, utility should not be defined only in terms of consumption and leisure, as in the previous case. Instead, the concept of utility can be extended to include an emotional component reflecting anticipated dividends and capital gains. For example, at node n_t, the household's utility would have as arguments consumption $c(n_t)$, leisure $L(n_t) - l(n_t)$, and a measure of future portfolio performance based on the dividend payouts $x_j(n_t)D_j(n_{t+1})$ and capital gains $x_j(n_t)(Q_j(n_{t+1}) - Q_j(n_t))$.

Consider a candidate formulation for the subutility associated with node n_t having the following form:

$$u^c(c(n_t), L(n_t) - l(n_t)) \; + \sum [v^d(n_{t+1})u^f(x(n_t)D_j(n_{t+1}))$$
$$+ v^g(n_{t+1})u^f(x_j(n_t)(Q_j(n_{t+1}) - Q_j(n_t)))] \qquad (11.8)$$

where the summations in Equation 11.8 are over securities j and nodes n_{t+1}, which are successor nodes to n_t. The terms $\{v^d\}$ denote the weights that apply to dividends and the terms $\{v^g\}$ denote the weights that apply to capital gains. The function u^f connotes the utility from anticipating how well the portfolio will perform in the future, which in this formulation refers only to the next date.

Expression 11.8 captures the idea that dividends and capital gains contribute separately to utility associated with anticipation. In addition, the weights might differ between dividend payouts and capital gains, meaning $v^d(n_{t+1}) \neq v^g(n_{t+1})$, as weights in prospect theory differ across risk profiles. This might stem directly from the subcertainty property identified in Kahneman and Tversky (1979) but might also stem from the rank-dependent feature developed in Tversky and Kahneman (1992).

With subutility defined according to Equation 11.8, household preferences no longer need to be indifferent to how the sum $D_j(n_t)) + Q_j(n_t)$ decomposes. If both components are positive, then concavity of u^f implies that the household would prefer to segregate its gains into dividends and capital gains rather than to accept only dividends or only capital gains. This feature is an application of the first point about hedonic editing mentioned previously.

Notice that expression 11.8 imposes segregation. In a pure hedonic editing framework, the choice to integrate or segregate comes as an option. The household compares $[v^d(n_{t+1})u^f(x(n_t)D_j(n_{t+1})) + v^g(n_{t+1})u^f(x_j(n_t)(Q_j(n_{t+1}) - Q_j(n_t)))]$ with its integrated counterpart $v^t(n_{t+1})u^f(x(n_t)(D_j(n_{t+1})) + (Q_j(n_{t+1}) - Q_j(n_t))$ and chooses the frame associated with the larger value. Formally capturing this feature entails replacing the term being summed in Equation 11.8 with the maximum of the two terms discussed in this paragraph.

The prospect theory aspect of the model captures the idea of a bird-in-the-hand effect so frequently mentioned in media discussions about dividends. For the expression to apply, dividends would have to be risk free or approximately so. In this respect, the combination of subcertainty and hedonic editing provides theoretical justification for the following feature: Some households might view the risk profile of two stocks differently, even those differing only in their dividend payouts but are otherwise identical in terms of return distribution.

Kahneman and Tversky's (1979) original conception of prospect theory was in terms of regret. They subsequently modified the theory to focus on gains and losses but continued to stress the importance of regret as a psychological concept.

Regret is the emotion a person feels when making a decision and learning subsequently that a different decision would have been superior. Kahneman and Tversky (1982) suggest that the amount of regret experienced depends on the ease with which a person can plausibly imagine having taken a different decision. They emphasize that when a person departs from what for him or her would be conventional behavior and the decision turns out badly, then regret is high. However, when a person follows behavior that is conventional for him or her and the outcome is unfavorable, regret will tend to be small if not zero. The rationale behind this feature is that the person would not find taking a different decision plausible.

The behavioral life cycle and prospect theoretic elements of the framework emphasize the importance of dividend income being stable over time. Stability is important in the BLC because retired households rely on dividend income in their I accounts to finance consumption. If dividend income is volatile and unpredictable, households using self-control heuristics that forbid dipping into capital might face the choice of either accepting volatile consumption or breaking the rule. If dividend income is volatile and unpredictable, the benefits of hedonic editing and subcertainty will diminish. In addition, prospect theory emphasizes that people experience losses much more intensely than they do gains of the same magnitude. Therefore, in the behavioral approach, households react very negatively to cuts or omissions in dividend payouts.

Shefrin and Statman (1984) suggest that households selling stock to finance consumption on an infrequent basis might expose themselves to regret, if the particular stock sold rises in value after the sale. They suggest adding a term to subutility to reflect the amount of regret experienced. This term would be in addition to terms appearing in Equation 11.8 and based on the difference between the household portfolio decision $x(n_t)$ actually chosen and the portfolio decision $x'(n_t)$ that would have been chosen to allow the same consumption level to have been financed by dividends. The key issue here is that financing consumer expenditures out of dividend income might induce less regret than selling stock. This is because using dividends to finance consumption is common, but selling stock to finance consumption is less conventional.

The preceding discussion focuses entirely on cash dividends as opposed to stock dividends. In theory, shareholders can use stock dividends to finance consumption without appearing to dip into capital. Stock dividends also provide for natural segregation. However, from a psychological perspective, stock dividends look less like income and more like equity than cash dividends.

As to testable hypotheses, the discussion in this section predicts that dividend yield of household portfolios will be positively correlated with their aversion to loss (or risk) and their aversion to regret.

EMPIRICAL EVIDENCE

The Shefrin-Statman (1984) framework suggests several hypotheses about the behavioral basis for dividend preference. The BLC aspects point to a connection between consumption and dividends, along with a clientele effect. The hedonic-editing aspects point to a connection between stock market downturns and dividends. About 20 years after being proposed, these hypotheses have come to be tested, with the overall results being supportive of the behavioral approach. This section discusses the nature of the empirical evidence.

Dividends and Consumption

Baker, Nagel, and Wurgler (2007) provide the strongest evidence for a connection between consumption and dividends. Their analysis makes use of two types of data sets: the Consumer Expenditure Survey (CEX) from the Bureau of Labor Statistics and brokerage account data. The CEX provides panel data on household consumption, income, wealth, dividends, and demographic information. The brokerage data provide information about how individual investors behave when they receive dividends.

The CEX data used by Baker et al. (2007) cover the period 1988–2001 and involve 3,272 household-year observations. Total expenditure including durables is about $50,000 (measured in December 2001 dollars). Total income, which includes dividends but not capital gains, has a mean of $56,789. Financial wealth is typically around a third of total wealth. For the mean household, interest income is $1,207 and dividend income is $891. On average, interest and dividends account for 4 percent and 2 percent of total income, respectively. The distribution is skewed, with the median household reporting zero dividend income.

The BLC predicts that the marginal propensity to consume from the I account exceeds the marginal propensity to consume from the A account. Shefrin and Statman (1984) suggest that dividends flow through the I account and that capital gains flow through the A account. This implies that the marginal propensity to consume from dividend income is about the same as the marginal propensity to consume from total income, which in turn exceeds the marginal propensity to consume from capital gains.

Baker et al. (2007) estimate that the marginal propensity to consume from dividend income is 0.49, the same as the marginal propensity to consume out of total income, whereas the marginal propensity to consume from total current-year returns is close to zero.

Dividends and Withdrawals

Barber and Odean (2000) introduced the second data set that Baker et al. (2007) analyze. The data, which cover household portfolios, contain monthly position statements and trading activity for a sample of 78,000 households that had accounts at a large discount brokerage firm. The analysis covers the period January 1991 to December 1996.

The mean account value in the Barber-Odean data set is $54,400 and the median is $28,400. For the mean household, about 83 percent of this value stems from holdings of common stock and 14 percent stems from holdings of mutual funds. The average total monthly return is 1.11 percent. Notably, the average dividend income per month is 0.20 percent of the beginning-of-month portfolio value. In about one-half of household-months, dividend income is positive. Here, 78 percent of dividend income is from ordinary dividends, with the remainder from mutual funds. Special dividends are infrequent but typically large.

Households using dividend income to finance consumption must first withdraw those dividends from their brokerage accounts. The Barber-Odean (2000) data provide an opportunity to investigate the connection between ordinary dividends and net withdrawals. Baker et al. (2007) report a positive relationship between net withdrawals and ordinary dividends that is close to one-for-one for small dividends. This statement does not apply to mutual fund dividends, which appear to be automatically invested.

Notably, households only withdraw a portion of large dividends. In this regard, the BLC stipulates that households require much less willpower to save large windfalls that find their way into the I account or for that matter the A account. Therefore, they might increase consumption in the face of a windfall (e.g., a special dividend) but still be able to save most of it. Baker et al. (2007) report that households reinvest very large special dividends, suggesting that households allocate these amounts to the A account, effectively treating them as capital.

In accordance with the BLC, Baker et al. (2007) report a much smaller effect for capital gains than for dividends. Specifically, regardless of the level of capital gains, median contemporaneous net withdrawals are close to zero. On average, the marginal propensity to withdraw contemporaneous dividends is 0.35 and the marginal propensity to withdraw ordinary dividends is 0.9. In contrast, the marginal propensity to withdraw capital gains is 0.02. Still, the size of capital gains is sufficiently large that the aggregate effect of that 0.02 is fairly sizable.

Baker et al. (2007) note that investors withdraw mutual fund dividends at a much lower rate, presumably because mutual fund investors use automatic reinvestment policies. The authors also note that investors withdraw small special dividends at roughly the same rate as investors withdraw ordinary dividends, but they mostly reinvest large special dividends.

A key feature of the Shefrin-Statman (1984) framework is that households view ordinary dividends as predictable, similar in nature to pension income, Social Security payments, interest payments, and labor income. This is because households choose portfolios with the intent to consume ordinary dividends. According to Baker et al. (2007), ordinary dividends, scaled by beginning-of-period portfolio wealth, are predictable. They find that dividends lagged by one year explain 57 percent of the variation in ordinary dividends. Moreover, the combination of dividends lagged one year and dividends lagged three months explain 81 percent of the variation. Baker et al. also report that mutual fund dividends are less predictable than ordinary stock dividends, and that special dividends are unpredictable.

Dividends are not completely predictable. For this reason, the question is worth asking whether households attempt to smooth consumption or whether they consume the unpredictable component as well as the predictable component. Baker et al. (2007) investigate this issue by adding the 12-month lag of dividends to their analysis of withdrawals, to control for the predictable component. They find that lagged dividends explain a portion of withdrawals but that their inclusion has no discernable effect on the impact of contemporaneous dividends. Similar statements apply to the CEX data, although dividends are less predictable in that data set than in the Barber and Odean (2000) data set.

The work of Rantapuska and Kaustia (2007) provides additional information about reinvestment behavior associated with ordinary dividends, special dividends, and tender offers. Their study uses Finnish data from the Finnish Central Securities Depositary (FCSD). A virtue of these data is that the FCSD records every transaction involving Finnish securities on an account basis. Rantapuska and Kaustia use transactions between 1995 and 2002. Their data include transactions by households and various nonhousehold investors.

The main finding from the Finnish data is that investors reinvest less than 1 percent of dividend payments within ten days of receiving payment. Some of this behavior can be attributed to the dividends being small, which does not justify the transaction costs of reinvestment. However, investors are also averse to reinvesting larger ordinary dividends, where transaction costs are not a major issue. Here reinvestment rates lie in the range of 4 percent to 8 percent.

Reinvestment rates are larger for special dividends and tender offers. Surprisingly, the associated reinvestment rates for special dividends and tender offers are not large. For special dividends, the reinvestment rate is about 8 percent and for tender offers it is about 13 percent. In fact, 57 percent of households choose not to reinvest either special dividends or tender offer proceeds within 10 days of receipt.

Clientele Effects Involving Age, Retirement Status, and Income

The behavioral theory of dividends predicts how both ordinary dividends and special dividends will affect consumption. The theory also predicts how the demand for dividends will vary over the household life cycle, depending on a household's needs to replace labor income. In particular, behavioral theory predicts that older, retired households will find dividends more attractive than younger households that are still in the workforce. Moreover, households that have few options for replacing labor income after retirement will find dividends especially attractive. Low-income households are similar to older, retired households. For both groups, the shadow price of current income is high, and yet both are trying to protect the balances in their asset accounts. In this respect, demand for dividends will be negatively related to income.

Behavioral dividend theory predicts that clienteles will form around age, retirement status, and low income. Graham and Kumar (2006) document how the demand for dividends depends on age, retirement status, and income. As with Baker et al. (2007), Graham and Kumar analyze the data used in Barber and Odean (2000).

Demographic information including age, income, occupation, marital status, and sex is available for a subset of 31,260 of the 77,995 households in the sample. Graham and Kumar (2006) focus on the behavior of older and low-income investors. They partition households by age, income, and occupation. For age, the partition boundaries are below 45 (younger), between 45 and 65, and above 65 (older). For income, the partition boundaries are annual household income below $40,000 (low income), between $40,000 and $75,000, and above $75,000 (high income). For occupation, the partition boundaries are professional, nonprofessional, and retired.

About 15 percent of investors in their sample are at least 65 years of age and about 17 percent of them have annual income below $40,000. Older investors hold larger portfolios than their younger counterparts ($55,685 versus $24,402, respectively), and their portfolios contain more stocks (six versus four, respectively). Older investors also turn their portfolios over at a lower rate than younger investors (monthly portfolio turnover of 4.46 percent versus 5.36 percent, respectively).

Graham and Kumar (2006) measure the preference for dividends using portfolio dividend yield. They report that irrespective of income, older households prefer dividend-paying stocks over non-dividend-paying stocks. For younger households, those with low income exhibit a somewhat stronger preference for dividend-paying stocks than households with higher income. Moreover, the preference for dividends is relatively stable, with dividend yields of individual investors' portfolios changing slowly over time. These findings support the predictions of behavioral dividend theory about the impact of age and income.

In terms of stock selection, Graham and Kumar (2006) report that older, retired investors hold about 80 percent of their portfolios in dividend-paying stocks, while younger investors hold about 65 percent of their portfolios in dividend-paying stocks. In particular, older investors with low incomes attach more weight to utility stocks than do younger investors with high incomes. The reverse is true for the stocks of firms in the computers and business services industries. This pattern is consistent with the idea that older, low-income investors focus more on industries with a reputation for paying higher dividends.

Further support for dividend clienteles stems from Graham and Kumar's (2006) analysis of household trading behavior. They report that households trade around dividend events such as ex-dividend days, dividend announcement dates, and dividend initiations. Before the ex-dividend date, households that are older or have less income are net buyers of stock. These households also increase their holdings after dividend initiations and exhibit abnormal buying behavior after dividend announcements. These behavior patterns appear to affect the prices for the stocks of small firms, where individual investors' trades play an especially important role.

Consistent with the predictions of behavioral dividend theory, retirement status increases the demand for dividends. Graham and Kumar (2006) regress portfolio yield on a series of variables including age and a retirement status dummy. They report that the age variable has a positive and significant coefficient estimate (0.038 with a t-statistic of 4.22), while the dummy for retirement status has a coefficient estimate of 0.010 with a t-statistic of 2.03.

Dong, Robinson, and Veld (2005) develop panel data from a survey of individual investors in the Netherlands. On a weekly basis, their survey asked questions about personal finance and consumption matters. Of the 2,035 survey respondents, 555 own or previously owned shares in exchange-listed companies or investment funds. Of these investors, less than 20 percent own individual stocks. Also, 40 percent of the investors are at least 55 years of age and 20 percent are at least 65 years of age.

Consistent with the findings of Graham and Kumar (2006) and Baker et al. (2007), Dong et al. (2005) find that consumption from dividends is confined to investors who are either older or have low incomes. Outside this group, individual investors do not consume a large portion of their dividends but instead reinvest their dividend income. In contrast to the findings reported by Baker et al., they find that the propensity to consume from dividend income is less than from regular income.

Dong et al. (2005) assert that the findings described previously run counter to the behavioral predictions from Shefrin and Statman (1984). However, as pointed out earlier, behavioral theory does not predict that all households consume dividends. Instead, behavioral theory only predicts that older, retired households and low-income households favor dividend-paying stocks to finance consumption. Younger investors with moderate to high incomes have little need to finance consumption with dividends.

According to Dong et al. (2005), their findings support the behavioral prediction for stock dividends. They find that in cases where firms cannot pay a cash dividend, investors indicate that they would prefer companies to pay a stock dividend as opposed to no dividends. This is a framing effect, because stock dividends involve costs but do not increase the fundamental value of investors' positions. As Dong et al. (p. 124) indicate, "In principle stock dividends are no more than stock splits."

Taxes and Transaction Costs

Shefrin and Statman (1984) argue that psychological elements are germane to the preference for dividends, not that taxes and transaction costs are irrelevant. In this regard, Graham and Kumar (2006) find strong evidence that taxes are important. In the aggregate, individual investors have a negative preference for dividends. Only the older, retired households with low income have a strong preference for dividends. Younger households tend to hold dividend-paying stocks in tax-deferred accounts instead of taxable accounts. However, for older investors, whose income is taxed at lower rates than that of younger investors, the situation is different. The dividend yields associated with their taxable accounts is about the same as the dividend yields associated with their tax-deferred accounts.

Baker et al. (2007) investigate the extent to which taxes and transaction costs might drive their findings. They point out that households are not particularly adept at tax minimization. In particular, for all months of the year except December, households display the disposition effect, selling their winning stocks too quickly and holding their losing stocks too long (Shefrin and Statman, 1985; Odean, 1998). Graham and Kumar (2006) also find that the disposition effect does not drive their findings. Baker et al. also ask whether households might be using dividend income to cover taxes rather than consumption. Yet they find that households tend to withdraw far more dividend income than would be necessary to cover taxes.

Transaction costs do not explain the Baker et al. (2007) findings because transaction costs tend to be higher for smaller portfolios in which odd-lot trading plays a larger role. Empirically, the propensity to withdraw dividends does not depend on portfolio size. In addition, Baker et al. report that high-turnover investors have the same propensity to withdraw dividends as low-turnover investors. High-turnover investors can reinvest unwanted dividends at little, if any, marginal cost.

Catering, Perceptions about Risk and Return, and Tolerance for Risk

On April 23, 2001, in the wake of the collapse of the technology stock bubble, *Barron's* ran an article with the title "Bird in the Hand." Journalist Jennifer Ablan reports that individual investors moved away from dividend-paying stocks during the 1990s bull market, mentioning the unfavorable tax treatment of dividends along with the fact that dividend-paying companies might have had few opportunities for growth and capital appreciation. However, she reports that investors were reversing themselves after the bubble collapsed. As she notes (p. 22) "the idea of a steady stream of cash income combined with the opportunity for capital appreciation suddenly doesn't seem like such a bad idea."

In addition to the tech bubble bursting, Ablan (2001) reports that tobacco stocks have been replacing electric utilities as reliable dividend payers. In this regard, utility dividends have decreased in predictability as a result of deregulation in the market for electricity. There are at least two behavioral issues that underlie the *Barron's* discussion. The first involves hedonic editing, with its decomposition of total return into a dividend yield and capital gain. The second is a belief that non-dividend-paying stocks were offering an unfavorable risk-return profile. Regarding the latter, investors exhibit sentiment to the extent that their views about the risk-return profile are erroneous.

Graham and Kumar (2006) present evidence about the first behavioral issue. They suggest that the degree of diversification in an investor's portfolio reflects that investor's aversion to risk. Risk-tolerant investors are more willing to hold less diversified portfolios. Graham and Kumar report a positive correlation between portfolio dividend yield and degree of diversification. They also find that the relationship is weak for low-income investors and older investors. The reason for the weak relationship is that such investors primarily rely on dividends to finance consumption expenditures not to exploit hedonic editing. However, the findings suggest that for younger investors with moderate to high incomes, hedonic editing rather than consumption is the primary reason for favoring dividend-paying stocks.

Evidence presented by Dong et al. (2005) runs counter to the predictions of hedonic editing. The respondents to their survey do not view high-dividend-paying stocks as less risky than low-dividend-paying stocks; if anything, they find the reverse.

Baker and Wurgler (2004a, 2004b) develop a theory in which firms choose their payouts to cater to investor sentiment. When sentiment leads investor preference for dividends to decrease, firms respond by delaying dividend initiation. When sentiment leads investor preference for dividends to increase, firms respond by initiating dividends. (Chapter 13 provides a detailed discussion of catering theory.)

CONCLUSIONS

This chapter develops a behaviorally based theory for why individual investors find dividends attractive and presents a combination of anecdotal and empirical evidence providing strong support for the theory. Behavioral dividend theory explains the impact of age, retirement status, and income on the relationship between consumer expenditures and the preference for dividends, and a psychological approach to dividend theory explains the relationship between tolerance for risk and the preference for dividends.

REFERENCES

Ablan, Jennifer. 2001. "Bird in the Hand: Suddenly, Dividend Stocks Don't Look So Old-fashioned, After All." *Barron's*, April 23, 22.

Baker, Malcolm, and Jeffrey Wurgler. 2004a. "Appearing and Disappearing Dividends: The Link to Catering Incentives." *Journal of Financial Economics* 73:2, 271–288.

Baker, Malcolm, and Jeffrey Wurgler. 2004b. "A Catering Theory of Dividends." *Journal of Finance* 59:3, 1125–1165.

Baker, Malcolm, Stefan Nagel, and Jeffrey Wurgler. 2007. "The Effect of Dividends on Consumption." *Brookings Papers on Economic Activity*, 277–291.

Barber, Brad, and Terrance Odean. 2000. "Trading Is Hazardous to Your Wealth: The Common Stock Investment Performance of Individual Investors." *Journal of Finance* 55:2, 773–806.

Clements, Jonathan. 2000. "The Party Seems to Be Over, Now What? It's Time to Adjust Your Investment Strategy to a More Lackluster Market." *Wall Street Journal*, Personal Finance & Spending, September 8, 28.

Clements, Jonathan. 2007. "When Retirement Experts Talk, Why Doesn't Anybody Listen?" *Wall Street Journal*, Getting Going, June 20, D1.

Crenshaw, Albert. 1994. "A Cautionary Tale of Inheritance and Second Chances; Susan Strange Had It All Figured Out—Before the Divorce, the Will Change and the Financial Planner Hit." *Washington Post*, May 29, h05.

De Aenlle, Conrad. 2006. "Is It Time for Dividends to Get Some Respect?" *New York Times*, Sunday Money: Investing, June 11, 6.

Dong, Ming, Chris Robinson, and Chris Veld. 2005. "Why Individual Investors Want Dividends." *Journal of Corporate Finance* 12:1, 121–158.

Graham, John, and Alok Kumar. 2006. "Dividend Preference of Retail Investors: Do Dividend Clienteles Exist?" *Journal of Finance* 6:3, 1305–1336.

Jones, Ceri. 2005. "In an Uncertain Climate, Dividends Are a Safe Bet." *Independent*, Trading Strategies, May 7, 14.

Kahneman, Daniel, and Amos Tversky. 1979. "Prospect Theory: An Analysis of Decision Making under Risk." *Econometrica* 47:2, 263–291.

Kahneman, Daniel, and Amos Tversky. 1982. "The Psychology of Preferences." *Scientific American* 246:1: 160–173.

McClure, Samuel, David Laibson, George Loewenstein, and Jonathan Cohen. 2004. "Separate Neural Systems: Value Immediate and Delayed Monetary Rewards." *Science* 306:15, 503–507.

Miller, Merton. 1988. "The Modigliani-Miller Propositions after Thirty Years." *Journal of Economic Perspectives* 2:4, 99–120.

Odean, Terrance. 1998. "Are Investors Reluctant to Realize Their Losses?" *Journal of Finance* 53:5, 1775–1798.

Rantapuska, Elias, and Markuu Kaustia. 2007. "Do Investors Reinvest Dividends and Tender Offer Proceeds?" Working Paper, Helsinki School of Economics, Finland.

Shefrin, Hersh, and Meir Statman. 1984. "Explaining Investor Preference for Cash Dividends." *Journal of Financial Economics* 13:2, 253–282.

Shefrin, Hersh, and Meir Statman. 1985. "The Disposition to Sell Winners Too Early and Ride Losers Too Long: Theory and Evidence." *Journal of Finance* 40:3, 777–790.

Shefrin, Hersh, and Richard Thaler. 1988. "The Behavioral Life Cycle Hypothesis." *Economic Inquiry* 26:4, 609–643.

Thaler, Richard, and Shlomo Benartzi. 2004. "Save More Tomorrow: Using Behavioral Economics to Increase Employee Savings." *Journal of Political Economy* 112:1, Part 2, S164–S187.

Thaler, Richard, and Eric Johnson. 1991. "Gambling with the House Money and Trying to Break Even: The Effects of Prior Outcomes on Risky Choice." In *Quasi-Rational Economics*, ed. Richard H. Thaler, 48–73. New York: Russell Sage Foundation.

Thaler, Richard, and Hersh Shefrin. 1981. "An Economic Theory of Self Control." *Journal of Political Economy* 89:2, 392–406.

Tversky, Amos, and Daniel Kahneman. 1992. "Advances in Prospect Theory: Cumulative Representation of Uncertainty." *Journal of Risk and Uncertainty* 5:4, 297–323.

ABOUT THE AUTHOR

Hersh Shefrin is Mario L. Belotti Professor of Finance at Santa Clara University. He has been studying the influence of psychology on economic and financial behavioral since the mid-1970s. In 1984, *Journal of Financial Economics* published an article he coauthored with Meir Statman, offering the first behavioral explanation for why investors find dividends attractive. The article applies the elements of behavioral decision making to a major puzzle in finance. He has authored several books. *Beyond Greed and Fear* provides a systematic treatment of behavioral finance. *A Behavioral Approach to Asset Pricing* develops a general unified behavioral pricing kernel treatment of asset pricing. *Behavioral Corporate Finance* is the first textbook with the purpose of teaching students the relevance of behavioral concepts to corporate finance.

CHAPTER 12

The Firm Life Cycle Theory of Dividends

LAARNI T. BULAN
Assistant Professor of Finance, International Business School and the Economics Department, Brandeis University

NARAYANAN SUBRAMANIAN
Senior Manager, Cornerstone Research

INTRODUCTION

The firm life cycle theory of dividends is based on the notion that as a firm matures, its ability to generate cash overtakes its ability to find profitable investment opportunities. Eventually, the optimal choice is for the firm to distribute its free cash flow to shareholders in the form of dividends.

According to the firm life cycle theory of dividends, a young firm faces a relatively large investment opportunity set but is not sufficiently profitable to be able to meet all its financing needs through internally generated cash. In addition, it faces substantial hurdles in raising capital from external sources. As a result, the firm will conserve cash by forgoing dividend payments to shareholders. Over time, after a period of growth, the firm reaches the maturity stage in its life cycle. At this point, the firm's investment opportunity set is diminished, its growth and profitability have flattened, systematic risk has declined, and the firm generates more cash internally than it can profitably invest. Eventually, the firm begins paying dividends to distribute its earnings to shareholders. The extent to which a mature firm distributes earnings to shareholders instead of investing them internally is a function of the extent to which the interests of its managers are aligned with those of its shareholders.

The life cycle theory of dividends predicts that a firm will begin paying dividends when its growth rate and profitability are expected to decline in the future. This is in sharp contrast to the signaling theory of dividends, which predicts that a firm will pay dividends to signal to the market that its growth and profitability

The authors thank Harry DeAngelo for helpful comments on an earlier draft of this chapter.

prospects have improved (i.e., that dividend initiations and increases convey "good news").

The empirical evidence on dividend initiations and changes generally supports the life cycle theory of dividends but is contrary to the signaling theory. Benartzi, Michaely, and Thaler (1997) find that dividend increases are not followed by an increase in the earnings growth rate, while dividend reductions are associated with an improvement in the growth rate. Grullon, Michaely, and Swaminathan (2002) report that firm profitability declines after a dividend increase and rises after a dividend decrease.

Bulan, Subramanian, and Tanlu (2007) document that firms initiate dividends after reaching maturity in their life cycles. Initiators are firms that have grown larger, are more profitable, have greater cash reserves, and have fewer growth opportunities than do noninitiators at the same stage in their life cycles. They also find that no significant improvement in profitability or growth occurs around the initiation. DeAngelo, DeAngelo, and Stulz (2006) present evidence that the probability that a firm pays dividends is significantly related to the mix of (internally) earned capital and (externally) contributed capital in its capital structure. Firms with a greater proportion of earned capital are more likely to be dividend payers. The evidence on the change in systematic risk around dividend changes is ambiguous. While Grullon et al. (2002) provide evidence that firms that increase dividends experience a decline in systematic risk, Bulan et al. (2007) find that systematic risk does not decline after dividend initiations.

The remainder of the chapter provides a discussion of the theory and empirical evidence in greater detail. The chapter begins with a brief overview of the theory of the firm's life cycle and how dividends fit in the life cycle, followed by the empirical evidence on dividend policy as it relates to the life cycle theory. The chapter concludes with an assessment of the theory vis-à-vis the evidence and provides a discussion of avenues for future research.

THE LIFE CYCLE THEORY OF THE FIRM

Mueller (1972) proposed a formal theory that a firm has a relatively well-defined life cycle, which is fundamental to the firm life cycle theory of dividends. His main focus is on the agency problem within the firm, namely, the question of whether the managers of a firm maximize shareholder value or pursue growth for the firm's own sake and overinvest in assets contrary to shareholder interests. However, he clearly recognizes the implications of the analysis for dividend policy and discusses the empirical evidence on shareholder preference for dividends in this context. Thus, studying the life cycle theory of the firm as proposed by Mueller is meaningful.

Drawing on the work of Knight (1921) and Schumpeter (1934), Mueller (1972) posits that a firm originates in an attempt to exploit an innovation involving a new product, process, or marketing or organizational technique. In its initial stages, the firm invests all available resources in developing the innovation and improving its profitability. The firm's growth is likely to be slow until it successfully sorts out "teething issues" and establishes a foothold in the market. Thereafter, the enterprise will grow rapidly, as it enters new markets and expands its customer base before any major competition can arise. The agency problem is either absent or not significant at these initial stages for three reasons. First, the firm faces so many opportunities for profitable investment that the pursuit of growth is also consistent with the pursuit of profits. Second, unable to meet all its financing needs through internal cash generation, the firm is forced to tap external capital markets and is therefore subject to market monitoring and discipline. Third, the entrepreneur or manager still retains a sufficiently high fraction of the firm's shares for his or her interests to be well aligned with those of the other suppliers of capital.

After a while, competitors begin to enter the market, adopting and improving on the pioneering firm's innovations. As existing markets become saturated and new markets harder to find, the growth of the firm begins to slow down. To maintain growth and profitability, the firm needs to generate innovations. However, as the firm grows as an organization, its ability to process information deteriorates, and the risk-taking incentives of the average manager diminish. These factors place a limit on the ability of a large firm to grow through innovations. As a result, the firm eventually reaches a point at which it lacks profitable investment opportunities for the cash generated from its existing operations. At this mature stage, a shareholder-value-maximizing firm would begin distributing its earnings to its shareholders. Eventually, when all the existing operations of the firm are on the verge of becoming unprofitable, a value-maximizing firm would liquidate all assets and distribute the proceeds to its shareholders. However, when the managers of a firm do not pursue strict value maximization but are rather interested in expanding the size of the firm to reap perks and other rewards, the distribution of earnings to shareholders will deviate from the optimal policy.

In summary, under the life cycle theory proposed by Mueller (1972), the typical firm will display an S-shaped growth pattern, with a period of slow growth at start-up leading to a period of rapid growth and eventually to maturity and stagnation or slow growth. The next section discusses corporate dividend policy in this framework.

DIVIDENDS IN THE FIRM'S LIFE CYCLE

Mueller (1972) also traces the implications of the life cycle theory of the firm to dividend policy. As previously discussed, the optimal dividend policy at a value-maximizing firm in his framework is to retain all earnings in the rapid growth phase and to pay out 100 percent of the earnings at maturity. Using a static discounted cash flow model of equity valuation provides one means of understanding this optimal dividend policy.

A Simple Static Model of Optimal Dividend Policy

Consider a highly simplified constant growth model of a firm of the type found in many valuation textbooks, such as that of Bodie, Kane, and Marcus (2005). The firm is infinitely lived and is fully equity financed. The number of shares outstanding is normalized to one for ease of exposition. The firm's return on assets in place is equal to its return on equity (ROE). In every period, the firm has access to a set of fresh investment opportunities with expected return equal to ROE. To focus on the payout decision, we abstract from external financing issues by assuming that the firm does not access external capital.

Let E_0 denote the equity base at the end of year 0. In year 1, the firm earns an amount e_1 given by $(ROE)(E_0)$. Assuming a constant payout ratio of d, the dividend amount for year 1, denoted by D_1, is de_1, and the amount of retained earnings for the period is $(e_1 - D_1)$.

The firm invests the retained earnings in new assets that provide a rate of return of ROE. Hence, total earnings for year 2 are $e_2 = ROE(E_0 + e_1 - D_1) = e_1 + ROE(1 - d)e_1 = (1 + g)e_1$, where g is the growth rate of earnings, given by

$$g = (e_2 - e_1)/e_1 = ROE(1 - d). \tag{12.1}$$

Extending this logic, the earnings of the firm in year t are $e_t = e_1(1 + g)^{(t-1)}$, and the dividend amount paid in year t is $D_t = de_1(1 + g)^{(t-1)}$. The value of the firm at time 0, given by the present value of future dividends, is therefore equal to $V_0 = \sum D_t/(1 + k)^t = \sum de_1(1 + g)^{(t-1)}/(1 + k)^t$, where the summation is from $t = 1$ to infinity.

Assuming for a moment that $g < k$, and substituting for g from Equation 1, the value of the firm is given by

$$V_0 = de_1/(k - g) = de_1/[k - ROE(1 - d)]. \tag{12.2}$$

Equation 12.2 relates the value of the firm to its dividend policy. Based on Equation 12.2, when ROE is greater than k, the value of the firm increases as the payout ratio d decreases. (However, to be consistent with the assumption that $g < k$, this applies only for $d > 1 - k/ROE$.) When ROE is less than k, the value of the firm increases with the payout ratio. Thus, the optimal dividend policy is to maintain a 0 percent payout ratio when $ROE > k$ and a 100 percent payout ratio when $ROE < k$.

The intuition for this optimal policy is exactly the same as that which underlies Mueller's (1972) argument that a value-maximizing firm should maintain a zero payout ratio at the initial stages and increase the payout to 100 percent upon reaching maturity. Essentially, when the firm's investments promise a rate of return (ROE) higher than the firm's cost of capital (k), the firm should reinvest all of its earnings in new assets. This is likely to be true for young firms that are in the process of expanding the market for their innovations. But when the expected return on the firm's investments is less than the firm's cost of capital (k), the optimal policy for the firm is to pay out all of its earnings to shareholders. This is likely to be true for firms that have exploited all profitable opportunities for their innovations and reached maturity in their life cycles.

The model of the firm described, though static and highly simplified, is useful in understanding the differences in dividend policy between young firms and mature firms. When combined with a description of the factors driving the changes in the investment opportunity set (i.e., ROE or marginal return on investment), and the cost of capital as a firm matures, the model will provide a complete life cycle–based explanation of dividends.

In the context of Mueller's (1972) life cycle theory of the firm, one explanation for the decline in the marginal return on investment as a firm grows larger is based on the hypothesis that the ability of an organization to process information and maintain risk-taking incentives declines as the firm matures. The change in cost of capital as a firm grows requires a more detailed analysis, which follows in the next section.

Cost of Capital over the Firm's Life Cycle

The cost of capital that a firm faces will vary over its life cycle as a result of changes in risk, information asymmetry, and the extent of the agency problem.

Risk

Grullon et al. (2002) present evidence supporting the hypothesis that the systematic risk of firms declines around dividend increases. They explain the decline as caused by a decline in the number of growth options, including compound options, held by the firm. This is, of course, a joint explanation for a reduction in both the cost of capital and the return on investment with maturity. Therefore, it does not, by itself, explain why firm maturity should shift dividend policy in the direction of higher payouts. A better understanding of the link between maturity and payout policy requires analysis of the changes in the level of information asymmetry and the extent of the agency problem over the firm's life cycle.

Information Asymmetry

When a firm is young and relatively unknown, substantial information asymmetry exists between its insiders and outside investors. As a result, raising capital from external sources is costly. At the same time, the firm's investment needs are likely to exceed the cash flow from its operations, which implies that its financing comes from external sources at the margin. As a result, the firm faces a high cost of capital. As the firm becomes more established and well known, investors gain better knowledge about its assets and its management, and the level of information asymmetry decreases. Correspondingly, the firm's cost of external capital decreases. In the context of dividend policy, this implies that as a firm matures, its management has less need to conserve cash for potential future projects and is, therefore, in a better position to make dividend payments.

The Agency Problem

The assumption that a firm derives its dividend policy from the objective of shareholder-value maximization may be appropriate for a small entrepreneur-managed firm in which the manager holds a substantial fraction of the firm's shares and the suppliers of capital are able to monitor the manager closely and take steps to prevent value-destroying activities. However, the professional managers who are employed at large corporations typically do not hold large fractions of the company's stock. In addition, the diffused nature of shareholding at a large corporation implies that the average shareholder may not have the power to control the management effectively. Mueller (1972) notes that this separation of ownership and control in large corporations implies that managers of these firms may have lower incentives to maximize shareholder value than the entrepreneur-manager. He hypothesizes that managers of large corporations will consequently aim to maximize firm size and growth rather than market value, and will therefore invest more and pay lower dividends than a shareholder-value-maximizing management. (Jensen and Meckling (1976) provide a detailed treatment of this agency problem.)

Mueller (1972, p. 208) links dividend policy to the firm's life cycle, stating that the "freedom to pursue growth, and the management-stockholder conflict that accompanies it, appear only over time as the firm expands and matures." On a similar note, Jensen (1986) observes that the shareholder-manager conflict is particularly severe in firms with large free cash flow (i.e., cash flow in excess of investment opportunities), coining the phrase "agency cost of free cash flow" to denote this problem. The management of a firm with a large free cash flow may be tempted to waste the cash by awarding itself excessive perks and benefits. Another potential problem with high levels of free cash flow is "tunneling." That is, at firms that are part of a business group controlled by one main shareholder, the controlling shareholder may be tempted to divert cash flow from firms in which he or she has low cash flow rights to firms in which he or she has high cash flow rights.

DeAngelo and DeAngelo (2006) and DeAngelo et al. (2006) characterize the agency cost of free cash flow as a cost associated with retention, which becomes progressively more severe as the firm becomes mature. Grullon et al. (2002) also recognize that the agency problem becomes important in the mature stage of a firm's life cycle. One view is that the agency cost of free cash flow is more usefully considered a part of the cost of capital of the firm. In an efficient market, investors will incorporate the possibility that the management might waste a portion of the returns on the firm's investments (whether the wastage occurs through consumption of perks by the management or diversion of profits through tunneling) and demand a correspondingly higher expected return or yield on the firm's securities when the agency cost is higher. Whether the agency cost is viewed as a cost of retention or an element of the cost of capital, the implication for the life cycle theory of dividends is the same—as a firm matures, it generates more cash than can profitably be invested, and the optimal dividend policy becomes one of investing less and paying out more to shareholders.

Finally, the exact point at which a firm may shift from being a non–dividend payer to a dividend payer may depend on various factors, including the severity of the agency problem, its corporate governance, and the market for corporate control. DeAngelo et al. (2006) emphasize this, and in support, they present evidence that there is no cutoff or trigger point based on the ratio of retained earnings to total assets beyond which a firm would necessarily start paying dividends.

EMPIRICAL EVIDENCE

This section provides a discussion of the empirical evidence in support of the life cycle theory of dividends. Early empirical studies on dividend policy in the life cycle context attempt to compare the rates of return on dividends and retained earnings at young and mature companies and industries. According to Mueller (1972), shareholders' preference for dividends over retained earnings (especially in mature industries), documented in many studies, indicates that shareholders tend to believe that firms overinvest for the sake of growth and maintain dividend levels below optimum. Grabowski and Mueller (1975) take a similar static approach, focusing on a comparison of the market valuation of retained earnings and dividend payments in mature companies against nonmature companies. These studies do not address the question of whether firms delay initiating dividends beyond the optimal point, and only indirectly deal with the question of whether firms pay lower dividends than optimal after initiation. As discussed here, subsequent studies address these questions more directly by examining the market reaction to dividend initiations and dividend changes.

Life Cycle Factors and the Propensity to Pay Dividends

Until recently, few studies directly tested the firm life cycle theory of dividends. Most studies focused on other theories of dividend policy, such as the signaling and clientele hypotheses, with most of the evidence being contrary to the predictions of those theories. The recent interest in the life cycle theory of dividends may perhaps be traced to Fama and French's (2001) study of the dividend payment behavior of publicly traded U.S. firms. They investigate the patterns and determinants of payout policy over the 1926–1999 period. Their results point to life cycle factors playing a major role in the decision to pay cash dividends. In particular, their findings show that dividend-paying firms are large and highly profitable. These firms have retained earnings that are sufficient to cover their capital investments. On the other hand, firms that have never paid dividends are small and not as profitable as dividend-paying firms. These firms have many investment opportunities that require external financing because their capital spending is far greater than their earnings. Thus, dividend-paying firms have the characteristics of mature firms, while firms that have never paid dividends have the characteristics of young, fast-growing firms.

Furthermore, Fama and French (2001) find that dividend payment propensity decreased in the latter decades of their sample and attribute this, in part, to a surge in new listings after 1978, with the new lists being dominated by firms with strong investment opportunities, low profitability, and high growth rates (i.e., firms in the early high-growth phase of their life cycles). In summary, this study shows a significant relationship between the overall patterns of dividend payment and firm characteristics that determine a firm's life cycle stage.

DeAngelo et al. (2006) attempt to explicitly test the life cycle theory of dividends by analyzing the relationship between dividend payment propensity and the mix of earned and contributed capital. They measure the mix of earned and contributed capital by the ratio of retained earnings to total equity or total assets of the firm. They assert that this ratio is a good proxy for a firm's life cycle stage because it captures the extent to which a firm relies on internally generated and external capital. When firms are in their high-growth phase, they rely heavily on external sources to finance their investments because their earnings capacity is low. Therefore, this ratio will be low for young high-growth firms. In contrast, firms in their mature stage will have high cash flows and few investment opportunities, and will largely be self-financing. Hence, for mature firms, this ratio will be high. The authors test the firm life cycle theory of dividends by relating dividend payment propensity to the mix of retained earnings to contributed capital.

Using a sample of publicly traded U.S. firms in the period 1972–2002, De Angelo et al. (2006) find support for the theory. They document a positive relationship between the proportion of dividend-paying firms and the ratio of retained earnings to total equity and total assets, after controlling for firm characteristics such as profitability, growth, firm size, leverage, cash balances, and dividend history. Thus, a firm is more likely to be a dividend payer when its main source of financing is internally generated earnings. They also find similar results for dividend initiations and omissions.

Denis and Osobov (2008) extend the evidence to five other countries, namely, Canada, United Kingdom, Germany, France, and Japan. In those five countries as well as in the United States, they find that the propensity to pay dividends is strongly associated with the ratio of retained earnings to total equity. However, von Eije and Megginson (2008) report no such association between the ratio of retained earnings to total equity and the propensity to pay dividends in their study of dividends and repurchases at firms listed in fifteen European Union countries. But they do find that firm age, size, and past profitability are positively related to the propensity to pay dividends as predicted by the life cycle theory.

Skinner (2007) studies corporate payout policy including dividends and repurchases and finds that firms are increasingly using repurchases in place of dividends to payout cash flow. He finds that for a large group of firms that payout earnings through dividends and repurchases, the level of repurchases is driven by earnings over two- or three-year windows, which is supportive of the life cycle theory. However, the annual relationship is weaker, leading Skinner to suggest that managers time repurchases within those windows on the basis of other considerations, such as taking advantage of a low stock price, offsetting dilution associated with employee stock options, managing reported earnings, and distributing excess cash.

Life Cycle Factors and Dividend Changes

Grullon et al. (2002) propose that firm maturity and the accompanying decline in systematic risk has important implications for dividend policy. Echoing the arguments discussed in the previous sections, they state that firm maturity is associated with high cash flows but fewer investment opportunities. At the same time, there is a decline in the systematic risk of the firm, as the number of growth options, including compound options, held by the firm have decreased. Consequently, as a firm matures, its earnings growth would slow down and its systematic risk and profitability (return on assets) would decline. This, in turn, brings about a reduction in the reinvestment rate (the reinvestment of retained earnings) of the firm and an increase in dividend payout. Thus, an increase in dividend payout signals the transition of the firm from a high-growth phase to a low-growth phase, or the mature phase, in its life cycle. The announcement effect of dividend changes, specifically the positive stock price reaction to dividend increases, is then explained by the change in systematic risk rather than profitability.

To test their maturity hypothesis, or what is essentially the firm life cycle theory of dividends, Grullon et al. (2002) use a sample of New York (NYSE) and American (AMEX) stock-exchange-listed firms that increased or decreased their dividends during the period 1967–1993. One of their main findings is the existence of a relationship between dividend changes and changes in risk. They show that systematic risk declines for dividend-increasing firms and increases for dividend-decreasing firms. In addition, they find a significant relationship between the positive announcement effect associated with dividend increases and the decline in the firm's systematic risk. In terms of profitability, Grullon et al. find that the return on assets of dividend-increasing firms declines after the dividend increase. In summary, their evidence supports the firm life cycle theory. Dividend increases signal a decline in risk and profitability as the firm has reached a more mature stage in its life cycle.

Life Cycle Factors and Dividend Initiations

Empirical tests of the traditional signaling theories of dividends rely on the information content of a change in dividend policy. If, indeed, dividend increases or decreases represent significant changes in firm characteristics, then there should be even more significant changes in firm characteristics around dividend initiations since initiations, by definition, occur only once in the firm's life cycle. This is the premise behind Bulan et al.'s (2007) analysis of the timing of dividend initiations in a firm's life cycle. They study how firm characteristics evolve over time as a firm moves toward dividend initiation. The authors estimate a firm's propensity to initiate a dividend as a function of firm characteristics relative to other firms that are at the same stage in their life cycles but that have never paid dividends. Their data cover publicly traded U.S. corporations during the period 1963–2001.

Bulan et al. (2007) find evidence supportive of the firm life cycle theory of dividends. Dividend initiators are firms that are larger, more profitable, and have higher cash balances but fewer growth opportunities than firms in the same life cycle stage that have never paid dividends. Thus, dividend initiators are mature firms. They find further evidence of firm maturity in the type of payout policy that firms adopt. Prior work by Jagannathan, Stephens, and Weisbach (2000) and Guay and Harford (2000) shows that firms use stock repurchases to pay out volatile cash flows but use regular cash dividends to pay out permanent cash flows. Their evidence shows a positive relationship between repurchasing activity and the probability of initiating a dividend (i.e., repeated repurchases indicate that a firm is moving toward maturity as its cash flows stabilize). The firm ultimately pays out its excess cash flows in the form of cash dividends.

Contrary to Grullon et al.'s (2002) evidence for dividend increases, Bulan et al. (2007) do not find evidence fully supporting the risk-signaling aspect of the life cycle theory of dividends. While firms that initiate dividends are mature firms, they show that the event of dividend initiation itself does not signal a change in the firm's life cycle characteristics. They find that there is no significant difference in sales growth or risk in the pre- and postinitiation periods. In addition, Bulan et al. report no evidence that life cycle factors account for the positive market reaction to dividend initiation announcements. Instead, their findings indicate that firms choose an opportune time to initiate a dividend upon reaching maturity. This opportune time to initiate a dividend depends on the market sentiment for dividend-paying stocks measured by Baker and Wurgler's (2004) dividend premium.

Dividend Initiation in the Life Cycle of a Firm: The Case of Microsoft

Microsoft Corp.'s announcement of its first cash dividend on January 16, 2003, illustrates the maturation of the firm and the timing of its dividend initiation.

Microsoft had its initial public offering (IPO) in 1986 and initiated dividends 17 years after its IPO. Figure 12.1 depicts the change in some key variables for the company over the period, specifically, the growth rate of sales, return on assets (profitability), ratio of cash to assets, and ratio of capital expenditures to assets. Each variable is industry-adjusted by subtracting the industry mean.

As Figure 12.1 shows, Microsoft grew faster than the industry average in the period until 1993. However, since then, Microsoft has grown more slowly than the average. The company's profitability was volatile in the first half of this period but appears to have stabilized after 1995. While the company was spending more on capital expenditures (relative to assets) than the industry average until the mid-1990s, Microsoft has since been spending less than the average firm in the industry. Finally, the company has held a much greater level of cash than the industry average. All these indicators point to maturation of the company around 1995. Thus, Microsoft had the characteristics of a dividend payer, but it did not declare a dividend for another eight years. Consistent with the empirical evidence, Microsoft initiated a dividend when it was already mature. The company's maturation, however, did not coincide with its dividend initiation.

One possible explanation for the timing of Microsoft's initiation is the reduction in the tax rate on dividends. At that time, investors anticipated a tax cut,

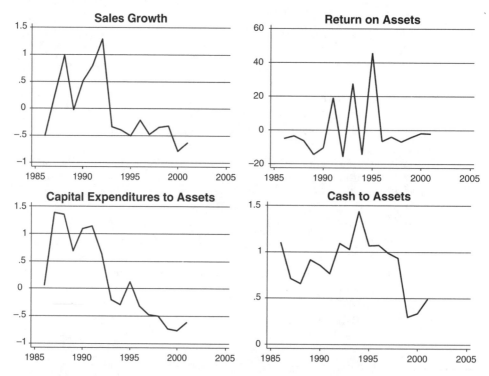

Figure 12.1 The Case of Microsoft

These panels present (clockwise from top left) sales growth, return on assets, cash to assets, and capital expenditures to assets for Microsoft Corporation from 1986 to 2002. All measures are industry adjusted using Microsoft's major industry group (SIC code 73 or Business Services).

although it had not yet been passed into law. Another possibility is the market sentiment for dividend-paying stocks measured by Baker and Wurgler's (2004) dividend premium. In the years 2001 and 2002, with the stock market downturn, there was a sharp rise in the dividend premium, with the premium being positive in 2002. Following this change in sentiment, Microsoft initiated dividends in January 2003.

CONCLUSIONS

The firm life cycle theory of dividends relates the optimal dividend policy of a firm to where a firm is in its life cycle. The basic model presented in this chapter encapsulates the essence of the theory. A firm determines its optimal dividend policy by the relationship between its ROE and its cost of capital (k), which, in turn, is determined by the firm's life cycle stage. A young firm in its high-growth stage has many profitable investment opportunities but low cash flows. Thus, the firm's ROE $> k$ and the optimal payout ratio is zero. A mature firm has high cash flows but far fewer investment opportunities. Therefore, the firm's ROE $< k$ and the optimal payout ratio is 100 percent. The theory predicts that the trade-off between the costs and benefits of raising new capital in relation to its investment opportunity set determine changes in dividend policy. More specifically, the theory predicts that a firm will begin paying dividends when it transitions from a high-growth phase to a mature (slower-growth) phase in its life cycle. A decline in the firm's growth rate, profitability, and risk usually indicates this transition. Hence, a change in dividend policy signals a life cycle change within the firm.

Overall, the empirical evidence favors the firm life cycle theory of dividends in terms of dividend payment propensity and life cycle characteristics. Firms in the early stages of their life cycles rarely pay dividends, while firms in the mature stage are likely to be dividend payers. Moreover, the decision to pay the first regular cash dividend is usually made contingent on having reached maturity. Other factors not predicted by this theory seem to determine the exact timing of the dividend initiation. The evidence is more ambiguous on the signaling aspect of the theory that changes in dividend policy signal that a firm has transitioned from one life cycle stage to another.

Consequently, there is much room for future work. How can researchers reconcile the evidence that dividend initiation does not signal life cycle changes but dividend increases (and decreases) do? In our view, dividend initiation represents a much more important change in dividend policy than does the increase or decrease of an existing dividend rate. Hence, precisely how different are they in a life cycle context? How can researchers characterize this difference? The evidence presented on dividend initiations also suggests that other factors and other theories outside of a life cycle explanation account for the positive announcement effect of dividend initiations. Might these same factors also be present for dividend increases or decreases after controlling for the firm's life cycle? For example, in related work, DeAngelo, DeAngelo, and Stultz (2008) find that the decision by firms to issue seasoned equity reflects both market timing and life cycle motives. Perhaps a richer, more unified (and of course more complex) theory of dividend policy with the life cycle framework as its backbone can generate more of the empirical regularities that are observed in the literature.

REFERENCES

Baker, Malcolm and Jeffrey Wurgler. 2004. "A Catering Theory of Dividends." *Journal of Finance* 59:3, 1125–1165.

Benartzi, Shlomo, Roni Michaely, and Richard Thaler. 1997. "Do Changes in Dividends Signal the Future or the Past?" *Journal of Finance* 52:3, 1007–1034.

Bodie, Zvi, Alex Kane, and Alan J. Marcus. 2005. *Investments*, 6th ed. New York: McGraw-Hill/Irwin.

Bulan, Laarni, Narayanan Subramanian, and Lloyd Tanlu. 2007. "On the Timing of Dividend Initiations." *Financial Management* 36:4, 31–65.

DeAngelo, Harry, and Linda DeAngelo. 2006. "The Irrelevance of the MM Dividend Irrelevance Theorem." *Journal of Financial Economics* 79:2, 293–315.

DeAngelo, Harry, Linda DeAngelo, and René Stulz. 2006. "Dividend Policy and the Earned/Contributed Capital Mix: A Test of the Life-Cycle Theory." *Journal of Financial Economics* 81:2, 227–254.

DeAngelo, Harry, Linda DeAngelo, and René Stulz. 2008. "Seasoned Equity Offerings, Market Timing, and the Corporate Lifecycle." Working Paper, University of California, Los Angeles.

Denis, David J., and Igor Osobov. 2008. "Why Do Firms Pay Dividends? International Evidence on the Determinants of Dividend Policy." *Journal of Financial Economics* 89:1, 62–82.

Fama, Eugene G., and Kenneth R. French. 2001. "Disappearing Dividends: Changing Firm Characteristics or Lower Propensity to Pay?" *Journal of Financial Economics* 60:1, 3–43.

Grabowski, Henry G., and Dennis C. Mueller. 1975. "Life Cycle Effects on Corporate Returns on Retentions." *The Review of Economics and Statistics* 20:3, 199–219.

Grullon, Gustavo, Roni Michaely, and Bhaskaran Swaminathan. 2002. "Are Dividend Changes a Sign of Firm Maturity?" *Journal of Business* 75:3, 387–424.

Guay, Wayne, and Jarrad Harford. 2000. "The Cash Flow Permanence and Information Content of Dividend Increases versus Repurchases." *Journal of Financial Economics* 57:3, 385–415.

Jagannathan, Murali, Clifford P. Stephens, and Michael S. Weisbach. 2000. "Financial Flexibility and the Choice between Dividends and Stock Repurchases." *Journal of Financial Economics* 57:3, 355–384.

Jensen, Michael C. 1986. "Agency Cost of Free Cash Flow, Corporate Finance, and Takeovers." *American Economic Review* 76:2, 323–329.

Jensen, Michael C., and William H. Meckling. 1976. "Theory of the Firm: Managerial Behavior, Agency Costs and Ownership Structure." *Journal of Financial Economics* 3:4, 305–360.

Knight, Frank H. 1921. *Risk, Uncertainty, and Profit*. New York: Hart, Schaffner, and Mary.

Mueller, Dennis C. 1972. "A Life Cycle Theory of the Firm," *Journal of Industrial Economics* 20:3, 199–219.

Myers, Stewart C., and Nicholas S. Majluf. 1984. "Corporate Financing and Investment Decisions When Firms Have Information that Investors Do Not Have." *Journal of Financial Economics* 13:2, 187–221.

Schumpeter, Joseph A. 1934. *The Theory of Economic Development*. Cambridge, MA: Harvard University Press.

Skinner, Douglas. 2007. "The Evolving Relation between Earnings, Dividends, and Stock Repurchases." *Journal of Financial Economics* 87:3, 582–609.

von Eije, J. Henk, and William L. Megginson. 2008. "Dividends and Share Repurchases in the European Union." *Journal of Financial Economics* 89:2, 347–374.

ABOUT THE AUTHORS

Laarni T. Bulan is an assistant professor of finance at the International Business School and the Economics Department of Brandeis University. She teaches the core MA/MBA course in international corporate finance. Her research is in the area of empirical corporate finance and covers topics in dividend policy, capital structure, executive compensation, corporate governance, and real options. Her current interests also include the effects of deregulation on corporate governance and on corporate financial policies. She holds a Ph.D. in finance from Columbia University.

Narayanan Subramanian is a senior manager at Cornerstone Research, an economic consultancy firm, where he specializes in projects involving financial economics. He has consulted on cases related to initial public offerings, employee stock options, and market efficiency, among other issues. Before joining Cornerstone Research in the fall of 2005, he was an assistant professor at the International Business School of Brandeis University. He has published articles in peer-reviewed journals on topics including executive compensation, dividend policy, risk, and intrapreneurship. He holds a Ph.D. in economics from Brown University.

CHAPTER 13

The Catering Theory of Dividends

MARGOT DE ROOIJ
Researcher

LUC RENNEBOOG
Professor of Corporate Finance, Tilburg University

INTRODUCTION

Black (1976, p. 8) argues, "The harder we look at the dividend picture, the more it seems like a puzzle, with pieces that just do not fit together." Explaining dividend policy has been one of the most controversial topics in corporate finance. According to Allen and Michaely (2003), the word *policy* indicates that dividends do not develop in a random and arbitrary manner and that some consistency over time is present. After the irrelevance proposition of Miller and Modigliani (1961), in which dividend policies are equivalent and no policy can increase shareholders' wealth in perfect capital markets, academics developed alternative theories for dividends in imperfect markets. Today, no consensus exists among researchers on the subject of dividend policy. The popular view is that the issue of dividend payment is important (Ross, Westerfield, and Jaffe, 2002), as evidenced by the amount of money involved and the repeated nature of the dividend payout decision. In addition, Allen and Michaely note that dividend decisions interact with investment and financial decisions.

Although many studies examine dividend policy, few examine the time-series trends. Fama and French (2001) document evidence of a major time-series shift in dividend policy of U.S. industrial companies. Specifically, they report a meaningful decline in the fraction of firms that pay dividends. They find that while 66.5 percent of listed firms paid dividends in 1978 only 20.8 percent did so in 1999. Fama and French show that this dramatic decline is due in part to changing firm characteristics of typical publicly traded companies. Fueled by new listings, the population of publicly traded companies changed to smaller firms with low (or negative) profits and high-growth opportunities, which are less likely to pay dividends. However,

The authors are grateful for useful comments from Jacob Flori, Filip De Monte, Marc Goergen, Marina Martynova, Greg Trojanowski, and Chendi Zhang.

even after controlling for this effect, firms have become less likely to pay dividends. Fama and French call the phenomenon of a lower propensity to pay the disappearing dividends. The dynamics of dividends are apparently different in continental Europe because there is less evidence of reduced dividends and dividend policy is less rigid than in Anglo-American countries. For instance, Goergen, Renneboog, and da Silva (2005) show that the dividend policy of German firms closely follows the changes in cash flows.

Baker and Wurgler (2002) investigate the causes for the declining propensity to pay dividends in the United States. They examine various explanations based on agency costs, asymmetric information, the issue of management stock options, tax-code awareness, dividend clienteles, and catering to investor sentiment. Their results suggest that catering incentives best explain the fluctuations in the propensity to pay dividends. According to this catering theory, firms cater to irrational investor demand for the categories of dividend-paying and growth stocks to boost share prices above their fundamental values (Baker, Ruback, and Wurgler, 2005). According to this behavioral finance motive, investors' psychological characteristics play a role in financial markets, and the irrational behavior of investors bounds the effectiveness of arbitrage. Likewise, managerial financing and investment decisions are rational responses to clients and markets.

Long (1978) gives some early indication that the catering motive can help to explain dividend policy. He finds that Citizen Utilities' shareholders price cash-dividend share classes differently from stock-dividend share classes, although these payouts are of equal value as set down in an amendment to the corporate charter. In addition, the relative price of the two types of shares fluctuates substantially over time. Poterba (1986) and Hubbard and Michaely (1997) conclude that traditional dividend theories cannot explain these fluctuations. These findings imply that cash dividends are an important characteristic to investors and introduce the possibility of a catering motivation for paying cash dividends.

This chapter surveys the literature on the catering theory of dividends as initiated by Baker and Wurgler (2004a) and has the following organization. The next section presents the basic model underlying the catering theory of dividends followed by extensions to the basic catering model based on dividend levels and frequency. Next, the chapter investigates the role of catering in relation to other dividend theories such as signaling and agency, and it then presents summaries of previous empirical evidence on the catering theory. The final section presents the conclusions.

BAKER AND WURGLER'S CATERING THEORY OF DIVIDENDS

Baker and Wurgler (2004a) develop a catering theory of dividends. Their empirical model is a discrete model in which investors categorize firms as dividend payers or non–dividend payers. Baker and Wurgler describe their model with the help of three essential assumptions. First, they argue that for psychological or institutional reasons, investor demand for dividend-paying stocks is uninformed and varies over time. Second, they assume that Modigliani-Miller style arbitrage fails to prevent this investor demand from driving apart the price of dividend payers and non–dividend payers. Third, Baker and Wurgler hold that managers rationally cater to investor demand for dividends by paying dividends when investors place a premium on dividend-paying stocks. In other words, non-dividend-paying firms initiate dividends when the shares of existing dividend-paying firms are trading at a premium relative to those of non-dividend-paying firms, in an attempt to increase their market values. Firms omit dividends when the shares of existing dividend payers are trading at a discount. As a result, prices of dividend-paying firms relative to non-dividend-paying firms (the so-called dividend premium) are high in high-demand years and low in low-demand years.

The Model

This section summarizes the catering theory of dividends as proposed by Baker and Wurgler (2004a). A firm has Q shares outstanding. At the terminal date $t = 1$, the firm pays a liquidating distribution of $V = F + \varepsilon$. F is the expected fundamental value of the firm, and ε is a standard normal random variable with mean zero. At $t = 0$, the manager chooses to pay an interim dividend per share of $d \in \{0, 1\}$. As there is a cost related to the issuance of dividends (c), the dividend payment reduces the firm's liquidation value by $d(1 + c)$.

There are two types of investors, category investors and arbitrageurs, who have aggregate risk tolerance per period of respectively γ and γ^A. Category investors care about whether firms pay dividends. As in the study of Barberis and Shleifer (2003), this type of investor places dividend payers in different investment categories. Baker and Wurgler give several motives that could explain the demand for the category of dividend payers. One motive involves the existence of dividend clienteles as developed by Black and Scholes (1974) and Allen, Bernardo, and Welch (2000), while another concerns the idea that dividend payers are less risky. Dividends are more salient signals when investors use them to infer management plans or to combat self-control problems as proposed by Thaler and Shefrin (1981) and Shefrin and Statman (1984).

Baker and Wurgler (2004a) model the demand of category investors through irrational expectations about the terminal distribution. They assume that category investors do not recognize c and misestimate the mean (not the variance) of the liquidating distributions of payers (V^D) and nonpayers (V^G). The arbitrageurs unbiasedly expect the liquidating distribution to be F if the firm does not pay a dividend and $F - cd$ if it pays a dividend. With limited arbitrage due to the risk aversion of arbitrageurs (γ^A), the misperceptions of category investors cause the relative prices of payers and nonpayers to differ.

At $t = 0$, demand from investor group $k(k = C$ for category investors, $k = A$ for arbitrageurs), where $E^C(V) = V(d; D)$ and $E^A(V) = F - cd$ (Li and Lie, 2006, p. 296) equals

$$D_0^k = \gamma^k \left(E^k(V) - P_0 \right). \tag{13.1}$$

Filling in the market-clearing condition $D_0^C + D_0^A = Q$ leads to prices of dividend payers (P^D) and growth firms (P^G) (Baker and Wurgler, 2004a, p. 1129).

$$P_0 = \begin{cases} P_0^D \equiv \dfrac{\gamma}{\gamma + \gamma^A} V^D + \dfrac{\gamma^A}{\gamma + \gamma^A}(F - c) - \dfrac{Q}{\gamma + \gamma^A} & (13.2) \\[3ex] P_0^G \equiv \dfrac{\gamma}{\gamma + \gamma^A} V^G + \dfrac{\gamma^A}{\gamma + \gamma^A} F - \dfrac{Q}{\gamma + \gamma^A} & (13.3) \end{cases}$$

On the basis of the prices, the manager chooses whether to pay dividends.

The manager is risk neutral and cares about the current share price and the value of total distributions, which he or she can influence via the cost c. In this short-run inefficient market, the manager has to decide to maximize either a firm's long-run fundamental value as determined by investment policy or its short-run price as affected by category investor demand and obtained through catering. The decision depends on the manager's horizon (λ) and how much of a trade-off exists between these objectives. The manager's problem is to maximize $\max_d(1 - \lambda)P_0 + \lambda(-dc)$. This results in the solution

$$P_0^D - P_0^G \equiv \frac{\gamma}{\gamma + \gamma^A}(V^D - V^G) - \frac{\gamma^A}{\gamma + \gamma^A}c \geq \left(\frac{\lambda}{1 - \lambda}\right)c. \qquad (13.4)$$

The first term in the middle of Equation 13.4 represents the immediate positive price impact of changing categories between payers and nonpayers. The second term is the immediate negative price impact of the arbitrageurs' recognition of the cost, c. The manager pays a dividend if the premium on dividend payers (the dividend premium) is positive and exceeds the long-run cost, which is the term to the right of the inequality (Equation 13.4). The propensity to pay dividends increases in the dividend premium, decreases in the cost c, decreases in the prevalence of arbitrage, and decreases in the manager's horizon (λ). The announcement effects of dividend initiations are positive and increasing in the dividend premium.

The model can be extended to address the negative announcement effect of omissions, documented by many others such as Healy and Palepu (1998) and Michaely, Thaler, and Womack (1995). This extension introduces former dividend-paying firms. Category investors neglect these stocks and such stocks only attract arbitrageurs, such that the price equals

$$P_0^{FD} = F - \frac{Q}{\gamma^A}. \qquad (13.5)$$

While the decision to initiate dividends is still governed by Equation 13.4, the model with former payers can incorporate the persistence of dividends (the propensity to continue):

$$P_0^D - P_0^{FD} \equiv \frac{\gamma}{\gamma + \gamma^A}\left(V^D - \left(F - \frac{Q}{\gamma^A}\right)\right) - \frac{\gamma^A}{\gamma + \gamma^A}c \geq \left(\frac{\lambda}{1 - \lambda}\right)c. \qquad (13.6)$$

Like the propensity to initiate dividends, the propensity to continue paying dividends increases in the dividend premium and decreases in the cost, c. The new insight is that dividend continuation may be attractive even when dividend initiations are not. If γ^A or c is small and V^D and V^G fall on opposite sides of F, Equation 13.6 is satisfied whenever Equation 13.4 is satisfied. Even if initiating dividends is unattractive, current dividend payers may continue to pay if the price impact of omitting is large. This category also suggests why some firms initiate (reinitiate) dividends even when the dividend premium is negative and why such initiations can still have a positive announcement effect.

The third category of former payers also helps to address the negative announcement effect of dividend omissions. Consider an intermediate time period between $t = 0$ and $t = 1$, in which neglected former payers face a positive probability of being recategorized as growth firms. In this setting, dividend payers may choose to omit a dividend at $t = 0$ even when Equation 13.6 is not satisfied. They suffer a short-run negative announcement effect, but the expected value of being recategorized as a growth firm may be valuable.

Proxies Capturing the Dividend Premium

To measure the difference between market prices of firms with similar investment policies but with different dividend policies, Baker and Wurgler (2004a) define several proxies reflecting the dividend premium. They measure the dividend premium by means of four proxies, which they expect can explain the observed time-series variation in dividend payment.

The first and main proxy (the dividend premium) is based on the market valuations of dividend payers and non–dividend payers: The market-to-book ratio is equal to book assets minus book equity plus market equity divided by book value of assets. Book equity is defined as stockholders' equity minus preferred-stock liquidating value plus balance-sheet deferred taxes and investment tax credit minus postretirement assets. The market equity is stock price times the number of shares outstanding at the end of the calendar year. The ratio is equally or value weighted across dividend payers and nonpayers. The dividend premium (P_t^{D-ND}) is the difference between the log-normally distributed average market-to-book ratio of dividend payers and non–dividend payers:

$$P_t^{D-ND} = \ln\left(\sum_i w_{ti}^d \frac{V_{ti}^d}{A_{ti}^d}\right) - \ln\left(\sum_i w_{ti}^{nd} \frac{V_{ti}^{nd}}{A_{ti}^{nd}}\right) \qquad (13.7)$$

where:

P_t^{D-ND} = Dividend premium in year t,
w_{ti}^d = Weight of firm i in the subset of payers in year t,
V_{ti}^d = Market value of firm i in the subset of payers in year t,
A_{ti}^d = Book value of firm i in the subset of payers in year t,
w_{ti}^{nd} = Weight of firm i in the subset of nonpayers in year t,
V_{ti}^{nd} = Market value of firm i in the subset of nonpayers in year t, and
A_{ti}^{nd} = Book value of firm i in the subset of nonpayers in year t.

Baker and Wurgler (2004a) argue that investor sentiment partially drives the dividend premium. For example, when investors are positive about growth opportunities, they prefer non-dividend-paying stocks, and such a preference drives up the prices of these stocks. When investors seek safety, they will ask for safe dividend-paying stocks, and this preference augments the prices of these stocks.

They use three other proxies. The second proxy is the price difference between Citizens Utilities' cash-dividend and stock-dividend share classes over the period 1962–1989, which are different in form but not in payout. The third proxy is the average three-day announcement effect of recent dividend initiations. The prediction is that if investors like to receive dividends, they will react more positively to dividend initiations, which can be observed by the announcement effect. The fourth proxy is the future excess return of payers over nonpayers. If firms initiate dividends to exploit market mispricing, there will be a negative relationship between this difference and the dividend initiation rate.

Dividend Payment Variables

In the catering model, investors categorize firms on the basis of whether they pay dividends. The following capture the dividend payment dynamics:

$$Initiate_t = \frac{New\ Payers_t}{Nonpayers_{t-1} - Delist\ Nonpayers_t} \tag{13.8}$$

$$Continue_t = \frac{Old\ Payers_t}{Payers_{t-1} - Delist\ Payers_t} \tag{13.9}$$

$$Listpay_t = \frac{List\ Payers_t}{List\ Payers_t + List\ Nonpayers_t} \tag{13.10}$$

The continuation rate is 1 minus the rate at which firms omit dividends. The variables used in the previous equations can be defined as follows:

Payers = Total number of payers
New payers = Number of initiators among last year's nonpayers
Old payers = Number of payers that also paid last year
List payers = Number of payers this year that were not in the sample last year
New nonpayers = Number of firms omitting dividends among last year's payers
Delist payers = Number of last year's payers not in the sample this year

Baker and Wurgler's Empirical Evidence

Dividend Payout

Focusing on firms over the period 1962–2000, Baker and Wurgler (2004a) relate the dividend premium to aggregate levels of dividend initiations and continuations. They report empirical univariate evidence that the first three dividend premium proxies mentioned previously are strongly positively correlated with the rate of dividend initiation. In a multivariate framework that includes these three proxies, only the first proxy of the dividend premium (Equation 13.7) shows a significant, positive relationship. The fourth proxy shows a negative relationship with the initiation rate of dividends, which indicates a relationship between an increase in the dividend-initiation rate and lower future stock returns of dividend payers compared to those of non–dividend payers.

There is a significant, positive relationship between the dividend premium and the continuation rate. Dividend payers are more likely to continue the payment of dividends when their share prices are higher. The reverse is also true: When dividends trade at a discount, dividend payers are more likely to omit the dividend payment. The fourth proxy, future excess return, shows a significant, negative relationship to the continuation rate of dividends.

The results also hold after controlling for the time trend, share repurchases, and several firm characteristics such as firm size, profitability, and investment opportunities. The dividend premium is positively related to the aggregate rate of initiation, continuation, and payment of dividends by newly listed firms.

Baker and Wurgler (2004a) also investigate other sources of time-varying demand for dividend payments. They do not find evidence in support of traditional dividend clienteles resulting from taxes, transaction costs, or institutional investment constraints, as suggested by Black and Scholes (1974). Still, there is a positive relationship between the dividend premium and the closed-end fund discount, a measure of investor sentiment used by Zweig (1973) and Lee, Shleifer, and Thaler (1991). This further substantiates the idea that investor sentiment is the basis for the demand for dividends.

The Propensity to Pay

Baker and Wurgler (2004b) use the methodology of Fama and French (2001) to categorize four trends in the propensity to pay dividends in the period 1963–2000. The first trend during 1963–1967 shows a positive dividend premium that corresponds with an increase in the propensity to pay. During 1968–1970, the premium becomes negative and coincides with the propensity to pay dividends. For 1970–1977, there is a misfit between the dividend premium and the propensity to pay. The authors explain this phenomenon by referring to the dividend controls of the Nixon era, which kept the propensity to pay low in relation to the dividend premium. Finally, 1978 marks the start of the fourth trend that ends in 2000, in which the propensity to pay decreases and the dividend premium becomes and remains negative. Using univariate regressions, Baker and Wurgler find that the dividend premium and changes in the propensity to pay predict the relative returns of dividend-paying and non-dividend-paying stocks.

In addition, Baker and Wurgler (2004b) find evidence consistent with catering from a returns analysis. When dividend initiations prevail relative to dividend omissions, returns on dividend payers are relatively low over the next one to three years and vice versa. This is in line with the idea that relative returns are associated with a real or perceived mispricing driven by investor demand and is consistent with the catering theory of dividends. The authors show that when sentiment for growth stocks is high, dividend premiums are negative and non–dividend payers attract investors. A high premium reflects that investors are attracted to safe dividend payers when sentiment for growth stocks is low. These results suggest that managers cater to investor demand based on investor sentiment.

EXTENSIONS TO THE CATERING THEORY OF DIVIDENDS

Li and Lie (2006) extend the catering theory of dividends by investigating changes in dividend levels in the United States. Ferris, Noronha, and Unlu (2006a) investigate the relationship between dividend payment frequency and catering for the United Kingdom.

Dividend Levels

Li and Lie (2006) indicate that the managers in the Baker and Wurgler (2004a) model can only decide whether to pay dividends but cannot decide how much to pay. Li and Lie view this as a serious shortcoming, as managers are more often confronted with decisions about changes in dividend levels than decisions about dividend initiations and omissions. Using a sample of U.S. firms that increased or decreased dividends between 1963 and 2000, they find that both the decision to change the dividend and the magnitude of the change are related to the premium that the capital market places on dividends. The magnitude of dividend increases (decreases) shows a positive (negative) relationship with the dividend premium. As share repurchases are significantly and negatively related to the dividend premium, Li and Lie state that firms increasing cash payouts will augment the dividends when the dividend premium is high and repurchase shares when the dividend premium is low.

Although Baker and Wurgler (2004a) do not find a statistically significant relationship between the dividend premium and the average announcement effect of recent dividend initiations, Li and Lie (2006) show that the stock market's reaction to dividend changes depends on the dividend premium. The evidence that the announcement returns for dividend increases are positively related to the dividend premium and that the announcement returns for dividend decreases are negatively related confirms this idea. The catering model assumes that the force driving catering incentives are managers who intend to maximize their firms' market values. Hence, for the catering theory to be valid, the capital market must reward managers for taking the demand for dividends to heart when making decisions about dividend policy. Thus, the announcement effect is an important measure to validate the catering theory.

When comparing the results of Baker and Wurgler (2004a) with those of Li and Lie (2006), decisions about dividend initiations and dividend omissions are clearly more sensitive to the dividend premium than decisions about dividend increases and decreases. This is in line with the study of Lie (2005), who confirms that the average announcement returns of dividend omissions are larger than the average announcement returns of dividend decreases. Li and Lie explain this result with the help of the catering theory: Managers are more likely to acknowledge the dividend premium if the reward (in terms of the market valuation of a firm's equity) is higher.

In contrast to the findings of Li and Lie (2006), Baker and Wurgler (2004a) find no significant correlation between dividend increases and the dividend premium when controlling for firm characteristics. When they control for the dividend yield directly, the effect of the dividend premium on the dividend initiation rate is even larger. Baker and Wurgler view the lack of a correlation between dividend changes and dividend premium as evidence of the catering effect. Li and Lie, however, show that investor sentiment is similar by level of dividend payment, and so they interpret the significant relation they find between dividend payout levels and the dividend premium as evidence of catering.

Hoberg and Prabhala (2006) challenge the findings of the catering theory of dividends. In line with Baker and Wurgler (2004a), Hoberg and Prabhala do not find a significant relationship between dividend increases and the dividend premium for U.S. firms over the period 1963–2000. They argue that the difference in methodologies employed explains the contrary results. Hoberg and Prabhala point out that the studies of Fama and French (2001), Baker and Wurgler (2004a), and Denis and Osobov (2005) use the two-step Fama-MacBeth method to capture panel data issues such as clustering and correlation. When applying the specification that assumes independence of observations as used by Li and Lie (2006), Hoberg and Prabhala (2006) find a significant relationship between dividend changes and the dividend premium, but the significance of this result disappears when they adjust the standard errors for clustering by year.

The Frequency of Dividend Payments

Using a sample of 21 civil law countries and 11 common law countries over the period 1996–2003, Ferris et al. (2006a) research the structure and determinants of the dividend-payment frequency. The dividend-payment frequency premium is higher in civil law countries than in common law countries. This implies that dividend payments are more important to investors who live in civil law countries, which are characterized by lower investor protection in which managers may be more inclined to expropriate earnings for private purposes. Ferris et al. conclude that catering incentives are present and influence the frequency of dividend payments.

THE ROLE OF CATERING IN EXPLAINING OTHER DIVIDEND THEORIES

Several theories, such as those based on taxes and clienteles, asymmetric information and signaling, and agency costs are applied to dividend policy. The following provides a discussion of the studies relating one of these theories to the catering theory of dividends.

Asymmetric Information and Signaling

In a recent study, Li and Zhao (2008) find a significant negative relationship between asymmetric information and dividend policy for U.S. firms over the period 1983–2003. They also recognize that catering could explain dividend policy and include this variable in their model that estimates the decision to pay dividends. When they include year dummies and a firm-risk variable in their model, the parameter estimate of the dividend premium is significantly negative. When they exclude the year dummies and firm-risk variable, the coefficient on the dividend premium becomes significant and positive. This corroborates the idea that the dividend premium captures the temporal variation in market sentiment.

Ali and Urcan (2006) study the relationship between dividend increases and unexpected earnings changes for U.S. firms over the period 1963–2000. According to the dividend signaling theory, dividend increases reveal new information to the capital markets about higher profitability (see, e.g., Bhattacharya, 1979; John and Williams, 1985; Miller and Rock, 1985). When taking into account the catering effect of dividends, firms will increase dividends as a response to a high-dividend premium, even when they do not expect future earnings to be higher. When controlling for catering incentives, Ali and Urcan find that a significant, positive relationship exists between dividend increases and unexpected changes in future earnings in low-dividend premium years. This finding is in line with the signaling theory of dividends. However, the relationship between dividend increases and unexpected changes in future earnings is insignificant in high-dividend-premium years, which is consistent with the notion that managers cater to investor demand for dividends.

Using a sample of 11,730 U.S. firms, Bulan, Subramanian, and Tanlu (2007) examine the timing of and differences in dividend payments and initiations over the life cycle of a firm. Contrary to the predictions of the signaling theory about dividend initiations, no significant improvement occurs in the profitability and investment opportunities around dividend initiations. Also, there is no significant decline in risk around dividend initiations. Therefore, alternative explanations must exist for the positive announcements returns of initiations.

Using the catering theory of dividends, Bulan et al. (2007) investigate whether investor sentiment can trigger these positive returns. In contrast to Baker and Wurgler (2004a), who study the aggregate rate of initiations including resumptions in dividend payments by old dividend payers, Bulan et al. focus on firm-specific characteristics that influence dividend initiation decisions. When all other firm characteristics are equal, they show that companies are more likely to initiate dividends when the dividend premium level is high. Using hazard regressions, they also document the effect of changes in the dividend premium on the likelihood of dividend initiation. Their evidence on changes is weaker than that on levels. Bulan et al. contend that a combination of the maturity and catering theory can explain the timing of dividend initiations. Mature firms, characterized by a high level of profitability and low growth rates, show a higher propensity to initiate dividends. A high-dividend premium will give even more rise to dividend initiations.

Agency Models

Denis and Osobov (2005) find a declining propensity to pay dividends in Canada, the United Kingdom, Germany, France, and Japan. They argue that the dividend premium may also be viewed as a measure of the relative growth opportunities of dividend payers and non–dividend payers. When the dividend premium is high, growth opportunities for dividend payers are better relative to those of non–dividend payers. When the dividend premium for dividend payers is low relative to non–dividend payers, the agency cost theory hypothesizes that non–dividend payers are less likely to initiate dividends. Denis and Osobov fail to reject the catering theory, indicating that the evidence is for all cases consistent with an agency cost explanation for dividends.

EVIDENCE FROM EMPIRICAL STUDIES

In addition to the studies that clearly focus on specific dividend theories to explain dividend policy, several other studies investigate the catering theory of dividends. These studies, using samples of U.S., U.K., European, and cross-country firms, show mixed evidence for the catering theory as proposed by Baker and Wurgler (2004a). Table 13.1 presents a summary of such studies.

U.S. Evidence

Hoberg and Prabhala (2005, 2006) argue that the catering theory is not the right theory to explain disappearing and reappearing dividends. Using the sample and methodology of Fama and French (2001), Hoberg and Prabhala find that neo-classical finance variables such as risk, cash flows, and information influence the dividend premium. In particular, idiosyncratic risk significantly explains the propensity to pay dividends, and it accounts for about a third of the cross-sectional variance in the models explaining the disappearing dividends. There is evidence of a catering effect, but it disappears when controlling for risk. Hoberg and Prabhala (2006) maintain that the dividend premium in Baker and Wurgler (2004a) measures the risk differential between dividend payers and non–dividend payers. In summary, because all variables give rise to varying prices for reasons other than behavioral ones, this evidence calls into question the catering view of firms' dividend policies. In contrast, using a sample with 11,730 U.S. firm-year observations over the period 1963–2001, Bulan et al. (2007) find that the dividend premium still affects the propensity to initiate dividends, even after controlling for idiosyncratic risk.

Hsieh and Wang (2006) study the determinants of the trends in aggregate corporate payout policy for U.S. industrial firms. As part of their research, they investigate whether investor preferences influence payout. In three out of six regressions, they find a significantly positive relation between the dividend premium and the payout ratio.

In a logistic regression using 5,875 U.S. observations from 1979 to 1998, Kale, Kini, and Payne (2006) consider several major theories of dividends: residual, tax, transaction costs, clientele, agency, and signaling. In varying degrees, they find evidence for most theories. They also investigate the effect of the catering theory of dividends. Supporting the catering theory of Baker and Wurgler (2004a), they disclose a positive relationship between the dividend premium and the decision to initiate dividends.

Julio and Ikenberry (2004) find a decline in the number of U.S. industrial firms paying dividends. They discuss five basic causes of this change in dividend policy, including one based on the catering theory of dividends. Although some findings indicate that firms respond to investor demand for dividends, their results show limited empirical support for the catering theory after correcting for firm size

Table 13.1 Overview of Empirical Studies Investigating the Catering Theory of Dividends

Study	Country	Sample Period	Focus	Measure	Dependent Variable	Independent Variables	Supports Catering
Panel A. U.S. and U.K. Studies							
Baker and Wurgler (2004a)	U.S.	1962–2000	DI, DC, NL	BW (EW/VW, BV)	1. DIR, DCR, NLR 2. DIR, DCR, NLR 3. PTI, PTC, PTL	1. P_{t-1}^{D-ND} 2. M/B, DY, Tax, YR 3. NYP, M/B, dA, E/A '	Yes
Baker and Wurgler (2004b)	U.S.	1963–2000	PTP	BW (EW/VW, BV)	1. dPTP 2. $r_D - r_{ND}$	1. P_{t-1}^{D-ND}, M/B, Nixon 2. P_{t-1}^{D-ND}, dPTP	Yes
Julio and Ikenberry (2004)	U.S.	1984–1999	DL	BW (VW, BV)	n.a.	N.A.	No
Hoberg and Prabhala (2005, 2006)	U.S.	1963–2000	PTP	BW (VW, BV)	1. dPTP 2. dPTI 3. AR 4. dDL, dE 5. dPTP	1. P_{t-1}^{D-ND}, AG, E/A, NYP, M/B, Risk, Nixon 2. P_{t-1}^{D-ND}, AG, E/A, NYP, M/B, Risk, Nixon 3. P_{t-1}^{D-ND}, Nixon 4. P_{t-1}^{D-ND}, Nixon 5. P_{t-1}^{D-ND}, HMLβ, SMBβ, MKTβ, Risk, Nixon	No
Ali and Urcan (2006)	U.S.	1963–2000	DI	BW (VW, BV)	1. $((E_1-E_0)/BV_{-1})$	1. P_{t-1}^{D-ND}, dDL, DFE, $((E_1-E_0)/BV_{-1})$	Yes
Kale, Kini, and Payne (2006)	U.S.	1979–1998	DI	BW (VW, BV)	1. DI 2. DY	1. P_t^{D-ND}, M/B, CX/TA, RD/TA, Debt, βA, Resstd, OI, UP, α, Undrep, Probseo, Own, Pbalown, Turn, Age, NYP, SR 2. P_t^{D-ND}, M/B, CX/TA, RD/TA, Debt, βA, Resstd, OI, UP, α, Undrep, Probseo, Own, Pbalown, Turn, Age, NYP, SR	Yes

Li and Lie (2006)	U.S.	1963–2000	Dinc, Ddec	BW (VW, BV)	1. Dinc, Ddec, SR 2. dDiv/S 3. AR	1. P_{t-1}^{D-ND}, DY, Mrktcap, Debt, Cash, M/B, OI 2. P_t^{D-ND}, DY, Mrktcap, Debt, Cash, M/B, OI 3. P_t^{D-ND}, DY, Mrktcap, dDL	Yes
Bulan, Subramanian, and Tanlu (2007)	U.S.	1963–2001	DI	BW (EW, BV)	1. DI 2. AR	1. P_t^{D-ND}, TA, SG, CX/TA, Cash, ROA, M/B, MKTβ, SMBβ, HMLβ 2. P_t^{D-ND}, DY, TA, SG, CX/TA, Cash, ROA, M/B, MKTβ, SMBβ, HMLβ, SD, SR	Inconclusive
Li and Zhao (2007)	U.S.	1983–2003	DP	BW (VW, BV)	1. DP, DIR, DInc, DL	1. P_t^{D-ND}, E/A, M/B, AG, NYP, FE, FD, SRa, Own	Inconclusive
Renneboog and Trojanowski (2005)	U.K.	1992–1998	PP	Tobin's Q	1. DP	1. MrktVal, ROA, AG, Debt, Own	No
Ferris, Sen, and Yui (2006)	U.K.	1988–2002	PTP	BW (EW, BV)	1. dPTP	1. P_{t-1}^{D-ND}, time, tax	Yes
Panel B. Studies from Other Countries and Regions							
Neves (2006)	9 Eurozone countries (Germany, France, the Netherlands, Spain, Belgium, Portugal, Ireland, Austria, Italy)	1986–2003	DL	Error term of market model	1. DL	1. P_t^{D-ND}, FCF, Debt, OI, Tang, TA	Yes

(*Continued*)

Table 13.1 (*Continued*)

Study	Country	Sample Period	Focus	Measure	Dependent Variable	Independent Variables	Supports Catering
Savov and Weber (2006)	Germany	1982–2003	Dinc	BW (EW/VW, MV)	1. Dinc	1. P_t^{D-ND}, size, dA, M/B, E/A, E_{t-1}/A_{t-1}, –EBIT, Debt, CX/TA, Div_{t-1}/TA_{t-1}	No
Dennis and Osobov (2005, 2007)	Canada, U.K., Germany, France, and Japan	1989–2002	DI, DC, NL, PTP	BW (EW, BV)	1. DIR, DCR, NLR 2. dPTP	1. P_{t-1}^{D-N} 2. $P_{t-1}^{D-ND\ D}$	Inconclusive
Ferris, Noronha, and Unlu (2006)	21 civil law countries, 11 common law countries	1996–2003	DPF	BW (EW, BV)	1. DPF	1. P_{t-1}^{D-ND}, OI, Div/E, TA, M/B, AG, ROA	Yes
Twu and Shen (2006)	31 countries	1998–2000	PTP	BW (VW, BV)	1. DPP 2. PTP	1. P_t^{D-ND} 2. P_{t-1}^{D-ND}, Mrktcap, OwnCon, Protect, Tax	Yes
Renneboog and de Rooij (2008)	The Netherlands	1993–2006	DI, DC, NL, PTP, DL, Dinc, Ddec.	BW (VW/EW, MV/BV)	1. PTP 2. PTI 3. PTC 4. PTL	1. Size, Tobin's Q, Asset growth, ROA 2. Size, Tobin's Q, Asset growth, ROA 3. Size, Tobin's Q, Asset growth, ROA 4. Size, Tobin's Q, Asset growth, ROA	Yes Yes Yes Yes
von Eije and Megginson (2008)	15 European Union countries (U.K., Denmark, Sweden, France, Italy, Spain, Greece, Portugal, Belgium, the Netherlands, Luxembourg, Germany, Austria, Iceland, Finland)	1989–2003	DP	BW (EW, BV)	1. PTP 2. DL	1. dP_T^{D-ND}, MrktVal, E, dA, Stds, Inc, Law, dLev, Euro, Yr 2. dP_T^{D-ND}, MrktVal, E, dA, Stds, Inc, Law, dLev, Euro, Yr	

This table provides an overview of empirical studies that investigate the catering theory of dividends and shows only the basic models of these studies that include a proxy for the catering effect of dividends. *Focus* indicates the aspect of dividend policy to which the paper is devoted. *Measure* reflects the proxy that is used to capture the catering effect of dividends. The table uses the following notations:

Focus: DI, dividend initiation; DC, dividend continuation; NL, new listing; PTP, propensity to pay; DL, dividend level; Dinc, dividend increase; Ddec, dividend decrease; DP, dividend policy; PP, payout policy; DPF, dividend payment frequency.

Measure catering effect: BW, the Baker and Wurgler dividend premium; EW, equally weighted; VW, value weighted; BV, book value weighted; MV, market value weighted.

Dependent variable: DIR, dividend initiation rate; DCR, dividend continuation rate; NLR, new list rate; PTI, propensity to initiate; PTC, propensity to continue; PTL, propensity to list; dPTP, change in propensity to pay; $r_D - r_{ND}$, future excess returns of dividend payers and nonpayers; dPTI, change in propensity to initiate; AR, abnormal announcement return; dDL, change in dividend level; dE, change in earnings level; $\frac{E_1 - E_0}{BV_{-1}}$, future earnings changes; DI, dividend initiation; DY, dividend yield; Dinc, dividend increase; Ddec, dividend decrease; SR, share repurchase; dDiv/S, absolute changes in dividend standardized by preannouncement stock price; DP, dividend payer; DL, dividend level; DPF, dividend payment frequency; DPP, dividend payer percentage; PTP, propensity to pay.

Independent variables: P_t^{D-ND}, dividend premium; M/B, market-to-book; DY, dividend yield; Tax, tax law indicators; YR, year; NYP, NYSE percentile; dA, change assets; E/A, earnings before interest and taxes standardized by total assets; Nixon, Nixon era control; dPTP, change in propensity to pay; AG, asset growth; Risk, idiosyncratic risk; HMLβ, firm-specific exposure to the HML risk factor; SMBβ, firm-specific exposure to the SMB risk factor; MKTβ, firm-specific exposure to the market risk factor; dDL, change in dividend level; DFE, deviation profitability from expected value; $\frac{E_0 - E_{-1}}{BV_{-1}}$, past earnings changes; TA, total assets; SG, sales growth; CX/TA, capital expenditures standardized by total assets; Cash, cash standardized by total assets; ROA, return on assets; SP, special dividend; SR, share repurchase; RD/TA, R&D expenditures standardized by total assets; Debt, debt standardized by total assets; βA, βequity of the firm's stock divided by 1 plus the debt-equity ratio; Resstd, MSE of the market model; OI, operating income standardized by total assets; UP, return to the IPO on the offer date; α, fraction of firm equity retained by the original owner in the IPO; Undrep, updated IPO underwriter reputation measure; Probseo, probability that the firm issues equity in hw two years following the observaton year; Own, institutional ownership; Pbalown, predicted value of the percentage of the firm's equity owned by balanced mutual funds; Turn, ratio of annual trading volume to shares outstanding; Age, one plus the number of years elapsed between the observation year and the IPO year; Mrktcap, market capitalization; FE, forecast error; FD, forecast dispersion; SRa, share repurchase amount; MrktVal, market value; Time, time trends; FCF, free cash flow; Tang, tangible fixed assets; E_{t-1}/A_{t-1}, lagged value of earnings before interest and taxes standardized by total assets; Div_{t-1}/TA_{t-1}, dividends standardized by total assets; dP_t^{D-ND}, change in dividend premium; E, earnings; Stds, standard deviation of net income related to actual annual sales; Inc, year of incorporation; Law, common versus civil law indicator; dLev, change in leverage ratio; Euro, Euro country dummy; Div/E, dividends standardized by earnings; OwnCon, ownership concentration; Protect, investor protection.

and age. Banerjee, Gatchev, and Spindt (2005) explain the declining propensity to pay dividends in the United States by an increase in market liquidity. The idea is that dividend payments allow investors to cash out and avoid transaction costs at the same time. They find evidence consistent with the hypothesis that firms cater (possibly through market valuation) to investors' liquidity preferences. Bulan et al. (2007) affirm that dividend initiations are more likely when market illiquidity is higher, but the change in illiquidity is not a predictor of dividend initiations.

Fenn and Liang (2001) show a relationship between the declining propensity to pay and the growth in the number of management stock options in the United States. As the value of management stock options is negatively related to the payment of dividends, options will reduce the demand for dividend payments, as indicated by Lambert, Lanen, and Larcker (1989). Consistent with the findings of Fenn and Liang, dividend initiations are less likely when the number of management stock options is higher, although the change in management stock options is not a significant predictor of initiations. Baker and Wurgler (2002) do not find evidence that the number of management stock options leads to a decline in the propensity to pay dividends. However, the growth in the number of stock options may have helped spread the declining propensity to pay after it had already started. When controlling for stock options, Bulan et al. (2007) still report evidence that the likelihood of dividend initiation is higher for mature firms facing a high dividend premium.

U.K. Evidence

Renneboog and Trojanowski (2005) examine the payout policy of both dividends and share repurchases of firms listed on the London Stock Exchange during the 1990s. Although they do not specifically test the catering theory, one of their robustness checks is the one-year lagged difference in Tobin's Q between dividend payers and non–dividend payers, which is a proxy for the dividend premium. Given that this proxy is negative, they de facto disclose some evidence against the catering theory of dividends.

Ferris, Sen, and Yui (2006b) demonstrate that the percentage of firms paying dividends in the United Kingdom declined from 75.9 percent to 54.5 percent over the period 1988–2001. As Smith and Watts (1992), Gaver and Gaver (1993), and Barclay, Smith, and Watts (1995) argue that firm size, profitability, and investment opportunities determine dividend policies, Ferris et al. control for these factors. They still find evidence of a declining propensity to pay. The reason for the decline is due to neither a tax effect nor the substitution of dividends by share repurchases. The authors contend that a shift in catering incentives most likely explains the changes in dividend policy. However, Denis and Osobov (2008) show that much variation exists in the dividend premium over the years 1995–2000 in the Ferris et al. (2006b) study and that the last two years of their sample period drive the conclusion that catering incentives play a role. A decreasing propensity to pay with a coinciding reduction in the dividend premium only occurs in 2001 and 2002. Therefore, Denis and Osobov argue that only limited evidence exists favoring the catering theory in the United Kingdom.

European Evidence

Neves (2006) studies the catering theory of dividends for Eurozone countries over the period 1986–2003. Using a new dividend model that includes a firm-level variable that proxies for catering, she finds evidence consistent with the catering theory of dividends after controlling for characteristics such as free cash flow, leverage, earnings, tangible fixed assets, and size. In addition, she examines the interaction effects between several firm characteristics and catering. Investor sentiment has a positive impact on dividend payout only for firms with a considerable amount of liquid assets. In firms with low liquid assets, she finds no evidence of catering. As previously discussed, dividends convey information about a firm's prospects. Neves finds that investors' preferences for dividend payouts only positively influence the payout ratios of firms with valuable investment opportunities. In such firms, investors have strong expectations about receiving higher dividends. Firms with a higher level of free cash flows, which are more prone to overinvestment, cater more strongly to investors' preferences for dividends.

Examining the dividend policy of 15 European Union firms over 1989–2003, von Eije and Megginson (2008) argue that characteristics such as firm age, size, and having headquarters in a common law country significantly increase the likelihood that dividends are paid and the amount of dividends paid. The catering variable's coefficient in the regressions measuring the propensity to pay varies over different periods and is only significantly positive over the period 1994–1998. In the regressions estimating the amount of dividends paid, the catering variable always has a positive sign but is only significant during the period 1989–1993.

Savov and Weber (2006) examine the determinants of dividend policy in Germany. Their models show negative coefficients for the value-weighted dividend premium and positive ones for the equally weighted measures, but both are insignificant. As the dividend premium may present the expected growth of the company, they run a regression controlling for the current growth rate. The coefficients of the dividend premium are negative and remain statistically insignificant. The authors argue that differences in German and U.S. corporate governance regimes may cause this finding.

La Porta, Lopez-de-Silanes, Shleifer, and Vishny (2000a) report that minority shareholders in civil law countries suffer from a reduced level of investor protection compared to minority shareholders located in common law countries. For investors in civil law firms, dividend payments are of greater importance because they reflect another dimension of their ability to extract cash from management in a less protective environment. Denis and Osobov (2005) find weak evidence of catering in common law countries. For civil law countries, the coefficients on the dividend premium are opposite from the predictions of the catering theory of dividends. In contrast, these coefficients are consistent with an agency cost explanation of dividend policy.

According to Renneboog and Szilagyi (2007), shareholder power is curbed in the majority of Dutch-listed firms because of the existence of the structured corporate regime (which transfers most shareholder power, e.g., approval of the accounts, to the supervisory board), priority or preference shares and other antitakeover mechanisms, and certificates (which strip the voting power of shares). In this context, an interesting topic to investigate is whether firms cater for investor sentiment by adopting a specific dividend policy. Renneboog and de Rooij (2008) show that the value-weighted dividend premium is positively related to dividend initiations and continuations even after controlling for possible agency problems (proxied by size, investment opportunities, and profitability). This relationship is still upheld when shareholder power is substantially reduced (as in the cases mentioned previously). Renneboog and de Rooij argue that firms initiate dividend catering to compensate shareholders for the fact that they have few rights.

Cross-Country Evidence

Institutional variables such as taxation, transaction costs, and institutional investment constraints can motivate dividend clienteles. Therefore, Twu and Shen (2006) examine whether dividend premiums hinge on the institutional framework. They claim that institutional variables can alter the weight that managers put on dividend premiums when deciding about dividend policy. Twu and Shen examine the following four institutional variables:

1. *Capital market development*: Dividend payments enable a firm to obtain favorable financing terms. Managers are stimulated to cater to the demand for dividends when they depend on the capital market for external financing (John and Williams, 1985).
2. *Legal investor protection*: Dividend payments are more likely when the degree of legal investor protection is higher (La Porta et al., 2000a).
3. *Taxes*: Dividends are more informative if the tax rate on dividends is higher, such that managers are more willing to cater to investor demand.
4. *Ownership concentration*: Controlling owners may neglect minority shareholders, which negatively affects the importance of the dividend premium (La Porta et al., 2000b).

The empirical results in Twu and Shen (2006) confirm that the first three variables have a positive effect on the importance of the dividend premium, whereas the fourth variable has a negative impact.

BEYOND CATERING FOR INVESTORS' SENTIMENTS

Split-Capital Closed-End Funds

Gemmill (2005) explores 634 split-capital closed-end funds to test the catering theory of dividends. These funds offer high yields by stripping equity portfolios into separately listed capital and dividend shares. In the late 1990s, issues of split-capital closed-end funds were prevalent in the United Kingdom. The rising stock market in this period caused a decline in the dividend yield, which resulted in the growth of high-yield split-capital closed-end funds. Gemmill maintains that salient features such as the dividend yield cause investor demand. Hence, high-yield fund issues can be regarded as a catering response for the time-varying dividend preferences. This supports the study of Lee et al. (1991), who argue that investors behave irrationally when buying closed-end funds.

Share Repurchases

Whereas Baker and Wurgler (2004a) only examine catering for dividends, Fairchild and Zhang (2005) develop a theoretical model in which a firm decides between catering for investors' preferences for dividends or share repurchases. They show that the size of the repurchasing premium and dividend premium and the managers' time horizon influence catering incentives. Gaspar, Massa, Matos, Patgiri, and Rehman (2004) hypothesize that managers use share buybacks to cater to the preference of short-term investors. They include the dividend premium to check whether this variable influences the use of share buybacks and find a weak negative relation between share buybacks and the dividend premium. According to Bulan et al. (2007), the repurchase probability is negatively related to the dividend premium, which is consistent with the finding of Li and Lie (2006). Dittmar and Dittmar (2004) argue that share repurchases replace dividends. To control for motives that may explain dividend policy, they include a dividend premium to capture time-varying preferences for dividends. Still, the dividend premium is not significant.

Catering Theory of Earnings Management

Lai (2004) uses the catering theory to explain the well-documented analyst bias. He argues that analysts are largely influenced by investors in that analysts cater to investors' beliefs. Employing the essential elements of the Baker and Wurgler (2004a) model, Rajgopal, Shivakumar, and Simpson (2007) develop a catering theory of earnings management. This theory assumes that managers cater to investors' earnings optimism by increasing abnormal accruals. They define abnormal accruals as the difference between normal and total accruals. Total accruals are the difference between income before extraordinary items and net cash flow from operating activities. They compute normal accruals with help of several alternative accruals models. The results suggest that managers recognize that investor attitudes toward earnings surprises change over time such that managers can cater to these shifts in attitudes.

WHY DO INVESTORS' PREFERENCES FOR DIVIDENDS CHANGE OVER TIME?

With evidence supporting catering incentives as an explanation for dividend payout, the question as to why investor demand changes over time still remains unsolved. Shefrin and Statman (1984) extend the work by Thaler and Shefrin (1981) and develop the behavioral life cycle theory of dividends. This theory relies on psychological reasons such as regret aversion, mental accounting, prospect theory, and self-control problems to explain why investors prefer dividends over capital gains. These elements could vary over time, leading to changing investor demand.

Baker and Wurgler (2004a) argue that the dividend premium reflects the preference for safe dividend payers over risky non-dividend-paying growth firms. These preferences rise in times when markets decline and fall when markets grow. Fuller and Goldstein (2003) investigate whether investors prefer dividend-paying stocks to non-dividend-paying stocks in market downturns. They show that dividend payers have higher returns than non-dividend payers in declining markets, which can be explained by the fact that investors seek the safety of dividend-paying firms.

CONCLUSIONS

Researchers have proposed many dividend theories about dividend payout decisions. This chapter reviews the catering theory of dividends, which is a recent theory based on investor sentiment. Catering theory stresses the importance of investor sentiment in decisions about dividend policies. Managers cater to investor demand by paying dividends when investors prefer dividend-paying firms and by not paying dividends (or reducing the dividend) when investors prefer non-dividend-paying companies. The dividend premium captures the relative market valuation of dividend payers versus nonpayers.

Michaely et al. (1995) document some evidence of a positive long-run price drift after dividend initiation announcements. If the catering theory of dividends were true, one would expect long-term stock returns to be negative for firms that cater to time the market successfully. This prediction from the catering theory of dividends seems to contradict not only the study of Michaely et al. (1995) but also those of Benartzi, Michaely, and Thaler (1997), Grullon, Michaely, and Swaminathan (2002), and Hoberg and Prabhala (2006), who find a significant, positive price drift after dividend-increase announcements.

The catering theory of dividends assumes that some investors are uninformed. As individuals seem to be more prone to sentiment compared to professionals, one would expect the theory to work better for firms in which individuals have larger ownership stakes. Hoberg and Prabhala (2006) find no support for this prediction as institutions, which are more likely to be informed, are more likely to hold stocks after dividend initiations. Like Grinstein and Michaely (2005), Hoberg and Prabhala (2006) argue that this could reflect the impact of prudent-man investing in the United States. Because researchers have not fully investigated the issue of the impact of ownership, this topic constitutes a prominent area for future research.

Baker et al. (2005) indicate that the original model does not explain the aggregate fluctuations in the level of dividends. It is more a theory to describe whether firms pay dividends and not about how much they pay. Still, Li and Lie (2006) extend the catering theory beyond dividend initiations/omissions and include changes in dividends. This increases the practical relevance of the model, as managers are more often confronted with decisions about changes in dividend levels than decisions about dividend initiations and omissions. To enhance the relevance of the theory, researchers should focus future efforts on the effects of catering to changes in dividend levels.

Several studies question whether the dividend premium is a reliable measure to capture investor sentiment, as the premium seems to capture future earnings growth of dividend payers relative to non–dividend payers. As argued by Hoberg and Prabhala (2006), a future challenge in the field of catering for dividends will be to develop clean proxies that can capture behavioral factors. There is still room for testing the cross-sectional predictions of the catering model, especially the effect of managerial horizons and/or costs of arbitrage.

The existing studies investigating the catering effect of dividends largely focus on the United States and to a lesser extent the United Kingdom. The empirical results summarized in Table 13.1 are far from conclusive or unanimous as to whether the catering theory of dividends can explain the dividend payout.

Despite these mixed findings, some general conclusions emerge. First, the announcement effects for dividend initiations are more strongly positive than the announcement effects of dividend increases. Therefore, the catering theory seems to explain dividend initiations better than dividend omissions. Second, because individual firm characteristics still play an important role in determining dividend policy, they should be integrated with investors' sentiment to explain dividend policy. Finally, the validity of the catering theory of dividends is confined not only to countries with strong investor protections but also to those with weaker investor protections.

REFERENCES

Ali, Ashiq, and Oktay Urcan. 2006. "Dividend Increases and Future Profitability." Working Paper, University of Texas at Dallas.

Allen, Franklin, Antonio E. Bernardo, and Ivo Welch. 2000. "A Theory of Dividends Based on Tax Clienteles." *Journal of Finance* 55:6, 2499–2536.

Allen, Franklin, and Roni Michaely. 2003. "Payout Policy." In *Handbook of the Economics of Finance 1A*, ed. George M. Constantinides, Milton Harris, and René Stulz, 337–429. Amsterdam: North-Holland-Elsevier.

Baker, Malcolm, Richard S. Ruback, and Jeffrey Wurgler. 2005. "Behavioral Corporate Finance: A Survey." Working Paper, National Bureau of Economic Research.

Baker, Malcolm, and Jeffrey Wurgler. 2002. "Why Are Dividends Disappearing? An Empirical Analysis." Working Paper, Harvard Business School.

Baker, Malcolm, and Jeffrey Wurgler. 2004a. "A Catering Theory of Dividends." *Journal of Finance* 59:3, 1125–1165.

Baker, Malcolm, and Jeffrey Wurgler. 2004b. "Appearing and Disappearing Dividends: The Link to Catering Incentives." *Journal of Financial Economics* 73:2, 271–288.

Banerjee, Suman, Vladimir A. Gatchev, and Paul A. Spindt. 2005. "Stock Market Liquidity and Firm Dividend Policy." Working Paper, Tulane University.

Barberis, Nicholas, and Andrei Shleifer. 2003. "Style Investing." *Journal of Financial Economics* 68:2, 161–199.

Barclay, Michael J., Clifford W. Smith, and Ross L. Watts. 1995. "The Determinants of Corporate Leverage and Dividend Policies." *Journal of Applied Corporate Finance* 7:4, 4–19.

Benartzi, Shlomo, Roni Michaely, and Richard Thaler. 1997. "Do Changes in Dividend Signal the Future or the Past?" *Journal of Finance* 52:3, 1007–1034.

Bhattacharya, Sudipto. 1979. "Imperfect Information, Dividend Policy and 'the Bird in the Hand' Fallacy." *Bell Journal of Economics* 10:1, 259–270.

Black, Fischer. 1976. "The Dividend Puzzle." *Journal of Portfolio Management* 2:2, 5–8.

Black, Fischer, and Myron Scholes. 1974. "The Effects of Dividend Yield and Dividend Policy on Common Stock Prices and Returns." *Journal of Financial Economics* 1:1, 1–22.

Bulan, Laarni, Narayanan Subramanian, and Lloyd Tanlu. 2007. "On the Timing of Dividend Initiations." *Financial Management* 36:4, 31–65.

Denis, David J., and Igor Osobov. 2005. "Disappearing Dividends, Catering Incentives and Agency Costs: International Evidence." Working Paper, Purdue University.

Denis, David J., and Igor Osobov. 2008. "Why Do Firms Pay Dividends? International Evidence on the Determinants of Dividend Policy." *Journal of Financial Economics* 89:1, 62–82.

Dittmar, Amy K., and Robert F. Dittmar. 2004. "Stock Repurchase Waves: An Explanation of the Trends in Aggregate Corporate Payout Policy." Working Paper, University of Michigan Business School.

Fairchild, Richard, and Ganggang Zhang. 2005. "Repurchase and Dividend Catering, Managerial Myopia, and Long-Run Value-Destruction." Working Paper, University of Bath.

Fama, Eugene F., and Kenneth R. French. 2001. "Disappearing Dividends: Changing Firm Characteristics or Lower Propensity to Pay?" *Journal of Financial Economics* 60:1, 3–43.

Fenn, George W., and Nellie Liang. 2001. "Corporate Payout Policy and Managerial Stock Incentives." *Journal of Financial Economics* 60:1, 45–72.

Ferris, Stephen P., Gregory Noronha, and Emre Unlu. 2006a. "The More, the Merrier: An International Analysis of the Frequency of Dividend Payment." Working Paper, University of Missouri–Columbia.

Ferris, Stephen P., Nilanjan Sen, and Ho Pei Yui. 2006b. "God Save the Queen and Her Dividends: Corporate Payouts in the United Kingdom." *Journal of Business* 79:3, 1149–1173.

Fuller, Kathleen, and Michael Goldstein. 2003. "Dividend Policy and Market Movements." Working Paper, University of Georgia.

Gaspar, José-Miguel, Massimo Massa, Pedro Matos, Rajdeep Patgiri, and Zahid Rehman. 2004. "Can Buybacks Be a Product of Shorter Shareholder Horizons?" Discussion Paper, INSEAD.

Gaver, Jennifer J., and Kenneth M. Gaver. 1993. "Additional Evidence on the Association between the Investment Opportunity Set and Corporate Financing, Dividend and Compensation Policies." *Journal of Accounting and Economics* 16:1/3, 125–160.

Gemmill, Gordon. 2005. "Catering for Dividends by Stripping Mutual-Fund Portfolios." Working Paper, University of Warwick.

Goergen, Marc, Luc Renneboog, and Luis Correia da Silva. 2005. "When Do German Firms Change Their Dividends?" *Journal of Corporate Finance* 11:1/2, 375–399.

Grinstein, Yaniv, and Roni Michaely. 2005. "Institutional Holdings and Payout Policy." *Journal of Finance* 60:3, 1389–1426.

Grullon, Gustavo, Roni Michaely, and Bhaskaran Swaminathan. 2002. "Are Dividend Changes a Sign of Maturity?" *Journal of Business* 75:3, 378–424.

Healy, Paul M., and Krishna G. Palepu. 1998. "Earnings Information Conveyed by Dividend Initiations and Omissions." *Journal of Financial Economics* 21:2, 149–175.

Hoberg, Gerard, and Nagpurnanand R. Prabhala. 2005. "Disappearing Dividends: The Importance of Idiosyncratic Risk and the Irrelevance of Catering." Working Paper, University of Maryland.

Hoberg, Gerard, and Nagpurnanand R. Prabhala. 2006. "Dividend Policy, Risk, and Catering." Working Paper, University of Maryland.

Hsieh, Jim, and Qinghai Wang. 2006. "Determinants of the Trends in Aggregate Corporate Payout Policy." Working Paper, George Mason University.

Hubbard, Jeff, and Roni Michaely. 1997. "Do Investors Ignore Dividend Taxation? A Reexamination of the Citizens Utilities Case." *Journal of Financial and Quantitative Analysis* 32:1, 117–135.

John, Kose, and Joseph Williams. 1985. "Dividends, Dilution, and Taxes: A Signalling Equilibrium." *Journal of Finance* 40:4, 1053–1070.

Julio, Brandon, and David L. Ikenberry. 2004. "Reappearing Dividends." *Journal of Applied Corporate Finance* 16:4, 89–100.

Kale, Jayant R., Omesh Kini, and Janet D. Payne. 2006. "On the Dividend Initiation Decisions of Newly Public Firms." Working Paper, Georgia State University.

La Porta, Rafael, Florencio Lopez-de-Silanes, Andrei Shleifer, and Robert W. Vishny. 2000a. "Investor Protection and Corporate Governance." *Journal of Financial Economics* 58:1/2, 3–27.

La Porta, Rafael, Florencio Lopez-de-Silanes, Andrei Shleifer, and Robert W. Vishny. 2000b. "Agency Problems and Dividend Policies around the World." *Journal of Finance* 55:1, 1–33.

Lai, Richard Kum-yew. 2004. "A Catering Theory of Analyst Bias." Working Paper, Harvard Business School.

Lambert, Richard A., Willliam A. Lanen, and David F. Larcker. 1989. "Executive Stock Options Plans and Corporate Dividend Policy." *Journal of Financial and Quantitative Analysis* 24:4, 409–425.

Lee, Charles M., Andrei Shleifer, and Richard H. Thaler. 1991. "Investor Sentiment and the Closed-End Fund Puzzle." *Journal of Finance* 46:1, 75–110.

Li, Kai, and Xinlei Zhao. 2008. "Asymmetric Information and Dividend Policy." *Financial Management*, forthcoming.

Li, Wei, and Erik Lie. 2006. "Dividend Changes and Catering Incentives." *Journal of Financial Economics* 80:2, 293–308.

Lie, Erik. 2005. "Operating Performance Following Dividend Decreases and Omissions." *Journal of Corporate Finance* 12:1, 27–53.

Long, John B., Jr. 1978. "The Market Valuation of Cash Dividends: A Case to Consider." *Journal of Financial Economics* 6:2/3, 235–264.

Michaely, Roni, Richard H. Thaler, and Kent L. Womack. 1995. "Price Reactions to Dividend Initiations and Omissions: Overreaction or Drift?" *Journal of Finance* 50:2, 573–608.

Miller, Merton H., and Franco Modigliani. 1961. "Dividend Policy, Growth, and the Valuation of Shares." *Journal of Business* 34:4, 411–433.

Miller, Merton H., and Kevin Rock. 1985. "Dividend Policy under Asymmetric Information." *Journal of Finance* 40:4, 1031–1051.

Neves, Elisabete. 2006. "Dividends: New Evidence on the Catering Theory." Working Paper, Universidad de Salamanca.

Poterba, James M. 1986. "The Market Valuation of Cash Dividends." *Journal of Financial Economics* 15:3, 395–405.

Rajgopal, Shiva, Lakshmanan Shivakumar, and Ana Simpson. 2007. "A Catering Theory of Earnings Management." Working Paper, University of Washington Business School.

Renneboog, Luc, and Margot de Rooij. 2008. "Dividend Policy Catering for Investor Sentiment in Firms with Poor Shareholder Rights." Working Paper, Tilburg University.

Renneboog, Luc, and Peter G. Szilagyi. 2007. "How Relevant Is Dividend Policy under Low Shareholder Protection?" Working Paper, Tilburg University.

Renneboog, Luc, and Grzegorz Trojanowski. 2005. "Patterns in Payout Policy and Payout Channel Choice of U.K. Firms in the 1990s." Working Paper, Tilburg University.

Ross, Stephen A., Randolph W. Westerfield, and Jeffrey Jaffe. 2002. *Corporate Finance*. New York: McGraw Hill.

Savov, Sava, and Martin Weber. 2006. "Fundamentals or Market Movements: What Drives the Dividend Decision?" Working Paper, University of Mannheim.

Shefrin, Hersh M., and Meir Statman. 1984. "Explaining Investor Preferences for Cash Dividends." *Journal of Financial Economics* 13:2, 253–282.

Smith, Clifford W., Jr., and Ross L. Watts. 1992. "The Investment Opportunity Set and Corporate Financing, Dividend, and Compensation Policies." *Journal of Financial Economics* 32:3, 263–292.

Thaler, Richard H., and Hersh M. Shefrin. 1981. "An Economic Theory of Self-Control." *Journal of Political Economy* 89:2, 392–406.

Twu, Mia, and Chin-Hsiang Shen. 2006. "Catering to Dividend Demand and the Institutional Variables of Capital Markets." Working Paper, Chengchi University.

von Eije, J. Henk, and William L. Megginson. 2008. "Dividend Policy and Share Repurchases in the European Union." *Journal of Financial Economics* 89:2, 347–374.

Zweig, Martin E. 1973. "An Investor Expectations Stock Price Predictive Model Using Closed-End Fund Premiums." *Journal of Finance* 28:1, 67–78.

ABOUT THE AUTHORS

Margot de Rooij is a researcher and Ph.D. student at Tilburg University. . She graduated with with a MPhil degree in finance from the Judge Business School at University of Cambridge and with a B.Sc. degree in business administration and an M.Sc. degree in investment analysis from Tilburg University. While at Tilburg University, she worked on buyer-supplier relationships. Her current research interests are corporate finance, dividend policy, and behavioral finance.

Luc Renneboog is professor of corporate finance at Tilburg University, and a research fellow at CentER (Tilburg) and ECGI (Brussels). He graduated from the University of Leuven with degrees in management engineering (B.Sc./M.Sc.) and in philosophy (BA), from the University of Chicago with an MBA, and from the London Business School with a Ph.D. in financial economics. He held appointments at the Universities of Leuven and Oxford, and visiting appointments at LBS (London), EUI Institute (Florence), HEC (Paris), and Venice University. He has published in *Journal of Finance*, *Journal of Financial* Intermediation, *Journal of Corporate Finance*, *Journal of Banking and Finance*, *European Financial Management*, and others. He has coauthored and edited books on corporate governance, dividend policy, and venture capital. His interests are corporate finance, corporate governance, insider trading, and law and economics.

PART III

Share Repurchases

CHAPTER 14

Stock Repurchases: Theory and Evidence, Part 1

JIM HSIEH
Associate Professor of Finance, George Mason University

QINGHAI WANG
Associate Professor of Finance, Georgia Institute of Technology

INTRODUCTION

Corporations can distribute capital to their shareholders by means of cash dividends or share repurchases or a combination of both. Historically, dividends have been the dominant form of payout. Recent articles studying the trends in corporate payouts, however, indicate a structural change in the way that firms pay out cash to their shareholders. Most notably, Fama and French (2001) document a large decline in the proportion of publicly traded firms that paid dividends over the period 1978–1999. DeAngelo, DeAngelo, and Skinner (2004) show that despite the decrease in the number of U.S. firms paying dividends, the real dollar value of aggregate dividends from those dividend-paying firms has actually increased. Grullon and Michaely (2002) and Hsieh and Wang (2007) further indicate the substitution effect between dividends and share repurchases over time. In particular, an increasing number of U.S. firms have gradually substituted repurchases for dividends.

Figure 14.1 plots the percentage of firms paying out cash as dividends or repurchases from 1972 to 2003. Overall, the portion of dividend payers to all industrial firms has decreased over time. In 1972, 57 percent of firms paid dividends, and this percentage peaked at 71 percent in 1977. The percentage then steadily declined to 22 percent in 2003. In contrast, the portion of firms repurchasing shares was stable before 1997, within the range of 22 percent to 34 percent. It increased sharply to 41 percent in 1999 and then decreased to 36 percent in 2003. Since 1996, share repurchases have replaced dividends as the dominant form of payout.

How much did firms pay out historically? Figure 14.2A shows that the aggregate ratio of payout to past five-year average earnings has increased over time. The change is especially dramatic for repurchases. Figure 14.2B shows that the aggregate ratio of dividends to total assets decreases during the sample period, while the repurchase ratio still exhibits an upward trend. From the time trend of corporate payout, share repurchases have apparently become the preferred form for corporations to disburse cash flows to shareholders.

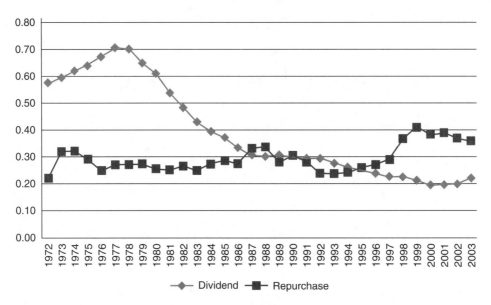

Figure 14.1   Percentage of U.S. Industrial Firms with Positive Dividends
or Share Repurchases
This figure plots the percentage of U.S. industrial firms in the universe of CRSP and Compustat
databases with positive dividends or share repurchases from 1972 to 2003. The percentages exclude
utilities (SIC codes 4900–4949) and financial firms (SIC codes 6000–6999).
Source: Hsieh and Wang (2007).

This chapter provides a synthesis of the theories and empirical findings of
share repurchases. The chapter begins by providing a discussion of mechanisms
used to repurchase shares followed by a discussion of why firms conduct share-
repurchase programs. The next section further discusses determinants of corporate
payout choice between dividends and share repurchases. The last section presents
concluding remarks about the overall findings.

SHARE REPURCHASE METHODS

Firms can buy back their shares through five different mechanisms: (1) fixed-price
tender offers, (2) Dutch-auction tender offers, (3) open-market share repurchases,
(4) transferable put-rights distributions, and (5) targeted stock repurchases. In a
fixed-price tender offer, the company offers to purchase a prespecified percentage
of shares at a predetermined price within a time period. The prespecified price is
usually higher than the market price at the time of the offer, such that the premium
offered provides a sufficient incentive for shareholders to tender their shares. If the
tender offer is oversubscribed, the firm can either buy back additional shares or
simply repurchase shares from the interested shareholders on a pro rata basis. If
the offer is undersubscribed, the firm can terminate the offer, extend the tendering
period, or simply buy back the shares tendered.

The process for a Dutch-auction tender offer is essentially the same as a fixed-
price offer, but in a Dutch auction, the firm only specifies a price range for the

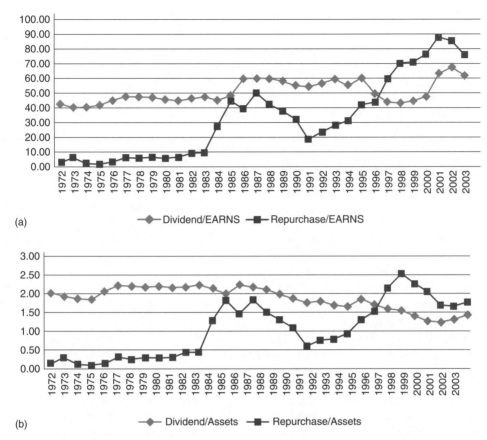

(a)

(b)

Figure 14.2 Aggregate Dividend Ratios and Repurchase Ratios for U.S. Industrial Firms
These two panels plot the aggregate ratios of payout to past five-year earnings (top graph) and to total assets (bottom graph), respectively. All variables are aggregated for all CRSP/Compustat firms each year. EARN5 is the average earnings in the past five years.
Source: Hsieh and Wang (2007).

repurchase rather than a fixed price. Each participating shareholder submits a price and the number of shares to be tendered. The firm accumulates all offers and ranks them by the submitted prices. The minimum price at which the firm can buy all of the prespecified number of shares is then set as the final offer price. All shares tendered at or below the final offer price will be bought back at that price while shares tendered above the final offer price will be returned to their owners.

In an open-market share repurchase, the company buys back a predetermined dollar amount of shares (rather than the number of shares) in the open market within a certain period of time, typically two to three years. Unlike fixed-price or Dutch-auction tender offers, firms announcing open-market repurchase programs are not obligated to buy back any shares in the market. In fact, Stephens and Weisbach (1998) document that for a sample of 450 open-market repurchase programs announced during the period 1981–1990, only 57 percent of the sampled firms repurchased the number of originally targeted shares within three years after announcements, and 10 percent of the firms reacquired less than 5 percent of targeted shares.

Another difference between open-market repurchase programs and fixed-price and Dutch-auction tender offers is that firms employing the latter two approaches can retire a large portion of shares within a short period. Thus, to some extent, fixed-price and Dutch-auction tender offers are better mechanisms than open-market repurchases for companies to quickly adjust their capital structure or to fend off a potential takeover threat.

The fourth share-repurchasing method is targeted stock repurchases, also called privately negotiated or negotiated-premium repurchases. In a targeted stock repurchase, the company buys back a large block of shares from a shareholder or a group of shareholders at a premium. Firms commonly use this procedure, termed *greenmail*, to repel a hostile or unwanted takeover threat. Nevertheless, not all of the targeted stock repurchases are for antitakeover purpose. In some instances, firms could use targeted stock repurchases to retire a large block of shares from a block holder.

Existing studies show that the financial market reacts differently to control-related and non-control-related targeted repurchases. On average, control-related targeted repurchases are associated with negative announcement returns for the repurchasing firms (see, e.g., Bradley and Wakeman, 1983; Dann and DeAngelo, 1988; Klein and Rosenfeld, 1988; Mikkelson and Ruback, 1991). In contrast, Chang and Hertzel (2004) show that non-control-related targeted repurchases earn positive returns for the repurchasing firms. The negative stock-price reaction is consistent with the argument that control-related targeted repurchases entrench management, while the positive reaction is more in line with the argument that non-control-related targeted repurchases improve the concentrated ownership structure of the firm. (For theories, see Shleifer and Vishny, 1986; Stulz, 1988; for empirical evidence, see, e.g., Demsetz and Lehn, 1985; Morck, Shleifer, and Vishny, 1988; Wruck, 1989; McConnell and Servaes, 1990).

The fifth repurchasing method is transferable put-rights distributions (TPRs). In a TPR, the firm issues put options to each shareholder in proportion to the number of shares owned. Each TPR gives the shareholder the right to sell one share back to the company at a predetermined price within a certain period. For instance, if the firm desired to repurchase 20 percent of total shares outstanding, each shareholder would receive one TPR per five shares owned. Shareholders with high reservation prices, which indicate an unwillingness to tender their shares, can sell their TPRs to those with low reservation prices in the open market. As Kale, Noe, and Gay (1989) argue, TPRs have at least two advantages over fixed-price tender offers. First, because investors with high reservation prices can keep their shares and sell TPRs to low-reservation-price investors, who in turn are willing to sell shares back to the company, the firm's ownership will result in a greater portion of high-reservation-price shareholders after the repurchase transaction. This effectively increases the cost of a hostile takeover by a potential raider. Second, given investors' heterogeneous tax status, investors with higher tax liabilities from tendering can keep their shares and sell TPRs to those with lower tax liabilities. This will lead to higher tax efficiency.

Since the early 1980s, open-market repurchases have become the most dominant form of all repurchasing mechanisms. As evidenced by Grullon and Ikenberry

(2000), open-market repurchases accounted for around 91 percent of the combined market value of the first three repurchase methods announced between 1980 and 1999. Thus, unless noticed, this chapter focuses mostly on open-market share repurchases.

POTENTIAL MOTIVES FOR SHARE REPURCHASES

Why do firms conduct share-repurchase programs? The seminal work of Miller and Modigliani (1961) (hereafter MM) shows that in a perfect market, corporate payout policy should not have any meaningful impact on firm value as long as corporate investment policy remains constant. Their theoretical study suggests several possible channels through which corporate payout policy affects firm value. The literature on share repurchases studies the motives that influence firms' repurchase activity by relaxing one or more of MM's assumptions and examining the economic significance of those assumptions. The remainder of this chapter examines three potential motives for share repurchases: (1) regulatory and tax considerations, (2) agency costs of free cash flows, (3) and signaling or undervaluation. Chapter 15 examines three additional motives: (4) capital structure, (5) takeover deterrence, and (6) employee stock options.

Regulation and Taxes

As shown in Figure 14.2, the level of share repurchases was much lower than that of dividends before 1984. The ratio of aggregate dividends to earnings was within the range of 40 percent to 50 percent during the period 1972–1983, while the ratio of aggregate repurchases to earnings was below 10 percent. Since the mid-1980s, share repurchases have increased dramatically. The surge was at least partially attributed to regulatory changes in 1982 by the Securities and Exchange Commission (SEC) and several other changes in tax policies since the 1970s. In particular, corporations repurchasing their own stocks were mainly governed by the antimanipulative provisions of the Securities Exchange Act (SEA) of 1934. This regulation exposed firms to certain risk of being charged with intentional stock-price manipulation. As a result, firms were reluctant to repurchase shares.

In 1982, the SEC responded to the constraints in the SEA of 1934 and adopted Rule 10b-18. Because the rule essentially provides a safe harbor for firms to buy back shares, many companies initiated open-market repurchase programs after the implementation of the rule in 1982. In addition, several policy changes regarding share-repurchase programs occurred before the adoption of Rule 10b-18. Grullon and Michaely (2002) report that because of the introduction of Rule 10b-18, firms have gradually substituted repurchases for dividends.

Another regulation-related event was the Tax Reform Act (TRA) of 1986. Because the TRA eliminated special treatments for capital gains, it essentially raised the tax rate on capital gains and made share repurchases less attractive relative to cash dividends. If the 1986 TRA resulted in a shift in payout policy, a significant increase in dividends and/or decrease in share repurchases should occur after the adoption of the TRA. The current evidence produces mixed results. Consistent with the conjecture that corporate payout policy responds to tax law changes, Lie and Lie (1999) find in the cross-sectional analysis that after TRA, firms are less likely to choose repurchases or self-tender offers than regular or special dividends as a means of disbursing cash. In contrast, Bagwell and Shoven (1989) and Hsieh and Wang (2007) provide time-series evidence that the aggregate dividend ratio has remained stable since the early 1980s, but the aggregate repurchase ratio has increased over time, a pattern inconsistent with the effectiveness of TRA.

In addition to regulatory and tax-law changes, differential tax rates (or tax-rate changes) are also a major determinant of corporate payout policy. In a perfect market without taxes, dividends and share repurchases are perfect substitutes. In reality, dividends are taxed at least at the same rates as repurchases because the former are taxed as ordinary income while the latter are taxed as capital gains. Thus, from a tax perspective, dividends have a substantial disadvantage relative to repurchases. The general theme in existing theories is to understand whether and why a firm chooses a certain form of payout to accommodate the heterogeneous tax status of its shareholders (the tax clientele effect) and how tax-rational investors respond to the firm's payout decisions.

Allen, Bernardo, and Welch (2000) assume that different groups of investors not only are taxed differently but also have different incentives to become more informed about corporate policies. Firms pay out cash as dividends rather than repurchases to attract larger and presumably better-informed investors, typically institutional investors. Further, institutional investors might prefer dividends to repurchases either because of the prudent-man laws (Del Guercio, 1996) or because many of them, such as pension funds and foundations, are at least partially tax exempted.

In contrast, Brennan and Thakor (1990) theorize that informed investors can exploit their information advantage when firms repurchase shares. Informed investors include institutional investors, block holders, and corporate insiders such as executives and directors. Such investors are unable to do so when firms pay out extra cash in the form of dividends. As a result, uninformed investors prefer dividends to repurchases despite the fact that dividends are more heavily taxed than repurchases. Conversely, informed investors prefer repurchases because they can profit at the cost of uninformed investors when firms repurchase shares. Supporting the theory of Brennan and Thakor, Barclay and Smith (1988) report that dividends are the dominant form of payout because individual, uninformed investors have a strong preference toward them. Moreover, they argue that firms do not substitute share repurchases for cash dividends because of the nontrivial costs from the information disparity between managers and uninformed investors. Those costs, in turn, reduce liquidity of the firm's shares, increase its cost of capital, and eventually reduce its market value.

Several studies provide evidence supporting the tax clientele effect. For example, Lie and Lie (1999) study the impact of personal taxation on firms' choice between share repurchases and dividends. Using several proxies for the marginal tax rates faced by investors, they find that managers are more likely to disburse cash to shareholders via repurchases, provided those shareholders have lower tax rates on capital gains than on dividends. They also report that managers are more likely to consider tax implications on shareholder wealth when holdings by institutional investors are high.

Grinstein and Michaely (2005) focus on the relationship between institutional ownership and corporate payout policy. Some but not all of their results support tax clienteles. Specifically, they show that corporate payouts affect institutional holdings but not vice versa. Further, institutional investors are attracted to firms that repurchase shares regularly but not to firms that pay high dividends. This finding is more in line with Brennan and Thakor (1990) than with Allen et al. (2000).

A survey study by Brav, Graham, Harvey, and Michaely (2005) reveals that financial executives do not view corporate payout policy as an effective mechanism to attract a particular investor clientele. They do not use their payouts to alter the proportion of different kinds of investors. Responding executives also believe that dividends are attractive to individual investors but both dividends and repurchases are equally attractive to institutions. This seems inconsistent with both Brennan and Thakor (1990) and Allen et al. (2000). Brav et al. also document that those executives do not consider taxation as a dominant factor in their payout decisions. After the 2003 dividend tax cut, a follow-up survey reinforces the second-order importance of taxation in their payout decisions. In particular, more than two-thirds of the executives surveyed mentioned that the 2003 dividend tax cut is unlikely to change their dividend and repurchase decisions.

As discussed earlier, the majority of studies address whether a firm sets a payout policy to accommodate the heterogeneous tax status of its shareholders. Is it plausible, however, that corporate executives and directors institute payout policy to suit their own interests? Clearly corporate insiders not only determine corporate payout policy but also are affected by disparate tax treatments between dividends and share repurchases. As indicated in Hsieh and Wang (2008), insiders usually face considerable tax liabilities for the dividends they receive. Thus, conceivably insiders' substantial exposure to dividend taxes would give them strong incentives to prefer share repurchases rather than dividends. Consistent with this conjecture, Hsieh and Wang find a positive relationship between insiders' implied tax liabilities from their shareholdings and firms' propensity to employ share repurchases as the form of payout.

Agency Costs of Free Cash Flows

Theories

There are three main findings related to share-price movements around the period when firms announce share repurchase programs. First, Vermaelen (1981) and Ikenberry, Lakonishok, and Vermaelen (1995) document that repurchasing firms usually experience negative share price returns leading up to the announcement.

Second, evidence shows that firms conducting share repurchases earn significantly positive announcement returns (Dann 1981; Vermaelen, 1981; Asquith and Mullins, 1986; Lakonishok and Vermaelen, 1990; Comment and Jarrell, 1991; Ikenberry et al., 1995; Stephens and Weisbach, 1998; Nohel and Tarhan, 1998). For instance, using a sample of 591 open-market repurchases from 1981 to 1990, Stephens and Weisbach document an average price reaction of about 2.7 percent over a three-day event window starting the day before the announcement. Nohel and Tarhan report an average three-day announcement return of 7.6 percent for a sample of 242 tender offers between 1978 and 1991. Ikenberry et al. find a positive relationship between the extent of the share-price change and the size of the repurchase program.

Third, Ikenberry et al. (1995) also find a post-repurchase announcement drift for repurchasing firms. In particular, they show that repurchasing firms, on average, earn 12.1 percent buy-and-hold abnormal returns over the four years after the announcement. High book-to-market stocks experience a more pronounced drift, in which the average abnormal return is a substantial 45.3 percent. Peyer and Vermaelen (2008) extend the study of Ikenberry et al. and document that the post-repurchase announcement drift persists over time.

The market-price movements around share repurchase announcements are consistent with at least two possible explanations: (1) firms buy back shares to mitigate the conflicts of interest between management and shareholders (free cash flows) and (2) firms use share repurchases to signal their future growth prospects (signaling). This section provides a discussion of studies related to free cash flows and the next section provides a discussion of articles related to signaling.

Agency theories recognize that managers can adjust corporate decisions to advance their own benefits (Jensen and Meckling, 1976). Of central concern is that when a firm's extra capital is more than enough to finance its investment opportunities, managers could consume the excess cash by investing in negative net present value projects (the overinvestment problem) or increase their own compensations instead of returning the extra cash to shareholders. Easterbrook (1984) and Jensen (1986) argue that shareholders should control the discretionary cash available to management to mitigate managerial expropriation of outside shareholders. One way to accomplish this is to increase the level of payout. Further, firms that are ideal candidates to incur agency costs of free cash flow or to overinvest are those with few growth opportunities. Therefore, applying the previous argument in the content of repurchases, the expectation is that firms with high levels of excess cash flows and/or with few growth opportunities should repurchase shares. The positive market reaction to repurchase announcements should also be greater for companies that are more likely to overinvest.

Another reasonable argument is that firms can also pay out extra cash as dividends. To some extent, dividends provide more credible signals to the market than share repurchases because firms usually are reluctant to cut dividends once initiated (Michaely, Thaler, and Womack, 1995). In contrast, firms can terminate share-repurchase programs at any time. Repurchases, however, might be associated with different benefits than dividends. Brennan and Thakor (1990) and Lucas and McDonald (1998) present theories in which investors prefer share repurchases to cash dividends in large distributions and larger repurchases are better news than smaller repurchases or dividends.

In addition, when a firm has excess cash flows and few investment opportunities, its growth rate of capital expenditures and return on investment are likely to be stable or even decline after its repurchase (Grullon and Michaely, 2004). A share repurchase along with few growth options could also signal the mature stage of the firm. This implies a decrease in the riskiness of the expected future cash flows or a reduction in cost of capital after a repurchase. Accordingly, the theories of free cash flows indicate that firms repurchasing shares should be associated with insignificant changes or even decreases in capital expenditures, return on investment, and cost of capital.

Empirical Support
Overall, existing empirical evidence provides support for free cash flow explanations. Dittmar (2000) investigates how a firm's level of cash flow affects its decision

to repurchase stock. Studying the levels of cash and cash flows for all U.S. industrial firms from 1977 to 1996, she finds that, after controlling for investment opportunities, firms repurchase stock to distribute excess capital. Lie (2000) documents a positive mean announcement return of 8 percent for a sample of 207 self-tender offers from 1981 through 1994. The levels of cash flows in those firms are higher than the median values of their industry peers before the offer announcements. He also finds higher announcement returns for firms with a low Tobin's Q (a proxy for investment opportunities) than for those with a high Tobin's Q. His evidence is consistent with the argument that large disbursements via self-tender offers effectively restrain the overinvestment problem.

Stephens and Weisbach (1998) reach a similar conclusion. In particular, they examine actual quarterly share repurchases for a sample of repurchase programs announced between 1981 and 1990 and present evidence that both expected and unexpected cash flows are positively correlated with the levels of repurchases. They define expected quarterly cash flow as the cash flow for the corresponding quarter from the previous year and unexpected quarterly cash flow as the seasonal first differences or the current quarter's cash flow minus the expected quarterly cash flow. Their results suggest that because of the flexibility inherent in repurchase programs, managers can adjust their share repurchases according to the cash flow fluctuation.

The aforementioned studies provide support for the positive relationship between repurchases and the level of cash flows. Two studies investigate changes in operating performance and in firm risk around repurchases. Nohel and Tarhan (1998) examine the determinants of post-repurchase operating performance for a sample of 242 fixed-price and Dutch auction tender offers from 1978 to 1991. They measure operating performance as the ratio of cash flow to market value of total assets. Their results show that the improvement of post-repurchase performance only occurs in low-growth (low-Tobin's-Q) firms. Those firms improve their performance by selling assets instead of investing in growth opportunities. Further, companies do not increase capital expenditures from three years before to three years after repurchases. They interpret their results as consistent with the free cash flow hypothesis.

Grullon and Michaely (2004) study firm performance and risk changes for a comprehensive sample of 2,735 open-market share repurchases from 1980 through 2000. Consistent with the findings in Nohel and Tarhan (1998), Grullon and Michaely also show that repurchasing firms experience profitability and investment decline within three years after repurchases. In addition, the average value of repurchasing firms' costs of capital also decreases from 16 percent to about 14 percent in the three years after the year of repurchase announcements.

As revealed in Brav et al. (2005), views from those surveyed financial executives are mostly consistent with the empirical evidence in academic studies. The managers tend to use share repurchases to reduce excess cash holdings, confirming the agency cost concerns. In addition, firms are more likely to buy back shares when few good investment opportunities are available. Taken together, the existing evidence provides strong support for the free cash flow hypothesis. The positive announcement returns for firms conducting share repurchases and the subsequent changes in operating performance and systematic risk are consistent with the notion that firms repurchase shares in response to their accumulated free cash flows and declining growth opportunities.

A recent theory by DeAngelo and DeAngelo (2006a) suggests that firms' propensity to pay dividends corresponds to their different life cycle stages. Companies use capital to fund growth opportunities in the growing stage. This explains why they have minimum extra capital to pay out as dividends. As firms mature, they become good candidates to pay dividends. DeAngelo, DeAngelo, and Stulz (2006) present dividend-related evidence supporting the life cycle theory. Whether the theory applies in the case of share repurchases requires future research.

SIGNALING AND UNDERVALUATION

Theories

In the MM (1961) world, capital markets are perfect, and managers and outside stakeholders share the same information set. In reality, managers possess more knowledge about the future prospects of the firm than outside shareholders. The asymmetric information between managers and outside investors provides incentives for managers to convey their assessment to the market if they believe the company's stock is undervalued. Researchers have long considered payouts a costly but effective signal about the prospects of the firm. The signaling hypothesis is among the most popular explanations for corporate payout policy. This section provides a review of existing theories and empirical evidence related to the signaling hypothesis. As discussed here, the signaling hypothesis offers different testable implications than the free cash flow hypothesis discussed in the previous section.

Bhattacharya (1979) proposes a model that assumes (1) outside investors have imperfect information about firm's expected cash flows, (2) dividends are taxed at a higher rate than capital gains, and (3) firm's commitment to paying dividends is a credible signal; otherwise, the company has to seek outside funding with additional transaction costs. In this setting, investors might underestimate (or simply cannot realize) firms' future profitability and paying cash dividends to shareholders incurs nontrivial signaling costs. In equilibrium, only the high-quality firm can signal the future profitability while the low-quality firm cannot because of the substantial tax liability and transaction costs associated with seeking external funding. Interestingly, in Bhattacharya's model, share repurchases can be perfectly substituted for a cash dividend. Thus, only the high-quality firm can conduct a share buyback, which also signals the firm's future cash flow. This can explain why share repurchases, on average, are associated with positive announcement returns. One drawback of the model is that it does not elaborate why managers choose payouts to signal their own valuation of the firm.

Miller and Rock (1985) develop an alternative two-period signaling model that considers dividend and investment policies together under asymmetric information. At time zero, the firm invests in a production function generating earnings for a dividend payment and a new round of investment at time one. Information asymmetry occurs at time one because only managers and directors, but not outside investors, can observe the earnings. The difference in information content about earnings leads to different estimates of the firm value. Investors can only form their estimate of the firm's future earnings based on the realized earnings and dividend amount at time one. This provides an opportunity for the low-quality firm to increase its dividend such that investors could be misled and overestimate its prospects. For the high-quality firm to solve this problem, it needs to increase its dividend level high enough such that the low-quality firm cannot match. In a separating equilibrium, only the high-quality firm can pay a higher level of dividend which in turn signals a higher level of investment and subsequent earnings. In Miller and Rock (1985), cash dividends and share repurchases can also be substituted. The major difference between Bhattacharya (1979) and Miller and Rock (1985) pertains to signaling costs. In Bhattacharya's model, the main signaling cost is the transaction cost of additional external financing, whereas in Miller and Rock's model, the cost is to forego future investment.

Williams (1988) incorporates financial assets in his signaling model and studies the interaction between dividends and investments in real and financial assets. The model assumes that each firm has its private information about the return on real assets while investors only observe the sources and uses of funds in net sale of new stock, dividends, and investments. In equilibrium, each firm invests to maximize the welfare of its shareholders, sells stock to finance the investment, and distributes dividends to its shareholders. Williams's theory offers an explanation of why firms raise capital in the market and distribute dividends to shareholders at the same time. Another prediction from the model is that firms with more valuable private information distribute larger dividends. Furthermore, the difference between Miller and Rock (1985) and Williams (1988) is that the signaling cost in the former model is the underinvestment cost, while the cost in the latter model is the payout amount.

The aforementioned studies consider cash dividends and share repurchases as substitutes. Several papers intend to distinguish between these two payout methods and explain why firms prefer one method over the other as a signaling device. Ofer and Thakor (1987) offer a model in which managers can choose either cash dividends or tender-offer repurchases to signal their firms' true values. They model tender-offer repurchases rather than open-market repurchases. Ofer and Thakor argue that open-market repurchases should contain less information than do tender-offer repurchases.

The model attempts to explain why a tender-offer repurchase, on average, receives a more positive stock-price reaction than does a dividend increase. In the setting, outside investors are risk-neutral while managers are risk-averse and hold a certain portion of their own company's shares. Managers' compensation is also contingent on their firm's stock performance. Another key assumption is that managers are not allowed to trade their share holdings during a share repurchase. There exists only one type of cost associated with cash dividends: the potential cost of seeking external financing for investment opportunities. Repurchases, however, have two types of cost: the cost of external financing and the cost associated with managers' undiversified holdings. The latter occurs because managers' shares are nontradable and account for a relatively greater percentage of total shares outstanding after repurchases. This increased risk exposure represents another nontrivial cost.

Ofer and Thakor (1987) show that managers choose cash dividends to signal their private information about future prospects when the disparity between a firm's intrinsic value and its market valuation is small. On the other hand, when the disparity is large or when the firm is severely undervalued, managers are more likely to employ share repurchases as the signaling device. As a result, repurchases have greater information content than dividends. This is why firms do not frequently use repurchases, but when used, the amount tends to be large. In contrast, dividend-paying firms usually pay dividends regularly (typically quarterly in the United States) with a smaller amount.

Hausch and Seward (1993) also consider a firm's signaling choice between deterministic cash dividends and stochastic stock repurchases. In contrast to Ofer and Thakor (1987), Hausch and Seward assume that (1) managers do not own their own firm's shares and that (2) both managers and outside investors are asymmetrically informed about each other. Thus, managers possess some private information, but they do not know any shareholder's minimum assessed value about the firm's stock. The model suggests that the more deviation between intrinsic value and market valuation (or more undervaluation) does not necessarily lead the firm to choose share repurchases. Rather, the model predicts that the firm's choice between dividends and repurchases depends on the property of cash disbursements from the firm's production function. If the production function generates deterministic (stochastic) cash disbursements, then the firm is more likely to choose dividends (repurchases).

Chowdhry and Nanda (1994) propose a signaling model in which managers have more timely information about the firm's future cash flows than outside investors. The model suggests that a firm pays out extra cash as a dividend to mitigate the free cash flow problem (Jensen, 1986) and carries the remaining cash to the next periods. A repurchase is not an attractive means of disbursing cash because of the premium the company has to pay to buy back shares. The only occasion when the firm is willing to repurchase shares is when the market substantially undervalues its stock relative to managers' own evaluation. Although Chowdhry and Nanda make several different assumptions, their model, as in other signaling models, generates a common feature that when managers perceive the firm's stock is undervalued, they are more likely to use share repurchases. The model also predicts a positive relationship between the size of the stock repurchase in the current period and both the level of dividends in the previous period and the level of unexpected earnings in this period.

The previous models show how firms signal with cash distributions and when they choose between cash dividends and stock repurchases. Several researchers have proposed theories to explain share repurchases alone. Vermaelen (1984) analyzes tender-offer repurchases under a standard signaling framework. His model assumes a link between managerial compensation and the signaling function. Thus, when managers have private information about the difference between the intrinsic value of the firm and the current market value before the tender-offer announcement, they have incentives to signal the difference to maximize the value of their compensation package. Managers signal their private information via the premiums offered, the target fraction of shares to be repurchased, and the fraction of their own share holdings. The model indicates possible relationships between tender-offer repurchases and perceived managerial benefits.

Constantinides and Grundy (1989) also investigate the signaling role of stock repurchases and its relationship with corporate investment and financing policies. Again, management has private information about the firm's future prospects. If the firm has insufficient capital to finance the investment optimally, management has to signal to the market about the firm's growth opportunities and to maximize the stock value by selecting the level of investment and the form of outside financing. In a signaling equilibrium with optimal investment, the firm chooses the form of financing and uses the proceeds to finance the investment and to initiate a stock repurchase.

Persons (1997) presents an information-asymmetry model by incorporating shareholders' heterogeneous reservation values as in Hausch and Seward (1993). Both papers share similar features about employing repurchases as the signaling device. However, two major differences exist between these two models. First, Hausch and Seward stipulate that managers choose the number of targeted shares (Dutch-auction tender offers) while Persons allows managers to choose both the number of shares and the purchase price (fixed-price tender offers). Second, Hausch and Seward's model assumes that managers have private information about current cash flows while they possess information about the firm's future cash flows in Persons' model. In addition, Persons argues that tender offer repurchases are more efficient signaling mechanisms than other strategies such as dividends.

In summary, although theoretical articles on the signaling role of share repurchases make different assumptions, they share a common feature. That is, information asymmetry between management and outside investors provides incentives for firms to announce share-repurchase programs to signal managers' private information about their companies. Those signaling models suggest that firms employ repurchases to signal their current or future favorable financial positions and prospects. The next section provides a discussion of the existing empirical work that investigates the predictions from those theories.

Empirical Support

Although certain variations in modeling exist, signaling models provide similar implications. In particular, they predict that firms use repurchases to signal market undervaluation about firms' current performance or to reveal information about firms' future earnings and cash flows. Because earlier theoretical work identifies information signaling as the major motivation for firms to repurchase shares, the signaling hypothesis has been among the most tested explanations for repurchases. The positive announcement returns for repurchasing firms documented in numerous studies generally supports the first possibility: the undervaluation story.

Surprisingly, the existing and especially the most recent empirical studies present mixed evidence for the second possibility: signaling future earnings and profitability. Earlier articles present strong evidence for the signaling hypothesis, while more recent papers using more comprehensive samples find little support. Moreover, it is important to note that to some extent, the signaling hypothesis and the agency-based free cash flow hypothesis (discussed in the previous section) provide different, or even opposite, testable implications. The signaling hypothesis suggests that repurchasing firms should increase their future earnings and improve subsequent profitability. In contrast, the free cash flow hypothesis predicts that firms distribute excess cash via repurchases in response to decreasing growth opportunities and profitability. Given that the findings from existing studies support the free cash flow hypothesis, those articles essentially provide evidence to reject the signaling hypothesis. This section proceeds by first looking at the earlier studies.

Comment and Jarrell (1991) extend research in announcement returns for repurchasing firms and attempt to distinguish the signal strength among three forms of repurchases. They argue that open-market repurchases and Dutch-auction tender offers provide weaker signals of undervaluation than fixed-price tender offers. In a fixed-price tender offer, management specifies a single purchase price, which also reveals its reservation value. In contrast, in a Dutch auction, outside investors are actively involved in selecting their tendering prices, while management in the repurchasing firm only reveals partial information. In an open-market repurchase, management announces the program and buys back shares from the market during an extensive period. Thus, fixed-price tender offers may provide more credible signals than the other two repurchase mechanisms. Consistent with this conjecture, fixed-price tender offers, on average, are associated with higher offer premiums and announcement returns than are Dutch-auctions and open-market repurchases. The average abnormal announcement return is 11 percent for fixed-price tender offers while the return is only 8 percent for Dutch auctions and 2 percent for open-market repurchases.

A study by Kamma, Kanatas, and Raymar (1992) also investigates the differences in announcement returns between Dutch auctions and fixed-price tender offers. They find that fixed-price tender offers pay higher premiums than do Dutch auctions. The total returns are higher in Dutch auctions than fixed-price tender offers after controlling for tender and firm characteristics.

One way to verify Comment and Jarrell's argument that fixed-price tender offers reveal more credible information than Dutch auctions or open-market repurchases is to examine how managers trade their own shares around repurchase announcements. If repurchase programs contain favorable information about firms' prospects, abnormally high (low) levels of buying (selling) from managers should occur before repurchase announcements. In addition, the magnitude should be more significant for fixed-price tender offers than the other two alternatives, as the former usually signal more credible information. Consistent with this prediction, Lee, Mikkelson, and Partch (1992) find that, on average, managers from the repurchasing firms tend to buy more or sell fewer of their own firms' shares six months before repurchase announcements. More important, the abnormal trading only occurs in fixed-price tender offers but not in Dutch auctions. The difference in managers' trading between fixed-price tender offers and Dutch auctions suggests that the two types of repurchases might convey different information about the firms' future prospects.

Extending the research by Comment and Jarrell (1991) and Lee et al. (1992), Lie and McConnell (1998) examine whether firms conducting fixed-price or Dutch-auction tender offers also exhibit any systematic differences in future earnings growth. Their argument is that if fixed-price tender offers reveal more favorable information than Dutch auctions, there should be greater earnings improvement for firms using fixed-price offers than for those using Dutch auctions. By using a more expanded sample from 1981 through 1994 and three different benchmarks for earnings improvement, Lie and McConnell find some evidence of earnings improvement following both types of tender-offer repurchases. The difference between these two types, however, is insignificant. In contrast to Comment and Jarrell, Lie and McConnell find no difference in abnormal announcement returns between fixed-price and Dutch-auction tender offers.

Denis (1990) investigates firms using open-market and tender-offer repurchases as well as special dividends as defensive devices to deter hostile takeovers.

He finds that although many hostile takeovers in his sample did not succeed, the target management implemented major restructuring initiatives after the contest such as divestitures or asset sales. Because the subsequent improvement in firm performance might simply be an ultimate response to control contest, the signaling hypothesis has difficulties explaining such situations.

Dann, Masulis, and Mayers (1991) examine a sample of 122 tender offers by 101 firms from 1969 through 1978 and show that those firms are associated with a positive earnings surprise over the concurrent and subsequent two years after announcements. Those firms also experience a reduction in the cost of equity capital. Announcement returns are positively correlated with the magnitude of earnings surprise. Overall, Dann et al. conclude that tender-offer announcements convey information about current and future earnings.

Hertzel and Jain (1991) extend this line of research and reach a similar conclusion. Specifically, their study using a sample of 226 tender offers over the period 1970–1984 shows that those tender-offer announcements convey favorable information about firms' future earnings. They further show that analysts tend to revise upward their forecasts for the repurchasing firms after the announcements. A new result from their study is that the market-price reactions around the announcements are only correlated with short-term revisions but not with long-term revisions. This suggests that tender-offer repurchases might contain primarily transitory changes in earnings.

Stephens and Weisbach (1998) find some support for both the undervaluation and free cash flows hypotheses based on a sample of open-market share repurchases. In particular, they show a negative relationship between the magnitude of a firm's repurchase in one quarter and the performance of its stock in the prior quarter. Thus, managers have more incentives to repurchase shares when they perceive their firm is undervalued. Further, their estimated quarterly repurchase amount is also positively correlated with both the expected and the surprise components of the firm's quarterly cash flows, indicating that firms adjust their repurchase amount in accordance with the changes in the firm's cash level.

Grullon and Michaely (2004) provide evidence consistent with the free cash flows hypothesis but not with the signaling hypothesis. Specifically, they do not find that firms undertaking open-market repurchase programs experience a significant increase in earnings or profitability. In fact, their sampled repurchasing firms underperform in several performance metrics relative to their non-repurchasing peers. They also document that firms with shrinking investment opportunity sets and sufficient free cash flows are more likely to initiate open-market repurchase programs.

Nohel and Tarhan (1998) provide corroborative results that repurchasing firms experiencing improvement in operating performance are those with low Tobin's Q. They demonstrate that the three-year median post-repurchase cumulative operating performance is 23.3 percent for low-Q firms and –1.94 percent for high-Q firms. More important, the low-Q firms achieve positive performance by restructuring their business rather than by increasing capital expenditures. Again, their findings are inconsistent with the signaling hypothesis.

The survey study by Brav et al. (2005) also finds little support for the standard signaling hypothesis. While financial executives agree that dividend and repurchase announcements convey information to investors, they do not believe that corporate payouts are a costly signal or dividends and repurchases provide different information contents. More important, they reject the notion that firms pay out extra cash via dividends or repurchases to reveal management's evaluation about the firm's true worth or to signal their higher firm value than their competitors. Thus, corporations seemingly use payouts to convey information, but the information content in the payout policy requires further investigation.

In contrast to Nohel and Tarhan (1998) and Grullon and Michaely (2004), Lie (2005) documents significant improvement in post-repurchase operating performance. He uses quarterly data rather than annual data used in other studies and sorts out whether firms immediately repurchase shares after announcement. Lie shows that among the firms announcing the 4,729 open-market repurchase programs during the period 1981–2000, only those implementing the repurchase program experience positive performance changes. The improvement mostly occurs within two quarters and persists for two years after the announcement quarter.

Most of the empirical studies examine the wealth effects of repurchases on stockholders. A related but less addressed question is whether and how repurchases affect bondholders' wealth. Dann (1981) appears to be the first to study this issue. Using 143 cash-tender offers over the period 1962–1976, he finds significantly positive announcement returns for stockholders, convertible debt holders, and convertible preferred stockholders. However, there was no significant wealth change for straight debt holders.

Maxwell and Stephens (2003) provide a more updated study on this subject. Using a sample of 945 repurchase announcements with bond data available over the period 1973–1997, they find a significantly negative abnormal bond-price reaction to repurchase announcements. The magnitude is even more negative for larger repurchase programs and for firms with non-investment-grade debt. These findings indicate a wealth transfer from bondholders to stockholders. Interestingly, although the bond value decreases after the repurchase announcement, Maxwell and Stephens further report that the positive announcement return for stockholders more than offsets the negative wealth change for bondholders, resulting in a positive net change in firm value. Consequently, the evidence suggests that the market still views open-market repurchases as positive signals beyond the effect of wealth transfer.

CONCLUSIONS

So far, the first part of this chapter has provided a discussion of the existing theoretical and empirical analyses of the first three motives for share repurchases: (1) regulatory and tax environments, (2) free cash flows, and (3) signaling. Current research suggests that firms change their payout policy in response to tax law changes. Specifically, firms have gradually substituted repurchases for dividends since the adoption of Rule 10b-18.

The results for the payout-tax clientele effect, however, are mixed. Although several theories indicate that firms change their payouts to satisfy the heterogeneous tax status of their shareholders or to attract different types of investors, empirical studies offer insufficient evidence to support those arguments.

In contrast, current studies support the notion that firms use share repurchases as a mechanism to mitigate the agency costs of free cash flows. Several studies demonstrate that firms with abnormally high levels of cash flows and/or few investment opportunities are more likely to initiate share repurchase programs and return extra cash to shareholders. Finally, the existing, especially the latest, studies provide mixed support for the signaling hypothesis. Researchers believe that managers use share repurchases to reveal their own private information about their companies. Yet the information content of the signal is ambiguous. This area deserves further investigation.

REFERENCES

Allen, Franklin, Antonio Bernardo, and Ivo Welch. 2000. "A Theory of Dividends Based on Tax Clientele." *Journal of Finance* 55:6, 2499–2536.

Asquith, Paul, and David Mullins. 1986. "Signaling with Dividends, Stock Repurchases, and Equity Issues." *Financial Management* 15:3, 27–44.

Bagwell, Laurie S., and John B. Shoven. 1989. "Cash Distributions to Shareholders." *Journal of Economic Perspectives* 3:3, 129–140.

Barclay, Michael J., and Clifford W. Smith, Jr. 1988. "Corporate Payout Policy: Cash Dividends versus Open-Market Repurchases." *Journal of Financial Economics* 22:1, 61–82.

Bhattacharya, Sudipto. 1979. "Imperfect Information, Dividend Policy, and 'the Bird in the Hand' Fallacy." *Bell Journal of Economics* 10:1, 259–270.

Bradley, Michael, and L. MacDonald Wakeman. 1983. "The Wealth Effects of Targeted Share Repurchases." *Journal of Financial Economics* 11:1, 301–328.

Brav, Alon, John R. Graham, Campbell R. Harvey, and Roni Michaely. 2005. "Payout Policy in the 21st Century." *Journal of Financial Economics* 77:3, 483–527.

Brennan, Michael, and Anjan Thakor. 1990. "Shareholder Preferences and Dividend Policy." *Journal of Finance* 45:4, 993–1019.

Chang, Saeyoung, and Michael Hertzel. 2004. "Equity Ownership and Firm Value: Evidence from Targeted Stock Repurchases." *Financial Review* 39:3, 389–407.

Chowdhry, Bhagwan, and Vikram Nanda. 1994. "Repurchase Premia as a Reason for Dividends: A Dynamic Model of Corporate Payout Policies." *Review of Financial Studies* 7:2, 321–350.

Comment, Robert, and Gregg Jarrell. 1991. "The Relative Signaling Power of Dutch-Auction and Fixed-Price Self-Tender Offers and Open-Market Share Repurchases." *Journal of Finance* 46:4, 1243–1271.

Constantinides, George, and Bruce Grundy. 1989. "Optimal Investment with Stock Repurchases and Financing as Signals." *Review of Financial Studies* 2:4, 445–465.

Dann, Larry Y. 1981. "Common Stock Repurchases: An Analysis of Returns to Bondholders and Stockholders." *Journal of Financial Economics* 9:1, 113–138.

Dann, Larry Y., and Harry DeAngelo. 1988. "Corporate Financial Policy and Corporate Control: A Study of Defensive Adjustments in Asset and Ownership Structure." *Journal of Financial Economics* 20:1, 87–127.

Dann, Larry Y., Ronald W. Masulis, and David Mayers. 1991. "Repurchase Tender Offers and Earnings Information." *Journal of Accounting and Economics* 14:3, 217–251.

DeAngelo, Harry, and Linda DeAngelo. 2006a. "The Irrelevance of the MM Dividend Irrelevance Theorem." *Journal of Financial Economics* 79:2, 293–316.

DeAngelo, Harry, Linda DeAngelo, and Douglas J. Skinner. 2004. "Are Dividends Disappearing? Dividend Concentration and the Consolidation of Earnings." *Journal of Financial Economics* 72:3, 425–456.

DeAngelo, Harry, Linda DeAngelo, and Rene M. Stulz. 2006. "Dividend Policy and the Earned/Contributed Capital Mix: A Test of the Lifecycle Theory." *Journal of Financial Economics* 81:2, 227–254.

Del Guercio, Diane. 1996. "The Distorting Effect of the Prudent-Man Laws on Institutional Equity Investments." *Journal of Financial Economics* 40:1, 31–62.

Denis, David. 1990. "Defensive Changes in Corporate Payout Policy: Share Repurchase and Special Dividends." *Journal of Finance* 45:5, 1433–1456.

Demsetz, Harold, and Kenneth Lehn. 1985. "The Structure of Corporate Ownership: Causes and Consequences." *Journal of Political Economy* 93:6, 1155–1177.

Dittmar, Amy K. 2000. "Why Do Firms Repurchase Stock?" *Journal of Business* 73:3, 331–355.

Easterbrook, Frank H. 1984. "Two Agency-Cost Explanations of Dividends." *American Economic Review* 74:4, 650–659.

Fama, Eugene F., and Kenneth R. French. 2001. "Disappearing Dividends: Changing Firm Characteristics or Lower Propensity to Pay?" *Journal of Financial Economics* 60:1, 3–43.

Grinstein, Yaniv, and Roni Michaely. 2005. "Institutional Holdings and Payout Policy." *Journal of Finance* 60:3, 1389–1426.

Grullon, Gustavo, and David L. Ikenberry. 2000. "What Do We Know about Stock Repurchases?" *Journal of Applied Corporate Finance* 13:1, 31–51.

Grullon, Gustavo, and Roni Michaely. 2002. "Dividends, Repurchases, and the Substitution Hypothesis." *Journal of Finance* 57:4, 1649–1684.

Grullon, Gustavo, and Roni Michaely. 2004. "The Information Content of Share Repurchase Programs." *Journal of Finance* 59:2, 651–680.

Hausch, Donald, and James Seward. 1993. "Signaling with Dividends and Share Repurchases: A Choice between Deterministic and Stochastic Cash Disbursements." *Review of Financial Studies* 6:1, 121–154.

Hertzel, Michael, and Prem Jain. 1991. "Earnings and Risk Changes around Stock Repurchase Tender Offers." *Journal of Accounting and Economics* 14:3, 253–274.

Hsieh, Jim, and Qinghai Wang. 2007. "Disappearing Dividends and Trends in Corporate Payouts." Working Paper, George Mason University and Georgia Institute of Technology.

Hsieh, Jim, and Qinghai Wang. 2008. "Insiders' Tax Preferences and Firm's Choice between Dividends and Share Repurchases." *Journal of Financial and Quantitative Analysis* 43:1, 213–244.

Ikenberry, David, Josef Lakonishok, and Theo Vermaelen. 1995. "Market Underreaction to Open Market Share Repurchases." *Journal of Financial Economics* 39:2/3, 181–208.

Jensen, Michael C. 1986. "Agency Costs of Free Cash Flow, Corporate Finance, and Takeovers." *American Economic Review* 76:2, 323–329.

Jensen, Michael C., and William H. Meckling. 1976. "Theory of the Firm: Managerial Behavior, Agency Costs and Ownership Structure." *Journal of Financial Economics* 3:4, 305–360.

Kale, Jayant R., Thomas H. Noe, and Gerald D. Gay. 1989. "Share Repurchase through Transferable Put Rights." *Journal of Financial Economics* 25:1, 141–160.

Kamma, Sreenivas, George Kanatas, and Steven Raymar. 1992. "Dutch Auction versus Fixed-Price Self-Tender Offers for Common Stock." *Journal of Financial Intermediation* 2:3, 277–307.

Klein, April, and James Rosenfeld. 1988. "Targeted Share Repurchases and Top Management Changes." *Journal of Financial Economics* 20:1/2, 493–506.

Lakonishok, Josef, and Theo Vermaelen. 1990. "Anomalous Price Behavior around Repurchase Tender Offers." *Journal of Finance* 45:2, 455–477.

Lee, D. Scott, Wayne H. Mikkelson, and Megan M. Partch. 1992. "Managers' Trading around Stock Repurchases." *Journal of Finance* 47:5, 1947–1961.

Lie, Erik, and Heidi J. Lie. 1999. "The Role of Personal Taxes in Corporate Decisions: An Empirical Analysis of Share Repurchases and Dividends." *Journal of Financial and Quantitative Analysis* 34:4, 533–552.

Lie, Erik. 2000. "Excess Funds and Agency Problems: An Empirical Study of Incremental Cash Disbursements." *Review of Financial Studies* 13:1, 219–248.

Lie, Erik. 2005. "Operating Performance Following Open Market Share Repurchase Announcements." *Journal of Accounting and Economics* 39:4, 411–436.

Lie, Erik, and John J. McConnell. 1998. "Earnings Signals in Fixed Price and Dutch Auction Self-tender Offers." *Journal of Financial Economics* 49:2, 161–186.

Lucas, Deborah J., and Robert L. McDonald. 1998. "Shareholder Heterogeneity, Adverse Selection, and Payout Policy." *Journal of Financial and Quantitative Analysis* 33:2, 233–253.

Maxwell, William F., and Clifford P. Stephens. 2003. "The Wealth Effects of Repurchases on Bondholders." *Journal of Finance* 58:2, 895–919.

McConnell, John J., and Henri Servaes. 1990. "Additional Evidence on Equity Ownership and Corporate Value." *Journal of Financial Economics* 27:2, 595–612.

Michaely, Roni, Richard H. Thaler, and Kent Womack. 1995. "Price Reactions to Dividend Initiations and Omissions: Overreaction or Drift?" *Journal of Finance* 50:2, 573–608.

Mikkelson, Wayne H., and Richard S. Ruback. 1991. "Targeted Repurchases and Common Stock Returns." *RAND Journal of Economics* 22:4, 544–561.

Miller, Merton H., and Franco Modigliani. 1961. "Dividend Policy, Growth, and the Valuation of Shares." *Journal of Business* 34:4, 411–433.

Miller, Merton, and Kevin Rock. 1985. "Dividend Policy under Asymmetric Information." *Journal of Finance* 40:4, 1031–1051.

Morck, Randall, Andrei Shleifer, and Robert Vishny. 1988. "Management Ownership and Market Valuation: An Empirical Analysis." *Journal of Financial Economics* 20:1/2, 293–315.

Nohel, Tom, and Vefa Tarhan. 1998. "Share Repurchases and Firm Performance: New Evidence on the Agency Costs of Free Cash Flow." *Journal of Financial Economics* 49:1, 187–222.

Ofer, Aharon R., and Anjan Thakor. 1987. "A Theory of Stock Price Responses to Alternative Corporate Cash Disbursement Methods: Stock Repurchases and Dividends." *Journal of Finance* 42:2, 365–394.

Persons, John C. 1997. "Heterogeneous Shareholders and Signaling with Share Repurchases." *Journal of Corporate Finance* 3:3, 221–249.

Peyer, Urs, and Theo Vermaelen. 2008. "The Nature and Persistence of Buyback Anomalies." *Review of Financial Studies*, forthcoming.

Shleifer, Andrei, and Robert Vishny. 1986. "Large Shareholders and Corporate Control." *Journal of Political Economy* 94:3, 461–488.

Stephens, Clifford, and Michael Weisbach. 1998. "Actual Share Reacquisitions in Open Market Repurchases Programs." *Journal of Finance* 53:1, 313–333.

Stulz, René M. 1988. "Managerial Control of Voting Rights: Financing Policies and the Market for Corporate Control." *Journal of Financial Economics* 20:1, 25–54.

Vermaelen, Theo. 1981. "Common Stock Repurchases and Market Signaling: An Empirical Study." *Journal of Financial Economics* 9:1, 139–183.

Vermaelen, Theo. 1984. "Repurchase Tender Offers, Signaling, and Managerial Incentives." *Journal of Financial and Quantitative Analysis* 19:2, 163–181.

Williams, John. 1988. "Efficient Signaling with Dividends, Investments, and Stock Repurchases." *Journal of Finance* 43:3, 737–747.

Wruck, Karen H. 1989. "Equity Ownership Concentration and Firm Value: Evidence from Private Equity Financings." *Journal of Financial Economics* 23:1, 3–28.

ABOUT THE AUTHORS

Jim Hsieh is an associate professor of finance at George Mason University. He received an MBA from University of Rochester, a MS in computational finance from Carnegie Mellon University, and a Ph.D. in finance from Ohio State University. His research focuses on corporate finance, particularly corporate restructuring decisions, corporate governance, and corporate payout policy. His research interests also include the investment behavior of institutional and individual investors as well as how the decision making of financial analysts interacts with other market participants. Hsieh's work has been cited in several trade publications, such as the *New York Times, Smart Money,* and *Bloomberg.* He has published his research in *Journal of Financial Economics, Journal of Financial and Quantitative Analysis,* and *Journal of Banking and Finance.*

Qinghai Wang is an associate professor of finance at the Georgia Institute of Technology. He received his Ph.D. from the Fisher College of Business, Ohio State University. His research focuses on the investment decisions and portfolio choices of institutional and individual investors and the impact of their behaviors on asset prices and market efficiency. His research interests also include behavioral aspects of corporate decision making and corporate governance, shareholder voting and the role of investors in corporate governance, and corporate payout policy. Wang's work has been published in *Journal of Finance, Journal of Financial Economics, Journal of Business,* and *Journal of Financial and Quantitative Analysis.* He has presented his research at various academic conferences, and his work has been cited in news publications such as the *New York Times* and *CFO* magazine.

CHAPTER 15

Stock Repurchases: Theory and Evidence, Part 2

JIM HSIEH
Associate Professor of Finance, George Mason University

QINGHAI WANG
Associate Professor of Finance, Georgia Institute of Technology

INTRODUCTION

This chapter continues the review of the theoretical and empirical studies on share repurchases. It provides a discussion of three other motives that influence firms' repurchase decisions: capital structure, takeover deterrence, and employee stock options. Overall, the existing research provides support for these three hypotheses. In addition, the chapter discusses why firms prefer one method of payout to another—cash dividends versus stock repurchases.

MOTIVES FOR SHARE REPURCHASE

Capital Structure

Two views dominate the literature in capital structure. The first view, called the pecking-order theory, contends that because of adverse selection, firms choose their financing mechanisms according to the following sequence: internal capital, external debt, and external equity (Myers and Majluf, 1984). The second view suggests that firms' leverage ratios adjust slowly toward their targets (for more recent studies, see, e.g., Fama and French, 2002; Leary and Roberts, 2005; Flannery and Rangan, 2006). Assuming that an optimal debt ratio exists, a firm could adjust its capital structure toward the target by issuing equity or reducing debt (to decrease leverage) and by issuing debt or repurchasing equity (to increase leverage).

Dittmar (2000) tests this theory by using a simple specification:

$$\text{Repurchase}_{it} = \alpha_{it} + \beta_1 \text{Leverage}_{i(t-1)} + \beta_2 X_{i(t-1)} + \varepsilon_{it}, \tag{15.1}$$

where *Repurchase* is the dollar amount of repurchases scaled by the prior year market value of equity; *Leverage* is the difference between the firm's net debt-to-asset ratio and its target ratio; and X is a vector of variables that could also influence corporate repurchase decisions. If the optimal capital structure affects a firm's decision to buy back shares, the prior-year leverage ratio will be lower for repurchasing firms than for nonrepurchasing firms, and the coefficient of *Leverage* will be negative. Consistent with this hypothesis, Dittmar finds that lower-leveraged firms are more likely to repurchase shares to increase their leverage ratios.

Hovakimian, Opler, and Titman (2001) also test the impact of an optimal debt ratio on firms' repurchasing decisions. They employ the following specification that explicitly takes into account the fact that firms' target ratios might change over time:

$$\text{Leverage}_{it} = \alpha W_{it} + \eta_{it} \tag{15.2a}$$

$$(\text{Debt/Equity Choice})_{it} = \beta \text{LeverageDeficit}_{it-1} + \gamma X_{it-1} + \varepsilon_{it}, \tag{15.2b}$$

where W and X are vectors of variables that could affect the leverage ratio and the debt-equity choice, respectively. Equation 15.2a estimates the target leverage ratio. *LeverageDeficit* is the difference between the firm's current leverage ratio and its estimated target from 15.2a. Equation 15.2b investigates whether a firm's leverage deficit influences its debt-equity choice. Using a total of 11,136 security issues and 7,366 repurchases during the period 1979–1997, the authors find that firms tend to use stock repurchases and debt retirements to move their debt ratios toward the targets.

The existing studies investigating the relationship between corporate capital structure and payout policy usually assume that firms have certain levels of the debt ratio in mind and use various securities as tools to adjust to their targets by issuing or repurchasing those securities. In this setting, researchers treat capital structure policy as the primary financial decision while repurchasing (or payout) policy is simply a subordinate decision. In contrast, DeAngelo and DeAngelo (2006) argue that firms' underlying economic fundamentals could determine both capital structure and payout policies simultaneously. The authors argue that firms constantly face the trade-off between mitigating free cash flow (FCF) problems and maintaining financial flexibility. To control agency problems, FCF-generating firms have to make regular cash distributions to equity holders and bondholders. At the same time, firms have to develop potential sources of future financial flexibility in response to unexpected earnings shortfalls. Thus, a firm's capital structure is a reflection of its ongoing decisions to build and draw down its cash flow reservoir while controlling for potential agency problems.

Takeover Deterrence

Theories

Another commonly cited motive for share repurchasing is to fend off hostile takeover bids. Managers use repurchases to serve as a takeover repellent to an unwanted bid by signaling firm value or increasing the cost of purchasing remaining shares outstanding. Bagnoli, Gordon, and Lipman (1989) propose a signaling model that, under information asymmetry, the firm's managers have private information about their ability to run the company and the true firm value.

Raiders also know their ability to run the company and the new firm value if they acquire the company. The shareholders do not know any of the three factors: the ability of managers, the ability of raiders, and the true or new value of the firm. Another assumption is that managers want to retain their jobs; thus, they are willing to engage in defensive techniques and to pay a high repurchase premium. Consequently, a tender-offer repurchase reveals the managers' private information about the quality of the firm's assets and its future value.

Another positive signal comes from an announced takeover bid, which essentially reveals the new firm's value if the raider takes over and restructures the firm. The model predicts that the stock price (1) increases after a takeover announcement, (2) increases as the raider's bid price increases for a successful takeover, and (3) remains high and becomes riskier than before the bid announcement for a failed takeover. Another implication of the theory is that managers can reveal their own valuation and dissuade shareholders from tendering their shares to the raiders so that the takeover bid eventually fails.

Bagwell (1991) develops an equilibrium model using repurchases as a takeover deterrent in the presence of heterogeneous valuations from shareholders. The model assumes that there are two firms: an acquiring firm and a target firm. In contrast to Bagnoli et al. (1989), Bagwell's model does not assume information asymmetry. Instead, the target firm value is common knowledge regardless of the bid outcome. The model has two time periods. At time one, the target management decides the form of payout: cash dividend versus share repurchase. At time two, the potential bidding firm decides whether to launch a takeover bid. At time one, if the firm decides to disburse cash via dividend, it distributes the amount to shareholders on a pro rata basis. On the other hand, for a tender-offer repurchase, shareholders who are willing to tender their shares are those with low valuations about the target firm. This is owing to the assumption that shareholders have heterogeneous valuations and that the supply curve for target shares is upward sloping.

Bagwell (1992) and Brown and Ryngaert (1992) provide evidence that firms face upward-sloping supply curves when they conduct Dutch-auction tender-offer repurchases. Consequently, the target firm consists of shareholders with high valuations after share repurchase; thereby, this effectively increases the cost of taking over the target. The implication from the model is that when the firm's managers expect a potential takeover bid, they are more likely to employ a share repurchase as a deterrent. In addition, the probability of distributing cash via repurchase increases when shareholder heterogeneity is high.

Harris and Raviv (1988) also model share repurchases as takeover deterrents but from a different perspective. They posit that the target management uses short-term capital structure changes as an antitakeover mechanism by changing the ownership structure of the firm. In particular, incumbent (target) managers can increase the firm's leverage ratio by exchanging debt for equity. This will result in a substantial shift in voting power from shareholders with low valuation to those with high valuation because the former are more likely to tender their shares. The increase in the leverage ratio could also improve target firm performance because of the reduction in free cash flows (Jensen, 1986).

Stulz (1988) provides a similar argument explaining how firms could use stock repurchases to deter hostile takeover bids through voting. Instead of focusing on shareholders' voting rights, he suggests that repurchases effectively increase managers' control of voting rights and increase the difficulty for potential bidders to acquire enough control. The theory indicates that repurchases reduce the resources for target managers to invest in negative net-present-value projects but also implies that managerial entrenchment could happen in target firms after repurchases. If the latter effect dominates the former, repurchases used as an antitakeover device should be associated with negative announcement returns; otherwise, the announcement returns will be positive.

Sinha (1991) presents an information-based theory in which a potential target uses debt-financed stock repurchase to fend off hostile takeover threats. In the model setup, outside investors do not know the level of investment. Thus, without any takeover threat, managers could allocate resources originally for funding growth opportunities to perquisite consumption. With potential takeover bids, managers use debt-financed repurchases to bond themselves from wasting resources. The model provides two testable implications. First, the announcement returns for debt-financed repurchases in response to takeover threats should be positive. Second, a high period of repurchases should accompany a high period of takeover activity.

EMPIRICAL RESULTS

Overall, the existing empirical findings support the idea that firms use repurchases to deter unwanted takeover bids. Yet the impact of such motivation on shareholder wealth is ambiguous. Dann and DeAngelo (1983) provide some early evidence that firms repurchase shares from blockholders and reach standstill agreements to reduce competition for corporate control. Using 81 deals between 1977 and 1980, they find that targeted stock repurchases and standstill agreements are associated with negative announcement returns for nonparticipating stockholders. Their results support the view of managerial entrenchment. The disappearance of takeover threat in the capital market induces greater managerial shirking and perquisite consumption at shareholders' expense.

Klein and Rosenfeld (1988) present evidence that firms conducting targeted share repurchases experience abnormal management turnover within one year after repurchases. They interpret their findings as supporting the view that internal corporate control mechanisms are also effective in monitoring top managers' behavior. Denis (1990) studies top management turnover for a sample of firms conducting tender-offer and open-market repurchases to fend off takeover threats and reports similar results.

Bradley and Wakeman (1983) also document the negative announcement returns on targeted share repurchases. Using 61 companies repurchasing large blocks of shares for the period 1974–1980, they show that the wealth loss for the nonparticipating shareholders is about 1 percent to 2 percent. Repurchases that terminate potential takeover bids are associated with an even more negative average return (−13 percent).

Dann and DeAngelo (1988) provide evidence on targeted share repurchases for firms engaging in takeover contests. In particular, they find that the average announcement return is about −2 percent to −3 percent for firms responding to hostile bids with defensive changes in asset and ownership structure. Their results support the models by Harris and Raviv (1988) and Stulz (1988). Dann and DeAngelo further document that those hostile takeovers do not prevail in many cases in which target management implements planned restructurings, a result consistent with the theory proposed by Bagnoli et al. (1989).

Mikkelson and Ruback (1991) dispute the argument that targeted share repurchases reduce nonparticipating shareholders' wealth. Specifically, they recognize that a targeted repurchase is the outcome of an ongoing takeover process. Most studies only estimate the change in shareholder wealth around the repurchase announcements. Mikkelson and Ruback suggest that the change in shareholder wealth for a targeted firm should be measured starting from the initial accumulation of the block shares through its repurchase announcement. Tracking 111 targeted repurchases from 1980 through 1983, the authors estimate total stock-price effect of the block shareholdings and repurchases. They report mean abnormal returns for repurchasing firms in four different periods during the process. The returns are 5.34 percent from the date when a block holder buys the target shares until two days before the initial 13D filing, 3.68 percent around the initial 13D filing, 3.33 percent from the filing date until the date the firm announced a targeted repurchase, and −3.52 percent for the announcement return of the repurchase. The series of returns results in an average return of 7.37 percent. Evidently, the positive return for the whole takeover process indicates that block holders' actions benefit stockholders, even for nonparticipating shareholders.

Denis (1990) investigates the effectiveness of defensive payouts announced in response to hostile takeovers. The sample consists of 40 repurchases and nine special dividends after actual or rumored takeover bids between 1980 and 1987. His evidence suggests that share repurchases and special dividends are effective antitakeover devices because many repurchasing firms remain independent after the contest. Even so, firms are more likely to experience large changes in both the capital structure and the structure of voting rights after defensive payouts. This supports the theories of Harris and Raviv (1988) and Stulz (1988).

Lie and Lie (1999) test whether managers more frequently select self-tender offers or special dividends as the takeover defense. Their sample consists of 213 self-tender offers and 433 special dividends announced between 1981 and 1994. They hypothesize that firms facing takeover threats should employ tender-offer repurchases because there is no reason to believe that special dividends can effectively deter hostile bids. In contrast to this conjecture, Lie and Lie find little evidence that firms are more likely to use tender-offer repurchases than special dividends to fend off potential outside threats.

Dittmar (2000) also examines whether firms use stock repurchases to deter takeovers. She includes in Equation 15.1 a dummy variable that equals 1 if the repurchasing firm is the target of an announced or rumored takeover attempt in the previous or current year of repurchase announcement. Dittmar then regresses the dollar volume of repurchase against this dummy variable along with other variables. The regressions show that the takeover dummy is significant in 6 of the 15 years of the sample period. Many of the significant years coincide with restructuring waves in the late 1980s. At most, the evidence suggests that only some repurchases during that period are in response to an increased takeover threat, but those beyond that period are not.

As discussed, many studies document that tender offers and targeted share repurchases serve as effective devices to repel unwanted takeover bids. Although Denis (1990) and Dittmar (2000) present some evidence that firms could also use open-market repurchases to deter hostile takeovers, such repurchases are not as popular as other repurchase mechanisms in response to hostile corporate control activity. A worthwhile research topic would be to investigate whether open-market repurchases play the same role as other repurchase mechanisms. One possibility is that firms use tender-offer repurchases to deter takeover attempts but use open-market repurchases for other purposes. As previously mentioned, firms can use fixed-price and Dutch-auction tender offers to retire a large percentage of shares within a short period. In contrast, firms tend to buy back shares within an extended time period after initiating open-market repurchase programs. Thus, fixed-price and Dutch-auction tender offers may be better antitakeover mechanisms than open-market repurchases if companies are pressured to quickly thwart takeover attempts.

A counterargument is that all different types of repurchases are effective in repelling hostile takeovers, but firms use them at different stages over the duration of the contest. Billett and Xue (2007) argue that firms initiate tender offers in the midst of hostile attempts for corporate control while firms conduct open-market stock repurchases in anticipation of possible bids. Thus, existing studies that simply examine whether open-market repurchases follow takeover events cannot capture the effectiveness of those repurchases in repelling unsolicited raiders. Instead, Billett and Xue employ a two-stage regression system to estimate the deterrent effect of open-market repurchases. Specifically, they estimate in the first equation the ex ante probability of the repurchasing firm becoming a takeover target. Then, in the second equation, they regress share repurchase activity on the perceived threat of a takeover. Using a large sample of repurchasing firms from 1985 to 1996, they show that open-market repurchases exhibit strong takeover deterrent effect. Apparently, firms undertake repurchase programs when they perceive the possibility of becoming takeover targets.

Another innovation from Billett and Xue (2007) is that they adopt a censored quantile regression (CQR) model to estimate the relationship between repurchase activity and estimated probability of becoming a target in the second equation. They argue that both Tobit and CQR models can be used to estimate repurchase activity, which is left censored at zero. The CQR model, however, generates more consistent coefficient estimates under regular conditions. Powell (1986) provides more details about the CQR estimation.

Stock-Option Grants and Earnings Management

Evidence shows that aggregate payout ratios have increased substantially since 1992, a period coinciding with the growing popularity of option grants in executive and employee compensation packages. A relationship could exist between the upward trend of share repurchases and the increasing portion of option grants in executive and employee compensations. In particular, the popularity of option-based compensations could influence corporate payouts in three different ways. First, agency theories suggest that option grants to corporate executives could better align the interests of managers and shareholders. As a result, an increase in total payouts may occur. Second, because of the potential dilution of earnings per share (EPS) from option exercises, firms may buy back shares to offset such dilution. Third, option grants may cause a structural change in corporate payouts. Because dividend yields decrease the share prices and the corresponding option values in the compensation arrangement, managers might be reluctant to employ cash dividends as the form of payout and instead prefer share repurchases.

Lambert, Lanen, and Larcker (1989) find a correlation between the adoption of an executive stock option plan and a substantial reduction in the level of cash dividends. Extending Lambert et al.'s argument suggests that managers should have strong incentives to substitute repurchases for dividends when managers are heavily compensated with option grants. Consistent with this conjecture, Jolls (1998) documents that firms with greater option grants in executive compensation are more likely to repurchase shares than are those with fewer option grants. Furthermore, Jolls finds no relationship between firms' adoption of restricted stock in executive compensations and their propensity to repurchase shares. Because restricted stock, unlike options, does not dilute EPS, Jolls concludes that preventing EPS dilution is one of the major motives for firms to initiate open-market repurchase programs.

Weisbenner (2000) also documents similar relationships between firms' repurchase decisions and their option-based compensations by using various sample firms in the S&P 500, MidCap 400, and Forbes 500 at the end of 1994. He further shows that the size of a firm's option grant is a strong predictor of its subsequent share repurchases. This relationship, however, does not exist between the option holdings of the top five executives and the company's repurchases. Weisbenner argues that stock options granted to top executives affect corporate payouts differently than options granted to other employees. Specifically, when firms grant a large scale of options to employees, they use repurchases to minimize the impact of option exercises on EPS dilution. This increases share repurchases and total payouts. On the other hand, when the option holdings of top executives are high, firms are more likely to retain earnings and reduce dividend payout to raise the executives' option value.

Both Jolls (1998) and Weisbenner (2000) study firms' decisions on repurchases and the choice between repurchases and other cash-distribution alternatives. Fenn and Liang (2001) investigate the impact of managerial options on the level of corporate payouts. They also extend their study by including managerial stock ownership and examine whether these two different types of ownership provide different incentives for corporate payouts. Using the Execucomp database for 1993–1997, Fenn and Liang first present evidence that managerial stock holdings are associated with higher payouts for firms with potentially greater agency costs. This suggests that managerial stock holdings help mitigate the free cash flow problems in those firms. They also show that higher managerial option holdings are associated with lower dividends and higher repurchases. This finding is consistent with that of Lambert et al. (1989), which suggests that firms increase repurchases at the expense of dividends. Finally, Fenn and Liang report that managerial option ownership is negatively related to firms' total payouts, a result supporting the notion that managers use share repurchases for their own benefits.

Similar to Weisbenner (2000) and Fenn and Liang (2001), Kahle (2002) examines how stock-option grants affect corporate repurchase decisions. To better measure managerial incentives, she considers both exercised and exercisable options for all employees of the firm from the year before until the year after the repurchase. She also links repurchase announcement returns with option grants to estimate market reaction on management repurchase decisions. Consistent with the argument in

Weisbenner and Fenn and Liang, Kahle presents strong evidence that firms repurchase shares to fund employees' exercisable options such that firms can reduce earnings dilution. Her evidence shows a high correlation between the number of shares actually repurchased and the number of options exercisable. Kahle further documents that firms' repurchase decisions are influenced by whether managers' wealth would be affected by dividend payment. The market, however, appears to recognize firms' repurchase decisions to fund employees' option exercises and to protect managers' own wealth. The announcement return is lower for repurchasing firms with large numbers of option grants.

Moreover, given the premise that share prices are sensitive to reported EPS, managers could employ share repurchase programs to manage earnings. In doing so, managers can effectively reduce the impact of diluting EPS caused by option exercises. Burgstahler and Dichev (1997), Andrade (1999), and Degeorge, Patel, and Zeckhauser (1999) among others provide empirical evidence that links EPS with stock valuation. Bens, Nagar, Skinner, and Wong (2003) find strong evidence that managerial incentives to manage diluted EPS affect stock repurchase decisions. Managers increase the level of share repurchases when facing a potentially dilutive effect of employee stock options. More important, they increase repurchases when earnings are below the level required to achieve the desired rate of EPS growth. Further, managers' decisions to buy back shares are not associated with actual employee stock options exercises, suggesting that earnings management might play a more important role than employee option exercises.

Gong, Louis, and Sun (2008) also provide a link between earnings management and share repurchases. They document significant improvements in long-term operating performance after firms repurchase their own shares. The significant change in performance, however, is absent from traditional signaling or free cash flow arguments. Instead, they show that firms purposely deflate earnings (with negative abnormal accruals) before repurchase announcements. Negative abnormal accruals are associated with higher future stock and operating performance. Gong et al. further report that the situation is even more severe for firms with higher executive ownership. Overall, their findings reveal that managers with more share holdings have greater incentives to manage earnings downward before announcing repurchases so that they will receive more personal benefits.

CASH DIVIDENDS VERSUS STOCK REPURCHASES

What determines a firm's form of payout? If cash dividends and stock repurchases are perfect substitutes, there should be random patterns in the use of repurchases and dividends. Conversely, if firms have preferences toward alternative payout mechanisms over time, some systematic trends in payouts should exist. As shown in Figure 14.1 in the previous chapter, fewer U.S. firms have distributed extra cash as dividends since the early 1980s. In contrast, Figure 14.2 in the previous chapter depicts a picture that firms have increased their repurchases over time. Evidence from Grullon and Michaely (2002) indicates that firms have gradually substituted repurchases for dividends. Clearly, the time trends in repurchases and dividends are not random. But what might drive these structural changes in corporate payouts?

The differential tax treatments between capital gains and dividends generally favor repurchases. But even if the tax rates on capital gains and dividends are the same (as in the late 1980s and after 2003), investors could still prefer share repurchases because of the timing ability and flexibility embedded in repurchase programs. Further, theories discussed in the previous sections suggest that dividends and repurchases could have different effects in reducing free cash flows, revealing information, or playing different roles as takeover deterrents. A logical question to ask then is, Can these theories explain the firm's payout choice between dividends and repurchases? If so, can they also help explain the observed time trend in corporate payouts?

Because the government usually taxes cash dividends more heavily than share repurchases, several earlier articles such as those of Ofer and Thakor (1987), Barclay and Smith (1988), and Brennan and Thakor (1990) attempt to explain why many firms choose dividends rather than repurchases to distribute extra cash. Those studies attempted to model the trade-offs of signaling benefits and potential costs associated with these two forms of payouts.

Besides the signaling consideration, firms could use different payout methods to attract the types of investors they desire (the clientele effect). For example, Allen, Bernardo, and Welch (2000) provide a theory that firms use dividends rather than share repurchases to attract large, better-informed investors.

In addition, from the regulatory and tax perspective, firms could adjust their payouts or change their payout methods as a response to regulatory changes. The previous section describes the impact of two major regulatory changes on corporate repurchase policy. In particular, after the government adopted Rule 10b-18, firms started to initiate more share repurchase programs. The regulatory changes, however, might not be able to fully explain the increasing popularity of share repurchases. Other factors might play a more important role on the increasing trend of repurchases. For instance, some believe that a factor contributing to the surge in repurchases in the mid-1990s was the growing use of executive option grants in compensation package.

On the taxation side, existing research suggests that firms could set their payout policy to accommodate the heterogeneous tax status of their shareholders (see, e.g., Lie and Lie, 1999) or to minimize insiders' own tax liability (Hsieh and Wang, 2008). In addition, using the 2003 dividend tax cut as an exogenous shock, Brown, Liang, and Weisbenner (2007) document that firms with higher executive ownership are more likely to increase dividends. This result is consistent with Hsieh and Wang's argument. Thus, firms may choose dividends or repurchases to satisfy the tax situation of their shareholders or insiders.

Another possibility is that firms change their payout methods to respond to changes in firms' characteristics. For example, Jagannathan, Stephens, and Weisbach (2000) as well as Guay and Harford (2000) assert that cash flow permanence and variability could determine corporate payouts. Firms paying out cash via dividends have higher permanent cash flows, while firms repurchasing shares have higher temporary cash flows. In addition, repurchasing firms have greater cash flow volatility than dividend-paying firms. These results imply that firms use dividends to respond to permanent earnings increases and repurchases to distribute intermittent cash windfalls. In summary, existing research points out that various motives such as regulatory and tax changes and firm attributes significantly influence a firm's method of payout. Although several existing articles provide some answers about this issue, the topic deserves further investigation.

CONCLUSIONS

Corporate payout policy is one of the most researched areas in the finance literature. This chapter reviews the existing studies on corporate repurchase decisions.
Most researchers agree that several factors are important in explaining why firms
initiate share repurchase programs. Chapters 14 and 15 identify the six most studied motives for share repurchases: (1) regulatory and tax environments, (2) free
cash flows, (3) signaling and undervaluation, (4) capital structure, (5) takeover deterrence, and (6) employee stock options. Most theories are built to capture the first
three motives. For example, for the payout-tax clientele effect, researchers assume
that firms deal with the trade-off between higher tax liability of dividends and
higher adverse selection cost of repurchases. In addition, under the free cash flow
hypothesis, firms pay out extra cash via dividends or repurchases to mitigate the
conflicts of interest between managers and shareholders. In the signaling hypothesis, firms use repurchases to signal their current undervaluation or future earnings.

Despite strong and clear theoretical predictions for the first three motives,
the empirical support mostly goes to the tax and free cash flow explanations.
Although the signaling motive was among the earliest identified, the existing
empirical findings are ambiguous. Numerous empirical studies document positive
announcement returns for repurchasing firms, a result consistent with the notion
that firms use repurchases to signal the market undervaluation of their firms.
The existing studies, however, cannot provide a definitive answer about whether
the information content of the signal goes beyond the announcement quarter.
Several studies provide evidence of positive performance changes after repurchase
announcements, while others reveal insignificant or even negative performance
changes. Hence, this issue appears to merit additional work. Furthermore, an
important extension from the signaling hypothesis would be to examine why
the market does not fully comprehend the signal around the periods when firms
announce repurchases. As several studies show, firms, especially those with high
book-to-market ratios, experience a positive postrepurchase-announcement drift.
Overall, the market seems to initially underreact to the repurchase news. A recent
study by Peyer and Vermaelen (2008) indicates several possible explanations.

Another area for future research is the theoretical work specifically for the last
three motives. At this point, most of the theories attempt to model taxation, free
cash flow, or signaling and undervaluation considerations. For the last three motives (capital structure, takeover deterrence, and employee stock options), specific
theories are lacking. Although researchers propose several theories for the cases in
which firms use repurchase programs to deter hostile bids, most of the testable predictions for the last three factors are derived from other more generalized theories.
A possible specific theory to develop is a more cohesive explanation of corporate
payout and capital structure policies. As DeAngelo and DeAngelo (2006) observe,
existing theories imply that corporations establish their target capital structure
first and then employ cash payout (via dividends or share repurchases) or security
issuance to adjust to their predetermined targets. DeAngelo and DeAngelo argue
that firms simultaneously determine corporate capital structure and payout policy.

Finally, open-market repurchases have replaced cash dividends to become the
dominant form of payout since the past decade. Although several recent studies
investigate the determinants of corporate payout choices, this area remains largely

unexplored. Further, although firms have gradually paid out more cash through share repurchases, an important question to address is whether the evidenced substitution effect between repurchases and dividends has caused firms to reduce dividends simultaneously such that the total payout remains stable or if the effect has provided incentives for firms to increase the total payouts. If the latter is shown to be more accurate, what motivates firms to increase total payouts? Addressing these issues should also provide a better understanding about how corporate payout policy interacts with investment and other financial policies.

REFERENCES

Allen, Franklin, Antonio Bernardo, and Ivo Welch. 2000. "A Theory of Dividends Based on Tax Clientele." *Journal of Finance* 55:6, 2499–2536.

Andrade, Gregor. 1999. "Do Appearances Matter? The Impact of EPS Accretion and Dilution on Stock Prices." Working Paper, Harvard Business School.

Bagnoli, Mark, Roger Gordon, and Barton L. Lipman. 1989. "Stock Repurchases as a Takeover Defense." *Review of Financial Studies* 2:3, 423–443.

Bagwell, Laurie S. 1991. "Share Repurchase and Takeover Deterrence." *RAND Journal of Economics* 22:1, 72–88.

Bagwell, Laurie S. 1992. "Dutch Auction Repurchases: An Analysis of Shareholder Heterogeneity." *Journal of Finance* 47:1, 71–105.

Barclay, Michael J., and Clifford W. Smith, Jr. 1988. "Corporate Payout Policy: Cash Dividends versus Open-Market Repurchases." *Journal of Financial Economics* 22:1, 61–82.

Bens, Daniel, Venky Nagar, Douglas J. Skinner, and M. H. Franco Wong. 2003. "Employee Stock Options, EPS Dilution, and Stock Repurchases." *Journal of Accounting and Economics* 36:1, 51–90.

Billett, Matthew T., and Hui Xue. 2007. "The Takeover Deterrent Effect of Open Market Share Repurchases." *Journal of Finance* 62:4, 1827–1850.

Bradley, Michael, and L. MacDonald Wakeman. 1983. "The Wealth Effects of Targeted Share Repurchases." *Journal of Financial Economics* 11:1, 301–328.

Brennan, Michael, and Anjan Thakor. 1990. "Shareholder Preferences and Dividend Policy." *Journal of Finance* 45:4, 993–1019.

Brown, David T., and Michael D. Ryngaert. 1992. "The Determinants of Tendering Rates in Interfirm and Self-Tender Offers." *Journal of Business* 65:4, 529–556.

Brown, Jeffrey R., Nellie Liang, and Scott Weisbenner. 2007. "Executive Financial Incentives and Payout Policy: Firm Responses to the 2003 Dividend Tax Cut." *Journal of Finance* 62: 4, 1935–1965.

Burgstahler, David, and Ilia Dichev. 1997. "Earnings Management to Avoid Earnings Decreases and Losses." *Journal of Accounting and Economics* 24:1, 99–126.

Dann, Larry Y., and Harry DeAngelo. 1983. "Standstill Agreements, Privately Negotiated Stock Repurchases, and the Market for Corporate Control." *Journal of Financial Economics* 11:1, 275–300.

Dann, Larry Y., and Harry DeAngelo. 1988. "Corporate Financial Policy and Corporate Control: A Study of Defensive Adjustments in Asset and Ownership Structure." *Journal of Financial Economics* 20:1, 87–127.

DeAngelo, Harry, and Linda DeAngelo. 2006. "Capital Structure, Payout Policy, and Financial Flexibility." Working Paper, University of Southern California.

Degeorge, Francois, Jayendu Patel, and Richard Zeckhauser. 1999. "Earnings Management to Exceed Thresholds." *Journal of Business* 72:1, 1–33.

Denis, David. 1990. "Defensive Changes in Corporate Payout Policy: Share Repurchase and Special Dividends." *Journal of Finance* 45:5, 1433–1456.

Dittmar, Amy K., 2000. "Why Do Firms Repurchase Stock?" *Journal of Business* 73:3, 331–355.

Fama, Eugene F., and Kenneth R. French. 2002. "Testing Trade-off and Pecking Order Predictions about Dividends and Debt." *Review of Financial Studies* 15:1, 1–33.

Fenn, George W., and Nellie Liang. 2001. "Corporate Payout Policy and Managerial Stock Incentives." *Journal of Financial Economics* 60:1, 45–72.

Flannery, Mark, and Kasturi Rangan. 2006. "Partial Adjustment toward Target Capital Structures." *Journal of Financial Economics* 79:3, 469–506.

Gong, Guojin, Henock Louis, and Amy X. Sun. 2008. "Earnings Management and Firm Performance Following Open-Market Repurchases." *Journal of Finance* 63:2, 947–986.

Grullon, Gustavo, and Roni Michaely. 2002. "Dividends, Repurchases, and the Substitution Hypothesis." *Journal of Finance* 57:4, 1649–1684.

Guay, Wayne, and Jarrad Harford. 2000. "The Cash-Flow Permanence and Information Content of Dividend Increases versus Repurchases." *Journal of Financial Economics* 57:3, 385–415.

Harris, Milton, and Artur Raviv. 1988. "Corporate Control Contests and Capital Structure." *Journal of Financial Economics* 20:1, 55–86.

Hovakimian, Armen, Tim Opler, and Sheridan Titman. 2001. "The Debt-Equity Choice." *Journal of Financial and Qualitative Analysis* 36:1, 1–24.

Hsieh, Jim, and Qinghai Wang. 2008. "Insiders' Tax Preferences and Firm's Choice between Dividends and Share Repurchases." *Journal of Financial and Quantitative Analysis* 43:1, 213–244.

Jagannathan, Murali, Clifford P. Stephens, and Michael S. Weisbach. 2000. "Financial Flexibility and the Choice between Dividends and Stock Repurchases." *Journal of Financial Economics* 57:3, 355–384.

Jensen, Michael C. 1986. "Agency Costs of Free Cash Flow, Corporate Finance, and Takeovers." *American Economic Review* 76:2, 323–329.

Jolls, Christine. 1998. "Stock Repurchases and Incentive Compensation." National Bureau of Economic Research Working Paper No. 6467.

Kahle, Kathleen M. 2002. "When a Buyback Isn't a Buyback: Open Market Repurchases and Employee Options." *Journal of Financial Economics* 63:2, 235–261.

Klein, April, and James Rosenfeld. 1988. "Targeted Share Repurchases and Top Management Changes." *Journal of Financial Economics* 20:1/2, 493–506.

Lambert, Richard A., William N. Lanen, and David F. Larcker. 1989. "Executive Stock Option Plans and Corporate Dividend Policy." *Journal of Financial and Quantitative Analysis* 24:4, 409–425.

Leary, Mark T., and Michael R. Roberts. 2005. "Do Firms Rebalance Their Capital Structures?" *Journal of Finance* 60:6, 2575–2619.

Lie, Erik, and Heidi J. Lie. 1999. "The Role of Personal Taxes in Corporate Decisions: An Empirical Analysis of Share Repurchases and Dividends." *Journal of Financial and Quantitative Analysis* 34:4, 533–552.

Mikkelson, Wayne H., and Richard S. Ruback. 1991. "Targeted Repurchases and Common Stock Returns." *RAND Journal of Economics* 22:4, 544–561.

Myers, Stewart C., and Nicholas S. Majluf. 1984. "Corporate Financing and Investment Decisions When Firms Have Information Those Investors Do Not Have." *Journal of Financial Economics* 13:1, 187–221.

Ofer, Aharon R., and Anjan Thakor. 1987. "A Theory of Stock Price Responses to Alternative Corporate Cash Disbursement Methods: Stock Repurchases and Dividends." *Journal of Finance* 42:2, 365–394.

Peyer, Urs, and Theo Vermaelen. 2008. "The Nature and Persistence of Buyback Anomalies." *Review of Financial Studies*, forthcoming.

Powell, James L. 1986. "Censored Regression Quantiles." *Journal of Econometrics* 32:1, 143–155.

Sinha, Sidharth. 1991. "Share Repurchase as a Takeover Defense." *Journal of Financial and Quantitative Analysis* 26:2, 233–244.

Stulz, René M. 1988. "Managerial Control of Voting Rights: Financing Policies and the Market for Corporate Control." *Journal of Financial Economics* 20:1, 25–54.

Weisbenner, Scott J. 2000. "Corporate Share Repurchases in the 1990s: What Role Do Stock Options Play?" FEDS Working Paper 2000-29.

ABOUT THE AUTHORS

Jim Hsieh is an associate professor of finance at George Mason University. He received a MBA from University of Rochester, an MS in computational finance from Carnegie Mellon University, and a Ph.D. in finance from Ohio State University. His research focuses on corporate finance, particularly corporate restructuring decisions, corporate governance, and corporate payout policy. His research interests also include the investment behavior of institutional and individual investors as well as how the decision making of financial analysts interacts with other market participants. Hsieh's work has been cited in several trade publications, such as the *New York Times*, *Smart Money*, and *Bloomberg*. He has published his research in *Journal of Financial Economics*, *Journal of Financial and Quantitative Analysis*, and *Journal of Banking and Finance*.

Qinghai Wang is an associate professor of finance at the Georgia Institute of Technology. He received his Ph.D. from Fisher College of Business, Ohio State University. His research focuses on the investment decisions and portfolio choices of institutional and individual investors and the impact of their behaviors on asset prices and market efficiency. His research interests also include behavioral aspects of corporate decision making and corporate governance, shareholder voting and the role of investors in corporate governance, and corporate payout policy. Wang's work has been published in *Journal of Finance*, *Journal of Financial Economics*, *Journal of Business*, and *Journal of Financial and Quantitative Analysis*. He has presented his research at various academic conferences and his work has been cited in news publications such as the *New York Times* and *CFO* magazine.

CHAPTER 16

Stock Repurchases and Dividends: Trade-Offs and Trends

BRADFORD CORNELL
Visiting Professor of Financial Economics, California Institute of Technology, and Senior
Consultant, CRA International

INTRODUCTION

The distributions that corporations make to their shareholders determine the ultimate value of equity. Firms make such distributions using three methods: (1) dividends, (2) share repurchases, and (3) a corporate control transaction that involves the redemption of shares. This chapter focuses on repurchases but does not examine corporate control transactions because they are relatively rare and idiosyncratic events and, therefore, not a method for routine distributions to shareholders. The same is not true of dividends, which compete with repurchases as an avenue for routine distribution of cash. In fact, one of the central questions related to repurchases is how companies divide intended payouts to shareholders between repurchases and dividends and what factors influence that choice. By necessity, this chapter revisits some aspects of the dividend decision previously discussed in earlier chapters.

The starting point of an analysis of repurchases and dividends is the fundamental work of Miller and Modigliani (1961) (hereafter MM). What MM make clear is that the value of a firm is determined primarily, if not exclusively, by the company's operations. For example, in perfect markets with no taxes, MM show that operations are the sole determinant of value. This implies that the determination of the size of payouts and the division of payouts between dividends and repurchases are likely to be second-order considerations for most companies. The main story of value creation occurs elsewhere. The fact that the division of payouts is typically a second-order consideration has implications for understanding both the theoretical work on repurchases and the empirical data.

With that in mind, this chapter proceeds as follows. The next section presents historical data on repurchases and dividends, followed by discussions of how to measure repurchases and the methods firms use to repurchase shares. Other sections examine how to incorporate repurchases into basic valuation models, analyze the factors that affect the trade-off between dividends and repurchases, and discuss theoretical models of the repurchase decision. The final section presents the conclusions.

REPURCHASES AND DIVIDENDS: THE HISTORICAL RECORD

Figure 16.1 presents the historical record of inflation-adjusted dividends and repurchases for nonfinancial U.S. corporations during the period 1971–2005. The figure is based on data provided by Roni Michaely and updates the information presented in Boudoukh, Michaely, Richardson, and Roberts (2007). The most dramatic aspect of the figure is the relentless rise of repurchases both in absolute numbers and relative to dividends beginning in the early 1980s. As Figure 16.1 shows, repurchases are not a substantial source of cash distributions before 1982. In fact, netting out new issues, repurchases are negative. By 2005, however, gross repurchases had surpassed dividends and markedly exceeded new issues.

Figure 16.1 should not be interpreted as implying that firms either pay dividends or repurchase shares. To the contrary, Grullon and Michaely (2002) report that dividend-paying firms account for nearly 90 percent of the total dollars spent on repurchases. This is due in part to the fact that dividend-paying firms are, on average, much larger and have much greater free cash flow than firms that do not pay dividends. For example, between 2004 and 2007 Time Warner paid billions in dividends while simultaneously repurchasing more than $20 billion in stock.

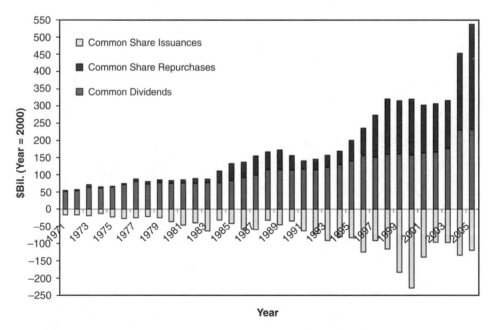

Figure 16.1 Deflated Aggregate Dividends, Share Repurchases, and Share Issuances for Nonfinancial Publicly Trade Firms from 1971 to 2005
Source: Figure created from data provided by Roni Michaely.

Grullon and Michaely (2002) also observe that hidden within the aggregate data is another important fact. Defining the initiation of cash distributions as the first time that a firm pays dividends or repurchases shares, there has been a marked change in initiation behavior. In the early 1970s, only 27 percent of the firms initiating payouts did so by repurchasing shares. By 1981, that percentage rose to 81 percent and approached 90 percent in 2005. This trend suggests that repurchases as a fraction of total shareholder payouts will continue to grow as these firms mature.

MEASURING REPURCHASES

Measuring dividends is typically straightforward. As Lintner (1956) observed more than 50 years ago, and as remains true today, most companies set a dividend policy and change it infrequently. Thus, the stability of dividends enables investors to speak of the current dividend and the dividend yield. With respect to repurchases, the situation is not so clear cut for two reasons.

First, companies rarely have a repurchase policy that involves anything like the fixed regularity of dividend policy. Indeed, evidence presented later in this chapter suggests that the opportunity to constantly adjust the level of repurchases is one reason for the growing preference for repurchases. Thus, while a repurchase yield can be defined by dividing annualized historical repurchases by equity market capitalization, the result must be interpreted with caution. Just because a firm repurchased a given number of shares in the past does not mean it will continue to repurchase shares at the same rate in the future. Even firms that announce their intention to spend a given amount of funds on repurchases rarely commit to a specific timetable and frequently alter the targeted expenditure. Second, at an even more basic level, ambiguity arises with respect to measuring the magnitude of repurchases that have actually occurred.

To begin with the second issue, Stephens and Weisbach (1998) discuss three methods for measuring the size of repurchases: (1) the gross (or net) dollar amount spent on repurchases as reported in a company's cash flow statement; (2) the change in a company's holding of Treasury stock as reported by Compustat; and (3) the change in the number of shares outstanding as reported on the Center for Research in Security Prices (CRSP) or Compustat databases. Each of these approaches can yield quite different estimates of the magnitude of repurchase activity.

Empirical studies on repurchase activity most commonly use the first approach. By construction, it properly reports the number of dollars spent on repurchases. The repurchase data presented in Figure 16.1 are based on this measure of repurchase activity. Dollar repurchases also provide a common basis for comparing dividends and repurchases. However, translating these dollar repurchases, which are reported in the cash flow statement, to share repurchases can be difficult because the financial statements do not provide the repurchase price. The cash flow statement also reflects funds spent repurchasing equity securities other than common stock. In practice, repurchases rarely involve such other securities.

Fama and French (2001) argue for the second measure on the grounds that changes in Treasury stock capture the cumulative effects of stock repurchases and reissues. In addition, new issues of stock (seasoned equity offerings) do not affect this method. As Allen and Michaely (2003) note, however, using Treasury stock to measure repurchases has several drawbacks. If firms retire the shares they repurchase, the number of shares outstanding decreases but the number of Treasury shares does not decline, so repurchases are understated. Allen and Michaely also argue that Treasury holdings understate repurchases because they do not change when firms repurchase and reissue stock. In this regard, their concern that changes in Treasury stock understate repurchases highlights the importance of knowing the purpose for which repurchases are being measured. If the goal is simply to document repurchase activity, then gross repurchases are the correct measure, as Allen and Michaely suggest. Yet if the goal is to measure aggregate distributions to shareholders in addition to dividends, then net repurchases, taking account of possible differences between repurchase and reissue prices, is the proper measure.

The third measure, namely, the change in the number of shares outstanding, has the benefit of being a net measure but the drawback of being affected by secondary issuances. To the extent that repurchases are offset by secondary issues, they do not represent net distributions to shareholders. In addition, the change in shares outstanding provides no information about the price at which firms may repurchase or reissue shares. Therefore, it fails to measure cash distributions to shareholders.

In conclusion, the dollar amount spent on repurchases is the most widely used and generally the most useful measure of repurchase activity. Yet a situation in which the number of shares repurchased is an important consideration requires using an alternative approach because data on repurchase prices are rarely available.

METHODS FOR REPURCHASING SHARES

Firms use three primary types of transactions to repurchase shares: (1) open-market share repurchases, (2) fixed-price tender offers, and (3) Dutch auctions.

Open-Market Repurchases

In an open-market share repurchase, firms simply buy back their shares in the open market. Historically, this practice has been a matter of regulatory and legal dispute for the reason that firms might use repurchases to manipulate their share price. For this reason, understanding the recent trend toward open-market repurchases as the preferred form of payout to shareholders requires a brief review of regulatory history.

In the United States, the antimanipulative provisions of the Securities Exchange Act of 1934 govern share repurchases. As a result, historically, companies have been concerned that repurchasing could lead to regulatory actions or civil litigation under that act. As part of an ongoing effort to deregulate securities markets in the early 1980s, the Securities and Exchange Commission (SEC) adopted Rule 10b-18 in 1982. This rule provides specific guidelines that, if followed, would allow firms to repurchase their shares without fear of prosecution under the 1934 act. The two key guidelines are that firms announce their repurchase programs in advance and limit their repurchases to a specified daily maximum.

Grullon and Michaely (2002) convincingly argue that the revision of the act led to a trend toward repurchases that developed after the adoption of Rule

10b-18. Although difficult to see in Figure 16.1, Grullon and Michaely report that the aggregate amount of cash spent on share repurchase programs tripled in 1983. They observe that after adoption of Rule 10b-18, John Shad, who was then chairman of the SEC, noted that without the change, companies were effectively inhibited from making big open-market buys. The passage of the rule removed that deterrent.

Fixed-Price Tender Offers

In a fixed-price tender offer, a firm offers to buy a portion of its shares at a prespec-ified price. The tender offer, which an investment bank typically manages, also specifies the number of shares sought and the duration of the offer. If the offer is oversubscribed, the company commonly reserves the right to buy additional shares. If the offer is undersubscribed, the company has the choice of buying the shares tendered or canceling the offer.

Dutch Auctions

In a Dutch auction, the company specifies the number of shares it wants to buy and a range of prices. Shareholders interested in selling submit a proposal containing a price and the number of shares they want to tender at that price. The firm examines all the offers and computes the minimum price at which it can buy the stated number of shares. All the tendering shareholders receive the calculated price, even if they submitted a tender at a lower price.

Before the introduction of Rule 10b-18, fixed-price offers and Dutch auctions were relatively common methods for repurchasing stock because they did not raise the specter of manipulation to the same degree as open-market purchases. Since passage of Rule 10b-18, both methods have become uncommon because they lack the flexibility associated with open-market purchases. Whereas firms must complete fixed-price offers and Dutch auctions in a short period of time, usually a month or less, open-market programs have horizons that often extend for three years or more. During that time the purchasing company has much discretion regarding when it chooses to repurchase shares, and even how many shares it will repurchase. For these reasons, open-market purchases have become the predominant form of share repurchases. By 1998, open-market purchases accounted for more than 95 percent of the dollar value of shares repurchased. Firms now use fixed-price offers and Dutch auctions only when they need to buy a large quantity of stock in a short period of time.

REPURCHASES VERSUS DIVIDENDS: TRADE-OFFS AND TRENDS

Without going into the formality of decision theory, distinguishing between the two types of decisions is useful. On one hand, some decisions are important but easy to make. For example, deciding whether to drive down an icy mountain road at high speed is clearly a critical decision but hardly a difficult one. On the other hand, deciding whether to order chicken or steak for dinner may be a difficult decision for someone equally disposed to both despite the fact that the consequences may be trivial. Evidence supports the view that decisions regarding the form of payout are of the second type. That is, they are not particularly important because they have a small impact on firm value. Consequently, considerations that are not particularly important to the functioning or valuation of a corporation determine the ultimate choice of payout method. Yet these conditions are sufficient to shift the balance in favor of one form of payout over another.

The ultimate size of repurchases depends on two variables: (1) the level of payout and (2) the division of payout. The focus here is on the division of the payout. In that context, the aggregate payout decision can be treated as exogenous. Yet mentioning the main factors that affect aggregate payout is also important. The primary one is the existence of free cash flow. As Allen and Michaely (2003) report, large payouts occur when companies have more cash flow than they need to follow their business plan. For this reason, most repurchasing firms are mature, low-growth firms that repurchase shares because of limited investment opportunities relative to cash flow. More specifically, the evidence shows that repurchasing firms experience a reduction in operating performance, have excess cash, and invest less in the years after the announcement of a repurchase program.

With that in mind, the main factors that researchers suggest as determining the trade-off between repurchases and dividends are (1) taxes, (2) managerial flexibility, (3) management of earnings per share, (4) management of employee stock options, and (5) defense against hostile takeovers.

Taxes

A discussion of the trade-off between dividends and repurchases inevitably begins with taxes. Compared to dividends, repurchases offer shareholders two tax advantages. First, repurchases are taxed at the capital gains rate, which is typically lower than the rate at which dividends are taxed. Second, repurchases allow investors to take advantage of the fact that they pay capital gains taxes only after realizing the gains. Therefore, investors who do not need the cash can hold their shares and benefit from the price appreciation associated with the repurchase without paying a tax. In addition, repurchases allow investors to take advantage of the tax-timing option. That is, investors can realize gains at optimal times such as when they have offsetting capital losses.

From a tax perspective, repurchases appear to dominant dividends, but a problem exits. Assuming that Congress intends to tax payouts to equity holders, if the substitution of repurchases for dividends becomes too pronounced, an adjustment in the tax rules is possible. Recognition of this possibility may serve to restrain the use of repurchases. From a game theoretic perspective, the rationale is unclear as to why any individual company would refrain from using repurchases in place of dividends simply because in the aggregate such decisions may lead to a change in the tax law.

A detailed survey of corporate chief financial officers (CFOs) by Brav, Graham, Harvey, and Michaely (2005) administered while dividends were taxed at federal rates of up to 40 percent and the maximum long-term capital gains tax was 20 percent reveals that CFOs believe that taxes are not a primary consideration in choosing between dividends and repurchases. Only 29.1 percent of the firms actively repurchasing shares cite personal taxes as an important factor affecting the number of shares repurchased. Ironically, the CFOs note that if there were a class of investors that they believe prefers dividends it is retail investors, the very investors who face the largest personal tax disadvantage.

Managerial Flexibility

Lintner (1956) argues that firms are highly reluctant to cut dividends. According to Brav et al. (2005) that viewpoint is equally applicable today. Executives they interviewed relate stories of selling assets, dismissing a large number of employees, borrowing heavily, or even bypassing positive net present value (NPV) projects before cutting dividends. Executives base this behavior on their belief that the stock market punishes firms that cut dividends. More specifically, the executives claim that the market reacts asymmetrically. Dividend increases are not particularly good news, but dividend cuts are bad news. For that reason, the executives believe that they have little flexibility to manage dividends. They have to set dividends at a level that the firms could comfortably maintain even in bad times. This requires limiting the dividend during good times. Conversely, the managers express markedly different views about repurchases. They believe that the market is much more willing to accept a reduction in a repurchase program than a dividend cut. For this reason, they view repurchases as being more flexible than dividends. The firm could increase dividends in good times and cut back dividends as a critical benefit of repurchases compared to dividends.

Another aspect of the flexibility provided by repurchases is that the executives can base the repurchase decision on the price of the company's stock. For instance, in the Brav et al. (2005) survey, 90 percent of the firms with low price-earnings (P/E) ratios state that market undervaluation could lead to repurchase. The $20 billion dollar repurchase by Time Warner referred to earlier was catalyzed by Carl Icahn's claim that the stock was undervalued.

Brav et al. (2005) also do not find evidence to support the hypothesis that managers target a repurchase ratio or repurchase yield. Only 4 percent of the managers interviewed state that they set repurchases as a percentage of earnings. More commonly, firms would target and announce a fixed dollar value of repurchases if they set a specific target at all. This increases the difficulty of applying valuation models that include a repurchase yield. Applying standard growth models requires translating a fixed dollar amount of repurchases into a repurchase rate.

Management of Earnings per Share

One surprise emerging from the Brav et al. (2005) survey is the importance that financial officers place on the management of earnings per share (EPS). Finance theory teaches that holding constant the free cash flow that a firm is producing and altering the EPS by changing the shares outstanding is of no economic significance. Nonetheless, three-fourths of the survey respondents indicate that increasing EPS by reducing shares outstanding is an important component of the repurchase decision. Despite the importance placed on repurchases as a tool for managing EPS, many executives appear confused about the impact of repurchases on EPS—believing that repurchases automatically reduce dilution and, thereby, increase EPS. In fact, a repurchase will only increase EPS if the funds used for the repurchase would not earn their cost of capital if reinvested by the firm.

Management of Employee Stock Options

Another problem related to dilution is the management of employee stock-option plans. Many companies adjust their repurchase programs to prevent earnings dilution that might otherwise be caused by employee stock plans. Two-thirds of the executives in the Brav et al. (2005) survey report that offsetting option-related dilution is either an important or a very important factor affecting the company's repurchase decision. On the other hand, virtually no support exists for the hypothesis that companies repurchase rather than pay dividends because employee stock options are not dividend protected.

Defense against Hostile Takeovers

Finally, management can use repurchases as a defense against a hostile takeover. As Stulz (1988) describes, by buying back stock from investors who value shares the least, a company can increase the expected premium that others must pay to acquire control. However, this motive for repurchases is likely to come into play only in the rare instances of hostile takeovers. It cannot explain the general shift toward repurchases observed in Figure 16.1. Nonetheless, this motive is another aspect of the flexibility that repurchases give management in comparison to dividends.

In summary, repurchases represent a dominant form of payout when compared to dividends. On every dimension considered, managers consider repurchases equivalent to or superior to dividends as a means of distributing cash to shareholders. First, repurchases offer a tax advantage, at least to some investors. Second, managers perceive repurchases as more flexible because they can scale back repurchase programs without bearing the costs associated with a dividend cut. Third, managers can use repurchases to manage EPS. Fourth, repurchases serve as a way to offset the potentially dilutive impact of employee stock-option programs. Last, managers can accelerate repurchases as a takeover defense should a hostile takeover threat emerge.

In light of this dominance, firms that consider initiating a payout overwhelming favor repurchases over dividends. In fact, among smaller, more growth-oriented firms, Brav et al. (2005) report that more than 90 percent of the companies would choose repurchases if they initiated a payout program. Given the predominance of such firms among new listings, this suggests that the trend toward repurchases and away from dividends is likely to continue in the near future. Fama and French (2004) provide data on new listings.

As noted previously, the trend toward repurchases depends on the continued passivity of the Internal Revenue Service (IRS). If the popularity of repurchases continues to rise, there may come a point at which Congress and the IRS conclude that tax revenues are being affected to such an extent that some corrective action is necessary. To date, the IRS has never taxed a repurchase as ordinary income on the grounds that it is a dividend in disguise, even for firms that repurchase shares on a regular basis.

THEORETICAL MODELS OF THE REPURCHASE DECISION

The level of repurchases depends on two factors—the level of aggregate payout and the division of that payout between repurchase and dividends. Thus far, this chapter has focused on the question of the division of the payout. Yet a full understanding of repurchases requires at least a short discussion of aggregate payout. Of course, the primary determinant of payout is having free cash flow to distribute. The level of free cash flow, in turn, depends primarily on factors related to firm size and firm profitability, which are not the subject of this chapter. The finance literature addresses the following question: Given a certain level of distributable free cash flow, what determines the amount that the firm actually distributes?

Once again, the starting point for the analysis is the classic contribution of MM (1961). Recall that according to MM the payout is a residual. On the basis of its business plan, the firm determines its cash needs, including requirements for capital expenditures. Any cash generated by operations in excess of this is potentially available for payout. If the firm is already holding the optimal level of cash and marketable securities as part of its business plan, then presumably the firm pays the excess cash to shareholders.

With respect to repurchases, the analysis presented previously suggests that the MM theory well describes repurchase behavior. The key here is the perceived flexibility of repurchases discussed in the previous section. Because managers believe that they can increase or decrease repurchases without any asymmetric cost, the firm can adjust the repurchase level as the free cash flow produced by operations varies. Dividends are more vexing because managers see dividend cuts as very costly. As noted previously, firms may alter their business plans or capital raising plans to keep the dividend constant. This makes the level of dividend payments difficult to reconcile with the residual payout theory of MM. But as stressed throughout this chapter, this inflexibility of dividends is a major reason for the trend toward repurchases as the preferred method of payout. Even dividend-paying firms, by combining repurchases with dividends, as many firms do, can maintain flexibility by adjusting the repurchase component of the total payout in response to changing free cash flow.

Over the years, researchers have extended the MM theory to take account of factors that may affect payouts other than the level of residual free cash flow. The two most widely analyzed approaches are the signaling models and the free cash flow models. Because of the prominence of these theories, each is reviewed briefly despite the fact that neither deals explicitly with repurchases.

Following the creative work of Spence (1973), economists began to interpret disparate phenomena as examples of signaling. In finance, the first application of signaling theory was to the payout decision. According to the signaling theory as developed originally by Bhattacharya (1979) and Miller and Rock (1985), firms adjust payouts to signal their prospects. These articles focus on dividends, but because researchers treat dividends and repurchases symmetrically, they are more generally theories of payouts. For the payout to serve as a signal, there must be a cost that prevents firms with weak future prospects from copying the signal sent by stronger firms. This requires that there be dissipative costs associated with payouts. Bhattacharya posits that the dissipative costs arise because increasing payout forces the firm into the capital market more frequently, thus resulting in increased financing costs. In the Miller and Rock model, the higher payout associated with the signal leads to costly distortions of the investment financing decision.

The basis of signaling theory is conscious decision making by management. Managers have to assess the prospects of the firm and then, if they view them as good, send the appropriate signal to the market via the payout decision. Furthermore, managers must conclude that sending the signal is the most reliable method for communicating information about future prospects to the market.

One source of empirical support of the signaling theories is the widely documented fact that when firms increase payouts stock prices rise on average. For example, Michaely, Thaler, and Womack (1995) report that this is true for dividends, and Lakonishok and Vermaelen (1995) find that it holds for repurchases. Too much should not be made of this alleged empirical support. When researchers derived the signaling theories, they were already aware that of the association between unexpected increases in payouts and positive residual returns. In fact, researchers partly designed signaling theories to explain the rise in stock prices associated with announcement of payout increases. A more independent test of the theory is to examine whether company operations improve following payout increases. Here the evidence is very weak. For example, Benartzi, Michaely, and Thaler (1997, p. 1008) report that their empirical analysis reveals, "There is no evidence of a positive relation between dividend changes and future earnings changes."

In addition to this empirical difficulty, signaling theories suffer from a conceptual flaw. Why is management so concerned about next period's stock price that it bears real costs, in terms of a payout greater than that which would be optimal in the standard MM framework to send a signal? Presumably the stock price will rise to reflect the company's opportunities as those opportunities become clear to the market over time. Therefore, managers could avoid dissipative costs by allowing the performance of the firm to be revealed in due course.

The other major innovation in payout theory is the agency approach to the management of free cash flow. As described by Jensen (1986), managers of public companies have an incentive to allocate free cash flow to activities, such as perk consumption or empire building, which benefit them at the expense of shareholders. If equity holders can minimize the cash that management controls, they can limit such discretionary spending. One way to solve this agency problem is to increase cash payouts. This theory represents a departure from the MM view that financing and operating decision are independent because payouts alter investment decision making by constraining the choices of management, albeit in a value-creating manner.

Basic agency theory is deficient in that it requires management to make a decision, increasing payout, which is implicitly assumed, to be counter to its interest. Accordingly, there must be some disciplinary mechanism, or ex post benefit to management, sufficient to induce management to increase the payout as suggested by the theory. One possibility is that the board of directors monitors and constrains managers in this regard. But if that is the case, why does the firm have to engage in the costly behavior of distributing more than the optimal amount of cash? Why can investment behavior not be constrained directly? A related question is, Why do firms use payouts rather than an increase in debt to constrain overinvestment? Debt covenants include restrictions that are difficult to circumvent compared to altering payout policy and, therefore, should be more effective devices for constraining overinvestment.

In some sense, debate over the signaling and agency theories has become falsely complicated. Because payout choices are conscious decisions of senior management endorsed by the board of directors, there is a simple way to test payout theories. Ask the relevant parties. Managers and directors would know if they are using payouts to distinguish themselves from their competitors or to show the market that they are placing constraints on free cash flow. Furthermore, managers and directors would have no reason to falsely claim that they are not using such mechanisms. Managers of weak firms may falsely claim that they are using such mechanisms, but that is a different question. In fact, such deception would introduce a new, and presumably costly, source of asymmetric information.

In this regard, the interviews conducted by Brav et al. (2005) are particularly instructive. In response to questions about payouts, managers universally declare that payout decisions are not influenced by the attempt to distinguish the firm from competitors or to constrain the investment opportunity set of management.

In short, the evidence suggests that the exotic theorizing that followed the original work of MM, while intellectually creative, has not done much to further our understanding of the payout decision. A combination of the MM theory with the view that dividend cuts are costly but that repurchases can be altered at little expense is sufficient to explain recent trends in payout policy and is consistent with the stated views of management. Neither signaling theory nor agency theory of free cash flow control appears to add much to this basic theory. The one question that the MM theory does not resolve is why managers see dividend cuts as so costly. Other chapters of this book address that question.

REPURCHASES AND VALUATION

As Grullon and Michaely (2002) note, dividends and repurchases are commonly considered competing methods for distributing cash to shareholders. Because these distributions are the ultimate source of shareholder value, exploring how to take account of repurchases in basic valuation models is worthwhile. What complicates the analysis, even in basic models, is that repurchases are not pro rata distributions to current shareholders. The distribution of cash occurs simultaneously with a reduction in shares outstanding that alters all the per share magnitudes. Furthermore, the magnitude of repurchase activity may vary over time in a fashion that complicates valuation.

Highlighting the impact of repurchases on valuation models requires using the simplest possible analytical framework. Specifically, following Cornell (2005), this framework assumes certainty, constant parameters through time with the exception of the level of repurchases, and a discount rate equal to the rate of return on investment so no growth options exist. Consequently, any growth is due to reinvestment of retained earnings. Furthermore, the model does not explicitly take account of taxes, although earnings could be interpreted as being on an after-tax basis. In particular, individual income taxes, which provide one motive for repurchases, are not incorporated.

When there are no share repurchases, so that shares outstanding remain constant, the basic constant growth dividend discount model applies, so that

$$P_0 = Div_1/(k - g), \tag{16.1}$$

where

$$g = b \times k. \tag{16.2}$$

In Equations 16.1 and 16.2, P_0 is the current share price, Div_1 is the end of period dividend, g is the growth rate of earnings, b is the earnings retention rate, and k is the cost of equity capital, which equals the return on investment.

To focus on the valuation impact of repurchases, assume that repurchased shares are retired or added to Treasury stock. This assumption implies that repurchases have no impact other than to distribute cash to shareholders. To account for repurchases, assume that the firm divides funds available for payout, $(1 - b) \times X$, between dividends with fraction, d, and repurchases, with fraction $(1 - d)$.

When analyzing repurchases, timing conventions are important. Here using the standard MM conventions can be confusing when applied to repurchases. The convention requires that just after the payment of dividends and just before the repurchase, the value of the firm is equal to the period zero value, plus retained earnings, plus funds earmarked for the repurchase. Therefore, the repurchase price equals this value divided by the shares outstanding, N_0.

$$\text{Repurchase price} = [P_0 + b \times X_1 + (1 - b) \times (1 - d) \times X_1]/N_0. \tag{16.3}$$

The number of shares repurchased equals the funds available for repurchase divided by the repurchase price, or

$$\text{Shares repurchased} = (1 - b) \times (1 - d) \times X_1/\text{Repurchase price}. \tag{16.4}$$

After the repurchase, the period 1 value of the firm falls to $P_0 + b \times X_1$, but the price remains the same because the number of shares outstanding falls to N_1 due to the repurchase.

Given the foregoing, suppose that a firm initiates a program where a fraction of the funds $(1 - d)$, originally earmarked for dividends, is instead used to repurchase shares. This causes the dividends per share to drop each by a factor of d from Div_t to $d \times Div_t$. Applying the standard dividend valuation model to the new, lower dividend stream provides the appearance that the value of the firm, at least as measured by the present value of dividends, also drops by a factor of d.

At first blush, this seems to imply that the per share dividend valuation will fall when initiating repurchases. The inference is incorrect because the repurchase program leads to a continual decline in the number of shares outstanding. This negative dilution means that per share quantities including dividends will grow faster than aggregate quantities. The higher growth rate precisely offsets the lower payout leaving the share price unchanged.

More specifically, with repurchases, dividends per share fall to $d \times DPS$, but the per share growth rate (gps) exceeds the aggregate dividend growth rate (g), as given by the following relation:

$$(1 + gps) = (1 + g)/(1 + gn) - 1, \tag{16.5}$$

where gn is the growth in the number of shares outstanding. If repurchases are positive, gn is negative, so that $gps > g$. Therefore, the per share valuation equation is given by

$$P_0 = d \times DPS_1/(k - gps). \tag{16.6}$$

For the two valuations to be equivalent, the following relation must exist:

$$1/(k - g) = d/(k - gps). \tag{16.7}$$

Rearranging this implies that

$$gps = (1 - d)(k - g) + g. \tag{16.8}$$

Although algebraically tedious, the process is straightforward, to show that solving for the rate of growth in shares outstanding that results from repurchases (gn) and substituting it into Equation 16.5 also leads to Equation 16.8. Therefore, the negative dilution precisely offsets the lower dividend payout, leaving per share values unchanged.

Defining the repurchase rate as $Repur_1/P_0$, where $Repur_1$ equals the repurchases per share, it is also the case that $(1 - d)(k - g) = Repur_1/V_0$. Substituting this relation into Equation 16.8 gives,

$$gps = Repur_1/V_0 + g. \tag{16.9}$$

Equation 16.9 says that the growth rate in per share magnitudes equals the aggregate growth rate in earnings due to reinvestment of retained earnings plus the repurchase yield. Using the repurchase yield is the simplest way to move between aggregate growth rates and per share growth rates.

The foregoing highlights the previously mentioned problem with defining repurchases. Although the repurchase rate increases growth in per share magnitudes, what is the appropriate definition of the repurchase rate? Unlike dividends payments that are largely invariant, repurchases can be highly volatile. Because the valuation model is forward looking, the correct repurchase yield is the ratio of expected future repurchases to the current market value of equity. Presumably estimation of this ratio requires examining historical data on repurchases and/or analyzing announced repurchase programs. The volatility of repurchase programs requires exercising care to ensure that past repurchase activity is indicative of what will occur in the future.

The analysis also highlights the importance of working properly with per share magnitudes when estimating growth. For instance, the growth rate in dividends per share must explicitly take account of the dilution associated with repurchases. In addition, the forecast pro forma financial statements, which serve as the basis for cash flow forecasts, must explicitly account for expected repurchases.

The simplified framework used to analyze repurchases thus far rules out the possibility that substituting repurchases for dividends affects the value of the firm. Without tax effects and without information or agency costs, dividends and repurchases are perfect substitutes. The practical question is how much value creation is likely to be associated with a shift from dividends to repurchases when relaxing these assumptions. The answer is very little.

To begin, the beneficial tax effects are small and may not even apply to the marginal investor. Clearly, the tax effects do not apply to tax exempt investors such as pension funds. In addition, corporate investors may actually prefer dividends because of the manner in which certain dividends are taxed at the corporate level. Even in the case of individual investors, the tax benefits are likely to be small particularly in light of the recent reductions in the tax rate on dividends.

Second, although management may prefer the flexibility associated with re-purchases, there is no clear cash flow benefit associated with that flexibility. In fact, the benefits that do exist may accrue to managers rather than shareholders in the form of making their job easier. The one exception to this conclusion is the possibility that the flexibility associated with repurchases allows management to time transactions and to buy the company's own stock at favorable prices. To date, little evidence exists that the practice of attempting to time repurchases is widespread or that when it does occur that it is successful.

CONCLUSIONS

The bottom line is this. Since the passage in 1982 of SEC Rule 10b-18, which greatly reduced the legal risk associated with repurchases, there has been a pronounced trend toward repurchases as the preferred form of payout to shareholders. This trend can be understood in light of the classic work of MM (1961). In the MM framework, company payouts are the residual. They represent the funds available to distribute to shareholders after meeting all the cash needs of the firm's business plan. Managers do not consider dividends the most effective tool in this context. In their minds, dividends lack flexibility because of the large costs, real or perceived, associated with cutting them. These costs imply that manage-ment will only choose to pay dividends at rates that it believes can be sustained over the long run. This perceived cost of dividend cuts places limits on man-agement flexibility that using repurchases can avoid. Interviews reveal that man-agers view this added flexibility as the major benefit of repurchases compared to dividends.

Besides providing payout flexibility, repurchases offer other benefits not pro-vided by dividends. First, managers can increase or decrease repurchases in light of perceived under or overvaluation of the company's stock. If management has superior information about the true value of the firm, timing repurchases can be value enhancing. Second, managers can use repurchases to influence EPS. Though finance theory is skeptical about why they would want to manage EPS, managers themselves see this as an important objective. Third, managers can use repurchases to offset the potential dilution associated with employee stock option programs. Once again, why such an offset should be beneficial is unclear. Finally, managers can use repurchases as a defense mechanism in the environment of hostile takeovers.

In light of all these benefits compared with other forms of payout, firms planning to initiate payouts tend to overwhelmingly favor repurchases. Therefore, as these new firms mature, the trend toward repurchases should continue.

With respect to the aggregate level of payouts, of which repurchases are a fraction researchers has advanced complex theoretical models to enhance the basic MM theory. The two most prominent theories involve signaling and agency. Although an active debate continues on these theories, the analysis presented here suggests that they do not add much to our understanding of repurchases.

Finally, in the context of valuation models, repurchases add several wrinkles. First, managers must take care to properly estimate growth rates on a per share basis because the negative dilution associated with repurchases drives a wedge between per share growth rates and aggregate growth rates. Second, they must account for the more variable nature of repurchases. Because repurchases are more flexible than dividends, repurchase rates are more variable than dividend yields. This makes estimating growth rates more difficult.

REFERENCES

Allen, Franklin, and Roni Michaely. 2003. "Payout Policy." In *North-Holland Handbook of Economics*, ed. George Constantinides, Milton Harris, and René Stulz, 337–429. Amsterdam: Elsevier–North Holland.

Benartzi, Shlomo, Roni Michaely, and Richard Thaler. 1997. "Do Changes in Dividends Signal the Future of the Past? *Journal of Finance* 52:3, 1007–1043.

Bhattacharya, Sudipto. 1979. "Imperfect Information, Dividend Policy, and 'The Bird in the Hand Fallacy.'" *Bell Journal of Economics* 10:1, 259–270.

Boudoukh, Jacob, Roni Michaely, Matthew Richardson, and Michael R. Roberts. 2007. "On the Importance of Measuring Payout Yield: Implications for Empirical Asset Pricing." *Journal of Finance* 62:2, 877–915.

Brav, Alon, John R. Graham, Campbell R. Harvey, and Roni Michaely. 2005. "Payout Policy in the 21st Century." *Journal of Financial Economics* 77:3, 483–527.

Cornell, Bradford. 2005. "Dividends, Stock Repurchases and Valuation." *Journal of Applied Finance* 15:2, 13–24.

Fama, Eugene F., and Kenneth R. French. 2001. "Disappearing Dividends: Changing Firm Characteristics or Lower Propensity to Pay?" *Journal of Financial Economics* 60:1, 3–43.

Fama, Eugene F., and Kenneth R. French. 2004. "New Lists: Fundamentals and Survival Rates." *Journal of Financial Economics* 73:2, 229–269.

Grullon, Gustavo, and Roni Michaely. 2002. "Dividends, Share Repurchase and the Substitution Hypothesis." *Journal of Finance* 57:4, 1649–1684.

Jensen, Michael C. 1986. "Agency Costs of Free Cash Flow, Corporate Finance, and Takeovers." *American Economic Review* 76:2, 323–329.

Lakonishok, Joseph, and Theo Vermaelen. 1995. "Market Underreaction to Open Market Share Repurchases." *Journal of Financial Economics* 39:2, 181–208.

Lintner, John. 1956. "Distribution of Incomes of Corporations among Dividends, Retained Earnings and Taxes." *American Economic Review* 46:1, 97–113.

Michaely, Roni, Richard H. Thaler, and Kent Womack. 1995. "Price Reactions to Dividend Initiations and Omissions: Overreaction or Drift?" *Journal of Finance* 50:2, 573–608.

Miller, Merton, and Franco Modigliani. 1961. "Dividend Policy, Growth and the Valuation of Shares." *Journal of Business* 34:4, 411–433.

Miller, Merton, and Kevin Rock. 1985. "Dividend Policy under Asymmetric Information." *Journal of Finance* 40:4, 1031–1051.

Spence, Michael. 1973. "Job Market Signaling." *Quarterly Journal of Economics* 87:3, 355–374.

Stephens, Clifford P., and Michael S. Weisbach. 1998. "Actual Share Reacquisition in Open Market Repurchase Programs." *Journal of Finance* 53:1, 313–333.

Stulz, René M. 1988. "Managerial Control of Voting Rights: Financing Policies and the Market for Corporate Control." *Journal of Financial Economics* 20:1, 181–208.

ABOUT THE AUTHOR

Bradford Cornell is a visiting professor of financial economics, California Institute of Technology, and a senior consultant with CRA International, a worldwide finance and economics consulting firm. Before joining the Caltech faculty, he was the Bank of America Professor of Finance at Anderson Graduate School of Management, University of California, Los Angeles. Cornell has published more than 80 peer-reviewed articles on a wide variety of financial topics. He is also the author of *Corporate Valuation: Tools for Effective Appraisal and Decision Making* and *The Equity Risk Premium and the Long-Run Future of the Stock Market*. Cornell has served as an associate editor of 10 academic journals. He is a past director and vice president of the Western Finance Association and a past director of the American Finance Association.

CHAPTER 17

Beating the Market with Share Buybacks

THEO VERMAELEN
Schroders Chaired Professor in International Finance and Asset Management, INSEAD

INTRODUCTION

The purpose of this chapter is to show that, on average, markets react inefficiently to various buyback methods such as fixed-price tender offers, open-market buybacks, and private repurchase. This allows investors to beat the market on the basis of publicly available information. Apparently, the market underreacts to buyback news because the market is skeptical about managers' ability to time the market.

A share repurchase is a nexus of corporate finance. Management may consider a share repurchase a payout decision or as a capital structure decision in the same way as a dividend payment. However, in contrast to a dividend payment, a share buyback is also an investment decision. Thus, finding that Brav, Graham, Harvey, and Michaely (2005) report the major motivation for share buybacks as undervaluation or good investment is not surprising. This market-timing hypothesis assumes that markets underreact to the repurchase announcement; this is in contrast to signaling models, which assume that a change in dividend policy fully reveals the manager's inside information. If the market reacted efficiently, the stock would no longer be undervalued after the buyback announcement, eliminating the possibility of engaging in market timing. Whether managers can time the market is an empirical question. Indeed, managers, infected with hubris, could be overconfident about the future and refuse to accept reality. The repurchase is then simply an act of desperate defiance.

Academic studies traditionally examine only short-term returns because of a strong prior belief in semistrong efficient markets. Figure 17.1, which is based on the sample used by Peyer and Vermaelen (2005), shows evidence on short-term announcement returns for four different buyback methods. The figure illustrates the cumulative abnormal returns (CARs) from 60 days before the announcement until 60 days afterward for four different buyback samples: 303 fixed-price tender offers, 251 Dutch-auction tender offers, 6,470 open-market repurchases, and 737 private repurchases, all announced between 1984 and 2001. In a fixed-price tender offer a company offers to repurchase its shares at a fixed price for a specific number of shares. In a Dutch auction, a company offers to buy back a specific number of shares within a price range. In an open-market buyback program, the company

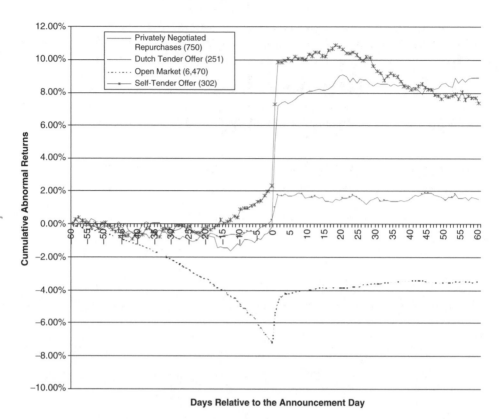

Figure 17.1 Share Repurchase and Market Response: Cumulative Abnormal Returns 60 Days before and after the Announcement Date

The figure shows the cumulative average abnormal return 60 days before and after the announcement for four subsamples of buybacks: open-market repurchases, fixed-price or self-tender offers, Dutch-auction tender offers, and privately negotiated transactions. The basis of the sample is data used by Peyer and Vermaelen (2005).

announces that it plans to buy back shares from time to time in the open market. Finally, in a private repurchase, the company announces that it is buying back shares from a large investor.

Figure 17.1 shows that, regardless of the repurchase method, stock prices increase around the announcement. The market reaction seems to be positively correlated with the repurchase premium. In the sample of fixed-price tender offers, the average repurchase premium is 23 percent, significantly greater than the 15 percent premium paid in Dutch-auction tender offers. In private repurchases, the average premium is only 2 percent. Although there are many potential reasons for the stock-price increase, the fact that the repurchase premium is the most important determinant of the stock price response is consistent with the signaling hypothesis of share repurchases. In other words, companies tend to buy back stock when their shares are undervalued. Paying a larger premium results in a larger cost to nonselling shareholders (who typically include the management) of false signaling. Consequently, paying a premium is a credible signal.

The purpose of this chapter is to more closely examine the rationality of the price behavior in Figure 17.1. The chapter begins by examining the price behavior of fixed-price and Dutch-auction repurchase tender offers around the announcement and expiration of the offer. Next, the chapter presents evidence on the long-term returns in tender offers, open-market repurchase programs, and private repurchases. Finally, the chapter discusses some real-life experience of the author with exploiting the buyback anomaly through the launch of the KBC buyback fund.

ANOMALOUS PRICE BEHAVIOR AROUND REPURCHASE TENDER OFFERS

The problem with the signaling hypothesis for fixed-price repurchase tender offers is that the repurchase premium of 23 percent is significantly larger than the cumulative average abnormal return of 8 percent to the nontendering shareholders (see Figure 17.1). As managers typically do not tender, they seem to incur a substantial wealth loss by overpaying for their own shares. One explanation consistent with efficient markets is that managers get some offsetting signaling benefits. For example, by increasing the stock price, bidders will be discouraged from making a takeover bid for the company, thereby allowing the managers to keep their jobs. Alternatively, the market may underreact so that the real gap between the repurchase premium and the fair value of the stock is much smaller than the market's estimate around the announcement. If the last hypothesis is true, one should be able to make excess returns by buying shares after the expiration of repurchase tender offers.

Lakonishok and Vermaelen (1990) examine long-term price behavior after 258 fixed-price tender offers announced between 1962 and 1986. They find that buying shares one month after the expiration and holding them for two years generates excess returns of 8 percent. They calculate excess returns by comparing the returns of the buyback company with the returns of a portfolio of control firms with similar size and beta. Lakonishok and Vermaelen report a cumulative abnormal return from the month before the announcement until the month after expiration of approximately 14 percent (significantly higher than the 8 percent reported in Figure 17.1). If the market had been efficient, stock prices should have risen to 22 percent, not 14 percent. Note that this level corresponds to the repurchase premium observed in their sample. As a result, when companies offer to repurchase their shares at a specific price, that price is a good estimate of the fair value of the stock. However, the market seems to underreact and be too skeptical about the often-stated managerial belief that the shares are undervalued or a good investment. On closer inspection, Lakonishok and Vermaelen report that the abnormal returns seem to be confined to small firms, which makes sense given that smaller firms are more likely undervalued.

Measuring long-term returns raises several methodological and statistical issues. In particular, long-term abnormal returns are sensitive to the model of normal returns. Therefore, researchers can criticize the results because any test of market efficiency is a joint test of efficiency and a model of market equilibrium. The possibility exists that an omitted repurchase risk factor, something that would comfort proponents of market efficiency, explains the excess returns observed. The early tests of Lakonishok and Vermaelen (1990) are adjusted for size and the market but not for book-to-market, a factor that Fama and French (1993) find to be significantly related to future returns. However, using the sample data from Figure 17.1, they repeat the tests using the three-factor Fama-French model as the benchmark and find essentially the same results. Louis and White (2007) report significant three-year postexpiration excess returns of 31 percent for fixed-price tender offers and 24.7 percent for Dutch-auction tender offers. They use Carhart's (1997) four-factor model and their sample consists of tender offers between 1981 and 2001. Hence, the market seems to underreact to tender offers and is too skeptical about the repurchase signal.

Researchers can test market underreaction to tender offers in a more direct way: buying shares after the announcement of a tender offer and tendering them to the company. To avoid arbitrage profits, the stock price after the announcement of a fixed-price tender offer should be equal to

$$P_A = P_T(F_p/F_t) + (1 - F_p/F_t)P_E, \tag{17.1}$$

where F_p and F_t are the expected fraction of shares repurchased and tendered, respectively, and P_E is now the expected price after expiration of the offer. Indeed, the marginal investor who tenders shares can expect that the company repurchases a fraction, F_p/F_t, of the investor's shares. For example, if the offer is undersubscribed, the company will repurchase all shares tendered. Thus, the expectation is that the stock price during the tender offer is equal to P_T. To the extent that the company repurchases at a higher price than the price expected after expiration, stock prices will fall after the expiration, which is consistent with the fall in the CARs in Figure 17.1 after 25 days when the first offers start expiring.

However, Lakonishok and Vermaelen (1990) report that prices are not consistent with zero-arbitrage profits: a simple strategy that involves (1) buying shares six days before the expiration of the fixed-price tender offer whenever the stock price is at least 3 percent below the tender price and tendering them to the firm and (2) selling the nonrepurchased shares after expiration, which generates excess returns of 9 percent, on average. This return is substantial considering that the investment period is less than two weeks. Lakonishok and Vermaelen's database covers the period 1974–1986.

Peyer and Vermaelen (2008) find almost identical results when they use 1986–2001 data to replicate the Lakonishok and Vermaelen (1990) study. Moreover, Peyer and Vermaelen find some evidence that the market seems to price stocks as if the average investor, not the marginal investor, sets market prices according to Equation 17.2:

$$P_A = F_p P_t + (1 - F_p)P_E. \tag{17.2}$$

In other words, investors believe that everyone tenders, which seems reasonable considering that the repurchase premium is substantially greater than the postexpiration price. However, the true puzzle is that very few investors tender. For example, Lakonishok and Vermaelen (1990) report that corporations repurchase 86 percent of all shares tendered, although they only buy back 16.4 percent of all the shares outstanding. Lücke and Pindur (2002) document similar tendering behavior and comparable large excess returns from buying and tendering in 22

French fixed-price tender offers. As a result, one way to interpret the evidence is that the market prices stocks as if investors are rational, but in reality, they are not.

The behavior of the cumulative average abnormal return around Dutch-auction tender offers in Figure 17.1 also seems to be inconsistent with market efficiency. On average, companies pay a repurchase premium of 15 percent, which is greater than the 8 percent abnormal return observed after the announcement. Such behavior would be consistent with market efficiency if one would observe a large price drop after the expiration date and there would be much prorationing (i.e., the firm repurchases only a small fraction of the shares tendered by the marginal shareholder). However, the reality is different: Figure 17.1 shows no large price drop after the expiration date and typically the prorationing in Dutch-auction tender offers is minimal. This is not surprising because market participants, not the company, set the premium.

Kadapakkam and Sarabjeet (1994) also report mispricing around Dutch-auction tender offers. They implement a simple strategy of buying and tendering shares two days before the announcement. Their results show significant average abnormal returns of 2.89 percent and positive abnormal profits in 72 percent of cases. Gay, Kale, and Noe (1996) model bidding strategies in Dutch auctions and argue that investors tend to bid above their reservation price to earn an expected profit, which may explain why the repurchase price is higher than the postexpiration price. Their model only considers two strategies: tendering or holding on to the stock. They overlook a third alternative, which is selling the stock before the expiration of the offer. Their model cannot explain why investors systematically choose to sell stock at prices below what they could obtain from tendering their shares.

Thus, a repurchase tender offer anomaly exists: market prices before the expiration of either fixed-price or Dutch-auction tender offers are too low. Investors would be better off tendering their shares rather than selling in the open market. The reason for the persistence of this anomaly may result from repurchase tender offers being relatively rare events. Alternatively, investors may believe that when a firm offers to buy back stock at $20, the stock should be at least worth $20. Therefore, the optimal strategy in this case is to hold the stock. However, considering that tendering does not involve transactions cost, the optimal strategy in this case is to tender and use the proceeds to reinvest in the stock.

Gray (2005) provides evidence discouraging to arbitrageurs because if they buy and tender, the fraction of shares tendered will increase, and the return will fall. In an extreme case, if arbitrageurs were to buy all the shares and tender them, the market would be efficient and excess returns will go to zero. Yet Gray's arguments are partially inconsistent: on the one hand, he assumes correctly that arbitrageurs care about wealth maximization, but on the other hand, he complains that when wealth increases, excess returns for the arbitrageur will fall. This is comparable to a preference of 2 percent on $1 million rather than 20 percent on $1,000.

MARKET UNDERREACTION AFTER OPEN-MARKET BUYBACK ANNOUNCEMENTS

Open-market repurchases are not firm commitments. They are authorizations rather than obligations to repurchase stock. Therefore, if markets are efficient, companies would announce open-market repurchase programs, and prices would

move to fair value. However, if the motivation for a share repurchase is undervaluation (i.e., buying back stock when it is cheap), no actual repurchases would take
place. As Stephens and Weisbach (1998) document, firms complete the vast majority of open-market repurchase programs. Managers generally believe the market
underreacts to buyback announcements. Thus, in the case of open-market repurchase programs, the management is irrational and overoptimistic or the market
underreacts.

Ikenberry, Lakonishok, and Vermaelen (1995) examine long-term excess returns after 1,289 open-market repurchase programs announced between 1980 and
1990. They test a strategy of buying companies that announce open-market share
buyback authorizations and holding the shares for four years (48 months). To
compute abnormal returns, Ikenberry et al. employ four benchmarks: (1) a value-
weighted stock market index (i.e., the S&P 500), (2) an equally weighted market
index, (3) a portfolio with the same size, and (4) a book-to-market ratio. Depending
on the method used to compute normal returns, long-term cumulative average abnormal returns vary between 6 percent and 12 percent. Of course, undervaluation
does not drive all repurchases.

Taking this discrepancy into account, Ikenberry et al. (1995) partition the sample using a proxy (i.e., the book-to-market ratio) assumed to be positively correlated with the likelihood that undervaluation motivates the repurchase. Ikenberry
et al. construct five portfolios based on the book-to-market ratio at the time of
the repurchase and calculate buy-and-hold returns for four years after the buyback announcement. They then compare these returns with returns of portfolios
of nonrepurchasing firms with similar book-to-market and size.

Figures 17.2a and 17.2b show, respectively, show the results for the bottom
book-to-market quintile (the glamour stocks) and the top book-to-market quintile
(the value stocks). As shown, glamour buyback stocks do not outperform their peer
group. But after four years, value buyback stocks outperform other value firms by
45 percent. This result is consistent with the hypothesis that value buyback stocks

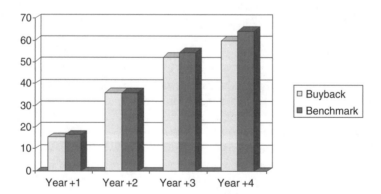

Figure 17.2a   Total Return up to Four Years after the Repurchase: Growth Stocks
The figure shows the buy-and-hold return (from one year until four years after the repurchase announcement) for a sample of repurchasing firms classified as glamour stocks (i.e., companies with
high market-to-book ratios). The portfolio of buyback stocks is compared with a benchmark of nonrepurchasing companies with similar market-to-book ratios. The figure is constructed using data from
Ikenberry et al. (1995, Table 4).

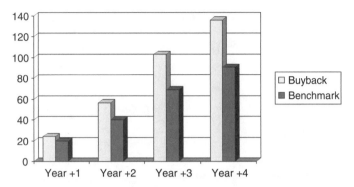

Figure 17.2b Total Return up to Four Years after the Repurchase: Value Stocks
The figure shows the buy-and-hold return (from one year until four years after the repurchase announcement) for a sample of repurchasing firms classified as value stocks (i.e., companies with low market-to-book ratios). The portfolio of buyback stocks is compared with a benchmark of nonrepurchasing companies with similar market-to-book ratios. The figure is constructed using data from Ikenberry et al. (1995, Table 4).

are more likely to be undervalued than glamour stocks and that companies can take advantage of this undervaluation. Ikenberry et al. (1995) do not observe any excess returns during the first year after the buyback announcement. Therefore, managers apparently do not have inside information about events that will become publicly known in the near future. The undervaluation is a result of the fact that stock prices do not reflect the long-term prospects of the company.

Mitchell and Stafford (2000) criticize Ikenberry et al. (1995) for equally weighting instead of value weighting all of the events. Mitchell and Stafford show the abnormal returns disappear when they value weight the events. Loughran and Ritter (2000) note that while value weighting provides a clearer picture about whether the anomaly is an economically important event, the method is biased against finding abnormal returns. Small firms, which fewer analysts follow, are more likely to be undervalued than large firms. If one would build a portfolio to exploit the anomaly, the weighting should be based on the inverse of market capitalization, which contradicts Mitchell and Stafford.

Fama (1998) points out that the research question to be answered should determine the type of weighting. For an investor, the relevant research question is, What can I expect if I buy shares in a company that announces a buyback program? Thus, equally weighting events seems appropriate. Mitchell and Stafford (2000) also criticize the buy-and-hold abnormal return methodology of Ikenberry et al. (1995) and argue that it is biased because of industry clustering. They recommend that researchers use the calendar-time portfolio approach recommended by Fama (1998). Schwert (2003) shows that even if anomalies exist during a period in which they are identified, the activities of practitioners, who implement strategies to take advantage of anomalous behavior, can cause anomalies to disappear. Consistent with this argument, Schwert documents that several anomalies have disappeared after the publication of articles that highlighted such anomalies, perhaps rendering repurchase anomalies invalid in a contemporary context.

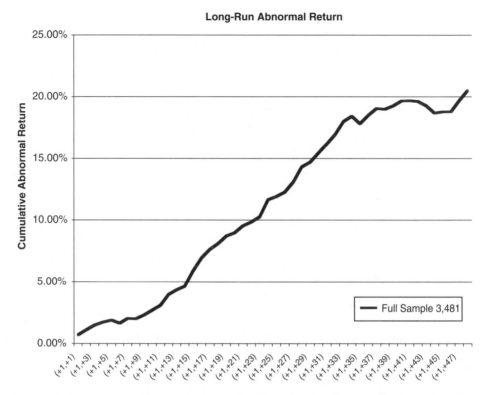

Figure 17.3 Long-Run Abnormal Return after Open-Market Share Repurchases from 1 to 48 Months after the Announcement

This figure shows the cumulative average abnormal return from the month after the buyback announcement until 48 months afterwards. The sample consists of 3,481 open-market repurchase programs announced between 1990 and 2001. Abnormal returns are calculated using the Fama-French three-factor model.

Source: Peyer and Vermaelen (2008).

Peyer and Vermaelen (2008) address these concerns by reexamining the Ikenberry et al. (1995) anomaly with a fresh 11-year data set, employing Fama's (1998) proposed methodology. On the basis of a sample of 3,465 observations, Peyer and Vermaelen confirm the results by Ikenberry et al. Figure 17.3 shows the cumulative abnormal returns for the total sample: On average, buyback stocks outperform the three-factor Fama-French model by 20 percent after three years. When splitting the sample according to book-to-market at the time of the repurchase, Figure 17.4 indicates that value buyback stocks (i.e., stocks in the highest book-to-market quintile) significantly outperform glamour buyback stocks (i.e., stocks in the lowest book-to-market quintile).

Moreover, Peyer and Vermaelen (2008) examine whether other proxies for the likelihood of undervaluation such as market cap, stated motivations for the buyback and past price behavior are better predictors of future excess returns. They combine these three indicators, together with book-to-market, in an undervaluation index, which ranges from 4 to 20. A portfolio containing all buyback

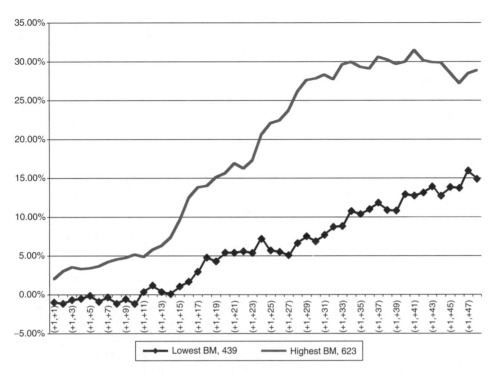

Figure 17.4 Long-Run Abnormal Return after Open-Market Share Repurchases from 1 to 48 Months after the Repurchase Announcement: Value versus Growth Stocks

This figure shows the cumulative average abnormal return from the month after the buyback announcement until 48 months afterward for two subsamples. The first sample (solid line) consists of all firms in the highest book-to-market quintile (value stocks). The second sample (interrupted line) consists of all firms in the lowest book-to-market quintile (glamour stocks). Abnormal returns are calculated using the Fama-French three-factor model.

Source: Peyer and Vermaelen (2008).

announcements with an index larger than 15 beats the Fama-French benchmark by 50 percent three years after the buyback announcement. Moreover, the strategy is stable over time. In particular, on the basis of buybacks announced between 1991 and 2002, a portfolio of 50 buyback stocks with the highest undervaluation index during the year beats the Fama-French benchmark as well as the S&P 500 during the next four years.

Although each indicator is correlated with future excess returns, the best individual predictor is the abnormal return the six months before the repurchase announcement. The sample of the 20 percent most beaten-down stocks outperforms the Fama-French (1993) benchmark by about 45 percent in the four years after the repurchase. Figure 17.5 illustrates this finding as well as the abnormal price behavior during the four years following the repurchase announcement for five quintiles formed on the basis of the abnormal price behavior during the six months preceding the announcement. Consistent with Ikenberry et al. (1995), the cumulative excess returns only become economically significant after two years.

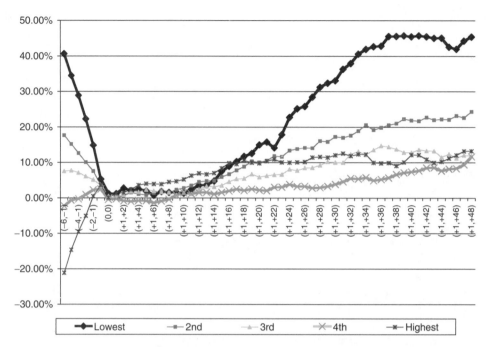

Figure 17.5 Long-Run Abnormal Return and Prior Returns: Cumulative Abnormal Returns from 6 Months before to 48 months after the Repurchase Announcement

The figure presents cumulative excess returns based on the Fama-French three-factor model from six months before the buyback announcement until 48 months afterward. The portfolios (quintiles) presented are formed based on the raw returns of stocks in the six months before the open-market repurchase announcement relative to the distribution of all CRSP firm's stock returns over the same time period.

Source: Peyer and Vermaelen (2008).

The fact that past price behavior is the main driver of future returns is consistent with the overreaction hypothesis. Markets overreact to some bad news and management takes advantage of this overreaction. Peyer and Vermaelen (2008) document a source of bad news. On average, analyst downgrade buyback stocks during the six months before the repurchase. This downgrade results from the fact that companies miss their earnings forecasts. As a result of missing this forecast, analysts also lower their forecasts of long-term earnings. According to Peyer and Vermaelen, this is a mistake because long-term forecasts have a significantly negative bias. This story can explain why this buyback anomaly exists for 25 years: Buyback stocks have negative momentum and are downgraded by analysts. Buying buyback stocks means going against analyst downgrades and momentum, something which, in general, is a bad investment strategy. As a result, investors are reluctant to join the company in purchasing the shares of the firm. The evidence shows that managers do not have inside information but simply disagree with the market's interpretation of publicly available information. In general, the results support the critique on the financial sector as being obsessed with short-term earnings. Practitioners tend to attach too much weight to short-term results because they use earnings multiples in valuation.

All the results discussed so far are based on U.S. data. Subsequent research finds economically and statistically significant long-run abnormal returns in Canada (Ikenberry, Lakonishok, and Vermaelen, 2000), the United Kingdom (Lasfer, 2002; Oswald and Young, 2004), and Hong Kong (Zhang, 2005). Because Canadian firms must disclose the number of shares repurchased each month, Ikenberry et al. (2000) can directly test the market-timing hypothesis. They find that companies that announce a repurchase but do not complete it experience significant excess returns in the year after the open-market authorization announcement and zero excess returns in the following two years. Still, firms that complete the repurchase in the year after the authorization announcement experience zero excess returns during that year but positive excess returns during the following years. Such a pattern is consistent with a market-timing story: Companies complete a buyback as long as the market has not become efficient. The evidence is clearly inconsistent with theories assuming that share prices should only go up if the repurchase takes place. Zhang (2005), who employs the same methodology as Ikenberry et al. (1995) using data from Hong Kong, finds similar results; long-term excess returns are significantly positive for value stocks but not for growth stocks.

Lasfer (2002) presents a surprising finding showing that long-term excess returns in continental Europe are significantly negative. Lasfer explains the difference in results by the lack of minority shareholder protection in continental Europe (note that a repurchase strengthens the control of the remaining stockholders) and lower information asymmetries in European firms. Because continental European share repurchase activity is a recent phenomenon, several years are likely to pass before researchers can conduct more definitive long-term event studies.

PRIVATE REPURCHASES AND LONG-TERM RETURNS

Corporations occasionally repurchase shares from a large investor. Studies by Dann and DeAngelo (1983),Bradley and Wakeman (1983), Klein and Rosenfeld (1988), Denis (1990), and Mikkelson and Ruback (1991) all report significant negative announcement returns, despite companies paying repurchase premiums around 20 percent. The general interpretation of these studies is that private repurchases are greenmail, which is a defensive measure to fight a takeover. If the repurchase is a pure wealth transfer to selling shareholders, the total weighted average return to selling and remaining shareholders should be zero. Therefore, when a company buys back shares from a private investor at a premium, stock prices should fall, reflecting this wealth transfer.

Peyer and Vermaelen (2005) examine more recent data and a broader sample of 737 private repurchases. Unlike previous research, they find the following: (1) private repurchases generate positive announcement returns of around 2 percent; (2) firms repurchase stock at an average discount of 13 percent in 45 percent of the sample; and (3) greenmail transactions have all but disappeared since 1990. They also contend that researchers should not aggregate all the transactions but separate them into four categories: greenmail transactions, repurchases at a premium, repurchases at market prices, and repurchases at a discount. The most value-creating transactions are the nongreenmail repurchases at a premium.

When examining long-term returns, researchers also observe market under-reaction in private repurchases. Moreover, the underreaction occurs regardless of whether the firm buys back the shares at a premium, a discount or market prices. Even greenmail transactions, in which the initial announcement return is negative, are followed by positive long-term excess returns, which largely compensate for the premiums paid to potential hostile bidders. This is the only case where the market does not only underreacts but also reacts in the wrong way. Rather than consider a greenmail transaction as signaling a stock's undervaluation, investors consider the transaction as evidence of non-value-maximizing behavior or the elimination of a potential takeover bid. The result on greenmail transactions show that one should make a clear distinction between two questions: (1) Why do managers repurchase stock? and (2) When do managers repurchase stock? Managers repurchase shares for various reasons (especially in private transactions), but regardless of the reason, they repurchase when the stock is cheap. Thus, the puzzle of underreaction to buyback announcement remains despite investigation by numerous researchers.

BEATING THE MARKET WITH BUYBACKS: FROM THEORY TO PRACTICE

In January 1995, a participant in an executive program was impressed by the buyback story and gave me $2 million to construct a buyback fund. I constructed a buyback portfolio of 25 stocks by April 1, 1995, using the book-to-market indicator and reported the results of the strategy in November 1997. From April 1995 until October 1997, the return on the portfolio of buyback stocks was 168 percent, significantly higher than the 93 percent of the S&P 500. Table 17.1 shows the composition of the portfolio and the return for each stock. Although most of the stocks were small-cap stocks, small caps underperformed large caps during the holding period. As a result, the small firm effect could not explain the large excess return. The strategy only works on average. For example, one company (Best Products) went bankrupt and four companies were acquired. If investors view a repurchase as a signal of a stock's undervaluation, a buyback may put a firm on the radar screen of potential bidders.

In August 1998, I launched the KBC Equity Buyback America fund, an open-ended mutual fund, in cooperation with the Belgian bank KBC. This fund invested in stocks that had announced an open-market share buyback during the previous six months and where the buyback seemed to be driven by undervaluation, using measures such as market-to-book ratios, statements in press releases, and prior stock-price behavior. I was responsible for the portfolio selection of the fund until February 2004. Table 17.2 shows the performance of all U.S. mutual funds sold in Belgium on February 13, 2004. Regardless of the look-back period (one, three, or five years), the KBC buyback fund had the highest buy-and-hold return, a result difficult to explain by anything but luck. According to Standard & Poor's, the Sharpe ratio of the fund over the three-year look-back period was the highest of all 71 comparable funds sold in Belgium. Over the five-year look-back period, the fund's Sharpe ratio was the second largest of the 41 surviving funds. Thus, the strategy can be implemented in practice.

Table 17.1 Performance of a Sample Buyback Portfolio, April 1, 1995–October 21, 1997

	Purchase Price	October 21	Return (%)	Market Cap ($million)
Interco (FBN)	7.00	18.00	157.00	900.00
Control Data (*)	7.00	21.50	207.00	NA
Garan	16.00	24.00	50.00	120.00
Decorator Industries	5.00	10.00	100.00	29.00
Shoe Carnival	4.50	7.75	72.00	100.00
Best Products	6.75	0.00	−100.00	NA
Pacific Gas & Electric	25.00	24.00	−4.00	9300.00
Aeroflex	3.75	12.00	220.00	170.00
First Harrisburg (*)	11.50		91.00	NA
Harley Industries	3.25	22.00	315.00	50.00
Westco Bank Co.	11.50	13.05	143.00	71.00
Life RE	19.25	28.00	183.00	743.00
Lakeview Financial	7.50	54.50	220.00	1110.00
Bank of Boston	32.00	24.00	176.00	12600.00
Midwest Bank Co.	24.00	88.00	108.00	14.00
Mead	52.00	50.00	41.00	3820.00
Hudson General	17.50	73.50	166.00	79.00
Twin Disc	24.00	46.50	36.00	91.00
Bairnco	4.75	32.75	132.00	100.00
PXRE	25.00	11.00	30.00	448.00
Fibreboard (*)	23.00	32.75	169.00	NA
Ross Stores	5.25	62.00	605.00	1770.00
Central Garden & Pet Stores	4.00	37.00	600.00	492.00
Ameresco	7.00	28.00	407.00	1260.00
Patrick Industries (*)	11.00	35.50	86.00	NA
		20.50		
Average			168	

Table 17.1 represents the results of an investment strategy to buy 25 stocks that announced buybacks between January 1 and April 1, 1995, and that traded below book value at the time of the buyback. The assumption is that all stocks in the portfolio were sold on October 21 1997. The asterisk indicates that the company was taken over before October 21. In that case, the assumption is that the proceeds of the sale are invested in the S&P 500 index.

CONCLUSIONS

The most popular reason managers give for repurchasing stock is undervaluation. The evidence of long-term event studies in the three countries where share repurchases are the most popular (United States, Canada, and the United Kingdom) is consistent with the hypothesis that, at least on average, managers can take advantage of an undervalued stock price. This evidence, in combination with the negative long-term returns observed after equity issues noted by Loughran and Ritter (2000), supports the hypothesis that managers have timing ability. Companies repurchase stock when they are undervalued and issue shares when they are overvalued. Information asymmetries create opportunities to take advantage of uninformed investors and benefit the existing long-term stockholders.

Table 17.2   Total Return of KBC Equity Buyback Fund (America) Measured in February 2004, over Different Investment Horizons: One, Three, and Five Years

	1 Year	3 Years	5 Years
KBC Equity Fund Buyback America C	67.92	10.03	78.21
KBC Equity Fund Buyback America D	66.56	7.60	73.30
Fidelity Funds American Growth Fund	54.14	−0.13	57.98
MLIIF US Opportunities Fund Class A (USD)	55.09	−4.98	57.46
MLIIF US Basic Value Fund Class A (USD)	45.95	5.15	36.35
Threadneedle Investment Funds ICVC American Select Growth	37.97	−21.91	19.58
MLIIF Basic Value Fund Class A (EUR)	23.68	−25.56	18.74
Threadneedle Investment Funds ICVC American Growth	35.76	−20.12	11.61
Parvest USA C	46.17	−13.90	11.35
Aberdeen Global American Growth Fund A	34.41	−22.24	9.36
Parvest USA D	43.74	−17.63	4.06
Aberdeen Global American Growth Fund B	33.00	−25.54	3.96
Credit Agricole Funds USA Private	32.81	−17.57	−2.80
Credit Agricole Funds USA Classic	32.68	−17.72	−3.02
JP Morgan Fleming Investment Funds JPMF US Select Equity Fund X	39.99	−10.59	−4.04

The table shows the total return of the best performing U.S. stock mutual funds sold in Belgium and the Netherlands on February 1, 2004. The table presents the total return one, three, and five years back. The table shows that the KBC buyback fund beats all its competitors over all investment horizons.
Source: http://www.destandaard.be.

Managers should no longer be discouraged by the efficient market hypothesis that tells them to trust market prices. Instead, they should be emboldened by the fact that sometimes the market is wrong. Stock repurchases allow managers to take advantage of market inefficiencies. An inefficient market is no longer a problem, but it creates an opportunity, at least for those firms who can afford to take advantage of this opportunity without compromising their strategic plans (Jensen, 2004). In other words, firms that have excess cash and debt capacity should exploit the opportunities provided by an occasionally inefficient market. Timing works only if the market underreacts to the buyback decision. However, timing the market also means that investors can potentially earn excess returns by buying companies that are repurchasing their undervalued stock.

REFERENCES

Bradley, Michael, and Lee Wakeman. 1983. "The Wealth Effects of Targeted Share Repurchases." *Journal of Financial Economics* 11:1–4, 301–328.

Brav, Alon, John R. Graham, Campbell R. Harvey, and Roni Michaely. 2005. "Payout Policy in the 21st Century." *Journal of Financial Economics* 77:3, 483–528.

Carhart, Mark. 1997. "On Persistence in Mutual Fund Performance." *Journal of Finance* 52:1, 57–82.

Dann, Larry, and Harry DeAngelo. 1983. "Standstill Agreements, Privately Negotiated Stock Repurchases and the Market for Corporate Control." *Journal of Financial Economics* 11:1–4, 275–300.

Denis, David J. 1990. "Defensive Changes in Corporate Payout Policy: Share Repurchases and Special Dividends." *Journal of Finance* 45:5, 1433–1456.

Fama, Eugene. 1998. "Market Efficiency, Long-term Returns and Behavioral Finance." *Journal of Financial Economics* 49:3, 283–306.

Fama, Eugene, and Kenneth French. 1993. "Common Risk Facts in the Returns of Bonds and Stocks." *Journal of Financial Economics* 33:1, 3–56.

Gay, Gerald D., Jayant R. Kale, and Thomas N. Noe. 1996. "Dutch Auction Share Repurchases." *Economica* 63:249, 57–80.

Gray, Wesley. 2005. "The Self-tender Repurchase Anomaly." Working Paper, University of Chicago.

Ikenberry, David, Josef Lakonishok, and Theo Vermaelen. 1995. "Market Underreaction to Open Market Repurchases." *Journal of Financial Economics* 39:2–3, 181–208.

Ikenberry, David, Josef Lakonishok, and Theo Vermaelen. 2000. "Stock Repurchases in Canada: Performance and Strategic Trading." *Journal of Finance* 55:5, 2373–2397.

Jensen, Michael. 2004. "The Agency Costs of Overvalued Equity and the Current State of Corporate Finance." *European Financial Management* 10:5, 545–548.

Kadapakkam, Palani-Rajan, and Seth Sarabjeet. 1994. "Trading Profits in Dutch Auction Tender Offers." *Journal of Finance* 43:1, 294–306.

Klein, April, and James Rosenfeld. 1988. "The Impact of Targeted Repurchases on the Wealth of the Non-participating Shareholders." *Journal of Financial Research* 11:2, 89–97.

Lakonishok, Joseph, and Theo Vermaelen. 1990. "Anomalous Price Behavior around Repurchase Tender Offers." *Journal of Finance* 45:2, 455–477.

Lasfer, M. Ameziane. 2002. "The Market Valuation of Share Repurchases in Europe." Working Paper, City University Business School.

Loughran, Tim, and Jay Ritter. 2000. "Uniformly Least Powerful Test of Market Efficiency." *Journal of Financial Economics* 55:3, 361–389.

Louis, Henock, and Hal White. 2007. "Do Managers Intentionally Use Repurchase Tender Offers to Signal Private Information? Evidence from Firm Financial Reporting Behavior." *Journal of Financial Economics* 85:1, 205–233.

Lücke, Marc-Olivier, and Daniel Pindur. 2002. "Riding the Hat Curve: Why Shareholders Should Tender Their Shares in Repurchase Programs." *Financial Markets and Portfolio Management* 16:3, 358–377.

Mikkelson, Wayne H., and Richard S. Ruback. 1991. "Targeted Repurchases and Common Stock Returns." *RAND Journal of Economics* 20:4, 544–561.

Mitchell, Mark, and Eric Stafford. 2000. "Managerial Decisions and Long-term Stock Price Performance." *Journal of Business* 73:3, 287–329.

Oswald, David, and Steve Young. 2004. "What Role Taxes and Regulation? A Second Look at Open Market Repurchase Activity in the United Kingdom." *Journal of Business Finance and Accounting* 31:1–2, 257–292.

Peyer, Urs, and Theo Vermaelen. 2005. "The Many Facets of Privately Negotiated Share Repurchases." *Journal of Financial Economics* 75:2, 361–395.

Peyer, Urs, and Theo Vermaelen. 2008. "The Nature and Persistence of Buyback Anomalies." *RFS Advance Access* published March 27, 2008, doi:10.1093/rfs/hhn024.

Schwert, G. William. 2003. "Anomalies and Market Efficiency." In *Handbook of the Economics of Finance*, ed. George Constantinides, Milton Harris, and René M. Stulz, 937–972. Amsterdam: Elsevier/North Holland.

Standard & Poor's. http://www.funds-sp.com.

Stephens, Clifford, and Michael Weisbach. 1998. "Actual Share Reacquisitions in Open Market Repurchase Programs." *Journal of Finance* 53:1, 313–333.

Zhang, Hong. 2005. "Share Price Performance following Actual Repurchases." *Journal of Banking and Finance* 29:7, 1887–1901.

ABOUT THE AUTHOR

Theo Vermaelen received his Ph.D. in business administration from the University of Chicago in 1980. He has been a member of the faculty at the University of British Columbia and the Catholic University of Leuven and, since 1987, he is Schroders Chaired Professor in International Finance and Asset Management, INSEAD. He has published more than 40 articles, many of them in leading journals such as *Journal of Finance*, *Journal of Financial Economics*, and *Review of Financial Studies*. Although he has published on a variety of topics in corporate finance and asset management, he has written more than 10 articles and a book on share buybacks. While his original research centers on corporate finance, his recent research focuses on the asset management implications of corporate financial decisions, in particular share buybacks. He applied his research ideas by launching the first buyback fund in cooperation with KBC in 1998. He is also coeditor of *Journal of Empirical Finance* and program director at the Amsterdam Institute of Finance, a leading financial training institute.

PART IV

Other Distribution Methods

CHAPTER 18

Special Dividends

MICHAEL GOMBOLA
Professor of Finance and Department Head, Drexel University

FENG-YING LIU
Professor of Finance, Rider University

INTRODUCTION

Special dividends, also known as specially designated dividends (SDDs), have traditionally served as a means of distributing cash to shareholders without raising expectations of such payments continuing. Management and shareholders are well aware that the reaction to dividend changes is asymmetric. That is, a small increase in the price of the company's stock typically accompanies a dividend increase, whereas a major negative impact on share price often accompanies a dividend decrease. Consequently, managers are reluctant to increase regular dividends unless they believe they can maintain the dividend at least for the foreseeable future.

Consider the dilemma faced by a firm with a large cash influx. Such a large cash influx could come from various sources, including operating cash flows at the peak of the business cycle but before a downturn, sale of a subsidiary or other large asset sale, or receipt of the proceeds from a legal settlement. The firm might have limited investment opportunities for using the cash in any of the three examples but cannot afford to maintain indefinitely a higher dividend payment. At the peak of the economic cycle, managers do not expect earnings to continue at the same level, and sales of subsidiaries or proceeds from legal settlements do not provide ongoing sources of funding for dividends.

A feasible solution to the dilemma is to pay a special dividend. By paying an SDD, managers do not raise shareholder expectations of future SDDs, and the firm does not suffer a decline in share price if it does not maintain the dividend in subsequent years. The declaration of an SDD comes with an implicit disclaimer that the firm might not continue this form of dividend in the future.

For example, Microsoft paid a large special dividend in 2004. Microsoft had not paid a regular dividend from its inception until 2003. Over that time, the firm retained cash from its operations sufficient to build up a cash reserve in excess of $75 billion. Microsoft announced a dividend of $0.08 per share on January 16, 2003, the first cash dividend ever paid by that company, followed by another announcement nine months later, on September 12, 2003, of a dividend amounting to $0.16 per share. Ten months later, on July 20, 2004, Microsoft announced a special dividend of $3 per share together with a regular quarterly dividend of $0.08 per share for the first quarter of fiscal year 2005. The firm combined news of the special dividend and regular dividend with an announcement of a stock repurchase plan approximately equivalent in size to the special dividend. The size of the special dividend, $32 billion in total, signaled a renewed interest by shareholders and managers in SDDs. Such interest had waned considerably before that time.

The role that SDDs play in dividend policy has evolved over the past 50 years. In the 1950s, nearly half of the companies on the New York Stock Exchange (NYSE) paid special dividends, which constituted about 20 percent of all dividends paid. One explanation for the prominence of special dividends was the prevalence of large cyclical industrial companies needing to return cash to shareholders, who were predominantly wealthy individual investors. Firms could modify payments over the economic cycle to fit the available cash. Many companies paid SDDs, except during recessionary periods, while others used SDDs as a precursor to increases in regular dividends. Since the 1980s, the frequency of SDDs waned as the popularity of stock repurchases increased, but repurchases did not necessarily serve as a replacement for SDDs. More recently, firms have used SDDs as a tool in financial restructuring, either as a takeover defense or as a component of changing the capital structure, as well as the more traditional role of distributing excess cash to shareholders.

This chapter begins with a chronological view of the role of SDDs and the changing application by companies, followed by a discussion of the information content of SDDs. Next, the chapter presents a comparison of SDDs and share repurchases, followed by a discussion of some academic literature on the information content of SDDs and of share repurchases. Finally, the chapter concludes with two cases of recent special dividend payments—one to implement a drastic change in capital structure and the other to reduce a firm's vulnerability as a takeover target.

HISTORICAL PAYMENT PATTERNS OF SPECIAL DIVIDENDS

Fifty years ago, the 30 companies in the Dow Jones Industrial Average were typically large industrial companies with cyclical earnings. General Motors, Sears Roebuck, Swift, International Harvester, Exxon, and Corning Glass were among the many companies that frequently paid SDDs. Their shareholders were more likely to be wealthy individuals whose lifestyle was supplemented by the dividends received from their investments. In 1950, almost half of all dividend-paying NYSE firms paid SDDs. By 1995, the percentage of dividend-paying NYSE firms that paid SDDs had fallen to 1.4 percent.

Today, the typical shareholder is a financial institution in which the receipt of dividends has little effect on its cash flow because the frequent purchases and sales can readily generate liquidity. Only a handful of companies now pay SDDs, and those that do tend to be smaller and less seasoned. The size of SDDs relative to regular dividends has also changed. During the 1950s, SDDs were generally smaller than the regular annual dividend. More recently, SDDs tend to be greater than the regular dividends. The example of Microsoft paying a regular dividend of $0.08 per share per quarter together with a special dividend of $3 per share is an example of the trend toward greater and less frequent SDDs. The recent SDDs are sufficiently large to allow the issuing company to make a statement that its shareholder will recognize.

General Motors is a good example of a company suited to paying SDDs. Its sales of automobiles and its resulting earnings tend to be cyclical with high earnings during boom years and much lower earnings and cash flows during a recession. When the economy was in recession in 1974 and 1975, General Motors paid no special dividend and was paying a regular dividend of $0.30 per quarter. During the next four years from 1976 to 1979, with a good economy and an increase in the sales of automobiles, the firm was able to pay a special dividend in addition to its regular dividend. Notably, in 1976, the first of these years of good earnings, its special dividend of $1.20 declared in November was the same size as four quarterly dividend payments of $0.30 each.

General Motors followed its large special dividend declared in November 1976 by an increase in the regular quarterly dividend to $0.425 declared in February 1977, together with a continuation of the $1.20 special dividend in November 1977, for a total dividend declaration of $1.625. The next year, General Motors raised its regular dividend further, with a quarterly dividend of $0.50 declared in February 1978 and another special dividend declared in November 1978. By 1980, with a softening of the economy and interest rates rising to historically high levels, the firm did not declare a special dividend in November, and the regular dividend reverted to the $0.30 that had been declared and paid per quarter in 1975. General Motors has not paid a special dividend since 1978.

The example of General Motors in the 1970s illustrates the use of SDDs to smooth out payments to shareholders and of the substitutability of regular and special dividends. The resumption of a special dividend payment presaged an increase in the regular dividend, and the elimination of the special dividend came before reducing the regular dividend. Apparently, the board of directors of General Motors was using both regular and special dividends as a means of the changing payout to shareholders. Management started to increase the payout by paying a special dividend in a year with good sales and earnings. If the good sales and earnings continued, management would confirm the higher payout by increasing the regular dividend payout that took the place of the SDD, at least in part. At the end of the economic cycle, management would cut or eliminate first the SDD, followed by reducing the regular quarterly dividend, if lower sales and earnings continued.

Companies less vulnerable to the economic cycle also employed the substitutability of regular and special dividends. In the 1960s and 1970s, Eastman Kodak was a growth company with consistently rising earnings and cash flows. It paid SDDs virtually without exception during those decades. The company would increase the SDD first, followed by increasing the regular dividend to a new level. Management would not eliminate the SDD after the increase in the regular dividend but would reduce the SDD by an amount approximately equal to the increase in the regular dividend. Eastman Kodak continued this practice of paying an SDD even through the early 1980s, which was a period of high inflation combined with recession. The firm paid the last SDD in 1986 followed by an increase in the regular dividend in the years 1987 to 1989, which brought the payout level beyond the combination of regular and special that it achieved in the mid-1980s.

During the time that Eastman Kodak paid SDDs, the company paid an SDD almost every year. General Motors paid SDDs in every year that the economy was expanding. Because these firms paid SDDs so frequently, labeling them as "special" would be misleading. Perhaps a better term would be *year-end*, which is a more apt descriptor of their payment. Outside the United States (e.g., in the United Kingdom), firms often pay a smaller dividend at midyear and a larger dividend at year-end.

Distinguishing between regular and special dividends supposedly provides different signals to investors and shareholders. Investors and shareholders should be able to count on regular dividends but not on special dividends. They expect firms to maintain an increase in regular dividends and impose severe consequences to the share price if firms do not maintain a regular dividend. On the other hand, the special dividend is supposed to be a way of providing a onetime distribution to shareholders. Shareholders should be using only regular dividends rather than SDDs as a signal of the firm's long-term ability to generate earnings and cash flows.

The behavior of General Motors and Eastman Kodak is at odds with the accepted distinction between regular and special dividends. If firms consistently pay SDDs, as in the case of Eastman Kodak, or if SDDs behave as predictors of regular dividends, as in the case of either General Motors or Eastman Kodak, the distinction between regular dividends and SDDs becomes meaningless. If investors come to anticipate a recurring SDD or anticipate an increase in the regular dividend from the payment of an SDD, the application of *special* to these dividends becomes perverse. The discontinuation of the recurring SDD or the failure to increase the regular dividend after paying an SDD would meet with the same market reaction as the discontinuation or reduction of a regular dividend. In this instance, SDDs and regular dividends become indistinguishable except for the additional confusion to shareholders from naming some of the dividends as *special*. Not surprisingly, management has learned to apply the term to dividends that were truly special and not just regular dividends under another name.

The decline in payment of SDDs took place at about the same time that stock repurchases became a more common financial practice. Before 1980, stock repurchases were relatively rare until the Securities and Exchange Commission (SEC) issued safe-harbor rules protecting repurchasing firms from lawsuits. The repurchasing company could have some indication that its current price is below the true value of the company, which is one of the primary reasons for a repurchase. The repurchasing company could then run afoul of insider-trading provisions, which could lead to recovery of foregone profits by sellers in a repurchase.

Tax treatment of stock repurchases is generally more favorable than dividends, either regular or special. Before the Tax Reform Act of 1980, rates on unearned income such as dividends or interest could be as high as 70 percent, whereas rates were limited to 50 percent on earned income from wages and salaries. Net long-term capital gains received a 50 percent exclusion from income, a considerable advantage over receipt of dividend income. Because of this tax benefit, an argument could be made that repurchases would supplant special dividends. However, because of the recurring nature of special dividends, they would run into the danger of being treated as "essentially equivalent to a dividend" under the provisions of Section 303 of the Internal Revenue Code.

The decline in popularity of SDDs being coincident with the increased popularity of repurchases may not have been due to the replacement of SDDs by stock repurchases. Stock repurchases, particularly fixed-price tender offers, occur much less frequently today than did SDDs during the heyday of specials. An annual stock repurchase recurring over several consecutive years, if treated as equivalent to a dividend, would cause tax problems for the many shareholders in a large public company.

Instead of SDDs being converted into repurchases, a more appropriate way to view the situation is to consider repurchases as being converted into SDDs. The previous practice of paying SDDs has largely been converted into the payment of regular dividends. SDDs, exemplified by the $3 per share ($32 billion in total) special dividend paid by Microsoft, have become infrequent onetime payments designed to raise awareness and make a statement about the company.

The reduction in frequency of SDDs after 1990 does not suggest their demise. Although they are less frequently observed, SDDs have become larger measured in either total dollars or relative to market value of the firm's equity. During the period 1990–1995, nearly 20 percent of SDDs were greater than 5 percent of the equity value of the firm. The special dividend declared by Domino's Pizza, for example, was $13.50 per share when its stock price was just over $30 per share. Other examples include a $6-per-share special dividend by TD Ameritrade when its stock was $25 per share, a $10 per share dividend by Health Management Associates, and a SDD of $7 per share by Marcus Corporation.

The motivation for each SDD was different. In the case of Marcus Corporation, the $7-per-share SDD represented much of the proceeds from its sale of the Baymont chain of hotels to La Quinta Corp. Marcus Corporation used the sale proceeds of $387 million to pay for the $213 million SDD and to pay down the firm's debt level. On the day of the announcement of the SDD, the firm's stock price rose 16 percent and continued to rise another 30 percent in the six months or so after the dividend announcement. Marcus had no better use for the proceeds than to distribute them to shareholders and was acting in the shareholders' best interest. Thus, the motivation for the SDD was prudent, as reflected in higher earnings and profits after distributing the special dividend.

The motivation for the $10 per share SDD paid by Health Management Associates also differed. That company was the takeover target by a private equity firm. Since buyout specialists try to use the target's own cash to pay interest payments on debt used to finance the takeover, eliminating the target's cash balance reduces the attractiveness of the firm as a takeover target. Health Management Associates took the process a step further by taking on debt to finance the SDD rather than using its available cash balance. Because acquirers typically finance takeovers largely using debt, the presence of debt reduces the ability of the private equity firm to finance the acquisition by debt.

When a target uses an SDD as a takeover defense, the ultimate effect on share price, as with other takeover defenses, is often negative. Reducing the probability of a takeover also reduces the chances that the bidder will pay a premium price for the target. If the current price reflects the probability of takeover at a premium price, then lowering that probability will also reduce the current stock price.

The next section discusses several empirical studies that show that the market reaction to a special dividend is generally positive. Researchers have not fully resolved the reason for the positive price reaction or the information content conveyed by a special dividend. Four different explanations, not necessarily mutually exclusive, could contribute to the information content of a special dividend announcement. The next section also provides a discussion of these four explanations.

THE INFORMATION CONTENT OF SPECIAL DIVIDENDS

Investors typically consider the announcement of a special dividend as good news. Several academic studies measure the stock price change associated with the announcement of a special dividend and find a positive stock price reaction. An early study by Brickley (1983) finds that stock prices increase by about 2 percent when firms announce unanticipated SDDs. In his study, he concentrates on firms with unanticipated special dividends by limiting his sample to firms that had not paid SDDs in the two years before the announcement.

A more recent study by DeAngelo, DeAngelo, and Skinner (2000) finds a positive market reaction even under more general circumstances. They show that for companies declaring SDDs in successive years, the market reaction is still positive even when payment in several successive years could lead to investors anticipating the special dividend announcement. DeAngelo et al. also find that investors still positively view the announcement of a special dividend, even though it represents a reduction in the amount of the special dividend relative to the payment of a previous year.

According to DeAngelo et al. (2000), the market reaction to a reduction in a special dividend is positive as long as the firm does not cut its regular dividend payment. This finding provides strong support for the rationale of differentiating between special dividends and regular dividends. Reducing or eliminating regular dividends is associated with sharp declines in stock prices. This indicates that declaring a regular dividend comes with an implicit promise that the firm will continue to make such payments. Identifying a payment as a special dividend does not carry that implicit promise. Instead, it carries an implicit caveat that management might not continue the special dividend in subsequent years. Investors apparently understand the managerial practice of distinguishing between regular and special dividends as shown by their reaction and interpretation of the announcements to regular and special dividends.

The positive reaction to the announcement of a special dividend is at odds with two possible negative interpretations of a special dividend announcement. The first of these negative interpretations is that the firm lacks investment opportunities. Declaration and payment of a special dividend implies that the firm has more cash available than it needs to fund its good investment opportunities. If a firm has more cash than necessary to fund investment opportunities, this could have good implications for cash generation or bad implications for investment opportunities. From this standpoint, the same point could be made about a stock repurchase or payment of a special dividend. In either case, the distribution of unneeded cash could have implications about the level of investment opportunities. However, if investors are already aware of the level of investment opportunities, a repurchase or special dividend should provide no new information. If special dividend paying firms are mature and their market prices depend more on the ability to generate cash from existing assets than on taking advantage of future investment opportunities, the announcement of a special dividend should have limited impact on how investors perceive those future investment opportunities.

The other negative implication of paying a special dividend is that the firm is trying to protect itself from a potential takeover. A company with substantial cash in its coffers is an attractive target for a leveraged buyout. In a leveraged buyout, a management group or an outside investor acquires the firm's assets using high levels of debt financing. Using a high level of debt financing to acquire the firm's assets has potential merit if the firm has sufficient cash to maintain interest payments on that debt. If the target firm has sufficient cash on hand and can generate substantial cash from its operations, financing the leveraged buyout can be virtually bootstrapped from its own assets.

Because the purchaser in a leveraged buyout pays a substantial premium to acquire the entire firm, any action that lowers the probability of a takeover, including payment of a special dividend, should have a negative impact on the stock price. On the other hand, if investors are unaware of the possibility of a takeover, the takeover defense could indicate that the company has become in play for a takeover. This upward revision of the probability of a takeover would be associated with a positive stock price reaction.

There are three common explanations for the positive market reaction to a special dividend announcement. Investors and shareholders could interpret the news of a firm paying a special dividend in several ways. The alternative explanations for this interpretation are (1) a reduction in the agency problems associated with holding and generating free cash flow, (2) a signal of improving company earnings, and (3) a wealth transfer from bondholders to stockholders.

An Agency Cost Explanation

The first of these three explanations is perhaps the most appealing and is the traditional interpretation of special dividend announcements. Distribution of free cash allows shareholders access to cash that otherwise would be sitting in the corporation's coffers. Not appropriately investing these cash flows is at best inefficient. Worse, management could waste the funds by undertaking projects with poor prospects or by generating perquisites for management. A rich company with considerable cash available could easily justify paying exorbitantly high salaries to management or acquiring assets primarily for management's use such as jet planes or vacation properties.

The agency problem explanation would predict that companies combining high levels of free cash flow with poor investment opportunities would have the strongest positive reaction to the announcement of a special dividend. Academic studies often measure the firm's level of investment opportunities by the ratio of the market value of the firm's stock to its book value or, by a related measure, Tobin's Q, which is the ratio of the market value of a firm's assets to the replacement cost of those assets. A firm perceived to have poorer investment opportunities should have a lower market-to-book ratio and a lower Tobin's Q value.

Howe, He, and Kao (1992) conduct a study to try to explain the market reaction to a special dividend announcement. They do not find any significant difference between the market reactions to special dividend announcements by companies with high versus low Tobin's Q. A later study by Gombola and Liu (1999) applies similar methodology to a somewhat larger sample of special dividend announcements. They find a statistically significant difference between the companies with the greatest potential agency problems of free cash flow as compared to companies with the lowest potential agency problems of free cash. Such results support the agency problem explanation for the market reaction to a special dividend announcement.

Lie (2000) provides support for the agency cost explanation. He shows that firms paying large special dividends have cash flows and cash balances that exceed industry norms. He finds a relationship between the size of the excess funds and the market reaction to the special dividend announcement, as would be predicted by an agency cost explanation. Several authors offer an alternative explanation (conditional signaling) for the market reaction to a special dividend announcement. The next section offers a review of this explanation.

A Signaling Explanation

The signaling explanation of the market reaction to a special dividend announcement lies in the interpretation that management is telling shareholders that the firm is doing well, perhaps better than expectations, at least for the short term. Managers can provide information to shareholders in several ways. Making a statement might not convince shareholders of improved prospects because words are cheap and managers can lie to protect their own positions. Accounting income is subject to a variety of interpretations, some of which allow managers to recognize income long before receiving cash. Cash flow, however, is more difficult to manipulate. To pay a regular or special dividend, managers must have the cash available. The signal of improved future performance becomes much more credible when combining words or accounting income with cash to be distributed to shareholders.

The historical tendency for firms to precede increases in regular dividends with payments of a larger special dividend supports the signaling explanation for SDDs. In the past, many firms paid SDDs year after year, which decreased the novelty of these special dividends. An increase in the regular dividend typically followed an increase in the special dividend, and an increase in the regular dividend should be an unambiguous indicator that the firm's fortunes have improved at least for the foreseeable future. For a firm that pays SDDs regularly, an increase in the special dividend may suggest that the firm's prospects have improved perhaps permanently.

Gombola and Liu (1999) provide empirical support for the signaling hypothesis. Their study begins by noting the difficulty in distinguishing between an increase in stock price due to a reduction in agency costs of free cash flow and an increase in stock price from conditional signaling. The conditional signaling explanation follows from the consideration that good news is better for companies from whom good news is unexpected. Investors typically do not expect companies with inferior investment opportunities, which are companies with low market-to-book or low Tobin's Q, to be able to generate strong positive earnings or cash flow growth. When these low-expectation companies announce a dividend increase or a special dividend, a greater revision in expectations of future earnings and cash flows occurs than for companies that already have good investor expectations for earnings and cash flow growth. Similarly, companies perceived as having good investment opportunities requiring financing could surprise investors unfavorably if they actually need less financing than expected and have funds available to pay a special dividend. In this case, a lesser market reaction for those firms with greater investment opportunities would be indistinguishable from a lesser market reaction due to the lesser agency problems of free cash flow for these firms with greater investment opportunities.

To distinguish between the conditional signaling explanation and the agency cost reduction explanation, Gombola and Liu (1999) examine the change in analysts' earnings forecasts associated with the dividend. A reduction in agency problems might eventually lead to better earnings in the longer term but probably not in the shorter term. A signal indicating that a firm has improved earnings and cash flow should be reflected in an upward revision in analyst forecasts of earnings.

Gombola and Liu (1999) find a significant upward revision in earnings forecasts by analysts for the current year—the fiscal year of the special dividend—but not for the year following the special dividend and not for long-term growth in earnings. The signal from the announcement of a special dividend is confined to the short-term prospects of the firm and has no implications for longer-term earnings and cash flows. These findings are surprising in that the business community typically considers a reduction in agency problems of free cash flow to be the purpose of a special dividend and the source of the positive market reaction to the announcement of a special dividend. Although the finding is at first troubling, short-term improvement in cash flows, but not necessarily long-term, is consistent with distinguishing between special and regular dividends. Identifying a dividend as nonrecurring limits shareholder expectations of continuing payments in future years from future cash flows. Thus, a special dividend could indicate that the current year would be particularly good, but the good current prospects might not carry over to future years.

Instead of looking prospectively at the effect on analyst earnings forecasts, Crutchley, Hudson, and Jensen (2003) look at the time pattern of actual earnings for companies paying SDDs. They find that firms announcing SDDs have unexpectedly high earnings in the year of the special dividend announcement. They also find evidence of high levels of earnings in the year preceding announcement of a special dividend. The high earnings level does not carry over to the following years. Instead, earnings tend to decline unexpectedly in the year after the special dividend announcement. Studying the long-term stock performance after the special dividend, they find no evidence that firms announcing a special dividend underperform or outperform the general market after the announcement of the special dividend. There is evidence that the stock of firms paying SDDs outperforms the market in the year before the dividend announcement but not after the announcement. These results are all consistent with the idea that firms pay SDDs when they have a very good year, a year that exceeds shareholder expectations but that might not be repeated in the near future.

A survey of CFOs by Baker, Mukherjee, and Powell (2005) provides similar evidence that is consistent with the empirical evidence from stock market prices, earnings announcements, and earnings forecasts. Responses from their survey are 72.5 percent in agreement and 12.5 percent in disagreement with the statement—the stock market generally views an announcement of an unexpected SDD as conveying information about a firm's short-term (current) earnings. Only 35 percent of respondents agree with the statement and 30 percent disagree with the statement that the stock market generally views an announcement of an unexpected SDD as conveying positive information about a firm's long-term (future) earnings prospects.

Wealth Transfer Considerations

Another possible explanation for the positive market reaction to the announcement of a special dividend is the wealth-transfer hypothesis. Distribution of cash (or any other asset) reduces the creditworthiness of the firm and its credit rating because fewer assets are available to support the firm's debt. With fewer assets and the same amount of debt outstanding, leverage ratios, such as debt to equity and debt to assets, will fall. Interest coverage ratios such as times interest earned (operating income before taxes/interest expense) will also fall with fewer assets generating cash and income. In an extreme case, distributing all of the firm's assets to the shareholders in a dividend-in-kind will eliminate the value of the debt completely thus transferring the entire asset value of the firm to the shareholders. Even in less extreme cases, an increase in the value of the firm's equity will offset the reduction in credit rating and value of the debt. The total value of the firm remains the same, but the proportionate claim of the bondholders and stockholders changes in favor of the stockholders.

A study by Jayaraman and Shastri (1988) examines the wealth transfer hypothesis by looking at the change in debt value and the change in equity value around the announcement of a special dividend. They find no evidence of a significant decline in bond value accompanying the increase in stock value that is observed with the announcement of a special dividend. The upward revision in analyst forecasts and the unexpected high announced actual earnings also support a signaling explanation rather than a wealth-transfer explanation.

Overall, the empirical evidence provides substantial support for a signaling explanation, although reduction in agency costs cannot be eliminated as a contributing explanation for the market reaction to a special dividend announcement. None of the available empirical evidence from stock market data, earnings data, or management surveys contradicts the agency cost explanation. The evidence provides very strong support that SDDs provide a positive signal of good earnings to investors but does not rule out the reduction in agency cost as a contributing factor.

SPECIAL DIVIDENDS AND SHARE REPURCHASES

When a firm has cash beyond the needs of its investment, either payment of a special dividend or share repurchases could serve as alternative means of effecting that distribution. These alternatives differ in how investors and shareholders perceive them in terms of their information content and in terms of their tax consequences. In addition, there could be some clientele differences between repurchasing firms and firms that pay SDDs. Chhachhi and Davidson (1997) find that firms paying SDDs pay larger regular dividends and have greater insider ownership than repurchasing firms.

Information Content of Special Dividends and Share Repurchases

The similarities in the market reaction between announcing an open-market share repurchase and a special dividend payment are striking. In the case of the announcement of an open-market share repurchase program or a special dividend, the abnormal return for the days around the announcement is about 2.5 percent and the upward revision in earnings forecast for current-year earnings is roughly 1.5 percent of share price. The difference in reception lies primarily for fixed price or Dutch-auction repurchase announcements, where the market reaction lies in the range of 8 percent to 10 percent and the earnings forecast revision is 3 percent to 5 percent of stock price.

At first, the similarity between investors' interpretation of an open-market share repurchase and a special dividend implies that they are close substitutes. Further consideration reveals some differences between the two. An open-market share repurchase announcement indicates that the announcing firm plans to buy back some of its stock in the open market at some point in the future. The text of the announcement can contain phrases such as "from time to time" or "as market conditions permit." There is no explicit or even implicit obligation to carry through with an actual repurchase plan, and the number of shares that firm actually repurchases remains in doubt. The firm does not have to make a formal announcement that it has canceled plans to complete the announced repurchase plan.

In the case of SDDs, the announcement is a declaration of the amount of the dividend and the date of record for its payment. The likelihood of cancellation is negligible, perhaps no more than the cancellation of payment of a regular dividend that the firm has already declared. Similarly, for a fixed price or Dutch-auction tender-offer repurchase, a company registers the repurchase with the SEC, which requires a firm, noncancelable offer of repurchase under the exact terms specified in the repurchase prospectus. Therefore, the similarity in investor reaction to a special dividend and an open-market share repurchase announcement should not be taken as an indication that the two are equivalent or substitutable for one another. The special dividend is a bird in the hand of a cash distribution to shareholders whereas the open-market share repurchase announcement is a bird in the bush of a cash distribution that shareholders might never receive.

Examining the differences in long-term returns between SDDs and open-market share repurchases shows substantial differences. Research evidence typically shows significant positive long-term returns after share repurchases, either open-market repurchases or tender offer share repurchases, but no significant long-term returns following special dividends (Ikenberry, Lakonishok, and Vermaelen, 1995; Peyer and Vermaelen, 2008). The implication is that managers employ a share repurchase when there is extra cash available and when they believe that the stock is undervalued. When the stock is not undervalued, managers use a special dividend to distribute extra cash. This difference is borne out in the results of the survey by Baker, Mukherjee, and Powell (2005). In response to the statement "firms tend to repurchase shares instead of using SDDs when managers believe their firm's stock is underpriced," 92.9 percent of respondents agree with the statement and 7.1 percent offer no opinion. None of the respondents disagree with the statement.

Tax Consequences

The difference in tax consequences between special dividends (or dividends of any sort) and stock repurchases varies across tax regimes in different countries and varies over time within countries. In the United States, the tax consequences of dividends and capital gains have varied widely from the very high, almost penalty rate of 70 percent in the 1970s to the 15 percent rate in force over the past few years. Rates on capital gains have also varied from an exclusion of half of long-term capital gains to full taxation to a 15 percent rate currently in effect on long-term capital gains. With a 15 percent rate applicable to both dividends and realized capital gains, tax differences between receiving dividends, including SDDs and receiving capital gains from stock repurchases have narrowed to the least difference since the imposition of income taxation.

Two additional tax consequences for dividends need to be taken into account in the case of SDDs. First, the first consequence is the dividends-received exclusion for corporate recipients of dividends. The purpose of this exclusion is to alleviate the multiple taxation of income, first at the corporate level and then at the investor level. If corporate recipients did not receive this exclusion, there would be triple taxation of the same income.

The second tax consequence is the possibility that the special dividend represents a partial of total return of capital for the recipient. SDDs can be large either in absolute amount or relative to the current earnings of the company. Given the differences in calculating earnings for tax and corporate reporting purposes, the firm can pay a special dividend that exceeds the current year's net income and the firm's retained earnings available for tax purposes. In this case, part or the entire dividend received represents a return of capital rather than of current income. The portion of the dividend deemed to be a return of capital escapes taxation, but the return reduces the cost basis of shares held and increases the capital gain realized in the future when investors sell their shares.

The potential tax treatment for shareholders could influence the managerial choice between a special dividend and a stock repurchase. Firms whose shareholders have experienced substantial price appreciation would have little difference between the capital gain from a share repurchase, on which only the gain is taxed, and a special dividend, which is all taxed at dividend rates. On the other hand, when shareholders have not enjoyed much price appreciation and the stock is languishing (particularly if the market underestimates the true value of the company), a stock repurchase would be a much more tax-efficient means of distributing cash to shareholders.

Special Dividends in Financial Restructuring

Although companies typically pay SDDs when they have amassed extra cash in excess of their need to acquire productive assets, firms need not have surplus cash to pay a special dividend. Instead, even cash-strapped firms with access to borrowing capacity can issue debt and use the proceeds to pay a special dividend to shareholders. Management could use such a financial tactic to create a quick change in the firm's capital structure. This change in capital structure could be designed to protect the firm against an unwelcome takeover, to reduce the company's cost of capital, or to ward off complaints of inefficient management. Such recapitalizations can involve large debt increases and large special dividend payments relative to the value of the company's stock. Of course, just as is the case of a regular dividend, the stock price will fall on the ex-dividend date by the amount of the special dividend and shareholders will typically face a tax bill on the special dividend received. The fall in stock price and the extra tax bill could be as large as $10 or $15 per share.

To the extent that a firm can benefit from the tax deductibility of debt, the substitution of debt for equity in the firm's capital structure can produce a lower cost of capital and higher valuation. The effectiveness of this tactic is subject to much controversy because no clear-cut evidence exists that additional borrowing can lower the cost of capital. This is particularly true when the tax benefits of additional borrowing are offset to some extent by the increased tax payments due from shareholders as a result of the special dividend. For a firm with extremely low debt, moving toward a capital structure that mirrors the industry standard and enjoying the benefits of lower capital cost accrues some benefit. Few firms have employed this tactic for the express purpose of lowering their capital cost. Although many underleveraged firms could employ this tactic, they prefer to refrain from adding debt to their capital structure. Perhaps some of the reluctance to add debt to enjoy lower capital costs is due to the reduced balance sheet strength and reduced financial flexibility from heavy borrowing.

Domino's Pizza announced in April 2007 that it had effected a recapitalization by borrowing $1.85 billion and paying a special dividend of $13.50 a share. This special dividend was more than a third of the firm's price per share at the time of the recapitalization announcement. The large increase in debt would move the firm to a capital structure that is similar to a leveraged buyout firm.

Financial restructuring can also serve as an effective tactic in protecting against an unwelcome takeover. Eliminating a firm's cash and taking on additional debt makes the firm a much less attractive target for a takeover since the firm will not have available cash to support the financing of a leveraged buyout. For example, Health Management Associates declared a $10 per share special dividend financed by additional debt in order to ward off a takeover. As would be expected, the stock price fell by the amount of the special dividend on the ex-dividend date. Even after the ex-dividend date, the company's stock has not performed well and has languished in the postrestructuring period. This anecdotal evidence suggests that using a special dividend to ward off a takeover can be of more benefit to an entrenched management than to the firm's shareholders. However, Denis (1990) finds that even defensive special dividend payments are associated with increased shareholder wealth.

Any dividend, regular or special, can reduce the agency problem of free cash flow because fewer resources are available for management to waste or to use for their own benefit. A special dividend in a leveraged restructuring can provide an immediate and substantial reduction in agency problems through the distribution of cash and through the discipline imposed by mandatory interest payments on the debt employed to bring about the restructuring. At the same time, management is "throwing a bone" to shareholders who might have received little from the company in the recent past. Management could use such a restructuring as a signal that the firm will be run much more tightly and efficiently than previously as mandated by additional debt payments.

The empirical evidence by Smith (1986) suggests that investors react favorably to a leveraged restructuring with a positive market reaction observed for those restructurings that firms do not use for defense against takeovers. Management can undertake restructurings with a stock repurchase or a special dividend. Samples of restructurings using SDDs tend to be smaller than those where management uses the debt proceeds to buy back new common stock, indicating that firms tend to use stock repurchases more commonly than special dividends to achieve a restructuring.

CONCLUSIONS

Special dividends receive the *special* designation to inform shareholders that the dividend might not be continued into the future. Historically, firms paid SDDs much more often than they do today with some firms paying special dividends year after year. In these cases, payment of SDDs and increases in payments of SDDs were precursors to increases in regular dividends. Today, firms pay SDDs much less frequently but such dividends tend to be larger in size, particularly relative to the size of the payer.

SDDs can provide the benefit of reducing the agency costs of free cash flow. Removing cash from managerial discretion reduces management ability to waste cash on poor projects or use it for managerial perquisites. Empirical evidence indicates that SDDs can also serve as a signal to shareholders that the company is experiencing particularly strong earnings and cash flow. This signal appears to be limited to current-year performance and appears to have no implications for the longer-term prospects of the firm.

SDDs and share repurchases both serve as a means of distributing surplus cash to shareholders. Managers tend to choose share repurchases when they believe that shareholders perceive their company's stock as undervalued. Some differences in tax considerations between the alternatives could also affect the managerial decision as to whether to pay a special dividend or to repurchase common stock. Managers can also use both SDDs and stock repurchases in leveraged restructurings where the firm issues debt to raise cash and then distributes that cash through either a stock repurchase or a special dividend. Leveraged restructurings provide a means to impose self-discipline on management or to ward off a takeover threat. Investors view the former motive more favorably than the latter.

REFERENCES

Baker, H. Kent, Tarun K. Mukherjee, and Gary E Powell. 2005. "Distributing Excess Cash: The Role of Specially Designated Dividends." *Financial Services Review* 14:2, 111–131.

Brickley, James A. 1983. "Shareholder Wealth, Information Signaling and the Specially Designated Dividend: An Empirical Study." *Journal of Financial Economics* 12:2, 187–209.

Chhachhi, Indudeep S., and Wallace N. Davidson III. 1997. "A Comparison of the Market Reaction to Specially Designated Dividends and Tender Offer Stock Repurchases." *Financial Management* 26:3, 89–96.

Crutchley, Claire E., Carl D. Hudson, and Marlin R. H. Jensen. 2003. "Special Dividends: What Do They Tell Investors About Future Performance?" *Financial Services Review* 12:2, 129–141.

DeAngelo, Harry, Linda DeAngelo, and Douglas J. Skinner. 2000. "Special Dividends and the Evolution of Dividend Signaling." *Journal of Financial Economics* 57:3, 309–354.

Denis, David J. 1990. "Defensive Changes in Corporate Payout Policy: Share Repurchases and Special Dividends." *Journal of Finance* 45:5, 1433–1456.

Gombola, Michael J., and Feng-Ying Liu. 1999. "The Signaling Power of Specially Designated Dividends." *Journal of Financial and Quantitative Analysis* 34:3 409–424.

Howe, Keith M., Jia He, and G. Wenchi Kao. 1992. "One-Time Cash Flow Announcements and Free Cash Flow Theory: Share Repurchases and Special Dividends." *Journal of Finance*, 47:5, 1963–1975.

Ikenberry, David, Josef Lakonishok, and Theo Vermaelen. 1995. "Market Underreaction to Open Market Share Repurchases." *Journal of Financial Economics* 39:2/3, 181–208.

Jayaraman, Narayanan, and Kuldeep Shastri. 1988. "The Valuation Impacts of Specially Designated Dividends." *Journal of Financial and Quantitative Analysis* 23:3, 301–312.

Lie, Erik. 2000. "Excess Funds and Agency Problems: An Empirical Study of Incremental Cash Disbursements." *Review of Financial Studies* 13:1, 219–247.

Peyer, Urs, and Theo Vermaelen. 2008. "The Nature and Persistence of Buyback Anomalies." *Review of Financial Studies*, forthcoming.

Smith, Clifford W., Jr. 1986. "Investment Banking and the Capital Acquisition Process." *Journal of Financial Economics*, 15:1/2, 3–29.

ABOUT THE AUTHORS

Michael Gombola is professor of finance and department head at Drexel University and previously served as interim accounting department head. Before joining Drexel, Gombola was on the faculties of the University of Connecticut and Southern Illinois University. He received an undergraduate degree from Clemson University, a Ph.D. from the University of South Carolina, and the certified cash manager designation from the Treasury Management Association. His research interests are in corporate finance and investments. His research has been published in more than a dozen journals, including *Journal of Financial and Quantitative Analysis*, *Financial Management*, *Journal of Financial Research*, *Financial Review*, *Financial Analysts Journal*, and *Journal of International Business Studies*. He is active in several academic associations and served two terms on the board of directors for the Eastern Finance Association and as its program vice president. Gombola has been a reviewer for 18 refereed journals and the National Science Foundation.

Feng-Ying Liu is professor of finance at Rider University. She has been on the faculty at Rider University since 1988. Her research interests are in corporate finance and investments. She received her undergraduate degree from National Taiwan University, her MBA and Ph.D. degrees from Drexel University, and the certified treasury professional designation from the Treasury Management Association. Her corporate experience includes three years with the Export-Import Bank of China and NCR in Taiwan. Her publications have appeared in journals such as *Journal of Financial and Quantitative Analysis*, *Financial Management*, *Journal of Financial Research*, *Financial Review*, and *Journal of Business Finance and Accounting*.

CHAPTER 19

Stock Splits, Stock Dividends, and Reverse Stock Splits

DAVID MICHAYLUK
Associate Professor, University of Technology, Sydney

INTRODUCTION

The common equity ownership of a publicly traded company is divided into shares, and each share represents an equal portion of ownership. The number of shares relative to the total outstanding shares indicates the proportion of the company that each shareholder owns. This chapter deals with the phenomena where management alters the total number of shares so that the value of an individual share changes even though theoretically the company as a whole does not change in total value. These cosmetic changes neither alter the portion of the company owned by each shareholder nor change the future cash flows of the firm.

What makes these actions interesting is that the market reacts to these events and empirical studies show the presence of abnormal stock-price changes at the announcement and sometimes at the ex-date. These puzzling reactions suggest that the partitioning of ownership and the determination of the value of a single share affect the total value of the equity of a firm. This empirical finding seems counterintuitive. Beginning with the first event study in finance, researchers hypothesized several potential explanations. This chapter examines three different changes in the partitioning of equity ownership.

- A *stock split* occurs when the management of a firm decides to give new shares to the owners of existing shares. A stock split is usually expressed as ratio, such as two for one, where the owner of every share receives an additional share. For example, in a three-for-one stock split, the holder of 100 shares before the split would receive 200 additional shares and be left with 300 shares after the split. Theoretically, the holder of a $90 share that splits three for one will be left with three shares each worth $30.
- A *stock dividend* occurs when the owner of each share also receives additional stock in the company thereby maintaining the same proportion of shares. A stock dividend is usually less than a stock split and is expressed as a percentage such as a 5 percent stock dividend. The usual break between stock dividends and stock splits is at the 25 percent ratio where anything below 25 percent is a stock dividend. A 25 percent stock dividend is actually

a five-for-four stock split. An example of a 10 percent stock dividend for the holder of 200 shares is that the holder would receive an additional 20 shares. If the stock dividend results in fractional shares, the firm can pay that amount in cash rather than shares. The accounting treatment of stock dividends in the United States requires reducing the retained earnings account and increasing the share capital account by the amount of the stock dividend, thereby leaving a lower amount of funds available to pay dividends.

- A *reverse stock split* happens when existing shares are grouped together to form a smaller number of new shares in a specific proportion. A reverse stock split is usually expressed as a ratio such as four for one or ten for one, but the ratio can be even larger. For example, in a 100-for-1 reverse stock split, a shareholder that owned 200 shares would receive two new shares after the reverse stock split. If the reverse stock split results in fractional shares, the firm usually pays the value of those shares in cash.

In these three situations, each shareholder maintains the same proportion of ownership of the firm since the ownership pie is simply sliced into a larger or smaller number of pieces.

This chapter provides a review of the empirical evidence about the stock market price reaction to these three corporate actions and examines the explanatory hypotheses set forth in the literature. The chapter also contains a review of the implications for investors and managers.

STOCK SPLITS

Stock splits divide existing shares into new shares so that the proportional ownership of each shareholder does not change. The phenomenon is of particular interest because the new share price is usually greater than would be expected by simply dividing the old share price by the new number of shares. This section examines the empirical evidence of the abnormal price increase as well as the source of this increase in value.

Empirical Evidence

Fama, Fisher, Jensen, and Roll (1969) wrote the seminal paper on stock splits and the first finance event study. In this study, they fail to separate stock dividends and stock splits. Other researchers criticize them for not removing announcements that occurred at the same time. Using monthly returns, Fama et al. report positive residuals for stock splits in the months around the split. Copeland (1979) suggests that other information released at the same time causes the observed price changes around a stock split.

Subsequent researchers including Lamoureux and Poon (1987) and Grinblatt, Masulis, and Titman (1984) test Copeland's (1979) conjecture by removing the announcements that occurred near the same time as the stock split. They report that the stock splits alone resulted in a 3 percent abnormal return on the announcement date and a 0.8 percent return on the ex-date (the actual date of the change to the new number of shares and pricing structure). Using a clean sample of stock splits with no other earnings or cash dividend information at the same time, they find that the abnormal returns are similar, thereby ruling out the simultaneous other information release explanation.

Some evidence exists that before and after stock splits, splitting firms have higher growth in earnings and dividends. Lakonishok and Lev (1987) suggest that firms execute stock splits after they have experienced an unusual growth in earnings and stock prices in the past so stock splits are a result of this unusual performance. McNichols and Dravid (1990) find that the difference between the actual and forecasted earnings following a stock split tends to be correlated with the size of the split factor. When the split factor is larger, the earnings are better. Ikenberry and Ramnath (2002) report that financial analysts tend to underestimate splitting firms' earnings, and then the market tends to initially underreact to information, which accounts for a positive postsplit abnormal return drift of 9 percent. The differences between splitting and nonsplitting stocks may be apparent even before stock splits. Ezzell and Rubiales (1975) use measures of growth as well as basic financial statement information to discriminate between stocks in advance of the stock split.

There are mixed findings about liquidity changes around stock splits. The strongest result is the increase in volatility following stock splits, possibly due to the lower price and higher proportional tick size. Ohlson and Penman (1985), Dubofsky (1991), Koski (1998), and French and Foster (2002) find that return volatility increases by about 30 percent after a stock split, and this increase is persistent for as long as a year after the ex-date.

For share volume, researchers report an increase in volume, a decrease in volume, and no change in volume. Lakonishok and Lev (1987) find no increase in volume after stock splits, but they do indicate there may be other aspects of marketability, such as the composition of shareholders, that undergo a change after stock splits. Maloney and Mulherin (1992) also find no increase in trading volume after stock splits. They also confirm an increase in both the ownership base and the number of small trades after stock splits. Lamoureux and Poon (1987) show that both the number of shareholders and transactions as well as the raw volume of shares increase after a stock split. Mukherji, Kim, and Walker (1997) also find an increase in the number of shareholders after a stock split, but they note that the proportion of institutional ownership remains unchanged following a stock split.

Copeland (1979) documents a drop in the split-adjusted volume and concludes that liquidity actually declines following a stock split. In contrast, Desai, Nimalendran, and Venkataraman (1998) observe an increase in trading volume after stock splits. Conroy, Harris, and Benet (1990) find that another measure of liquidity, the percentage bid-ask spread, tends to increase after a stock split. Easley, O'Hara, and Saar (2001) confirm an increase in the percentage bid-ask spread after stock splits. They also find that the number of executed limit orders increases after stock splits, and they interpret this finding as an increase in informed trading. Similarly, Schultz (2000) finds that the minimum bid-ask spread is wider after a stock split. Overall, these mixed results on liquidity are inconclusive.

Researchers have also investigated long-run stock performance after stock splits. Desai and Jain (1997) find that the one- and three-year average buy- and-hold abnormal returns after the stock split announcement month are 7 percent and 12 percent, respectively. They suggest that these results indicate that the market underreacts to the stock split announcement. In contrast, Byun and Rozeff (2003) examine long-run performance using reference portfolios, but they fail to find significant abnormal performance. Boehme and Danielsen (2007) also find no long-run abnormal returns after considering industry momentum, and they attribute the positive abnormal return drift to market frictions.

Levels of risk may change after stock splits. Both Lamoureux and Poon (1987) and Brennan and Copeland (1988a) identify a permanent increase in beta following stock splits. Conversely, Wiggins (1992) finds that the decay in the beta change after stock splits is larger when lengthening the measurement interval. He finds no statistically significant difference between betas before and after stock splits. Please see here Table 19.1.

Table 19.1   Stock Split Empirical Literature

Author	Date	Sample	Key Results
Fama, Fisher, Jensen, and Roll	1969	940 stock splits in 1927–1959	Event study methodology provides a new way to measure the effect of an event on the price of stock. Abnormal returns occur around stock splits using monthly data.
Ezzell and Rubiales	1975	875 stock split firms in 1966–1971	Split firms are more likely to issue splits again.
Grinblatt, Masulis, and Titman	1984	1,140 stock splits in 1967–1976	Positive abnormal returns follow stock splits.
Ohlson and Penman	1985	1,257 stock splits on the NYSE in 1962–1981	Volatility Increases after stock splits.
Lamoureux and Poon	1987	213 stock splits on the NYSE and AMEX in 1962–1985	Stock splits increase trading activity and increase the tax-option value of the stock. A permanent increase in beta follows stock splits.
Lakonishok and Lev	1987	1,015 stock splits in 1963–1982	The study provides support for the normal trading range and signaling explanations for stock splits.
Brennan and Copeland	1988b	1,034 stock splits	Signaling explains a large proportion of the abnormal announcement returns around stock splits.
Sheikh	1989	Optionable stocks in 1976–1986	Return volatility increases after stock splits but does not support the trading-range hypothesis.
Maloney and Mulherin	1992	446 stock splits on the NASDAQ in 1984–1996	Stock splits do increase split-adjusted volume but do result in a larger number of small trades.
McNichols and Dravid	1990	1,376 stock splits and dividends in 1976–1983	Managers choose the stock split factor as a signal about future earnings.
Wiggins	1992	2,300 stock splits on the NYSE and AMEX in 1962–1989	Beta does not change after stock splits when the measurement interval is sufficiently lengthy.

Table 19.1   (*Continued*)

Author	Date	Sample	Key Results
Ikenberry, Rankine, and Stice	1996	1,275 stock splits on the NYSE and AMEX in 1975–1990	The market underreacts to stock splits resulting in a positive drift of 8 percent for 1 year and 12 percent for 3 years. Managers self-select stock splits when optimistic.
Desai and Jain	1997	5,596 stock splits on the NYSE, AMEX, and NASDAQ in 1976–1991	Stock splits result in 1-year buy-and-hold abnormal returns of 7 percent and 3-year buy-and-hold abnormal return of 12 percent. Underreaction to the stock split occurs and a positive association exists between announcement and long-run abnormal returns with an increase in dividends.
Koski	1998	317 stock splits on the NYSE in 1987–1989	Variance increases after stock splits even after controlling for the bid-ask spread and price discreteness.
Easley, O'Hara, and Saar	2001	75 stock splits on the NYSE in 1995	An increase in uninformed traders and an increase in executed limit orders occur as a result of stock splits but an increase in the costs of executing market orders also results due to higher bid-ask spreads.
Ikenberry and Ramnath	2002	3,028 stock splits on the NYSE, AMEX, and NASDAQ in 1988–1997	Financial analysts underestimate earnings of split firms, which accounts for the positive abnormal drift of 9 percent in the first year after the stock split.

This table reports the authors, year of publication, sample details, and key results of widely cited research studies that empirically examine stock splits.

Explanatory Hypotheses

The first theories propose two broad explanations for stock splits: the information-signaling hypothesis and the optimal-price-range hypothesis. Subsequent research further extends the optimal-price-range hypothesis, as there are implications for liquidity and stock volatility. Many other explanations, which are not necessarily mutually exclusive, also exist.

The Signaling Hypothesis

The information signaling argument, put forth by Copeland (1979), Grinblatt, Masulis, and Titman (1984), and Brennan and Copeland (1988b), claims that managers use costly stock splits to convey private information to the market about the current and future performance of the firm. Grinblatt et al. suggest that managers do not use stock splits to move the firm's stock price back to a preferred trading range unless this action reflects favorable future prospects. This argument is consistent with a positive stock market reaction and increases in earnings and/or dividends around the stock split.

The Optimal-Trading-Range or Liquidity Hypothesis

The optimal-price-range hypothesis offered by Grinblatt et al. (1984) suggests that if managers have negative information, they will not issue stock splits because such information will lower the price. Therefore, managers issue stock splits when they believe the only way to reduce the price to the norm is by a stock split. Lakonishok and Lev (1987) propose another version on the optimal-trading-range hypothesis. They suggest that industry norms exist for financial ratios and that managers use stock splits to adjust prices to reflect these norms. Conroy et al. (1990) consider a specific price range to be optimal. They reason that stocks with prices in this range are more liquid because they have lower brokerage fees as a percent of traded value and are more affordable for small investors because they can buy round lots of shares. If the nominal price range is lower, the stock is more attractive to retail investors, who want to minimize transaction costs, and the number of these investors would increase. The liquidity aspect of the optimal trading range confounds the explanation. Therefore, some researchers contend that the two hypotheses are separable but interrelated. Baker and Powell (1993) survey managers and 70 percent cite a preferred price range or a stock's liquidity as the reason for the stock split.

Does support for the optimal-trading-range and higher-liquidity hypotheses negate the signaling hypothesis? Dennis (2003) tries to disentangle the two by examining the trading of an index stock that undergoes a stock split. Because no signaling exists in this situation, all postsplit trading differences are attributable to liquidity changes. Dennis finds that the bid-ask spread increases and the daily volume is unchanged, but the frequency, individual share volume and dollar value of small trades all increase after the index stock split. Muscarella and Vetsuypens (1996) examine cases when American Depository Receipts (ADRs) split in the United States. They find that the stock price increases on the announcement of an ADR stock split even when there is no accompanying stock split in the firm's home market. They, along with Kryzanowski and Zhang (1996) and Schultz (2000), identify an increase in the number of small trades after stock splits, and this provides support for the liquidity hypothesis.

The Optimal-Tick-Size Hypothesis

Angel (1997) suggests that the mandated minimum tick size (before decimalization) would increase the costs of trading shares when lowering a stock's price. Therefore, stock splits are a way of balancing an increase in transaction costs for traders through a larger bid-ask spread with the increase in limit-order traders who would enter the market if the bid-ask spread were large. Thus, this hypothesis represents a trade-off between these two measures of liquidity that would determine the optimal price. Companies could perform a stock split to lower their stock price to attract more institutional traders who would respond to the larger bid-ask spread. With the move to decimalization, the large bid-ask spreads created by the binding minimum tick size is no longer in place so this hypothesis may no longer be as relevant.

The Self-Selection Hypothesis

Ikenberry, Rankine, and Stice (1996) synthesize both the trading range and the signaling hypotheses to suggest that stock splits realign prices to a lower trading range, but managers self-select by conditioning the decision to undergo a stock split on expected future performance. This appears to be similar to the Grinblatt et al. (1984) argument that managers will not perform stock splits if negative information exists that will cause the stock price to drop below the optimal range in the future.

The Neglected-Firm Hypothesis

Arbel and Swanson (1993) suggest that if minimal information exists about a firm, then the press neglects that firm. If a firm then announces a stock split, this information draws attention and interest to the firm. This argument is compelling in a stock universe of thousands of firms, but it does not explain why well-known firms would undergo stock splits.

The Tax-Option-Value Hypothesis

According to Constantinides (1984), one effect of the higher volatility after stock splits is that the stock has a higher tax-option value. A stock with a price that fluctuates wildly presents its holder with the opportunity to realize short-term losses or long-term gains to reestablish short-term status. Lamoureux and Poon (1987) suggest that an increase in noise trading raises the tax-option value of the stock, and the market reacts to this increase in value at the announcement date. Dhatt, Kim, and Mukherji (1997) test this hypothesis around the tax reform in 1986 and find evidence that is inconsistent with the tax-option hypothesis.

Inconvenience Hypothesis

Nayar and Rozeff (2001) suggest that the inconvenience of a recording date for stock splits results in a negative abnormal return at the record date and a positive abnormal return at the ex-date. Angel, Brooks, and Mathew (2004) support this hypothesis by examining trading in when-issued shares (shares that are traded in advance of the stock split as if the split had already happened).

Despite the various explanations suggested and more than three decades of study, researchers have yet to reach a consensus why managers decide to initiate stock splits. Support exists for the two main hypotheses (information signaling and optimal price range), which are not likely mutually exclusive. Perhaps by asking managers why they initiate stock splits, this survey evidence may help to explain which of the hypotheses is more important to which types of managers.

STOCK DIVIDENDS

Because stock dividends provide a proportional increase in the number of shares for each shareholder, the proportional ownership for each shareholder does not change. Similar to stock splits, the new share price is higher than what would be expected by simply dividing the old share price by the new number of shares. The accounting treatment for stock dividends differs from that of stock splits. With a stock dividend, a portion of the retained earnings transfers to the share capital. This section examines the empirical evidence of the abnormal price increase as well as the source of this increase in value.

Empirical Evidence

Although stock dividends involve the distribution of fewer shares to owners than stock splits, the same argument that cosmetic changes should not affect value applies to firms that pay stock dividends. Researchers have investigated the stock market reaction to the announcement of the stock dividend and at the date when the firm pays the stock dividend (the ex-date) (see Table 19.2).

The Announcement Date

In the first event study in finance, Fama et al. (1969) identify a positive announcement effect but do not separately examine stock dividends and stock splits. Also, they do not separate these events from announcements of cash dividends or other information. Foster and Vickrey (1978) and Woolridge (1983b) isolate stock dividends and also report positive excess returns at the announcement date. Grinblatt et al. (1984) remove contemporaneous announcements and confirm a positive stock market reaction at the announcement of about 5 percent.

Table 19.2   Stock Dividend Empirical Literature

Author	Date	Sample	Key Results
Grinblatt, Masulis, and Titman	1984	301 stock dividends in 1967–1976	Stock dividends are similar to stock splits.
Lakonishok and Lev	1987	1,257 stock dividends in 1963–1982	Stock dividends are different from stock splits and a declining phenomenon. The difference may be due to stock dividends being a substitute for low cash dividends.
McNichols and Dravid	1990	1,376 stock splits and dividends in 1976–1983	Managers choose the stock split factor as a signal about future earnings.
Koski	1998	44 stock dividends on the NYSE in 1987–1989	Variance increases after stock dividends even after controlling for the bid-ask spread and price discreteness.

This table reports the authors, years of publication, sample details, and key results of widely cited research articles that empirically examine stock dividends.

Lakonishok and Lev (1987) compare characteristics of firms that paid a stock dividend with firms that underwent a stock split. They find that the two groups differ substantially. Compared to nondistributing firms, firms paying stock dividends are smaller than the population of firms. Lakonishok and Lev also observe that stock-dividend firms are not concentrated in specific industries. They compare firms that paid a stock dividend with control firms that did not pay any stock dividends. They document that firms paying stock dividends have somewhat higher preannouncement earnings growth than control firms. Yet for many of the subperiods, the earnings differences between the stock-dividend-paying firms and the control firms are not statistically significant. Regular dividend differences are minimal between firms paying and not paying stock dividends. In some subperiods, the non-stock-dividend-paying firms paid higher cash dividends. The above-average earnings growth in the preannouncement period does not translate to cash dividends.

The Ex-Date

Empirical tests of ex-date stock dividends by Barker (1959) find that the actual price drop on the stock dividend ex-date is 97.4 percent of the calculated dilution price decline. Because the price drop is less than expected, this indicates an increase in overall firm value. Woolridge (1983a) confirms that the total shareholder wealth increases on the ex-date since again, the new share price does not fully adjust to the stock distribution. He also finds that small (less than 6 percent) stock-dividend-paying firms have the largest abnormally positive stock market reaction on the ex-date, suggesting that the large one-eighth tick size ($0.125) may prevent the full price adjustment of the stock price. In contrast, Foster and Vickrey (1978) do not find any change in company value on the ex-date, but their sample size of 82 events is small. Eades, Hess, and Kim (1984) confirm a positive ex-date abnormal return, but their sample includes both stock dividends and stock splits. Grinblatt et al. (1984) remove events with confounding news and document positive excess returns on the ex-date for stock dividends of about 1.9 percent.

Other empirical studies examine the liquidity changes after a stock dividend. Dravid (1987) finds that unlike stock splits, stock volatility does not increase for firms that undergo a stock dividend. In contrast, Koski (1998) shows an increase in the variance of weekly returns after a stock dividend, even after controlling for bid-ask spreads and price discreteness. Kamara and Koski (2001) include stock dividends in their study and find that the increase in small traders accounts for the increase in standard deviation of returns. They also find feedback in that the increased volatility leads to the increased small trading.

Other empirical studies examine risk changes after stock splits. For example, Bar-Yosef and Brown (1977) find a decrease in the level of stock risk, while Ohlson and Penman (1985) and Sheikh (1989) find an increase in risk.

Explanatory Hypotheses

A common explanation for issuing stock dividends, often found in finance textbooks, is that stock dividends are a temporary replacement for cash dividends. Lakonishok and Lev (1987) indicate that the rationale for regarding a stock dividend as a substitute is unclear. Researchers offer many hypotheses to explain the positive reaction to stock dividends. These explanations are similar to those for stock splits but include the retained-earnings hypothesis, trading-range hypothesis, attention hypothesis, increase-in-cash-dividends hypothesis, and signaling hypothesis.

The Retained-Earnings Hypothesis

The retained-earnings hypothesis proposed Barker (1959) and reiterated by Grinblatt et al. (1984) and Rankine and Stice (1997) suggests that paying a stock dividend requires firms to subtract the value of the newly distributed shares from retained earnings (earned surplus) and to add the amount to the firm's capital account. This transfer from retained earnings places restrictions on the availability to pay cash dividends. Therefore, the act of a stock dividend may provide information that management believes future earnings will be sufficient to compensate for the reduction in retained earnings. This argument only applies to stock distributions of less than 25 percent because any greater amount is treated as a stock split, and stock splits do not affect retained earnings. Grinblatt et al. partition their sample of stock distributions into stock dividends and stock splits and show that the larger abnormal return to stock dividends provides support for the retained-earnings hypothesis.

The Trading-Range Hypothesis

Barker (1959) suggests that stock dividends, like stock splits, help bring the common stock price into a more popular price range. Grinblatt et al. (1984) suggest that, given the cost associated with stock dividends, managers will not increase the number of shares if they possess negative information about future growth. They conjecture that once the firm releases the negative information, its stock price will decline. Therefore, managers will not pay a stock dividend to reduce an abnormally high price if the new price is not sustainable. Although this argument is similar to that for stock splits, the scale is lower, which would be valid for stock prices that are only 20 percent higher than the optimal range. This hypothesis suggests the existence of a precise optimal trading range.

The Attention Hypothesis

The attention hypothesis proposed by Grinblatt et al. (1984) suggests that management of underpriced firms wants to bring attention to the firm to trigger reassessment by analysts of the firm's cash flows. Conventional news releases would not suffice because information may be released to competitors, and a liability may exist in the event if that the information communicated in news releases is incorrect. These types of announcements may be less revealing to competitors and less libelous because managers do not release any specific information.

The Increase-in-Cash-Dividends Hypothesis

According to the increase-in-cash-dividends hypothesis, the total amount of cash dividends per share may not change, but the additional shares would require the firm to pay out more cash. This explanation is valid if the firm does not alter the amount of cash dividends despite an increase in the number of shares resulting from a stock dividend. Grinblatt et al. (1984) report no support for this explanation because they find a positive stock dividend announcement effect even for those stocks that do not pay cash dividends.

The Signaling Hypothesis

Building on the Spence (1973) signaling framework, Grinblatt et al. (1984) offer several signaling-based explanations for stock dividends. They relate the retained-earnings hypothesis to a signal that firms cannot be successfully mimicked without commensurate increases in future earnings to support the reduction in retained earnings and additional shares. Again, the act of a stock dividend is the costly action that less successful firms cannot easily copy.

Stock dividends appear to be stock splits but with a smaller magnitude. However, the accounting treatments differ between stock dividends and stock splits. Stock dividends require the shifting of retained earnings into a capital stock account that firms cannot pay out to shareholders. The accounting treatment for stock dividends protects this portion of the equity capital and requires other cash flows to pay cash dividends and firm expenses. By contrast, none of the amounts in the capital accounts changes as a result of a stock split. Instead, the number of shares increases with a corresponding decrease in the par value of each share. This explanation is believable when a firm is young, but it becomes increasingly questionable when the retained-earnings account dwarfs the other capital accounts. Other explanations include those that are relevant for stock splits but on a smaller scale. Stock dividends appear to be becoming less important in recent years, and researchers may never agree to consensus explanation for stock dividends.

REVERSE STOCK SPLITS

Although reverse stock splits decrease the number of shares, existing shareholders still retain the same proportional investment in the company. Reverse stock splits are of interest because the adjusted share price is typically less than the original share price multiplied by the multiple of the reverse stock split. This section examines the empirical evidence surrounding these value-destroying transactions as well as the explanatory hypotheses for the decline in value.

Empirical Evidence

In an early study, Woolridge and Chambers (1983) report significantly negative abnormal returns over the announcement period for reverse stock splits. Although Peterson and Peterson (1992) find overall negative abnormal returns, they document some positive wealth effects for those companies forced to undergo a reverse stock split. Spudeck and Moyer (1985) and Desai and Jain (1997) confirm negative returns. Other studies by Lamoureux and Poon (1987) and Koski (2007) find that volatility decreases after reverse stock splits, thereby reducing the tax-option value of the stock. Desai and Jain investigate long-run performance following reverse stock splits and report negative long-run abnormal returns using one- and

Table 19.3   Reverse Stock Split Empirical Literature

Author	Date	Sample	Key Results
Woolridge and Chambers	1983	57 reverse stock splits on the NYSE and AMEX in 1973–1983	Abnormal returns around reverse split announcements are about –7 percent.
Lamoureux and Poon	1987	49 reverse stock splits on the NYSE and AMEX in 1962–1985	Reverse stock splits reduce activity and reduce the tax-option value of the stock.
Maloney and Mulherin	1992	446 1.25 for 1 or greater reverse stock splits on NASDAQ in 1984–1996	Negative abnormal returns are associated with reverse stock splits.
Peterson and Peterson	1992	1,057 reverse stock splits on the NYSE, AMEX, and NASDAQ in 1973–1989	Riskiness declines for stocks that underwent a reverse stock split.
Han	1995	136 reverse stock splits on the NYSE, AMEX, and NASDAQ in 1963–1990	Liquidity improves after reverse stock splits.
Desai and Jain	1997	76 reverse stock splits in 1976–1991	Reverse stock splits result in 1-year buy-and-hold abnormal returns of –10.76 percent and 3-year buy-and-hold abnormal return of –33.90 percent. An underreaction to the split event occurs.
Martell and Webb	2008	1,668 reverse stock splits on the NYSE, AMEX, and NASDAQ in 1972–2003	Performance after reverse stock splits is better in poor overall stock market conditions.

This table reports the authors, years of publication, sample details, and key results of widely cited research articles that empirically examine reverse stock splits.

three-year buy-and-hold returns. This study shows a return magnitude of –11 percent and –34 percent returns for the one- and three-year returns, respectively (see Table 19.3).

Explanatory Hypotheses

Researchers offer several reasons for managers choosing to have their company stock undergo a reverse stock split. Common explanations include complying with different listing and institutional rules, reducing transaction costs and increasing liquidity, allowing stock marginability, signaling, and removing costly small stockholders.

Complying with Listing and Institutional Rules

Some view a reverse stock split as a last-ditch effort to artificially maintain a firm's stock market listing or to delay bankruptcy. Stock exchanges such as the New York Stock Exchange (NYSE) and NASDAQ have set the minimum stock price at $1 calculated as the average over a 30-day trading period.

Reducing Transaction Costs and Increased Liquidity

Han (1995) shows that after reverse stock splits, stock liquidity improves with lower bid-ask spreads, higher trading volume, and fewer nontrading days. Using a sample of 136 NYSE/AMEX and NASDAQ firms in the period 1963–1990, Han shows the average abnormal return around the announcement date is about –5 percent. Using control firms (matched on price and industry), the evidence shows that the proportional bid-ask spread decreases from 11.12 percent to 6.94 percent for stocks that underwent a reverse stock split. The average standardized split adjusted trading volume also increases after reverse stock splits. No changes occur in the control groups.

Allowing Stock Marginability

Exchanges typically require a minimum price of $5 for investors to buy stock on margin. Han (1995, p. 160) cites the National Realty one-for-five reverse stock split on the NYSE where the company disclosed that the reverse stock split was "intended to decrease the transaction costs of trading . . . and to increase the price enough to allow buyers to purchase the shares on margin." In addition, institutional investors, who are subject to prudent-man rules when investing clients' money, often consider stocks with prices less than $5 as too risky.

Signaling

The market reaction to the announcement of reverse stock splits typically results in short-term negative abnormal returns. Although the market may view reverse stock splits as negative signals, managers are unlikely to willingly signal negative information. However, some companies may experience stock-price increases after reverse stock splits. The information conveyed may be related to the motivation for the reverse stock split that investors may view as positive. For example, investors may view removing costly small shareholders as a positive signal if it is going to reduce future shareholder servicing costs.

Removing Costly Small Shareholders

Firms may undertake a reverse stock split to force holders of small amounts of stock to relinquish their stock back to the company. For example, a 100-for-1 reverse stock split forces all stockholders with less than 100 shares to give back their shares to the company in return for cash. Peterson and Peterson (1992) indicate that this action will eliminate small shareholders and reduce the costs of servicing these shareholders.

Similar to stock splits, some firms undertake reverse stock splits to move their stock price into a more appropriate range as a means of attracting investors. This forced price movement is associated with negative returns because it implies that the firm cannot accomplish this action through increases in earnings. According to Martell and Webb (2008), an unusually high number of NASDAQ stocks engaged in reverse splits after the decline in NASDAQ prices in 2000.

IMPLICATIONS FOR INVESTORS

Abnormal positive returns are typically associated with stock dividends and stock splits, but can investors profit if they do not already own the stock at the time of the announcement? Charest (1978) reports that a simple three-month buy-and-hold strategy with the purchase at the end of the month of the stock-split declaration resulted in abnormal returns of about 1.5 percent. Before rushing to buy firms that undergo stock splits, the question remains as to whether 1.5 percent is economically meaningful especially when considering transaction costs and risk. A strong implication for investors is that stock splits are associated with firms whose managers believe a high stock price is sustainable. If managers artificially cause the nominal price to drop, they place themselves under more scrutiny in the event that the future stock price drops below the optimal price range. These positive signals from managers suggest strong firm performance in the future.

Reverse stock splits, on the other hand, are associated with negative abnormal returns. Because managers of these firms are resorting to artificially increasing the stock price, the message is that the firm is unable to increase the price through normal operations. This information may be associated with poor long-term prospects so shareholders should be cautious with these firms.

IMPLICATIONS FOR MANAGERS

Evidence shows an association between stock splits and improvements in earnings and dividends. In addition, some managers use stock splits to bring a company's stock price back within an optimal trading range. In a survey of chief financial officers of firms that split their stock, Baker and Gallagher (1980) confirm the trading-range hypothesis by finding that 94 percent of respondents agree with this rationale for stock splits. If performance improvements are sustainable, a stock split may be an appropriate way to communicate this information to existing and prospective shareholders.

Furthermore, stock dividends may be another way of providing information to investors but on a smaller scale. Because of the accounting requirement to shift retained earnings to capital accounts, this action indicates that the firm does not need the capital for cash flow. In addition, this method of conveying information may be particularly relevant for young firms with little retained earnings.

By contrast, because reverse stock splits typically convey negative information, managers are unlikely to willingly convey this information to the market. The challenge to managers contemplating a reverse stock split is to avoid the negative connotation. One approach may be to indicate the reasons for engaging in the reverse stock split as a way of counteracting the negative connotation. For example, if the goal is to improve shareholder interest in the firm, this rationale is not necessarily negative.

CONCLUSIONS

This chapter examines the costly process of altering the number of shares in a publicly traded company through stock splits, stock dividends, and reverse stock splits. These actions appear to be purely cosmetic, such as changing the number of pieces into which a pie is cut. Because the action is costly and changes the price of an individual share, stock market participants react to the change. Individual prices do matter to individual shareholders because high prices may reduce affordability and affect transaction costs. Likewise, minimum prices for stock exchange listings and prudent-man investors also place a lower bound on individual share prices. Combining these constraints with managers who act as agents for owners and who want to convey positive information suggests that this area of research will continue for many years.

REFERENCES

Angel, James J. 1997. "Tick Size, Share Prices, and Stock Splits." *Journal of Finance* 52:2, 655–681.

Angel, James J., Raymond M. Brooks, and Prem G. Mathew. 2004. "When-issued Shares, Small Trades, and the Variance of Returns around Stock Splits." *Journal of Financial Research* 27:3, 415–433.

Arbel, Avner, and Gene Swanson. 1993. "The Role of Information in Stock Splits Announcement Effects." *Quarterly Journal of Business and Economics* 32:2, 14–25.

Baker, H. Kent, and Patricia L. Gallagher. 1980. "Management's View of Stock Splits." *Financial Management* 9:2, 73–77.

Baker, H. Kent, and Gary E. Powell. 1993. "Further Evidence on Managerial Motives for Stock Splits. *Quarterly Journal of Business and Economics* 32:3, 20–31.

Barker, C. Austin. 1959. "Price Changes of Stock-dividend Shares at Ex-dividend Dates." *Journal of Finance* 14:3, 373–378.

Bar-Yosef, Sasson, and Lawrence D. Brown. 1977. "A Reexamination of Stock Splits Using Moving Betas." *Journal of Finance* 32:4, 1069–1080.

Boehme, Rodney D., and Bartley R. Danielsen. 2007. "Stock-Split Post-Announcement Returns: Underreaction or Market Friction?" *Financial Review* 42:4, 485–506.

Brennan, Michael J., and Thomas E. Copeland. 1988a. "Beta Changes around Stock Splits: A Note." *Journal of Finance* 43:4, 1009–1013.

Brennan, Michael J., and Thomas E. Copeland. 1988b. "Stock Splits, Stock Prices, and Transaction Costs." *Journal of Financial Economics* 22:1, 83–102.

Byun, Jinho, and Michael S. Rozeff. 2003. "Long-run Performance after Stock Splits: 1927 to 1996." *Journal of Finance* 58:3, 1063–1085.

Charest, Guy. 1978. "Split Information, Stock Returns and Market Efficiency." *Journal of Financial Economics* 6:2/3, 265–296.

Conroy, Robert M., Robert S. Harris, and Bruce A. Benet. 1990. "The Effects of Stock Splits on Bid-ask Spreads." *Journal of Finance* 45:4, 1285–1295.

Constantinides, George M. 1984. "Optimal Stock Trading with Personal Taxes." *Journal of Financial Economics* 13:1, 65–89.

Copeland, Thomas E. 1979. "Liquidity Changes following Stock Splits." *Journal of Finance* 34:1, 115–141.

Dennis, Patrick. 2003. "Stock Splits and Liquidity: The Case of the Nasdaq-100 Index Tracking Stock." *Financial Review* 38:3, 415–433.

Desai, Hemang, and Prem C. Jain. 1997. "Long-run Common Stock Returns following Stock Splits and Reverse Splits." *Journal of Business* 70:3, 409–433.

Desai, Anand S., M. Nimalendran, and S. Venkataraman. 1998. "Changes in Trading Activities following Stock Splits and Their Effect on Volatility and the Adverse-Information Component of the Bid-ask Spread." *Journal of Financial Research* 21:2, 159–183.

Dhatt, Manjeet S., Yong H. Kim, and Sandip Mukherji. 1997. "Did the 1986 Tax Reform Act Affect Market Reactions to Stock Splits? A Test of the Tax-option Hypothesis." *Financial Review* 32:2, 240–271.

Dravid, Ajay R. 1987. "A Note on the Behavior of Stock Returns around Ex-Dates of Stock Distributions." *Journal of Finance* 42:1, 163–168.

Dubofsky, David A. 1991. "Volatility Increases Subsequent to NYSE and AMEX Stock Splits." *Journal of Finance* 46:1, 421–431.

Eades, Kenneth M., Patrick J. Hess, and E. Han Kim. 1984. "On Interpreting Security Returns during the Ex-dividend Period." *Journal of Financial Economics* 13:1, 3–34.

Easley, David, Maureen O'Hara, and Gideon Saar. 2001. "How Stock Splits Affect Trading: A Microstructure Approach." *Journal of Financial and Quantitative Analysis* 36:1, 25–51.

Ezzell, John R., and Carlos Rubiales. 1975. "An Empirical Analysis of the Determinants of Stock Splits." *Financial Review* 10:1, 21–30.

Fama, Eugene F., Lawrence Fisher, Michael C. Jensen, and Richard Roll. 1969. "The Adjustment of Stock Prices to New Information." *International Economic Review* 10:1, 1–21.

Foster, Taylor W. III, and Don Vickrey. 1978. "The Information Content of Stock Dividend Announcements." *Accounting Review* 53:2, 360–370.

French, Dan W., and Taylor W. Foster III. 2002. "Does Price Discreteness Affect the Increase in Return Volatility Following Stock Splits?" *Financial Review* 37:2, 281–293.

Grinblatt, Mark, Ronald W. Masulis, and Sheridan Titman. 1984. "The Valuation Effects of Stock Splits and Stock Dividends." *Journal of Financial Economics* 13:4, 461–490.

Han, Ki C. 1995. "The Effects of Reverse Splits on the Liquidity of the Stock." *Journal of Financial and Quantitative Analysis* 30:1, 159–169.

Ikenberry, David L., and Sundaresh Ramnath. 2002. "Underreaction to Self-Selected News Events: The Case if Stock Splits." *Review of Financial Studies* 15:2, 489–526.

Ikenberry, David L., Graeme Rankine, and Earl K. Stice. 1996. "What Do Stock Splits Really Signal?" *Journal of Financial and Quantitative Analysis* 31:3, 357–375.

Kamara, Avraham, and Jennifer L. Koski. 2001. "Volatility, Autocorrelations, and Trading Activity after Stock Splits." *Journal of Financial Markets* 4:1, 163–184.

Koski, Jennifer L. 1998. "Measurement Effects and the Variance of Returns after Stock Splits and Stock Dividends." *Review of Financial Studies* 11:1, 143–162.

Koski, Jennifer L. 2007. "Does Volatility Decrease after Reverse Stock Splits?" *Journal of Financial Research* 30:2, 217–235.

Kryzanowski, Lawrence, and Hao Zhang. 1996. "Trading Patterns of Small and Large Traders around Stock Split Ex-Dates." *Journal of Financial Research* 19:1, 75–90.

Lakonishok, Joseph, and Baruch Lev. 1987. "Stock Splits and Stock Dividends: Why, Who, and When." *Journal of Finance* 42:4, 913–932.

Lamoureux, Christopher G., and Percy Poon. 1987. "The Market Reaction to Stock Splits." *Journal of Finance* 42:5, 1347–1370.

Maloney, Michael T., and J. Harold Mulherin 1992. "The Effects of Splitting on the Ex: A Microstructure Reconciliation." *Financial Management* 21:4, 44–59.

Martell, Terrence F., and Gwendolyn P. Webb. 2008. "The Performance of Stocks that Are Reverse Split." *Review of Quantitative Finance and Accounting* 30:3, 253–279.

McNichols, Maureen, and Ajay Dravid. 1990. "Stock Dividends, Stock Splits, and Signaling." *Journal of Finance* 45:3, 857–880.

Mukherji, Sadip, Yong H. Kim, and Michael C. Walker. 1997. "The Effect of Stock Splits on the Ownership Structure of Firms." *Journal of Corporate Finance* 3:2, 167–188.

Muscarella, Chris J., and Michael R. Vetsuypens. 1996. "Stock Splits: Signaling or Liquidity? The Case of ADR 'Solo-Splits'." *Journal of Financial Economics* 42:1, 3–26.

Nayar, Nandukumar, and Michael S. Rozeff. 2001. "Record Date, When-issued, and Ex-date Effects in Stock Splits." *Journal of Financial and Quantitative Analysis* 36:1, 119–139.

Ohlson, James A., and Stephen H. Penman. 1985. "Volatility Increases Subsequent to Stock Splits: An Empirical Aberration." *Journal of Financial Economics* 14:2, 251–266.

Peterson, David R., and Pamela P. Peterson. 1992. "A Further Understanding of Stock Distributions: The Case of Reverse Stock Splits." *Journal of Financial Research* 40:1, 189–205.

Rankine, Graeme, and Earl K. Stice. 1997. "The Market Reaction to the Choice of Accounting Method for Stock Splits and Large Stock Dividends." *Journal of Financial and Quantitative Analysis* 32:2, 161–182.

Schultz, Paul. 2000. "Stock Splits, Tick Size, and Sponsorship." *Journal of Finance* 55:1, 429–450.

Sheikh, Aamir M. 1989. "Stock Splits, Volatility Increases, and Implied Volatilities." *Journal of Finance* 44:5, 1361–1372.

Spence, A. Michael. 1973. "Job Market Signaling." *Quarterly Journal of Economics* 87:3, 355–374.

Spudeck, Raymond E., and R. Charles Moyer. 1985. "Reverse Splits and Shareholder Wealth: The Impact of Commissions." *Financial Management* 14:4, 52–56.

Wiggins, James B. 1992. "Beta Changes around Stock Splits Revisited." *Journal of Financial and Quantitative Analysis* 27:4, 631–640.

Woolridge, J. Randall. 1983a. "Ex-date Stock Price Adjustment to Stock Dividends: A Note." *Journal of Finance* 38:1, 247–255.

Woolridge, J. Randall. 1983b. "Stock Dividends as Signals." *Journal of Financial Research* 6:1, 1–12.

Woolridge, J. Randall, and Donald R. Chambers. 1983. "Reverse Splits and Shareholder Wealth." *Financial Management* 12:3, 5–15.

ABOUT THE AUTHOR

David Michayluk is an associate professor at the University of Technology, Sydney. He obtained his Ph.D. at Louisiana State University in 1998 for his work on intraday price formation and bid-ask spread components on the New York Stock Exchange and the Paris Bourse. Michayluk is a founding coeditor of the *International Journal of Managerial Finance* and a chartered accountant in Canada. He previously held faculty positions at the University of New South Wales and the University of Rhode Island and has also taught at the University of Saskatchewan and Bond University South Africa. His research interests include market microstructure and corporate finance, with a special interest in stock market liquidity measurement.

CHAPTER 20

Dividend Reinvestment Plans

WEI HE
Instructor of Finance, Mississippi State University

INTRODUCTION

Dividend reinvestment plans (DRIPs) are options for shareholders to reinvest their dividends back to the companies by purchasing shares or fractional shares. Today, more than 2,000 companies offer DRIPs directly or through transfer agents. Although mutual funds and closed-end funds have provided DRIPs since the 1940s, non–investment companies initiated DRIPs through a U.S. Securities and Exchange Commission (SEC) regulation revision in 1968. Allegheny Power was the first utility company that started its DRIP to allow individual shareholders to increase their share holdings without brokerage fees.

There are three types of DRIPs classified by different sources of shares: (1) open-market DRIPs, where the firm uses reinvested dividends to buy its outstanding shares in the open market to satisfy the needs of participating shareholders; (2) new-issue DRIPs, where the firm raises capital by selling new shares to participating shareholders; and (3) a combination of open-market and new-issue DRIPs.

Before 1972, all DRIP-participating companies used open-market plans, and the financial and utility industries offered the majority of DRIPs. For market-based plans, participating firms used the dividends available for reinvestment to buy shares in the open market and resell them to shareholders at low or no cost. In 1973, utilities started new-issue plans to satisfy their needs for shares by using the authorized but unissued shares or treasury stock in providing shares to participating shareholders. Long Island Lighting was the first company to offer the new-issue DRIP, and AT&T was the first firm to implement a new-issue DRIP with a discount feature to investors.

The purpose of this chapter is threefold: (1) to discuss the benefits and drawbacks of DRIPs from the viewpoint of investors and participating companies; (2) to review the financial theory and empirical evidence related to DRIPs; and (3) to make suggestions to corporations and investors on the applications of DRIPs in other investment alternatives.

The organization of the chapter is as follows. The first section describes the characteristics of DRIPs and direct stock purchase plans, followed by a comparison of the benefits and weaknesses of DRIPs from the investors' point of view. Next, the chapter presents various motives of companies for adopting DRIPs, followed by a review of the theory and empirical evidence on DRIPs. The remaining sections include a discussion of the implications of DRIPs to corporations and investors, observations on future research in DRIPs, and concluding remarks.

CHARACTERISTICS OF DRIPs AND DIRECT STOCK PURCHASE PLANS

Small investors are attracted to DRIPs because they often require a small investment, sometimes as little as $10, depending on the plan. These plans are typically commission free and sometimes offer a feature allowing investors to buy additional shares at a discount, often around 5 percent of current market value. Other features of DRIPs may include optional cash payments, partial reinvestment of dividends, and automatic reinvestment through an investor's checking account (Baker and Johnson, 1989).

Investors need to own at least a share of the company's stock before they can participate in DRIPs. The following example indicates how a DRIP works. Wal-Mart Stores set up its DRIP through Temper Enrollment Service, which helps investors obtain shares required for enrollment in a DRIP and open the plan account. Currently, Wal-Mart requires only one share to be qualified and investors can invest additional cash of $50 up to $150,000 per year into shares on top of the dividends reinvested. There is no brokerage fee on the optional cash purchase with automatic withdrawal from a checking account, but investors still need to pay $1 per transaction plus $0.10 per share. Some companies charge no fee on the optional cash purchase. For example, 3M Company specifies a minimum of $10 and a maximum of $10,000 per quarter for optional cash investment with automatic withdrawal through a checking account without a transaction fee.

Company-Operated and Brokerage-Operated DRIPs

Companies themselves, transfer agents, or brokerage firms can operate DRIPs. Company-operated DRIPs are often administered by personnel in corporate headquarters who deal directly with investors. The company's public relations department, which handles all plan materials, promotes company-operated DRIPs. There are some restrictions on the specific time for share purchases, often quarterly. On the plan settlement date, DRIP-participating firms take shares from their reserves or treasury stock account to satisfy the needs of shareholders at the current market price. When investors want to sell shares, they can sell directly to the company.

The management of DRIPs can be so cumbersome that many corporations use the service of a transfer agent to handle all DRIP-related activities. Transfer agent–operated DRIPs involve a bank or financial institution, such as ChaseMellon Shareholder Services or Boston EquiServe, which takes over the administration activities and enjoys economies of scale. Transfer agents provide investors information about DRIPs, including enrollment forms and telephone numbers to sign up for DRIPs and transfer funds on behalf of participating investors.

Brokerage-operated DRIPs are more flexible and allow dividend reinvestment at any time. Some brokerages offer the investors the opportunity to reinvest dividends even if a company does not offer a formal DRIP directly. To meet the investors' demand for shares, the brokerage firm buys directly from the secondary market and adds these shares to the investor's brokerage account. However, one drawback of brokerage-operated DRIPs is that they do not allow optional cash purchases but only dividends.

Steps in DRIP Investing

As previously mentioned, investors need to hold at least a share in the company to be qualified to participate in a DRIP. The shares should be under the investor's name rather than the street name in the case of brokerage-operated DRIPs. Before making a commitment to participate in a DRIP, investors should review the prospectus, which describes all features of the plan such as the discount granted on dividend reinvestment purchases, tax consequences of participation, and service charges, if any. Several web sites, such as www.directinvesting.com, www.dripcentral.com, and www.sharebuilder.com, can help investors select DRIP-participating companies with order information on more than 1,600 companies that offer DRIPs. Investors can also request enrollment materials from the Direct Purchase Plan Clearinghouse, a free service that provides investors with the ability to request prospectuses from companies that offer DRIPs or direct stock purchase plans.

Evolution of Direct Stock Purchase Plans

Another type of direct investing plan is the direct stock purchase plan (DSPP), which permits investors to buy initial shares directly from the company or its transfer agency without commissioned brokers. Investors can make a one-time purchase or sign up for a periodic purchase plan with optional cash purchases. A DSPP enables an investor to be a first-time buyer without owning a share of stock, unlike the case of DRIPs. On December 1, 1994, the SEC granted Rule 10b-6, subject to certain conditions, to facilitate the availability of DSPPs to investors. The regulation change simplifies the development process and filing procedures of DSPPs, which in turn encourages corporate participation.

Baker, Khan, and Mukherjee (2002) survey managers of 267 U.S. companies with DSPPs in 1999 to determine their reasons for establishing the plans. Based on 73 responses, the evidence shows that companies offer DSPPs to attract small investors at low cost. Bank-sponsored DSPPs can help companies promote their DSPPs because a bank is more effective in distributing the plan materials to its regular customers than a participating firm, even though unsolicited advertising material can be sent to the audience under a registered DSPP. About 60 percent to 70 percent of companies offering DSPPs are bank sponsored.

Currently, more than 2,000 companies offer DRIPs, DSPPs, or both. The proliferation of web sites such as www.directinvesting.com and www.sharebuilder.com make the direct stock purchase more accessible. However, the federal government prohibits companies from promoting DSPPs. Investors who surf DRIP web sites may fail to identify companies that offer DSPPs. MacQuarrie (1995) reports that an issuer cannot make blanket mailings to the general public, although an issuer can place tombstone advertisements. This explains why investors do not find specific information about the DSPPs on a company's investor relations page. The future trend of DRIPs is that companies will offer both DRIPs and DSPPs to investors.

STRENGTHS AND WEAKNESSES OF DRIPs: THE INVESTOR'S PERSPECTIVE

Strengths of DRIPs from the Investor's Perspective

Several key features of DRIPs, such as no commissions, dollar-cost averaging, and purchase discounts, provide benefits to investors. By bypassing brokers, most plans offer investors no transaction costs when reinvesting dividends. This feature is especially attractive to small investors, who may participate by purchasing fractional shares. DRIPs also enable investors to take advantage of dollar-cost averaging to build up wealth over the long term at a reduced cost. Dollar-cost averaging is an investment strategy that involves averaging stock prices when investors acquire shares on a regular basis. While investors buy some shares when prices are high, they obtain other shares when prices are low. Assuming that stock prices generally rise over time, investors would experience a low average cost of their investment.

Other attractive features of DRIPs are the discount feature, optional cash purchase, and automatic reinvestment from checking accounts. The discount offered by some DRIPs usually ranges from 1 percent to 10 percent below prevailing market prices of shares. While DRIP companies initially required that shareholders reinvest only the dividends, now most companies allow cash purchase in addition to the dividend reinvestment amount. The optional cash purchase plan is a voluntary purchase option to make additional investment beyond the dividend amount at no cost or a fee for an amount sometimes as low as $10. In some plans, investors are also able to invest partial or full dividends through an automatic transfer from their checking accounts.

Weaknesses of DRIPs from the Investor's Perspective

Because of some specific restrictions, DRIPs have drawbacks. While purchasing stocks without a broker appears attractive, market timing is not possible with DRIPs because the reinvestment of dividends takes place on predetermined dates. The advantages given to traditional investors, such as information sharing with brokers and keeping securities in street names, are unavailable to DRIP participants. Unlike regular investors, DRIP investors have no control over the purchase prices. DRIP investors tend to have limited portfolio diversification unless they join the DRIP of each stock in their portfolios.

DRIP investors also need to keep records of the cost basis of purchases for tax purposes, which can be cumbersome given the frequency of purchases. They must also monitor the plan for term changes. The calculations may become complicated when investors trade shares often or when the company changes the cost basis. Another drawback involves taxes. There is no tax advantage for reinvested dividends, which are included in taxable income and subject to the same taxes as for cash dividends. Although investors do not have a tax advantage by participating in DRIPs, the savings from commissions and discounts may partially offset the tax payment. Thus, investors may still be better off by participating in DRIPs.

MOTIVATIONS OF COMPANIES FOR OFFERING DRIPs

Both investors and participating corporations benefit from DRIPs. Corporations offer DRIPs to achieve several objectives, such as reducing the cost of capital, lessening the negative effects of issuing new capital, broadening and strengthening the shareholder base, and improving stakeholder relations.

Reduce Capital Costs

Corporations offering DRIPs can either buy shares in the open market or issue new shares to meet the needs of participating investors. While open-market DRIPs provide no new injection of capital, firms may be able to raise capital at lower cost under new-issue DRIPs than through an underwriter, by avoiding flotation cost and underwriting fees. Scholes and Wolfson (1989), Roden and Stripling (1996), and Bierman (2001) all agree that new-issue DRIPs may serve as an alternative to a seasoned equity issue. The benefits of avoiding underwriting fees may outweigh the discounts, if any, granted to DRIP investors. Thus, raising capital through a DRIP may be cheaper than other financing alternatives.

From the viewpoint of investors, raising capital under a DRIP instead of a seasoned equity offering has its weaknesses. When firms raise money through underwriters, the security market provides scrutiny and reduces agency costs because underwriters perform a detailed analysis on the financial position of the firm. Without underwriter certification on an issue in the case of new-issue DRIPs, investors may undertake greater investment risk.

Lessen the Negative Effects of Issuing Shares

New-issue DRIPs provide companies with a continuous flow of capital and enable them to avoid the negative signaling effects often associated with seasoned equity issues. One explanation for the negative market reaction to seasoned equity issues is the unfavorable information conveyed to the market about the firm's future earnings and investment potential. Investors may also question the firm's motives for offering seasoned equity. For example, investors may believe that the company has private information and may sell equity to take advantage of overvalued stocks. The fact that firms with new-issue DRIPs raise funds on a continuous basis by using authorized but unissued shares rather than issuing stocks at a specific time mitigates the problem of asymmetric information. As a result, the market reaction to these periodic and smaller issuances is likely to be less negative.

In addition, DRIPs are flexible. If a firm does not need equity funds, it may resort to the open market to buy shares for DRIP investors rather than issue new equity. The firm may choose a specific plan according to their magnitude of capital needs at the time. This explains why most DRIP firms derive shares through both the open market and new issues.

Broaden and Strengthen the Shareholder Base

Companies often establish DRIPs to broaden and stabilize their shareholder base by attracting small investors. DRIP investors typically are small, passive, stable, or buy-and-hold investors. Highly regulated corporations tend to prefer buy-and-hold investors for improved public relations and political influence. Another motivation for offering DRIP involves managerial entrenchment. Having a diffuse shareholder base with many small investors is an advantage to management because such investors usually do not monitor managerial behavior as stringently as institutional investors. Small investors, such as DRIP participants, may lack the time or resources needed to monitor managerial behavior. Instead, they typically vote with management or do not bother to vote, which leads to the ratification of management's plans or decisions.

Improve Stakeholder Relations

DRIPs can serve as a mechanism to create goodwill and build loyalty among investors, customers, and employees. In a competitive environment in which customers have a variety of choices, building company loyalty becomes increasingly important. Having a DRIP conveys a message to investors that a company cares about them and provides a service to those who want to increase their stake in the company on a regular basis and at a low cost.

Participating firms may also enjoy economies of scale because promotional materials about DRIPs may include information on the company's future prospects and its products and services. By turning shareholders into customers, the firm may be able to boost sales because shareholders are likely to consume more of its products or services. In addition, DRIPs may serve as a means of attracting employees to become shareholders because the plans help strengthen employee loyalty and align managerial and shareholder interests.

Although such motivations drive firms to establish DRIPs, several factors may discourage them from offering DRIPs. First, the start-up and maintenance costs of DRIPs can be high. Administrating the plans and educating investors about DRIP policies can also be costly. Second, firms may dilute their earnings per share when issuing new shares under new-issue DRIPs. Third, conflicts of interest created between participants and nonparticipants of DRIPs may impair investor relations because participants may buy additional shares at a discount below the current price. Thus, DRIPs may appeal to long-term investors but may not be attractive to all shareholders.

THEORIES AND EMPIRICAL EVIDENCE ON DRIPs

Various studies examine the impact of DRIPs on firm value and shareholder wealth. The following section discusses the market reaction to DRIP announcements, factors affecting the participating rate of DRIP investors and corporate decisions to initiate and discontinue DRIPs, and factors determining the choice between open-market and new-issue DRIPs.

Market Reaction to DRIP Announcements

At first glance, DRIPs should not affect shareholders' value because such plans should not change the firm's investment decisions or risks. However, viewing DRIPs as an extension of dividend policy may affect value because of investors' different perceptions of the benefits and costs associated with DRIPs. Consistent with the signaling hypothesis, the market might respond positively if it views the announcement of DRIPs as a signal of favorable prospects of the firm. For example, if investors agree that new-issue DRIPs are a relatively low-cost source of financing, the price of the firm's stock should rise shortly after announcing such a plan.

Conflicting evidence exists about the effect of DRIP announcements, which often arise from sampling and model specification differences. When using event study methodology to determine the presence of excess returns, one difficulty involves identifying the exact announcement date for DRIPs. In addition, the benchmarks used in excess return calculations differ among studies. Consequently, the presence of contradictory evidence involving the relationship between DRIP announcements and firm value is common. While most studies (Dubofsky and Bierman, 1988; Scholes and Wolfson, 1989; Perumpral, Keown, and Pinkerton, 1991; Ogden, 1994; Roden and Stripling, 1996) find positive abnormal returns around DRIP announcements, Dhillon, Lasser, and Ramirez (1992) report negative evidence. Table 20.1 summarizes the findings on the market reactions to DRIP announcements.

Table 20.1 Summary of Market Reactions to DRIP Announcements

Study by Author	Year	Sample with Positive Reaction	Sample Period
Hansen, Pinkerton, and Keown	1985	Adjusted present value method framework	NA
Dubofsky and Bierman	1988	33 utilities and 20 nonutilities offering discount DRIP	1975–1983
Scholes and Wolfson	1989	Utilities and nonutilities compared with Salomon Brothers bank stock index	1984–1988
Perumpral, Keown, and Pinkerton	1991	160 DRIP companies (114 market plans, 43 original issue plans, and 50 discount plans)	1968–1980
Dammon and Spatt	1992	The case of Southwestern Bell Corp.	NA
Ogden	1994	Utilities and nonutilities compared with non-DRIP firms	1980–1989
Roden and Stripling	1996	31 utility firms with DRIPs	1971–1981
		Sample with Negative Reaction	
Peterson, Peterson, and Moore	1987	70 nonutility (neutral) and 48 utility firms before May 1981	1976–1983
Dhillon, Lasser, and Ramirez	1992	76 industrial firms and 71 utilities	1976–1987

This table summarizes the findings of studies on market reactions to DRIP announcements by sample and sample period.

Peterson, Peterson, and Moore (1987) find mixed evidence when partitioning their sample of firms into three subsamples around the enactment of the Economic Recovery Tax Act of May 1981. This act permitted DRIP participating shareholders to exclude $750 of dividends reinvested in utilities from taxable income ($1,500 for joint returns) from 1981 to 1985. Utility firms implementing plans before May 1981 show significant negative excess returns, but nonutility firms have insignificant abnormal returns. The post July 1981 sample of utility firms experience insignificant positive returns.

In contrast, using a sample of utility firms before May 1981, Roden and Stripling (1996) find significant positive excess returns. They attribute the contradiction to the use of different event dates. Specifically, Peterson et al. (1987) examine a one-day window around SEC filings for new shares. The information on the filing dates is not new as the dates usually follow formation and announcement of DRIPs. Thus, the change in security returns and shareholder wealth is not significant. The evidence by Roden and Stripling is consistent with the explanation that DRIPs are an efficient way to raise equity financing.

Dubofsky and Bierman (1988) examine a three-day window surrounding the announcement of discount DRIPs using a sample of 53 firms, both utility and nonutility firms, and find significant positive excess returns. From the perspective of capital structure, Dubofsky and Bierman conclude that their findings support the hypothesis that DRIP firms are moving toward a more optimal capital structure by adding equity capital and lowering the debt-to-equity ratio. The internal financing aspects of DRIPs that result from lower transaction costs and underwriting fees convey positive information when announced.

Scholes and Wolfson (1989) report an excess return of 12 percent on a portfolio of firms with DRIPs compared with Salomon Brothers banks stock index during 1984 and 1988. Ogden (1994) compares a sample of DRIP firms with a sample of non-DRIP firms for the period 1980–1989. The results show that firms with DRIPs provide higher excess returns. Perumpral, Keown, and Pinkerton (1991) find similar results to those of Dubofsky and Bierman (1988). Chang and Nichols (1992) find evidence consistent with Peterson et al. (1987) about qualifying utilities (see Table 20.1).

There are two major views on the announcement effects of DRIPs. One approach uses discount theory to explain the market reaction. This theory suggests that an optimal discount exists to attract new shareholders but does not excessively increase the cost of equity financing. For companies offering a discount above the optimal level, the market reaction should be negative. For companies offering a discount at or below the optimal level, the market reaction should be insignificant.

Another approach to explain the wealth effect of DRIP announcement is a continuation of the "dividend puzzle," which attempts to explain why corporations pay dividends. Dividend irrelevance theory, as set forth by Miller and Modigliani (1961), states that under certain conditions, such as without transaction costs and taxes, dividend policy should not matter. If transaction costs and taxes both exist, retaining earnings and repurchases are more desirable than paying cash dividends. According to Myers's (1984) pecking-order theory of capital structure, firms use external financing only after they exhaust internal sources of funds.

The choice between retaining earnings and raising capital by DRIPs is a strategic decision because shareholders have to pay taxes on reinvested dividends but not on retained earnings. Bierman (1997) indicates that, with taxes, using DRIPs is inferior to retaining earnings because shareholders pay taxes on both the dividend and the discount. An explanation for this situation is that the firm must satisfy the needs of shareholders who want cash dividends as well as those who prefer dividend reinvestment. DRIPs serve as an option for the long-term investors and as a way to raise equity capital when the firm does not retain enough earnings.

However, the practice of new-issue DRIPs is not in conflict with the pecking-order theory of financing because DRIPs are a combination of external sources of funds raised from new issues and internal sources of funds supplied by participating shareholders. According to the signaling effect of dividend policy, dividend payout serves as a signal to current and future earnings due to information asymmetry between managers and investors. Although low dividend payout implies that the firm retains more earnings for future growth, it may also signal that the firm expects lower earnings. DRIPs provide firms with an alternative to avoid the negative signal by paying an acceptable level of dividends and, at the same time, retaining the dividends reinvested. Especially when a participating company believes that its shares are undervalued, the firm may buy shares in the open market to create a demand for its shares and convey the information to its shareholders. Under such conditions, the market reaction should be positive.

Factors Determining the Choice between Open-Market and New-Issue DRIPs

Although most firms with DRIPs enjoy the flexibility of using both an open-market plan and new issues to provide shares for DRIP participants, some firms tend to prefer one to the other at different times. The availability of internal sources of funds may trigger firms to adopt new-issue DRIPs or a combination of open-market and new-issue DRIPs to raise external equity capital needed to support growth. Given the negative signaling effect arising from information asymmetry associated with new equity offerings, new-issue DRIPs serve as a better alternative to external financing. The firm can transfer the benefit of avoiding the negative effect to existing shareholders because they are the ones who reinvest their dividends. The following section discusses the factors determining the firm's choice between new-issue and open-market DRIPs.

Historical Dividend Policy
Historical dividend policy affects the level of retained earnings and therefore determines the needs for external financing by DRIPs. A firm experiencing higher financial growth often has immediate need for capital and a history of high retained earnings and low dividend payout ratio. Finnerty (1989) and Tamule, Bubnys, and Sugrue (1993) support the notion that firms with a low dividend payout ratio tend to use new-issue DRIPs to raise external capital and gradually increase their dividend payout ratios over time. In contrast, Baker and Seippel (1980) report that open-market DRIP firms tend to have high dividend payout ratios and low growth. The difference can be attributed to different sample firms at different time periods.

Cash Flow from Operations

The current cash flow condition can be a factor determining the choice between open-market and new-issue DRIPs. Firms with sufficient cash flows may purchase shares in the open market to satisfy the needs of DRIPs. On the other hand, firms with low free cash flows from operations may prefer new-issue DRIPs to open-market DRIPs to raise capital from the market.

Ownership Structure

Another factor influencing the decision between open-market and new-issue DRIPs is the existing ownership structure. While institutional investors are major advocates of corporate activism, managers in firms with relatively more institutional investors may prefer to use new-issue DRIPs to increase the proportion of individual shareholders to alleviate the monitoring pressure from institutional investors. This is consistent with the corporate motive of adopting DRIPs to broaden the shareholder base. In contrast, firms with a low proportion of institutional investors may go to the open market to acquire shares from existing shareholders, all other factors being the same.

Capital Structure

Open-market DRIPs may have no impact on capital structure unless investors expect the firm to redistribute treasury stock. An unexpected change in leverage can lead to wealth transfer from stockholders to bondholders. In an imperfect financial market with taxes and transaction costs, DRIPs have a direct impact on capital structure, as new equity raised by new-issue DRIPs increases the equity base and lowers the debt-to-equity ratio. Theoretically, an optimal level of debt exists that maximizes the firm's value where the marginal profit from tax shields of debt equals the marginal cost of bankruptcy and agency problems. If a firm is moving toward its optimal capital structure by enlarging its equity base through DRIPs, a positive market reaction should occur. On the other hand, if a firm is underutilizing its financial leverage, additional equity capital raised by DRIPs would not create value. Nevertheless, when firms are approaching their debt capacity, DRIPs supported by authorized but unissued shares can serve as an alternative to raising external funds and reduce reliance on debt financing. Firms with high leverage approaching capacity are likely to use new-issue DRIPs to meet their capital shortage. Open-market DRIPs are more suitable for the firms with relatively low debt ratios.

Factors Affecting the Participation Rates of DRIPs

The development of DRIPs over the past four decades indicates the attractiveness of DRIPs among investors. Four factors contribute to the participation rate of shareholders: discount features, voluntary purchase options, tax considerations, and dividend clientele of investors.

Discount Features

The discount feature of DRIPs is attractive to most shareholders because it allows them to buy shares at a discount to the prevailing market price. Companies that sponsor DRIPs treat the purchase discount as a way to reward loyal shareholders. Therefore, the participation rates of DRIPs may vary with the level of the price discount offered. Baker and Johnson (1989) and Todd and Domian (1997) report that the discount feature of DRIPs leads to higher participation rates. In an examination of the market reaction to the announcement of discount DRIPs for utilities and nonutilities, Lyroudi (1998) reports that shareholders consider the discount feature favorably.

Despite the positive responses of shareholders to discount features, controversy surrounds the adoption of discount DRIPs among corporations. Some researchers contend that a discount DRIP may cause wealth redistribution from nonparticipating shareholders, who need cash dividends for consumption, to participating shareholders, who reinvest dividends. When the discount offered is greater than the average flotation cost of issuing new shares, the firm might have offered so much discount that it puts nonparticipating shareholders at a disadvantage. Under new-issue DRIPs, however, all shareholders including both participating and nonparticipating shareholders would benefit from the avoidance of negative market reactions to external financing if the discount is below the average flotation cost. The participating shareholders may gain at the expense of the investment banker rather than the nonparticipating shareholders. Consequently, the net effect of the discount feature on share value depends on whether the benefit of discount DRIPs outweighs the cost.

Empirically, Finnerty (1989) supports the wealth transfer argument in that the price discount inherent in some DRIPs results in a transfer of wealth from nonparticipating shareholders to participating shareholders. Therefore, the announcement effects are nonpositive, and the amount of wealth transfer depends on the level of price discount. Nevertheless, Hansen, Pinkerton, and Keown (1985), who view the price discount as a flotation cost of a new issue, find support for the opposite view of wealth transfer.

Voluntary Purchase Options

Most DRIPs are associated with the voluntary purchase options (VPOs) that allow shareholders to voluntarily buy additional shares supplied by the participating companies through open-market purchases or issuance of new shares. The shareholders pay a price specified in the DRIP's prospectus (e.g., the average of daily closing stock prices over the last five trading days of the month) if new shares are issued, or the average price paid by the companies for the shares acquired in the open market. Dammon and Spatt (1992) state that the design of the purchase price for newly issued shares may create valuable options for investors because they can use the available stock information to decide whether to buy additional shares. Dammon and Spatt analyze the value of the VPO in both theory and practice and conclude that the incremental value of the VPO is comparable to a direct discount of 3 percent to 5 percent under plausible conditions. Yet the value of the VPO is reduced due to the investment limits specified by most DRIPs and the availability of complete stock-price information. The probability of exercising the VPO declines as the end of the year approaches and when obtaining complete stock information is costly. Therefore, the expectation is that investors would participate more actively in DRIPs when market conditions enable more savings and before the investment limits approach.

Tax Considerations

A change in tax policy or regulation should affect the participation rate of DRIPs. Currently, the U.S. tax rate on reinvested dividends under DRIPs is the same as cash dividends. Disregarding brokerage fees and discounts, the tax treatment of funds reinvested through a DRIP is the same as for cash dividends. This situation is unlike the case of stock dividends, where investors can delay their tax payments until they sell the shares. During one period the tax treatment differed between cash dividends and reinvested dividends. The Economic Recovery Tax Act of 1981 permitted excluding from taxable income up to $750 ($1,500 if married, filing jointly) of dividends reinvested in qualified utilities from July 1981 to 1985. A qualified utility under the act was a utility firm that used new issues to satisfy the needs for DRIPs. This tax benefit motivated many utilities to adopt DRIPs. Chang and Nichols (1992) find an increased DRIP participation rate for qualifying utility firms after the tax reform. Therefore, a future change in tax law that taxes reinvested dividends at the same rate as stock dividends may increase the participation of DRIPs.

Dividend Clientele

According to the dividend clientele effect, firms attract investors who favor a particular dividend policy. Thus, firms with different dividend policies would appeal to different groups of investors or dividend clienteles. For example, firms paying stable and predictable dividends would mainly attract investors seeking stability and income. For that reason, stocks of utility companies with high dividends are likely to attract individual investors seeking income and institutional investors such as pension plans that pay little or no taxes. Investors who do not need current income should prefer firms paying little or no dividends. DRIP investors are typically long-term investors who count on cost averaging and discount features of reinvested dividends. An implication of the clientele effect is that investors who prefer the reinvestment features under DRIPs should forego the consumption opportunities and reinvest their dividends. Hence, the participation rates of firms with low dividend payout ratios should be high.

Factors Influencing the Adoption of DRIPs

Several studies attempt to examine the characteristics of DRIP firms associated with adopting DRIPs (Pettway and Malone, 1973; Chang and Nichols, 1992; Tamule, Bubnys, and Sugrue, 1993; Mukherjee, Baker, and Hingorani, 2002; DeGennaro, 2003; Chiang, Frankfurter, and Kosedag, 2005; Boehm and DeGennaro, 2007). Table 20.2 provides a summary of empirical studies on the characteristics of firms adopting DRIPs. From a corporate perspective, researchers often contend that firms should adopt DRIPs when they can bring some benefits and discontinue the plans when such benefits no longer exist. For example, Mukherjee et al. study the financial characteristics of a sample of 55 firms adopting new-issue plans and 31 firms discontinuing DRIPs. Their results support the notion that firms initiate new-issue DRIPs to raise funds and discontinue them when the need for external funding diminishes. Overall, the factors determining the timing and eagerness to establish DRIPs include the stage of the business cycle, firm size, leverage ratios, and managerial entrenchment considerations.

Stage of the Business Cycle

Common stages of a firm's life cycle are start-up, growth, maturity, and decline. During the start-up stage, firms usually pay no dividends because they need cash to fund operating and investing activities. During the growth stage, firms' sales and cash flow grow rapidly. At this stage, firms often have a low-dividend payout policy. During the maturity stage, firms usually have sufficient cash flow but limited investment opportunities; thus, they tend to pay out a higher percentage of earnings as dividends. Finally, during the decline stage, firms experience negative growth in both revenue and cash flow. Dividend payments tend to be generous.

The firms sponsoring DRIPs, especially those with new-issue plans, are likely those needing funds from dividends reinvested, which they would otherwise pay out as cash. The studies on the financial characteristics of DRIP firms (as shown in Table 20.2) generally support that DRIP sponsoring firms tend to have high dividend payout ratios, dividend yields, and return on assets. Consistent with the findings, Mukherjee et al. (2002) conclude that firms in the later phase of rapid expansion and decline stages prefer to retain some earnings initially paid out as dividends to facilitate future growth by establishing new-issue DRIPs. Nevertheless, the evidence on the growth potential is mixed when measured by price-to-earnings and market-to-book ratios (Pettway and Malone, 1973; Tamule et al., 1993; Mukherjee et al., 2002; DeGennaro, 2003; Chiang et al., 2005; Boehm and DeGennaro, 2007).

Firm Size

Several early studies document that larger firms are more likely to offer DRIPs. For example, Pettway and Malone (1973) indicate that shareholder participation increases with increasing firm size, increasing price-to-earnings ratios, and declining leverage. In a survey conducted by Baker and Seippel (1981) involving DRIPs of 88 utility firms, they report that DRIP firms are, on average, much larger than non-DRIP firms. At that time, the largest industry group adopting DRIPs involved regulated electric and gas companies.

Chang and Nichols (1992) and DeGennaro (2003) report that DRIP firms tend to be larger firms when measured by total assets than non-DRIP firms. For instance, DeGennaro finds that average DRIP firms in 1999 are more than five times larger than non-DRIP firms. Large firms may have an advantage in sponsoring DRIPs because of economics of scale. The average cost of providing DRIPs is lower per participating shareholder for larger firms than for smaller firms as the total administrative expenses of DRIPs are about the same. Thus, firms offering DRIPs have a history of dividend payouts and now want to attract investors to reinvest their dividends. Firms at the introduction stage are typically too small to pay dividends or to sponsor DRIPs. These observations are consistent with evidence from Mukherjee et al. (2002), who find that large firms at the latter phase of expansion or the decline stage are more likely to adopt DRIPs.

Leverage

There are two opposing arguments on the relation between leverage and initiation of DRIPs. On one side, high leverage firms are likely to offer new-issue DRIPs because they are approaching their limit of debt capital and may have to rely on

Table 20.2 Studies on the Characteristics of Firms Adopting DRIPs

Characteristics	PM (1973)	CN (1992)	TBS (1993)	MBH (2002)	DG (2003)	CFK (2005)	BD (2007)
Total assets	H	H			H		
Sales		H			H**		H**
Market value of equity		H					
Sales growth rate						L**	
Asset growth rate				H**			
Payout ratio	H		L*		H***	H***	H**
Debt to net worth	L						
Dividend yield		H***			H***		H***
Net profit margin					H***	L	H***
Average stock return				H*			
Long-term debt to market value of equity		H***					
Debt–net worth ratio	L						
Debt ratio			H*	H*	H		H
Market-to-book ratio			L	H	L	H	L
Price-to-earnings ratio	L				L	L	L
Return on assets					H***	H	H**
Return on equity						H	H
Free cash flow						H	
Beta				H*		L	
Earning per share			L		H	L	H
Institutional ownership				H**		H	
Insider ownership			H**			L***	
Number of common shareholders					H**		H**
Number of common shares outstanding	H						H
Number of common shares traded					L**		L
Number of employees					H**		H

This table summarizes the characteristics of firms adopting DRIPs compared with non-DRIP firms. PM is the Pettway and Malone (1973) study of 205 firms with DRIPs and non-DRIPs before 1972. CN is the Chang and Nichols (1992) study of the financial variables of 50 utility firms as of fiscal year-end 1980. TBS is the Tamule, Bubnys, and Sugrue (1993) study of 76 open-market and 82 new-issue plans in 1988. MBH is the Mukherjee, Baker, and Hingorani (2002) study on 68 DRIP companies and matching firms. DG is the DeGennaro (2003) study of 906 DRIP companies in 1999 compared with 906 non-DRIP companies. CFK is the Chiang, Frankfurter, and Kosedag (2005) study of 206 DRIP firms. BD is the Boehm and DeGennaro (2007) study of 852 DRIP companies in 1999 and 852 non-DRIP companies. H indicates the variable for DRIP firms is higher than that for non-DRIP firms. L indicates that the variable for DRIP firms is lower than that for non-DRIP firms. $^*p < .10.$ $^{**}p < .05.$ $^{***}p < .01.$

DRIPs to raise additional equity. New-issue DRIPs appear to be a source of low-cost equity financing because of the mitigation of the negative impact of information asymmetry associated with seasoned equity offerings. The counterargument is an extension of the business cycle argument in which DRIP-adopting firms are likely those with high growth rates and lower levels of leverage than non-DRIP firms. Empirical studies on this topic (Tamule et al., 1993; Mukherjee et al., 2002; DeGennaro,

2003; Boehm and DeGennaro, 2007) typically support the notion that DRIP firms have higher leverage as measured by the debt-to-asset ratio than matching firms without DRIPs. An exception is the early study by Pettway and Malone (1973), which reports that DRIP firms tend to have low leverage as measured by the ratio of debt to net worth.

Managerial Entrenchment

Managerial entrenchment relates to broadening the shareholder base to dilute the control of institutional investors and to alleviate institutional activism. As previously discussed, DRIPs tend to attract small individual shareholders who are likely to be long-term investors who follow a buy-and-hold strategy. Such investors have little initiative to monitor management as actively as institutional investors. Evidence from Steinbart and Swanson (1998) is consistent with the managerial motive for initiating new-issue DRIPs to attract small investors. Mukherjee et al. (2002) and Chiang et al. (2005) also provide support that DRIP firms have greater institutional ownership than non-DRIP firms and issue new shares to mitigate the control of institutional investors.

Predicting the Adoption or Discontinuation of DRIPs

Boehm and DeGennaro (2007) use a discrete model to determine which type of firm adopts DRIPs and to predict whether companies will have a plan in the future. Their results are based on a study of 852 firms for 1999 and 2004. They show that variables measuring the ability to pay dividends, dividend yield, managerial entrenchment, and industry classification affect the likelihood that a firm has a DRIP. In addition, firms discontinuing their DRIPs are those that do not foresee or rely on the benefits of DRIPs. Boehm and DeGennaro also find supporting evidence that misclassified companies are likely to switch their plan. If a firm's financial records suggest that it should have a DRIP in place but does not, the model predicts that the firm would be more likely to initiate the plan than the other companies in the sample. Conversely, if a firm does have a DRIP but financial data suggest that it should not, the company may discontinue the plan in the future.

IMPLICATIONS OF DRIPs

The increasing popularity of DRIPs has some implications for both corporations and investors. Expected changes in economic and tax policy should affect the proliferation of DRIPs. Some positive influences are expected on the wealth effects for investors and other investment opportunities such as exchange-traded funds (ETFs).

DRIPs and Changes in Tax Laws

DRIPs are likely to remain attractive because the Bush administration extended the tax relief on capital gains and dividends to 2010. The 5/15 plan refers to reduced tax rates on dividends and capital gains to 15 percent if taxpayers are in the 25 percent income-tax bracket or higher, or 5 percent if taxpayers are in the 15 percent or lower tax bracket. Furthermore, the administration proposed to remove double taxation by eliminating shareholder-level taxes on dividends and retained earnings. The tax relief on the dividends reinvested may be lowered to the same level for stock dividends or even eliminated. The tax relief should prompt more companies to pay dividends, thereby benefiting DRIP investors.

Implication of DRIPs for Stock Value and Liquidity

Some characterize DRIP investors as long-term investors who rely on dollar averaging to build their wealth. Yet Todd and Domian (1997) find that some DRIP participants might not be buy-and-hold investors but instead are interested in trading stocks after their reinvesting dividends at a discount when trading volume is likely to increase. Based on 55 survey responses, Todd and Domian find that the participation rate has some positive impact on trading volume. Determining the impact requires additional research.

Another buying pressure for the firm's stock comes from open-market DRIPs. For such firms, the frequent purchase of stock in the secondary market leads to improved liquidity. Such buying activity on a regular basis should provide some price support to the shares and temper volatility. An implication is that a firm should opt to use the reinvested dividends from an open-market plan to increase liquidity and boost share value when the firm's shares are undervalued, while using new-issue DRIPs when the shares are overvalued and the firm is in need of cash flow. By adopting DRIPs, firms obtain flexibility to enhance liquidity and provide greater price stability whenever needed.

Implications of DRIPs for Other Investment Alternatives

The use of DRIPs as an investment tool has implications for the development of other investment alternatives. The nature of a DRIP encourages investors to invest periodically, which is consistent with the principle of long-term investing for retirement. Historically, DRIPs have been an extension of retirement investment in which employees buy the company's shares on a regular basis through its employee stock purchase plan. The survey results of Baker et al. (2002) indicate a growing interest in participating in DSPPs if the plans can be linked to retirement plans such as individual retirement accounts (IRAs). Assuming the ability to link DSPPs or DRIPs to retirement plans such as 401(k) accounts, investors can increase their retirement portfolios by investing in individual stocks on a continuous basis. This would provide companies with additional cash flows to use for growth and other purposes. Future technological developments may make such investments easier if such transactions can be done securely through the Internet.

Another implication of DRIPs is on the development of ETFs. The popularity and growth of ETFs have increased dramatically in recent years. Similar to mutual funds, ETFs are a basket of stocks that track the performance of specific indexes or sectors. The ETFs trade intraday like stocks but unlike mutual funds, which trade at the end of each day. Investors can neither trade ETFs without a broker nor buy them directly from the company, despite that some ETFs offer a dividend reinvestment option for existing shareholders. Investors need to pay commissions on ETFs similar to the fees associated with trading common stock.

NASDAQ Global Funds has proposed that NASDAQ 100 ETFs trade without a broker. If this proposal is successful, other index ETFs may follow to give investors more options. These options include buying initial shares directly from a transfer agent, who will accumulate the investments, and reinvesting on behalf of the investors, as is the case for direct stock purchase plan. This move of ETFs toward a direct purchase plan would enable investors to enjoy a low-cost investment with benefits of dollar-cost averaging as in DRIPs.

FUTURE RESEARCH IN DRIPs

Despite much research on DRIPs, future avenues include an in-depth study of participating investors with respect to tax reforms, the impact of corporate governance system on the choice of DRIPs, time-series analysis of the benefits of DRIPs to firms and investors, and international evidence.

Researchers also need to update the impact of economic or tax reform on DRIPs. Evidence is missing on the profile and participation rate of DRIP investors within different personal-income-tax brackets. Conducting a time-series analysis of participation rates or other decision factors around tax reform would also be worthwhile. Although the extant literature indicates that many foreign companies have adopted DRIPs through their American Depositary Receipts, the international evidence on the evolution of DRIPs is not widely available. Thus, research should explore international DRIPs or DSPPs.

Another area to investigate is the role of corporate governance in DRIP initiation and discontinuation decisions. If managers have a substantial stake in companies that sponsor DRIPs, they are likely to take advantage of the same benefits as existing shareholders. Managers may be more interested in using new-issue DRIPs to raise capital. On the other hand, if the insider ownership is relatively low, managers may prefer open-market DRIPs to acquire shares, all else being equal. In addition, conducting a time series analysis of corporate governance variables and other financial characteristics may help explain why firms initiate and discontinue DRIPs at different periods and how the market reacts to the discontinuation of DRIPs.

CONCLUSIONS

For the past four decades, DRIPs have provided an investment option for shareholders and a source of equity financing for some corporations. The plans benefit small investors because of the features offered, including convenience, low cost, additional cash investments, potential discounts, and dollar-cost averaging. DRIPs also are a strategic tool for some firms to reduce their cost of capital, broaden their shareholder base, and strengthen stakeholder relations. With expected tax reforms on the elimination of taxes at the shareholder level and use of DRIPs and DSPPs in individual retirement accounts, direct investment and reinvestment will continue to be popular with investors and corporate managers.

REFERENCES

Baker, H. Kent, and Martha C. Johnson. 1989. "Dividend Reinvestment Plans among Utilities: A Survey of Current Practices." *Midwestern Journal of Business and Economics* 4:1, 55–67.

Baker, H. Kent, Walayet A. Khan, and Tarun K. Mukherjee. 2002. "Direct Investing: The Role of Stock Purchase Plans." *Financial Services Review* 11:1, 47–63.

Baker, H. Kent, and William H. Seippel. 1980. "Dividend Reinvestment Plans Win Wide Currency." *Harvard Business Review* 58:6, 182–186.

Baker, H. Kent, and William H. Seippel. 1981. "The Use of Dividend Reinvestment Plans by Utilities." *Akron Business and Economic Review* 12:1, 35–41.

Bierman, J. Harold. 1997. "The Dividend Reinvestment Plan Puzzle." *Applied Financial Economics* 7:3, 267–271.

Bierman, J. Harold. 2001. *Increasing Shareholder Value: Distribution Policy, a Corporate Finance Challenge.* Boston: Kluwer Academic Publishers.

Boehm, Thomas P., and Ramon P. DeGennaro. 2007. "A Discrete Choice Model of Dividend Reinvestment Plans: Classification and Prediction." Working Paper, Federal Reserve Bank of Atlanta.

Chang, Otta H., and Donald R. Nichols. 1992. "Tax Incentives and Capital Structures: The Case of the Dividend Reinvestment Plan." *Journal of Accounting Research* 30:1, 109–125.

Chiang, Kevin, George M. Frankfurter, and Arman Kosedag. 2005. "Exploratory Analyses of Dividend Reinvestment Plans and Some Comparisons." *International Review of Financial Analysis* 14:5, 570–586.

Dammon, Robert M., and Chester S. Spatt. 1992. "An Option-Theoretic Approach to the Valuation of Dividend Reinvestment and Voluntary Purchase Plans." *Journal of Finance* 47:1 331–347.

DeGennaro, Ramon P. 2003. "Direct Investments in Securities: A Primer." *Economic Review: Federal Reserve Bank of Atlanta* 88:1, 1–14.

Dhillon, Upinder S., Dennis J. Lasser, and Gabriel G. Ramirez. 1992. "Dividend Reinvestment Plans: An Empirical Analysis." *Review of Quantitative Finance and Accounting* 2:2, 205–213.

Dubofsky, David A., and Leonard Bierman. 1988. "The Effect of Discount Dividend Reinvestment Plan Announcements on Equity Value." *Akron Business and Economic Review* 19:2, 58–68.

Finnerty, John. 1989. "New-Issue Dividend Reinvestment Plans and the Cost of Equity Capital." *Journal of Business Research* 18:2, 127–139.

Hansen, Robert S., John M. Pinkerton, and Arthur J. Keown. 1985. "On Dividend Reinvestment Plans: The Adoption Decision and Stockholder Wealth Effects." *Review of Business and Economic Research* 20:2, 1–10.

Lyroudi, Katerina. 1998. "The Dividend Reinvestment Plans with a Price Discount: Theoretical and Empirical 1998 Evidence." *Corporate Finance Review* 12:4, 6–20.

MacQuarrie, Steve. 1995. "And Now, Direct to the Public." *Financial Executive* 11:6, 35–39.

Miller, Merton H., and Franco Modigliani. 1961. "Dividend Policy, Growth, and the Valuation of Shares." *Journal of Business* 34:4, 411–433.

Mukherjee, Tarun K., H. Kent Baker, and Vineeta L. Hingorani. 2002. "Why Firms Adopt and Discontinue New-Issue Dividend Reinvestment Plans." *Journal of Economics and Finance* 26:3, 284–296.

Myers, Stewart C. 1984. "The Capital Structure Puzzle." *Journal of Finance* 39:3, 575–592.

Ogden, Joseph P. 1994. "A Dividend Payment Effect in Stock Returns." *Financial Review* 29:3, 345–349.

Perumpral, Shalini, Arthur J. Keown, and John Pinkerton. 1991. "Market Reaction to the Formulation of Automatic Dividend Reinvestment Plans." *Review of Business and Economic Research* 26:2, 48–58.

Peterson, Pamela P., David R. Peterson, and Norman H. Moore. 1987. "The Adoption of New-Issue Dividend Plans and Shareholder Wealth." *Financial Review* 22:2, 221–232.

Pettway, Richard H., and R. Phil Malone. 1973. "Automatic Dividend Reinvestment Plans of Nonfinancial Corporations." *Financial Management* 2:4, 11–18.

Roden, Foster, and Tom Stripling. 1996. "Dividend Reinvestment Plans as Efficient Methods of Raising Equity Financing." *Review of Financial Economics* 5:1, 91–100.

Scholes, Myron S., and Mark A. Wolfson. 1989. "Decentralized Investment Banking: The Case of Discount Dividend Reinvestment Plans and Stock Purchase Plans." *Journal of Financial Economics* 24:1, 7–35.

Steinbart, Paul John, and Zane Swanson. 1998. "'No-Load' Dividend Reinvestment Plans." *Review of Financial Economics* 7:2, 121–141.

Tamule, Harold B., Edward L. Bubnys, and Timothy F. Sugrue. 1993. "Dividend Reinvestment Plans and Pecking Order Capital Structure Behavior: An Empirical Investigation." *Journal of Economics and Finance* 17:1, 91–101.

Todd, Janet M., and Dale L. Domian 1997. "Participation Rates of Dividend Reinvestment Plans: Differences between Utility and Nonutility Firms." *Review of Financial Economics* 6:2, 121–135.

ABOUT THE AUTHOR

Wei He is an instructor of finance at Mississippi State University. She earned her Ph.D. in financial economics at the University of New Orleans. Before joining Mississippi State University, she taught at the University of Texas of the Permian Basin, the University of New Orleans, and Assumption University of Thailand. Her teaching interests are primarily in corporate finance, entrepreneurial and small business finance, international finance, and financial statements analysis. He's research interests include corporate restructuring choices, corporate governance issues, dividend reinvestment plans, and corporate investment and financing decisions. She has published in *Journal of Economics and Finance*, *Journal of Entrepreneurial Finance and Business Ventures*, and *International Journal of Business Research*.

PART V

Survey Evidence on Dividends and Dividend Policy

CHAPTER 21

Cash Dividends and Stock Repurchases

GARY E. POWELL
Associate Professor of Finance, Queens University of Charlotte

INTRODUCTION

Interest in survey research in corporate finance dates back more than 50 years as researchers have sought to better understand managerial decision making. Survey research provides perhaps its greatest value in managerial decision areas in which theoretical and empirical research efforts have not provided sufficient explanations and guidance for corporate managers. In such cases, surveys may help offer a better understanding of the gray areas where theory meets practice.

Dividend policy represents a particularly interesting area for survey research. Do managers believe that dividend policy affects firm value? If so, what factors do they believe determine a firm's optimal dividend payout policy? These issues have puzzled researchers and corporate managers for decades. The common notion before the seminal work of Miller and Modigliani (1961) was that higher dividend payouts led to higher stock valuations. Graham and Dodd (1951) and Gordon (1959) provide early arguments that an increase in dividend payout would increase a firm's stock price and lower its cost of equity.

A few years later, Miller and Modigliani (1961) presented a compelling and widely accepted argument that, in a world of perfect capital markets, dividend policy is irrelevant. In such a world, a firm cannot increase its stock price by altering its dividend payout policy. Still others, including Blume (1980), Litzenberger and Ramaswamy (1982), and Ang and Peterson (1985), argue that stocks with high dividend payouts have higher costs of equity and therefore lower stock prices. The lack of consensus among researchers and practitioners led Black (1976, p. 5) to conclude that "the harder we look at the dividend picture, the more it seems like a puzzle, with pieces that don't fit together."

An extensive body of theoretical and empirical research focuses on this dividend puzzle. This research attempts to explain why dividends may matter in a world with taxes, asymmetric information, and transaction, flotation, and agency costs. Researchers in the field of dividend policy have made progress toward providing a better understanding of the various pieces to the puzzle. Yet, as Baker, Powell, and Veit (2000, p. 255) note, "Despite a voluminous amount of research, we still do not have all the answer to the dividend puzzle." In particular, managers are left with general and sometimes conflicting views about whether they can have an optimal dividend payout and about which factors are most important in determining that payout. Fortunately, survey research has helped to provide important insights into the dividend puzzle by shedding light on how managers view various aspects of dividend policy. Survey research has also offered important insights on whether managers' views align with the theoretical explanations for why firms pay dividends and the factors that are important in setting a firm's dividend payout pattern.

Since the mid-1980s firms have increasingly used share repurchases to distribute cash to shareholders. A dramatic increase in share repurchases during the past two decades has coincided with a decreasing proportion of firms paying cash dividends. Because some view cash dividends and share repurchases as alternative means for firms to distribute cash to shareholders, this chapter also focuses on survey research on share repurchases to better understand managers' views about cash distributions to shareholders.

The remainder of this chapter has the following organization. The first section focuses on reviews of survey research that primarily examine managers' views about the determinants of a firm's dividend payout policy and whether dividend payouts affect firm value. Lintner's (1956) seminal study on dividend policy receives particular attention, as does Baker, Farrelly, and Edelman's (1985) study that examines a larger sample of managers of New York Stock Exchange (NYSE)–listed firms to learn their views about the determinants of dividend payout policy. This section also briefly summarizes several survey research studies that focus on NASDAQ-listed firms as well as firms listed on international exchanges.

The next section focuses on survey research studies involving share repurchases. This section takes a close look at the Baker, Gallagher, and Morgan (1981), Wansley, Lane, and Sarkar (1989), and Baker, Powell, and Veit (2003) surveys. The final section reviews the Brav, Graham, Harvey, and Michaely (2005) survey, which examines comprehensive payout policy by considering both dividend and share-repurchase policies.

SURVEY RESEARCH ON DIVIDEND POLICY

Lintner's Seminal Study

Lintner (1956) provides some of the earliest and most important survey evidence focusing on managers' views on dividend policy. From an initial sample of 600 large, well-established industrial companies, Lintner chose 28 firms for follow-up intensive interviews. For each firm, his method includes in-depth personal interviews with several senior managers who are responsible for their firm's dividend decisions. His sample mainly consists of presidents, vice presidents of finance, treasurers, and directors. Lintner inquires about their views on 15 variables, which he identifies through the finance literature as those likely to have an impact on a firm's dividend policy including firm size, capital expenditures, earnings stability, and ownership by control groups.

From these interviews, Lintner (1956) reports that managers believe that shareholders prefer stable dividend payments that reflect stability and gradual growth. Managers also perceive that having to reverse a dividend increase is highly undesirable. Therefore, when earnings increase, firms do not immediately increase their dividends commensurately to achieve the previous payout ratio. Instead, managers need time to determine the permanence of any earnings increases. Firms therefore tend to increase their dividends gradually toward a target payout ratio to avoid any sudden changes in dividends should the earnings increase not be permanent.

On the basis of these findings, Lintner (1956) develops a behavioral model indicating that the change in a firm's dividend is a function of the target dividend payout less the previous period's dividend payout, multiplied by a speed-of-adjustment factor. He argues that firms adjust their dividend payouts slowly toward a firm-specific target payout.

Baker, Farrelly, and Edelman's Follow-up Survey

Nearly 30 years later, Baker, Farrelly, and Edelman (1985) provide an important survey-based study that not only examines whether Lintner's results still explain management's views about dividend policy but also incorporates more recent theoretical explanations and motives for why firms pay dividends. They survey the chief financial officers (CFOs) of 562 NYSE-listed firms, asking which factors they consider most important in determining their firm's dividend policy. Baker et al. also attempt to better understand these managers' perceptions of the signaling and clientele effects, motives often hypothesized in the academic literature as explanations for why firms pay dividends. Finally, Baker et al. want to determine whether managers' views about the determinants of dividend policy differ by type of industry. To address this issue, they divide their sample into three industry groups: 309 manufacturing firms, 103 wholesale and retail firms, and 150 utilities. Using a mail questionnaire sent to each firm, they obtain 318 usable responses, representing a 56.6 percent response rate.

The first section of the Baker et al. (1985) survey instrument contains 15 closed-end statements about the importance of factors that each firm used in determining its dividend policy. Many of these factors correspond to those identified by Lintner (1956) that are likely to influence a firm's dividend policy. Their survey asks respondents to indicate the level of importance for the 15 factors using a five-point scale from 0 = "no importance" to 4 = "maximum importance." On the basis of the mean response for each question, Baker et al. report that the most highly ranked determinants are the anticipated level of a firm's future earnings and the pattern of past dividends. These findings are consistent with Lintner's prior research findings. The third and fourth most highly ranked determinants in shaping a firm's dividend policy are the availability of cash flow and the concern of maintaining or increasing stock price.

The second section of the Baker et al. (1985) survey consists of 18 closed-end statements about theoretical issues involving corporate dividend policy. The survey also asks respondents to indicate their general opinion about each statement based on a seven-point disagree/agree scale from −3 = "strongly disagree" to 3 = "strongly agree." Two of the most highly ranked statements are that a firm should avoid making changes in its dividend rates that might soon have to be reversed, and a firm should strive to maintain an uninterrupted record of dividend payments. Baker et al.'s evidence also shows that respondents generally agree that a firm should have a target payout ratio and should periodically adjust the payout toward the target. Again, these results strongly support Lintner's (1956) previous findings.

Baker et al. (1985) find little or no support for a few of Lintner's (1956) findings. Namely, Lintner reports that managers focus on the change in the existing rate of dividend payout not on the dollar amount and that investment opportunities generally have little effect on modifying the pattern of dividend behavior. In the Baker et al. survey, managers express no strong opinion on these two factors.

Another objective of the Baker et al. (1985) study is to learn managers' opinions on several important theoretical issues. They report managers fairly strongly believe that dividend payout affects common stock prices, results that do not support Miller and Modigliani's (1961) hypothesis that dividend policy has no effect on firm value in a world of perfect capital markets. Yet these results would be consistent if market imperfections caused a firm's dividend policy to affect its value. One such imperfection, asymmetry of information between managers and outsiders, may give managers incentives to signal information to outsiders through certain actions, such as unexpected increases in dividends. Managers may use dividends to signal to outsiders that they have favorable inside information about the firm's future prospects, especially the belief that future cash flows will be sufficient to maintain the increased dividend.

Baker et al. (1985) find fairly strong support for using dividends as a signal. They report that responding managers agree that dividend payments provide a signaling device of future company prospects and that the market uses dividend announcements as information for assessing security value. They also report that respondents generally agree that a firm should adequately disclose the reasons for changes in dividend policy to investors. These three results taken together support a signaling explanation for paying dividends.

Baker et al. (1985) also examine a clientele-effect explanation for dividend-payout policy in which investors who have similar payout preferences buy stocks that satisfy their preferences and thereby create a clientele for that type of payout. They find mixed agreement with a series of statements related to the clientele effect. Specifically, their evidence shows that respondents believe that investors have different perceptions of the relative risk related to dividends and retained earnings and thus are not indifferent between dividends and capital gains. Respondents, however, express only slight agreement with the notion that firms attract certain stockholders with dividend policies appropriate to that stockholder's tax environment and that management should be responsive to its shareholders' dividend preferences.

Finally, Baker et al. (1985) test for differences in the responses among three industry groups (manufacturing, wholesale and retail, and utilities). Among the responding companies, the results show that the dividend payout ratio for utilities (70.3 percent) is much higher than for manufacturing (36.6 percent) and wholesale and retail (36.1 percent). On the basis of these differences in dividend payouts, the evidence shows that many of the respondents' opinions from the utilities differ significantly from those of the other two industry groups. Baker et al. hypothesize that the regulated environment in which utilities operate helps to explain many of these differences and suggests that segregating utilities from nonregulated firms when examining dividend policy may be worthwhile.

Baker and Powell's Survey of NYSE-Listed Firms

The Lintner (1956) and Baker et al. (1985) studies provide a useful foundation for how managers view dividend policy. In an attempt to update the results and determine whether changes in these views occur in response to more recent theoretical and empirical studies about dividends, Baker and Powell (1999) survey the CFOs of 603 NYSE-listed firms that paid a cash dividend in at least one year during the period 1994–1995. As does that of Baker et al. (1985), their sample includes three industry groups—manufacturing, wholesale and retail, and utilities. Their 198 usable responses represent a 32.9 percent response rate. The survey instrument contains 26 closed-end statements relating to dividend policy.

In response to the question "Do corporate managers believe that dividends are relevant?" Baker and Powell (1999) generally find that corporate managers believe that dividends are relevant. Consistent with Baker et al. (1985), this evidence does not support Miller and Modigliani's (1961) seminal research that argues for dividend irrelevance. In particular, most respondents agree that a change in dividend policy affects both a firm's value and its cost of capital. More than 90 percent of the responding managers also agree that an optimal dividend policy strikes a balance between current dividends and future growth that maximizes stock price and that a firm should formulate its dividend policy to produce maximum value for shareholders. These results support the survey findings of Baker et al. (1985).

Baker and Powell (1999) also ask, "What explanations of dividends do managers tend to favor?" Their survey includes closed-end statements related to four explanations of dividend policy: (1) the bird in the hand, (2) signaling, (3) tax preference, and (4) agency. Of these four explanations, the evidence shows the highest level of agreement with signaling. Specifically, respondents agree, on average, that investors not only regard dividend changes as signals of a firm's future prospects but also use dividend announcements as information to assess a firm's stock value. Respondents also agree that dividend changes convey some unanticipated information to the market.

The Baker and Powell (1999) survey indicates mixed support for the tax-preference explanation for paying dividends. Respondents generally agree that a firm should be responsive to the dividend preferences of its shareholders and that firms attract investors if such firms that have dividend policies appropriate to the investors' particular tax circumstances. Yet managers surveyed appear uncertain about whether firms that pay high (low) dividends attract investors in high (low) tax brackets. Respondents are also unsure about whether investors prefer that a firm retains funds over paying dividends because of the tax advantages associated with capital gains.

In addition, the Baker and Powell (1999) survey shows mixed support for the agency theory explanation. While more than 90 percent of respondents agree that paying dividends forces a firm to seek more external financing, thereby subjecting the firm to the scrutiny of outside investors, respondents do not view dividend payments as a bonding mechanism that encourages managers to act in the interest of outside shareholders. Moreover, the evidence shows practically no support for the bird-in-the-hand explanation for paying dividends.

Baker and Powell (1999) also ask managers to answer the question, "How do firms set the amount of dividends that they pay?" Their findings are consistent with

Lintner's (1956) previous results. In particular, nearly 85 percent of respondents believe that a firm should avoid changing its regular dividend if managers might have to reverse the change in a year or so. About 75 percent agree that a firm should strive to maintain steady or modestly growing dividends and maintain an uninterrupted record of dividend payments.

Finally, the authors report very few differences in the responses among the three industry groups to the various statements. They conclude that the views of management do not vary substantially by industry type. These findings contrast sharply with the earlier findings by Baker et al. (1985). Baker and Powell (1999) speculate that these new findings are reasonable given that utilities now operate in a more competitive environment than in previous decades.

Baker and Powell's Longitudinal Study

Baker and Powell (2000) take a closer look at the factors influencing the dividend policy of NYSE-listed firms. Using the survey instrument and results from the Baker and Powell (1999) study, they perform a longitudinal analysis to ascertain whether the factors that determine dividend policy differ between 1983 and 1997. They take the survey data for the 1983 base year from Baker et al. (1985) and for 1997 from Baker and Powell (1999).

Baker and Powell (2000) find few changes over time in managers' views of the determinants of dividend policy. The top-ranked factors in both surveys are the level of current and expected future earnings, the pattern or continuity of past dividends, and the concern about maintaining or increasing stock price. The continued importance of the first two factors also indicates that Lintner's (1956) findings continue to describe how managers view dividend policy.

The authors find a few changes in the relative rankings of factors between 1983 and 1997 but suggest that these changes occur in some of the less-important factors. In particular, respondents rank the availability of cash and projections about the future state of the economy higher in importance in the 1983 study than in the 1997 study. Baker and Powell (2000) hypothesize that the higher inflation, tighter credit, and less robust growth in the early 1980s may have caused managers to pay closer attention to macroeconomic projections in the earlier time frame.

Baker and Powell (2000) take a closer look at whether the views of managers about the determinants of dividend policy differ between the regulated utilities and the less regulated manufacturing and wholesale and retail industries. On the basis of the 1997 survey-response data, they find that industry type appears to influence the importance that respondents place on some determinants of dividend policy. The greatest difference among the three industry groups involves investor preferences. Respondents from the utilities rank the "needs of current shareholders such as the desire for current income" factor sixth in importance among 20 factors, while respondents from the manufacturing and wholesale and retail industries rank the "current income" factor ninth and twelfth, respectively.

Respondents from utility firms also express a greater desire to pay out in the long run a given fraction of earnings and a greater preference to pay dividends instead of undertaking risky reinvestment of earnings than the other two industries. Baker and Powell (2000) suggest that the risk preferences of managers combined with shareholders' desires for current income likely have greater influence on dividend-policy decisions for managers of utilities than for managers of firms in the other industry groups.

Not surprisingly, given the regulated environment of utilities, their evidence shows that respondents from the utilities express greater concern about maintaining a target capital structure than respondents from the other industries. Baker and Powell (2000) argue that this finding may be caused by some regulators who apply a target capital structure rather than the utility's current observed capital structure when determining that utility's weighted average cost of capital. Such enforcement would likely cause these managers to pay closer attention to dividend policy to the extent that it affects a firm's need to seek external financing and its resulting capital structure. Finally, respondents from utilities express a greater desire to conform to industry dividend practice than respondents from the other industries. These results confirm those reported earlier in Baker et al. (1985).

Baker, Veit, and Powell's Survey of NASDAQ Firms

Baker, Veit, and Powell (2001) examine the factors influencing the dividend-policy decisions of NASDAQ firms. Using a mail questionnaire, they survey CFOs of the 630 firms whose stock traded on NASDAQ that paid cash dividends each quarter during calendar years 1996 and 1997. Their final sample of 188 responses represents a 29.8 percent response rate.

A key finding is that the four most highly ranked factors when making dividend decisions are the firm's (1) pattern of past dividends, (2) stability of earnings, (3) level of current earnings, and (4) level of expected future earnings. This evidence shows that managers of NASDAQ firms consistently report the same factors as being important determinants of their firms' dividend policy as managers of NYSE-listed firms as reported by Baker et al. (1985) and Baker and Powell (1999). The results also support Lintner's (1956) behavioral model in explaining the dividend-policy decisions of NASDAQ firms.

Other U.S. Surveys of Dividends and Dividend Policy

Other surveys on various aspects of dividend policy contribute to understanding how firms determine their dividend payouts. Farrelly, Baker, and Edelman (1986) investigate the views of corporate policy makers on how they establish their firm's dividend policy. The evidence shows that the views of policymakers of high-payout, regulated utilities differ from the views of low-payout, unregulated firms in manufacturing and wholesale and retail industries. The authors also find strong support for Lintner's (1956) findings and the notion that policy makers believe that dividend policy affects the value of their firm's common stock.

Baker and Farrelly (1988) document the opinions of dividend achievers, which they define as firms having unbroken records of at least ten consecutive years of increasing dividends. Their evidence indicates that dividend achievers generally place a greater emphasis on the importance of dividend stability and its impact on stock price than other firms. Farrelly and Baker (1989) survey portfolio managers and security analysts to learn their views on dividend policy and receive 130 responses. The respondents not only believe a dividend increase positively affects a firm's stock price but also indicate a preference for capital gains over dividends as a source of investment returns.

Pruitt and Gitman (1991) survey financial managers of the 1,000 largest U.S. firms. On the basis of 114 responses, they document that the most important influences on a firm's dividend policy include the firm's current and past profits, the year-to-year variability of earnings, the growth in earnings, and the dividends paid in prior years. Pruitt and Gitman find no evidence that a firm's investment and financing actions drive its dividend decision.

Baker, Mukherjee, and Powell (2005) conduct a mail survey of top managers of 343 NYSE, AMEX, and NASDAQ firms that issued at least one specially designated dividend (SDD) between 1994 and 2001. Specially designated dividends include cash dividends labeled by management as "extra," "special," or "year-end." Based on 45 usable responses (39 NASDAQ, four AMEX, and two NYSE), their results show that firms tend to pay SDDs when they experience strong earnings and cash flows and therefore want to increase the yield to their shareholders. A substantial proportion of the respondents report that they distribute excess cash using multiple methods: regular dividend increases, share repurchases, and special dividends.

Baker et al.'s (2005) survey results lend support to the signaling explanation for disbursing excess funds, while the free cash flow and wealth-transfer explanations receive little or no support. Specifically, respondents believe that SDDs generally convey positive information about a firm's short-term (current) earnings, and the stock market generally reacts positively to the unexpected announcements of an SDD. Their evidence also suggests that SDD announcements indicate current excess performance not expected improvements in long-run performance.

Finally, respondents do not perceive a negative relation between the frequency that a firm declares SDDs and the market reaction to the announcements. Firms declaring SDDs typically make small special payments, which result in a modest stock-price reaction. The market tends to respond more positively to large, nonrecurring specials. Hence, the views of respondents tend to differ markedly from the results of several empirical studies documenting a negative relationship between the frequency of SDDs and the stock-price reaction.

Non-U.S. Surveys of Dividends and Dividend Policy

Numerous studies extend dividend survey research internationally. Partington (1989) examines the variables influencing the dividend policy of Australian firms. The questionnaire consists of 20 statements about dividend policy to 152 large firms from the Sydney Stock Exchange Industrial List. On the basis of 93 responses, which represent a 61.2 percent response rate, Partington finds that Australian managers believe the most important determinant of dividend payment amounts is the level of firm profits. He finds that more than 90 percent of responding managers perceive that an increase or decrease in profits has an important influence on future dividend levels. He also finds that share price, stability of dividends, and stability of earnings are important factors for determining dividends. Partington observes that 93 percent of responding managers agree that a cut in dividends will adversely affect a firm's share price. His evidence shows that about 75 percent believe that investors prefer dividends to an increase, as profits increase without considering the reinvestment opportunities for the firm. Finally, he finds that managers pay little attention to the tax status of their shareholders.

More recently, Dhanani (2005) surveys the top 800 London Stock Exchange and the top 200 Alternative Investment Market (AIM) companies, as measured by sales turnover, to examine the relevance and importance of various theories of dividend policy for U.K. firms. He obtains a 16.4 percent response rate from a mail survey questionnaire containing 26 closed-end statements related to various dividend hypotheses. Dhanani finds strong support that U.K. managers believe that dividend policy is relevant for maximizing shareholder wealth. He documents strong support for signaling and ownership structure motivations for paying dividends and weak support for agency and financing and investment decision motivations. He finds that companies generally disagree with the notion of a residual dividend policy. Finally, Dhanani notes that U.K. managers place less emphasis on using dividends to value a firm and to send signals about future firm performance.

Baker, Mukherjee, and Paskelian (2006) survey managers of 121 Norwegian firms listed on the Oslo Stock Exchange that paid dividends in 2003 about their views on dividend policy. The 33 usable responses represent a response rate of 27.3 percent. Their results indicate that the most important factors influencing the dividend policy of Norwegian firms are the level of current and expected future earnings, the stability of earnings, the current degree of financial leverage, and liquidity constraints. Baker et al. also find that the relative importance Norwegian managers place on earnings in determining dividend policy is similar to that reported by U.S. managers in several previous studies. By contrast, the authors discover that U.S. managers generally rank the pattern of past dividends as more important than do Norwegian managers. On the other hand, Baker et al. find that Norwegian managers view legal rules and constraints as more important than do their U.S. counterparts and attribute this finding to the greater degree of government regulation that firms face in Norway.

Baker, Saadi, Dutta, and Gandhi (2007) survey managers of 291 dividend-paying firms listed on the Toronto Stock Exchange (TSX). They report that Canadian dividend-paying firms are significantly larger, are more profitable, have greater cash reserves and ownership concentration, and have fewer growth opportunities than their non-dividend-paying counterparts. Canadian managers express their belief that dividend policy affects firm value. Baker et al. cite the most important factors influencing dividend policy as the level of current and expected future earnings, the stability of earnings, and the pattern of past dividends. Canadian managers also express strong support for the signaling and life cycle explanations for paying dividends. The bird-in-the-hand, tax-preference, clientele, agency-cost, and catering explanations generally receive little or no support. These managers also express little agreement with the residual-dividend policy theory.

A few key points are worth noting before transitioning to reviewing surveys that focus on share repurchases. The seminal Lintner (1956) and Baker et al. (1985) survey-based studies provide the broad basis for understanding management's views about dividend policy. Lintner reports that managers believe that shareholders prefer stable dividend payments, set their dividend levels to avoid having to reverse dividend increases, and therefore only gradually increase dividends toward a target payout ratio when earnings increase. Baker et al. find broad support for Lintner's prior research and for signaling as a motive for dividend increases, but they report mixed support for a clientele effect that could motivate how firms set their dividend policies.

SURVEY RESEARCH ON SHARE REPURCHASES
Baker, Gallagher, and Morgan's Study

Disbursing cash to shareholders via share repurchases has increased dramatically in the United States since the mid-1980s. Because managers may choose between dividends and share repurchases to payout cash to shareholders, understanding management's views of share repurchases is important. Baker, Gallagher, and Morgan (1981) survey the CFOs of NYSE-listed firms to better understand managers' reasons for repurchasing stock. The authors employ a split sample of firms. Their repurchase group includes a random sample of 150 NYSE firms that had changes in treasury stock between December 1977 and May 1979. The nonrepurchase group consists of a random sample of 150 NYSE firms that did not repurchase stock during that period. Their mail survey consists of 25 closed-end statements and six multiple choice or open-end questions to the CFOs of both groups. Using a seven-point semantic differential scale, the survey asks managers to indicate their level of agreement with these statements and questions, using their own firm as a frame of reference. The authors receive 146 responses (73 from the repurchase group and 63 from the nonrepurchase group), resulting in a response rate of 48.7 percent.

Based on the mean score of the level of agreement on the 25 closed-end statements, Baker et al. (1981) find that managers of both groups share similar opinions about share repurchases. In particular, respondents from both groups, on average, believe that (1) share repurchases make a good investment when their firm's stock price is depressed; (2) repurchasing shares positively affects earnings per share and stock price by reducing the number of shares outstanding; (3) stock repurchases may have a harmful effect on the firm's capital structure through the resulting increase in debt ratios; and (4) firms repurchase shares to fund stock-option privileges and employee-bonus plans. Baker et al. note that this latter motive for repurchasing shares takes precedence over other reasons commonly given, such as acquiring shares for mergers and acquisitions, conversions of preferred stock or debentures, tax benefits to shareholders, and gaining greater internal control.

Baker et al. (1981) ask managers from the repurchasing group whether they regard their recent share repurchases as a dividend, investment, or financing decision. In addition, the respondents could indicate "other" and write in a different response. About half (50.7 percent) view stock repurchases as an investment decision, 15.1 percent view share repurchases as a financing decision, and none view repurchases as a dividend decision. In the "other" category, another 20.5 percent view repurchases as a means for acquiring shares for employee stock options and bonuses. This latter finding reflects an important difference between the theoretical notions in the academic finance literature and the views of financial managers.

Motives for Repurchases

In the years following the Baker et al. (1981) survey, researchers have developed and empirically tested several motives for share repurchases. Grullon and Ikenberry (2000) provide five theoretical explanations for repurchases including (1) a signaling explanation; (2) an explanation based on agency cost of free cash flows; (3) a capital market allocation hypothesis; (4) a tax-motivated substitution of repurchases for dividends reason, and (5) a capital structure adjustment explanation. A brief discussion of each explanation follows.

Miller and Rock (1985) propose a signaling-theory explanation in which managers use share repurchases to convey to the market positive private information about the firms' future cash flow prospects. Managers have incentives to signal the information to their shareholders through dividends or share repurchases. Easterbrook (1984) and Jensen (1986) purport that by paying dividends, firms can reduce the agency costs associated with the free cash flows that are under managers' control by distributing cash to shareholders. Thus, share repurchases can also reduce these agency costs.

Another explanation for repurchasing shares is the capital-market allocations hypothesis. This theory posits that firms with limited investment opportunities disburse cash via share repurchases to shareholders who then reinvest the funds in shares of other firms that have ample productive investment opportunities. According to this hypothesis, managers disburse the cash to shareholders through share repurchases to invest elsewhere because these shareholders have a broader view of productive opportunities in the economy than the firm's management. Nohel and Tarhan (1998) find empirical support for this explanation for share repurchases.

Other potential motivations for share repurchases include a tax-motivated substitution for dividends and a capital-structure-adjustments explanation. According to the former, shareholders pay fewer taxes when firms disburse cash to shareholders by repurchasing shares instead of paying dividends. While the full amount of a dividend is taxable as ordinary income, the government taxes only capital gains incurred by shareholders, often at lower long-term capital-gains tax rates. According to the latter explanation, firms may repurchase shares to provide a quick adjustment that brings their capital structure to a desired range.

Wansley, Lane, and Sarkar's Study

Surveys provide important insights about management's views of the proposed motives for share repurchases. Wansley, Lane, and Sarkar (1989) use a mail survey to contact CFOs of 620 large U.S. corporations. After eliminating surveys with unanswered questions, their final sample consists of 140 survey respondents, resulting in a 22.6 percent response rate. The majority of these respondents (98) represent repurchasing firms. The survey asks recipients to indicate their level of agreement with a series of closed-end statements based on a seven-point disagree/agree scale. The questionnaire contains 17 closed-end statements on the reasons for repurchasing shares and 11 statements on the determinants of premiums in tender-offer repurchases.

Among the repurchasing and nonrepurchasing groups, the highest-ranked statement under reasons for repurchasing shares is the belief that managers view their firm's shares as undervalued. The second highest reason for the repurchasing group (and third highest for the nonrepurchasing group) is the belief that repurchases serve as a method to signal investors about confidence in the future level of earnings and stock prices. For the repurchasing group, the next highest reason for repurchasing shares is to use repurchases as a means to increase the firm's leverage. Nonrepurchasing firms, however, rank this as the eleventh most important reason.

Other reasons both groups rank as important are to use excess cash to remove an overhanging block of stock, to use repurchases as a substitute for cash dividends, to buy out minority shareholders, to bring the firm to the attention of the market through press announcements of the repurchase, and to increase the percentage of insider holdings.

The four most highly ranked statements dealing with the determinants of premiums in tender-offer repurchases indicate that premiums are greater when (1) the share repurchase is part of a strategy to avoid a takeover; (2) the management has confidence in future earnings and stock prices; (3) the repurchase represents a greater percentage of shares outstanding; and (4) the firm offers debt securities instead of cash. The ranking order for these statements is similar for both groups.

Tsetsekos, Kaufman, and Gitman's Study

Tsetsekos, Kaufman, and Gitman (1991) survey 1,000 firms consisting of the Fortune 500 firms and 500 firms selected from the Compustat database. Respondents returned 183 surveys with answers to at least half of the questions, a response rate of 18.3 percent. The authors find that the motives for repurchases differ from those found by Baker et al. (1981). In particular, the most highly cited motive for repurchasing shares is to change the firm's capital structure followed by to increase the stock price.

Tsetsekos et al. (1991) also ask managers about their opinions on a series of statements. Respondents generally agree that (1) stock repurchases should not be undertaken at the expense of profitable capital spending plans; (2) greenmail is harmful to remaining shareholders; and (3) repurchases serve as a signal to the market that management believes the stock is undervalued. Managers generally disagree that firms should implement stock repurchase plans only during periods when stock prices are declining. Furthermore, they disagree that repurchases benefit participating shareholders more than nonparticipating shareholders.

Baker, Powell, and Veit's Study

Baker, Powell, and Veit (2003) survey 642 top financial executives of firms that repurchased shares between January 1998 and September 1999. Their 218 usable responses represent a 34.0 percent response rate. Nearly half of the respondents report their current position as CFO; others include vice president of finance, vice president and CFO, and vice president and treasurer. More than 90 percent report involvement in their firm's decision to repurchase shares of common stock.

Using a series of questions, Baker et al. (2003) characterize their sample of responding firms and their recent repurchase. The results show that most (89.8 percent) use open-market repurchases. Other methods, including target block repurchases, Dutch-auction tender offers, and fixed-price tender offers, represent only a small percentage of the share repurchases. Given the overwhelming proportion of share repurchases via the open-market repurchase method, Baker et al. limit their analysis to the 194 responses from firms that conducted their share repurchases in this manner. Firms finance their open-market repurchases primarily with cash (71.1 percent) and new short-term debt (19.1 percent). The use of cash to fund most repurchases supports the capital-market hypothesis proposed by Grullon and Ikenberry (2000).

The majority of respondents (74.6 percent) indicate that a low (undervalued) stock price is the most important circumstance leading to their firm's most recent share repurchase. Baker et al. (2003) conclude that this finding supports the signaling hypothesis, in which managers use share repurchases to signal the market about their belief that the firm's shares are undervalued. A lack of profitable investment opportunities is the second most cited reason for repurchases.

Baker et al. (2003) also ask managers to rate the level of importance of 20 reasons for their particular firm's most recent share repurchase using a four-point scale where 0 = "none," 1 = "low," 2 = "moderate," and 3 = "high." Respondents also could write in another reason not listed on the survey. On the basis of the mean value of responses, the five most highly rated reasons are to (1) add value to shareholders, (2) acquire stock at a bargain price, (3) increase earnings per share, (4) increase the stock price, and (5) make the best use of cash.

Baker et al. (2003) also find evidence of a decline in importance of the signaling explanation since the earlier surveys by Baker et al. (1981) and Wansley et al. (1989). In their 2003 study, Baker et al. find that managers attribute relatively minor importance to conveying positive information possessed by management to the market in the firm's decision to initiate a share repurchase. Only 12.4 percent of respondents attribute a high level of importance to this reason. Respondents indicate an even lower level of importance to another signaling-related statement, namely, gaining publicity through press announcements about the repurchase. In their 1989 survey, Wansley et al. report that the second most important reason cited by managers for their recent share repurchases is to signal investors about management's confidence about the company's future.

Baker et al. (2003) also find evidence that several other motives may have declined in importance. Baker et al. (1981) report an important reason for repurchasing shares is to provide for stock-option privileges or bonuses for employees. They also find strong support for the rationale that managers believe stock repurchases can remove a large block of stock overhanging the market. Yet Baker et al. (2003) report decreased support for these reasons. They also find some motives for repurchasing shares may have increased. In particular, they report stronger support for repurchasing shares to change a firm's capital structure and as a tax-efficient way to distribute funds to shareholders.

Baker, Veit, and Powell's Study

Baker, Veit, and Powell (2003) extend the results from a section of the Baker et al. (2003) survey to learn management's views about the false signals given to the market when firms announce share repurchases and fail to follow through with them. Responding managers report that repurchasing fewer shares than announced is a common practice. In general, respondents also express their belief that the intentional repurchase of fewer shares than announced is unethical because it sends a false signal to the market and damages the firm's credibility with its shareholders. Managers believe that in cases where firms repurchase fewer shares than announced, the firms should disclose both the reasons for not repurchasing the stated amount and the shortfall amount.

COMPREHENSIVE PAYOUT SURVEY RESEARCH

None of the survey research efforts reviewed in the previous sections considers a comprehensive payout approach, with cash dividends and share repurchases receiving relatively equal emphasis in survey questions and statements. Brav et al. (2005) identify this shortcoming and survey 384 financial executives to determine the factors that are important in determining both a firm's dividend and its share repurchase decisions. In their survey instrument, they ask managers many identical questions about both dividends and share repurchases. They also conduct in-depth interviews with 23 executives to gain additional insights.

Brav et al. (2005) confirm results that managers set their dividend policy conservatively. About 94 percent of respondents from companies that paid dividends agree strongly or very strongly that their firms try to avoid reducing dividends. In addition, 88 percent agree strongly or very strongly that reducing dividends has negative consequences. The pattern of payout and the level of past dividends also matter. Evidence shows that 88 percent of the respondents agree strongly or very strongly that they consider the level of dividends per share paid in recent quarters when choosing today's dividend policy, and 84 percent report that maintaining consistency with historical dividend policy is an important or a very important factor in their dividend policy. Brav et al. also find that dividends tend to change in response to permanent changes in earnings, with nearly 70 percent of respondents listing the stability of future earnings as an important factor affecting their dividend policy. These results strongly support some of Lintner's (1956) major findings discussed earlier.

Brav et al. (2005) learn that respondents express similar beliefs to some of these same statements when applied to share repurchases. Nearly two-thirds of respondents also report that the stability of cash flows and sustainable changes in earnings are important or very important factors affecting share repurchases (as well as cash dividend policy). Yet their evidence shows greater differences between opinions about dividends and share repurchases for temporary increases in earnings. While about two-thirds of responding executives indicate that a temporary increase in earnings is an important factor for share repurchases, only 8.4 percent indicate that it is an important factor for dividend policy. Their findings also show that excess cash on the balance sheet is a more important factor for share repurchases than for cash dividends. Managers do not believe that negative consequences follow reductions in share repurchases or that maintaining consistency with historical repurchase patterns is important or very important. Personal interviews confirm that financial executives consider repurchases as more flexible than dividends in that the market is more receptive to reductions in the former.

Brav et al.'s (2005) personal interviews with 23 financial executives also provide insights about dividend and share repurchase policies. Some executives told stories of heavy borrowing, selling assets, large layoffs, and bypassing profitable investment opportunities to avoid cutting dividends. Managers also note an asymmetry in that the penalties from reducing dividends are more severe than any rewards from similar increases in dividends. Finally, executives report that many of their firms would like to cut dividends but feel constrained from doing so by their historical dividend policy. Some managers, however, look for so-called stealth cuts in situations where they hope the market does not notice. For example, one executive's firm waited to reduce its dividend level until other competitors reduced theirs, referring to it as a form of air cover. Others report that they can make dividend cuts when their firms split their stock by reducing their postsplit total dividend payouts.

When asked about their dividend targets, managers view various dividend targets, including targeting earnings per share (40 percent of respondents), dividend payout (28 percent), growth in dividends per share (27 percent), and dividend yield (13 percent). Brav et al.'s (2005) analysis indicates that larger, mature firms with large steady cash flows tend to target the growth in dividends per share, while smaller, more indebted, and less profitable firms have a tendency to not target a payout ratio or growth in dividends.

Brav et al. (2005) also ask managers about any targets they have in mind when their firms repurchase shares. They find that only 4 percent target a repurchase payout ratio; instead, the largest group (about 40 percent) reports that it targets the dollar value of repurchases. Another 22 percent indicate that they do not target repurchases at all. Firms do not appear to have specific targets in mind with a share repurchase. Rather, the authors find that managers use share repurchases to target other types of variables or policies such as the number of shares needed for employee stock-option exercises, the debt ratio, and the amount of excess cash.

Finally, Brav et al. (2005) survey the financial executives to learn their views about factors that may affect dividend policy, namely taxes, clienteles, agency conflicts, and information signaling. Responses from interviews and surveys indicate that taxes are not a primary factor or determinant of dividend policy. When asked if the lowering of personal tax rates on dividends would increase their dividend levels, most (70 percent) disclose it would not. The results show some evidence for a clientele effect with almost half of responding CFOs indicating their belief that paying dividends is an important or very important factor in attracting retail investors to purchase their stock. Yet the authors report that these managers do not believe dividend payments affect institutional investors' choices about which stocks to hold. In addition, they find no evidence that managers pay dividends to attract institutional monitoring.

Brav et al. (2005) discover very little support for managers using dividends or share repurchases to avoid the agency costs of free cash flows. They report that 87 percent and 80 percent believe that the discipline imposed by paying dividends or repurchasing shares, respectively, is not an important factor that affects a firm's payout policy.

Both interviews and survey responses provide strong evidence that managers believe dividends and share repurchases convey information to investors. In particular, about 80 percent believe that dividend decisions signal information to investors, while 85 percent believe that repurchase decisions signal information. The personal interviews confirm the views that dividends and share repurchases provide important signals to investors regarding management's confidence about the future. Brav et al. (2005) find some differences in opinion among managers about whether the signal provided information about the mean of the distribution of future earnings or about the riskiness (uncertainty) of this distribution. Interviewed managers stress the importance of payout signals to align with other direct communications with the investment community.

Brav et al. (2005) ask additional questions that allow them to better understand how managers view the various costs associated with making a dividend a costly signal. They find very little support that firms employ dividends as a costly signal or to make their firm look better than its competitors. Moreover, only 17.9 percent of the CFOs from dividend-paying firms agree or strongly agree (and 60 percent disagree) that they use dividends to signal to investors that the firm is strong enough to bear the costs of external finance if it is needed. Slightly less than 17 percent agree that they pay dividends as a signal that their stock is valuable enough that investors should buy despite the personal tax disadvantage to the investors. Only 9 percent agree that their firms pay dividends to signal to investors that their firm is strong enough to pass up profitable (positive net present value) investment projects. Not surprisingly, when the authors ask the same questions substituting share repurchases for dividends, they find even lower support for using repurchases as costly signals to investors.

Finally, 86.4 percent of respondents agree or strongly agree that firms initiate or accelerate share repurchases when their share price is low by historical standards. In the personal interviews, about half of CFOs admit that their firm tracks their repurchase timing and find that their firm can beat the market by $1 to $2 per share over a typical year. Survey responses do not indicate that firms tie dividend levels to stock prices.

De Jong, van Dijk, and Veld (2003) examine the dividend and share repurchase policies of Canadian firms. Their mail survey went to the 500 largest nonfinancial Canadian TSX-listed firms and resulted in 191 usable responses (38.2 percent response rate). Their study differs markedly from other survey research in that they collect information about firms from the questionnaire and then use the data to empirically investigate dividend and share repurchase policies using logit models. De Jong et al. find evidence supporting a two-step process in which firms first decide whether to payout cash and then decide on the form of payout. The firm's level of free cash flows drives the initial payout decision. Tax and behavioral preferences drive the choice to pay dividends, while tax preference drives the choice to disburse cash via share repurchases.

CONCLUSIONS

This chapter provides a summary and overview of survey research studies related to cash dividends and share repurchases. Lintner's (1956) findings that managers smooth dividend payments, avoid having to reverse dividend increases, and do not immediately increase their dividends in response to earnings increases continue to be strongly supported by later survey research efforts both in the United States and abroad. Managers also offer the strongest agreement with a signaling explanation as a motivation for paying dividends, but tax clientele and agency explanations receive little or no support in most survey research studies. Contrary to Miller and Modigliani's (1961) dividend irrelevance argument, most survey research indicates that managers believe dividend policy is relevant in maximizing a firm's share price.

Survey research reveals that managers typically believe that a low (undervalued) stock price is the most important circumstance leading to their firm's most recent share repurchase. Other reasons for repurchasing shares are to add value to shareholders, acquire stock at a bargain price, increase earnings per share, increase the stock price, and make the best use of cash. Managers also believe that repurchasing shares positively affects earnings per share and stock price by reducing the number of shares outstanding, but that increases in leverage that often accompany stock repurchases may have a harmful effect on the firm's capital structure. Survey research also provides support for a signaling hypothesis where managers use share repurchases to signal the market about their belief that the firm's shares are undervalued.

A recent study by Brav et al. (2005) reveals some important differences in management's beliefs about dividends and share repurchases. While about two-thirds of responding executives indicate that a temporary increase in earnings is an important factor for share repurchases, less than 10 percent believe it is an important factor for dividend policy. Brav et al. find that excess cash on the balance sheet is a more important factor for share repurchases than for cash dividends. They report that managers do not believe that negative consequences follow reductions in share repurchases, or that maintaining consistency with historical repurchase patterns is important. Managers also believe that share repurchases are more flexible than dividends because the market is more receptive to reductions in the former.

REFERENCES

Ang, James S., and David R. Peterson. 1985. "Return, Risk, and Yield: Evidence from Ex Ante Data." *Journal of Finance* 40:2, 537–548.

Baker, H. Kent, and Gail E. Farrelly. 1988. "Dividend Achievers: A Behavioral Perspective." *Akron Business and Economic Review* 19:1, 79–92.

Baker, H. Kent, Gail E. Farrelly, and Richard B. Edelman. 1985. "A Survey of Management Views on Dividend Policy." *Financial Management* 14:3, 78–84.

Baker, H. Kent, Patricia L. Gallagher, and Karen E. Morgan. 1981. "Management's View of Stock Repurchase Programs." *Journal of Financial Research* 4:3, 233–247.

Baker, H. Kent, Tarun K. Mukherjee, and Ohannes Paskelian. 2006. "How Norwegian Managers View Dividend Policy." *Global Finance Journal* 17:1, 155–176.

Baker, H. Kent, Tarun K. Mukherjee, and Gary E. Powell. 2005. "Distributing Excess Cash: The Role of Specially Designated Dividends." *Financial Services Review* 14:1, 111–131.

Baker, H. Kent, and Gary E. Powell. 1999. "How Corporate Managers View Dividend Policy." *Quarterly Journal of Business and Economics* 38:2, 17–35.

Baker, H. Kent, and Gary E. Powell. 2000. "Determinants of Corporate Dividend Policy: A Survey of NYSE Firms." *Financial Practice and Education* 10:1, 29–40.

Baker, H. Kent, Gary E. Powell, and E. Theodore Veit. 2000. "Revisiting the Dividend Puzzle: Do All of the Pieces Now Fit?" *Review of Financial Economics* 11:4, 241–261.

Baker, H. Kent, Gary E. Powell, and E. Theodore Veit. 2003. "Why Companies Use Open-Market Repurchases: A Managerial Perspective." *Quarterly Review of Economics and Finance* 43:3, 483–504.

Baker, H. Kent, Samir Saadi, Shantanu Dutta, and Devinder Gandhi. 2007. "The Perception of Dividends by Canadian Managers: New Survey Evidence." *International Journal of Managerial Finance* 3:1, 70–91.

Baker, H. Kent, E. Theodore Veit, and Gary E. Powell. 2001. "Factors Influencing Dividend Policy Decisions of Nasdaq Firms." *Financial Review* 38:3, 19–38.

Baker, H. Kent, E. Theodore Veit, and Gary E. Powell. 2003. "Stock Repurchases and False Signals." *Journal of Applied Business Research* 19:2, 33–46.

Black, Fischer. 1976. "The Dividend Puzzle." *Journal of Portfolio Management* 2:2, 3–8.

Blume, Marshall. 1980. "Stock Return and Dividend Yield: Some More Evidence." *Review of Economics and Statistics* 62:4, 567–577.

Brav, Alon, John R. Graham, Campbell R. Harvey, and Roni Michaely. 2005. "Payout Policy in the 21st Century." *Journal of Financial Economics* 77:3, 483–527.

De Jong, Abe, Ronald van Dijk, and Chris Veld. 2003. "The Dividend and Share Repurchase Policies of Canadian Firms: Empirical Evidence Based on an Alternative Research Design." *International Review of Financial Analysis* 12:4, 349–377.

Dhanani, Alpa. 2005. "Corporate Dividend Policy: The Views of British Financial Managers." *Journal of Business Finance & Accounting* 32:7–8, 1625–1672.

Easterbrook, Frank. H. 1984. "Two Agency-Cost Explanations of Dividends." *American Economic Review* 74:4, 650–659.

Farrelly, Gail E., and H. Kent Baker. 1989. "Corporate Dividends: Views of Institutional Investors." *Akron Business and Economic Review* 20:2, 89–100.

Farrelly, Gail E., H. Kent Baker, and Richard B. Edelman. 1986. "Corporate Dividends: Views of the Policy Makers." *Akron Business and Economic Review* 17:4, 62–73.

Gordon, Myron. 1959. "Dividends, Earnings, and Stock Prices." *Review of Economics and Statistics* 41:2, 99–105.

Graham, Benjamin, and David Dodd. 1951. *Security Analysis: Principles and Techniques.* 3rd ed. New York: McGraw-Hill.

Grullon, Gustavo, and David L. Ikenberry. 2000. "What Do We Know about Corporate Repurchases?" *Journal of Applied Corporate Finance* 13:1, 31–51.

Jensen, Michael. 1986. "Agency Costs of Free Cash Flow." *American Economic Review* 76:2, 323–329.

Lintner, John. 1956. "Distribution of Incomes of Corporations among Dividends, Retained Earnings and Taxes." *American Economic Review* 46:2, 97–113.

Litzenberger, Robert H., and Krishna Ramaswamy. 1982. "The Effects of Dividends on Common Stock Prices: Tax Effects or Information Effects." *Journal of Finance* 37:2, 429–443.

Miller, Merton H., and Franco Modigliani. 1961. "Dividend Policy, Growth and the Valuation of Shares." *Journal of Business* 48:3, 261–297.

Miller, Merton H., and Kevin Rock. 1985. "Dividend Policy under Asymmetric Information." *Journal of Finance* 40:4, 1031–1051.

Nohel, Tom, and Vefa Tarhan. 1998. "Share Repurchases and Firm Performance: New Evidence on the Agency Costs of Free Cash Flow." *Journal of Financial Economics* 49:2, 187–222.

Partington, Graham H. 1989. "Variables Influencing Dividend Policy in Australia: Survey Results." *Journal of Business Finance & Accounting* 16:2, 165–182.

Pruitt, Stephen W., and Larry J. Gitman. 1991. "The Interactions between the Investment, Financing, and Dividend Decisions of Major U.S. Firms." *Financial Review* 26:3, 409–430.

Tsetsekos, George P., Daniel J. Kaufman, and Lawrence J. Gitman. 1991. "A Survey of Stock Repurchase Motivations and Practices of Major U.S Corporations." *Journal of Applied Business Research* 7:3, 15–20.

Wansley, James W., William R. Lane, and Salil Sarkar. 1989. "Managements' View on Share Repurchase and Tender Offer Premiums." *Financial Management* 18:3, 97–110.

ABOUT THE AUTHOR

Gary E. Powell, CFA, is an associate professor of finance at Queens University of Charlotte. He has published more than 20 articles in journals including *Financial*

Management, Financial Review, Review of Financial Economics, Quarterly Review of Economics and Finance, and *Journal of Applied Business Research,* in such areas as dividend policy, share repurchases, stock splits, exchange listing, market anomalies, and corporate social responsibility. He also coauthored a book *Understanding Financial Management* (Blackwell Publishing, 2005). Powell has also been a financial consultant and trainer in many developing countries in areas related to project finance, privatization, regulation of utilities, and capital market development. He received a DBA in finance and an MA in economics from Kent State University. Powell is also a chartered financial analyst charter holder.

CHAPTER 22

Stock Splits, Stock Dividends, and Dividend Reinvestment Plans

HALIL KIYMAZ
Associate Professor of Finance, Crummer Graduate School of Business, Rollins College

INTRODUCTION

A major topic of academic inquiry involves stock splits, stock dividends, and dividend reinvestment plans (DRIPs). Such inquiry is part of a much larger dividend puzzle. As previously discussed in this book, considerable debate still exists as to whether dividend policy affects firm value. This controversy also relates to stock splits and stock dividends and to a lesser degree to DRIPs. As Frankfurter and Wood (2003, p. 205) note, the subject of stock splits and stock dividends "is sometimes referred to as a tearing of a large piece of paper into several smaller pieces and the factor's reaction of the market to such an activity." Although stock distributions are seemingly cosmetic changes, these distributions are more than what they initially appear to be. Yet explaining their favorable market reaction is difficult because so many other events occur simultaneously.

This chapter synthesizes the survey evidence on dividend-policy-related issues involving stock splits, stock dividends, and DRIPs. Much of the academic literature attempts to explain the rationale for these other methods of distribution. Such explanations persist in the literature despite inconsistencies in the empirical evidence. The chapter also focuses on the surveys dealing with the perceptions of both those who initiate stock splits or dividends or DRIPs and those who receive stock splits or dividends or participate in DRIPs. Each section first discusses plausible explanations followed by the survey findings of managers. The chapter begins by briefly reviewing the issue of whether dividend policy affects firm value.

OVERVIEW OF DIVIDEND POLICY AND FIRM VALUE

As previously discussed in this book, the impact of dividend policy on firm value has received much attention from both academicians and practitioners. The literature contains hundreds of published and unpublished studies on dividend policy.

The mixed empirical results are unable to show clearly that dividend payments increase the value of a firm. This may result from an inability of researchers to isolate the noise in the statistics to detect the impact of dividends on firm value. From the practitioners' perspective, firms appear to behave as though dividend policy affects firm value. Hence, documenting the views of practitioners on whether dividend policy matters is important. Three broad views tend to dominate research on dividend policy and firm value.

One view is that dividends are irrelevant. In irrelevance theory, firm value stems from the choice of asset mix and risks assumed and not from the financing sources of these assets. Therefore, the firm's basic earning power and business risks are main factors determining firm value. In this case, shareholders would be indifferent to dividend policy. Miller and Modigliani (1961) (hereafter MM) suggest that dividend policy has no impact on the value of a firm in a world without taxes, transaction costs, or other market imperfections. If a firm does not pay dividends, shareholders can sell stock to create dividends. Conversely, if a firm pays a higher dividend than shareholders desire, they can use the undesired dividends to buy additional shares. Yet dividends may be relevant when market imperfections exist. In their irrelevance argument, MM propose that investors form their portfolios to reduce transaction costs and taxes. Thus, each firm attracts a specific clientele of investors who have similar tax and cost objectives.

The second group argues that dividends are relevant and affect firm value. That is, higher dividend payments result in higher stock prices because they provide information about the firm's future prospects. MM (1961) assume that investors and managers have identical information about the firm's earnings and dividends. In reality, managers have better information about their firm's future prospect than investors. Management tends to increase dividends only if it believes the firm can maintain higher dividends. From the investors' perspective, a higher dividend payout announcement signals that management expects higher cash flows or earnings. If this occurs, an increase in stock prices may be associated with a public announcement of a dividend increase. The dividend announcement will influence the stock prices if it provides information to investors unavailable from any other sources. Thus, the information asymmetry between management and investor may cause a dividend decision to influence stock prices.

A third view is the tax preference theory. According to this theory, dividends matter. However, dividends can reduce value when they are too high, and investors may pay a higher price for low-payout firms. This view suggests that the best interest of the firm is served from not paying any dividends because of the tax disadvantage of ordinary income over capital gains. Historically, the tax rates on cash dividends have generally been higher than on capital gains to the investors. The U.S. tax changes that occurred in 2003 reduced the tax rate on dividend income to the same rate as on long-term capital gains. Nevertheless, the tax effect on capital gains is still more favorable than on dividend income due to the time-value effect. This is because the taxation of capital gains occurs later than dividends. Furthermore, if an individual holds a stock until death, no capital-gains tax is due. As a result of these tax advantages, investors may prefer that firms minimize dividends. This view essentially argues that dividends matter but that they have a negative effect on stock prices.

STOCK SPLITS

Nature of Stock Splits

A stock split refers to a corporate action that increases the number of shares in a public company. The accounting treatment requires adjusting the price of the shares such that before- and after-market capitalization of the company remains the same and dilution does not occur. In the United States, accountants treat stock splits and stock dividends differently. Accounting for stock dividends requires reducing the retained earnings and increasing the common stock and paid-in capital accounts to take into account the market value of additional stocks distributed. Stock splits, on the other hand, do not require any adjustment in retained earnings but require an adjustment in the number of shares. The accounting profession recommends treating stock distributions of greater than 20 percent to 25 percent as stock splits. In a similar manner, the New York Stock Exchange treats distributions of 25 percent or greater as stock splits.

A stock split may look like a cosmetic accounting change that reduces the stock's par value but does not change the total value of the firm. However, studies show that stock splits have an impact on firms, including generating excess returns on the announcement day and higher expected growth rates in earnings, increasing risk and reducing the liquidity of shares. For example, Fama, Fisher, Jensen, and Roll (1969) among others find an association between stock splits and abnormal returns. Bar-Yosef and Brown (1977) and Lamoureux and Poon (1987) also report positive abnormal returns on the ex-date of firms announcing stock splits.

Explanations for Issuing Stock Splits

The literature provides various explanations for stock splits. Some of the more popular explanations include the information asymmetry hypothesis, the optimal trading range hypothesis, and the liquidity hypothesis. Baker, Phillips, and Power (1995) provide a good discussion of these hypotheses. The following discussion reviews these different hypotheses.

The Information Asymmetry Hypothesis

According to the information asymmetry hypothesis, management may use financial decisions to convey favorable information to investors. This hypothesis poses that managers usually have better information about a firm's future than outsiders, and their actions will signal information to investors. In the case of stock splits, the information asymmetry hypothesis of Brennan and Copeland (1988) proposes that managers use their inside information to determine the split ratios from which investors predict the private information held by management. The split ratios cannot be too high because the cost associated with lower stock prices limits them. Similarly, increasing transaction costs per dollar limits managers who do not have favorable private information from using stock splits. Brennan and Copeland report that both the number of shares outstanding after the split and target stock prices provide signals to investors about management's private information.

Empirical evidence on the information asymmetry hypothesis is mixed. For example, Dowen (1990) rejects this hypothesis, whereas McNichols and Dravid (1990) support it. These studies consider analysts' forecasts and the size of the distribution.

Another version of the information asymmetry hypothesis is the attention-getting hypothesis. Grinblatt, Masulis, and Titman (1984) contend that managers use stock splits to get attention from analysts and institutional investors to trigger a revaluation of their firms. This attention generated by stock splits will also increase pricing efficiency as institutional investors use new information more than individual investors. The reported positive returns for firms either stock dividends or splits support the attention-getting hypothesis.

Szewczyk and Tsetsekos (1992, 1993) investigate the relationship between ownership structure and stock splits announcements. While Szewczyk and Tsetsekos (1992) focus on institutional ownership, Szewczyk and Tsetsekos (1993) look at the managerial ownership of firms announcing stock splits. With respect to institutional ownership, Szewczyk and Tsetsekos (1992) find an inverse relation between the stock-price reaction around the announcement of stock splits and the degree of institutional ownership. The abnormal returns of firms with high institutional ownership are almost twice as high as those for firms with low institutional ownership. Similarly, their findings associated with managerial ownership structure show that firms with higher managerial ownership experience lower abnormal returns during the announcement of stock splits. They interpret their findings as providing support for the information asymmetry hypothesis that stock splits have less informational value for firms with a high managerial ownership structure.

The Optimal-Trading-Range Hypothesis

Another explanation for stock splits is the optimal-pricing-range hypothesis. Lakonishok and Lev (1987) suggest that managers should use stock splits to get a firm's stock price to an optimal range. They also contend that having a lower price would increase the firm's ownership base. Individual investors prefer lower stock prices because the cost of buying stock is less in round lots (multiples of 100 shares) than in odd lots. On the other hand, Lakonishok and Lev note that institutional investors may prefer higher stock prices as fixed per-share transaction costs reduce the cost for a given dollar-value transaction. Industry norms may also influence managers who want to use splits to adjust stock prices to such norms.

For example, Lakonishok and Lev (1987) report that managers choose split factors to adjust their stock prices toward a marketwide or industrywide price average. Similarly, McNichols and Dravid (1990) find that managers have some range of trading in mind when they decide on stock splits. They further report an inverse relationship between the split factor and the market value of a firm's stock implying higher trading ranges for larger firms.

The Liquidity Hypothesis

A relationship may also exist between the optimal pricing range and improved liquidity. Splitting firms can potentially make their shares more attractive to investors by lowering stock prices, which, in turn, may increase both the number of trades and owners. On the other hand, the average size of the trade might decline.

Empirical evidence on the impact of stock splits on liquidity is mixed. Elgers and Murray (1985) and Murray (1985) report that stock splits do not increase short-term trading activity and Conroy, Harris, and Benet (1990) show the shareholder liquidity is worse after stock split. Yet Lakonishok and Lev (1987) and Maloney and Mulherin (1992) find that stock splits increase the number of shareholders and cause higher trading volume. Murray (1985) reports that firms issuing stock dividends experience a decrease in trading volume, which suggests a decrease in liquidity. Findings show that stock splits do not result in an increase in short-term trading activities. Furthermore, Murray finds no evidence that stock splits significantly reduce trading volume. Maloney and Mulherin (1992) examine 446 NASDAQ firms splitting stocks during the period 1984–1990 and find a relationship between changes in liquidity and price increases on the split ex-date. They report higher volume, more trades, and increased shareholders following stock splits.

Survey Studies on Stock Splits

Table 22.1 contains key information on various stock split surveys. Baker and Gallagher (1980) investigate the rationale for stock splits and compare the reasons managers give for issuing stock splits instead of stock dividends. Their survey involves a matched sample of 100 NYSE-listed and control firms. Their response rate is 64 percent and 63 percent for the sample and control group, respectively. The same statements receive the highest ranking in both groups. In rank order, these statements are (1) stock splits enable small stockholders to purchase round lots more easily; (2) stock splits keep a firm's stock price in an optimal price range; (3) stock splits increase the number of shareholders in the firm; (4) stock splits make stocks more attractive to investors by increasing the number of shares outstanding; and (5) stock prices do not fully adjust to an occasional stock split, thereby increasing the market value of the stock.

The reasons given by the stock-split group for issuing stock splits include the following: (1) stock splits lead to a lower share price, which provides a better trading range and attracts small investors; and (2) stock splits increase the number of shares outstanding, which improves the liquidity of trading. In contrast, the most common reasons given by the control group for not issuing stock splits include the following: (1) the firm's stock price currently is in its optimal range; (2) the firm's stock price is too low; and (3) there is a lack of interest or no reason for issuing stock splits.

Baker and Powell (1993) examine managerial motives for issuing stock splits by analyzing the survey data from 136 respondent firms listed on the NYSE and AMEX. The study investigates three major research questions. First, why do some managers continue to support stock splits given the associated costs and the apparently limited benefits of the distributions to stockholders? Next, what is the preferred trading range of firms issuing stock splits? Finally, does this range differ for stocks with small versus large stock splits?

The survey results show that the most important issue related to stock splits is to move the firm's stock into a preferred trading range. The second most highly ranked issue is to enable small investors to buy shares in round lots. Other important issues include making shares more attractive to investors by lowering the stock

Table 22.1   Survey Studies and Findings on Stock Splits

Panel A. Survey Studies on Stock Splits

Authors	Net Sample	Response Rate (%)	Industry/Sample Source
Baker and Gallagher (1980)	63 split 64 control	63.0 64.0	Two groups: 100 firms with stock splits during 1978 and 100 randomly selected firms without stock splits as a control group
Baker and Powell (1993)	136	54.8	NYSE and AMEX firms

Panel B. Results of Survey Studies on Stock Splits

Authors	Major Findings	
	Reasons to Split Stocks	**Reasons Not to Split Stocks**
Baker and Gallagher (1980)	Enable small stockholders to purchase round lots more easily, keep a firm's stock price in an optimal price range, increase the number of shareholders in the firm, and make stocks more attractive to investors by increasing the number of shares outstanding.	Stock price currently is in its optimal range, the firm's stock price is too low, and no reason for issuing stock splits.
Baker and Powell (1993)	Move firm's stock into a preferred trading range, increase a stock's liquidity, signal optimistic managerial expectations about the future, and attract more investors. The preferred trading range of the responding stock split firms is from $20 to $35, which differs significantly between small and large stock splits.	NA

This table outlines the sample description of survey studies on stock splits and summarizes the major findings of these studies.

price, signaling optimistic managerial expectations about the future, and attracting more investors to increase a stock's liquidity. An implication of this evidence is that managers perceive that bringing the stock price into a better trading range increases the number of shareholders and the frequency of trading and thus may increase liquidity.

The Baker and Powell (1993) survey provides evidence on the motives for stock splits. The results show that managers believe that the most important motive for undertaking a stock split is moving the stock price into a better trading range (50.7 percent). The second most highly ranked motive is improving the liquidity of stocks (22.1 percent), followed by signaling optimistic managerial expectations about the future (14.0 percent). The findings of this survey are similar to those of Baker and Gallagher (1980). Both studies highlight the importance of identifying an optimal trading range, increasing the number of investors, and improving liquidity. The evidence also shows that the preferred trading range of the responding stock split firms is from $20 to $35, but this range differs substantially between small- and large-stock splits. Managers of firms having less than two-for-one splits express a lower preferred trading range than those with two-for-one or greater splits (about $18 to $29 versus $23 to $41, respectively). This is consistent with the notion that firms with higher stock prices tend to issue large splits but also prefer a higher trading range as a result of their higher market valuations.

STOCK DIVIDENDS

Nature of Stock Dividends

A stock dividend is a pro rata distribution of additional shares of a company's stock to common-stock owners. Firms may choose to conserve available cash by paying their shareholders with stock dividends instead of cash dividends. With stock dividends, firms recapitalize their earnings and issue new shares, which have no effect on their total assets and liabilities. Stock dividends are usually expressed as a percentage of the number of shares that the firm has outstanding. Shareholders who receive a stock dividend acquire more shares of the firm, but their wealth in the firm does not increase. Because the company's assets and liabilities remain the same, the price of the stock must necessarily decline to account for the dilution brought on by issuing more shares. After a firm issues a stock dividend, shareholders have more shares. However, their proportionate ownership interest in the firm remains the same and the market price of the individual shares declines proportionately. Firms may opt for stock dividends for various reasons, including inadequate cash or a desire to lower the price of the stock on a per share basis to prompt more trading and increase liquidity.

Explanations for Issuing Stock Dividends

Similar to stock splits, there are various explanations for stock dividends. These theory-inspired explanations include the signaling hypothesis, optimal-trading-range hypothesis, liquidity hypothesis, tax hypothesis, and cash substitution hypothesis. The following discussion provides an overview of these hypotheses.

The Signaling Hypothesis
According to signaling hypothesis, the dividend announcement conveys new information to the market about the firm's future cash flows separate from cash dividends. Several studies support this hypothesis. For example, Elgers and Murray (1985) report that firms moving from poor earnings years to better earnings years declare stock dividends. Similarly, Lakonishok and Lev (1987) find that an increase in cash dividends and trading volume often follows stock dividends announcements. Nichols (1981) and Woolridge (1983) examine the signaling hypothesis using the stock price reaction around the announcement of stock distributions. With a

sample of 113 firms, Nichols finds that an increasing abnormal return pattern occurs up to the announcement month, followed by a declining pattern in abnormal returns. His findings provide partial support to the signaling hypothesis. Woolridge follows a similar approach by examining the abnormal returns around 317 stock dividends announcements. He finds that larger stock dividends convey more information to investors, which supports the signaling theory of stock dividends.

The Optimal Trading Range Hypothesis

A second explanation for issuing stock dividends is to move a stock's price into an optimal or preferred trading range. A lower price range enables investors to buy round lots of a given stock. The implicit assumption is that the average investor's portfolio is not large enough to benefit from diversification; so buying round lot purchases at higher prices is not desirable.

Although some mixed empirical evidence exists on the trading-range hypothesis, most studies do not support the hypothesis. For example, Elgers and Murray (1985) investigate the motivations of stock distributions by using the distribution ratio as a dependent variable and various other potential motives, including keeping stock prices in a desired price range, as independent variables. The evidence shows that higher-priced stocks experience lower distribution ratios. This result does not support the trading-range hypothesis. Lakonishok and Lev (1987) examine 1,257 stock dividend announcements during the period 1963–1982 and report similar results. They also find that the stock dividend firms are smaller than the overall population in their sample.

The Liquidity Hypothesis

The third explanation for stock dividends relates to liquidity. The liquidity hypothesis proposes that stock dividends increase the liquidity of the firm by creating additional shares of stock. Accordingly, stock dividends enhance liquidity by increasing the proportion of shares traded and by decreasing the bid-ask spread. There is no empirical support for this hypothesis. For example, Murray (1985) reports that firms issuing stock dividends experience a decrease in trading volume, which suggests a decrease in liquidity. Lakonishok and Lev (1987) also report that trading volume does not increase as a result of stock dividends issuance.

The Tax Hypothesis

A fourth explanation involves the tax code and the ability of investors to defer their tax obligations. Cash dividends received by shareholders are taxable, and shareholders can delay any taxes on stock dividends until they sell the shares. Ang, Blackwell, and Megginson (1991) support this hypothesis. Their study on dual class (i.e., shares involving stock dividends and cash dividends) shows that the shares of stock-dividend firms sell at premium when a tax advantage exists for stocks dividends relative to cash dividends. An early study by Eades, Hess, and Kim (1984) reports similar results. They examine firms listed in the NYSE declaring a stock distribution between 1962 and 1980. Their findings of positive returns on the ex-dividend date, along with the positive abnormal returns on the taxable distribution firm portfolio, favor the tax-code explanation of stock dividends. Poterba

(1986) also reports that investors prefer the shares of firms issuing stock dividends relative to those paying cash dividends. Because tax preference may be a reason for behavior, this study provides partial support for the tax-code hypothesis.

The Cash-Substitution Hypothesis

The final explanation is that some investors may consider stock dividends as a substitute for cash conservation. A firm's financial health and its need to fund corporate activities such as expansion projects may constrain its ability to continue paying cash dividends. Accordingly, stock dividends may provide a substitute for cash dividends. The empirical studies provide weak support for this explanation. For example, Lakonishok and Lev (1987) find cash dividend yields between their sample of stock-dividend-paying firms and matching control group are similar three years before issuing stock dividends. However, in the month before the stock dividend announcement, the yield on stock-paying dividend firms is much smaller than that of the control group. This provides weak support for the cash substitution hypothesis. Yet Elgers and Murray (1985) find that a firm's liquidity position and earnings levels are unrelated to stock dividend payments, and consequently do not support the cash-substitution hypothesis.

Survey Studies on Stock Dividends

Table 22.2 contains a summary of major surveys on stock dividends. Eisemann and Moses (1978) conduct the first study that investigates why managers of NYSE-listed firms issue stock dividends. They compare these results to a sample of non-stock-dividend-paying NYSE firms. The survey results reveal that the principal motive for issuing stock dividends is the belief that such dividends increase the number of shareholders in the firm. Although managers of firms issuing stock dividends believe that increasing the number of shareholders also makes the stocks more attractive and eases the ability to sell new equity, the managers of nonissuing firms reject both arguments.

The primary reasons respondents give for not issuing stock dividends are the costs of new issues and the concern that institutional investors may eliminate firms that pay frequent stock dividends from their portfolios because handling costs makes these stocks unattractive. The respondents from both groups strongly endorse the idea that issuing stock conserves cash. This result is surprising because stock dividends will save cash only if they replace cash dividends. The study further investigates whether stock dividends increase after-tax returns to investors. The vast majority of dividend-paying firms report that paying stock dividends reduces investors' tax-liability or increases after-tax returns. This is because investors can sell their stock and pay only capital gains taxes on dividends in place of receiving cash dividends and paying taxes at ordinary income levels.

The non-dividend-paying group is evenly divided over the issue. While the dividend-paying group strongly agrees that stock dividends enable management to express confidence in the firm, suggesting that stock dividends may have some information content, the non-dividend-paying group expresses the opposite view. In their responses to an open-ended question, the major reasons surveyed managers give for issuing a stock dividend are as follows: to maintain an historical

Table 22.2   Survey Studies and Findings on Stock Dividends

Panel A. Survey Studies on Stock Dividends

Authors	Net Sample	Response Rate (%)	Industry/Sample Source
Eisemann and Moses (1978)	39	48.0	Two groups of NYSE firms: firms issuing and those not issuing stock dividends
Baker and Phillip (1993)	121	77.5	NYSE, AMEX, and NASDAQ firms
Frankfurter and Lane (1998)	127	34.7	Firms in CRSP

Panel B. Results of Survey Studies on Stock Dividends

Authors	Major Findings	
	Reasons to Issue Stock Dividends	Reasons Not to Issue Stock Dividends
Eisemann and Moses (1978)	Maintain company practice, conserve cash, increase yield to stockholders, and expand equity presentation.	High administrative cost, no change in net position of stockholders, dilution effect on earnings, stockholder preference for cash dividends to stock dividends, and low stock price.
Baker and Phillips (1993)	Have a positive psychological impact on investors, maintain company practice, signal optimistic expectations about the future, and increase trading volume.	Higher administrative costs as perceived by NYSE and AMEX managers of stock dividends compared to cash dividends.
Frankfurter and Lane (1998)	Meet stockholders' preference to receive a stock dividend, maintain a wide distribution of stocks, and increase the trading frequency of stock.	Lack of interest of stockholders and may create an obligation for a firm to issue a stock dividend again in the future.

This table outlines the sample description of survey studies on stock dividends and summarizes the major findings of these studies.

company practice, to conserve cash, to increase the yield to stockholders, to expand equity representation, and to express confidence in the firm.

In contrast, respondents from non-stock-dividend-paying firms report that their firms do not issue stock dividends for the following reasons: the high administrative costs, the inability of this practice to change the net position of stockholders, the effect of dilution on earnings, the preference of stockholders for cash dividends, the stock price being too high, and the bad earnings performance by the company. Finally, both the paying and nonpaying groups indicate that stock prices would not fully adjust to stock dividends.

Expanding and updating the study of Eisemann and Moses (1978), Baker and Phillips (1993) survey 312 NYSE, AMEX, and NASDAQ firms. Their study addresses two major research questions. First, why do some managers support stock dividends? Second, do managerial views about the issues and motives concerning stock dividends differ among the exchanges on which stocks trade? The survey results show that more than 95 percent of respondents agree that stock dividends have a positive psychological impact on investors receiving them.

Respondents also strongly agree with the statement that stock dividends convey favorable information about the firm's future prospects. For example, more than 68 percent of respondents agree that stock prices react positively to stock dividends announcements. More than 70 percent of respondents also believe that stock dividends are cosmetic changes and do not alter the firm's underlying risk and return characteristics. About 69 percent of respondents believe that stock prices do not fully adjust to an occasional small (less than 25 percent) stock dividend.

Baker and Phillips (1993) also investigate the motives for issuing stock dividends. The respondents view maintenance of the firm's historical practice of paying stock dividends as a top reason to issue stock dividends. Other motives include signaling optimistic managerial expectations about the future, increasing the trading volume, and increasing the total market value of the firm's stock. Eisemann and Moses (1978) report similar results.

Regarding explanations for paying stock dividends, Baker and Phillips (1993) report that the signaling hypothesis appears to be the most popular explanation among the surveyed managers. In fact, more than 78 percent of respondents indicate that stock dividends signal favorable information about the future of the firm. Although many of the statements yield similar results to those in Eisemann and Moses (1978), a few differences exist among these studies. For example, while the vast majority of respondents in the Eisemann and Moses study indicate that issuing stock dividends increases the number of shareholders in the firm and allows the firm to conserve cash, only a small percentage of respondents support these statements in the Baker and Phillips study.

When Baker and Phillips (1993) partition the sample by trading location and size of the stock dividends, the results show no statistically significant differences among the subgroups on many of the issues. The only statistically significant difference between the NYSE/AMEX and NASDAQ groups involves the costs associated with stock dividends. While respondents from NYSE/AMEX firms perceive that stock dividends are more expensive to administer than cash dividends, those from NASDAQ firms express less agreement with the statement. With respect to the frequency of stock dividends, the regular stock-dividend payers are much more likely than infrequent payers to agree that shareholders expect stock dividends to continue once initiated. Similarly, the dividend-paying group expresses higher agreement with the statement that discontinuing a policy of issuing regular stock dividends negatively affects stock prices.

Finally, with respect to the size of the dividends (less than 10 percent and between 10 percent and 25 percent), Baker and Phillips (1993) do not find any statistically significant differences between these two groups on any of the statements. The evidence suggests that managers of these subgroups mostly have similar views about various issues and motives for stock dividends with respect to trading location and size of the stock dividends. However, managers of firms paying regular stock dividends versus occasional stock dividends have major differences in their views about motives and other issues.

A more recent study by Frankfurter and Lane (1998) surveys financial managers of firms included in the Center for Research in Security Prices (CRSP) database to determine how managers perceive the benefits or shortcomings of stock dividends. The net sample includes a total of 127 firms representing a response rate of 34.7 percent. Frankfurter and Lane's findings show that managers generally agree on the following statements: their stockholders do not trade the stock often; institutional investors are sophisticated as far as stock dividends are concerned; stockholders like to receive stock dividends; and a wide distribution of stocks and increased trading frequency of stock are important to managers. The evidence also shows that these managers are neutral to the statements related to accounting and regulatory aspects of stock dividends. Managers disagree with numerous statements, including whether stockholders are interested in stock dividends, whether the rising stock price is a prerequisite for paying a stock dividend, and whether paying a stock dividend once is an obligation for a firm to pay again in the future.

DIVIDEND REINVESTMENT PLANS

The Nature of DRIPs

A dividend reinvestment plan (DRIP) is an equity investment option offered directly from the underlying company. Instead of receiving cash dividends, shareholders who opt to participate in the company plan receive additional shares of stock. These investors face a potential tax obligation on dividend income, whether they receive cash or additional shares of stock through reinvestment.

A DRIP allows plan participants to reinvest all or part of their cash dividends in shares typically without incurring brokerage fees or waiting to accumulate enough cash to buy a full share of stock. Some DRIPs are free of charge for participants, while others charge various fees. DRIPs are a popular means of investing because they enable investors to effectively take advantage of dollar-cost averaging with income in the form of corporate dividends. Investors receive a return in the form of dividend yield and earn a return if the stock appreciates during the period of ownership.

A limitation of using DRIPs is that the investor must keep track of the cost basis for many small purchases of stock and maintain records of these purchases. This ensures that the investor can accurately calculate the capital-gains tax when selling shares and document the cost basis to the Internal Revenue Service (IRS). This record keeping can become both burdensome for the investor participating in more than one DRIP for many years and costly if done by an accountant.

Reasons Firms Offer DRIPs

DRIP-participating sponsors have various objectives for their reinvestment programs. One objective is to improve shareholder relations, especially with individual investors, who are the targets for such plans. DRIPs may not appeal to institutional investors because they can obtain negotiated brokerage fees with their large purchase of securities. Some firms sponsor DRIPs to increase demand for the company stock by easing the process of buying shares by odd-lot investors. This may lead to improved investor relations, as shareholders now have the opportunity to increase their investments conveniently at an expense considerably less than a broker's fees on odd-lot purchases. The advantages to small shareholders participating in such plans include reduced commission rates, full use of funds committed to programs through fractional share ownership, and record-keeping services at low fees.

Another reason that firms establish DRIPs is to stabilize the stockholder base. DRIPs enable firms to broaden their ownership base, which in turn can provide several ways such as providing protection against takeovers. Firms often believe that shareholders who choose to participate in reinvestment plans are likely to retain their shares. Thus, firms expect that increasing the number of shareholders may have a stabilizing impact on their shareholder base.

A third reason for issuing DRIPs is to raise equity capital at a lower cost. New-issue DRIPs, as opposed to market plans, can provide periodic additions to equity capital. By using authorized but previously unissued shares in connection with DRIPs, firms can obtain regular cash inflows, and hence reduce their dependence on other external financing sources. Baker and Meeks (1990) provide the overview of the evolution of DRIPs.

Survey Studies on DRIPs

Table 22.3 lists the survey studies on DRIPs and summarizes the major findings. Pettway and Malone (1973) survey S&P 500 firms to ascertain the prevalence of automatic dividend reinvestment (ADR) plans among these firms, percentage of stockholder participation in the plans, and the expected influence of stockholder participation on future dividend policy. Among these firms, 92 had established ADR plans. Stockholder participation among responding companies typically ranges between 5 percent and 10 percent. The primary reason survey respondents cite for establishing ADR plans is to provide a service for those shareholders who want to save and not use the current dividend income for consumption. Only a few of the sampled financial managers indicate that strong shareholder participation would influence the firm's dividend payout policy. They also find that shareholder participation increases with increasing firm size, increasing price-earnings ratios, and declining leverage.

Baker and Seippel (1980, 1981) survey chief financial officers of NYSE- and AMEX-listed firms about their views on DRIPs. The net sample consists of 88 utility firms and 113 nonutility firms. While newly issued stocks are the main source of shares for utilities, nonutilities rely mostly on shares purchased in the open market. The majority of firms do not provide a discount to their participants, but about a third of the utilities let shareholders buy shares at less than market price. Utilities appear to allow more cash supplements to their plans than do nonutilities.

Survey participants from the Baker and Seippel (1980, 1981) surveys further highlight the advantages and disadvantages of DRIPs from the viewpoint of firms and investors. From a firm perspective, managers of utilities view the most important reason for establishing DRIPs as providing a way of raising equity capital followed by improving shareholder goodwill. Nonutility firms view DRIPs as a way of improving shareholder's goodwill and encouraging small shareholders to own a larger portion of the company. Managers of utilities view the major advantages to plan participants as allowing participants to acquire stocks at reduced

Table 22.3   Survey Studies and Findings on DRIPs

Panel A. Survey Studies on DRIPs

Authors	Net Sample	Response Rate (%)	Industry/Sample Source
Pettway and Malone (1973)	92	64.0	Manufacturing and utilities in S&P 500
Baker and Seippel (1980)	201	68.0	Two groups: 88 utilities and 113 other NYSE and AMEX firms
Fredman and Nichols (1980)	49	69.0	Electric utilities
Baker and Johnson (1988)	250	41.7	Manufacturing, financial, and utilities
Baker and Johnson (1989)	100	39.4	Utilities
Todd and Domian (1997)	55	37.3	Utilities and nonutilities

Panel B. Results of Survey Studies on DRIPs

Authors	Major Findings
Pettway and Malone (1973)	Major motive is to provide a service for those shareholders who want to save and not use the current dividend income for consumption. Strong shareholder participation would not influence a firm's dividend payout policy.
Baker and Seippel (1980)	*Utilities:* Major motives include raising equity capital, improving shareholder goodwill, and allowing participants to acquire stocks at a reduced fee. *Nonutilities:* Major motives include improving shareholder goodwill and encouraging small shareholders to own larger portion of the firm. *Utilities and nonutilities:* Disadvantages include paying taxes on reinvested dividends and maintaining detailed records for the tax purposes.
Fredman and Nichols (1980)	Major motives include raising new equity capital, providing shareholders a convenient way to invest, and improving shareholder loyalty.
Baker and Johnson (1988)	DRIPs improve relations with shareholders and do not reduce firm's flexibility to declare dividends. Compared to early periods, DRIP participation rates are higher and fewer firms use a discount feature.
Baker and Johnson (1989)	DRIPs improve relations with shareholders. Managers see DRIPs as an economical way to raise new capital. Compared to earlier periods, there are fewer new-issue plans and fewer firms using a discount feature.
Todd and Domian (1997)	Utility firms offer a discount and use new issues in their DRIPs significantly more than nonutility firms. Participation rates as a percentage of eligible shareholders are significantly higher than for firms that do not offer a discount. Participation rates tend to positively related to stock returns and have effect on trading volume.

This table outlines the sample description of survey studies on DRIPs and summarizes the major findings of these studies.

service fees and brokerage charges, as well as providing a convenient way to invest relatively small dividends that shareholders otherwise might spend. The order of advantage is reversed for nonutilities' perspective. Both utilities and nonutilities cite taxes as the major disadvantage to plan participants followed by the requirement of maintaining detailed records for tax purposes.

Fredman and Nichols (1980) also survey managers of electric utilities to determine the extent to which electric utilities use DRIPs, the problems facing the plans, and the advantages and disadvantages associated with DRIPs. The survey includes 49 electric utilities. When asked why they established DRIPs, respondents report raising new equity capital as the most important motive (28.1 percent). The next most popular responses are providing a convenient way for shareholders to reinvest (25.6 percent), followed by improving loyalty to shareholders (15.3 percent). The next most important reasons are to reduce cash dividend outflows (14.3 percent) and increase small shareholder positions (9.1 percent). Baker and Seippel (1980) report similar findings.

In the Fredman and Nichols (1980) study, more than half of the responding firms indicate that they have a discount feature that permits participants to buy shares at 5 percent below market value. While only 10 out of 45 firms completely absorb brokerage fees, 45 out of 48 firms pay the administrative fees, and 17 firms pay the safekeeping fees. The cash payments option also appears popular among electric utilities because all respondents state that they have cash payment-option plans. While 6 plans are on a maximum annual contribution basis, 35 are on a quarterly maximum, and 6 are on a monthly maximum. Only one firm indicates that it does not have a ceiling on cash payments. During the period of this study, the dollar ceiling on most popular quarterly plans was between $10,000 and $20,000. When asked how they assess their DRIPs with regard to the cost of the operation and administration, a vast majority (45 out of 49) respond that they are reasonable, and the remaining four state that they are expensive.

Baker and Johnson (1988) revisit DRIPs with the objective of updating the Baker and Seippel (1980) study. They justify the study by stating that dynamic changes have occurred since the initial studies and that these changes can influence these plans and the attitudes of management toward them. The study specifically investigates whether changes have occurred in the following: (1) management perceptions and attitudes about DRIP-related issues; (2) sources of stock for DRIPs; (3) participation rates; and (4) company use of DRIPs features. They also investigate whether plan features influence participation rates.

The Baker and Johnson (1988) survey results of 250 usable responses show a decline in the popularity of DRIPs after 1980, which supports the notion that DRIPs have reached the maturity of their life cycle. Further analysis reveals that respondents from both utility and nonutility firms believe that DRIPs improve relations with shareholders and do not reduce a company's flexibility in declaring dividends. Other findings include the reduction in the use of newly issued shares as a source of stock for their DRIPs by utilities (from 81 percent in 1979 to 61 percent in 1988) and an increase in newly issued shares by nonutilities (from 9.7 percent in 1979 to 30.8 percent in 1988). Evidence also indicates an increase in the participation rate. For example, firms with a participation rate of at least 20 percent rose from 6.8 percent in 1979 to 81.6 percent in 1988. This finding suggests that companies have been successful in marketing DRIPs to shareholders. Finally, a declining trend appears in the use of the discount feature among utilities from 36.4 percent in 1979 to 15.3 percent in 1988. Nonutilities report the opposite trend, from 8 percent to 26.6 percent during the same period.

Baker and Johnson (1989) survey 254 utilities to examine the perceptions and attitudes of utility managers on various DRIP issues, the impact of plan features on participation rates, and the changes in both participation rates and DRIPs characteristics since the 1970s. Survey results show a strong level of agreement with the statements that DRIPs improve relations with shareholders and are an economical way to raise new capital. The study reports that 61 percent of respondents use new-issue plans, a decline from the 82 percent reported in earlier studies. These findings suggest a trend away from using new-issue plans to market plans. The disadvantages of DRIPs to participating firms include the creation of administrative problems (49 percent), the dilution of equity value if shareholders sell new shares (30 percent), and the creation of high costs relative to the benefits received (11 percent).

The Baker and Johnson (1989) survey also asks questions about the perceived advantage and disadvantage to shareholders. The advantages of DRIPs to shareholders differ from those in previous studies. Providing a convenient way to invest relatively small dividends that shareholder might otherwise spend is the most widely cited advantage (50 percent), followed by providing inexpensive record-keeping and custodial services (19 percent). The perceived disadvantages to shareholders include reducing the control of shareholders over the price at which shares are purchased (49 percent), followed by requiring shareholders to pay income tax on the amount of dividends reinvested (26 percent).

Regarding the features offered by DRIPs, Baker and Johnson (1989) ask the participants about discounts, additional cash payments, split-share participation, types of funds reinvested, and street-name shareholders, as well as about payments of brokerage commissions, administrative fees, and safekeeping service charges. The most important plan feature appears to be discounts. However, only 15 percent of the responding firms offer discounts, which is down from about 40 percent in previous studies. Those offering discounts cite increased shareholder participation and increased dollar amount as major reasons for offering new plans. In addition, the results show that 63 percent of the responding firms allow split-share participation, 33 percent allow participation by street-name shareholders, and only 27 percent pay brokerage commissions, while 93 percent pay administration fees and 62 percent pay safekeeping service charges. Compared to previous studies, the percentage of firms allowing split-share participation and paying safekeeping fees has increased, while the percentage of firms paying brokerage commissions has declined.

Todd and Domian (1997) examine features of reinvestment plans and their relationship to participation rates by surveying 295 firms. Of the 110 surveys returned, the final usable sample includes 32 utilities and 23 nonutilities. Their analysis shows that firms in the utility group offer a discount and use new issues in their DRIPs significantly more than in the nonutility group. Furthermore, Todd and Domian report that participation rates as a percentage of eligible shareholders is significantly higher than for firms whose DRIPs do not offer a discount. The participation rates tend to be positively related to stock returns and have effect on trading volume.

CONCLUSIONS

Despite the mixed empirical evidence on the impact of dividend policy on firm value, managers behave as though dividend policy is relevant. This chapter documents the views of managers on dividend policy by synthesizing the survey evidence on stock splits, stock dividends, and DRIPs. These other distribution methods are part of the larger dividend puzzle.

Survey evidence shows that stock splits enable small stockholders to buy round lots more easily. Survey results also show that the major reasons for issuing stock splits include keeping a firm's stock price in an optimal price range, increasing the number of shareholders, making stocks more attractive to investors by increasing the number of shares outstanding, increasing liquidity, and signaling management's optimistic expectations about the firm's future prospects. Companies choosing not to split stocks perceive that their stock price currently is in its optimal trading range or too low. In addition, they have no reason for issuing stock splits.

The reasons respondents express in survey studies for issuing stock dividends include maintaining historical firm practice, conserving cash, increasing yield to stockholders, and expanding the amount of equity. Further, stock dividends have a positive psychological impact on investors and signal optimistic expectations about the future. Survey respondents indicate that the main reasons for not issuing stock dividends are high administrative costs, no change in the net position of stockholders, dilution effect on earnings, and stockholders' preference for cash over stock dividends.

Finally, the studies on DRIPs show that firms may benefit from these plans by raising equity capital through new-issue plans, improving shareholder goodwill, and allowing plan participants to acquire stocks at a reduced fee. Survey respondents cite taxes and maintenance of detailed tax records as major disadvantages of these plans.

Based on survey evidence highlighting management views on stock splits, stock dividends, and DRIPs, several conclusions emerge. First, managers behave as if there were an optimal dividend policy. Second, managers do not perceive that stock splits and stock dividends are merely cosmetic changes but rather benefit issuing firms in various ways. Third, managers generally believe that both stock splits and stock dividends signal their optimistic expectations about the future of the firm, suggesting that these forms of distribution may have some information content. Fourth, improving relations with stockholders appears to be important for most firms, as managers attempt to increase their shareholder base and retain their shareholders.

REFERENCES

Ang, James S., David W. Blackwell, and William L. Megginson. 1991. "The Effects of Taxes on the Relative Valuation of Dividends and Capital Gains: Evidence from Dual-Class British Investment Trusts." *Journal of Finance* 46:1, 383–399.

Baker, H. Kent, and Patricia L. Gallagher. 1980. "Management's View of Stock Splits." *Financial Management* 9:2, 73–77.

Baker, H. Kent, and Martha C. Johnson. 1988. "Dividend Reinvestment Plans: A Survey of Current Practices." *Journal of Midwest Finance Association* 17, 37–49.

Baker, H. Kent, and Martha C. Johnson. 1989. "Dividend Reinvestment Plans among Utilities: A Survey of Current Practices." *Midwestern Journal of Business and Economics* 5:3, 55–67.

Baker, H. Kent, and Sue E. Meeks. 1990. "The Evolution of Dividend Reinvestment Plans: 1968–1988." *Southern Business Review* 16:2, 1–11.

Baker, H. Kent, and Aaron L. Phillips. 1993. "Why Companies Issue Stock Dividends." *Financial Practice and Education* 3:2, 29–37.

Baker, H. Kent, Aaron L. Phillips, and Gary E. Powell. 1995. "The Stock Distribution Puzzle: A Synthesis of the Literature on Stock Splits and Stock Dividends." *Financial Practice and Education* 5:1, 24–27.

Baker, H. Kent, and Gary E. Powell. 1993. "Further Evidence on Managerial Motives for Stock Splits." *Quarterly Journal of Business and Economics* 32:3, 20–31.

Baker, H. Kent, and William F. Seippel. 1980. "Dividend Reinvestment Plans Win Wide Currency." *Harvard Business Review* 58:6, 182–186.

Baker, H. Kent, and William H. Seippel. 1981. "The Use of Dividend Reinvestment Plans by Utilities." *Akron Business and Economic Review* 12:1, 24–29.

Bar-Yosef, Sasson, and Lawrence D. Brown. 1977. "A Reexamination of Stock Splits Using Moving Betas." *Journal of Finance* 32:4, 1069–1080.

Brennan, Michael J., and Thomas E. Copeland. 1988. "Stock Split, Stock Prices and Transaction Costs." *Journal of Financial Economics* 22:1, 83–101.

Conroy, Robert M., Robert S. Harris, and Bruce A. Benet 1990. "The Effects of Stock Splits on Bid-Ask Spreads." *Journal of Finance* 45:4, 1285–1295.

Dowen, Richard J. 1990. "The Stock Split and Dividend Effect: Information or Price Pressure?" *Applied Economics* 22:7, 827–932.

Eades, Kenneth M., Patrick J. Hess, and E. Han Kim. 1984. "On Interpreting Security Returns during the Ex-Dividends Period." *Journal of Financial Economics* 13:1, 3–34.

Eisemann, Peter C., and Edward A. Moses. 1978. "Stock Dividends: Management's View." *Financial Analysts Journal* 34:4, 77–83.

Elgers, Pieter T., and Dennis Murray. 1985. "Financial Characteristics Related to Managements' Stock Split and Stock Dividends Decisions." *Journal of Business Finance and Accounting* 12:4, 543–551.

Fama, Eugene F., Lawrence Fisher, Michael C. Jensen, and Richard Roll. 1969. "The Adjustment of Stock Prices to New Information." *International Economic Review* 10:1, 1–21.

Frankfurter, George M., and William R. Lane. 1998. "The Perception of Stock Dividends." *Journal of Investing* 7:2, 32–40.

Frankfurter, George M., and Bob G. Wood, Jr. 2003. *Dividend Policy Theory and Practice*. London: Academic Press.

Fredman, Albert J., and John R. Nichols. 1980. "New Capital Dividend Reinvestment Plans of Electric Utilities." *Public Utilities Fortnightly* 105:5, 119–128.

Grinblatt, Mark S., Ronald W. Masulis, and Sheridan Titman. 1984. "The Valuation Effects of Stock Splits and Stock Dividends." *Journal of Financial Economics* 13:4, 461–190.

Lakonishok, Josef, and Baruch Lev. 1987. "Stock Splits and Stock Dividends: Why, Who, and When." *Journal of Finance* 42:4, 913–932.

Lamoureux, Christopher G., and Percy Poon. 1987. "The Market Reaction to Stock Splits." *Journal of Finance* 42:5, 1347–1370.

Maloney, Michael T., and J. Harold Mulherin. 1992. "The Effects of Splitting on the Ex: Microstructure Reconciliation." *Financial Management* 21:4, 44–59.

McNichols, Maureen, and Ajay Dravid. 1990. "Stock Dividends, Stock Splits, and Signaling." *Journal of Finance* 45:3, 857–879.

Miller, Merton H., and Franco Modigliani. 1961. "Dividend Policy, Growth, and the Valuation of Shares." *Journal of Business* 34:4, 411–433.

Murray, Dennis. 1985. "Further Evidence on the Liquidity Effects of Stock Splits and Stock Dividends." *Journal of Financial Research* 8:1, 59–67.

Nichols, William D. 1981. "Security Price Reaction to Occasional Small Stock Dividends." *Financial Review* 16:1, 54–62.

Pettway, Richard H., and R. Phil Malone. 1973. "Automatic Dividend Reinvestment Plans of Nonfinancial Corporations." *Financial Management* 2:4, 11–18.

Poterba, James M. 1986. "Market Value of Cash Dividends: The Citizen Utilities Case Reconsidered." *Journal of Financial Economics* 15:3, 395–405.

Szewczyk, Samuel H., and George P. Tsetsekos. 1992. "Stock Splits, Institutional Ownership, and the Flow of Information." Working Paper, Drexel University.

Szewczyk, Samuel H., and George P. Tsetsekos. 1993. "The Effects of Managerial Ownership on Stock Split-Induced Abnormal Returns." *Financial Review* 28:3, 351–370.

Todd, Janet M., and Dale L. Domian. 1997. "Participation Rates of Dividend Reinvestment Plans: Differences between Utility and Nonutility Firms." *Review of Financial Economics* 6:2, 121–135.

Woolridge, J. Randall. 1983. "Stock Dividends as Signals." *Journal of Financial Research* 6:1, 1–12.

ABOUT THE AUTHOR

Halil Kiymaz, CFA, is an associate professor of finance at the Crummer Graduate School of Business, Rollins College. Before joining the Crummer School, he taught at the University of Houston–Clear Lake, Bilkent University, and the University of New Orleans. His research interests include international mergers and acquisitions, emerging capital markets, linkages among capital markets of developing economics, dividend policy, mutual fund performances, initial public offerings, and financial management of multinationals. Kiymaz has published extensively in academic journals. His teaching area includes corporate finance, mergers and acquisitions, investment banking, and international financial management.

CHAPTER 23

Why Individual and Professional Investors Want Dividends

MING DONG
Associate Professor of Finance, Schulich School of Business, York University, Canada

CHRIS ROBINSON
Associate Professor of Finance, Atkinson School of Administrative Studies, York University

CHRIS VELD
Professor of Finance, University of Stirling in Scotland

INTRODUCTION

The finance literature abounds with theories of why investors want, do not want, or should not want corporations to pay dividends. Researchers from Lintner (1956) to Brav, Graham, Harvey, and Michaely (2005) ask financial managers why they pay dividends in an attempt to infer why investors want dividends. Other surveys asking managers about dividends include Baker, Farrelly, and Edelman (1985), Baker, Powell, and Veit (2002), De Jong, van Dijk, and Veld (2003), and Frankfurter et al. (2004).

Earlier research typically attempts to infer from share-price behavior around dividend announcements or share prices relative to dividend payouts why investors want dividends. What is missing is empirical evidence on how investors view dividends without taking any intermediary steps that require making assumptions before drawing inferences. The purpose of this chapter is to explore why individual investors want dividends and why professional or institutional investors want dividends when investing directly or indirectly on their behalf.

Two studies help to remedy this deficiency in the existing evidence regarding individual investors. Dong, Robinson, and Veld (2005) survey Dutch families who are regularly questioned about financial matters. Maditinos, Sevic, Theriou, and Tsinani (2007) use a survey of individual Greek investors to ask about their dividend preferences and beliefs. The key findings of these two surveys follow:

- The most strongly held belief, on average, in both countries is that investors want to receive cash dividends. Dividends appear relevant but the rationales for wanting them differ.
- Despite the previous statement, a sizable minority of investors are indifferent or do not want their shares to pay dividends.
- Investors in both countries agree with some theories but not others. More specifically, both studies find that dividend increases provide positive signals and that dividend decreases provide negative signals, which supports the signaling theory. On the other hand, they do not support agency theories and the behavioral explanation for cash dividends.
- The above observations hold on average, but for every theory, some investors are at the opposite ends of the agree-disagree scale. No single theory can explain why investors want dividends.

The earliest theories of why companies pay dividends and how they determine their policies developed from a casual empirical observation of how individual investors seem to behave. Because investors seem to want dividends, researchers developed theories to explain that observation. For example, Miller and Modigliani (1961) and Gordon (1962) apply formal modeling with different assumptions, but they still depict the behavior of individual investors.

The investment world has changed markedly since Miller and Modigliani (1961) and Gordon (1962) published their pathbreaking research. One major change is the rise of the holdings of institutional investors, who collectively hold a dominant position among investors in many countries. Examples of institutional holders include mutual funds, life insurance companies, hedge funds, and pension funds holding investments indirectly for individual investors; insurance companies, banks, and investment dealers holding shares for their own corporate portfolios; and portfolio managers holding investments that they manage directly on behalf of individual investors. Thus, the attitudes and beliefs about dividends held by the institutional investors are now important in investigating dividend theories. In addition, the attitudes of investment advisers who provide advice and transactions services to clients may also influence behavior toward dividends.

On the basis of interviews with investment advisers and money managers and a review of numerous financial analysts' reports that describe the attitudes and beliefs of institutional investors, we make the following observations:

- Advisers and money managers, except pension managers, believe that their clients prefer dividend-paying stocks.
- Analysts typically do not incorporate dividends into their written opinions.
- Advisers and money managers generally agree that dividend decisions provide information but they have a more complex and situation-contingent view of how to interpret them. While they view dividends as valuable signal about firm performance, they do not accept the simple signaling model that says that dividend increases signal good times and that decreases signal bad times.

The subsequent sections of this chapter summarize the existing evidence on individual investors' attitudes and beliefs and report on our research into the attitudes and beliefs of institutional investors.

WHY INDIVIDUAL INVESTORS WANT DIVIDENDS

As discussed in detail in other chapters in this book, many dividend theories exist. The following provides a brief summary of various explanations examined by Dong et al. (2005) and Maditinos et al. (2007).

Explanations Related to Cash Dividends

Dividend Irrelevance
Miller and Modigliani (1961) show that in a perfect and complete capital market the dividend policy of a firm does not affect its value. A stockholder can replicate any desired stream of payments by buying and selling common stock.

Taxes
In most countries dividends are taxed for individual investors as ordinary income. This generally creates a disadvantage for dividends compared to share repurchases because share repurchases can lead to income that is taxed as capital-gains income. Because capital gains are often taxed more favorably than ordinary income, taxes provide a disincentive for paying dividends. The situation differs between countries. In some countries, taxes provide a disadvantage for dividends, while in other countries individual investors are indifferent between dividends and share repurchases from a tax perspective.

Signaling
Bhattacharya (1979) and Miller and Rock (1985) argue that information asymmetries between firms and outside shareholders may induce a signaling role for dividends. The authors contend show that dividend payments communicate private information in a fully revealing manner. The most important element of signaling theory is that firms have to pay out funds regularly. Therefore, similar reasoning applies to recurrent share buybacks.

Recent literature suggests that the signaling role of dividends depends on the corporate governance structure. For example, Gugler (2003) finds that state-controlled firms in Austria smooth dividends, while family-owned firms do not show such smoothing. Gugler and Yurtoglu (2003) find that German companies, in which the ownership and control structures make the expropriation of minority shareholders more likely than for other firms, exhibit significantly greater negative wealth effects. Finally, Goergen, Renneboog, and Correia da Silva (2005) find that German firms with banks as their major shareholders are more willing to omit their dividends than are firms controlled by other types of shareholders.

Share buybacks may signal that the undervaluation of shares. Evidence by Comment and Jarrell (1991) as well as Ikenberry, Lakonishok, and Vermaelen (1995, 2000) show a significantly positive association between share buyback announcements and abnormal returns.

Agency Costs

According to Easterbrook (1984), dividends reduce the overinvestment problem even when free cash flow is already constrained, because paying dividends increases the frequency with which firms have to go to equity markets to raise capital. In the process of attracting new equity, firms subject themselves to the monitoring and disciplining of these markets, which lowers agency costs. Repurchasing common stock is an alternative to paying cash dividends. Both ways of paying out cash are useful to mitigate the agency problems raised by Easterbrook (1984) and Jensen (1986). Thus, a share repurchase creates a similar monitoring effect as cash dividends.

Free Cash Flow

Free cash flow is the cash flow that remains after a firm undertakes all positive net present value (NPV) projects. Jensen (1986) conjectures that managers aim to expand the size of the firm for their own prestige and compensation and thus may take on negative NPV projects instead of paying dividends. Black (1976) also argues that paying dividends can mitigate a potential overinvestment problem, because dividends reduce the amount of free cash flow.

Behavioral Explanation

Shefrin and Statman (1984) develop a behavioral life cycle theory of dividends based on self-control to prevent too much current consumption. People set up mental accounts, which are ways of dividing cash flow between the part that they can sustainably spend and the part that they must keep as capital to earn sustainable income. Equity investors mentally classify dividends, or that amount of cash flow, as the amount that they can spend. The effect should be especially strong for elderly (retired) investors, as they have little or no labor income and rely more heavily on income from their security holdings. Shefrin and Statman contend that support for their theory comes from evidence by Lease, Lewellen, and Schlarbaum (1976), who find that the elderly have a stronger preference for dividend-paying stocks than do younger investors.

Transaction Costs

Investors who want to receive regular income from their security holdings have a choice between buying dividend-paying stocks and cashing in the dividends and buying non-dividend-paying stocks and regularly selling part of their portfolios. As Allen and Michaely (2003) show for small individual investors, the transaction costs of cashing in the dividends may be substantially smaller than the transaction costs associated with selling part of their stock holding.

Uncertainty Resolution

Gordon (1961, 1962) argues that outside shareholders prefer a high dividend policy. Shareholders prefer a dividend today to a highly uncertain capital gain from a questionable future investment. The model seems to accord well with casual observations.

Reduce Accounting Manipulations
Companies may pay dividends because investors may perceive such firms as honest and less subject to accounting manipulations. For example, Laing (2002, p. 1) recommends that investors "embrace stocks that pay healthy dividends.... Healthy dividend payments also indicate that companies are generating real earnings rather than cooking the books."

Theories on Why Investors Want Stock Dividends

Taxes
Stock dividends are generally not taxed. This is not remarkable, as they are nothing more than a distribution of additional shares of stock.

Transaction Costs
Compared to using cash dividends to buy a firm's stock, stock dividends result in lower transaction costs because investors receive stock.

Behavioral Explanations
Shefrin and Statman (1984) argue that there are behavioral reasons to pay stock dividends. The reasons are especially compelling if the company does not want to pay a cash dividend because it does not have free cash flow. They argue that because stock dividends are labeled as dividends, investors who sell off and subsequently consume their stock dividends do not break the mental accounting rule to avoid consuming capital.

DUTCH AND GREEK SURVEYS

Dong et al. (2005) use a Dutch panel of consumers managed by CentERdata at Tilburg University. These consumers are representative of the Dutch population and answer questions on the Internet or a television connection each week. CentERdata managers are experts in questionnaire design and administration. In a survey of 2,723 panel members, CentERdata received responses from 2,035, resulting in a 75 percent response rate. Of the respondents, 555 owned investments directly and hence answered questions about dividends. Maditinos et al. (2007) emailed five copies of a questionnaire to each of 150 firms listed on the Athens Stock Exchange, asking each firm to send the questionnaires to their customers. Of the 750 customers, 248 (33 percent) responded.

Both studies use the same design. The survey consists of a series of questions designed to elicit responses about different theories or explanations of dividend policy. Almost all of the questions use a seven-point scale ranging from 1 = "completely disagree" (no, or definitely not) to 7 = "completely agree" (yes or definitely) with the midpoint of 4 being neutral. The tabulation of responses does not include responses that are "don't know" or "no opinion." Each study tests whether means and medians differ significantly from 4 (neutral) using t-statistics for means and binomial p-tests (based on the two-tail Fisher sign test) for medians. Table 23.1 summarizes the responses for selected questions and shows whether support exists for each theory, the mean score, and significance level. The two surveys contain

Table 23.1 Summary Results from Surveys of Individual Investors: The Netherlands and Greece

Theory	Support	Disagree (%) (1, 2, 3)	Neutral (%) (4)	Agree (%) (5, 6, 7)	Mean	Std. Dev.	Country
Panel A. Cash Dividends							
1. *Dividend relevance/irrelevance*: Do you want dividends?	Yes	12	27	61	4.98**	1.59	Netherlands
	Yes	8	13	79	5.23**	1.32	Greece
2. *Taxes*: Do they matter?	No	33	48	19	3.60**	1.52	Netherlands
(Note: Taxes should not matter in either the Netherlands or Greece because the tax codes do not tax dividends.)	Unreported						Greece
3. *Signaling*: Do dividend *increases* signal that performance will (1 = deteriorate strongly; 7 = improve strongly)?	Yes	4	45	51	4.67**	0.95	Netherlands
	Yes	2	19	79	5.28**	1.03	Greece
Do dividend *decreases* signal that performance will (1 = deteriorate strongly to 7 = improve strongly)?	Yes	42	52	6	3.56**	0.82	Netherlands
	Yes	79	19	2	2.57**	1.10	Greece
Does a share repurchase signal stock undervaluation?	Yes	19	35	46	4.36**	1.30	Netherlands
	Yes	17	18	65	4.80**	1.58	Greece
4. *Agency costs*: Do you want to receive dividends if the company has to issue new shares to pay for them?	No	74	19	7	2.40**	1.47	Netherlands
	No	37	28	35	3.95	1.65	Greece
Do you want to receive dividends if the company has to issue new debt to pay for them?	No	81	14	5	2.03**	1.34	Netherlands
	No	22	57	21	3.15**	1.10	Greece

Question					Mean	SD	Country
5. *Free cash flow:* Do you want to receive cash dividends because otherwise the company will invest the money unprofitably?	No	51	36	13	3.06**	1.54	Netherlands
	No	65	22	13	3.02**	1.57	Greece
6. *Behavioral explanation:* Would you for consumption purposes sell part of your stocks in a company that has always paid a dividend, if the management of that company would decide not to pay a dividend anymore?	No	61	23	16	2.87**	1.75	Netherlands
	No	47	41	12	3.50**	1.34	Greece
7. *Transaction costs:* Do you want dividends to save transaction costs of selling shares?	Yes	21	46	33	4.20**	1.55	Netherlands
	No	44	31	25	3.58**	1.69	Greece
8. *Uncertainty resolution:* Are dividend-paying shares less risky?	No	43	36	21	3.62**	1.33	Netherlands
	No	49	12	39	3.78	1.93	Greece
9. *Reduce accounting manipulations:* Do dividends assure earnings quality?	No	34	40	26	3.66**	1.60	Netherlands
	No	57	19	24	3.50**	1.76	Greece

(Continued)

Table 23.1 (*Continued*)

Theory	Support	Disagree (%) (1, 2, 3)	Neutral (%) (4)	Agree (%) (5, 6, 7)	Mean	Std. Dev.	Country
Panel B. Stock Dividends							
1. *Taxes*: If you only consider income taxes, do you prefer stock or cash dividends? (1 = cash dividends; 7 = stock dividends)	No	21	50	29	4.11	1.49	Netherlands
	Yes	25	68	7	3.74**	1.22	Greece
2. *Transaction costs*: Do you prefer stock dividends to cash dividends because of transaction costs, implying that investors reinvest cash dividends?	Yes	17	41	42	4.40*	1.51	Netherlands
	No	28	62	10	3.76**	1.21	Greece
3. *Behavioral explanation*: Do investors want stock dividends instead of a cash dividend when there is no free cash flow to pay a cash dividend?	Yes	17	27	56	4.72**	1.69	Netherlands
	Yes	14	11	75	5.03**	1.53	Greece

This table presents a summary of investors' responses to a dividend survey in the Netherlands (Dong et al., 2005) and Greece (Maditinos et al., 2007) using a seven-point scale ranging from 1 = "completely disagree" (no or definitely not) to 7 = "completely agree" (yes or definitely) with the midpoint of 4 being neutral. Std. Dev. is the standard deviation of the difference between the mean response and 4 (neutral). *p < .05 (two-tailed). **p < .01 (two-tailed).

additional details, including other questions for each theory and means partitioned by income (low/high) and age (more than and less than 55 years old). The Dutch study also includes a subsample split by education (university and no university education).

The results are generally similar between the two countries. As panel A of Table 23.1 shows, individual investors typically want to receive cash dividends (A1), which lends support to the dividend relevance theory. Not surprisingly, taxes are unimportant (A2). Under the Dutch income-tax system since January 1, 2001, rational individual investors in the Netherlands should be indifferent between receiving dividends and capital gains. The tax system now levies what is effectively a wealth tax, which is applied to the market value of capital. Individual Greek investors pay no tax on dividends. Hence, in both countries the unequal taxation of dividends is not an issue the way it is in many other markets. Strong support exists for signaling theory (A3). In addition, individual investors generally agree that share repurchases signal share undervaluation, which provides additional support for signaling theory. Results are mixed involving the role of transaction costs (A7). Dutch investors generally agree that they prefer dividends to save the transaction costs of selling shares, whereas the Greek investors do not.

There is a lack of support for several explanations for paying cash dividends, including agency cost (A4), free cash flow (A5), behavioral explanation, and uncertainty resolution (A8). Individual investors, on average, also do not believe that dividend payouts help protection against accounting manipulations (A9).

Panel B of Table 23.1 shows how individual investors view several statements involving stock dividends. With regard to taxes (B1) rational Dutch and Greek investors should be indifferent between cash and stock dividends because both countries treat cash and stock dividends in the same manner. Dutch investors confirm this result, but Greek investors do not. In terms of transaction costs (B2), Dutch investors prefer stock dividends over cash dividends. This result suggests that most investors reinvest their dividends. Greek investors prefer cash dividends over stock dividends, which suggests that they do not reinvest their dividends. When asked if they want stock dividends (another form of mental accounting) instead of a cash dividend when there is no free cash flow to pay a cash dividend (B3), both Dutch and Greek investors strongly prefer to receive stock dividends. Thus, the evidence on stock dividends provides some support for the behavioral finance theory of Shefrin and Statman (1984).

Although there are no statistical tests of whether the answers from the Dutch and Greek investors differ, the overall results indicate a high level of consistency in the direction of their responses. The findings suggest support for some explanations for paying dividends but not others. However, the mean of the responses hides substantial variability, as shown by the standard deviations in Table 23.1. Although the average response may differ from neutral (4), the views of individual investors indicate a range of beliefs about the relevance of dividends.

For example, consider the question of whether dividends are relevant. The median response is 5, and the sample mean and median are both greater than 4 at the 99 percent confidence level. Nonetheless, looking at the left-hand columns of Table 23.1 (Netherlands), the results show that 61 percent of respondents say that they want cash dividends (i.e., response = 5, 6, or 7), 27 percent are indifferent, and 12 percent do not want to receive dividends. Extending that 12 percent to an entire population of investors would result in many investors. The question of whether dividend-paying shares are less risky (Panel A, 8) shows a wide dispersion of responses: 21 percent of respondents agree that higher dividend-paying shares are less risky, 36 percent are neutral, and 43 percent do not believe that higher dividends translate into lower risk.

What this evidence involving individual investors seems to suggest is the coexistence of different beliefs about the relevance of dividends. In their review of numerous studies on dividend policy, Frankfurter and Wood (2002, p. 111) hold a similar view, concluding, "The results presented here are consistent with the contention that no dividend model, either separately or jointly with other models, is supported invariably." In a recent article, Graham and Kumar (2006) find that dividend clienteles exist for retail investors. They explain their findings on the basis of tax and age considerations, where behavioral considerations are likely to drive the age clienteles. The Dutch and Greek studies also may contain clientele effects in which different beliefs drive the results.

WHY PROFESSIONAL INVESTORS WANT DIVIDENDS

Methodology

This section provides evidence about the beliefs of professional or institutional investors involving dividends obtained from interviews. The section also attempts to develop a theory of how professional investors respond to dividend policy and dividend-payout decisions and how that relates to the individuals whom they are supposed to represent as agents. Glaser and Strauss (1967) provide the methodological basis, called grounded theory, for this section. Grounded theory is a qualitative method that embodies the commonsense basis for most social science research. Bettner, Robinson, and McGoun (1994) explain how qualitative research such as grounded theory can provide valuable contributions to finance research. Perhaps the earliest work on dividend policy based on grounded theory is Lintner (1956). His results have largely stood the test of time and are still widely accepted.

This section reports the results from three Canadian sources:

1. Semistructured interviews with five Canadian professional investors or money managers.
   - An investment adviser with one of the largest investment dealers in Canada who acts as a broker-agent to buy and sell securities and manages portfolios for individuals for an asset management fee.
   - A pension fund manager who is part of a team managing a company pension fund valued at more than $10 billion.
   - A founding partner and the head of research for a firm who manages portfolios for high net worth (greater than $500,000) clients as its primary business. The firm also manages several mutual funds and pension funds. Because both managers consistently agree completely, they represent a single interviewee called Private Manager 1.
   - Another senior money manager whose firm manages high-net-worth portfolios as its primary business but also manages one mutual fund and some pension funds. This manager is called Private Manager 2.

2. A review of documents consisting of 455 one-page analysts' reports on companies and eight detailed reports on four companies.
3. A Canadian focus group of relatively new investment advisers who work for a large investment dealer.

Qualitative methods such as grounded theory have more nuances than quantitative methods and require adjustments to fit the specific research problem. For this problem, the specific method has the following characteristics:

- The sample is not random but consists of professionals who represent the different facets of investing on behalf of others, clienteles, and institutional factors.
- The interview is a semistructured one lasting between one and two hours. The interviewer does not use a questionnaire and does not focus on questions about specific dividend theories. The goal of the interviews is to discover the decision models of professional investors without guiding them into predetermined paths. The following general question guides the conversation with each interviewee: How do dividend policies and payouts enter into your decisions on which shares to buy and sell? From that starting point the interviewer guides the discussion to keep it on track and to understand what the interviewee is saying.
- The sample is necessarily small because of the time-consuming nature of this research method.
- The interview is normally at the interviewee's place of business.
- The interviewer tapes the interview and a professional transcriber provides a written transcription. The written transcription is the empirical evidence for this study.

Evidence from Canadian Institutional Investors

Analysts
An analysis of 455 one-page summary reports on Canadian stocks and a few Australian mining companies published by RBC Dominion (2008), one of the largest investment dealers in Canada, provides insights into institutional investors. These reports represent 43 different principal analysts including 10 chartered financial analysts. The data include detailed analysts' reports on four companies by two of the same analysts written in early 2008 and four detailed reports on the same four companies by two analysts working for a different large Canadian investment dealer. The summary reports come directly from the detailed reports. The format and ranking systems of the two investment dealers' detailed reports are similar.

The evidence from all 463 reports is consistent with respect to the relevance of dividends to the analysts' rankings. Each report has a box containing four years of statistics, including 2006 and 2007 actual and 2008 and 2009 estimated. Each report contains information on dividends per share and dividend yield.

Analysts rank each company as "outperform," "sector perform," or "underperform" on the basis of comparison of the actual share price with their estimate of the true price per share. The ranking includes a risk qualifier: average, above average, or speculative. The analysts use a full range of valuation metrics, but none of the reports mentions the dividend growth model or uses dividend payout as part of the evaluation. Overall, the evidence suggests that the analysts do not view dividends as important to the investment decision. A caveat to this conclusion is that dividend policies or decisions may provide useful information for valuations despite that the reports do not mention such policies or decisions.

Interviewees and a Focus Group

The interviewees generally agree that dividends are relevant but differ on the reasons for dividend relevance. With the exception of the pension fund manager, the institutional investors strongly believe that their clients want dividends, which is consistent with the survey evidence of Brav et al. (2005). Because pension funds in Canada pay out a stream of income that is not differentiated by the original source, the pensioners are indifferent. This helps to explain why the pension fund manager does not believe that his clients care whether their stocks pay dividends. For the other subjects, the relevance for dividends is partly due to their clients' preferences. Dividend relevance is not just for cash flow but can also refer to other reasons investors want to buy dividend-paying shares. Institutional investors who have direct contact with the beneficial investors agree that their clients want dividend-paying stocks. For example, one money manager says:

> I think it's a tremendous source of solace to many clients, including many of our own clients, when markets go on volatile swings, to take comfort in the fact that they have a portfolio of stocks where there's a high degree of confidence in the dividend income, and that this will go up a bit each year.

On the basis of their own experience, the investment advisers interviewed agree that individual investors prefer to receive dividends to satisfy their comfort levels, not because dividends relate to the value of the stocks. In addition, the interviewees agree that dividends are relevant because they convey information. Their opinions are more sophisticated than a simple signaling mechanism. The information content of dividends is set within the context of the wider information set and how investors expect the company to behave. However, investment advisers do not view dividends as the most important part of the information, compared particularly with cash flows and forecasts of cash flows. For example, the pension manager uses dividend information as a minor part of the total information set: "To answer very succinctly, dividends are really a secondary and even a tertiary consideration. The philosophy of the fund is that dividends are not the primary consideration that we invest in equities."

The pension manager sees dividends as a confirmation of what he already sees in other evidence:

> For some companies, their value is well supported because of the dividends that they paid, but we would not buy a company because they pay high dividends.... If they had the capabilities of paying over the years, that gave you a little bit more confidence, and of course we love the consistency of dividends and even the very smooth trend of systematically increasing dividends year after year after year.

> The Gordon growth model, of course, is one tool that we use, but certainly we do not buy stocks on that basis. The approach that we took, I think, was a true fundamental analysis. We really studied the company; we did our pro forma cash flows; we studied the industry; and then we took it from there. I mean, to do a dividend growth model takes about two minutes to do, but it would take us months to do the cash projections.

Some interviewees believe that a dividend increase is always good news, while others are more cautious and stress the need to examine the specific economic environment. Some believe that dividend initiation may convey the adverse signal that the company has diminishing growth prospects. This diversity of opinion led to a somewhat heated debate in the focus group of investment advisers.

Private Manager 1 expresses this difficulty in interpreting dividend information:

We do detailed discounted cash flow models of all our investing companies by segment. So, if they do a big increase, say a 20% increase, and I can't reconcile the magnitude of that increase with the growth that we envision in those individual segments, you know, initially you're cynical. . . . A big spike up in payout ratios isn't necessarily a good thing.

The investment adviser views dividends as a means of determining the stability of a company:

One of the things I do is try and pick established companies that are profitable and that provide a little bit of stability to a portfolio that's intended to grow over time. And so one of the measures of a company that's profitable over time is whether the board of directors declares dividends and what those dividends are. So if the company is declaring regular dividends and those dividends are increasing each year, that is one measure of attractiveness for investment.

Overall, this evidence, while mixed, suggests that dividends are less important for share valuation than many individual investors think. Dividends appear irrelevant for the analysts. Yet investment advisers regard dividends as important, but primarily because individual clients seem to be happier with dividends. Although the money managers have different perspectives, they believe that dividends provide information. The cash flow from dividends is irrelevant both for the pension fund manager and for the individual money managers who are managing pension funds or mutual funds. There is some support for the signaling hypothesis.

The individual money managers and the investment advisers say that most of their clients reinvest part or all of their dividend income. Although retired investors are more likely to consume dividend income, many of them do not. Most of their retired and other clients leave the principal intact. Two money managers from the same firm believe that their clients should not consume more than their dividend income, which means that the clients allow the growth in value over time to remain in the account. Most clients want to leave bequests to their children. Therefore, the dividend payout of the firm becomes a control mechanism to ensure savings for the next generation. This opinion is consistent with the mental accounting of Shefrin and Statman (1984). On the other hand, the evidence from all the interviewees is that most clients do not spend or withdraw their dividend income but leave it to accumulate. Hence, these clients can control their spending without strictly limiting themselves to consuming only dividends.

Almost all interviewees support the view that a share buyback indicates the management believes the company's stock is undervalued. For example, Private Manager 2 says that he would not buy a dividend-paying stock if the stock never buys back its shares, because a company that never repurchase shares indicates overvaluation.

A final topic on which the interviewees seem to agree involves stock div-idends. They all agree that a stock dividend is nothing more than a cosmetic transaction. As one respondent notes: "Well, we all know a stock dividend is like a wooden nickel; it's not worth very much. It's an accounting illusion, just like a stock split."

CONCLUSIONS

The survey results of individual investors in the Netherlands and Greece are largely consistent. The responses of a majority of the respondents lend support to a few div-idend theories, but considerable variation exists in their views about each theory. Not surprisingly, respondents hold different beliefs about why dividends mat-ter. Although a majority of individual investors surveyed prefer dividend-paying stocks, others are indifferent or do not want to receive dividends. Similarly, the survey results suggest that individual investors often view a dividend increase as a positive signal about the future performance of the company, but this perception is not universal.

Generalizing the results from interviews with professional investors in Canada requires caution because the sample represents only small number of such investors from a single country. A broader sample is likely to be more reliable. Given this caveat, several key observations emerge from the interviews.

First, the Canadian professional investors interviewed typically agree that their clients want dividends in order to provide a sense of comfort. Second, they agree that dividends provide information but disagree on how to interpret a dividend increase or decrease. These professional investors go beyond a simple signaling model in which dividend increases are good and dividend decreases are bad to consider dividends in the context of the company, its industry, and management's actions.

In conclusion, research that tries to infer investor preferences for dividends from market-based studies is unlikely to fully resolve the dividend puzzle. Market prices cannot reject or fail to reject the validity of any dividend theory if people hold varying views about each theory. As evidence from survey research shows, alternative dividend theories coexist because respondents do no universally sup-port a single explanation of why firms pay dividends and why investors want them. Thus, both market- and survey-based streams of research can complement each another and provide insights into solving the dividend puzzle.

REFERENCES

Allen, Franklin, and Roni Michaely. 2003. "Payout Policy." In *North-Holland Handbook of Economics*, ed. George Constantinides, Milton Harris, and René M. Stulz, 337–429. Amsterdam: North-Holland.

Baker, H. Kent, Gail E. Farrelly, and Richard B. Edelman. 1985. "A Survey of Management Views on Dividend Policy." *Financial Management* 14:3, 78–83.

Baker, H. Kent, Gary E. Powell, and E. Theodore Veit. 2002. "Revisiting Managerial Perspectives on Dividend Policy." *Journal of Economics and Finance* 26:3, 267–283.

Bettner, Mark S., Chris Robinson, and Elton McGoun. 1994. "The Case for Qualitative Research in Finance." *International Review of Financial Analysis* 3:1, 1–18.

Bhattacharya, Sudipto. 1979. "Imperfect Information, Dividend Policy, and the 'Bird in the Hand' Fallacy." *Bell Journal of Economics* 10:1, 259–270.

Black, Fischer. 1976. "The Dividend Puzzle." *Journal of Portfolio Management* 2:2, 5–8.

Brav, Alon, John R. Graham, Campbell R. Harvey, and Roni Michaely. 2005. "Payout Policy in the 21st Century." *Journal of Financial Economics* 77:3, 483–527.

Comment, Robert, and Gregg Jarrell. 1991. "The Relative Signalling Power of Dutch-Auction and Fixed-Price Self-Tender Offers and Open-Market Share Repurchases." *Journal of Finance* 46:4, 1243–1271.

De Jong, Abe, Ronald van Dijk, and Chris Veld. 2003. "The Dividend and Share Repurchase Policies of Canadian Firms: Empirical Evidence Based on an Alternative Research Design." *International Review of Financial Analysis* 12:4, 349–377.

Dong, Ming, Chris Robinson, and Chris Veld. 2005. "Why Individual Investors Want Dividends." *Journal of Corporate Finance* 12:1, 121–158.

Easterbrook, Frank H. 1984. "Two Agency-Cost Explanations of Dividends." *American Economic Review* 74:4, 650–659.

Frankfurter, George M., Arman Kosedag, Kevin Chiang, David Collison, David M. Power, Hartmut Schmidt, Raymond So, and Mihail Topalov. 2004. "A Comparative Analysis of Perception of Dividends by Financial Managers." *Research in International Business and Finance* 18:1, 73–114.

Frankfurter, George M., and Bob G. Wood, Jr. 2002. "Dividend Policies and Their Empirical Tests." *International Review of Financial Analysis* 11:2, 111–138.

Glaser, Barney G., and Anselm L. Strauss. 1967. *The Discovery of Grounded Field Theory: Strategies for Qualitative Research*. Chicago: Aldine Press.

Goergen, Marc, Luc Renneboog, and Luis Correia da Silva. 2005. "When Do German Firms Change Their Dividends?" *Journal of Corporate Finance* 11:1–2, 375–399.

Gordon, Myron J. 1961. *The Investment, Financing, and Valuation of the Corporation*. Homewood, IL: Richard D. Irwin.

Gordon, Myron J. 1962. "The Savings Investment and Valuation of a Corporation." *Review of Economics and Statistics* 44:1, 37–51.

Graham, John R., and Alok Kumar. 2006. "Do Dividend Clienteles Exist? Evidence on Dividend Preferences of Retail Investors." *Journal of Finance* 61:3, 1305–1336.

Gugler, Klaus. 2003. "Corporate Governance, Dividend Payout Policy, and the Interrelation between Dividends, R&D, and Capital Investment." *Journal of Banking and Finance* 27:7, 1297–1321.

Gugler, Klaus, and B. Burcin Yurtoglu. 2003. "Corporate Governance and Dividend Payout Policy in Germany." *European Economic Review* 47:4, 731–758.

Ikenberry, David, Josef Lakonishok, and Theo Vermaelen. 1995. "Market Underreaction to Open Market Share Repurchases." *Journal of Financial Economics* 39:2–3, 181–208.

Ikenberry, David, Josef Lakonishok, and Theo Vermaelen. 2000. "Stock Repurchases in Canada: Performance and Strategic Trading." *Journal of Finance* 55:5, 2373–2398.

Jensen, Michael C. 1986. "Agency Costs of Free Cash Flow, Corporate Finance, and Takeovers." *American Economic Review* 76:2, 323–339.

Laing, Jonathan. 2002. "After the Bubble," *Barron's*, July 1, 2002, accessed at http://online.barrons.com/article/SB1025303425582899600.html.

Lease, Ronald C., Wilbur G. Lewellen, and Gary G. Schlarbaum. 1976. "Market Segmentation: Evidence on the Individual Investor." *Financial Analysts Journal* 32:5, 53–60.

Lintner, John. 1956. "Distribution of Incomes of Corporations among Dividends, Retained Earnings, and Taxes." *American Economic Review* 46:2, 97–113.

Maditinos, Dimitrios I., Zeljko Sevic, Nikolaos G. Theriou, and Alexandra V. Tsinani. 2007. "Individual Investors' Perceptions towards Dividends: The Case of Greece." *International Journal of Monetary Economics and Finance* 1:1, 18–31.

Miller, Merton, and Franco Modigliani. 1961. "Dividend Policy, Growth, and the Valuation of Shares." *Journal of Business* 34:4, 411–433.

Miller, Merton H., and Kevin Rock. 1985. "Dividend Policy under Asymmetric Information." *Journal of Finance* 40:4, 1031–1051.

RBC Dominion. 2008. *Fundamentals*. Toronto, Canada: RBC Dominion (Winter).

Shefrin, Hersh M., and Meir Statman. 1984. "Explaining Investor Preference for Cash Dividends." *Journal of Financial Economics* 13:2, 253–282.

ABOUT THE AUTHORS

Ming Dong, Ph.D., is an associate professor of finance at the Schulich School of Business, York University, Canada. He received his doctoral degree in finance from Ohio State University. He also holds a master's degree in physics from New York University. His main research areas include corporate finance and behavioral finance. Dong has published influential work in mergers and acquisitions in top journals, including *Journal of Finance* and *Journal of Financial Economics*. He has also worked in stock valuation modeling and option pricing. His recent interests include valuation of initial public offerings and market performance; determinants of public equity and debt issues; the effects of stock market misvaluation on corporate investments, new issues, and mergers; and the differences in firm and investor behavior between China and developed nations.

Chris Robinson, Ph.D., CA, CFP, teaches and researches in personal finance, financial statement analysis, environmental management, and alternative perspectives on finance and accounting. He received all his degrees from the University of Toronto and has taught at York University since 1983. His research has been published in finance, accounting, law, environment, and general business journals, including *Financial Analysts Journal*, *Journal of Corporate Finance*, *Canadian Journal of Administrative Science*, and *Canadian Business Law Journal*. His most recent research topics include dividends, regulation of payday lenders, stochastic retirement planning, and the impact of environmental considerations on the capital budgeting practices of forest companies and dry cleaners. His textbook *Personal Financial Planning*, coauthored with Kwok Ho, is used across Canada in both French and English. There is also a Dutch edition, coauthored with Chris Veld, a Chinese edition, and a U.S. edition. Mexican and U.K. editions are forthcoming.

Chris Veld, Ph.D., is a professor of finance at the University of Stirling in Scotland. He received all his degrees from Tilburg University in the Netherlands and taught at Tilburg University and Simon Fraser University in Vancouver before moving to Scotland. In addition, he has held visiting positions at McGill University in Montreal and at York University in Toronto. His research covers topics in corporate finance, investments, and derivative securities, and he has published in journals such as *Journal of Finance*, *Financial Management*, *Journal of Corporate Finance*, and *Journal of Banking and Finance*. Veld holds editorial board positions for *European Financial Management*, *Canadian Journal of Administrative Sciences*, and *Review of Futures Markets*. He also coauthored the Dutch version of *Personal Financial Planning* with Kwok Ho and Chris Robinson.

PART VI

Other Dividend Issues

CHAPTER 24

Why Firms Begin Paying Dividends: Value, Growth, and Life Cycle Effects

NEIL FARGHER
Professor of Accounting, The Australian National University, Canberra, Australia

ROBERT A. WEIGAND
Professor of Finance and holder of the Brenneman Professorship in Business Strategy, Washburn University, Topeka, Kansas

INTRODUCTION

This chapter investigates dividend initiations and the reasons firms begin paying regular cash dividends to shareholders. Since Miller and Modigliani (1961) (hereafter MM) published their seminal proof that a firm's dividend payout cannot directly affect its value, at least in perfect financial markets, researchers have proposed and tested numerous explanations for the convention of dividends. There are so many competing theories of dividends that Ang (1987, p. 55) observed, "We have moved from a position of not enough good reasons to explain why dividends are paid to one of too many."

Some have proposed that the difficulty in sorting through the arguments for dividends arises because they assume there is one unique explanation that applies to all firms. Baker, Powell, and Veit (2002, p. 256) note, "Each theory typically takes a 'one-size-fits-all' approach by trying to generalize the findings." More recently, Chiang, Frankfurter, Kosedag, and Wood (2006, p. 62) comment, "There might not be a single theoretical model blanket covering firm dividend behavior." These studies also assert that academic theories are more likely to be supported empirically when they correspond with managers' perceptions, as cataloged by various surveys conducted over the years. Moreover, although the reasons that firms engage in positive dividend events such as initiations, increases, and resumptions arise from substantially different circumstances, there have been few attempts, either theoretical or empirical, to distinguish among such events. Researchers usually

The authors appreciate comments provided by H. Kent Baker and Robert Irons.

assume the same theory is as applicable to a firm increasing its dividend as it is to a firm resuming dividends or initiating a payout for the first time.

This chapter reports the results of a study that takes a first step toward addressing a challenge put forth by Baker et al. (2002, p. 257): "researchers have identified all the key pieces of the dividend puzzle but need to focus their attention on developing firm-specific dividend models." It proposes that the signaling, agency, and risk explanations are best understood within a larger context proposed by Grullon, Michaely, and Swaminathan (2002), who hypothesize that dividend increases convey information about changes in a firm's life cycle—specifically, the transition from a faster growth phase to a slower growth, mature phase. The study asserts that the life cycle hypothesis is even more applicable to first-time dividend initiators than dividend increasers. The failure to account for this richer framework may explain some of the difficulty researchers have had in identifying a single best explanation for dividends, as averaging empirical variables such as stock returns, profits, and risk across entire samples obscures important differences in the reasons firms choose to engage in positive dividend events.

The remainder of this chapter has the following organization. The first section reviews the literature and develops hypotheses about dividend initiation. The next section describes the data and empirical methodology, followed by empirical findings. The final section provides the conclusions.

WHAT IS KNOWN ABOUT DIVIDENDS?

DeAngelo and DeAngelo (2006) present a critique of MM's (1961) proof that dividends do not affect the value of the firm in perfect markets. They claim the finding of dividend irrelevance results from MM's framework, which mandates 100 percent payouts. By relaxing this assumption, payout policy affects value in the same manner as investment policy. DeAngelo and DeAngelo argue that the irrelevance result is essentially hardwired into MM's assumptions, which makes their proof nothing more than an elegant tautology. They also claim that Black's (1976) dividend puzzle is a nonpuzzle, as it is based on MM's conclusions. DeAngelo and DeAngelo (p. 295) assert that MM and Black have "limited our vision about the importance of payout policy and sent researchers off searching for frictions that would make payout policy matter, while it has mattered all along."

DeAngelo and DeAngelo's (2006) critique suggests two distinct perspectives about dividends and valuation. The first perspective, which was widely held before MM (1961), is set forth by Graham and Dodd (1934), Williams (1938), Lintner (1956), and Gordon (1959). The idea is simple: Investors like dividends, and the bigger the better. More formally, dividends are the stream of expected future cash flows that give stocks their "intrinsic" value.

The second perspective, which prevails after MM (1961), is defined by researchers' quest for the reasons—all due to market imperfections—that firms engage in the practice of regular cash payouts. Lease, John, Kalay, Lowenstein, and Sarig (2000) set forth three major (tax-induced clienteles, signaling or asymmetric information, and agency costs) and three minor (transaction costs, flotation costs, and irrational investor behavior) explanations for dividend relevance. This chapter focuses on two of the three major explanations, signaling and agency costs, and includes a third, less-studied explanation, the relationship between dividend initiation and risk.

Recent research has proposed that dividends convey information about firm maturity. For example, DeAngelo, DeAngelo, and Stulz (2006) show the probability that a firm will pay dividends increases when there is more retained equity in its capital structure, which is typical of older, more established firms. Grullon et al. (2002) hypothesize that increases in dividends convey information about firms' transition from a faster-growth phase to a mature, slower growth phase. This life cycle hypothesis is likely to be even more applicable to the case of first-time dividend initiators than to that of firms increasing dividends. Successful dividend-paying firms increase dividends regularly, in some cases every year for periods lasting several decades. Any change in life cycle signaled by a dividend increase is likely to be incremental compared with the signal of changing firm maturity conveyed by a first-time dividend.

The goal of this chapter is to develop and test the idea that the signaling, agency, and risk explanations for dividends have different implications for growth and value stocks in the context of the life cycle hypothesis. For example, the market prices stocks with lower market-to-book (hereafter M/B) ratios for slower growth, implying that investors have already observed substantial evidence of a slowdown, such as decreases in earnings growth or capital spending as the firms' investment opportunity set diminishes. These companies are also less likely to be signaling future growth in profits and more likely to be completing the transition to a period of lower risk.

Conversely, stocks heading into dividend initiation with higher M/B ratios have expectations of faster growth in their prices. If the signaling explanation for dividends has any validity, future growth in profits should be evident among such firms. In addition, the higher M/B firms should invest more in capital expenditure than their lower M/B counterparts before dividend initiation. If capital spending slows after dividend initiation, as suggested by the life cycle hypothesis, these firms should have a more urgent need to begin disgorging excess cash.

Dividends and Signaling

One explanation of why firms pay dividends proposes corporate dividend policy reflects managers' expectations of future firm earnings, a specific application of an economic concept known as signaling, pioneered by Ackerloff (1970) and Spence (1973). Studies such as those of Bhattacharya (1979), Miller and Rock (1985), and John and Williams (1985) incorporate this idea into the finance literature on dividends and information. These theoretical models portray managers as intentionally communicating their positive expectations about future firm earnings via dividend initiations and increases. Dividends may serve as credible signals because rival firms with less positive prospects would have difficulty imitating a sustained dividend payout.

The focus of dividend signaling theories on future earnings is incompatible with Lintner's (1956) view of dividends, which Benartzi, Michaely, and Thaler (1997, p. 1032) call "the best description of the dividend setting process available." Lintner describes how managers conservatively smooth past and current earnings changes into the level of the firm's dividend. His findings indicate that managers believe dividends should be uninterrupted, related to permanent (rather than temporary) increases in profits, and be increased only when the level and stability of earnings make reducing future dividends unlikely.

Decades of evidence including surveys corroborates Lintner's views, including Fama and Babiak (1968), Baker, Farrelly, and Edelman (1985), Baker, Veit, and Powell (2001), and Brav, Graham, Harvey, and Michaely (2005). For example, the Brav et al. survey reveals that, among dividend-paying firms, 94 percent of respondents try to avoid reducing dividends, while 90 percent strive for a smooth dividend. Managers are also reluctant to make dividend decisions that might have to be reversed in the future (78 percent); they strive for consistency with historical dividend policy (84 percent); and they consider the expected stability of future earnings before increasing dividends (72 percent).

Yet empirical support for the signaling explanation of dividends is limited. Although some studies find a positive correlation between dividends and future earnings (Watts, 1973; Gonedes, 1978; Healy and Palepu, 1988; Nissim and Ziv, 2001), a substantial body of research fails to find such a relationship (Benartzi et al., 1997; Dyl and Weigand, 1998; Grullon et al., 2002; Koch and Sun, 2004; Grullon, Michaely, Benartzi, and Thaler, 2005). The general consensus among more recent studies of dividends and earnings is that past and current earnings growth provide the basis for the decision to initiate or raise the firm's dividend but not expected growth in future earnings. This does not mean that dividend payouts do not communicate information to markets. Instead, it means that the information may be more corroborative, confirming that recent earnings changes are permanent rather than predictive of future earnings growth, as suggested by earnings signaling models.

Survey evidence by Brav et al. (2005) also indicates a potential misalignment between signaling theory and managers' attitudes. Although 80 percent of managers in the study believe dividends convey information to investors, only 25 percent of respondents indicate they use dividends to look better than their competitors. Less than 5 percent report deliberately incurring the costs associated with raising external funds and foregoing new investments to distinguish their firm from rivals.

Lintner's (1956) dividend model and subsequent survey evidence suggest managers are conservative in their dividend decisions. Thus, dividend initiation is likely to be one of the most conservative dividend decisions of all, given managers' aversion to reversing dividend decisions, particularly ones that involve reducing or omitting the firm's payout. In addition, signaling models, which propose that managers base dividend decisions on expectations of future earnings growth, may be incompatible with Lintner's more conservative description of the dividend decision process. Therefore, a rising pattern of profits is likely to precede the dividend initiation year, similar to the pattern observed leading up to dividend increases (Benartzi et al., 1997; Grullon et al., 2002). Consistent with the Lintner model, profitability is likely to stabilize around this new, higher level. If there is any validity to the idea that dividend initiation signals higher future earnings, continued earnings growth should occur in high-M/B stocks, which have expectations of faster future growth embedded in their prices.

Agency Explanations for Dividends

Easterbrook (1984) argues that dividends provide investors with a way to monitor managerial behavior. Companies paying out cash that could be used to fund new investment must access capital markets more frequently than firms that do not.

This increased scrutiny by markets adds value as investors monitor managers' investment and operating decisions, which are the real drivers of value in a MM (1961) world. Jensen (1986) builds on Easterbrook's arguments by asserting dividends increase the value of mature firms that generate large cash flows because they limit managers' tendency to waste excess capital on low-return investments. Jensen believes in this free cash flow theory so strongly that he recommends that mature firms maximize their value by paying out all the free cash flow they cannot profitably reinvest. Siegel (2002) expands this line of thought by suggesting that historically high dividend payouts help limit the type of accounting fraud that has recently plagued the United States. He (p. A20) observes that with no Securities and Exchange Commission (SEC) or Financial Accounting Standards Board (FASB) providing oversight in the nineteenth century, investors demanded that firms provide "concrete evidence of real earnings" via regular dividend payments.

Mixed empirical evidence exists about whether dividends are successful in reducing agency costs, as agency costs are not directly observable and therefore are harder to correlate with a firm's dividend policy. A persuasive argument in the literature is the idea that managers and executives should not have access to too much of the firm's free cash flow for too long. In addition to possessing a considerable amount of commonsense appeal, various studies find empirical support for the idea (e.g., Lang and Litzenberger, 1989; Borokhovich, Brunarski, Harman, and Kehr, 2005; DeAngelo et al., 2006). Others fail to support it (e.g., Denis, Denis, and Sarin, 1994; Yoon and Starks, 1995). Evidence from the Brav et al.'s (2005) survey is largely unsupportive of agency and free cash flow motivations for paying dividends. Less than one-third of managers agree that they pay dividends to attract the monitoring benefits associated with higher institutional ownership, and only 13 percent believe paying out excess cash disciplines the firm to make more efficient decisions.

The current study tests for free cash flow, agency, and monitoring effects by observing changes in balance sheet cash, capital expenditure, and debt levels across high- and low-M/B firms. The expectation is that high-M/B firms have higher levels of cash and capital expenditure before dividend initiation. As predicted by the maturity hypothesis, these stocks are also likely to exhibit the greatest buildup and subsequent disgorgement of cash as they transition into a slower-growth phase, particularly if their capital spending slows around the announcement of their initial dividend. Conversely, another expectation is that the lower growth premium assigned to the value stocks implies lower levels of cash and capital expenditure and less of a cycle of cash buildup and disgorgement than the high-M/B stocks. This study also examines the use of debt three years before and after the initial dividend, to test Easterbrook's (1984) claim that firms access capital markets more frequently if they pay dividends. The expectation is that the greatest increase in debt should occur among the high-M/B firms, as they are most likely to be in need of new capital after they begin paying dividends.

Dividends and Risk

Researchers have proposed an association between dividend payments and lower risk. Venkatesh (1989) argues that stock return volatility should decrease after firms begin paying dividends because investors will focus more on the information content of dividend announcements and less on other news events, such as earnings announcements. Dyl and Weigand (1998) maintain that dividends convey information about lower risk more directly to markets, as managers decide to initiate or increase dividends when they believe the firm's earnings stream is not only permanently higher but also more stable and predictable. Grullon et al. (2002) argue that fundamental news about a firm concerns either its cash flows or discount rate, and the lack of support for cash flow signaling implies that the market response to positive dividend events must be a reaction to an expected change in risk.

Widespread empirical support exists for the idea that risk decreases after both dividend initiations and increases. The only question unresolved in the literature is whether the risk decrease involves total risk—both systematic and unsystematic risk—or is confined to only one of these components. Studies reporting a decrease in unsystematic risk after dividend initiation include Venkatesh (1989) and Dyl and Weigand (1998), while those finding a decrease in systematic risk after dividend increases include Bajaj and Vijh (1990), Boehme and Sorescu (2002), and Grullon et al. (2002).

The expectation is that low-M/B firms will have the greatest decrease in risk after dividend initiation. Their relative valuations imply that they have already entered the slower-growth, mature phase that Grullon et al. (2002) describe. As these stocks are unlikely to have as much cash to disgorge as their high-M/B counterparts, dividend initiation probably signals a safer, more stable stream of earnings out of which these firms can maintain regular dividend payments. Higher-M/B firms are less likely to experience a decrease in risk, at least to the same extent as low-M/B firms. These firms present a different profile to the market, announcing an initial dividend while still priced for faster future growth. The prediction is that any decrease in risk for high-M/B firms is probably still several years in the future as they evolve into more stable and predictable firms and resolve any uncertainty that remains regarding their spending plans and intentions to disgorge significant amounts of cash to their shareholders.

SAMPLE SELECTION AND EMPIRICAL METHODOLOGY

The sample for this study includes companies that initiate dividends between 1964 and 2000. Following Michaely et al. (1995), the sample excludes firms resuming dividend payments. The sample includes all NYSE and AMEX firms listed on the Center for Research in Security Prices (CRSP) database that pay four quarterly dividends (CRSP code 1232) for at least two consecutive years. To ensure adequate availability of pre-event data, the company must have been traded on the NYSE or AMEX for three years before the initiation of dividends.

After excluding all closed-end funds, real estate investment trusts (REITs), and American Depository Receipts, the sample consists of only CRSP security types 10 and 11, which also eliminates companies that pay monthly dividends. These initial criteria result in a sample of 766 dividend initiations over the period 1964–2000. The analysis also requires three years of Compustat data before and after the initiation year. The sample excludes 172 firms due to insufficient Compustat data, resulting in a final sample of 594 firms.

Table 24.1   Sample Distribution Firms Initiating Dividends between 1964 and 2000

Panel A. Distribution of Sample by Event Year

Year	Number of Firms Initiating Dividends	Number of Firms with Compustat Data	Year	Number of Firm Initiating Dividends	Number of Firms with Compustat Data
1964	15	4	1983	7	6
1965	32	7	1984	10	6
1966	14	2	1985	8	6
1967	10	9	1986	17	9
1968	9	6	1987	7	6
1969	6	2	1988	21	17
1970	9	7	1989	25	20
1971	13	11	1990	16	15
1972	26	24	1991	11	10
1973	42	34	1992	19	15
1974	35	29	1993	13	9
1975	82	71	1994	9	8
1976	96	78	1995	16	14
1977	73	63	1996	8	8
1978	31	26	1997	16	15
1979	21	16	1998	5	5
1980	13	11	1999	8	6
1981	10	9	2000	5	4
1982	8	6	Total	766	594

Panel B. Distribution of Sample by First Digit of SIC Code

First SIC Digit	Sample (%)	Number of Firms	First SIC Digit	Sample (%)	Number of Firms
1	9.9	59	5	14.0	83
2	15.8	94	6	8.4	50
3	32.5	193	7	8.7	52
4	4.9	29	8	5.7	34

This table presents the sample distribution classified by the event year in panel A and by the first digit of each firm's SIC code in panel B.

Descriptive Statistics

Panel A of Table 24.1 shows the distribution of the sample through time classified by dividend initiations into fiscal year based on the dividend initiation date. There is some clustering of dividend initiations in the period 1972–1978, similar to results reported by Baker and Wurgler (2004). The rate of dividend initiations is relatively low during the 1990s, consistent with Fama and French's (2001) finding that the propensity to pay dividends has been declining over time.

Panel B of Table 24.1 presents the distribution of the sample by the first digit of each firm's SIC code. Not surprisingly, there is clustering in SIC digits 2 and 3,

Table 24.2 Descriptive Statistics of Dividend Initiators

Variables	Year −1	Year 0	Year 1
Return on equity	37.1%	40.6%	39.2%
(before depreciation)	(24.8)	(31.7)	(31.3)
Return on assets	15.3	16.7	16.4
	(8.6)	(8.6)	(9.1)
Profit margin	15.5	16.3	15.6
	(14.8)	(18.5)	(23.2)
Debt to assets	20.2	18.9	19.6
	(17.1)	(16.8)	(16.9)
Market capitalization	$200,563	$298,049	$357,097
(thousands)	(948,843)	(1,990,007)	(2,841,137)
Market-to-book	1.6	1.7	1.8
	(1.5)	(1.8)	(1.9)

This table reports end-of-year mean descriptive statistics for the sample of 594 dividend initiators in years −1, 0, and 1 relative to the year of the dividend initiation announced. Standard deviations appear in parenthesis below the mean value of each metric. Return on equity = operating income before depreciation minus preferred dividends divided by shareholders equity. Return on assets = operating income before depreciation divided by total assets. Profit margin = operating income before depreciation divided by sales. Debt to assets = long-term debt divided by total assets. Market capitalization = end-of-year stock price multiplied by the number of shares of common stock outstanding. Market-to-book = year-end stock price per share divided by the book value of equity per share.

which cover the full spectrum of manufacturing firms. The stable cash flow streams and steady growth characteristic of these types of firms increase the likelihood that they will mature into regular dividend payers.

Table 24.2 reports descriptive statistics for the sample of firms during the year preceding, the year of, and the year after dividend initiation (years −1 to 1). Return on equity, return on assets, and profit margins indicate that the firms are consistently profitable, which is not surprising given the decision to begin regular dividend payouts. The firms use a moderate amount of debt, as indicated by their mean debt-to-assets ratio, and are relatively small, as evidenced by a mean market capitalization of less than half a billion dollars. The average market-to-book ratio is greater than one, suggesting the market ranks these firms' prospects as positive and above average.

Data Items and Definitions

The results include three-day (−1 to 1) cumulative excess stock returns around the dividend announcement, based on a single-index market model:

$$R_{it} = \alpha_i + \beta_i R_{mt} + \varepsilon_{it}. \tag{24.1}$$

Estimating the market model parameters involves using daily data from months −12 to −1 relative to the announcement month based on the CRSP value-weighted index of all NYSE and AMEX stocks. The study also reports cumulative monthly excess returns for the three years before and after the month in which the announcement takes place. The monthly excess returns are based on a three-factor model (Fama and French, 1993), which incorporates factors for size (SMB) and value (HML) in addition to the traditional market-risk premium ($MKTRF$):

$$R_{it} - RF_t = \alpha_i + \beta_i (MKTRF)_t + \lambda_i (SMB)_t + \gamma_i (HML)_t + \varepsilon_{it}. \qquad (24.2)$$

Equation 24.2 provides the basis for estimating pre- and postevent risk metrics. The source of the daily and monthly stock returns is the CRSP database. An online data library provided by French (2006) serves as the source for the time series of risk factors and the monthly risk-free rate.

Compustat serves as the basis for obtaining the following accounting data items for the seven-year period (years −3 to 3) surrounding the dividend initiation announcement year (year 0). These items followed by their annual data item numbers (in parentheses) are total assets (6), operating income before depreciation and amortization (13), book value of common equity (60), long-term debt (9), capital expenditures (128), and cash and short-term investments (1).

Following Barber and Lyon (1996), profitability is measured as return on assets (ROA), using operating income before depreciation and amortization in the numerator:

$$ROA_t = \frac{\text{operating income}_t}{\text{total assets}_t}. \qquad (24.3)$$

Firms' cash and short-term investments are measured relative to total assets:

$$Cash_t = \frac{\text{cash and short-term investments}_t}{\text{total assets}_t}, \qquad (24.4)$$

as are capital expenditures:

$$CapEx_t = \frac{\text{capital expenditures}_t}{\text{total assets}_t}. \qquad (24.5)$$

Firms' use of debt is measured as long-term debt relative to total assets:

$$Debt_t = \frac{\text{long-term debt}_t}{\text{total assets}_t}. \qquad (24.6)$$

EMPIRICAL RESULTS

Table 24.3 reports cumulative daily excess returns for the three-day window surrounding the dividend announcement and cumulative monthly excess returns over months −36 to −1 and 1 to 36 relative to the announcement month. To test whether the mean and median returns are different from zero, a t-statistic and a Wilcoxon rank-sum statistic, respectively, is used. Table 24.3 and the following tables report mean results in panel A and median results in panel B.

For the full sample of firms, the mean three-day excess announcement return equals 3.5 percent, which is significantly different from zero at the 1 percent level.

Table 24.3 Excess Stock Returns before and after Dividend Initiation

Panel A. Mean Excess Returns

	n	Days −1 to 1	Months −36 to −1	Months 1 to 36
Full sample	594	3.50%	10.51%	−3.09%
		(12.53**)	(4.09**)	(−1.08)
M/B Q₁	148	4.92	0.04	13.00
		(7.89**)	(0.01)	(2.55*)
M/B Q₂	149	4.02	0.42	−5.96
		(6.71*)	(0.10)	(−1.12)
M/B Q₃	148	3.09	11.73	−14.38
		(6.57**)	(2.08*)	(−2.38*)
M/B Q₄	149	1.94	29.97	−5.03
		(3.88**)	(5.61**)	(−0.79)

Panel B. Median Excess Returns

	n	Days −1 to 1	Months −36 to −1	Months 1 to 36
Full sample	594	2.13%	4.25%	−5.17%
		(5.87**)	(1.48)	(−0.63)
M/B Q₁	148	3.18	−2.28	12.60
		(3.55**)	(−0.28)	(1.34)
M/B Q₂	149	2.58	−3.87	−7.93
		(3.15**)	(−0.21)	(−0.60)
M/B Q₃	148	2.23	0.35	−21.31
		(2.99**)	(0.65)	(−3.42**)
M/B Q₄	149	0.70	25.92	−2.84
		(1.92)	(2.52*)	(−0.45)

$^{*}p < .05.$ $^{**}p < .01.$ This table reports mean and median cumulative excess returns from days −1 to 1 relative to the announcement (Equation 24.1), and cumulative excess monthly returns from months −36 to 1 and 1 to 36 relative to the announcement (Equation 24.2). Both t-tests (panel A) and Wilcoxon tests (panel B) are used to test if the mean or median returns, respectively, are significantly different from zero. Results are reported for the full sample of 594 dividend initiators and for quartiles sorted by each firm's M/B ratio in year −1 relative to the dividend initiation year (Q₁ = lowest M/B and Q₄ = highest M/B). The t-statistics (panel A) and z-statistics (panel B) are shown in parentheses.

The mean announcement return is comparable to the returns reported by previous research into the effects of dividend initiation. For example, Asquith and Mullins (1983) find two-day abnormal announcement returns of 3.7 percent, Healy and Palepu (1988) report two-day excess returns of 3.9 percent, and Michaely, Thaler, and Womack (1995) find three-day excess returns of 3.4 percent. The market apparently views the announcement of an initial dividend as good news regarding firms' future prospects.

Table 24.3 reports excess returns after sorting firms into equally sized quartiles by their M/B ratios from year −1 relative to the year of dividend initiation (with the lowest M/B firms in quartile 1 and the highest in quartile 4). Following Lang and Litzenberger (1989), M/B ratios serve as a proxy for firms' expected growth opportunities. The mean announcement returns are significant at the 1 percent level for all the quartiles. Returns decline monotonically as firms' M/B ratios rise. Stocks with lower M/B ratios, priced by the market for slower future growth, gain the most when they announce the intention to initiate regular dividend payments to shareholders. This result is also evident in the medians, as reported in panel B. The median announcement return for the high M/B stocks is only 0.70 percent, which is insignificantly different from zero. The findings provide support for the idea that the information content of a dividend initiation announcement is different for stocks priced for value and growth before the dividend event. These results are also consistent with Grullon et al.'s (2002) life cycle hypothesis, as the market places greater value on initial dividends paid by low-M/B, slower-growth firms.

Table 24.3 also reports patterns of longer-term excess returns pre- and postdividend. Firms initiating dividends earn excess returns of 10.5 percent over the three years preceding their first dividend and show no evidence of excess returns over the following three years. The pre-event results are similar to those reported by Michaely et al. (1995), who find that firms initiating dividends outperform by 15 percent in the year preceding the event. The postdividend results are substantially different, however. Michaely et al. report significant three-year postdividend excess returns of 25 percent, whereas our mean postdividend returns over the same period are insignificantly different from zero. The difference in the two studies is due to the use of different methodologies. Michaely et al. use market-adjusted returns, essentially subtracting the CRSP market index return from the average daily portfolio return, whereas the current study computes long-term excess returns using the three-factor Fama and French (1993) model shown as Equation 24.2. Long-term excess returns before and after dividend initiations do not appear nearly as large after adjusting for risk in this manner.

Table 24.3 shows the higher M/B firms, with mean and median cumulative excess returns of 30 percent and 26 percent, respectively, mainly earn positive excess returns preceding dividend initiation. However, the low-M/B stocks are the only quartile of firms that earn significantly positive excess returns on a risk-adjusted basis, equal to 13 percent over the three-year period after their initial dividend. Most of the other M/B quartiles have insignificant postdividend returns, with the exception of the third quartile, which underperforms after dividend initiation with risk-adjusted excess returns of −21 percent over the following three years. Overall, the findings suggest that after initiating dividends, firms settle into periods of steady performance, earning returns that are appropriate for their level of risk, consistent with the life cycle hypothesis.

Changes in Return on Assets

Table 24.4 reports mean and median return on assets (Equation 24.3) before and after dividend initiation for the full sample of firms and the M/B quartiles. The study tests whether the mean and median metrics from year −3 are significantly different from year 0 and whether the metrics from year 0 are significantly different from year 3, using a difference-between-the-means t-statistic and a nonparametric Mann-Whitney statistic, respectively.

In both means and medians, ROA for the full sample of firms increases significantly from years −3 to 0 and then exhibits a significant decline back to its pre-event level by year 3. The pattern is virtually identical to that reported by

Table 24.4   Return on Assets before and after Dividend Initiation

Panel A. Mean Return on Assets

	n	−3	−2	−1	0	1	2	3
Full sample	594	14.23%	14.11%	15.33%	16.72% (5.34**)	16.37%	15.22%	14.33% (−5.15**)
M/B Q$_1$	148	11.62	11.32	12.06	14.04 (3.99**)	14.20	13.43	12.47 (−3.51**)
M/B Q$_2$	149	13.86	12.80	14.30	16.27 (3.59**)	15.22	14.12	13.76 (−4.07**)
M/B Q$_3$	148	14.94	14.61	16.15	17.51 (3.33**)	17.17	15.59	14.45 (−3.75**)
M/B Q$_4$	149	17.56	19.63	20.93	20.16 (1.91)	19.78	18.30	16.85 (−1.76)

Panel B. Median Return on Assets

	n	−3	−2	−1	0	1	2	3
Full sample	594	13.50%	13.66%	14.70%	16.19% (6.94**)	15.71%	14.77%	14.17% (5.64**)
M/B Q$_1$	148	11.08	11.51	12.02	13.36 (4.09**)	14.26	13.10	13.04 (1.61)
M/B Q$_2$	149	13.32	13.20	14.20	16.09 (3.76**)	14.68	13.78	14.17 (3.78**)
M/B Q$_3$	148	14.49	15.02	15.70	16.79 (3.72**)	17.07	15.96	14.26 (3.69**)
M/B Q$_4$	149	15.65	17.86	19.80	20.42 (2.24*)	18.10	17.50	15.93 (3.65**)

$^*p < .05.$ $^{**}p < .01.$ This table reports mean and median return on assets (ROA) from years −3 to 3 relative to the year in which firms announce an initial dividend. The first reported t-statistic (panel A) and Mann-Whitney statistic test (panel B) test whether the mean or median ROA in year −3 is significantly different from year 0; the second reported statistics test if the mean or median ROA in year 0 is significantly different from year 3. Results are reported for the full sample of 594 dividend initiators and for quartiles sorted by each firm's M/B ratio in year −1 relative to the dividend initiation year (Q$_1$ = lowest M/B and Q$_4$ = highest M/B). The t-statistics (panel A) and z-statistics (panel B) are shown in parentheses.

Grullon et al. (2002) before and after dividend increases. The results indicate that the announcement of dividend initiation does not signal higher future profitability for firms and confirm Lintner's (1956) description of the conservative approach to dividend policy employed by managers, who wait to observe a permanently higher level of profitability before deciding to begin paying dividends.

    Mean and median ROA increases monotonically with firms' M/B ratios in years −3, 0, and 3. All quartiles exhibit the same pattern of increasing and decreasing ROA, although for the highest-M/B quartile the changes are only significant in medians. The results also show that the spread in profitability between the high- and low-M/B quartiles compresses from years −3 to 3. In other words, value stocks' mean and median ROA drifts higher, while growth stocks' ROA drifts lower. After

Table 24.5 Cash and Short-Term Investments before and after Dividend Initiation

Panel A. Mean Cash + Short-Term Investments to Total Assets

	n	−3	−2	−1	0	1	2	3
Full sample	594	10.38%	10.29%	10.96%	12.07% (3.56**)	10.69%	10.42%	10.01% (−3.60**)
M/B Q$_1$	148	6.86	6.79	7.39	8.24 (2.43**)	7.92	8.57	8.11 (−1.36)
M/B Q$_2$	149	10.08	10.26	10.21	12.00 (1.97*)	10.24	10.19	10.22 (−2.02*)
M/B Q$_3$	148	11.34	10.44	11.76	12.53 (1.57)	11.62	10.14	9.79 (−2.62**)
M/B Q$_4$	149	14.67	15.51	16.62	17.11 (1.65)	13.75	13.25	12.07 (−3.25**)

Panel B. Median Cash + Short-Term Investments to Total Assets

	n	−3	−2	−1	0	1	2	3
Full sample	594	6.26%	6.80%	6.92%	7.75% (4.46**)	6.63%	6.20%	5.78% (4.86**)
M/B Q$_1$	148	4.60	5.11	5.47	5.92 (3.03**)	5.12	5.28	4.99 (3.59**)
M/B Q$_2$	149	5.92	5.98	6.56	8.63 (2.78**)	6.30	5.35	4.88 (3.98**)
M/B Q$_3$	148	6.56	6.88	7.75	7.87 (2.00*)	7.44	6.23	5.94 (3.28**)
M/B Q$_4$	149	10.37	10.01	12.13	11.17 (1.52)	8.00	8.33	7.63 (3.71**)

*$p < .05$. **$p < .01$. This table reports the mean and median ratio of cash plus short-term investments to total assets from years −3 to 3 relative to the year in which firms announce an initial dividend. The first reported t-statistic (panel A) and Mann-Whitney statistic (panel B) test whether the mean or median cash + ST investments to total assets in year −3 is significantly different from year 0; the second reported statistics test if the mean or median cash + ST investments to total assets in year 0 is significantly different from year 3. Results are reported for the full sample of 594 dividend initiators and for quartiles sorted by each firm's M/B ratio in year −1 relative to the dividend initiation year (Q_1 = lowest M/B and Q_4 = highest M/B). The t-statistics (panel A) and z-statistics (panel B) are shown in parentheses.

dividend initiation, the extreme quartiles of stocks begin to resemble one another, once again consistent with the life cycle hypothesis. This pattern is also evident in other variables, as shown in the following tables.

Changes in Cash and Short-Term Investments

Table 24.5 reports changes in cash and short-term investments (Equation 24.4) before and after dividend initiation. The results show that firms' cash holdings and short-term investments increase from years −3 to 0 and decrease from years 0 to 3. The findings are significant for the full sample of firms in both means and medians and for most of the M/B quartiles, although the value stocks have less cash to disgorge than the growth stocks, and their drawdown of cash is only significant in medians.

Conversely, the buildup of cash is not significant for the highest-M/B firms, but as such firms already hold higher levels of cash predividend, their disgorgement of cash over years 0 to 3 is statistically significant. This provides further evidence that high- and low-M/B firms are in different life cycle stages as early as three years before they begin paying dividends. In addition to the profitability of the value stocks being lower than that of the growth stocks (Table 24.4), the value stocks hold half as much cash and short-term investments relative to total assets three years before dividend initiation. Moreover, as was the case for ROA, the results show that the differences are substantially reduced by the third year following an initial dividend. In both means and medians, the spread in the cash holdings of the growth stocks compresses closer to that of the value stocks. This further supports the idea that the low-M/B firms have fully transitioned into their mature phase before dividend initiation, and the growth stocks are just beginning this transition at the time of their initial dividend.

Changes in Capital Expenditure

Table 24.6 reports changes in capital expenditure (Equation 24.5) before and after dividend initiation. The findings show little change in capital expenditure for the full sample of firms. Stocks with higher M/B ratios have generally higher capital expenditures in years −3 and 0 relative to the event. Although none of the changes in the quartiles over time is statistically significant, the evidence shows the same compression in the spread across the high- and low-M/B quartiles as shown for the ROA and balance sheet cash. Starting in year −3 the high-M/B firms spend 3 percent to 4 percent more relative to total assets than do low-M/B firms, but by year 3 the spread is about 1 percent. This further supports the idea that the firms are at different life cycle stages before initiating dividends. Within three years after dividend initiation, firms that were formerly priced for faster growth exhibit the same reduction in capital spending as the lower-M/B firms.

Changes in Debt

This study tests Easterbrook's (1984) idea that firms paying dividends benefit from the increased monitoring that results from accessing capital markets more frequently. The conjecture is that firms with higher M/B ratios are more likely to need additional capital as they attempt to keep up with the higher growth expectations reflected in their stock prices. Table 24.7 reports the ratio of long-term debt to total assets (Equation 24.6) for all firms initiating dividends and for the M/B quartiles.

The evidence indicates no change in the overall use of debt for the full sample of firms, although the high-M/B firms' debt/assets ratio drifts downward from years −3 to 0 and then increases significantly from years 0 to 3. This is the only quartile of firms exhibiting a significant increase in the use of debt after initial dividend payments, which further supports the idea that the firms' growth prospects have not diminished to the same extent as lower-M/B firms already priced for slower growth.

Table 24.6 Capital Expenditure before and after Dividend Initiation

Panel A. Mean Capital Expenditure to Total Assets

	n	−3	−2	−1	0	1	2	3
Full sample	594	9.35%	8.30%	7.94%	8.03% (−0.91)	8.71%	8.84%	8.31% (0.16)
M/B Q$_1$	148	7.47	6.28	5.76	5.75 (−1.41)	6.76	7.85	7.05 (0.38)
M/B Q$_2$	149	8.68	7.33	7.17	7.41 (−0.94)	8.47	8.67	8.54 (0.37)
M/B Q$_3$	148	10.48	10.02	9.36	9.85 (−0.13)	9.75	9.83	9.32 (−1.04)
M/B Q$_4$	149	11.60	10.19	10.22	9.52 (−0.33)	10.18	8.97	8.19 (−0.22)

Panel B. Median Capital Expenditure to Total Assets

	n	−3	−2	−1	0	1	2	3
Full sample	594	6.05%	5.11%	5.07%	5.62% (1.02)	6.04%	6.41%	5.65% (1.06)
M/B Q$_1$	148	4.78	3.93	4.30	4.63 (0.12)	4.95	5.62	4.87 (1.30)
M/B Q$_2$	149	5.30	5.11	4.82	5.51 (0.14)	5.96	6.34	6.05 (0.35)
M/B Q$_3$	148	7.74	6.57	6.32	6.61 (0.74)	6.51	7.32	6.23 (1.48)
M/B Q$_4$	149	7.82	5.14	6.31	6.64 (1.17)	7.32	6.69	5.44 (1.29)

$^*p < .05.$ $^{**}p < .01.$ This table reports the mean and median ratio of capital expenditure to total assets from years −3 to 3 relative to the year in which firms announce an initial dividend. The first reported t-statistic (panel A) and Mann-Whitney statistic (panel B) test whether the mean or median capital expenditure to total assets in year −3 is significantly different from year 0; the second reported statistics test whether the mean or median capital expenditure to total assets in year 0 is significantly different from year 3. Results are reported for the full sample of 594 dividend initiators and for quartiles sorted by each firm's M/B ratio in year −1 relative to the dividend initiation year (Q$_1$ = lowest M/B and Q$_4$ = highest M/B). The t-statistics (panel A) and z-statistics (panel B) are shown in parentheses.

Changes in Risk

Table 24.8 reports changes in risk before and after firms begin paying dividends. The study compares the total volatility of monthly returns over months −36 to −1 to months 1 to 36, as well as the size (*SMB*), value (*HML*), and market-risk premium (*MKTRF*) factor loadings from Equation 24.2. For the full sample, both the mean and median total risk decline significantly in the postdividend period. The largest decrease in total risk accrues to the value quartiles. Yet total risk remains unchanged for the high-M/B quartile.

Regarding the Fama-French (1993) risk factors, for the full sample of firms, the *SMB* risk factor loading is lower postdividend initiation in both the means and medians. The results also reveal a significant decrease in the mean *MKTRF* risk

Table 24.7 Long-Term Debt to Total Assets before and after Dividend Initiation

Panel A. Mean Long-Term Debt to Total Assets

	n	−3	−2	−1	0	1	2	3
Full sample	594	21.59%	21.41%	20.22%	18.87% (−0.90)	19.56%	20.43%	21.28% (1.31)
M/B Q$_1$	148	22.60	22.05	21.49	21.11 (−0.21)	22.12	21.78	22.50 (0.98)
M/B Q$_2$	149	20.40	19.69	18.73	17.46 (−0.82)	18.76	19.99	20.81 (0.71)
M/B Q$_3$	148	23.06	22.85	21.82	19.97 (−0.59)	20.03	21.26	21.33 (0.07)
M/B Q$_4$	149	19.73	20.87	17.96	16.05 (−0.62)	16.54	18.34	20.45 (2.87**)

Panel B. Median Long-Term Debt to Total Assets

	n	−3	−2	−1	0	1	2	3
Full sample	594	19.00%	19.48%	17.47%	16.06% (0.10)	16.40%	18.57%	18.76% (1.01)
M/B Q$_1$	148	20.53	20.31	19.46	18.96 (0.42)	19.11	19.67	21.30 (1.41)
M/B Q$_2$	149	17.21	16.27	16.50	14.89 (0.25)	16.64	17.85	18.64 (0.47)
M/B Q$_3$	148	21.10	20.70	19.48	17.55 (0.12)	17.52	19.27	17.77 (0.25)
M/B Q$_4$	149	13.41	16.91	11.99	10.54 (0.32)	10.18	17.14	15.80 (3.40**)

*$p < .05$. **$p < .01$. This table reports the mean and median ratio of long-term debt to total assets from years −3 to 3 relative to the year in which firms announce an initial dividend. The first reported t-statistic (panel A) and Mann-Whitney statistic (panel B) test whether the mean or median debt to total assets in year −3 is significantly different from year 0; the second reported statistics test if the mean or median debt to total assets in year 0 is significantly different from year 3. Results are reported for the full sample of 594 dividend initiators and for quartiles sorted by each firm's M/B ratio in year −1 relative to the dividend initiation year (Q$_1$ = lowest M/B and Q$_4$ = highest M/B). The t-statistics (panel A) and z-statistics (panel B) are shown in parentheses.

factor. Systematic risk declines after the initiation of regular cash dividends. Firms in the low-M/B quartile experience the greatest risk decrease, with significant declines in their *MKTRF*, *SMB*, and *HML* factor loadings. There is no change in any of the systematic risk factors for the highest-M/B quartile. This provides additional support for the idea that leading up to dividend initiation the low-M/B firms are further along in the transition into their mature phase than the high-M/B firms.

Excess Returns and Changes in Risk and Return on Assets

This section provides the results of the multivariate regression used to test whether there is a relationship between the market reaction to dividend initiation and the changes in risk and profitability reported in previous sections. Following Grullon

Table 24.8 Risk before and after Dividend Initiation

Panel A. Changes in Mean Risk Measures

	σ pre	σ post	SMB pre	SMB post	HML pre	HML post	MKTRF pre	MKTRF post
Full sample	12.84%	11.69% (−4.99**)	1.25	1.09 (−2.47*)	0.23	0.16 (−1.13)	1.15	1.06 (−2.07*)
M/B Q₁	13.91	11.46 (−6.06**)	1.55	1.25 (−2.57*)	0.70	0.47 (−2.42*)	1.22	1.04 (−2.36*)
M/B Q₂	12.47	11.42 (−2.28*)	1.27	1.11 (−1.17)	0.28	0.29 (0.14)	1.04	1.06 (0.09)
M/B Q₃	12.79	11.64 (−2.02*)	1.10	0.96 (−2.28*)	0.14	−0.10 (−0.71)	1.21	1.11 (−0.20)
M/B Q₄	12.18	12.25 (0.87)	1.07	1.05 (−0.30)	−0.19	−0.02 (1.23)	1.13	1.06 (−0.73)

Panel B. Changes in Median Risk Measures

	σ pre	σ post	SMB pre	SMB post	HML pre	HML post	MKTRF pre	MKTRF post
Full sample	12.16%	11.02% (5.20**)	1.19	1.03 (2.42*)	0.23	0.12 (0.95)	1.12	1.04 (1.70)
M/B Q₁	13.37	11.02% (5.66**)	1.50	1.28 (2.61*)	0.72	0.48 (2.95**)	1.13	1.07 (1.53)
M/B Q₂	12.10	11.00% (1.79)	1.17	1.05 (0.84)	0.28	0.20 (0.27)	1.03	1.03 (0.14)
M/B Q₃	11.92	11.05% (1.77)	1.09	0.88 (1.79)	0.04	−0.09 (−0.21)	1.18	1.03 (0.15)
M/B Q₄	11.67	11.10% (1.61)	1.00	0.96 (1.34)	−0.41	−0.05 (1.95)	1.09	1.04 (0.35)

*$p < .05$. **$p < .01$. This table reports mean and median risk measures for the 36 months preceding and following the month in which firms announce an initial dividend. The t-statistics (panel A) and Mann-Whitney statistics (panel B) test whether the predividend mean or median risk measures (months −36 to 1) are different from in the postdividend period (months 1 to 36). Results are reported for the full sample of 594 dividend initiators and for quartiles sorted by each firm's M/B ratio in year −1 relative to the dividend initiation year (Q_1 = lowest M/B and Q_4 = highest M/B). The t-statistics (panel A) and z-statistics (panel B) are shown in parentheses.

et al. (2002), the study investigates the relationship between long-term returns after the dividend initiation announcement and changes in the variables presented previously. The study uses the functional form depicted as Equation 24.7:

$$ExRetPost_i = a + b_0 \Delta SMB_i + \sum\nolimits_{j=1}^{4} b_j \left(Q_j \times \Delta SMB_i \right) + c_0 \Delta HML_i$$

$$+ \sum\nolimits_{j=1}^{4} c_j \left(Q_j \times \Delta HML_i \right) + d_0 \Delta MKTRF_i$$

$$+ \sum\nolimits_{j=1}^{4} d_j \left(Q_j \times \Delta MKTRF_i \right) + e_0 \Delta ROA_i$$

$$+ \sum\nolimits_{j=1}^{4} e_j \left(Q_j \times \Delta ROA_i \right) + \varepsilon_i. \tag{24.7}$$

This equation models monthly cumulative excess returns from months 1 to 36 after the dividend announcement as a function of changes in systematic risk factors and the change in ROA shown previously. Each dependent variable also includes 0, 1 interactive indicator variables for the individual M/B quartile each firm occupies in our sample (the Q in Equation 24.7, designating quartiles 1, 2, and 4, with quartile 3 omitted to avoid the problem of perfect collinearity). This allows testing if the regression coefficients for each dependent variable are different for the high- and low-M/B quartiles (Q_1 vs. Q_4). Equation 24.7 variable definitions are as follows:

ExRetPost_i = the monthly cumulative excess return for firm i over months 1 to 36 (based on the three-factor model shown as Equation 24.2 following the month in which the firm announces dividend initiation.

ΔSMB_i = the change in the SMB risk factor loading for firm i, measured as the SMB coefficient from months 1 to 36 minus the SMB coefficient from months -36 to -1.

ΔHML_i = the change in the HML risk factor loading for firm i, measured as the HML coefficient from months 1 to 36 minus the HML coefficient from months -36 to -1.

$\Delta MKTRF_i$ = the change in the $MKTRF$ risk factor loading for firm i, measured as the $MKTRF$ coefficient from months 1 to 36 minus the $MKTRF$ coefficient from months -36 to -1.

ΔROA_i = the change in ROA for firm i, measured as ROA in year 3 minus ROA in year 0.

Q_j = a 0, 1 indicator variable that equals 1 if a firm in the sample is classified in M/B quartile 1, 2, or 4, and 0 otherwise.

Table 24.9 reports the results of the regression, which has an adjusted R^2 of 13.6 percent. The regression coefficient on the postdividend ΔSMB variable is positive and significant at the 5 percent level. This, of course, is the average coefficient for the full sample—the coefficient for quartiles 1, 2, and 4 are found by summing the ΔSMB coefficient with the coefficient on the interactive indicator variable for each quartile. The coefficients for each quartile suggest the relationship between postevent excess returns and the change in the ΔSMB risk factor is different, depending on firms' M/B ratios. The coefficients for quartiles 1, 2, and 4 are -0.059, 0.068, and 0.111, respectively. Moreover, the F-statistic (8.14) shows that quartile 1's coefficient is significantly lower than quartile 4's at the 1 percent level. Recall that the SMB risk factor declines after dividend initiation for all the quartiles. The negative coefficient for the low-M/B quartile therefore suggests that, controlling for changes in other risk factors and ROA, the reduction in these stocks' size premium positively influences postevent returns. The positive coefficient for the higher-M/B stocks suggests the lack of a significant decrease in the SMB risk factor contributes to their negative postevent returns. This is consistent with the life cycle idea that high- and low-M/B firms initiate dividends for different reasons, with the low-M/B firms exhibiting a decline in their SMB size premium risk factor.

Table 24.9 also shows the average coefficient on the ΔHML variable is negative and significant at the 5 percent level. Adding the indicator variables' coefficients to this value shows the coefficient becomes more negative for quartiles 1, 2, and 4, with values of -0.093, -0.150, and -0.194, respectively. There is a small difference

Table 24.9   Regressions of Excess Returns on Changes in Risk and Return on Assets

Variable	Regression Coefficient	t-statistic	F-statistic ($Q_1 = Q_4$)
Intercept	0.01881	0.60	
ΔSMB	0.08104	2.03*	
$Q_1 \times \Delta$SMB	−0.14017	−2.48*	
$Q_2 \times \Delta$SMB	−0.01352	−0.24	
$Q_4 \times \Delta$SMB	0.03034	0.51	8.14**
ΔHML	−0.08718	−2.32*	
$Q_1 \times \Delta$HML	−0.00618	−0.11	
$Q_2 \times \Delta$HML	−0.06238	−1.15	
$Q_4 \times \Delta$HML	−0.10717	−1.98*	3.20
ΔMKTRF	0.22117	3.47**	
$Q_1 \times \Delta$MKTRF	−0.23698	−2.55*	
$Q_2 \times \Delta$MKTRF	0.00181	0.02	
$Q_4 \times \Delta$MKTRF	−0.01406	−0.16	5.74*
ΔROA	2.26686	4.01**	
$Q_1 \times \Delta$ROA	−2.04421	−2.54*	
$Q_2 \times \Delta$ROA	−0.95201	−1.23	
$Q_4 \times \Delta$ROA	0.11461	0.15	8.09**

*$p < .05$. **$p < .01$. This table reports the regression of cumulative excess returns for the three years following dividend initiation on the change in systematic risk factors and ROA over the same three-year period. The regressions include interactive 0, 1 indicator variables that equal 1 if the firm is in M/B quartile 1, 2, or 4, and 0 otherwise (Q_1 = lowest M/B and Q_4 = highest M/B; quartile 3 is omitted to avoid perfect collinearity). The t-statistics test whether the regression coefficients are significantly different from 0, and the F-statistics test whether the regression coefficient on the first quartile interactive indicator variable is different from the coefficient on the fourth quartile interactive indicator variable.

in how the change in the *HML* value factor loading affects postevent returns between quartiles 1 and 4; the p-value for the F-statistic (3.20) is 0.07, just outside the conventional level for statistical significance, but the t-statistic on quartile 4's indicator variable is significant at the 5 percent level, confirming that the returns of the extreme value and growth quartiles exhibit different responses to this variable. Panels A and B of Table 24.8 show that only stocks in the high-M/B quartile exhibit an increase in the *HML* risk factor. The significantly negative coefficient in the regression indicates the rise in this risk factor also contributes to the negative post-event excess returns earned by the high-M/B firms.

The regression coefficient on the $\Delta MKTRF$ variable is positive and statistically significant at the 1 percent level, indicating decreases in this variable are associated with lower postevent returns. A different relationship exists between returns and $\Delta MKTRF$ across the quartiles ($F = 5.74$, significant at the 1 percent level). The coefficients for quartiles 1, 2, and 4 are −0.016, 0.223, and 0.207, respectively, indicating that the decline in the *MKTRF* risk factor positively influences the low-M/B quartile's postevent returns, while changes in this factor negatively influence the higher-M/B firms' postevent returns. Controlling for changes in ROA, the results show that value stocks' higher excess returns after dividend initiation are positively influenced by declines in systematic risk, while the minimal decrease in risk displayed by the high-M/B stocks contributes to their negative excess returns.

The coefficient on ΔROA is positive and significant at the 1 percent level, with the extreme M/B quartiles displaying a different relationship between postevent returns and changes in profitability ($F = 8.09$, significant at the 1 percent level). The coefficients on quartiles 1, 2, and 4 are 0.227, 1.315, and 2.381, respectively. As ROA generally declines after dividend initiation, the positive slope coefficient indicates that higher ROA positively influences postevent returns. The difference in the slope coefficients further suggests the postdividend returns of high-M/B firms are more sensitive to the influence of higher profitability, which is not surprising given their larger ROA following the initiation of dividends. The findings are once again consistent with the life cycle hypothesis, as the postdividend returns of the high-M/B stocks are positively influenced by their higher profitability, while the returns of the low-M/B stocks display less sensitivity to changes in profits.

CONCLUSIONS

This chapter investigates dividend initiation and firms' motivations for paying regular cash dividends to shareholders, allowing for interaction among the various dividend theories and taking individual firm characteristics into account. The chapter focuses on three established explanations for dividends—signaling, agency costs, and risk—and shows how these explanations are best understood in the context of Grullon et al.'s (2002) life cycle hypothesis, which proposes dividend initiation conveys information about firms' transition from a faster growth phase to a slower growth, mature phase. Evidence shows that firms initiating dividends are experiencing a change in their life cycles, but the changes are subtly different depending on whether a firm has fully transitioned into its mature phase at the time of the event (low M/B) or begins showing signs of slowing down following the event (high M/B).

The results reveal that low-M/B stocks display the strongest price reaction to a dividend initiation announcement, with excess announcement returns declining monotonically for higher-M/B firms, consistent with the life cycle hypothesis. The evidence shows that all firms' profitability (ROA) rises over the three years preceding the initiation of dividends but declines back to its pre-event level by year 3. This is unsupportive of signaling theory but is consistent with the slowdown in growth predicted by the life cycle hypothesis. High-M/B stocks hold higher levels of cash and engage in greater capital spending than do low-M/B stocks and disgorge substantially more of this cash after dividend initiation. In addition, the spread among the profitability, cash levels, and capital expenditures of the high- and low-M/B firms compresses after dividend initiation. This is driven mainly by a slowdown in the high-M/B firms, which more closely resembles that of the low-M/B firms by the third year following the event.

Low-M/B stocks exhibit significant decreases in their market, size, and value risk-factor loadings after dividend initiation, while high-M/B stocks display no change in systematic risk, which provides further support for the life cycle hypothesis. Moreover, the postdividend excess returns earned by low-M/B firms are related to the decrease in risk, while the returns of the high-M/B firms are related to their greater profitability after dividend initiation. Overall, there is strong support for the idea that firms initiating dividends are entering a more mature life cycle phase, with low-M/B firms having completed most of this transition predividend, and high-M/B firms just beginning to show signs of slowing down.

REFERENCES

Ackerloff, George. 1970. "The Market for Lemons: Quality Uncertainty and the Market Mechanism." *Quarterly Journal of Economics* 84:3, 488–500.

Ang, James S. 1987. "Do Dividends Matter? A Review of Corporate Dividend Theories and Evidence." Monograph Series in Finance and Economics. New York: Salomon Brothers Center for the Study of Financial Institutions and the Graduate School of Business Administration, New York University.

Asquith, Paul, and David W. Mullins. 1983. "The Impact of Initiating Dividend Payments on Shareholders' Wealth." *Journal of Business* 56:1, 77–96.

Bajaj, Mukesh B., and Anand M. Vijh. 1990. "Dividend Clienteles and the Information Content of Dividend Changes." *Journal of Financial Economics* 26:2, 193–219.

Baker, H. Kent, Gail E. Farrelly, and Richard B. Edelman. 1985. "A Survey of Management Views on Dividend Policy." *Financial Management* 14:3, 78–84.

Baker, H. Kent, Gary E. Powell, and E. Theodore Veit. 2002. "Revisiting the Dividend Puzzle: Do All the Pieces Now Fit?" *Review of Financial Economics* 11:4, 241–261.

Baker, H. Kent, E. Theodore Veit, and Gary E. Powell. 2001. "Factors Influencing Dividend Policy Decisions of Nasdaq." *Financial Review* 38:3, 19–38.

Baker, Malcolm, and Jeffrey Wurgler. 2004. "A Catering Theory of Dividends." *Journal of Finance* 59:3, 1125–1165.

Barber, Brad M., and John D. Lyon. 1996. "Detecting Abnormal Operating Performance: The Empirical Power and Specification of Test Statistics." *Journal of Financial Economics* 41:3, 359–399.

Benartzi, Shlomo, Roni Michaely, and Richard H. Thaler. 1997. "Do Changes in Dividends Signal the Future or the Past?" *Journal of Finance* 52:3, 1007–1034.

Bhattacharya, Sudipto. 1979. "Imperfect Information, Dividend Policy, and 'the Bird in the Hand' Fallacy." *Bell Journal of Economics* 10:1, 259–270.

Black, Fischer. 1976. "The Dividend Puzzle." *Journal of Portfolio Management* 2:2, 5–8.

Boehme, Rodney D., and Sorin M. Sorescu. 2002. "The Long-Run Performance Following Dividend Initiations and Resumptions: Underreaction or Product of Chance?" *Journal of Finance* 57:2, 871–900.

Borokhovich, Kenneth A., Kelly R. Brunarski, Yvette S. Harman, and James B. Kehr. 2005. "Dividends, Corporate Monitors and Agency Costs." *Financial Review* 40:1, 37–65.

Brav, Alon, John Graham, Campbell Harvey, and Roni Michaely. 2005. "Payout Policy in the 21st Century." *Journal of Financial Economics* 77:3, 483–527.

Chiang, Kevin, George M. Frankfurter, Arman Kosedag, and Bob G. Wood, Jr. 2006. "The Perception of Dividends by Professional Investors." *Managerial Finance* 32:1, 60–81.

DeAngelo, Harry, and Linda DeAngelo. 2006. "The Irrelevance of the MM Dividend Irrelevance Theorem." *Journal of Financial Economics* 79:2, 293–315.

DeAngelo, Harry, Linda DeAngelo, and René Stulz. 2006. "Dividend Policy and the Earned/Contributed Capital Mix: A Test of the Life-Cycle Theory." *Journal of Financial Economics* 81:2, 227–254.

Denis, Diane J., David J. Denis, and Atulya Sarin. 1994. "The Information Content of Dividend Changes: Cash Flow Signaling, Overinvestment and Dividend Clienteles." *Journal of Financial and Quantitative Analysis* 29:4, 567–587.

Dyl, Edward A., and Robert A. Weigand. 1998. "The Information Content of Dividend Initiations: Additional Evidence." *Financial Management* 27:3, 27–35.

Easterbrook, Frank. 1984. "Two Agency-Cost Explanations of Dividends." *American Economic Review* 74:4, 650–659.

Fama, Eugene F., and Harvey Babiak. 1968. "Dividend Policy: An Empirical Analysis." *Journal of the American Statistical Association* 63:324, 1132–1161.

Fama, Eugene F., and Kenneth R. French. 1993. "Common Risk Factors in the Returns on Stocks and Bonds." *Journal of Financial Economics* 33:1, 3–56.

Fama, Eugene F., and Kenneth R. French. 2001. "Disappearing Dividends: Changing Firm Characteristics or Lower Propensity to Pay?" *Journal of Financial Economics* 60:1, 3–43.

French, Kenneth R. 2006. *Data Library.* http://mba.tuck.dartmouth.edu/pages/faculty/ken.french/data_library.html.

Gonedes, Nicholas. 1978. "Corporate Signaling, External Accounting, and Capital Market Equilibrium: Evidence on Dividends, Income, and Extraordinary Items." *Journal of Accounting Research* 16:1, 26–79.

Gordon, Myron. 1959. "Earnings and Stock Prices." *Review of Economics and Statistics* 41:2, 99–105.

Graham, Benjamin, and David Dodd. 1934. *Security Analysis.* New York: McGraw-Hill.

Grullon, Gustavo, Roni Michaely, Schlomo Benartzi, and Richard Thaler. 2005. "Dividend Changes Do Not Signal Changes in Future Profitability." *Journal of Business* 78:5, 1659–1682.

Grullon, Gustavo, Roni Michaely, and Bhaskaran Swaminathan. 2002. "Are Dividend Changes a Sign of Firm Maturity?" *Journal of Business* 75:3, 387–424.

Healy, Paul M., and Krishna G. Palepu. 1988. "Earnings Information Conveyed by Dividend Initiations and Omissions." *Journal of Financial Economics* 21:2, 149–175.

Jensen, Michael C. 1986. "Agency Costs of Free Cash Flow, Corporate Finance, and Takeovers." *American Economic Review* 76:2, 323–329.

John, Kose, and John Williams. 1985. "Dividends, Dilution, and Taxes: A Signaling Equilibrium." *Journal of Finance* 40:4, 1053–1070.

Koch, Adam S., and Amy X. Sun. 2004. "Dividend Changes and the Persistence of Past Earnings Changes." *Journal of Finance* 59:5, 2093–2116.

Lang, Larry H. P., and Robert H. Litzenberger. 1989. "Dividend Announcements: Cash Flow Signaling vs. Free Cash Flow Hypothesis." *Journal of Financial Economics* 24:1, 181–192.

Lease, Ronald, Kose John, Avner Kalay, Uri Lowenstein, and Oded Sarig. 2000. *Dividend Policy: Its Impact on Firm Value.* Boston: Harvard Business School Press.

Lintner, John. 1956. "Distribution of Income of Corporations among Dividends, Retained Earnings and Taxes." *American Economic Review* 46:2, 97–113.

Michaely, Roni, Richard H. Thaler, and Kent L. Womack. 1995. "Price Reactions to Dividend Initiations and Omissions: Overreaction or Drift?" *Journal of Finance* 50:2, 573–608.

Miller, Merton, and Franco Modigliani. 1961. "Dividend Policy, Growth, and the Valuation of Shares." *Journal of Business* 34:4, 411–433.

Miller, Merton, and Kevin Rock. 1985. "Dividend Policy under Asymmetric Information." *Journal of Finance* 40:4, 1031–1052.

Nissim, Doron, and Amir Ziv. 2001. "Dividend Changes and Future Profitability." *Journal of Finance* 56:6, 2111–2133.

Siegel, Jeremy J. 2002. "The Dividend Deficit." *Wall Street Journal,* February 13, A20.

Spence, Michael. 1973. "Job Market Signaling." *Quarterly Journal of Economics* 87:3, 355–374.

Venkatesh, P. C. 1989. "The Impact of Dividend Initiation on the Information Content of Earnings Announcements and Returns Volatility." *Journal of Business* 62:2, 175–197.

Watts, Ross. 1973. "The Information Content of Dividends." *Journal of Business* 46:2, 191–211.

Williams, John Burr. 1938. *The Theory of Investment Value.* Cambridge, MA: Harvard University Press.

Yoon, Pyung Sig, and Laura T. Starks. 1995. "Signaling, Investment Opportunities, and Dividend Announcements." *Review of Financial Studies* 8:4, 995–101.

ABOUT THE AUTHORS

Neil Fargher, CPA, is a professor of accounting at The Australian National University in Canberra, Australia. His research interests include financial accounting and auditing with a particular interest in how risk is measured, how risk is communicated to the market, and how investors respond to such communication. Fargher's research relates to issues involving audit qualifications, leverage, derivatives, fair value accounting, and initial public offerings. Being fluent in both IFRS and U.S. GAAP and associated regulations, his work increasingly covers regulatory issues in Australian, U.S., and international markets. Before joining The Australian National University, Fargher taught at the University of New South Wales and the University of Oregon and has also taught as a guest at the University of Illinois and Guangzhou University. He had 10 years of experience in corporate accounting and information systems before undertaking a doctorate at the University of Arizona.

Robert A. Weigand is a professor of finance and Brenneman Professor of Business Strategy at Washburn University in Topeka, Kansas. Previously, he was on the faculties of Texas A&M University, the University of Colorado, and the University of South Florida. His research interests include dividend policy and the factors affecting long-term changes in risk and expected returns in financial markets. Weigand has authored more than 30 papers, book chapters, and articles. He is an active public speaker and offers consulting services and educational seminars for corporations and private clients. He holds a BS and Ph.D. in financial economics from the University of Arizona.

CHAPTER 25

Dividend Policy and Corporate Governance

SHANTANU DUTTA
Assistant Professor of Finance, University of Ontario Institute of Technology

SAMIR SAADI
Research Associate and Instructor of Finance, Telfer School of Management, University of Ottawa

INTRODUCTION

The issue of dividend policy has stimulated much debate among financial economists at least since the publication of Lintner's (1956) seminal work. To understand the rationale behind dividend policy, Lintner interviewed managers from 28 U.S. companies and found that (1) corporate dividend policy is determined by establishing a long-term target payout ratio, and (2) managers are reluctant to change dividend policy unless there is a long-term and sustainable change in a firm's future cash flow.

Modigliani and Miller (1958) and Miller and Modigliani (1961) (hearafter MM) challenge Lintner's practical approach to explaining a firm's dividend policy. According to MM, dividend policy is irrelevant in a frictionless market and has no consequences on shareholder wealth. By paying more dividends, a firm would reduce its retained earnings and capital gains, which in turn would leave shareholder wealth unchanged. Subsequently, Black (1976) questions the highly restrictive assumptions used in the MM model and shows that under the classical tax regime, in which capital gains have a tax advantage over dividend income, taxable individuals show preference for capital gains. Despite such disadvantages, some companies continue to pay reasonably large dividends to their shareholders.

In an attempt to explain the dividend puzzle, financial economists offer various theories, including signaling theory, tax-preference and dividend clientele theory, agency-costs theory, bird-in-the-hand theory, and catering theory (Baker, Saadi, Dutta, and Gandhi, 2007). In particular, signaling theory, as originally proposed by Bhattacharya (1979), has gained popularity in explaining the dividend puzzle. However, La Porta, Lopez-de-Silanes, Shleifer, and Vishny (2000, p. 2) find that

---

The authors thank H. Kent Baker, the editor, for his helpful comments and suggestions.

recent studies examining signaling theory show mixed results, as "current dividend changes do not help predict firms' future earnings growth."

Another theory that has gained momentum is the agency problem, which involves the separation of ownership and control (Jensen 1986; La Porta et al., 2000). As a result of differing goals and interests between owners (shareholders) and agents (managers), the payment of cash dividends could be an area of potential conflict between these two groups (White 1996). Agency theory predicts that in the absence of effective governance mechanisms, managers would expropriate cash and would not invest extra cash in profitable businesses or distribute dividends to shareholders. Despite its intuitive appeal, agency theory has received only limited attention until recently (La Porta et al. 2000; Bhattacharyya, Mawani, and Morrill, 2008).

This chapter provides a synthesis of the growing body of literature investigating the link between dividend policy and different corporate governance mechanisms under the agency model framework. The chapter provides a discussion of corporate governance and how it is a key to providing a deeper understanding of corporate dividend policy and a distinctive answer to the question of why firms pay dividends.

AGENCY THEORY AND RELEVANCE TO DIVIDEND POLICY

Agency theory predicts that outside shareholders prefer higher dividend payments because dividends reduce the opportunities for managers to squander cash. La Porta et al. (2000, p. 2) explain how agency approach differs from the traditional assumptions of the MM theorem with respect to two issues.

> First, the investment policy of the firm cannot be taken as independent of its dividend policy, and, in particular, paying out dividends may reduce the inefficiency of managerial investments. Second, and more subtly, the allocation of all the profits of the firm to shareholders on a pro rata basis cannot be taken for granted, and in particular the insiders may get preferential treatment through asset diversion, transfer prices, and theft—even holding the investment policy constant.

Therefore, the agency approach clarifies some novel issues by considering the practical scenario of the conflict between managers and outside shareholders. Because investors are not fully convinced of management's intensions, they are better off receiving extra cash from the firms in the form of dividends. This view prompts a closer examination of the relationship between the agency theory and dividend payments.

A few other firm-specific factors and macroeconomic variables influence the dividend expectation behavior of outside shareholders in the context of the agency problem. For example, if the internal corporate governance mechanism of a firm and the minority shareholder rights in an economy are strong, outside investors might be satisfied with lower dividend payments. Similarly, if a firm has genuine growth opportunities, management may receive less pressure from shareholders to pay dividends.

Easterbrook (1984) explains the role of dividends in reducing the agency costs of management. He bases his explanations on the assumption that managers are not perfect agents and try to pursue their own interests when they get such opportunities. This imperfect agent assumption leads to various agency costs. One is the cost of monitoring the managers, and the other is the risk aversion of managers. Monitoring costs become a major issue when a firm has a wide ownership base. In such a situation, the monitoring shareholders will bear the costs while all other shareholders will reap the benefits. Therefore, to have an effective monitoring mechanism, shareholders would prefer to have an external body monitor the managers. Dividend payments can help in the process. Dividend-paying firms often need to go to the market for additional capital, which subjects the firm's management to external scrutiny. Because suppliers of additional funds are good monitors of management, Easterbrook (1984, p. 654) notes that "the purchasers of stock will pay no more than the value of future profits under current management unless they are prepared to wage a takeover contest of some sort, which can be very costly."

Another agency cost relates to the risk-taking behavior of managers. Because managers sometimes have substantial personal wealth tied up in their firms, they might be unwilling to undertake riskier projects to benefit shareholders. Given the risk-return paradigm in finance, if risk-averse managers continue to invest in safe projects, the firm is likely to generate lower returns for the shareholders.

Managers can also reduce the firm's risk level by lowering the debt-equity ratio. If managers continue to rely on internal funds, the debt-equity ratio will decline. This will give an undue advantage to the existing debt holders because they have already scheduled their payoff structure on the basis of a higher risk level. Therefore, Easterbrook (1984) notes that as firms continue to finance projects using retained earnings, they will transfer wealth from shareholders to debt holders. Shareholders would like managers to take adequate risk within the limits set by creditor's contract. Yet motivating managers to invest in risky projects is not easy.

The literature often cites two mechanisms to alleviate this problem: structuring a manager's compensation package (discussed later) and making managers dependent on external financing sources for new projects or investments. Firms can achieve the latter by regularly paying dividends and limiting access by managers to internal financing sources for new projects. When a firm issues new securities, management generally uses professional services from financial intermediaries, such as investment bankers or underwriters, to structure a deal. At this stage, underwriters of stock or the lenders verify the risk-taking behavior of managers in the process of structuring a deal. If the managers are not taking adequate risk, the new security price will reflect this. However, transaction costs can play an important role if the firm relies on external financing too frequently.

Rozeff (1982) proposes an equilibrium model of dividend payout by combining agency and transaction costs and empirically tests the model. Rozeff presents arguments similar to Easterbrook (1984) with respect to agency costs and dividend payout ratio. In his model, Rozeff argues that agency costs will decrease as the firm increases the payout ratio (i.e., a firm pays more dividends). Alternatively, transaction costs will increase if the firm becomes more dependent on external financing. Minimizing the sum of these two costs leads to an optimal dividend policy.

In the empirical model, Rozeff (1982) uses two proxies for different dimensions of agency costs: insider ownership data to test the implication of monitoring costs and a firm's beta to test the implication of managers' risk-aversion behavior. The results show that firms pay higher dividends when insiders hold a lower fraction of the equity and/or a greater number of shareholders own the outside equity. This evidence supports the view that outside investors, who have little influence over management, want to give managers less opportunity to use retained earnings for future investment projects. Rozeff also finds that firms with higher betas (i.e., higher operating and financial risk) prefer lower dividend-payout ratios. This finding has implications for both agency costs and transaction costs. Managers in high-risk firms will try to avoid external financing in an attempt to restrict the firm's overall risk level. Further, high-risk firms will have a higher cost of external financing thus increasing the level of transaction costs of financing. Therefore, high-risk firms will have incentives to lower their dividend-payout ratios. Dempsey and Laber (1992) reexamine Rozeff's model and report similar results.

Jensen (1986) presents the free cash flow hypothesis in the context of agency theory. Cash reserves can provide funds for investment opportunities and can create an opportunity of expropriation by either management or controlling shareholders of a firm. Firms often accumulate much more cash than they require for normal business operations. Jensen contends that the presence of large free cash flows can compound a firm's agency problem by insulating managers from being monitored by external market forces. Managers who are intent on empire building may use excess cash in making poor investments such as nonproductive acquisitions instead of distributing cash to the firm's shareholders (Harford, 1999). Also, managers can derive personal benefits by using extra cash for non-business-related purposes or by participating in outright theft. The payment of higher dividends may reduce the agency cost of free cash flow because it would lower management's chance to expropriate or waste extra cash on value-decreasing projects.

The previous discussion suggests that a strong relationship may exist between agency costs and a firm's dividend policy. Figure 25.1 provides a summary of the

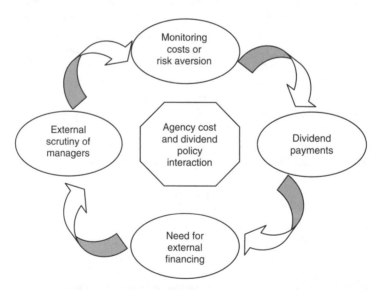

Figure 25.1   Agency Costs and Dividend Policy

To alleviate the two forms of agency costs (monitoring costs and the risk-aversion problem), shareholders should encourage or compel managers to pay higher dividends. This will force managers to enter the market to raise external financing and will subject them to external scrutiny. In turn, the whole process will discipline managers.

arguments. To alleviate the two forms of agency costs (i.e., monitoring costs and the risk-aversion problem), shareholders should encourage or compel managers to pay higher dividends. This will force managers to enter the market to raise external financing and will subject them to external scrutiny. In turn, the whole process will discipline managers.

The following sections on shareholder rights and legal environment, ownership structure, board composition, and executive compensation provide a discussion of corporate governance mechanisms, which may act as substitutes or complements to dividend policy. Of these governance mechanisms, shareholder rights and legal environment are external governance mechanisms, while the other three are internal governance mechanisms.

SHAREHOLDER RIGHTS AND LEGAL ENVIRONMENT

The previous sections show that dividend policy can play a vital role in alleviating agency problems between managers and outside shareholders. Yet controlling shareholders may also have incentives to expropriate other shareholder wealth. Taking a general view, both managers and controlling shareholders are insiders who attempt to expropriate shareholder wealth of others. Researchers also refer to these other shareholders as outsiders or minority shareholders, with substantially little voice in management. The identity of the insiders can differ across countries. In some countries, such as the United States and the United Kingdom, numerous shareholders own large, publicly listed companies. In these firms, managers typically control the firm and are insiders, but in other countries such as Korea, a family or an individual shareholder holds a large portion of a firm's equity. These shareholders often maintain substantial control over management and influence a firm's decision-making process. Managers in a majority of these firms are related to the controlling shareholder. Irrespective of the identity of insiders, La Porta et al. (2000) observe, minority shareholders are the ones who pay the price for agency problems.

Dividend payments serve as an indicator of the extent of a firm's agency problems. The failure of the minority shareholders to disgorge extra cash from a firm may lead to diversion of such resources by the managers or controlling shareholders. This adversely affects the interests of the minority or outside shareholders. La Porta et al. (2000) posit that a country's legal environment and shareholders' right affect a firm's dividend policy or outside shareholders' attempt to extract cash from the firm. The authors argue that the severity of agency problems differs across countries as a result of differences in legal environment and shareholder activism, which may affect the dividend payments. Therefore, examining a firm's dividend policy in the context of a country's legal environment and protection to minority shareholders is important. An effective legal environment depends on both the content of laws and the strictness of their enforcement. La Porta et al. report that common law countries generally provide the best legal protection to minority shareholders, whereas civil law countries grant the weakest protection to minority shareholders.

La Porta et al. (2000) offer two competing views in predicting the relationship between a firm's dividend policy and the strength of the legal protection and

shareholder rights. According to the first view, minority shareholders can benefit from the effectiveness of the legal system by forcing companies to distribute
cash in the form of dividends. The stronger the legal system, the easier minority
shareholders can get dividends. Under a strong and effective legal system, minority shareholders can take several steps to discourage insiders from expropriating
a substantial fraction of company earnings or existing wealth. For example, minority shareholders might use their voting powers to replace ineffective and/or
opportunistic directors, to take legal actions, or to sell shares to a potential hostile
acquirer. The possibility of such actions by the minority shareholders will discipline insiders. Thus, minority shareholders are likely to receive higher dividends
in a country with better legal protection. La Porta et al. term this the *outcome model*,
because under this view dividends represent an outcome of the quality of legal
protection available to the minority shareholders.

According to the second view, minority shareholders can benefit from the
managers' dependence on the external market for financing new projects or investments. To raise external funds from the market with relative ease, managers
need to portray themselves as custodians of minority shareholder rights. One way
to create such a reputation is to pay regular dividends. Because the firm will have
lower cash reserves once it pays dividends, little cash remains for insiders to expropriate. However, once a firm establishes such a reputation, it should guard this
standing because the firm may repeatedly need to enter financial markets.

Reliance on such a reputational mechanism is more critical in countries with
weaker legal protection available to the minority shareholders. As La Porta et al.
(2000, p. 7) argue, "In countries with stronger shareholder protection, in contrast,
the need for a reputational mechanism is weaker, and hence so is the need to
pay dividends." In other words, if this view holds, the firm will pay less (more)
dividends in countries with stronger (weaker) legal protection to minority shareholders. Because firms use dividends as substitutes for legal protection, La Porta
et al. term this mechanism as a *substitution model*.

The views discussed here would be incomplete if a firm's growth prospects
were ignored. Firms with higher growth prospects usually have more legitimacy
in paying less or no dividends. Therefore, the growth prospects of a firm will
influence the relationship between agency problems and dividend payments.
According to the outcome model, in a country with stronger legal protection, minority shareholders are likely to allow managers to use internal funds to respond
to investment opportunities. In such a legal environment, minority shareholders
are more assured of managers' intentions. Thus, in countries with stronger legal
protection for minority shareholders, other things being equal, dividend payments
are likely to be lower for high-growth versus low-growth companies. As La Porta
et al. (2000) note, such a relationship may not hold true in countries with weaker
legal protection because shareholders are more inclined to get whatever they can
from the firm.

According to the substitution model, firms use dividends as substitutes for
legal protection. Therefore, high-growth firms might need to pay higher dividends because they need to go to capital market more frequently than low-growth
firms. La Porta et al. (2000) examine 4,000 firms from 33 different countries to test
the validity of the outcome and substitution models. They report that firms operating in countries with stronger legal protection to minority shareholders pay

higher dividends. This finding supports the prediction of the outcome model. Further, their evidence shows that high-growth firms in these countries pay higher dividends than low-growth firms, again supporting the prediction of the outcome model.

After the La Porta et al. (2000) study, other researchers investigated the relationship between corporate governance and dividend policy in the context of a country's legal environment. For example, Mitton (2004) uses firm-specific corporate governance ratings developed by Credit Lyonnais Securities Asia (CLSA) for 365 firms from 19 emerging markets to study the impact of firm-level corporate governance mechanisms on dividend payouts. Mitton's study differs from La Porta et al.'s in one important way. Mitton focuses on firm-level corporate governance practices of a broad sample of firms, whereas La Porta et al. link dividend payment behavior to the country-level legal protection extended to the minority shareholders. Mitton (2004, p. 410) maintains that "if protection of minority shareholders does have a positive impact on dividend payouts, then the shareholder protection should help explain not just country-level differences in dividend payouts, but also firm-level differences in dividend payout within countries."

Mitton (2004) contends that firm-level protection extended to the minority shareholders should carry the same weight as the country-level protection in protecting minority shareholder rights. His evidence is consistent with the outcome model of dividends in that firms with stronger corporate governance practices have higher dividend payouts. In addition, the negative relationship between dividend payouts and growth opportunities is stronger among firms with better governance.

In the spirit of La Porta et al. (2000), Mitton (2004) also examines the impact of country level legal protection (civil law or common law country) on the dividend payments. He finds that firms in the countries with better legal protection (common law countries) pay higher dividends, and country-level investor protection and firm-level corporate governance complement each other. The results show that irrespective of the nature of the shareholder protection (whether at the firm-level or at the country-level), firms pay higher dividends whenever shareholders have better protection.

In another influential study, Faccio, Lang, and Young (2001) extend support for the outcome model. They study the dividend policies of firms from East Asia and Western Europe. Unlike U.S. firms, a family or a large shareholder controls a large number of firms operating in these two regions. Because of the concentrated ownership structure in both regions, controlling shareholders have the potential to expropriate the wealth of minority shareholders. Faccio et al. use dividend payments by the firms to measure the extent of expropriation. Their results show that firms pay more dividends in Western Europe than in East Asia, despite having similar ownership structures. In Western Europe, minority shareholders have better legal protection, which helps them to extract more dividends.

Yet conflicting empirical evidence exists on this issue. For example, Jiraporn and Ning (2006) examine the relationship between corporate governance and dividend payout policy by considering 3,732 U.S. firm-year observations. They use the governance index (known as the G-Index) developed by Gompers, Ishii, and Metrick (2003) as a proxy for the firm-level corporate governance strength. The basis of the G-Index is the number of corporate governance provisions in a firm that restricts shareholder rights. The higher the G-Index value, the lower is the strength of shareholder rights. Jiraporn and Ning report a positive relationship between a firm's G-Index and its dividend payout ratio. In other words, firms extending lesser protection to minority shareholders pay higher dividends.

This finding supports the prediction of the substitution model and differs from the findings of La Porta et al. (2000) and Mitton (2004). Jiraporn and Ning (2006) attribute this difference to the fact that the other two studies examine dividend policies across dissimilar legal systems around the world. In their study, Jiraporn and Ning investigate the relationship between corporate governance and dividend policy within a single country (i.e., the U.S. legal system).

EXECUTIVE COMPENSATION

The structure of executive compensation is another important element of a firm's agency costs. Bhattacharyya et al. (2008) contend that in equilibrium, high-quality managers should receive higher compensation compared to low-quality managers and should favor low dividend payments. Because high-quality managers find new avenues for positive net present value (NPV) projects, they want to invest excess cash in new projects. Core, Holthausen, and Larcker (1999) posit that a better approach would be to look into the chief executive officer's (CEO) excess pay to assess the governance impact on a firm's decision-making process.

Different views exist on how CEO excess pay may affect dividend policy. For example, firms in which CEOs have a higher level of excess pay are likely to retain more cash for expropriation. In addition, CEOs with excess pay favor higher dividend payments to gain more support from the shareholders. Few empirical studies in this area investigate either the relationship between CEO compensation and dividends or the effect of CEO excess pay. Consistent with the overall viewpoint of CEO compensation, Smith and Watts (1992) find that lower dividend yields are associated with higher levels of executive compensation after controlling for firm size and growth opportunities.

Bhattacharyya et al. (2008) examine 14,013 U.S. firm-year observations and find that CEOs' cash compensation, bonus, and options all individually affect a firm's retention ratio. The relationships are significant and positive. Alternatively, all the components of compensation negatively affect firm's payout policy. The findings suggest that good CEOs, who are well compensated, have good investment projects and choose not to pay higher dividends.

A competing viewpoint is the management entrenchment hypothesis. Compensation contracts that rely more heavily on non-equity-based components, such as cash compensation and bonuses, give more protection to managers for non-value-maximizing decisions. According to Hu and Kumar (2004), entrenched managers are likely to pay higher dividends to protect themselves against disciplinary sanctions by shareholders. Consistent with this hypothesis, they find a positive relationship between the likelihood of dividend payments and dividend yields as well as non-equity-based compensation.

Recently, stock options have become a major component of executive compensation packages. Stock options are contracts that give executives the right to buy a share of stock at a prespecified exercise or strike price for a prespecified term. Such options supposedly motivate managers to take appropriate actions to increase a firm's stock price, leading to long-term appreciation in firm value. The annual flow of CEO compensation in the 1980s was mainly in the form of cash salary and bonuses. Hall and Liebman (1998) report that only 30 percent of CEOs received new option grants in the 1980s. Bryan et al. (2000) and Murphy (1999) report, however, that the 1990s witnessed a large increase in equity-based compensation (stock options and restricted stock awards) for U.S. CEOs. Toward the latter part of the 1990s, Core and Guay (1999) found that more than 90 percent of CEOs held some form of equity grants and stock options, which contributed about one-third of the median CEO's equity portfolio.

Studies on stock options often examine their impact on firm value. The general consensus in the literature is that performance-based compensation for top managers leads to higher market value of a firm (Mehran, 1995; Carpenter and Sanders, 2002) and CEO pay has a strong relationship to firm performance (Yermack, 1996). A smaller body of literature links CEO stock options to a firm's dividend policy.

Lambert, Lanen, and Larker (1989) suggest that managers holding a substantial level of stock options in their firms will be less inclined to pay dividends. Standard option valuation models show that the value of executive stock options, such as call options, decreases if the firm pays dividends. Consistent with this viewpoint, Lambert et al. find that dividends decline relative to expected levels after the adoption of executive option plans. Similarly, studies by Hu and Kumar (2004) and Bhattacharyya et al. (2008) report a negative relation between stock options and dividend payments.

Although the arguments relating stock options and cash dividend payments are appealing, the overall effect of stock options on total payouts (cash payout and stock repurchase) is uncertain. As Fenn and Liang (2001, p. 47) argue, "ceteris paribus, management will be indifferent to retaining the proceeds from a reduction in dividends or using them to repurchase stock, as the value of their call options will be the same in either case." If managers want to maintain a target payout ratio, they can choose the right balance between cash dividends and stock repurchase (i.e., less cash dividends and more stock repurchase in the mix), which can help them achieve their goal of maintaining stock option value.

Fenn and Liang (2001) empirically examine the relationship between corporate payout policy and managerial stock incentives by using data on more than 1,100 nonfinancial firms during the period 1993–1997. Similar to Lambert et al. (1989), they report a strong negative relationship between dividends and management stock options. Further, Fenn and Liang find a statistically significant, positive relationship between repurchases and management stock options. The results have implications with respect to the choice of dividend payouts. Apparently, managers with substantial levels of stock options prefer to make stock repurchases at the expense of cash dividends.

White (1996) highlights another determinant of dividend payments by examining explicit provisions included in the compensation contract. As Healy (1985) points out, a relationship often exists between cash dividend payments and the annual pool of bonus reserves that firms distribute to managers. Such a mechanism encourages managers to pay more cash dividends. White examines this issue by using a sample of the largest companies in the oil and gas, defense and aerospace, and food-processing industries, where dividend-related agency costs are likely to be high. Consistent with her hypothesis, White finds a positive relationship between dividend provisions in the compensation contract and higher dividend payouts and yields as well as higher annual changes in dividend yields. She also reports that firms with potentially higher agency problems adopt such contractual provisions more often than those with a greater number of inside directors and low managerial ownership.

MANAGERIAL AND OUTSIDE BLOCKHOLDER OWNERSHIP

Managerial ownership has direct implications for the agency problem. As Jensen and Meckling (1976) note, managers become more aligned with shareholders' interest as their ownership increases. Because managerial ownership works as an alternative mechanism of corporate governance, firms with a higher level of managerial ownership tend to pay lower dividends. Mahadwartha (2007) contends that maintaining higher managerial ownership and a higher dividend payout ratio would be ineffective and costly because the intent of both mechanisms is to achieve the same goal of reducing the agency cost of equity.

Many empirical studies find a negative relationship between managerial ownership and dividend payout ratio (Crutchley and Hansen, 1989; Jensen, Solberg and Zorn, 1992; Eckbo and Verma, 1994; Hu and Kumar, 2004; Mahadwartha, 2007). Yet Fenn and Liang (2001) argue that the relationship between managerial ownership and dividend payouts is likely to depend on the extent of a firm's agency problem. Managerial ownership is likely to mitigate agency problems at companies with lower investment opportunities or excess free cash flow. Accordingly, Fenn and Liang find an association between managerial ownership and higher dividend payouts by firms with greater agency problems. Characteristics of these firms include low management stock ownership, few investment opportunities, and high free cash flows. Fenn and Liang do not find any significant relationship between managerial ownership and dividend payouts for the firms with relatively high managerial ownership, more investment opportunities, and limited cash flows.

Earlier studies caution about the methodological choices in determining the relationship between managerial ownership and dividend payouts. Demsetz and Lehn (1985) contend that managerial ownership is endogenously determined with value-maximizing behavior. Jensen et al. (1992) assert that managerial ownership, debt, and dividend policy are related both directly and indirectly through their association with operating characteristics of firms.

To distinguish these effects, Jensen et al. (1992) use a system of equations to examine the determinants of managerial ownership, debt, and dividend policy. They analyze cross-sectional firm data at two points in time—1982 (565 firms) and 1987 (632 firms)—by using a three-stage least squares methodology. Their results show that financial decisions and insider ownership are interdependent and insider ownership has a negative influence on a firm's debt and dividend levels.

Other studies use similar methodologies to examine the joint determination of managerial ownership, institutional ownership, capital structure, and dividend policy as related to a firm's agency costs. For example, Chen and Steiner (1999) show a substitution-monitoring effect between managerial ownership and each of three variables (dividend policy, institutional ownership, and debt policy). Crutchley, Jensen, Jahera, and Raymond (1999) use a simultaneous equation system to examine the joint determination of the aforementioned variables in 1987 to compare to the results of Jensen et al. (1992). Crutchley et al. add an institutional ownership variable and use 1993 to capture the increase in institutional activism in the early 1990s. They do not find any significant relationship between managerial ownership and dividends in the 1987 period. Their results also show little evidence that institutional ownership is a substitute monitoring device. In 1993, however, Crutchley et al. find a simultaneous system whereby both insider ownership and institutional ownership negatively affect a firm's dividend payments.

Outside block holders or large shareholders act as an alternate governance mechanism and monitor managerial activities. Therefore, firms with a substantial presence of outside block holders do not need to pay dividends to gain the confidence of shareholders if there are positive NPV projects for investment. Also, large shareholders may not need to rely on dividend payments to discipline managers because large shareholders have strong voting positions or board representations. Consistent with this view, Hu and Kumar (2004) find that the likelihood of dividend payments and dividend yields are negatively related to the fraction of total shares owned by the largest outside shareholders.

A competing viewpoint predicts a positive relationship between the ownership of large shareholders and dividend payments. According to Shleifer and Vishny (1986), large shareholders have greater incentives to monitor management. However, active involvement by large shareholders in monitoring managers is expensive and extends free-rider benefits to other shareholders. Accordingly, Zeckhauser and Pound (1990) maintain that large shareholders such as institutional holders are unlikely to monitor managers directly but instead force managers to pay dividends. Regular dividend payments compel managers to rely on external markets for additional funds, which subject them to external scrutiny. The tax implication for dividend income is also likely to influence the dividend expectations of large shareholders. In many countries including the United Kingdom and Canada, large institutional investors receive favorable tax treatment on dividend income. Thus, such investors prefer dividends to retention.

Using panel data, Short, Zhang, and Keasey (2002) examine the possible link between dividend payments and institutional ownership using a sample of 211 U.K. firms. They report a significant positive relation between dividend policy and institutional ownership. They attribute such findings to the preferential tax treatment given to institutional shareholders in the United Kingdom. Eckbo and Verma (1994) use a sample of 308 firms listed on the Toronto Stock Exchange to examine the impact of both relative ownership and voting power of institutional shareholders and managers on dividend policy. Their results show that cash dividend yield increases significantly with share ownership or voting power of corporate and institutional shareholders and decreases significantly with share ownership or voting power of managers.

BOARD STRUCTURE

The board of directors, which consists of both inside and outside members, is the most visible and legally articulated control mechanism for corporate governance. Fama (1980) and Fama and Jensen (1983) suggest that outside directors have an incentive to develop a good reputation in monitoring management because they compete with one another. As Subrahmanyam, Rangan, and Rosenstein (1997) note, shareholders expect outside (independent) directors to represent their interests by mitigating agency problems between managers and shareholders. Pfeffer (1981) contends that inside directors are loyal to the CEO because of the power that the CEO has over them. Accordingly, researchers generally view outside directors as independent and inside directors as influenced by top managers.

Despite the belief that outside directors are efficient monitors, the empirical results are mixed. While Xie, Davidson, and DaDalt (2003), Byrd and Hickman (1992) and Weisbach (1988) conclude that outside directors protect shareholders interests, Erickson, Park, Reising, and Shin (2005), among others, do not find a significant relationship between board independence and firm performance. In addition, Agrawal and Knoeber (1996) and Bhagat and Black (2002) find that outsiders have a negative effect on shareholders' welfare.

Some studies also investigate the relationship between board structure and compensation policy. Using a sample of 193 firms, Boyd (1994) finds a negative relationship between the ratio of insiders and CEO compensation. Grinstein and Hribar (2004) conclude that the ratio of insiders is not a significant determinant of bonuses perceived by CEOs in mergers and acquisitions. Using a sample of 153 manufacturing firms, Mehran (1995) reports that firms with more outside directors on the board employ a greater use of equity-based compensation. The mixed findings may result from a lack of independence of outside board members (Main, O'Reilly, and Wade, 1995), or a lack of time, expertise, or motivation to monitor management (Gilson and Kraakman, 1991). In most cases, the CEO influences the selection of board members. Shivdasani and Yermack (1999) show that the CEO has a direct influence in the directors' nomination process in more than 50 percent of the sample.

Other arguments exist as to how independent directors influence a firm's dividend policy. One view is that having a high proportion of outside board members improves the quality of corporate governance. Depending on the dynamics between shareholder rights and management intention, good corporate governance practices may lead to low or high dividend payments. In light of La Porta et al.'s (2000) arguments, researchers can view the role of directors on dividend policy in the context of an outcome model or a substitution model. According to the outcome model, board independence improves internal monitoring and increases the likelihood of taking actions against managerial wrongdoing. With the help of independent directors, minority shareholders can extract cash dividends more easily in a firm with better governance practices.

According to the substitution hypothesis, managers pay more dividends to minority shareholders if the firm's corporate governance practices are weak. In a firm with more agency costs (e.g., firms with more inside directors), managers prefer to maintain a good reputation in the market by paying dividends. Therefore, the substitution model predicts a negative relationship between board independence and dividend payment. This relationship implies that managers in a firm with an independent board will not feel undue pressure to distribute cash dividends as long as good investment opportunities exist. Hu and Kumar (2004) examine the impact of board independence on dividend payouts. Consistent with the prediction of the outcome model, they report a positive relationship between board independence and dividend payouts.

Few studies examine the market reactions to dividend change announcements and relate such reactions to board independence. According to Borokhovich,
Brunarski, Harman, and Kehr (2005), any surprises associated with dividend increases will be more effective in mitigating agency costs if firms have numerous
inside board members who are related to and controlled by managers. They use
a sample of U.S. firms with dividend surprises between 1992 and 1999 to test
this hypothesis. Borokhovich et al. find that, on average, firms with a majority of
strict outside directors on their boards experience significantly lower abnormal
returns around the dividend surprise dates. This finding supports the substitution
hypothesis.

CONCLUSIONS

In recent years, academics' and practitioners' interests in corporate governance
have increased markedly. The extant finance literature shows that shareholder-
manager agency conflicts strongly influence corporate financial policies such as
capital structure and dividend payouts (Hu and Kumar, 2004). Yet the literature on
the relationship between agency theory and dividend policy is limited but growing.
The failure of traditional theories, such as signaling, tax clientele, and bird in the
hand, in explaining the dividend puzzle has increased interest in agency theory as
an explanation of this phenomenon.

This chapter discusses different external and internal corporate governance
mechanisms that may influence a firm's dividend policy. The chapter also reviews
the literature on shareholder rights and legal environment that may influence
a firm's dividend policy. Numerous studies report a significant impact of these
factors on dividend policy. The majority of studies show that better legal protection
of minority shareholders leads to a higher level of dividend payments. However,
a few other studies find that managers operating in a weaker legal environment
pay higher dividends to maintain a good reputation in the market. The chapter
also reviews the literature on the effect of other traditional corporate governance
mechanisms such as managerial and block-holder ownership, compensation, and
board structure on dividend policy. Evidence tends to show that these variables
significantly affect a firm's dividend policy.

Limited evidence exists on the relationship between corporate governance
mechanisms and dividend policy. In many countries, regulatory authorities impose
stringent corporate governance regulations to protect minority shareholder rights.
These new developments are likely to affect dividend policy.

REFERENCES

Agrawal, Anup, and Charles R. Knoeber. 1996. "Firm Performance and Mechanisms to
    Control Agency Problems between Managers and Shareholders." *Journal of Financial and
    Quantitative Analysis* 31:3, 377–397.
Baker, H. Kent, Samir Saadi, Shantanu Dutta, and Devinder Gandhi. 2007. "The Perception
    of Dividends by Canadian Managers: New Survey Evidence." *International Journal of
    Managerial Finance* 3:1, 70–91.
Bhagat, Sanjai, and Bernard S. Black. 2002. "The Non-Correlation between Board Indepen-
    dence and Long-Term Firm Performance." *Journal of Corporation Law* 27:1, 231–274.

Bhattacharya, Sudipto. 1979. "Imperfect Information, Dividend Policy, and 'the Bird in the Hand' Fallacy." *Bell Journal of Economics* 10:1, 259–270.

Bhattacharyya, Nalinaksha, Amin Mawani, and Cameron Morrill. 2008. "Dividend Payout and Executive Compensation: Theory and Evidence." *Accounting and Finance* 48:4, 521–541.

Black, Fischer. 1976. "The Dividend Puzzle." *Journal of Portfolio Management* 2:2, 5–8.

Borokhovich, Kenneth A., Kelly R. Brunarski, Yvette Harman, and James B. Kehr. 2005. "Dividends, Corporate Monitors and Agency Costs." *Financial Review* 40:1, 37–65.

Boyd, Brian K. 1994. "Board Control and CEO Compensation." *Strategic Management Journal* 15:4, 335–344.

Bryan, Stephen, LeeSeok Hwang, and Steven Lilien. 2000. "CEO Stock-Based Compensation: An Empirical Analysis of Incentive-Intensity, Relative Mix, and Economic Determinants." *Journal of Business* 73:4, 661–693.

Byrd, John W., and Kent A. Hickman. 1992. "Do Outside Directors Monitor Managers? Evidence from Tender Offer Bids." *Journal of Financial Economics* 32:2, 195–221.

Carpenter, Mason A., and William Gerard Sanders. 2002. "Top Management Team Compensation: The Missing Link between CEO Pay and Firm Performance?" *Strategic Management Journal* 23:4, 367–375.

Chen, Carl R., and Thomas L. Steiner. 1999. "Managerial Ownership and Agency Conflicts: A Nonlinear Simultaneous Equation Analysis of Managerial Ownership, Risk Taking, Debt Policy, and Dividend Policy." *Financial Review* 34:1, 119–136.

Core, John, and Wayne Guay. 1999. "The Use of Equity Grants to Manage Optimal Equity Incentive Levels." Working Paper, Wharton School, University of Pennsylvania.

Core, John E., Robert W. Holthausen, and David F. Larcker 1999. "Corporate Governance, Chief Executive Officer Compensation, and Firm Performance." *Journal of Financial Economics* 51:3 371–406.

Crutchley, Claire E., and Robert S. Hansen. 1989. "A Test of the Agency Theory of Managerial Ownership, Corporate Leverage, and Corporate Dividends." *Financial Management* 18:4, 36–46.

Crutchley, Claire E., Marlin R. H. Jensen, John S. Jahera, Jr., and Jennie E. Raymond. 1999. "Agency Problems and the Simultaneity of Financial Decision Making: The Role of Institutional Ownership." *International Review of Financial Analysis* 8:2, 177–197.

Dempsey, Stephen J., and Gene Laber. 1992. "Effects of Agency and Transaction Costs on Dividend Payout Ratios: Further Evidence of the Agency-Transaction Cost Hypothesis." *Journal of Financial Research* 15:4, 317–321.

Demsetz, Harold, and Kenneth Lehn. 1985. "The Structure of Corporate Ownership: Causes and Consequences." *Journal of Political Economy* 93:6, 1155–1177.

Easterbrook, Frank H. 1984. "Two Agency-Cost Explanations of Dividends." *American Economic Review* 74:4, 650–659.

Eckbo, B. Espen, and Savita Verma. 1994. "Managerial Shareownership, Voting Power, and Cash Dividend Policy." *Journal of Corporate Finance* 1:1, 33–62.

Erickson, John, Yun W. Park, Joe Reising, and Hyun-Hun Shin. 2005. "Board Composition and Firm Value under Concentrated Ownership: The Canadian Evidence." *Pacific-Basin Finance Journal* 13:4, 387–410.

Faccio, Mara, Larry H. R. Lang, and Leslie Young. 2001. "Dividends and Expropriation." *American Economic Review* 91:1, 54–78.

Fama, Eugene F. 1980. "Agency Problems and the Theory of the Firm." *Journal of Political Economy* 88:2, 288–307.

Fama, Eugene F., and Michael Jensen. 1983. "Separation of Ownership and Control." *Journal of Law and Economics* 26:2, 301–325.

Fenn, George W., and Nellie Liang. 2001. "Corporate Payout Policy and Managerial Stock Incentives." *Journal of Financial Economics* 60:1, 45–72.

Gilson, Ronald J., and Reinier Kraakman. 1991. "Reinventing the Outside Director: An Agenda for Institutional Investors." *Stanford Law Review* 43:4, 863–906.

Gompers, Paul, Joy Ishii, and Andrew Metrick. 2003. "Corporate Governance and Equity Prices." *Quarterly Journal of Economics* 118:1, 107–155.

Grinstein, Yaniv, and Paul Hribar. 2004. "CEO Compensation and Incentives: Evidence from M&A Bonuses." *Journal of Financial Economics* 73:1, 119–143.

Hall, Brian J., and Jeffrey B. Liebman. 1998. "Are CEOs Really Paid Like Bureaucrats?" *Quarterly Journal of Economics* 113:3, 653–691.

Harford, Jarrad. 1999. "Corporate Cash Reserves and Acquisitions." *Journal of Finance* 54:6, 1969–1997.

Healy, Paul M. 1985. "The Effect of Bonus Schemes on Accounting Decisions." *Journal of Accounting and Economics* 7:1–3, 85–107.

Hu, Aidong, and Praveen Kumar. 2004. "Managerial Entrenchment and Payout Policy." *Journal of Financial and Quantitative Analysis* 39:4, 759–790.

Jensen, Gerald R., Donald P. Solberg, and Thomas S. Zorn. 1992. "Simultaneous Determination of Insider Ownership, Debt, and Dividend Policies." *Journal of Financial and Quantitative Analysis* 27:2, 247–263.

Jensen, Michael. 1986. "Agency Cost of Free Cash Flow, Corporate Finance, and Takeovers." *American Economic Review* 76:2, 323–329.

Jensen, Michael, and William Meckling. 1976. "Theory of the Firm: Managerial Behavior, Agency Costs and Ownership Structure." *Journal of Financial Economics* 3:4, 305–360.

Jiraporn, Pornsit, and Yixi Ning. 2006. "Dividend Policy, Shareholder Rights, and Corporate Governance." *Journal of Applied Finance* 16:2, 24–36.

Lambert, Richard A., William N. Lanen, and David F. Larker. 1989. "Executive Stock Option Plans and Corporate Dividend Policy." *Journal of Financial and Quantitative Analysis* 24:4, 409–425.

La Porta, Rafael, Florencio Lopez-de-Silanes, Andrei Shleifer, and Robert W. Vishny. 2000. "Agency Problems and Dividend Policies around the World." *Journal of Finance* 55:1, 1–33.

Lintner, John. 1956. "Distribution of Income of Corporations among Dividends, Retained Earnings, and Taxes." *American Economic Review* 46:2, 97–113.

Mahadwartha, Putu Anom. 2007. "The Association of Managerial Ownership with Dividend Policy and Leverage Policy: Indonesian Firms." SSRN Working Paper Series, http://ssrn.com/abstract=637061.

Main, Brian, Charles A. O'Reilly, and James Wade. 1995. "The CEO, the Board of Directors and Executive Compensation: Economic and Psychological Perspectives." *Industrial and Corporate Change* 4:2, 293–332.

Mehran, Hamid. 1995. "Executive Compensation Structure, Ownership and Firm Performance." *Journal of Financial Economics* 38:2, 163–184.

Miller, Merton, and Franco Modigliani. 1961. "Dividend Policy, Growth, and the Valuation of Shares." *Journal of Business* 34:4, 411–433.

Mitton, Todd. 2004. "Corporate Governance and Dividend Policy in Emerging Markets." *Emerging Markets Review* 5:4, 409–426.

Modigliani, Franco, and Merton Miller. 1958. "The Cost of Capital, Corporate Finance, and the Theory of Investment." *American Economic Review* 48:3, 261–297.

Murphy, Kevin J. 1999. " Executive Compensation." In *Handbook of Labor Economics 3B*, ed. Orley Ashenfelter and David Card, 2485–2563. New York: Elsevier Science North Holland.

Pfeffer, Jeffrey. 1981. *Power in Organizations*. Boston: Pitman.

Rozeff, Michael S. 1982. "Growth, Beta and Agency Costs as Determinants of Dividend Payout Ratios." *Journal of Financial Research* 5:3, 249–259.

Shivdasani, Anil, and David Yermack. 1999. "CEO Involvement in the Selection of New Board Members: An Empirical Analysis." *Journal of Finance* 54:5, 1829–1854.

Shleifer, Andrei, and Robert W. Vishny. 1986. "Large Shareholders and Corporate Control." *Journal of Political Economy* 94:3, 461–488.

Short, Helen, Hao Zhang, and Kevin Keasey. 2002. "The Link between Dividend Policy and Institutional Ownership." *Journal of Corporate Finance* 8:2, 105–122.

Smith, Clifford, Jr., and Ross L. Watts. 1992. "The Investment Opportunity Set and Corporate Financing, Dividend, and Compensation Policies." *Journal of Financial Economics* 32:3, 263–292.

Subrahmanyam, Vijaya, Nanda Rangan, and Stuart Rosenstein. 1997. "The Role of Outside Directors in Bank Acquisitions." *Financial Management* 26:3, 23–36.

Weisbach, Michael S. 1988. "Outside Directors and CEO Turnover." *Journal of Financial Economics* 20:1, 302–308.

White, Lourdes Ferreira. 1996. "Executive Compensation and Dividend Policy." *Journal of Corporate Finance* 2:4: 335–358.

Xie, Biao, Wallace N. Davidson III, and Peter J. DaDalt. 2003. "Earnings Management and Corporate Governance: The Role of the Board and the Audit Committee." *Journal of Corporate Finance* 9:3, 295–316.

Yermack, David D. 1996. "Higher Valuation of Companies with a Small Board of Directors." *Journal of Financial Economics* 40:2, 185–212.

Zeckhauser, Richard J., and John Pound. 1990. " Are Large Shareholders Effective Monitors? An Investigation of Share Ownership and Corporate Performance." In *Asymmetric Information, Corporate Finance and Investment*, ed. Glenn Hubbard, 149–180. Chicago: University of Chicago Press.

ABOUT THE AUTHORS

Shantanu Dutta is an assistant professor of finance at University of Ontario Institute of Technology (UOIT). Previously, he taught at St. Francis Xavier University, Nova Scotia, and Assumption University, Bangkok as a full-time faculty member. Before his career in academe, he served as a finance manager and project controller at Lafarge, a world leader in construction materials. Dutta's research focuses on corporate governance, mergers and acquisitions, market efficiency, dividend policy, and technology management. He has published in *Journal of Banking and Finance, Global Finance Journal, Canadian Investment Review, International Journal of Theoretical and Applied Finance, International Journal of Managerial Finance, International Journal of Technology Transfer*, and *International Journal of Global Energy Issues*. He has also participated and presented papers in many scholarly conferences. Dutta is a recipient of the Barclay Global Investor Canada Research Award.

Samir Saadi is a finance Ph.D. candidate at Queen's School of Business. He is also a research associate and part-time instructor of finance at the Telfer School of Management, University of Ottawa. His research interests include dividend policy, executive compensation, and international finance. Saadi is a recipient of several best-paper awards at national and international conferences. He has published in finance and applied economics journals, including *Journal of Multinational Financial Management, Journal of International Financial Markets, Institutions and Money, Global Finance Journal, Journal of Theoretical and Applied Finance, Review of Financial Economics*, and *International Journal of Managerial Finance*.

CHAPTER 26

Dividend Policy in Regulated Industries

ROSS DICKENS
Professor of Finance and Chair of the Department of Economics and Finance, University of South Alabama

INTRODUCTION

Compared to the voluminous work on nonregulated industries, research examining dividend policy in regulated industries is relatively sparse. Although many studies investigate the dividend policies of regulated firms, no universal agreement exists on which are regulated industries. Examples of regulated industries include commercial banking, savings and loans, investment banking, life insurance, property and casualty insurance, electric and gas utilities, real estate investment trusts (REITS), petroleum, telecommunications, railroads, airlines, and motor carriers. This chapter reviews published studies that consider dividend policy for firms in any of the preceding regulated industries. The chapter also includes a table providing a quick reference of the reviewed studies.

There are two underlying motives for studying regulated industries. First, because most dividend studies exclude regulated firms, researchers need to investigate whether dividend policies differ between regulated and nonregulated firms. Such research not only provides evidence to support or refute the idea that such differences exist but also offers insights into the dividend policies of regulated firms.

Second, researchers examine the dividend policies of regulated industries because doing so allows controls when investigating specific areas of dividend policy. For instance, most work examining the banking industry notes that regulatory oversight from the Federal Reserve, Federal Deposit Insurance Corporation (FDIC), and other regulators should theoretically reduce the importance of dividends in relation to some agency cost issues. Filbeck and Mullineaux (1993) provide an excellent discussion on this point. Another example is the requirement that REITs pay out a high percentage of earnings to avoid tax penalties. The required percentage was at least 95 percent at the time of most studies reported in the next section. This requirement should allow a purer focus on non-tax-related issues that may affect dividend policy.

Wansley (2003) examines the dividend policies of various regulated industries but does not review past studies in detail. Instead, he concentrates on providing newly developed descriptive evidence of the differences between the dividend policies of regulated and nonregulated firms both in terms of dividend payout and in terms of dividend yield. The following sections review Wansley's work along with that of others. Dividend policy research in regulated industries is most common in commercial banking followed by utilities, insurance, and REITs. A few studies examine the petroleum industry and multiple industry sectors.

LITERATURE REVIEW

This section groups studies by industry according to study type and chronological date of publication. The reviews include only published works with publication dates ranging from 1964 through 2003. Multiple dividend policy articles often appear after major changes in tax laws relating to dividend payments. Recently, researchers have presented several working papers at various academic meetings examining the impact of the Jobs and Growth Tax Relief Reconciliation Act of 2003. Publications from these papers may begin appearing in 2008. The examination in this chapter includes the following industry categories: banking, utilities, insurance, REITs, petroleum, and general (for studies examining multiple industries). Table 26.1 provides a quick reference for each study.

Banking

Dividend studies examining banking firms have various motivations. Along with the idea mentioned previously that banking regulators may lessen agency costs, much of the extant dividend literature on banking examines the impact of regulatory capital requirements on dividend policy. Early dividend studies in particular exclude banking.

Gupta and Walker (1975) provide the earliest banking-related study on dividend policy. They analyze data from 980 banking firms from 1965 to 1968 to identify variables that might explain the dividend policies of banks. They find a positive relationship between dividends and current profits, the change in profits from the prior year, the sum of profits over time, and the growth in total assets and liquidity. Their liquidity measure, however, is more of an illiquidity measure because its expected relationship to dividends is negative. The major conclusion is to present the coefficient estimates from the model that Gupta and Walker consider the best fit for the data. While current and past profits as well as asset growth are all related to dividends, the liquidity measure's influence (based on coefficient estimates) is much greater on dividends than on the other three variables.

Keen (1978) examines banks that cut their dividends. Starting with 28 banks that reduced dividends between 1974 and 1977, he matches 16 surviving firms for which he has data to 16 banking firms that did not cut dividends. This study presents evidence of how dividend cuts affect deposits, share price, and operating performance in general terms without reporting formal statistical tests for differences. Keen reports that dividend-cutting firms do not seem to lose an inordinate amount of deposits after cutting dividends. Also, the average share price of the sample banks was fairly stable after the cut announcement. Finally, the dividend-cutting banks improved their operating performance after the cut.

Table 26.1 Summary of Dividend Studies of Regulated Firms

Author(s)	Date	Sample Size	Summary of Key Findings
Panel A. Banking			
Gupta and Walker	1975	980	Dividends are related to profits, total asset growth, and liquidity.
Keen	1978	16	Dividend-cutting firms have stable deposits and share prices after cutting dividends.
Mayne	1980	>12,000	Dividends are related to total assets, income before security gains, equity, total asset growth, and holding company affiliation.
Keen	1983	21	Dividend-cutting firms have significantly negative cumulative abnormal returns after announcements.
Kennedy and Scott	1984	120	Dividends are related to firm size, number of shares outstanding, and various measures of geographic restriction.
Kennedy and Nunnally	1986	80	Dividends are related to prior-year dividends and the price-earnings ratio.
Graddy and Karna	1987	44	The market places a higher value on firms with lower dividend payouts.
Filbeck and Mullineaux	1993	246–484	Abnormal stock returns are positive for dividend increases and negative for dividend decreases.
Madura, McDaniel, and Wiant	1994	112	Abnormal stock returns are positive for dividend increases.
Black, Ketcham, and Schweitzer	1995	74	Abnormal stock returns are negative for announcements of dividend cuts in the short term but not the long term.
Boldin and Leggett	1995	207	Dividends are not related to geographic restriction or the banking model (regional, superregional, or money center).
Mercado-Mendez and Willey	1995	104	Dividend yield has a positive relationship to total assets, and dividends provide a way to decrease agency costs
Bessler and Nohel	1996	81	Abnormal stock returns are negative for announcements of dividend cuts with stronger reactions occurring for larger banks.
Casey and Dickens	2000	46–82	Dividends are positively related to capital; dividends increase after the marginal rate of dividend income decreases.
Panel B. Utilities			
Dhrymes and Kurz	1964	261	Dividends are related to sales more than to profit.
Higgins	1974	81	Little relationship exists between dividends and stock price or the cost of equity.
Lee	1976	116	Dividends and retained earnings measures should be considered together when studying stock prices.

(Continued)

Table 26.1 *(Continued)*

Author(s)	Date	Sample Size	Summary of Key Findings
Baker, Farrelly, and Edelman	1985	318	Managers of regulated and nonregulated (utilities) firms agree on the most important determinants of dividend policy (anticipated future earnings, past dividend pattern, cash availability, and impact on stock price) but differ on other determinants.
Edelman, Farrelly, and Baker	1985	318	Utility managers formally review dividend policies less often than nonregulated firms' managers.
Farrelly, Baker, and Edelman	1986	318	Utility managers report fewer instances of dividend payments affecting capital expenditures than managers of nonregulated firms.
Moyer, Rao, and Tripathy	1992	69	Dividend payments are higher the lower the regulatory setting.
Hansen, Kumar, and Shome	1994	70–81	Utility firms pay higher dividends than nonregulated firms; dividends serve as way to curb conflicts between stockholders and regulators.
Baker and Powell	1999	53–117	Utility and unregulated firms' dividend policy differ; utility policy is more influenced by stockholder preference and industry standards.
Baker and Powell	1999	198	Utility and nonregulated managers' survey opinions on dividend policy rarely significantly differ.
Panel C. Insurance			
Lee and Forbes	1980	34	Dividends are positively related to stock price from 1955 to 1968 but inconsistent from 1969 onward.
Harrington	1981	68	Insurers owned by holding companies pay higher dividends.
Lee and Forbes	1982	61	Dividends are related to last year's dividend, earnings, and equity-to-total assets.
Chen	1990	31–42	Insurance companies with a lower marginal tax rate prefer higher-dividend-yield stocks.
Akhigbe, Borde, and Madura	1993	759	Positive abnormal returns occur after dividend increase announcements, but returns differ by insurance company type.
Panel D. REITS			
Lee and Kau	1987	29	The dividend policies of REITs and non-REITs differ. Dividends increase the cost of capital.
Wang, Erickson, and Gau	1993	38–102	The determinants of the dividend payout of REITs and non-REIT are similar. Equity REITs pay greater dividends than mortgage REITs.
Bradley, Capozza, and Sequin	1998	75	Dividend increases (decreases) are associated with positive (negative) abnormal returns. The market reaction to dividend decreases is greater than for dividend increases.
Mooradian and Yang	2001	15–51	Dividends are greater at hotel-owning REITS than non-REITs. Compared to non-REITs, REITs maintain greater free cash flows before and after dividends.

Table 26.1 *(Continued)*

Author(s)	Date	Sample Size	Summary of Key Findings
Panel E. Petroleum			
Casey and Theis	1997	42	A significantly negative relationship exists between dividend payouts of petroleum firms and both insider ownership percentage and beta.
Panel F. Other			
Kennedy, O'Brien, and Horn	1987	Not reported	Little concern exists about the relationship between dividends and stock prices among utilities, telecommunications, and motor carriers.
Collins, Saxena, and Wansley	1996	500	The dividend policies of financial service firms do not differ significantly from those of unregulated firms but utilities have significantly higher payouts.
Wansley	2003	>2,000	Dividends are higher for REITs and utilities than for unregulated firms and dividends vary most among petroleum firms.

This table presents a summary of studies involving dividend policy issues of regulated firms in order of publication.

Mayne (1980) compares the dividend policies of banking firms owned by bank holding companies (BHCs) as compared to those outside the BHC framework. Using data from 1973 to 1976 from more than 12,000 banking firms, she finds banks affiliated with holding companies pay out significantly more in dividends than do their non-BHC counterparts. She models total dividends for each firm as dependent on total assets, income before securities gains, equity, the total assets growth rate, and a holding company dummy variable (with all variables expressed as a percentage of total assets except the holding company variable). All variables are highly significantly related to dividends in all years, as hypothesized. For example, total assets and growth show a negative relationship while all others have a positive relationship. Mayne's data set does not include the largest banking firms—those BHCs with more than $1 billion in total assets. At the time of the study, all banking companies with $1 billion or more in total assets used the holding company ownership form. As such, there were no non-BHC banks to compare in the largest asset segment. Thus, her study is the only one known to focus on "small" banking firms.

Keen (1983) uses a two-factor model, consisting of both a market index and a banking industry index and an early event-study methodology, to examine the abnormal weekly stock returns of 21 banks following the announcement of dividend cuts during the 1974–1977 period. His evidence reveals significantly negative cumulative abnormal returns (CARs) during the week of the announcement. Other tests provide support for the position that dividend cuts provide new information to the markets. Overall, Keen finds evidence supporting the idea that dividend policies provide a signal to the market even within the banking industry, where signaling could arguably be less important given the relatively high regulatory oversight.

Kennedy and Scott (1984) model the average dividend payout ratios of large banks for the years 1967–1976 as a function of 20 variables related to such banking-related measures as leverage, deposit makeup, geographic characteristics, size, and profitability. Starting with 120 of the largest banks in the United States, the authors use half of each year's sample to estimate a predictive model of dividend behavior based on discriminant analysis. They use the resulting model on the holdout sample to see how well the model predicts. The model's classification predictions are significant in 7 of the 11 variations tested. While determinants such as the size and the number of shares outstanding may be timeless indicators of dividend policy, other variables such as location may no longer be relevant. The passage of the Reigle-Neal Interstate Banking and Branching Act of 1994 eliminates geographic limitations, which were likely related to the regional proxies the authors use.

In a study closely related to Kennedy and Scott (1984), Kennedy and Nunnally (1986) examine dividend payout ratios for 1982–1983 using stepwise regression techniques to select the important determinants of payout ratios. The analyses use about 80 large banking firms, depending on the model specifications and data availability in each case. The prior year's dividend payout ratio and the stock's price-earnings (PE) ratio consistently enter the analyses as important determinant variables.

Graddy and Karna (1987) use the banking industry to test the hypothesis that capital gains are preferable to ordinary gains given tax savings. The study examines the payout ratios of 44 large banks over 1978 to 1980 by focusing on how taxes on dividends affect stock returns. The authors model each year's stock return as a function of the dividend payout ratio, which is split into six dichotomous groupings. The model's results generally support the hypothesis that the market places a greater value on lower dividend payouts.

The relatively early use of event-study methodology by Keen (1983) has four companions from the mid-1990s: Filbeck and Mullineaux (1993), Madura, McDaniel, and Wiant (1994), Black, Ketcham, and Schweitzer (1995), and Bessler and Nohel (1996). All use basic event-study methodology to examine the relationship between stock prices of banks and information on dividend policy information. The data periods of these four studies closely overlap.

Filbeck and Mullineaux (1993) examine a sample of 246 to 484 dividend changes from 1973 to 1987 by banking firms. The number of usable dividend announcements depends on the model specification employed. The methodology groups the dividend announcements into four categories: (1) an increase of 20 percent or more, (2) an increase between 10 percent and 20 percent, (3) an increase of less than 10 percent, and (4) a decrease or omission. In general, the results confirm their expectations. Specifically, two-day abnormal returns are significantly positive for announcements of dividend increases and significantly negative for decreases and omissions. In general, smaller dividend increases lead to less significant abnormal returns.

Madura, McDaniel, and Wiant (1994) examine stock return changes around 112 dividend change announcements from 25 BHCs during 1980–1989. Almost all of the dividend changes are positive with 99 of the 112 changes being increases of 5 percent or more. The CARs out to day 10 are significantly positive. Cross-sectional analysis of the CARs finds dividend yields and a measure of the infrequency of such announcements related in a positive manner. However, the overall cross-sectional analysis regression is not significant, which reduces confidence in the importance of the component results.

Black, Ketcham, and Schweitzer (1995) examine stock price reactions to cuts in banking firms' dividends during 1974–1987 and divide the cuts into 1974–1977 and 1978–1987. The early period allows general comparison to Keen (1978) and the later period is characterized as one in which dividend cuts were no longer such a surprising move. The study identifies 74 cuts from 37 banking firms. The banks' shares have significantly negative returns around the announcement date but have abnormal returns insignificantly different from 0% by day 30. The authors conclude that the stock-price reaction of banks to dividend cuts and omissions is no different than that of nonbanks. The CARs between the two test periods do not differ significantly.

The study further examines the determinants of stock abnormal returns. Black et al. (1995) model two-day event period excess returns as a function of the percentage cut in dividends, capital (defined as net worth to total assets), subordinated debt (defined as subordinated debt to total assets), a variable for stock-dividend amounts (when needed), and various information dummy variables (based on the source of information and other concurrent announcements). The regression using 1974–1977 data is not significant at the 5 percent level. The latter period's regression (1978–1987) is significant at the 5 percent level with the percentage cut in dividends and the existence of a stock dividend having the expected negative relationship to abnormal returns. The latter period's results may occur because the announcements are no longer a surprise as the model's variables can statistically explain their impact on stock prices.

The final banking study chiefly employing event-study methodology is Bessler and Nohel (1996). They investigate the stock price reaction to 81 dividend reductions and omissions by 56 commercial banks over the period 1974–1991 with the majority of the observations occurring in 1990 and 1991. Not surprisingly, the evidence shows negative abnormal returns (−8.02 percent) for the two-day event window. This reaction is not only greater than results reported for nonfinancial firms in other studies but also seemingly stronger than other negative announcements associated with the sample banks over the test period.

Bessler and Nohel (1996) also find that dividend cuts seem to be a greater surprise by yielding a more negative response for banking firms with higher capital standards. The finding that stock-price reactions are greater before increasing capital standards on December 1981 reinforces this result. Stock-price reactions are also greater for larger banking firms. This result is somewhat surprising, as signaling theory generally considers signals to be of greater value to smaller-sized firms. However, because the smallest banks in the survey have total assets of about $1 billion or more, interpreting the result requires caution because the sample contains no truly small banks.

The remaining bank-related studies do not have as their primary focus stock-price reactions to dividend announcements. Boldin and Leggett (1995) use 1989 data from 207 BHCs to examine dividends as a signal of quality. Neither geographic location nor basic banking model (regional, superregional, or money center) affect the quality of the bank. The study finds a positive relationship between bank-quality rating and the dollar amount of dividends but a negative relationship between bank-quality rating and the payout ratio. The interpretation is that higher dividends signal a better-quality bank, which is in line with signaling theory expectations, but higher payout ratios are associated with a lower-quality rating given the importance in the banking industry of retained earnings as a source of capital.

In a study examining agency costs for banking firms, Mercado-Mendez and Willey (1995) examine the 104 largest U.S. banks during 1985–1989. They use a dividend yield–inspired measure estimated as a function of earnings volatility, total assets, and a measure that attempts to incorporate managers' exposure to overinvestment in the managed firm. The authors relate manager exposure to personal wealth tied into general shareholders' returns through increased stock ownership, options, and other factors. The only variable with a significant relationship to the dividend yield is total assets, which has a positive relationship. Mercado-Mendez and Willey (p. 115) interpret this result to mean that banks use "more dividends to control for agency costs."

Casey and Dickens (2000) investigate the impact of the Tax Reform Act of 1986 on the dividend policies of banks. Using the basic Rozeff (1982) model, which considers dividend yield as a function of insider ownership, past revenue growth, forecasted revenue growth, the firm's systematic risk (beta), and the number of the firm's common stockholders, the study examines data covering 1982–1992. The results show that only two of the Rozeff variables (forecasted revenue growth and the number of stockholders) are significant in explaining dividend payout ratios of banks for the period. Given the robust results from other studies in estimating Rozeff's model over multiple industries and differing time periods, Casey and Dickens use this result as evidence that the dividend policies of banks differ from nonregulated firms. They modify the basic Rozeff model by adding a capital adequacy measure (equity divided by total assets) and a dummy variable to differentiate the periods before and after the Tax Reform Act's passage. The results offer support for banks' dividend payouts increasing after the top marginal tax rates on dividends decreased. The results also provide support for the hypothesis that banks with greater capital ratios have larger payout ratios.

Three general conclusions emerge from these studies regarding commercial banks and their dividend policies. First, stock-price reactions to dividend policy changes seem to be in line with nonbanking firms. Generally, short-term price reactions are in the same direction as the dividend change, but longer-term abnormal returns are generally insignificantly different from zero. Second, balance sheet and income statement variables such as total assets and income, which researchers theorize as related to dividend policy for nonbanking firms, are generally related for banking firms. Third, some dividend policy determinants of banks appear to be unique. Perhaps the best way to classify these unique factors is under the general heading of regulatory related such as capital and, historically, geographic constraints.

Utilities

Many utility studies focus only on electric utilities. One group of empirical studies includes Dhrymes and Kurz (1964), Higgins (1974), Lee (1976), Moyer, Rao, and Tripathy (1992), and Hansen, Kumar, and Shome (1994). A second groups consists of surveys by Baker, Farrelly, and Edelman (1985), Edelman, Farrelly, and Baker (1985), Farrelly, Baker, and Edelman (1986), and Baker and Powell (1999a, 1999b).

Some electric utilities are part of conglomerate corporations that own gas utilities and other types of firms.

Empirical Studies

Dhrymes and Kurz (1964) examine dividend policy of electric utilities using data from 1947–1959. The model examines payout ratios for 261 firms as a function of net profits, sales, investment level, capital structure (measured by long-term debt level), and liquidity. The results show that dividend payouts are more in line with sales levels than with profit levels for electric utilities of that era.

Higgins (1974) focuses mainly on stock valuation and cost of capital issues. At least for the period 1960–1968 for the electric utility industry, higher total dividends distributions are negative and significantly related to stock value in five of the nine years. Higgins (p. 1200) concludes that his results corroborate dividend irrelevancy theory "in strongly suggesting that dividends do not increase share prices." This evidence is particularly relevant for an industry in which many presume that dividend yield is important. He also reports evidence that a company's dividend payout has little impact on its estimated cost of equity capital.

Lee (1976) uses stock prices, retained earnings, and dividends from 116 electric utility firms for 1960–1969 to examine the impact of retained earnings and dividends on stock prices. Much of the article's motivation is to test for the proper functional form to best model any relationship. Specifically, Lee wants to determine whether the relationship is linear, logarithmic, or has a more general format. He finds that a general functional form incorporating both dividends and retained earnings provides a better result than using dividends and retained earnings independently of each other.

Moyer, Rao, and Tripathy (1992) use data from 69 electric utilities for the period 1978–1986. The model estimates dividend payout (or, in turn, dividend yield) as a function of the utilities' regulatory climate rating (above average, average, or below average), which is based on the adequacy of returns allowed on investments. Tests find that firms with average or below average ratings pay out more dividends. The relationships hold in the aggregate and in most years when estimated separately. The authors conclude that the results provide evidence of regulatory agencies' influencing dividend policies for electric utilities.

Hansen, Kumar, and Shome (1994) study dividend payout ratios for the periods 1980–1985 (81 firms) and 1986–1990 (70 firms). As predicted, the evidence shows that payout ratios of electric utilities are significantly greater than those of S&P 400 firms. The study estimates a model of utility firms' payout ratios as a function of a ranking (from 1 to 13) of stockholder/regulator conflict (with a higher ranking meaning less conflict), ownership concentration, flotation costs for new capital funds, and total asset growth rate. Consistent with their expectations, all variables are significantly negatively related to payout ratios. The authors interpret the results as evidence that dividends of utility firms serve as a method to reduce the stockholder/regulator conflict as opposed to serving as a signal of investment options or a method to reduce stockholder/management conflicts.

Survey Studies

Another group of studies uses survey methodology to examine the dividend policies of utility firms and other industry groups. Baker et al. (1985), Edelman et al.

(1985), and Farrelly et al. (1986) all examine survey responses from 114 utility firms, 147 manufacturing firms, and 57 wholesale/retail firms. The three studies share the same underlying survey. The three industry groups share the same top-four determinants of dividend policy—anticipated future earnings, past dividend pattern, cash availability, and impact on stock price—but not always in the same order of importance. Comparisons show utility firm managers' responses in regards to cash availability and, especially, the impact on stock prices to be different from the nonregulated firms.

Baker et al. (1985) ask managers to indicate the importance of 18 statements linked in theory to dividend policy. Respondents generally believe that dividends affect stock prices, serve as a signal, and are less risky than retained earnings. Tests support differences in opinions between managers of utility firms and nonregulated firms for half of the 18 theoretical statements. Thus, while respondents seem to agree on the major determinants of dividend policy, the rationale underlying those major determinants is arguably quite different for utility managers.

According to Edelman et al. (1985), utility managers are likely to review dividend policy in a formal manner only once a year. Conversely, managers of manufacturing and wholesale and retail firms are more likely to review dividend policies four times a year.

Farrelly et al. (1986) report a relevant finding about the relationship between investment and dividend policy decisions. While more than 90 percent of the managers from all three industries respond that they "never" or "almost never" forego capital investments because of pressures to pay dividends, managers of utility firms report the least disruption to investment from dividends. Only 3.5 percent of the responses from managers of utility firms report an inability to take investments "sometimes" compared to 8.2 percent of the responses from managers of manufacturing firms. The greatest disruption to investment appears to be for wholesale and retail firms. While these managers have only 3.5 percent of responses in the "sometimes" category, they also account for 3.5 percent of the responses in the "often" category. An implication of this evidence is that some seemingly important differences exist as to how utility managers consider dividends as opposed to managers of manufacturing and wholesale and retail firms.

Baker and Powell (1999a) survey managers of U.S.-based firms trading on the New York Stock Exchange (NYSE) to obtain their views on dividend policy for regulated (utility) versus nonregulated (manufacturing) firms. The authors base their analysis on 53 survey respondents for regulated and 117 for nonregulated firms. Both groups provide general support for the importance of four general explanations for dividend policy (signaling, bird in the hand, tax preference, and agency costs). Managers of the utility firms express significantly more support for three of the six signaling-related statements; both bird-in-the-hand statements; and one tax-preference and one agency-cost statement. Of the 20 factors possibly influencing dividend policy, statistically significant differences exist in responses from regulated versus nonregulated firms for seven factors: maintaining the stock price, desiring to pay out target fraction of earnings, meeting current shareholder needs, maintaining capital structure, conforming to industry dividend practice, projecting the future economy, and paying dividends over taking risky investments. Finally, Baker and Powell compare their results to those of earlier surveys and find that the rankings of the dividend determinants to be mostly stable but closer in the later survey.

In contrast, Baker and Powell (1999b) generally find little difference between managers of utility firms and managers of nonregulated firms regarding their opinions on the theoretical underpinnings of dividend policy. The survey of managers from manufacturing, wholesale and retail, and utility firms results in 198 responses. Managers from all three industry groups generally perceive that dividend policy affects firm value and that dividends are a signaling device. The authors offer an explanation for the lack of difference in managers' opinions when comparing across industries. Specifically, Baker and Powell posit that changes in the utilities industry brought about an environment with greater competition, which lessened the differences among the three industry groups.

Insurance

Studies focusing on the insurance industry generally divide data into different types of insurance companies. Lee and Forbes (1980, 1982) focus on non-life-insurance companies. Harrington (1981), Chen (1990), and Akhigbe, Borde, and Madura (1993) consider all types of insurance companies but control for separate groups such as life, property-liability, and other insurers.

Lee and Forbes (1980) examine the stock prices of 34 non-life-insurance companies as a function of dividends per share and retained earnings for 1955–1975. They find a consistent and significantly positive relationship between dividends and equity value for 1955–1968, but the relationship becomes inconsistent from 1969 forward. However, the validity of this evidence of the relationship between dividends and stock value is questionable because this relation is not robust to differing definitions of income.

Lee and Forbes (1982) examine dividend payout ratios and dividend yields of 61 non-life-insurance companies for 1955–1975. The authors use the same four income definitions as their 1980 study but consider three different ownership categories based on whether the majority of each company's common stock during the study period was owned by a single entity, acquired by a single entity, or never owned by a single entity. The results show that the variables best explaining the current dividend measures are dividends of the prior year, current earnings, and the firm's capacity ratio, which is a measurement of each firm's ability to pay dividends based on the relation of equity accounts to assets. Also, the coefficients of determination (R^2) differ significantly between the three ownership classifications. The R^2 estimation decreases the longer a single entity owned the majority of the company's stock during the study period. Finally, tests show non–life insurers take about two years to adjust dividend payout levels to target levels based on earnings.

Unlike Lee and Forbes (1980, 1982), Harrington (1981) focuses on life insurance companies instead of non-life-insurance companies. Using data from 1950 to 1974 to examine 68 publicly traded life insurance companies, he splits the data into two groups: wholly owned subsidiaries and non-wholly-owned subsidiaries. He uses a model to predict the level of dividends that the firm would have paid if it had not become a wholly owned subsidiary. The results show that life insurers acquired by another firm pay higher dividends than predicted. As such, he provides evidence of an association between holding company affiliation and increased dividend payments. This result is consistent with Mayne (1980), who finds that BHCs pay greater dividends than banking firms not within the BHC framework.

Chen (1990) focuses on dividend payouts. He uses dividend income from investments of insurance companies to test for tax-clientele effects. Examining California-based insurance companies, Chen compares 31 life insurers to 42 property-liability insurers. Because life insurers generally have lower marginal tax rates, Chen hypothesizes that life insurance companies prefer higher dividend income. Tests find evidence that life insurers prefer higher-dividend-yielding stocks, thus supporting tax-clientele theory.

One insurance-based study from the mid-1990s uses event-study methodology. Akhigbe, Borde, and Madura (1993) examine the impact of dividend increase announcements on the valuations of insurance companies. Using 253 announcements from 1969 through 1991 for life insurers (113 announcements), property-liability insurers (69), and other insurers (71), tests find significantly positive two-day returns for all insurer types along with 253 banking firms and 253 industrial firms used as a control group. Four-day stock returns are significantly, positively related to the announcements for all except life insurers and banks.

Examination of the two-day abnormal returns shows insurance companies' reactions are significantly greater than those of banking firms but insignificantly different from the industrial firms. "Other" insurers have greater two-day abnormal returns than bank or industrial firms, while life insurers have lower two-day abnormal returns than industrial companies but statistically have the same returns as banking firms. Property-liability insurers have two-day abnormal returns that are greater than banks but statistically similar to industrial companies. Akhigbe et al. (1993) speculate the different reactions of life insurance firms are due to their lower capitalization.

Real Estate Investment Trusts

REITs have unique dividend requirements in that they must pay out a very high percentage, usually 95 percent or more, of net income as dividends to maintain tax benefits. Thus, REITs serve as a unique data base to examine why payouts would be above the mandated level.

Lee and Kau (1987) examine 29 REITs for the period 1971–1981 and report their dividend payment behavior differs from that of industrial firms and insurance companies. Such a difference would justify eliminating REITs from studies examining dividend policy for general firms. The authors also report that increased dividend payments raise the cost of capital of REITs and, therefore, may decrease their stock values.

Wang, Erickson, and Gau (1993) examine dividend payouts for 102 equity and mortgage REITs using data from 1981 to 1988. They model dividend payout as a function of return on assets, an estimated Tobin's Q ratio, the growth rate of total assets, and a leverage ratio, as well as a dummy variable to separate equity and mortgage REITs. The authors hypothesize that all the variables, except the leverage ratio, will have a positive relationship to dividend payout. The model examines dividend payouts for 1985–1988 with samples ranging from 38 firms in 1985 to 71 firms in 1987. Only return on assets, asset growth, and leverage ratio variables are significant in any of the years modeled, but these variable do have the hypothesized relation to dividend payouts when significant. One interpretation of these results is that the dividend policies of REITs do not differ markedly from those of other firms. The tests also show equity REITs have significantly greater dividend payouts than mortgage REITs. The authors' explanation is that the expected cash flows of mortgage REITs should be easier to determine than equity REITs. As such, equity REITs would have higher monitoring costs for their owners, and the owners would require higher dividend payouts to reduce internal monitoring costs.

Similar to the other mid-1990s studies, Wang et al. (1993) also use event-study methodology to test for abnormal returns related to dividend announcements. Both equity and mortgage REIT stocks have significantly positive reactions to dividend increase announcements, while equity REITs have significantly negative reactions to dividend decrease announcements. Contrary to expectations, the share-price reaction of mortgage REITs to dividend decreases is insignificant.

Bradley, Capozza, and Seguin (1998) examine 75 REITs for the period 1985–1992 and find an inverse relationship between dividend payout ratios and cash flow volatility as well asset size and geographic diversification. Property-type diversification has no impact. Evidence shows that returns to shareholders increase with higher dividend payouts while controlling for changes in funds from operations and other items. Thus, a positive relationship exists between dividend payout and stock value. In addition, the study presents evidence that about 90 percent of the stock-price reaction to changes in dividend payouts occurs outside a three-day event window. Evidence also shows that the market punishes firms for cutting dividends more than it rewards them for increasing dividends. That is, stock returns are more severely negative in reaction to a dividend cut than they are positive in response to a dividend increase.

Mooradian and Yang (2001) examine dividend policies for 16 hotel REITs and 51 non-REIT hotel firms for the period 1993–1999. Not surprisingly, non-REIT firms have lower dividends and dividend-per-asset ratios than REIT firms, which pay 95 percent or more of their earnings as dividends. The study's comparison relates more to free cash flow, which is measured before and after considering dividend payouts, than to dividend payouts. Compared to REITS, non-REITs retain greater free cash flows before and after dividends.

Petroleum

Casey and Theis (1997) focus exclusively on dividend policy in the petroleum industry. Studies usually exclude the petroleum industry given accounting peculiarities that make comparing earnings per share to other industries difficult. The authors examine 42 firms (29 U.S.-based and 13 foreign-based) using data for 1992–1995 and employ a modified version of the Rozeff (1982) model. The results show a significantly negative relationship between the dividend payouts of petroleum firms and both insider ownership percentage, which is typical for other industries, and beta. The results provide evidence that the relationship between beta and financial leverage is not as strong in the petroleum industry as in other industries. Casey and Theis do not find a significant relationship between past and expected revenue growth rates. The authors contend that the industry's investment requirements are so large as to possibly render dividend policy a separate, all-but-unrelated management activity. The study's results again show the appropriateness of excluding some industries from earlier studies. The Rozeff model, which is often robust across industries and time periods, does not perform well for the petroleum industry.

General

Kennedy, O'Brien, and Horn (1987) report the results of a 1983 survey of executives working in the electrical utility, telecommunications, and motor carrier sectors. Respondents report that 55 percent of their companies have a formal payout ratio goal, but 36 percent do not even have an informal goal. Also, the survey respondents do not report much concern with any relationship between stock price and the dividend policies of their firms. The authors suggest that this response indicates that the executives do not believe that dividend policy is an important factor in determining stock price.

Collins, Saxena, and Wansley (1996) undertake a more general study that tries to control for various regulated industry types. Their study compares the dividend policy of regulated and nonregulated firms. The authors separate regulated firms into 45 utility firms (of which 29 are electrical and 16 are natural gas firms) and 53 financial services firms (of which 38 are banking and 15 insurance firms) as compared to 402 nonregulated firms from 21 different industries. The study follows Rozeff (1982) in modeling dividend payouts as a function of revenue growth (historical), revenue growth (predicted), systematic risk level (as measured by a beta estimate), the number of shareholders, and the percentage of outstanding stock held by insiders. Using a series of dummy variables within the general Rozeff framework, tests find the dividend payout ratios of financial services firms and unregulated firms are not statistically different. However, utility firms have a significantly higher payout ratio but payout less as insider ownership increases. The results suggest that research may not need to consider financial services firms different from unregulated firms because regulators may be serving as low-cost monitors of the firm's management.

Finally, Wansley (2003) reports dividend payout ratios for each year from 1980 to 2000 for eight industry categories: unregulated, petroleum, transportation, telecom, utilities, financial services (banking), insurance, and REITs. His study provides evidence that regulated firms have both higher dividend payouts and yields than unregulated firms. Utilities and REITs have higher levels than other regulated industries and petroleum firms have the greatest variation in dividend payout ratios. When Wansley eliminates firms that do not pay a dividend in a given year from the sample, there appears to be less difference between the regulated and nonregulated firms for all except utilities and REITs. Petroleum firms continue to have the greatest variation in dividend payout ratios. The findings require caution because Wansley does not include any tests for statistical significance.

FUTURE RESEARCH

There appear to be two major avenues for future dividend-policy study regarding regulated firms. For banking firms, a ripe area would be to explore how changes in regulatory capital definitions affect dividend policies. For both regulated and nonregulated firms, another potential research area would be to test whether the passage of various acts during the Bush administration, which lowered tax rates on most dividend income, affected dividend policies.

For commercial banks, there have been two phases of regulatory capital definitions that may influence dividend policies since 1991. First, the original Basel Accord (Basel 1) was enacted in the United States mainly through the FDIC Improvement Act of 1991 and applied to all commercial banks. Regulators are now in the process of implementing the Basel 1-A for noninternationally involved banks and Basel 2 for the largest 20 or so U.S. banks with substantial international operations. One way to judge whether the regulatory process is having an impact on the management of banking firms is to determine whether dividend payouts have changed over the last 15 or so years and whether any changes differ among the various regulatory categories of banking firms.

One complicating factor during the preceding period is the ongoing change in the marginal tax rates for capital gains versus ordinary income. The Jobs and Growth Tax Relief Reconciliation Act, which was signed into law on May 28, 2003, removes much of the disparity in taxation between capital gains and dividends by taxing both at the 15 percent level. Examining dividend policies to determine whether payout ratios have changed from before to after the Act's passage is an open avenue for all firm types. Despite this complication, the added restrictions on the regulated firms may allow more closely focusing on how tax changes affect dividend policy of regulated firms.

Another area suitable for research is to take any dividend study on nonregulated firms that excludes regulated industries and try to replicate the study for a regulated industry. The results would provide added evidence as to the uniqueness, if any, of the two groupings. Such evidence would help researchers decide whether they need to eliminate regulated firms from future analysis.

CONCLUSIONS

Although researchers have not examined the dividend policies of regulated firms to the extent of nonregulated firms, many studies exist in this area. Given its central importance to the economy, finding that the largest number of studies focuses on commercial banking is not surprising. Yet many studies exist for insurance, utilities, and REITs. Furthermore, avenues for future research appear to be open. Still, the best use of regulated firms to advance knowledge will likely be in some clever methodology that uses the regulatory oversight and special taxation rules that apply in these industries to examine specific dividend policy theories.

REFERENCES

Akhigbe, Aigbe, Stephen F. Borde, and Jeff Madura. 1993. "Dividend Policy and Signaling by Insurance Companies." *Journal of Risk and Insurance* 60:3, 413–428.

Baker, H. Kent, Gail E. Farrelly, and Richard B. Edelman. 1985. "A Survey of Management Views on Dividend Policy." *Financial Management* 14:3, 78–84.

Baker, H. Kent, and Gary E. Powell. 1999a. "Dividend Policy Issues in Regulated and Unregulated Firms: A Managerial Perspective." *Managerial Finance* 25:6, 1–20.

Baker, H. Kent, and Gary E. Powell. 1999b. "How Corporate Managers View Dividend Policy." *Quarterly Journal of Business and Economics* 38:2, 17–35.

Bessler, Wolfgang, and Tom Nohel. 1996. "The Stock-Market Reaction to Dividend Cuts and Omissions by Commercial Banks." *Journal of Banking and Finance* 20:9, 1485–1508.

Black, Harold A., David C. Ketcham, and Robert Schweitzer. 1995. "The Reaction of Bank Holding Company Stock Prices to Dividend Cuts and Omissions." *Mid-Atlantic Journal of Business* 31:3, 217–231.

Boldin, Robert, and Keith Leggett. 1995. "Bank Dividend Policy as a Signal of Bank Quality." *Financial Services Review* 4:1, 1–8.

Bradley, Michael, Dennis R. Capozza, and Paul J. Seguin. 1998. "Dividend Policy and Cash Flow Uncertainty." *Real Estate Economics* 26:4, 555–580.

Casey, K. Michael, and Ross N. Dickens. 2000. "The Effects of Tax and Regulatory Changes on Commercial Bank Dividend Policy." *Quarterly Review of Economics and Finance* 40:2, 279–293.

Casey, K. Michael, and John D. Theis. 1997. "A Note on the Determinants of Cash Flow Dividend Payout in the Petroleum Industry." *Journal of Energy Finance and Development* 2:2, 239–248.

Chen, Charng Yi. 1990. "Risk-Preferences and Tax-Induced Dividend Clienteles: Evidence from the Insurance Industry." *Journal of Risk and Insurance* 57:2, 199–219.

Collins, M. Cary, Atul Saxena, and James W. Wansley. 1996. "The Role of Insiders and Dividend Policy: A Comparison of Regulated and Unregulated Firms." *Journal of Financial and Strategic Decisions* 9:2, 1–9.

Dhrymes, Phoebus, and Mordecai Kurz. 1964. "On the Dividend Policy of Electric Utilities." *Review of Economics and Statistics* 465:1, 76–81.

Edelman, Richard B., Gail E. Farrelly, and H. Kent Baker. 1985. "Public Utility Dividend Policy: Time for a Change?" *Public Utilities Fortnightly* 115:4, 26–31.

Farrelly, Gail E., H. Kent Baker, and Richard B. Edelman. 1986. "Corporate Dividends: Views of Policymakers." *Akron Business and Economic Review*, 17:4, 62–74.

Filbeck, Greg, and Donald J. Mullineaux. 1993. "Regulatory Monitoring and the Impact of Bank Holding Company Dividend Changes on Equity Returns." *Financial Review* 28:3, 403–415.

Graddy, Duane B., and Adi S. Karna. 1987. "Dividend Aspirations, Regulatory Policy, and the Return on BHC Shares." *Akron Business and Economic Review* 18:4, 80–89.

Gupta, Manak C., and David A. Walker. 1975. "Dividend Disbursal Practices in Commercial Banking." *Journal of Financial and Quantitative Analysis* 10:3, 515–529.

Hansen, Robert S., Raman Kumar, and Dilip K. Shome. 1994. "Dividend Policy and Corporate Monitoring: Evidence from the Regulated Electric Industry." *Financial Management* 23:1, 16–22.

Harrington, Scott E. 1981. "Stock Life Insurer Shareholder Dividend Policy and Holding Company Affiliation." *Journal of Risk and Insurance* 48:4, 550–567.

Higgins, Robert C. 1974. "Growth, Dividend Policy and Capital Costs in the Electric Utility Industry." *Journal of Finance* 29:4, 1189–1201.

Keen, Howard, Jr. 1978. "Bank Dividend Cuts: Recent Experience and the Traditional View." *Business Review*, Federal Reserve Bank of Philadelphia, November/December, 5–13.

Keen, Howard, Jr. 1983. "The Impact of Dividend Cut Announcement on Bank Share Prices." *Journal of Bank Research* 13:4, 274–291.

Kennedy, William F., and Bennie H. Nunnally, Jr. 1986. "An Empirical Examination of Large Bank Dividend Payout Ratios, 1982–1983." *Financial Review* 21:3, 48.

Kennedy, William F., Thomas J. O'Brien, and Carl Horn, Jr. 1987. "Dividend Policy of Large Public Utilities: Results of a Nationwide Survey of Chief Executives." *Financial Review* 22:3, 69–70.

Kennedy, William F., and David F. Scott, Jr. 1984. "An Analysis of Large Bank Dividend Policy." *Review of Business and Economic Research* 20:1, 28–38.

Lee, Cheng F. 1976. "Functional Form and the Dividend Effect in the Electric Utility Industry." *Journal of Finance* 31:5, 1481–1486.

Lee, Cheng F., and Stephen W. Forbes. 1980. "Dividend Policy, Equity Value, and Cost of Capital Estimates for the Property and Liability Insurance Industry." *Journal of Risk and Insurance* 47:2, 205–222.

Lee, Cheng F., and Stephen W. Forbes. 1982. "Income Measures, Ownership, Capacity Ratios and the Dividend Decision of the Non-Life Insurance Industry: Some Empirical Evidence." *Journal of Risk and Insurance* 59:2, 269–289.

Lee, Cheng F., and James B. Kau. 1987. "Dividend Payment Behavior and Dividend Policy on REITs." *Quarterly Review of Economics and Business* 27:2, 6–21.

Madura, Jeff, William R. McDaniel, and Kenneth J. Wiant. 1994. "Dividend Policy and Signaling by Large Commercial Banks." *Review of Business Studies* 3:1, 1–14.

Mayne, Lucille S. 1980. "Bank Dividend Policy and Holding Company Affiliation." *Journal of Financial and Quantitative Analysis* 15:2, 469–480.

Mercado-Mendez, Jose, and Thomas Willey. 1995. "Agency Costs in the Banking Industry: An Examination of Ownership Behavior, Leverage, and Dividend Policies." *Journal of Economics and Finance* 19:3, 105–117.

Mooradian, Robert M., and Shiawee X. Yang. 2001. "Dividend Policy and Firm Performance: Hotel REITs vs. Non-REIT Hotel Companies." *Journal of Real Estate Portfolio Management* 7:1, 79–87.

Moyer, R. Charles, Ramesh Rao, and Niranjan Tripathy. 1992. "Dividend Policy and Regulatory Risk: A Test of the Smith Hypothesis." *Journal of Economics and Business* 44:2, 127–134.

Rozeff, Michael S. 1982. "Growth, Beta and Agency Costs as Determinants of Dividend Payout Ratios." *Journal of Financial Research* 5:3, 249–259.

Wang, Ko, John Erickson, and George W. Gau. 1993. "Dividend Policies and Dividend Announcement Effects for Real Estate Investment Trusts." *Journal of the American Real Estate and Urban Economics Association* 21:2, 185–201.

Wansley, James. 2003. " Dividend Policy of Regulated Industries." In *Dividend Policy Theory and Practice*, ed. George M. Frankfurter and Bob G. Wood Jr., 173–185. San Diego, CA: Academic Press.

ABOUT THE AUTHOR

Ross Dickens is a professor of finance and chair of the Department of Economics and Finance at the University of South Alabama. His teaching focuses mostly on corporate finance (undergraduate and graduate) and commercial banking courses. He received his Ph.D. in finance from the University of Tennessee, his MBA from the University of North Carolina, and his BS in business administration from Presbyterian College (South Carolina). He worked in the commercial banking industry in South Carolina before returning to graduate school. He has published articles in about 15 finance journals and authored *Contestable Markets Theory, Competition, and the United States Banking Industry* (Garland Publishing). His work includes three publications related to dividend policy in regulated industries.

CHAPTER 27

Dividend Policy in a Global Perspective

MARC GOERGEN
Professor of Finance, Cardiff Business School

LUC RENNEBOOG
Professor of Corporate Finance, Tilburg University

INTRODUCTION

This chapter examines the role of dividends and the patterns of dividend policy across various national settings. Empirical studies that have tested the validity of Lintner's (1956) model on dividend behavior find that the model generally works well across various countries. Rather than focus on these studies, which have already been reviewed extensively (for an overview, see, e.g., Lease, John, Kalay, Lowenstein, and Sarig, 2000),this chapter focuses on those theories and studies that refine Lintner's model as well as predict and document differences in payout policies across countries and/or companies. Indeed, some of the studies find marked differences, for example, in terms of the flexibility of dividends across countries (Goergen, Renneboog, and Correia da Silva, 2005; Andres, Betzer, Goergen, and Renneboog, 2007).

   Most of the comparative, cross-country studies on dividend policy focus on national characteristics such as corporate governance and political or legal systems. For example, a large body of the empirical finance literature documents that corporate control and ownership varies substantially across different countries. Combining this empirical evidence with the theories suggesting that dividends fulfill a corporate governance role, the expectation is that dividends play an entirely different role across various corporate governance regimes. Hence, the chapter starts by reviewing both the theoretical and empirical literature on the link between corporate governance and dividends. Some argue that the real driving force behind corporate governance is not corporate ownership and control, but law—in particular, the characteristics of a country's legal system—or politics, which in turn determine corporate control. As a result, this chapter also reviews what the theories

The authors are grateful to Marina Martynova, Reginald Liebert, Greg Trojanowski, Corneel Verdonck, and Chendi Zhang for helpful comments.

say about the role of dividends across various legal and political systems. This theoretical review is then followed by a discussion of the few empirical studies that attempt to test the validity of these theories. Finally, the chapter concludes with some policy recommendations and suggestions as to the future research agenda.

HOW DIVIDENDS LINK TO CORPORATE CONTROL AND OWNERSHIP

In the absence of agency problems and based on other restrictive assumptions, Miller and Modigliani (1961) show that dividends are irrelevant in terms of the firm's market value. Rozeff (1982), Easterbrook (1984), and Jensen (1986) were the first to argue that, in the presence of agency costs, dividends play an important role. Their theoretical framework explicitly assumes that ownership has been separated from control within the firm, as hypothesized by Berle and Means (1932). However, there is now a large body of the finance literature showing that firms based outside the United States and the United Kingdom do not normally experience such a separation as they remain under the control of one or several shareholders, even after going public (see, e.g., Goergen and Renneboog, 2003). Hence, in most of the world, dividends are likely to play a very different role from that hypothesized by the key theories in the area. The remainder of this section provides a review of the theories about the role of dividends in the presence of agency costs followed by a summary of the relevant empirical evidence.

The Theory

Despite the fact that both dividend policy and corporate governance are two of the most researched topics in finance, little theoretical work links the two. Further, as discussed shortly, the few theories on the relationship between corporate control and dividends tend to focus on one particular type of ownership (managerial ownership). However, apart from some U.S. and U.K. companies, managers for most other companies tend not to own any shares in their firm and control lies with a large shareholder.

Before reviewing the theories on dividends and control, an important fact to mention is that because of certain legal devices, which are available to companies in most countries including the United States, ownership is not necessarily equivalent to control. Such legal devices include dual class shares, which may consist of one class of shares with no or limited voting rights and another class of shares with full voting rights (see Correia da Silva, Goergen, and Renneboog, 2004, for an overview of other such legal devices). Therefore, a large shareholder can potentially own all the control rights (the voting stock) but share the cash flow rights with others. An example of a company that has such dual-class stock is the German sports-car manufacturer Porsche AG. The founding family owns all the voting stock, whereas the nonvoting stock is listed on the stock exchange and is widely held. Avoiding any confusion in what follows requires making a clear distinction between control and ownership. In particular, the term *control* refers to the ownership of control rights and the term *ownership* refers to the ownership of cash flow rights.

In their seminal book, *The Modern Corporation and Private Property*, Berle and Means (1932) argue that, as companies grow, ownership is separated from control. Beyond a certain size, the initial owners of the firm will no longer be able to finance the firm and will have to take the firm public to gain access to further financing. As the firm grows further, more investors will hold the firm's stock and each investor's holding in the firm will be too small to confer any reasonable level of control over the management. The dispersion of ownership then effectively puts the firm's management in control. Two groups end up controlling the firm: its management (the agent), who has no or little ownership in the firm, and dispersed shareholders (the principals), who own the firm but do not hold sufficient stakes to exercise control. Under such a scenario, there is a real danger that the management may not operate the firm in the best interests of the shareholders.

According to Rozeff (1982), dividends are one way of mitigating this principal-agent problem. Rozeff argues that there is a dividend-payout ratio that maximizes the firm's value. A firm achieves this optimal dividend-payout ratio at the point where it minimizes the sum of the agency costs and transaction costs of financing. Agency costs decrease with dividends whereas transaction costs increase with dividends. The minimization of the sum of these costs then produces a unique optimal dividend payout ratio for the firm.

Similarly, Jensen (1986) recognizes the corporate governance role of dividends. Managers, who have access to large free cash flows (cash flows exceeding the financing of all investment projects with positive net present values [NPVs]) may be tempted to spend these on negative NPV projects. Indeed, if left to their own devices, managers may pursue growth objectives rather than shareholder value maximization as they derive benefits from managing larger firms, such as increased social status. High dividends then become a way whereby managers keep free cash flows low and reduce the firm's agency costs.

While Rozeff's (1982) model implies a negative and monotonic relation between the dividend payout ratio and managerial ownership and control, Schooley and Barney (1994) suggest a nonmonotonic relationship between the two. They argue that this form of relationship is consistent with the corporate governance role of dividends, including the managerial entrenchment hypothesis advanced by Morck, Shleifer, and Vishny (1988). Morck et al. hypothesize that at lower levels, managerial ownership and control realign the interest of managers with those of the shareholders, whereas at intermediate levels, such ownership and control shield managers from the disciplinary action of their shareholders. At high levels of managerial ownership and control, managers' interests are then again in line with those of the other shareholders. On the basis of a sample of large U.S. firms, Morck et al. find that their hypothesis holds, as the link with firm value is positive for managerial ownership and control below 5 percent, is negative in the region of 5 percent and 25 percent, and is positive above 25 percent.

Easterbrook's (1984) spin on dividends as a corporate governance device is slightly different from that of Rozeff (1982) and Schooley and Barney (1994). According to Easterbrook, a high dividend payout will keep internal funds to a minimum and force the firm to raise new capital from the market at regular intervals. Each time the firm raises new funds, it subjects itself to the scrutiny of outsiders, including its investment banks, financial analysts, the financial press, and potential investors.

As already mentioned in the introduction to this chapter, the limited theory on the corporate governance role of dividends assumes a corporate governance framework that prevails in the United States and United Kingdom but that could not be more different from that found in the rest of the world. In particular, as shown in the next section, large shareholders such as families, banks, and governments tend to control companies outside the United States and United Kingdom. Hence, the agency problems are likely to be different from those hypothesized by the previous theoretical articles.

Indeed, the agency problems within companies from countries outside the United States and United Kingdom tend to be between the large controlling shareholder and the minority shareholders. In particular, the minority shareholders face the danger of being expropriated by the large shareholder. However, a large shareholder may also be beneficial, as this shareholder has the right incentives to monitor the management and thereby address the free-rider problem and the ensuing lack of monitoring that normally affects firms with dispersed control (Shleifer and Vishny, 1986). Goergen et al. (2005) argue that, given that dividends are a costly way of ensuring that managers run the firm in the interests of the shareholders, firms with a large shareholder may prefer to resort to less costly shareholder monitoring. Dividends would then be more flexible and play a less important role in firms with concentrated control than in those with dispersed control.

The Empirical Evidence

Before turning to reviewing the empirical evidence on the link between corporate control and dividend policy, assessing corporate control across the world is important. The European Corporate Governance Network (ECGN), the predecessor of the European Corporate Governance Institute (ECGI), undertook the first detailed cross-country study of corporate control, and Barca and Becht (2001) report the results from the study. The study analyzes the ultimate control of listed firms in Europe and the United States. *Ultimate control* is defined as the ownership of control rights via both direct holdings (holdings at the first tier) and indirect holdings (holdings at higher tiers). Hence, if a shareholder held shares in a listed company via both direct and indirect stakes, the study adds up the various stakes to arrive at the aggregate voting rights held by that shareholder.

While only about 2 percent of listed U.S. and U.K. firms have a majority shareholder, the study finds that in Europe the percentage of listed firms with such a shareholder ranges from about 26 percent (for Sweden) to 68 percent (for Austria). If the focus is on the presence of a shareholder controlling a blocking minority of 25 percent or more, 15 percent of listed firms in the United Kingdom and 5 to 8 percent of firms in the United States—depending on whether they are listed on the NYSE or NASDAQ—have such a shareholder compared to between 64 percent (for Sweden) and 94 percent (for Belgium) for continental Europe.

Given the marked differences in the concentration of control, the agency problems are likely to be very different. Goergen and Renneboog (2001) argue that the agency problem prevailing in the United Kingdom (and United States) is the classical agency problem between management and shareholders. By contrast, in the rest of the world, it is more likely to be a conflict of interests between the large controlling shareholder and minority shareholders. Barca and Becht (2001) also report that major differences exist between the types of shareholders that prevail in the United Kingdom and the rest of Europe. In the United Kingdom, the most important type of shareholder is institutional investors, followed by the management (see Goergen and Renneboog, 2001, for further details). In the rest of Europe, the most important shareholders are families or individuals, other companies, and the government.

Table 27.1 provides detailed data on the control structure of 221 German firms listed during 1984–1993. About 84 percent of German firms have a shareholder holding at least 25 percent of their voting equity and at least 40 percent have a majority shareholder. Given direct control, the most important type of large shareholder is other companies. However, given ultimate control (control via a chain of holdings), families are the most important type of large shareholder followed by banks and other companies.

The remainder of this section starts by reviewing the empirical evidence on the United States and United Kingdom, and then proceeds by reviewing the empirical evidence on the rest of the world.

The United States and United Kingdom

Using U.S. data, Rozeff (1982) tests his proposition that the dividend-payout ratio increases as the percentage of shares held by the management decreases. He finds empirical support in favor of his proposition. Other studies such as Dempsey and Laber (1992), Crutchley and Hansen (1989), Eckbo and Verma (1994), and Hu and Kumar (2004) provide further support for the U.S. case. However, Hu and Kumar also find that the relation disappears once they control for firm size.

Several papers investigate the validity of Easterbrook's (1984) thesis that a high dividend-payout ratio is a self-disciplinary mechanism forcing managers to raise equity on a regular basis, thereby subjecting themselves to the scrutiny of outsiders. For example, Born and Rimbey (1993) analyze a sample of 490 U.S. firms which, over the 1962–1989 period, either initiated dividends (474 firms) or reinitiated dividends (16 firms). Out of the 490 firms, 102 issued new equity during the 12 months preceding the dividend change. They find that firms raising capital experience lower abnormal returns at the dividend announcement than those not acquiring outside capital. Yet when they adjust for the size of the dividend, by using the dividend yield (the dividend over the stock price), they find that firms that raise external capital have higher abnormal returns than the other firms. Born and Rimbey interpret this as evidence in favor of Easterbrook (1984).

Filbeck and Mullineaux (1999) also test Easterbrook's thesis on a sample of U.S. banks. However, contrary to Born and Rimbey (1993), they do not find any support for the disciplinary role of dividends. Their interpretation of this contradictory result is that banks have less need for self-disciplinary mechanisms such as high dividends, given that they are already subject to intense monitoring by banking regulators.

Moh'd, Perry, and Rimbey (1995) test both Rozeff's (1982) and Easterbrook's (1984) hypotheses on 341 U.S. firms over the 1972–1989 period. Contrary to the previously mentioned studies, they use time-series data rather than a single cross-section. They also use various measures of the potential agency costs: management ownership, institutional ownership, and ownership concentration (measured by

Table 27.1   Control Structure of 221 German Industrial and Commercial Quoted Firms in 1984, 1989, and 1993

| | First-Tier Control | | | | Ultimate Control | | | |
| | ≥25% | | ≥50% | | ≥25% | | ≥50% | |
	%	N	%	N	%	N	%	N
Panel A. 1984								
A. Widely held	15.4	28	45.6	83	15.9	29	46.2	84
B. Closely held, the largest shareholder being								
1. Family	25.8	47	19.8	36	33.0	60	24.7	45
2. Industrial/commercial	25.8	47	18.7	34	11.0	20	8.2	15
3. State	4.4	8	3.3	6	7.7	14	5.5	10
4. Bank	12.1	22	2.7	5	15.9	29	5.5	10
5. Insurer	0.5	1	0	0	1.1	2	0	0
6. Foreign institution	6.0	11	4.9	9	8.2	15	7.1	13
7. Holding	9.3	17	4.4	8	0	0	0	0
8. Foundation	0.5	1	0.5	1	1.6	3	1.1	2
9. Unknown	0	0	0	0	5.5	10	1.6	3
Total	100	182	100	182	100	182	100	182
Panel B. 1989								
A. Widely held	15.8	35	41.2	91	16.3	36	41.6	92
B. Closely held, the largest shareholder being								
1. Family	26.7	59	22.6	50	36.2	80	29.4	65
2. Industrial/commercial	27.6	61	19.5	43	10.0	22	7.2	16
3. State	3.6	8	3.2	7	6.3	14	5.0	11
4. Bank	8.6	19	2.7	6	12.2	27	5.0	11
5. Insurer	0.5	1	0	0	0.5	1	0	0
6. Foreign institution	6.3	14	4.1	9	9.5	21	7.2	16
7. Holding	9.5	21	5.4	12	0.9	2	0	0
8. Foundation	1.4	3	1.4	3	2.7	6	1.8	4
9. Unknown	0	0	0	0	5.4	12	2.7	6
Total	100	221	100	221	100	221	100	221
Panel C. 1993								
A. Widely held	14.9	31	39.4	82	15.9	33	39.9	83
B. Closely held, the largest shareholder being:								
1. Family	22.1	46	16.3	34	32.7	68	25.0	52
2. Industrial/commercial	33.7	70	26.4	55	12.0	25	9.6	20
3. State	4.3	9	3.4	7	8.7	18	6.3	13
4. Bank	7.7	16	2.4	5	10.1	21	3.8	8
5. Insurer	1.9	4	0	0	1.9	4	0	0
6. Foreign institution	5.3	11	5.3	11	10.6	22	10.6	22
7. Holding	9.1	19	5.8	12	0.5	1	0.5	1
8. Foundation	1.0	2	1.0	2	1.9	4	1.4	3
9. Unknown	0	0	0	0	5.8	12	2.9	6
Total	100	208	100	208	100	208	100	208

Widely held firms are those that do not have any shareholder holding at least 25% or 50% of the voting shares. The sample size varies over the ten-year period as some firms in the sample are not quoted during the whole period and some went private or bankrupt.
Source: Goergen et al. (2005).

the natural logarithm of the number of shareholders). Moh'd et al. find support for both hypotheses. They also report that firms adjust their dividends to reflect changes in their agency costs and transaction costs.

Chen and Steiner (1999) place dividend policy in a wider context by estimating a simultaneous equations system for dividend policy, management ownership of voting rights, risk taking, and capital structure. For a cross-section of 784 U.S. firms for 1994, they find that management ownership and dividends are substitute mechanisms for reducing agency costs. Their result provides further support for Rozeff (1982).

Crutchley, Jensen, Jahera, and Raymond (1999) investigate the joint determination of dividends, leverage, management ownership, and institutional ownership for two cross-sections of more than 800 NYSE- and AMEX-listed firms for 1987 and 1993. They find that for 1987, dividend policy and institutional ownership are jointly determined and positively correlated. Contrary to Rozeff's prediction, insider ownership is not linked to dividends. Conversely, for 1993, they find a negative, convex link between the two, which supports Schooley and Barney's (1994) extension of Rozeff (1982).

In addition, the relationship between dividends and institutional ownership is also different. Dividends are now negatively determined by institutional ownership. Crutchley et al. (1999) explain the change in the relationship by the fact that institutional investors were more active shareholders in 1993 than in 1987. Similar to Crutchley et al., Schooley and Barney (1994) and Hamid, Prakash, and Smyser (1995) also report evidence in support of a nonlinear relationship between dividends and insider ownership. Finally, Zeckhauser and Pound (1990) do not find evidence that firms with large shareholders have lower dividend payouts.

Although banks in the United States are not allowed to hold equity stakes in industrial firms, they may still monitor the management of the firms to which they have made substantial loans. Low, Glorfeld, Hearth, and Rimbey's study (2001) suggests that this is indeed the case. They study the announcement effect of dividend omissions for two samples of large and small U.S. firms that omitted their dividend some time during 1978–1996. They find that, for small firms, the negative announcement reaction to a dividend omission is less substantial for firms with considerable bank debt than for those with little or no bank debt. They do not, however, find such a link for the large firms. Further, they report that nonbank debt reduces the negative price reaction to dividend omissions less than bank debt. Low et al. conclude that their results suggest that banks reduce informational asymmetries and agency problems.

In the case of the United Kingdom, Short, Zhang, and Keasey (2002) study the dividend policy of 211 firms from the Official List of the London Stock Exchange (LSE) over 1988–1992. They distinguish between managerial and institutional ownership of voting rights. Their measures of ownership are two dummy variables which equal one if managerial ownership and institutional ownership, respectively, exceed 5 percent; and zero otherwise. They find strong evidence that firms with institutional ownership have higher dividend payouts whereas those with managerial ownership have lower dividend payouts. They interpret their results as further evidence in favor of Rozeff (1982) and Easterbrook (1984). Short et al. argue that institutional shareholders impose high dividends on the firms in which they invest to force the latter regularly to raise external capital and to subject themselves to the scrutiny of outsiders.

Renneboog and Trojanowski (2005, 2007) provide further support for Rozeff (1982). They analyze a large panel of U.K. firms for the 1990s and find that the payout policy is significantly related to control concentration. They report that companies adjust their dividends to earnings changes only gradually, which is consistent with dividend smoothing, as documented in the literature. They claim that their results suggest a presence of the more general phenomenon of total payout smoothing. Indeed, while profitability drives the payout decision of the analyzed companies, the presence of strong block holders or block-holder coalitions weakens the relationship between the two. The reduced sensitivity of dividends to earnings under concentrated control suggests that controlling shareholders trade off the agency costs of free cash flow against the risk of underinvestment. In line with Rozeff (1982), strong block holders or block-holder coalitions mitigate the agency conflict between the management and shareholders and, consequently, reduce the need to limit the free cash flow within the firm. Although they find the impact of the voting power of shareholder coalitions on the payout ratio is consistently negative, the magnitude of this effect differs across the categories of block holders. In particular, industrial firms and individuals not connected with management are the categories of block holders that require the lowest payouts.

The Rest of the World

Given that corporate control exhibits very dissimilar patterns in the rest of the world, dividend policy is likely to play a substantially different role. The presence in most firms of large shareholders, who may perform monitoring tasks, may indeed reduce the need for dividends. In particular, a common view is that German firms have strong ties with their main bank, the so-called Hausbank (see, e.g., Edwards and Fischer, 1994; Becht and Boehmer, 2001; Franks and Mayer, 2001; Köke, 2004), which provides their debt capital. German banks also hold substantial stakes in larger firms, especially those without other large shareholders. In Japan, *keiretsus* consists of several firms grouped around a core bank, which provides financing to the members of the group (Kester, 1986; Prowse, 1990; Hoshi, Kashyap, and Scharfstein, 1990, 1991; Berglöf and Perotti, 1994). Given that German and Japanese banks own equity and debt capital in the firms with which they have strong ties, they also have the right incentives to monitor the management of the latter. Hence, firms with strong bank ties may be subject to less substantial agency problems.

Dewenter and Warther (1998) compare the dividend policies of Japanese and U.S. firms. They find that Japanese firms belonging to *keiretsus* are less reluctant to cut or omit their dividends and that the stock-price reaction is less substantial when they do so. Dewenter and Warther interpret this pattern as evidence that Japanese banks reduce asymmetric information and agency costs by monitoring the firms that are part of their *keiretsu*.

Goergen et al. (2005) study the flexibility of dividends in Germany. They distinguish among the following types of controlling shareholders: families, other German firms, the government, banks, insurance companies, foreign shareholders, holding companies, and charities. They find that, compared to U.S. firms (see DeAngelo, DeAngelo, and Skinner, 1992), German firms are much less reluctant to reduce or omit their dividend. For firms with at least five consecutive years of positive earnings preceding the loss, 80 percent of loss-making German firms omit their dividend in the year of the loss compared to only 15 percent of U.S. firms. Goergen et al. also find that bank-controlled firms are less reluctant to cut or omit their dividend than firms with other types of controlling shareholders and widely held firms. Similar to what Dewenter and Warther (1998) conclude for the case of Japanese firms, Goergen et al. conclude that bank-controlled German firms suffer less from asymmetric information and agency problems than other firms and therefore have less need for costly dividend signaling. Conversely, Gul and Kealey (1999) do not find that Korean *chaebols*, large conglomerates owned by families and banks, have a different dividend policy from that of firms controlled by other shareholders.

Gugler and Yurtoglu (2003) argue that dividends reflect the severity of the conflict of interests between the large controlling shareholder and the small shareholders. Based on 736 announcements of dividend changes by German firms over the period 1992–1997, they find that the dividend payout ratio decreases with the size of the stake held by the largest shareholder but increases with that held by the second largest shareholder. Similarly, the stock-price reaction at the announcement of a dividend cut is also more negative (but not significantly more negative) for firms with one large shareholder but no second large shareholder than for those firms with two large shareholders. Gugler and Yurtoglu also find that firms with violations of the one-share-one-vote rule—via pyramids of ownership and cross-shareholdings—have more negative announcement effects and lower dividend payout ratios than other firms.

Gugler and Yurtoglu (2003) reach several conclusions based on their results. While a large shareholder can have positive effects via increased monitoring of the management, the shareholder with uncontested control may also have negative effects via the expropriation of minority shareholders. However, their results do not tend to warrant their interpretation. They report that, in their sample of 266 German firms, the largest stake amounts to 50.1 percent on average (median of 50.1 percent) of the votes, whereas the second stake makes out on average only 18.3 percent of the votes (median of 10.0 percent). which is clearly below a blocking minority of 25 percent. Hence, why the second largest shareholder should have any power to prevent the largest shareholder from expropriating the minority shareholder should the latter wish to do so is not entirely clear. Gugler and Yurtoglu also find that majority firms without a large minority shareholder also have a higher (albeit not significantly higher) Tobin's Q than other firms. This finding also does not fit with their interpretation. Finally, the differences between the announcement effects of dividend changes are not statistically significant between majority-controlled firms with a large minority shareholder and those without one.

Gugler (2003) predicts that different types of large shareholders provide different levels of monitoring. He expects government-controlled firms to suffer the most from agency problems as these firms are ultimately controlled by the citizens who have even fewer incentives to monitor the management than small shareholders of privately-held firms. As a result, Gugler expects managers of government-controlled firms to pay out stable dividends and to have high dividend payouts to keep their principals happy. Conversely, as family-controlled firms are less likely to suffer from agency problems, their dividend policy is likely to be more flexible and their dividend payout ratio is likely to be lower. Gugler does not make any predictions as to the dividend policy of firms controlled by banks and foreign shareholders, as the ultimate controlling shareholder, who defines the dividend policy, may vary for these firms.

Gugler (2003) finds evidence for his predictions for a sample of 214 nonfinancial Austrian firms. Although these firms are among the 600 largest Austrian firms, most of them are not listed on the stock exchange. When investment opportunities are good, government-controlled firms have the highest and least flexible dividends, whereas family-controlled firms have the lowest dividends and also more flexible dividend policies. The dividend policy of foreign- and bank-controlled firms is somewhere between these two extremes. Finally, Gugler finds that for those firms with few investment opportunities dividends are high irrespective of their control structure. Similar to Gugler, Gul (1999) reports a positive link between the dividend payout ratio and government ownership for Chinese firms.

Summary

To summarize, only a limited amount of theory exists on the link between corporate control and dividend policy. In addition, the existing theory assumes that the agency problem within firms is the classical agency problem between the management and the shareholders. Therefore, most theoretical work tends to focus on the relation between managerial ownership and dividends. Given the concentration of corporate control outside the United States and United Kingdom, which results in the main agency problem being between the large controlling shareholder and the minority shareholders, the theory has limited applicability to the rest of the world.

In the case of the United States and United Kingdom, the empirical literature confirms that management ownership and dividends are substitute devices for reducing agency costs. There is also support for the thesis that firms use high dividend payouts as a self-disciplinary mechanism, as high dividends force them to raise capital regularly from the outside investors and subject themselves to the scrutiny of the latter. Empirical evidence from the rest of the world suggests that large shareholders also have an impact on payout policies. Evidence from German and Japanese firms shows that bank-controlled firms tend to have more flexible dividend policies than those with other types of controlling shareholders and widely held firms. Evidence from Austria and China also suggests that government-controlled firms pay out higher and more stable dividends than other firms.

DIVIDENDS, POLITICS, AND LAW

The previous section focused on national characteristics relating to corporate control and whether differences in corporate control have an impact on payout policies. This section starts by reviewing the theories arguing that a country's legal or political system determines corporate control. If the theories are valid, differences between legal and political systems will be the main explanatory factor for differences in corporate payout policies across countries. After providing a review of these theories, this section provides a discussion of the scant empirical evidence testing the predictions of these theories as to dividend policy.

The Theory

According to La Porta, Lopez-de-Silanes, Shleifer, and Vishny (1997, 1998, and 2000a), the quality of law drives corporate governance and corporate control. They distinguish between two broad families of law: common law and civil law. Common law accords an important role to the judges, who essentially create the law by setting precedents in court. Given the high discretionary power of judges under common law, La Porta et al. argue that this family of law is more flexible and therefore provides a higher degree of shareholder protection from managers. Conversely, civil law relies on extensive codes of law and limits the role of the judges to the interpretation of law texts in court. As a result, La Porta et al. believe that this family of law provides much weaker investor protection.

La Porta, Lopez-de-Silanes, Shleifer, and Vishny (1999) report that weak shareholder protection prevents the separation of ownership from control. They find that very few firms are widely held in countries with weak legal protection of investors. They argue that shareholders are reluctant to give up control as keeping control is the only way they can prevent the managers from expropriating their investment.

Martynova and Renneboog (2007) document the evolution of the main aspects of corporate governance regulation in Europe and the United States over a 15-year period. They find that corporate governance regulation in most Continental European countries was subject to substantial changes, especially during the period 1998–2002. Overall, (minority) shareholder protection increased at the expense of creditor protection. However, despite Continental European corporate (governance) law moving somewhat in the direction of U.K. law, many national differences are still upheld.

La Porta, Lopez-de-Silanes, Shleifer, and Vishny (2000b) propose an alternative thesis (the outcome thesis) to Easterbrook's thesis (1984). Easterbrook bases his thesis on the assumption that shareholders can enforce high dividend payout policies on the management and/or elect managers who will choose such payout policies. In contrast, La Porta et al. argue that, in countries with weak investor protection, shareholders cannot force the insiders to pay out enough cash and thereby limit the consumption of the firm's resources by the insiders. Hence, they expect that weak shareholder protection goes hand in hand with low dividend payouts and vice versa.

Conversely, Roe (2003) believes that the real driver of corporate governance is politics rather than law. He argues that left-wing governments exacerbate the classical agency problems between managers and shareholders. Left-wing governments tend to favor workers over investors, and they put in place policies that increase the power of the former within corporations. According to the principal-agent model, managers, if left unchecked, pursue growth objectives rather than the maximization of shareholder wealth. Indeed, managers derive certain benefits from running large firms, such as increased social recognition.

Furthermore, the literature on the determinants of managerial compensation suggests that the main determinant of management pay is firm size and not profitability. Similarly, workers prefer large firms over small ones as the former typically provide better working conditions and increased job security. As a result, under left-wing governments, the only way for investors to address the reinforced principal-agent problem is to keep large controlling stakes, enabling them to keep the management in check. In contrast, right-wing governments tend to favor investors over workers, and they formulate policies that improve investor protection. As a consequence, ownership and control of firms located in right-wing countries can easily be separated.

The Empirical Evidence

La Porta et al. (2000b) conduct the first extensive cross-country survey of dividend policy. Their sample covers 4,000 large firms from 33 different countries. They argue that the degree of shareholder protection in a given firm's country can serve as a proxy for potential agency problems. They find that firms from countries with good shareholder protection pay on average higher dividends and have a negative relationship between their dividend payout ratio and their investment opportunities (as measured by the sales growth). In contrast, the dividend ratios of firms from countries with weak shareholder protection are independent of their growth opportunities. La Porta et al. conclude that this is evidence of the agency costs of low shareholder protection.

Correia da Silva et al. (2004) question whether La Porta et al.'s (2002b) interpretation of their results is that straightforward. Using three different measures for the dividend payout ratio, La Porta et al. find that the patterns across countries vary markedly with each measure. The three different measures they use are the ratio of dividends over cash flows, the ratio of dividends over earnings, and that of dividends over sales.

Consistent with La Porta et al.'s (2002b) interpretation, the median for each measure is always significantly higher for the common law countries. However, several countries clearly stick out. In particular, two of the largest civil law economies, Germany and Japan, have dividend-payout ratios—if measured by dividends over earnings and dividends over cash flows—that are higher than the median payout ratio for the common law countries. Yet Taiwan, another civil law country, has a dividend payout amounting to between 2.5 and 6 times (depending on the measure) the level of the median dividend payout for the common law countries. In contrast, the common law country of Canada has a lower payout ratio than the median dividend payout of the civil law countries. Another criticism of the La Porta et al. study is the use of a single cross-section on dividend payout to attempt to derive generally valid conclusions. Indeed, as Goergen et al.'s (2005) study suggests, the payout policy of German firms is much more flexible than that of the U.S. and U.K. counterparts. Hence, basing the analysis on a single cross-section may not lead to generally valid conclusions.

Renneboog and Szilagyi (2006) study the impact of antishareholder provisions on dividend behavior. A well-known fact (see, e.g., La Porta et al., 2000a) is that firms in stakeholder-oriented regimes tend to adopt antishareholder devices that violate the one-share-one-vote rule. Most Dutch firms limit shareholder control by adopting poison pills and golden shares or by simply issuing nonvoting depository receipts (*certificates*). In addition, once Dutch firms reach a certain size, they are legally obliged to adopt an institutional form known as the structured regime, which automatically strips shareholders of most of their rights.

Renneboog and Szilagyi (2006) show that Dutch dividends tend to be low, fairly flexible, and correlated with operating cash flows. They argue that shareholders are often too weak to enforce optimal payout policies. Firms that adopt the structured regime and multinationals that voluntarily adopt it despite benefiting from an exemption pay even lower dividends and smooth dividends to a lesser extent. Firms that are majority owned by a foreign shareholder and are therefore free to adopt a mitigated form of the regime show signs of being tightly monitored but do not adopt a lower and smoother dividend payout. Renneboog and Szilagyi conclude that dividend policy and strong block-holder control are not substitute governance devices to curb agency problems. On the contrary, firms with a major shareholder pay higher dividends, and their dividend policy is more rigid. When antishareholder provisions erode shareholder power, dividend payout is typically lower and closely follows the cash flow stream.

Bank, Cheffins, and Goergen (2006) test Roe's (2003) politics thesis for the case of U.K. firms over the period 1950–2002. They argue that if Roe's thesis is valid, dividends will be higher under conservative governments than under Labour Party governments. They find much anecdotal evidence suggesting that various U.K. governments have targeted company dividends. For example, according to Bank et al. (p. 9), Winston Churchill, in 1951, as the conservative leader of the opposition, strongly criticized the Labour government for proposing to introduce compulsory controls on dividends:

> To win the extreme section of the trade union leaders to this policy [the then Chancellor of the Exchequer], proposed that dividends should . . . be frozen. Observe that this was not done on the merits, but because much of the driving power of the Socialist movement is derived from the jealousy and envy of others who think they are more fortunate than themselves.

Bank et al. (2006) use both direct and indirect measures of the political orientation of the party in power. They base their direct measures on Cusack and Engelhardt's (2004) politics indices. Their indirect measures include tax preference indices, measures of union power, and dummy variables indicating law changes and the presence of compulsory or voluntary dividend controls. However, Bank et al. do not find any consistent evidence in support of Roe's politics theory. Their lack of support of Roe (2003) is difficult to reconcile with the nature of the United Kingdom's political system, which ensures strong majority governments. In contrast, the political systems of other European countries frequently lead to coalition governments, which may have a weak power base. Hence, whereas for the United Kingdom the measurement of the political orientation of the government is a relatively straightforward exercise, this may not be the case for other countries. Testing Roe's thesis for countries other than the United Kingdom may be relatively more difficult.

Summary

This section reviews theories claiming that corporate governance across countries is not exogenous and is driven by certain factors. If the theories are correct, these factors, rather than corporate governance, determine dividend policy. These theories argue that the driving force behind corporate governance—and dividends—is either the quality of law or the political orientation of the government.

The legal theory advanced by La Porta et al. (1997) distinguishes between two broad families of law: common law and civil law. The perception is that common law is better at protecting investors than civil law. La Porta et al. (2000b) claim to find confirmation of their outcome thesis. According to this thesis, good legal protection enables shareholders to get managers to return enough cash to them and to limit on-the-job consumption by the latter. However, La Porta et al.'s interpretation of the results may be less straightforward than they claim. Indeed, payout policies change markedly depending on the measure used for the payout ratio and some of the larger national economies do not conform to their outcome thesis. Hence, the jury is still out on whether the quality of law—as measured by La Porta et al.—determines dividend policy.

Whereas La Porta et al. (2000a) believe that the quality of law determines corporate governance, Roe (2003) claims that politics is the main driving force behind corporate governance. He argues that right-wing governments prefer investors over workers and they will create laws that protect the former and/or reduce the power of the latter within firms. Hence, under right-wing governments, investors feel protected enough to permit the separation of ownership from control. Bank et al. (2006) argue that dividends should also be higher under right-wing governments. They test Roe's theory on the United Kingdom over 1950 to 2002 but do not find any consistent evidence that the political orientation of the party in power has any influence on corporate payout policies.

To conclude, no consensus exists about what determines corporate governance and, in turn, dividend policy across countries. There are also competing theories to the ones advanced by La Porta et al. (2000a) and Roe (2003), such as Pagano and Volpin (2005), who claim that neither law nor politics determines corporate governance but rather the proportionality of the voting system. They distinguish among the three social groups of workers, managers, and rentiers. The latter live off the income generated by their wealth. In a proportional voting system, parties target coherent social groups, such as those of the workers and managers, as they need a majority of votes to win the election. Such political systems result in strong workers' rights. On the contrary, weak workers' rights characterize a majoritarian system, which guarantees an election victory if the pivotal district is won over. Indeed, Pagano and Volpin argue that rentiers who, contrary to workers and managers, do not have a strong affiliation to a particular political party, populate the pivotal district. They find confirmation of their predictions as the proportionality of the voting system is positively correlated with employment protection and negatively correlated with investors' rights.

CONCLUSIONS

This chapter focuses on dividend policy in a global perspective and reviews the theories that explain differences in the behavior of firms and managers across countries. Such theories are those that relate dividend policy to corporate governance. As there is now ample empirical evidence that corporate control varies substantially between the United States and United Kingdom on one side and the rest of the world on the other side, the role of dividends and their level and flexibility should vary across countries. The limited evidence that exists suggests that dividend policy does indeed reflect the characteristics of national corporate governance regimes and the control structure of individual firms.

Other theories argue that corporate governance is not exogenous. That is, other factors, such as the type of legal or political system prevailing in a country determine corporate governance. Unfortunately, as yet, few empirical studies have tested the validity of these theories.

This lack of empirical evidence provides a fertile ground for further research. Also, as is the case with other research areas in finance, much existing research concentrates on the United States, and to a lesser extent, the United Kingdom, despite the pronounced idiosyncrasies of these two national systems. As Goergen (2007) argues, very little is known about the role of dividends across different corporate governance regimes despite the fact that various cross-national bodies have been advocating for the adoption of the shareholder model on a global level.

REFERENCES

Andres, Christian, Andre Betzer, Marc Goergen, and Luc Renneboog. 2007. "Dividend Policy of German Firms: A Dynamic Panel Data Analysis of Partial Adjustment Models." Working Paper, University of Sheffield.

Bank, Steven A., Brian R. Cheffins, and Marc Goergen. 2006. "*Dividends and Politics.*" ECGI–Law Working Paper 24/2004, available at SSRN: http://ssrn.com/abstract= 636523 or DOI: 10.2139/ssrn.636523.

Barca, Fabrizio, and Marco Becht. 2001. *The Control of Corporate Europe.* Oxford: Oxford University Press.

Becht, Marco, and Ekkehardt Boehmer. 2001. "Ownership and Voting Power in Germany." In *The Control of Corporate Europe*, ed. Fabrizio Barca and Marco Becht, 128–153. Oxford: Oxford University Press.

Berglöf, Erik, and Enrico Perotti. 1994. "The Governance Structure of the Japanese Financial Keiretsu." *Journal of Financial Economics* 36:2, 259–284.

Berle, Adolf A., and Gardiner C. Means. 1932. *The Modern Corporation and Private Property.* New York: Macmillan.

Born, Jeffery A., and James N. Rimbey. 1993. "A Test of the Easterbrook Hypothesis Regarding Dividend Payments and Agency Costs." *Journal of Financial Research* 16:3, 251–260.

Chen, Carl R., and Thomas L. Steiner. 1999. "Managerial Ownership and Agency Conflicts: A Nonlinear Simultaneous Equation Analysis of Managerial Ownership, Risk Taking, Debt Policy, and Dividend Policy." *Financial Review* 34:1, 119–136.

Correia da Silva, Luis M., Marc Goergen, and Luc Renneboog. 2004. *Dividend Policy and Corporate Governance.* Oxford: Oxford University Press.

Crutchley, Claire E., and Robert S. Hansen. 1989. "A Test of the Agency Theory of Managerial Ownership, Corporate Leverage and Corporate Dividends." *Financial Management* 18:4, 36–76.

Crutchley, Claire E., Marlin R. Jensen, John S. Jahera, and Jennie E. Raymond. 1999. "Agency Problems and the Simultaneity of Financial Decision Making: The Role of Institutional Ownership." *International Review of Financial Analysis* 8:2, 177–197.

Cusack, Thomas R., and Lutz Engelhardt. 2004. "Parties, Governments and Legislatures Data Set." http://www.wz-berlin.de/mp/ism/people/misc/cusack/d_sets.en.htm#data, accessed November 30, 2004.

DeAngelo, Harry, Linda DeAngelo, and Douglas Skinner. 1992. "Dividends and Losses." *Journal of Finance* 47:5, 1837–1863.

Dempsey, Steven J., and Gene Laber. 1992. "Effects of Agency and Transactions Costs on Dividend Payout Ratios: Further Evidence of the Agency-Transaction Cost Hypothesis." *Journal of Financial Research* 15:4, 317–321.

Dewenter, Kathryn L., and Vincent A. Warther. 1998. "Dividends, Asymmetric Information, and Agency Conflicts: Evidence from a Comparison of the Dividend Policies of Japanese and U.S. Firms." *Journal of Finance* 53:3, 879–904.

Easterbrook, Frank H. 1984. "Two Agency-Cost Explanations of Dividends." *American Economic Review* 74:4, 650–659.

Eckbo, B. Espen, and Sanita Verma. 1994. "Managerial Share Ownership, Voting Power, and Cash Dividend Policy." *Journal of Corporate Finance* 1:1, 33–62.

Edwards, Jeremy S., and Klaus Fischer. 1994. *Banks, Finance and Investment in Germany*. London: CEPR and Cambridge University Press.

Filbeck, Greg, and Donald J. Mullineaux. (1999). "Agency Costs and Dividend Payments: The Case of Bank Holding Companies." *Quarterly Review of Economics and Finance* 39:3, 409–418.

Franks, Julian R., and Colin P. Mayer. 2001. "Ownership and Control in Germany." *Review of Financial Studies* 14:4, 943–977.

Goergen, Marc. 2007. "What Do We Know about Different Systems of Corporate Governance?" *Journal of Corporate Law Studies* 7:1, 1–15.

Goergen, Marc, and Luc Renneboog. 2001. "Strong Managers and Passive Institutional Investors in the U.K." In *The Control of Corporate Europe*, ed. Fabrizio Barca and Marco Becht, 258–284. Oxford: Oxford University Press.

Goergen, Marc, and Luc Renneboog. 2003. "Why Are the Levels of Control (So) Different in German and U.K. companies? Evidence from Initial Public Offerings." *Journal of Law, Economics, and Organization* 19:1, 141–175.

Goergen, Marc, Luc Renneboog, and Luis M. Correia da Silva. 2005. "When Do German Firms Change Their Dividends?" *Journal of Corporate Finance* 11:1/2, 375–399.

Gugler, Klaus. 2003. "Corporate Governance, Dividend Payout Policy, and the Interrelation between Dividends and Capital Investment." *Journal of Banking and Finance* 27:7, 1297–1321.

Gugler, Klaus, and Burcin Yurtoglu. 2003. "Corporate Governance and Dividend Pay-out Policy in Germany." *European Economic Review* 47:4, 731–758.

Gul, Ferdinand A. 1999. "Government Share Ownership, Investment Opportunity Set and Corporate Policy Choices in China." *Pacific-Basin Finance Journal* 7:2, 157–172.

Gul, Ferdinand A., and Burch T. Kealey. 1999. "Chaebol, Investment Opportunity Set and Corporate Debt and Dividend Policies of Korean Companies." *Review of Quantitative Finance and Accounting* 13:4, 401–416.

Hamid, Shahid S., Arun J. Prakash, and Michael W. Smyser. 1995. "The Role of Managerial Demand and Ownership in the Determination of Dividend and Debt Policies of Mature Corporations." Working Paper, Florida International University.

Hoshi, Takeo, Anil Kashyap, and David Scharfstein. 1990. "The Role of Banks in Reducing the Costs of Financial Distress in Japan." *Journal of Financial Economics* 27:1, 67–88.

Hoshi, Takeo, Anil Kashyap, and David Scharfstein. 1991. "Corporate Structure, Liquidity, and Investment: Evidence from Japanese Industrial Groups." *Quarterly Journal of Economics* 106:1, 33–60.

Hu, Aidong, and Praveen Kumar. 2004. "Managerial Entrenchment and Payout Policy." *Journal of Financial and Quantitative Analysis* 39:4, 759–790.

Jensen, Michael C. 1986. "Agency Costs of Free Cash Flow, Corporate Finance and Takeovers." *American Economic Review* 76:2, 323–329.

Kester, W. Carl. 1986. "Capital and Ownership Structure: A Comparison of United States and Japanese Manufacturing Corporations." *Financial Management* 15, 5–16.

Köke, Jens. 2004. "The Market for Corporate Control in a Bank-based Economy: A Governance Device?" *Journal of Corporate Finance* 10:1, 53–80.

La Porta, Rafel, Florencio Lopez-de-Silanes, Andrei Shleifer, and Robert W. Vishny. 1997. "Legal Determinants of Finance." *Journal of Finance* 52:3, 1131–1150.

La Porta, Rafel, Florencio Lopez-de-Silanes, Andrei Shleifer, and Robert W. Vishny. 1998. "Law and Finance." *Journal of Political Economy* 106:6, 1113–1155.

La Porta, Rafel, Florencio Lopez-de-Silanes, Andrei Shleifer, and Robert W. Vishny. 1999. "Corporate Ownership around the World." *Journal of Finance* 54:2, 471–517.

La Porta, Rafel, Florencio Lopez-de-Silanes, Andrei Shleifer, and Robert W. Vishny. 2000a. "Investor Protection and Corporate Governance." *Journal of Financial Economics* 58:1–2, 3–27.

La Porta, Rafel, Florencio Lopez-de-Silanes, Andrei Shleifer, and Robert W. Vishny. 2000b. "Agency Problems and Dividend Policies around the World." *Journal of Finance* 55:1, 1–33.

Lease, Ronald, Kose John, Avner Kalay, Uri Lowenstein, and Oded Sarig. 2000. *Dividend Policy: Its Impact on Firm Value.* Oxford: Oxford University Press.

Lintner, John. 1956. "Distribution of Incomes of Corporations among Dividends, Retained Earnings and Taxes." *American Economic Review* 46:2, 97–113.

Low, Soo-Wah, Louis Glorfeld, Douglas Hearth, and James N. Rimbey. 2001. "The Link between Bank Monitoring and Corporate Dividend Policy: The Case of Dividend Omissions." *Journal of Banking and Finance* 25:11, 2069–2087.

Martynova, Marina, and Luc Renneboog. 2007. "A Corporate Governance Index: Convergence and Diversity of National Corporate Governance Regulations." Working Paper, Tilburg University.

Miller, Merton H., and Franco Modigliani. 1961. "Dividend Policy, Growth and the Valuation of Shares." *Journal of Business* 34:4, 411–433.

Moh'd, Mahmoud A., Larry G. Perry, and James N. Rimbey. 1995. "An Investigation of the Dynamic Relationship between Agency Theory and Dividend Policy." *Financial Review* 30:2, 367–385.

Morck, Randall, Andrei Shleifer, and Robert W. Vishny. 1988. "Managerial Ownership and Market Valuation: An Empirical Analysis." *Journal of Financial Economics* 20:1/2, 293–315.

Pagano, Marco, and Paolo F. Volpin. 2005. "The Political Economy of Corporate Governance." *American Economic Review* 95:5, 1005–1030.

Prowse, Stephen D. 1990. "Institutional Investment Patterns and Corporate Financial Behavior in the United States and Japan." *Journal of Financial Economics* 27:1, 43–66.

Renneboog, Luc, and Peter Szilagyi. 2006. "How Relevant Is Payout Policy under Low Shareholder Protection?" Discussion Paper CentER, Tilburg University and European Corporate Governance Institute.

Renneboog, Luc, and Greg Trojanowski. 2005. "Patterns in Payout and Channel Payout Choice of U.K. Firms in the 1990s." Discussion Paper CentER, Tilburg University.

Renneboog, Luc, and Greg Trojanowski. 2007. "Control Structures and Payout Policy." *Managerial Finance* 33:1, 43–64.

Roe, Mark J. 2003. *Political Determinants of Corporate Governance.* Oxford: Oxford University Press.

Rozeff, Michael S. 1982. "Growth, Beta and Agency Costs as Determinants of Dividend Payout Ratios." *Journal of Financial Research* 5:3, 249–259.

Schooley, Diane K., and L. Dwayne Barney. 1994. "Using Dividend Policy and Managerial Ownership to Reduce Agency Costs." *Journal of Financial Research* 17:3, 363–373.

Shleifer, Andrei, and Robert W. Vishny. 1986. "Large Shareholders and Corporate Control." *Journal of Political Economy* 94:3, 461–488.

Short, Helen, Hao Zhang, and Kevin Keasey. 2002. "The Link between Dividend Policy and Institutional Ownership." *Journal of Corporate Finance* 8:2, 105–122.

Zeckhauser, Richard J., and John Pound. 1990. "Are Large Shareholders Effective Monitors? An Investigation of Share Ownership and Corporate Performance." In *Asymmetric Information, Corporate Finance and Investment*, ed. R. Glenn Hubbard, 149–180. Chicago: University of Chicago Press.

ABOUT THE AUTHORS

Marc Goergen has a degree in economics from the Free University of Brussels, an MBA from Solvay Business School (Brussels), and a D.Phil. from the University of Oxford. He has held appointments at UMIST and the Universities of Manchester, Reading, and Sheffield. He holds a chair in finance at Cardiff Business School. His research interests are in international corporate governance, mergers and acquisitions, dividend policy, corporate investment models, insider trading, and initial public offerings. Goergen has widely published in academic journals, such as *European Financial Management*, *Journal of Corporate Finance*, *Journal of Finance*, *Journal of Financial Intermediation*, and *Journal of Law, Economics and Organization*. He has also contributed chapters to numerous books and written two books: *Corporate Governance and Financial Performance* (Edward Elgar) and *Dividend Policy and Corporate Governance* (Oxford University Press). Goergen is a research associate of the European Corporate Governance Institute.

Luc Renneboog is professor of corporate finance at Tilburg University and a research fellow at CentER (Tilburg) and ECGI (Brussels). He graduated from the University of Leuven with degrees in management engineering (B.Sc./M.Sc.) and in philosophy (BA), the University of Chicago with an MBA, and the London Business School with a Ph.D. in financial economics. He held appointments at the universities of Leuven and Oxford and visiting appointments at a.o. LBS (London), EUI Institute (Florence), HEC (Paris), and Venice University. Renneboog has published in *Journal of Finance*, *Journal of Financial Intermediation*, *Journal of Law and Economics*, *Journal of Corporate Finance*, *Journal of Banking and Finance*, *Journal of Law, Economics, and Organization*, and others. He has coauthored and edited books on corporate governance, dividend policy, and venture capital. His interests are corporate finance, corporate governance, insider trading, and law and economics.

CHAPTER 28

Dividend Policy in Emerging Markets

P. C. KUMAR
Emeritus Professor, Kogod School of Business, American University

MICHEL A. ROBE
Associate Professor of Finance, Kogod School of Business, American University

INTRODUCTION

Before the 1980s, discussions of financial markets usually took place in the context of developed nations. Since then, the markets of other countries have started to play increasingly important roles in global financial activity. Researchers and policy makers soon recognized that the markets of some developing countries offered fresh opportunities for improving portfolio performance (Errunza, 1977). In 1981, the International Finance Corporation coined the phrase "emerging financial markets" (EFMs) to reference a set of developing countries for which it had developed standardized stock market indices. According to Beim and Calomiris (2001, p. ix), the emergence of these markets connotes "the separation of financial systems from state domination through a process of liberalization."

Beim and Calomiris (2001, p. x) also note that EFMs constitute "some 50 experiments in privatizing economies and building financial systems, none perfect, with different emphases and different problems." Accordingly, much research exists on EFMs. The objective of this chapter is to synthesize and to place in perspective the part of that work focusing on corporate payout policies.

When setting their dividend policies, EFM firms face variations of the traditional determinants of corporate payout policies in developed financial markets (DFMs) plus several unique factors. There are legal constraints on the amounts that may, or must, be distributed to shareholders. Further, EFMs underwent, mostly in the first half of the past two decades, waves of privatization and of capital account liberalization that affected payout policies. Finally, EFMs are subject to greater macroeconomic volatility than DFMs. Indeed, many EFMs experienced, directly

---

The authors are grateful to H. Kent Baker, the editor, and to David Reiffen for comments and suggestions. They thank Elif Aksoy for her diligent research assistance.

or indirectly, one or more financial crises in the last decade. This chapter provides evidence that dividends payments are sensitive to these shocks.

The chapter proceeds as follows. The first section introduces the specific institutional factors that condition corporate payout policies in emerging markets. Next, the chapter provides a discussion of cross-country and single-country studies of dividend policies in these markets followed by evidence on the evolution of key descriptive statistics of dividend policies in 24 emerging markets in Eastern Europe, Asia, Latin America, and Africa. Finally, the chapter provides several conclusions and outlines avenues for future research.

INSTITUTIONAL FACTORS INFLUENCING CORPORATE PAYOUT POLICIES IN EFMs

The environment in which a firm operates conditions its behavior. There are three major areas in which EFMs differ from the United States: (1) legal constraints or mandates; (2) corporate governance and ownership structures, including the prevalence of government or foreign ownership; and (3) macroeconomic environment. These differences bring about substantially different dividend policies in EFMs.

Legal Constraints or Mandates

A source of potential divergence between corporate payout policies in emerging and other markets arises from possible legal restrictions on the maximum or minimum amounts that companies pay out to shareholders and from constraints on how these payments may take place.

Mandatory Dividends

Even in the United States, laws have at times directly influenced the amounts that corporations must return to their shareholders in the form of dividends. As Christie and Nanda (1994) note, the unexpected tax imposed on undistributed corporate profits in 1936 and the large dividend increases that ensued illustrate the sensitivity of payout to government policies. Allen and Michaely (2003) argue that modern U.S. laws discouraging or banning various types of institutional investors from investing in companies that pay little or no dividends are instrumental in the decision to pay out dividends despite the burden on individual investors in the form of additional taxes.

Corporate laws in a number of EFMs are more direct, in that they openly mandate minimum payout levels in the form of dividends. Examples of countries with minimum-dividend rules include Brazil, Chile, Colombia, Greece, and Venezuela (La Porta, Lopez-de-Silanes, Shleifer, and Vishny, 2000; Mitton, 2004; Castillo and Jakob, 2006). As Stulz and Williamson (2003) observe, no English-speaking or Protestant country has such rules. Some civil law countries that once had payout requirements now have rescinded them. For example, Adaoglu (1999) reports that Turkey stopped requiring cash dividends of at least 50 percent of profits after 1995.

Legality of Various Forms of Dividend Payout

Besides constraining the amounts distributed, regulations in many countries also influence the manner in which those distributions take place. Grullon and Michaely (2002) note that while U.S. laws have never explicitly prohibited share repurchases, programs for repurchasing shares did not take off until 1983. At that time, the U.S. Securities and Exchanges Commission (SEC) took actions to alleviate fears about its predisposition to take a pessimistic view of such programs.

Much has been made of the trends since the mid-1980s toward greater use of share repurchases by U.S. firms (Bagwell and Shoven, 1989; Fama and French, 2001) and greater concentration of the dividend flow within a subset of companies (Skinner, 2008). Outside the United States, share repurchases either have only recently been legalized or, in some cases, remain illegal. Even when allowed, share repurchases are typically subject to more restrictions. Constraints include preconditions to the adoption of a buyback program (e.g., requiring a vote of the shareholders as opposed to merely obtaining the approval of the board of directors); the size of the buyback (in many countries, at most 10 percent of outstanding shares may be repurchased); the treatment of repurchased shares (e.g., whether they must be canceled); limits on the resources that may be used to finance a buyback program; and limits on off-exchange transactions (International Organization of Securities Commissions, 2004; Vermaelen, 2005).

In DFMs, much of the shift toward legalization took place in the past decade. Exceptions include tiny Luxembourg, which authorized buybacks in 1915, and the United Kingdom, where repurchases became legal in 1981. Many other DFMs waited until more recently to legalize repurchases. Government authorities relaxed buyback laws in Australia in 1989; Ireland and Portugal in 1990; Switzerland in 1992; Japan in 1994 (although, in practice, tax laws continued to discourage repurchase programs until 1995); Denmark in 1995; Finland in 1997; France, Italy, and Germany in 1998; Norway in 1999; and Sweden in 2000 (Lasfer, 2000; Sabri, 2003; Kim, Schremper, and Varaiya, 2005; De Ridder, 2006). The belated legalization of buybacks in much of Western Europe is striking given that the European Commission published a directive recommending their legalization in 1976 (Vermaelen, 2005). Nevertheless, share repurchases now account for more than a third of the amounts that Western European companies distribute to their shareholders (von Eije and Megginson, 2008).

In EFMs, the 1990s also stand out as a decade that witnessed the widespread legalization of share repurchases. The first legal buyback in Hong Kong occurred in late 1991 (Brockman and Chung, 2001.; Firth and Yeung, 2005). Korea first permitted repurchases in 1994 (Jung, Lee, and Thornton, 2005; Joh and Ko, 2007). Brazil substantially relaxed its laws in 1997 (Saito, 2002). Other major EFMs have since allowed the practice, including Malaysia and Poland in 1997, Singapore and India in 1998, South Africa in 1999, Taiwan in 2000, and China in 2005 (Sabri, 2003; Gryglewicz, 2004; Chang, Lai, and Yu, 2005; Gupta, 2005; De Ridder, 2006; Chiao, Chih, Wang, and Hsu, 2007). Although repurchases are still modest in many EFMs (Liu, 2002), they have become frequent in Taiwan, Hong Kong, and South Korea. South Korea appears unique. By 2005, more than a quarter of all publicly listed Korean firms had repurchased some of their own shares, and in 2003, the amounts distributed through buybacks exceeded for the first time the amounts paid out as dividends (Joh and Ko, 2007). Some EFMs continued to prohibit buybacks under any circumstances—including Jordan, Oman, Lebanon, Morocco, and Saudi Arabia (Sabri, 2003) and even larger EFMs such as Chile (Pistor, Keinan, Kleinheisterkamp, and West, 2003) and Turkey.

Ownership Structure and Corporate Governance

The idea behind dividend signaling models is that high-quality firms pay higher dividends to reduce information disparities between managers and investors. In practice, however, there is only mixed evidence that signaling drives U.S. payout policies. Survey evidence, furthermore, suggests that privately held U.S. firms are even less likely to use dividends as signals (Brav, Graham, Harvey, and Michaely, 2005). Both of these empirical facts suggest that signaling considerations may have little relevance at EFM firms because many of the latter are owned by families or belong to corporate groups. Dewenter and Warther (1998) make a similar point for Japanese firms in general and *keiretsu* firms in particular.

In contrast, the typical ownership structures in EFMs should give a major role to agency considerations in explaining observed payout policies in these markets. First, although Morck and Yeung (2005) note that dividend taxation discourages pyramidal structures in the United States, this may not apply to EFMs because many EFM companies belong to industrial conglomerates or to family groups. If laws protecting external investors are weak or if their enforcement is lax, then the empirical question that arises is whether membership in an industry or a family group in those countries is associated with the expropriation of outside investors by dominant shareholders.

Second, despite rounds of privatizations in the past two decades, many EFM governments or government-controlled entities retain ownership stakes in some corporations. Thus, these governments' cash flow needs are a potentially important determinant of corporate payout policies, particularly if political authorities are unable or unwilling to sell shares to generate revenues.

Finally, while EFMs have historically restricted foreign ownership and penalized or banned dividend payments to foreign investors, many EFMs have liberalized capital account operations in the past 20 years. In many of those countries, one would expect changes in dividend policies reflecting the greater role played by foreign investors and multinationals.

Macroeconomic Conditions: Growth Rates, Volatility, and Crises

Fama and French (2001) find that U.S. firms with the strongest growth opportunities plow back most or all of the earnings they generate rather than distribute the cash as dividends. To the extent that growth opportunities are greater in EFMs than in mature economies, managers of EFM firms should be more willing than their DFM counterparts to adjust payout in response to changes in investment opportunity sets.

Another reason for EFM companies to have more volatile dividend policies relates to the economic environment in which they operate. Not only are macroeconomic fluctuations stronger and costlier in EFMs (Pallage and Robe, 2003), but EFM firms also have reduced access to international capital during domestic downturns and crises (Kaminsky, Reinhart, and Végh, 2004). Consequently, EFM shareholders should more readily accept dividend cuts following earnings shortfalls.

CROSS-COUNTRY STUDIES

Glen, Karmokolias, Miller, and Shah (1995) provide perhaps the earliest study of dividend policies in EFMs. According in part to a survey of financial market participants, they conclude that managers in EFMs emphasize target dividend payout ratios and attempt to achieve their targets even though this policy may generate volatility in the amounts distributed. In other words, there is less concern than in DFMs for preserving dividend levels.

More recent cross-country studies have emphasized agency-theoretic premises. At the core of this literature is the study by La Porta et al. (2000) that examines the relationship between investor protection and dividend policy. Subsequent contributions focus on extensions of La Porta et al., including the influences on dividend policies of ownership structure and control (Faccio, Lang, and Young, 2001); the organization of financial systems (Aivazian, Booth, and Cleary, 2003a, 2003b); and firm-level corporate governance (Mitton, 2004).

On Investor Protection, Legal Traditions, and Dividends

La Porta et al. (2000) test empirically whether agency considerations explain why firms pay dividends. They propose two alternative hypotheses of how corporate dividend policies may reveal agency problems. In their "substitute" theory, corporate insiders—conscious of their need to raise capital in the future from external markets—pay dividends to establish a reputation for fair treatment of minority shareholders. Under their alternative theory, dividends are the outcomes of minority investors' exercising their legal power to wrest resources from corporate insiders. According to the outcome hypothesis, any unseen and, hence, immeasurable decrease in agency costs may be attributed to improvements in the legal environment protecting the rights of investors.

The legal tradition of a country offers a clue as to the treatment of investors in that investors enjoy better legal protections in countries following the common law (Anglo-Saxon) tradition than in countries following the civil law tradition. La Porta et al. (2000) exploit this insight. Using a sample of 4,103 firms in 33 countries in the early 1990s, they find that various specifications of dividend payout ratios are generally higher in countries with common law traditions, thus lending support for the outcomes theory. In these common law countries, dividend payout ratios are higher for slow-growth companies than for high-growth companies. La Porta et al. (p. 18) conclude that "well-protected minority shareholders are willing to delay dividends in firms with good growth prospects."

On Ownership, Control and Dividends

Faccio et al. (2001) specifically examine how the structure of ownership and control influences dividend behavior in East Asian corporations within an agency-theoretic framework and with West European corporations as benchmarks. In the United States, financial markets are well regulated and transparent. Hence, the main agency problem is between managers and shareholders. In East Asia, where firms are often controlled by a family that also provides the top manager, the key conflict is between dominant and minority shareholders. Faccio et al. (p. 54) note that an "extraordinary concentration of control" is a major source of problems in East Asian corporate governance; and that "this control is obscured behind layers of corporations, hence insulated against the forces of competition on less-than-transparent capital markets." Thus, controlling shareholders can extract large personal benefits from projects that yield poor returns to their firms. Insiders can, for example, set unfair terms for sales of goods and services to other companies within the same group or for transfers of assets and control stakes between members of the same group. The role of dividends lies in reducing the net corporate wealth under insider control and thereby limiting the scope for insider expropriation.

Faccio et al. (2001) find that the payout ratios of Western European corporations are higher than those of their East Asian counterparts, which complements the La Porta et al. (2000) finding that greater legal protection brings about higher dividends. At the same time, Faccio et al. find that tightly affiliated corporations (those bound to a business group by a chain of control that entails at least 20 percent of the control rights at each link) pay significantly higher dividends than those having a lower ownership-control ratio. This finding suggests that investors expect expropriations at such firms and that corporations competing for capital must pay higher dividends to allay their concerns.

On the Organization of Financial Systems and Dividends

Aivazian et al. (2003a, 2003b) analyze dividend policy through the prism of institutional differences between countries that have adopted the Anglo-Saxon capital markets model and those following the "Continental-German-Japanese" banking model. Aivazian et al. (2003b, p. 103) argue that the orientation of a country's financial system should influence "the use of dividend policy as both a signal and a pre-commitment device."

Aivazian et al.'s (2003b) "substitute" hypothesis posits that dividends can substitute for direct communication with investors in the firm. Thus, dividend policy should be more important in firms operating in arm's-length capital markets (where debt is held by uninformed investors) than in relationship-based, bank-centric capital markets (where banks provide much of the financing and collect the relevant information on their own). Their alternative complement hypothesis posits that dividends reinforce rather than replace other factors in controlling problems arising from agency and adverse selection issues. Bank debt in general reduces both the moral hazard related to managerial behavior and the agency costs connected to insider actions. Nevertheless, in bank-centric countries where investor protection is poor, firms should still pay dividends if they are to attract equity capital.

Empirically, Aivazian et al. (2003b) find only mixed evidence that a country's financial system helps explain its firms' payout policies. Aivazian et al. (2003a) also report that, while the same variables as in the United States influence dividend policies in emerging markets, the sensitivities to these variables vary. Furthermore, predicting dividend changes using the Lintner (1956) dividend-smoothing model is more difficult for EFM firms than U.S. firms. As Aivazian et al. (2003b, p. 120) note, it appears that "the institutional structures of developing countries make corporate dividend policy a less viable mechanism for signaling future earnings and for reducing agency costs, than for U.S. firms operating in capital markets with arm's length transactions."

On Firm-Level Corporate Governance and Dividends

Mitton (2004) compares the respective effects of firm-level corporate governance and countrywide investor protections on dividend policy. Intuitively, a firm's corporate governance traditions add to its host country's investor protection laws in arming shareholders with more rights. As in La Porta et al.'s (2000) outcomes model, having greater rights should enable shareholders to force corporate insiders to disgorge cash through dividend payments.

Mitton (2004) finds that firms with better corporate governance ratings have higher dividend payouts. An increase in the corporate governance rating of unit standard deviation results in a 4 percent increase in the dividend payout. Analogous to the finding in La Porta et al. (2000), Mitton reports that firms with stronger corporate governance ratings exhibit a negative relationship between growth opportunities and dividends. However, while both countrywide investor protection and firm-level corporate governance have explanatory powers for corporate dividend payouts, the former variable is dominant. Furthermore, firm-level corporate governance has a positive relationship with dividend payouts in countries that offer strong investor protection. Mitton concludes that firm-level corporate governance and countrywide investor protection are complements rather than substitutes.

Summary of Empirical Cross-Country Findings

The La Porta et al. (2000) study serves as the core for studies relating to dividend policy in emerging markets. The legal tradition of a country plays a major part in protecting minority investors. La Porta et al. show that investors in countries whose legal framework follows the common law tradition exercise their rights to dividends as a way to prevent wasteful managerial discretionary expenditures. Mitton (2004) shows that, compared to country-wide investor protections, good corporate governance at the firm level has only a minor effect on dividend policy. From showing that even in EFMs corporations tightly controlled by a family or business group pay higher dividends compared to corporations with lower degrees of control, Faccio et al. (2001) conclude that dividends payments help allay the concerns of minority shareholders who otherwise would expect expropriation by dominant shareholders. Finally, the factors determining corporate dividends are broadly the same in bank-centric and market-centric emerging economies, although the degree of dividend sensitivity to firm-level financial variables differs between EFMs and the United States (Aivazian et al., 2003a, 2003b).

INDIVIDUAL COUNTRY STUDIES

This section synthesizes the results of 36 other studies on corporate payout policies in 19 individual EFMs. Table 28.1 lists these studies and identifies their main focus. Together, these studies highlight similarities, as well as the existence and

Table 28.1   Sample of Single-Country Studies of Payout Policies in EFMs

	Author	Date	Focus or Identifying Feature
Panel A. Latin America			
Argentina	Bebzcuk	2004*	General
Brazil	Anderson	1999**	Bond covenants' impact on dividends
Chile	Castillo and Jakob	2006**	Ex-dividend day behavior
Mexico	Price, Roman, and Rountree	2007*	Governance, legal reforms, and payout
Panel B. Emerging Europe			
Cyprus	Travlos, Trigeorgis, and Vafeas	2001**	Signaling, event study
Czech Republic	Bena and Hanousek	2008**	Large internal versus external shareholders
Poland	Gryglewicz	2004*	Stock buybacks versus dividends
	Kowalewski, Stetsyuk, and Talavera	2007*	Governance
Turkey	Adaoglu	1999**, 2000**	Dividend stability, legal mandates
	Yilmaz and Gulay	2006**	Information content, event study
Panel C. Africa and Middle East			
Egypt	Omran and Pointon	2004**	Trading frequency, Investment Opportunities
Jordan	Al-Malkawi	2007**	General; government stake
Oman	Al-Yahyaee, Pham, and Walter	2006*	General; government stake
Tunisia	Ben Naceur, Goaied, and Belanes	2006**	General
Panel D. Asia			
China	Wei, Zhang, and Xiao	2004**	Privatization
	Deng, Gan, and He	2007*	Governance, privatization
	Xu and Wang	1997*	Government stake
	Gul	1999a**	Investment opportunities, government stake
Hong Kong	Brockman and Chung	2001**	Share repurchases
	Ho, Lam, and Sami	2004**	IOS, director ownership
	Firth and Yeung	2005**	Share repurchases
India	Gupta	2005*	Share repurchases
	Kumar	2006**	Ownership structure
	Reddy	2002*	General
	Reddy and Rath	2005**	Disappearing dividends
	Som	2006***	Survey; corporate governance
Malaysia	Pandey	2001*	Investment Opportunities, Industry patterns
	Sun and Tong	2002**	Privatization and payout level

(Continued)

Table 28.1 (*Continued*)

	Author	**Date**	**Focus or Identifying Feature**
South Korea	Black, Jang, and Kim	2006**	Corporate governance
	Joh and Ko	2007*	Ownership structure and repurchases
	Jung, Lee, and Thornton	2005**	Stabilization funds and repurchases
	Kim, Kim, and Kwon	2007*	Large internal *versus* external shareholders
Taiwan	Chang, Lai, and Yu	2005**	Reaction to repurchase
	Chiao, Chih, Wang, and Hsu	2007*	Repurchases
Thailand	Ronapat and Evans	2005**	Disappearing dividends

This table provides a summary description of 36 single-country studies that analyze or discuss corporate payout policies in 19 different EFMs. The table lists these studies by continent and country and provides the relevant features of each study in terms of dividend research. One asterisk denotes a working paper, two asterisks denote a journal article, and three asterisks denote a book.

persistence of some important differences, between payout policies in EFMs and DFMs. Notably, Som's (2006) monograph on corporate governance and policies in India is the sole single-country study that includes survey data.

Similarities between EFMs and DFMs

Perhaps the strongest similarity between EFMs and DFMs is the link between growth opportunities and corporate payout behavior. Investment opportunities influence dividend policies in the United States (Smith and Watts, 1992), Western Europe (Denis and Osobov, 2008), and Japan (Gul, 1999b). Researchers report similar findings for Brazil (Anderson, 1999), Cyprus (Travlos, Trigeorgis, and Vafeas, 2001), China (Gul, 1999a), India (Kumar, 2006; Som, 2006), Hong Kong (Ho, Lam, and Sami, 2004), Malaysia (Pandey, 2001), Jordan (Al-Malkawi, 2007), Mexico (Price, Roman, and Rountree, 2007), Poland (Kowalewski, Stetsyuk, and Talavera, 2007), and actively traded firms in Egypt (Omran and Pointon, 2004). Investment opportunities influence dividend policies in EFMs for three reasons: (1) availability of good projects in high-growth economies, (2) difficulty in raising external equity capital, and (3) influence of controlling shareholders on directing funds to reinvestment rather than payout.

A second similarity is the decrease in the proportion of firms paying dividends. This decrease, well known in DFMs, has taken hold in several EFMs as well, including India (Reddy and Rath, 2005; Som, 2006), Jordan (Al-Malkawi, 2007), Thailand (Ronapat and Evans, 2005), and Turkey (Adaoglu, 2000). In most of these countries, as in the United States (Skinner, 2008), a key reason for the decrease seems to be the emergence of a large group of newer companies that have yet to pay dividends. Some EFMs have more local reasons for the drop in the fraction of dividend payers. An example is the abrogation of mandatory dividend laws in Turkey after 1995 (Yilmaz and Gulay, 2006).

A weaker similarity is the role that certain types of investors play in encouraging cash dividend payments. In the United States, empirical (Brav and Heaton, 1998) and survey evidence (Brav et al., 2005) indicate that a prudent-man consideration leads institutional investors to favor dividend payers. Some evidence exists that a related consideration may influence dividend decisions in countries with privatized pension systems, particularly in Latin America (Glen et al., 1995).

Differences between EFMs and DFMs

Alongside those similarities, the literature identifies significant differences between dividend policies in EFMs and DFMs. The most basic is the method of distributing corporate earnings to shareholders. Notwithstanding the legalization of share repurchases in many EFMs, repurchases have become common practice in only a few. Other than Taiwan, Hong Kong and especially South Korea, there is little evidence that stock buybacks are gaining much popularity in other EFMs.

Second, substantial differences in ownership structures between EFMs and DFMs lead to differences in their payout policies. For example, the government or a government-related entity is a key shareholder of at least some corporations in several EFMs. The notion that, ceteris paribus, state-controlled firms have different payout ratios is borne out by evidence from Jordan (Al-Malkawi, 2007), Oman (Al-Yahyaee, Pham, and Walter, 2006), the Philippines (Glen et al., 1995), Malaysia (Sun and Tong, 2002), and China (Xu and Wang, 1997; Gul, 1999a; Wei, Zhang, and Xiao, 2004; Deng, Gan, and He, 2007).

Another difference is that various EFM companies are subsidiaries of multinational companies from the United States and United Kingdom and tend to pay substantial, stable dividends (Lehmann and Mody, 2004). A third difference is that, in line with the evidence in Faccio et al. (2001) for Western Europe, the existence of large external (noncontrolling) shareholders affects dividend policy in some EFMs. In the Czech Republic, for example, the existence of a large outside shareholder has a positive effect on dividend payments (Bena and Hanousek, 2008). In Korea, there is similar evidence that outside block holders tend to switch their investments from passive to active when a firm's payout ratio is low, and such switches have resulted in increases in payout (Kim, Kim, and Kwon, 2007). Investors also value dividends more highly at well-governed Korean firms (Black, Jang, and Kim, 2006).

Finally, in addition to the de facto conditions (e.g., controlling versus outside shareholders) already discussed, various de jure conditions (e.g., different share classes, restrictions on foreign investors, differential taxation of dividends depending on the recipient) also have direct implications for dividend policy. In many Eastern European countries, for example, investors deprived of their voting rights get legal preferential treatment in terms of dividends (Berglöf and Pajuste, 2003). In Thailand, by contrast, foreign investors who exceed some legal ownership threshold lose not only their voting rights but also their dividend rights (Ronapat and Evans, 2005).

Third, EFMs have much greater exposure than DFMs to severe economic shocks. Hence, both controlling shareholders and managers are likely to push for dividends reductions when earnings fall. Researchers document this willingness to cut dividends in a broad set of EFMs including India (Reddy, 2002; Som, 2006), Jordan (Al-Malkawi, 2007), Oman (Al-Yahyaee et al., 2006), Tunisia (Ben Naceur,

Goaied, and Belanes, 2006), and Turkey (Adaoglu, 2000). Indeed, when a major financial crisis hits, evidence from Thailand (Ronapat and Evans, 2005; Bailey, Mao, and Sirodom, 2008) and Argentina (Bebzcuk, 2004) suggests that many companies simply omit dividends. The findings confirm the conclusion from cross-country studies that many EFM firms do not perceive dividend stability to be as essential as do their DFM counterparts.

A SIMPLE EMPIRICAL ANALYSIS

With the exception of Mitton (2004), whose data series end in 2001 for most firms, almost all EFM cross-country dividend studies use corporate data series ending in the early to mid-1990s. This section uses 1994–2004 data to document the evolution of corporate dividend policies in 24 EFMs during a momentous decade that saw the legalization of share repurchases in many countries, the privatization of state-owned enterprises, two major financial crises—Asia and Russia (1997–1998) and Argentina (2001–2002)—and the beginning of a renewed investment boom in EFMs.

The data used are from the 2005 Worldscope (EFMs) and 2007 Compustat (United States), excluding financial firms (1-digit SIC code 6) and firms with suspect data (missing or negative common dividends and/or negative figures for sales or total assets). Tables 28.2 through 28.5 provide summary statistics. Figure 28.1 plots the proportion of dividend-paying firms over time. Figure 28.2 presents the median payout ratios for dividend-paying firms. Figure 28.3 plots the median dividends-to-sales ratios for dividend-paying firms, while Figure 28.4 displays the same information for all firms in each country.

Dividends-to-sales ratios may be more robust than payout ratios for several reasons. First, as La Porta et al. (2000, p. 11) observe, "Sales are less dependent (than earnings) on accounting conventions, are harder to manipulate or smooth through accounting practices, and are less subject to theft." Second, even absent deliberate distortions of earnings, payout policy may not be intuitively obvious from a cursory examination of payout ratios in markets subject to significant volatility. This is because, when a firm's earnings are close to zero, a small change in earnings can make its payout ratio oscillate between very large positive and negative values. This issue is unlikely to matter much in DFMs where most dividends are paid by large and stable corporations that, unlike their EFM counterparts, are less often subject to major macroeconomic shocks. If corporate earnings drop precipitously in an EFM as a consequence of a macro shock and if companies do not cut their dividends substantially, then large swings should be expected in many companies' payout ratios. Dividends-to-sales ratios are immune to this problem and can better describe dividend policies during major economic downturns.

Proportion of Dividend-Paying Firms

The fraction of firms paying dividends has fallen somewhat in the United States (Fama and French, 2001; DeAngelo, DeAngelo, and Skinner, 2004) and in major DFMs (Dennis and Osobov, 2008). Figure 28.1 highlights several noteworthy facts about the proportion of dividend-paying firms in EFMs versus the United States.

Table 28.2 Dividend Payout Ratios — Summary Statistics for All Companies, 1994–2004

Country	1995–2004				1995–1999			2000–2004			Change: 90s to 00s	
	N	Mean	Median	Std. Dev	N	Mean	Median	N	Mean	Median	Mean	Median
Argentina	529	0.243	0	3.828	237	0.321	0.147	320	0.189	0	−0.132	−0.147
Brazil	2,095	0.263	0.132	5.992	840	0.227	0.238	1,334	0.291	0.132	0.065	−0.106
Chile	1,075	0.741	0.418	5.031	467	0.808	0.449	664	0.677	0.418	−0.132	−0.031
Colombia	223	0.617	0.414	1.985	118	0.698	0.380	123	0.508	0.414	−0.190	0.034
Czech Republic	317	0.447	0.000	3.159	162	0.172	0.000	155	0.735	0.000	0.563	0.000
Hong Kong	4,896	0.268	0	1.823	1,494	0.364	0.221	3,512	0.240	0	−0.124	−0.221
Hungary	232	0.349	0	1.051	98	0.249	0.036	139	0.419	0	0.170	−0.036
India	3,101	0.300	0.188	1.058	1,259	0.355	0.217	1,859	0.263	0.188	−0.092	−0.030
Indonesia	1,889	0.193	0	1.430	748	0.288	0.136	1,221	0.159	0	−0.130	−0.136
Jordan	36	0.587	0.616	0.388	5	0.802	0.698	31	0.553	0.616	−0.250	−0.082
South Korea	5,366	0.208	0	1.969	1,906	0.247	0.011	3,638	0.183	0	−0.064	−0.011
Malaysia	4,993	0.215	0.092	4.184	1,725	0.295	0.163	3,438	0.183	0.092	−0.112	−0.071
Mexico	998	0.455	0	9.900	498	0.821	0	558	0.112	0	−0.709	0
Morocco	64	2.067	0.558	8.345	14	0.327	0.315	50	2.554	0.558	2.227	0.243
Pakistan	839	0.282	0.102	0.907	447	0.230	0.001	459	0.335	0.102	0.105	0.101
Philippines	954	0.060	0	2.182	405	0.155	0	590	−0.001	0	−0.156	0
Poland	568	0.133	0	0.577	216	0.144	0	360	0.125	0	−0.019	0
Russian Federation	256	0.754	0.034	8.598	76	0.049	0.007	180	1.052	0.034	1.003	0.027
Singapore	3,158	0.397	0.094	3.512	959	0.330	0.213	2,294	0.417	0.094	0.087	−0.119
Slovenia	21	0.280	0.248	0.220	NA	NA	NA	21	0.280	0.248	NA	NA
South Africa	2,436	0.180	0.019	2.042	1,073	0.272	0.105	1,453	0.121	0.019	−0.151	−0.086
Taiwan	6,625	0.220	0	2.656	1,290	0.164	0	5,434	0.236	0	0.072	0
Thailand	2,748	0.464	0	3.314	1,166	0.738	0.194	1,743	0.313	0	−0.425	−0.194
Turkey	1,072	0.256	0	1.702	342	0.598	0.242	753	0.110	0	−0.488	−0.242
United States	81,318	0.166	0	4.1	44,452	0.168	0	36,866	0.162	0	−0.006	0

This table provides summary statistics for the ratio of cash dividends (excluding preferred dividends) to earnings (net income) in 24 EFMs and in the United States. The data are from the 2005 Worldscope (EFMs) or the 2007 Compustat (United States). For each year, ratios are for all firms in the relevant database including firms that did not pay regular dividends that year, except for financial firms (1-digit SIC code 6) and firms with suspect data (missing or negative common dividends and negative figures for sales or total assets).

510

Table 28.3 Dividend Payout Ratio: Summary Statistics for Dividend-Paying Companies Only, 1994–2004

Country	1995–2004				1995–1999			2000–2004			Change: 90s to 00s	
	N	Mean	Median	Std. Dev	N	Mean	Median	N	Mean	Median	Mean	Median
Argentina	212	0.607	6.038	0.526	124	0.550	0.526	88	0.686	0.445	0.135	−0.081
Brazil	1,232	0.448	7.810	0.348	475	0.343	0.348	757	0.513	0.343	0.170	−0.005
Chile	939	0.849	5.375	0.481	377	0.922	0.481	562	0.799	0.484	−0.123	0.004
Colombia	170	0.810	2.240	0.550	80	0.940	0.550	90	0.694	0.610	−0.246	0.060
Czech Republic	165	0.859	4.344	0.303	83	0.335	0.303	82	1.389	0.341	1.054	0.038
Hong Kong	2,520	0.521	2.515	0.353	979	0.480	0.353	1,541	0.547	0.362	0.067	0.009
Hungary	114	0.711	1.413	0.277	48	0.475	0.277	66	0.882	0.415	0.407	0.138
India	2,506	0.371	1.165	0.239	1,080	0.408	0.239	1,426	0.343	0.235	−0.065	−0.004
Indonesia	933	0.391	2.016	0.239	448	0.382	0.239	485	0.400	0.234	0.017	−0.006
Jordan	31	0.682	0.331	0.656	5	0.802	0.656	26	0.659	0.629	−0.144	−0.027
South Korea	3,119	0.358	2.573	0.167	1,086	0.417	0.167	2,033	0.327	0.177	−0.090	0.010
Malaysia	3,235	0.332	5.194	0.249	1,243	0.360	0.249	1,992	0.315	0.279	−0.045	0.030
Mexico	423	1.073	15.194	0.230	199	1.966	0.230	224	0.279	0.250	−1.687	0.021
Morocco	63	2.100	8.408	0.559	13	0.352	0.559	50	2.554	0.630	2.202	0.071
Pakistan	529	0.448	1.110	0.394	225	0.369	0.394	304	0.506	0.440	0.137	0.046
Philippines	293	0.196	3.938	0.218	145	0.399	0.218	148	−0.004	0.314	−0.403	0.096
Poland	204	0.370	0.917	0.227	95	0.321	0.227	109	0.412	0.300	0.091	0.073
Russian Federation	177	1.091	10.331	0.088	49	0.077	0.088	128	1.479	0.137	1.403	0.049
Singapore	2,013	0.623	4.383	0.284	715	0.417	0.284	1,298	0.736	0.294	0.319	0.010
Slovenia	17	0.346	0.190	0.281	NA	NA	NA	17	0.346	0.281	NA	NA
South Africa	1,353	0.324	2.731	0.268	629	0.416	0.268	724	0.244	0.271	−0.173	0.003
Taiwan	2,247	0.648	4.531	0.333	342	0.511	0.333	1,905	0.673	0.327	0.162	−0.006
Thailand	1,510	0.844	4.436	0.449	593	1.230	0.449	917	0.594	0.445	−0.636	−0.004
Turkey	449	0.612	2.589	0.358	233	0.824	0.358	216	0.382	0.380	−0.442	0.022
United States	25,060	0.538	7.373	0.322	14,149	0.529	0.322	10,911	0.549	0.323	0.020	0.001

This table provides summary statistics for the ratio of cash dividends (excluding preferred dividends) to earnings (net income) in 24 EFMs and in the United States. The data are from the 2005 Worldscope (EFMs) or the 2007 Compustat (United States). Ratios are for dividend-paying firms only, excluding financial firms (1-digit SIC code 6) and firms with suspect data (missing or negative common dividends and negative figures for sales or total assets).

Table 28.4 Dividends-to-Sales Ratio: Summary Statistics for All Companies, 1994–2004

Country	1995–2004				1995–1999			2000–2004			Change: 90s to 00s	
	N	Mean	Median	Std. Dev	N	Mean	Median	N	Mean	Median	Mean	Median
Argentina	166	0.060	0.044	0.064	238	0.049	0.017	68	0.028	0.044	−0.021	0.027
Brazil	1,101	0.038	0.025	0.044	841	0.027	0.009	680	0.027	0.025	0.000	0.016
Chile	792	0.077	0.040	0.110	468	0.090	0.044	465	0.033	0.040	−0.057	−0.004
Colombia	145	0.076	0.054	0.085	119	0.060	0.025	80	0.029	0.054	−0.031	0.029
Czech Republic	154	0.032	0.014	0.053	162	0.013	0.000	75	0.028	0.014	0.015	0.014
Hong Kong	2,250	0.054	0.031	0.073	1,494	0.044	0.018	1,370	0.039	0.031	−0.006	0.012
Hungary	100	0.036	0.027	0.030	98	0.018	0.005	55	0.038	0.027	0.021	0.022
India	2,387	0.025	0.018	0.029	1,259	0.022	0.016	1,360	0.022	0.018	−0.001	0.002
Indonesia	845	0.032	0.021	0.050	748	0.029	0.013	439	0.026	0.021	−0.003	0.008
Jordan	25	0.104	0.104	0.052	5	0.110	0.122	21	0.069	0.104	−0.041	−0.018
South Korea	2,934	0.010	0.007	0.014	1,911	0.004	0.002	1,933	0.011	0.007	0.006	0.005
Malaysia	2,942	0.039	0.020	0.066	1,725	0.036	0.015	1,794	0.019	0.020	−0.016	0.005
Mexico	390	0.027	0.015	0.030	498	0.016	0	207	0.020	0.015	0.004	0.015
Morocco	44	0.073	0.057	0.056	14	0.034	0.029	31	0.066	0.057	0.033	0.029
Pakistan	477	0.041	0.020	0.053	448	0.020	0.001	269	0.044	0.020	0.024	0.019
Philippines	270	0.042	0.019	0.084	408	0.014	0	132	0.026	0.019	0.011	0.019
Poland	189	0.017	0.012	0.023	216	0.006	0	97	0.023	0.012	0.016	0.012
Russian Federation	172	0.017	0.009	0.032	76	0.004	0.002	124	0.015	0.009	0.010	0.006
Singapore	1,829	0.033	0.017	0.051	959	0.026	0.013	1,171	0.027	0.017	0.001	0.004
Slovenia	17	0.017	0.006	0.016	NA	NA	NA	17	0.014	0.006	NA	NA
South Africa	1,283	0.029	0.014	0.055	1,075	0.021	0.006	679	0.032	0.014	0.011	0.009
Taiwan	1,998	0.036	0.024	0.040	1,292	0.013	0	1,691	0.026	0.024	0.013	0.024
Thailand	1,273	0.049	0.033	0.055	1,168	0.037	0.016	777	0.039	0.033	0.002	0.016
Turkey	394	0.049	0.030	0.069	342	0.038	0.021	190	0.040	0.030	0.001	0.008
United States	22,713	0.036	0.024	0.046	44,465	0.014	0	9,859	0.017	0.024	0.003	0.024

This table provides summary statistics for the ratio of cash dividends (excluding preferred dividends) to sales (net sales or revenues) in 24 EFMs and in the United States. The data are from the 2005 Worldscope (EFMs) or the 2007 Compustat (United States). For each year, ratios are for all firms in the relevant database including firms that did not pay regular dividends that year, excluding financial firms (1-digit SIC code 6) and firms with suspect data (missing or negative common dividends and negative figures for sales or total assets).

Table 28.5 Dividends-to-Sales Ratio: Summary Statistics for Dividend-Paying Companies, 1994–2004

Country	1995–2004				1995–1999			2000–2004			Change: 90s to 00s	
	N	Mean	Median	Std. Dev	N	Mean	Median	N	Mean	Median	Mean	Median
Argentina	212	0.079	0.052	0.087	124	0.083	0.052	88	0.074	0.045	-0.009	-0.007
Brazil	1,233	0.044	0.027	0.060	476	0.043	0.027	757	0.045	0.028	0.001	0.001
Chile	939	0.090	0.044	0.123	377	0.097	0.044	562	0.086	0.042	-0.011	-0.002
Colombia	170	0.079	0.057	0.085	80	0.074	0.057	90	0.085	0.057	0.011	0.000
Czech Republic	165	0.045	0.015	0.103	83	0.025	0.015	82	0.066	0.021	0.041	0.005
Hong Kong	2,520	0.061	0.032	0.087	979	0.058	0.032	1,541	0.063	0.033	0.005	0.000
Hungary	114	0.037	0.030	0.030	48	0.033	0.030	66	0.040	0.033	0.007	0.003
India	2,506	0.027	0.018	0.037	1,080	0.025	0.018	1,426	0.029	0.018	0.003	0.000
Indonesia	933	0.036	0.022	0.055	448	0.041	0.022	485	0.032	0.017	-0.008	-0.005
Jordan	31	0.105	0.108	0.054	5	0.110	0.108	26	0.104	0.106	-0.006	-0.002
South Korea	3,121	0.011	0.007	0.016	1,086	0.007	0.007	2,035	0.013	0.008	0.006	0.002
Malaysia	3,235	0.044	0.020	0.077	1,243	0.043	0.020	1,992	0.044	0.021	0.002	0.001
Mexico	423	0.032	0.016	0.042	199	0.033	0.016	224	0.031	0.015	-0.002	-0.001
Morocco	63	0.095	0.062	0.078	13	0.036	0.062	50	0.110	0.083	0.074	0.021
Pakistan	529	0.046	0.022	0.064	225	0.033	0.022	304	0.055	0.028	0.022	0.006
Philippines	293	0.055	0.022	0.109	145	0.036	0.022	148	0.074	0.033	0.038	0.011
Poland	204	0.021	0.013	0.038	95	0.014	0.013	109	0.027	0.014	0.014	0.001
Russian Federation	177	0.017	0.009	0.031	49	0.007	0.009	128	0.021	0.011	0.014	0.002
Singapore	2,013	0.040	0.018	0.069	715	0.031	0.018	1,298	0.044	0.019	0.013	0.001
Slovenia	17	0.017	0.006	0.016	NA	NA	NA	17	0.017	0.006	NA	NA
South Africa	1,353	0.032	0.015	0.062	629	0.030	0.015	724	0.034	0.016	0.004	0.001
Taiwan	2,249	0.039	0.025	0.049	344	0.044	0.025	1,905	0.039	0.024	-0.006	-0.001
Thailand	1,510	0.062	0.036	0.082	593	0.057	0.036	917	0.064	0.037	0.007	0.002
Turkey	449	0.052	0.030	0.073	233	0.052	0.030	216	0.052	0.027	-0.001	-0.003
United States	25,063	0.044	0.025	0.068	14,151	0.043	0.025	10,912	0.044	0.026	0.001	0.000

This table provides summary statistics for the ratio of cash dividends (excluding preferred dividends) to sales (net sales or revenues) in 24 EFMs and in the United States. The data are from the 2005 Worldscope (EFMs) or the 2007 Compustat (U.S.). Ratios are for dividend-paying firms only, excluding financial firms (1-digit SIC code 6) and firms with suspect data (missing or negative common dividends and negative figures for sales or total assets).

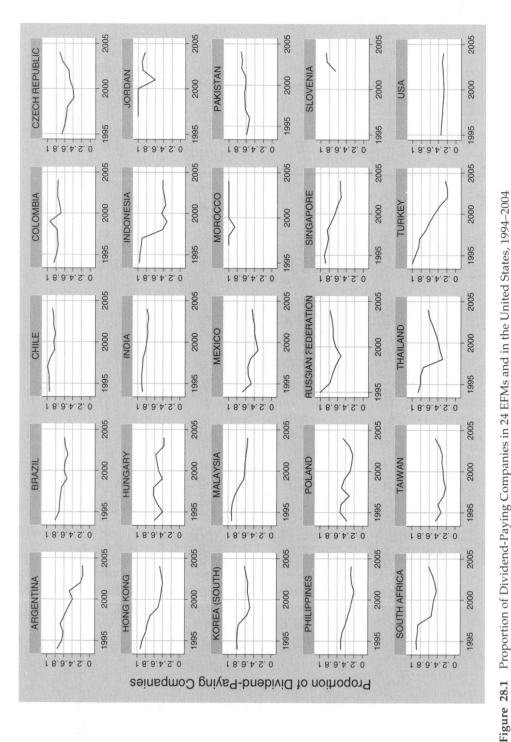

Figure 28.1 Proportion of Dividend-Paying Companies in 24 EFMs and in the United States, 1994–2004
This figure plots the proportion of dividend-paying companies in 24 EFMs and in the United States between 1994 and 2004. The data are from the 2005 Worldscope (EFMs) and 2007 Compustat (United States), excluding financial firms (1-digit SIC code 6) and firms with suspect data (missing or negative common dividends and negative figures for sales or total assets).

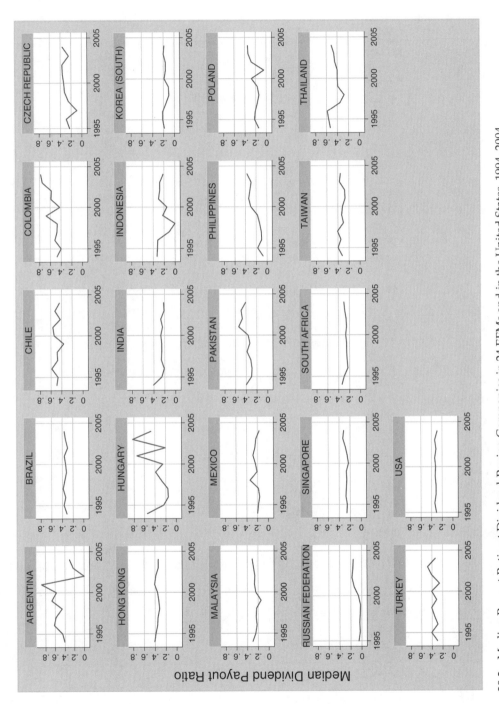

Figure 28.2 Median Payout Ratio at Dividend-Paying Companies in 24 EFMs and in the United States, 1994–2004

This figure plots the median ratio of cash dividends (excluding preferred dividends) to earnings (net income) in 24 EFMs and in the United States between 1994 and 2004. The data are from the 2005 Worldscope (EFMs) or the 2007 Compustat (United States). In any given year, the ratio is computed for dividend-paying firms only, excluding financial firms (1-digit SIC code 6) and firms with suspect data (missing or negative common dividends and negative figures for sales or total assets).

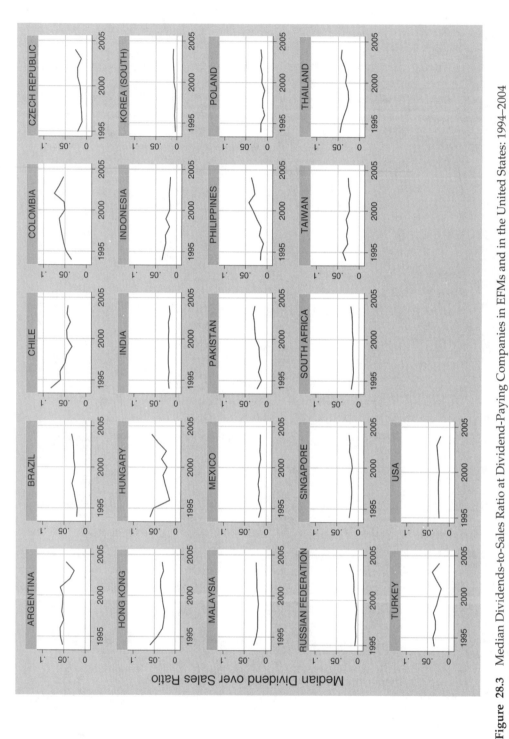

Figure 28.3 Median Dividends-to-Sales Ratio at Dividend-Paying Companies in EFMs and in the United States: 1994–2004

This figure plots the median ratio of cash dividends (excluding preferred dividends) to sales (net revenues or sales) in 24 EFMs and in the United States between 1994 and 2004. The data are from the 2005 Worldscope (EFMs) or the 2007 Compustat (U.S.). In any given year, the ratio is computed for dividend-paying firms only, excluding financial firms (1-digit SIC code 6) and firms with suspect data (missing or negative common dividends, and negative figures for sales or total assets).

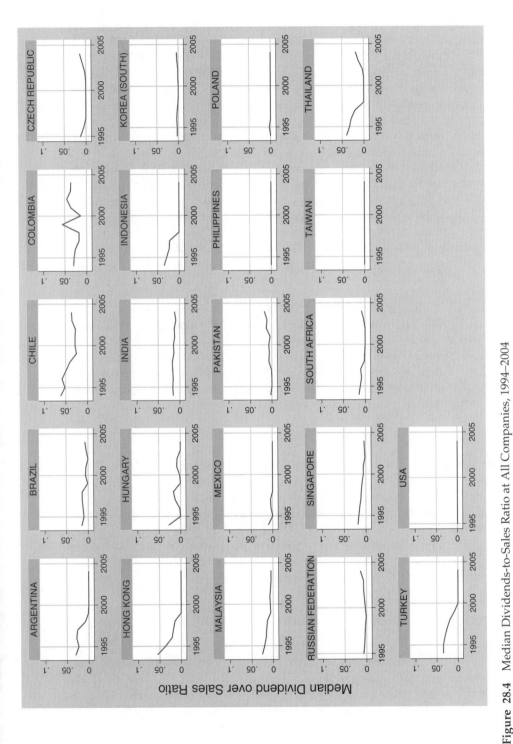

Figure 28.4 Median Dividends-to-Sales Ratio at All Companies, 1994–2004

This figure plots the median ratio of cash dividends (excluding preferred dividends) to sales ("net revenues or sales") in 24 EFMs and in the United States from 1994 to 2004. The data are from the 2005 Worldscope (EFMs) or 2007 Compustat (United States). In any given year, the ratio is computed for all firms including those that did not pay any regular dividends that year, but excluding financial firms (1-digit SIC code 6) and firms with suspect data (missing or negative common dividends and negative figures for sales or total assets).

517

Levels

The fraction of companies paying dividends has historically been much higher in EFMs than in the United States. This disparity continues through the period although the difference has shrunk somewhat. The proportion of U.S. dividend-paying firms hovers around 30 percent, declining almost continuously between 1994 and 2001 but increasing slightly after the burst of the Internet stock bubble. The first part of this pattern is consistent with the idea that numerous newly listed technology firms elected not to start paying dividends. The second part may reflect the disappearance of internet firms after the tech-stock bust, although a similar increase in dividend payout ratios also took place in Western Europe during that period (von Eije and Megginson, 2008).

In many EFMs, the proportion of dividend payers exceeds 80 percent of the companies in the data set. Brazil, Chile, and Colombia merit special mention as they require dividend payments from firms reporting positive earnings. Even excluding mandatory-dividend countries, a majority of firms in more than two-thirds of the EFMs pay dividends. In only three countries (Argentina, Philippines, and Turkey) is the proportion of dividend payers now slightly lower than in the United States.

Trends

In two Eastern European EFMs (Czech Republic and Poland), Pakistan, and Taiwan, trend reversals follow initial decreases in the proportion of dividend payers—so much so that the proportion of dividend payers is higher in 2004 than in 1995. In 13 of the 24 EFMs studied, however, the proportion of dividend-paying firms falls almost continuously—either moderately (Brazil, Jordan, South Korea, and Mexico) or rapidly (Argentina, Hong Kong, Indonesia, Malaysia, Philippines, Singapore, South Africa, Thailand, and Turkey).

Volatility

The proportion of dividend-paying firms fluctuates substantially more in EFMs than in the United States. Notably, this percentage dropped sharply after the Asian crisis of 1997–1998 in Malaysia (from more than 80 percent to about 60 percent), South Korea (from just under 80 percent to less than 50 percent), Indonesia (from 96 percent to 33 percent), Turkey (from 100 percent to 20 percent), and Thailand (from 76 percent to just over 30 percent). Similarly, the portion of dividend payers in Argentina fell by more than half in 2002 after the sovereign crisis and fell further in 2003.

Magnitude of Dividend Payments

Figure 28.1 shows that, on average, a greater fraction of EFMs firms pay dividends than do U.S. firms, while economic volatility in EFMs induces more variations in the patterns of dividend payments. Are EFM dividend payers more generous than their U.S. counterparts? The answers to this question are in Tables 28.2, 28.3, 28.4, and 28.5, and Figures 28.2, 28.3, and 28.4. Several findings emerge from these graphs.

Levels

The median payout ratio at U.S. dividend-paying firms varies between 30 percent and 35 percent. The figure is comparable in many of EFMs including Brazil, the Czech Republic, Hong Kong, Singapore, Taiwan, and Turkey. The U.S. ratio is slightly higher than in India, Indonesia, Malaysia, Mexico, the Philippines, Poland, South Africa, and South Korea, but smaller than the typical payout ratio in Argentina (except in 2001–2002), Chile and Colombia, where the payout ratio routinely exceeds 50 percent. The dividends-to-sales ratio at dividend-paying firms tells a similar story. In the United States, the median ratio is around 2.5 percent. About half of the EFMs studies have higher median dividends-to-sales ratios.

In the early 1990s, Glen et al. (1995) observed that dividend payout ratios are lower in EFMs than in DFMs. Tables 28.2 through 28.5 show that corporate dividend payout ratios in EFMs have become comparable to those in the United States. This finding could partly reflect greater internal resources and greater profitability at EFMs firms. In addition, an overall increase in dividend payout ratios may reflect improvements in minority shareholders' rights. Indeed, while the reported indicators for creditors' rights, financial transparency and corporate governance are generally inferior in EFMs to DFMs, there is evidence that many EFMs are making efforts to remedy these shortfalls (International Monetary Fund, 2005).

Trends

With the dividends-to-sales ratio trending slightly upward in a few countries (Colombia, Czech Republic, Hungary, Philippines, Poland, and Russia) and slightly downward in a few of the others (Chile, Hong Kong, and Indonesia), Figure 28.3 provides little evidence of a major secular change in payout ratios. Eastern European EFMs are the exception as Figures 28.2 and 28.3 show increased dividend payments. A comparison of the 1995–1999 and 2000–2004 subperiods in Tables 28.3 and 28.5 confirms these observations.

Volatility

Figure 28.1 shows that the proportion of dividend-paying firms fluctuates more strongly in EFMs than in the United States. Figures 28.2 to 28.4 also show that the ratios of dividends to earnings or to sales are more subject to change in EFMs. Figure 28.3 best illustrates this fact, as the median dividends-to-sales ratio for dividend payers as well as nonpayers drops to zero (or close to zero) in many EFMs after the Asian crisis in 1997–1998 (Hong Kong, South Korea, Malaysia, and Indonesia as well as in Argentina and Mexico). This apparent readiness to cut dividends is in line with the conclusions of several studies discussed earlier (Glen et al., 1995; Bebczuk, 2004; Som, 2006).

Market data show that the corporate bank liabilities in EFMs exceed their bond liabilities, which suggests that the countries may typically be characterized as bank-centric rather than capital market–centric (International Monetary Fund, 2005). Aivazian et al. (2003b) argue that dividends should be more predictable in arm's-length capital markets and less so in bank-centric markets. Evidence provided in the various figures and tables suggests that dividends paid by EFM corporations are in fact less predictable than in the U.S. control sample.

CONCLUSIONS

One objective of this chapter is to synthesize the extant research on dividend policies in emerging financial markets. This research shows that the environments conditioning or constraining corporate payout policies in these markets differ substantially from those in developed financial markets, specifically in terms of (1) legal mandates on the amounts that may be or *must* be paid out; (2) legislation relating to share repurchases, with most EFMs legalizing share repurchases only recently and with buybacks becoming common in just a few EFMs; (3) overall macroeconomic volatility; and (4) ownership structure.

Ownership structure, in particular, has a major impact on EFM firms' dividend policies. First, the presence of foreign and, especially, governmental owners influences managers' propensity to pay large, stable dividends. Second, at domestically owned EFM companies, the prevalence of concentrated ownership structures reduces the need for dividend payments as signals. Third, the generosity of corporate payout policies is generally higher in countries offering greater investor protections, thus lending support for the notion that dividends are the outcomes of minority investors' exercising their legal power to wrest resources from corporate insiders.

The second objective of this chapter is to present some empirical evidence on EFM dividend policies using recent data. The results show that the proportion of dividend-paying firms remains much higher in most EFMs than in the United States. While the proportion of dividend-paying firms has been relatively stable in the United States, this proportion fluctuates considerably over time in EFMs. The magnitude of dividend distributions, as measured by the dividend payout ratio and the dividends-to-sales ratio of dividend-paying firms, is now comparable in many EFMs and in the U.S. sample. Although there is little evidence of major secular changes in payout ratios at EFM firms, these ratios are more volatile in EFMs than in the United States. A cause for dividend instability is the volatile economic environment in which EFM firms operate—in particular, the financial crises experienced directly or indirectly by many EFMs in 1997 and 1998 and again in 2001–2002.

In sum, macroeconomic instability and ownership structure are key drivers of dividend policies in EFMs. This chapter shows the results of simple data analyses that are sufficiently revealing to enable a comparison of dividend policies in EFMs to those in the United States. The chapter also relates the figures derived to the global macroeconomic phenomena. A few extensions of this research may now be identified. While most studies have confined themselves to dividend payments, now that many EFMs permit share repurchases, an avenue of research would be to investigate whether repurchases and cash dividend payments are substitutes and/or complements. Next, the Lintner (1956) model, which explains current dividends in terms of past dividends and current earnings, has been a robust descriptor of dividend payments in the United States. Given the apparent volatility of their payout ratios, a useful extension would be to examine the kinds of models that could most effectively predict dividend payments in EFMs. Finally, the results of the data analyses provided in this study indicate that macroeconomic fluctuations affect dividend payments in EFMs. Thus, a worthwhile exercise would be to examine the time-series properties of dividend and earnings before and after the point when a crisis becomes apparent. More generally, changes in EFM corporate payout policies over the course of the business cycle seem worthy of study. The extent to which these EFM and DFM series differ should prove informative to the academic community, corporate managers, and policy makers who are concerned with the broader impacts of macroeconomic volatility.

REFERENCES

Adaoglu, Cahit. 1999. "Regulation Influence on the Dividend Policy of the Istanbul Stock Exchange (ISE) Corporations." *ISE Review* 3:11, 1–19.

Adaoglu, Cahit. 2000. "Instability in the Dividend Policy of the Istanbul Stock Exchange (ISE) Corporations: Evidence from an Emerging Market." *Emerging Markets Review* 1:3, 252–270.

Aivazian, Varouj A., Laurence Booth, and W. Sean Cleary. 2003a. "Do Firms in Emerging Markets Follow Different Dividend Policies from U.S. Firms?" *Journal of Financial Research* 26:3, 371–387.

Aivazian, Varouj A., Laurence Booth, and W. Sean Cleary. 2003b. "Dividend Policy and the Organization of Capital Markets." *Journal of Multinational Financial Management* 13:2, 101–121.

Allen, Franklin, and Roni Michaely. 2003. "Payout Policy." In *Handbook of the Economics of Finance 1A*, ed. George M. Constantinides, Milton Harris, and René M. Stulz, 337–429. Amsterdam: Elsevier/North-Holland.

Al-Malkawi, Husam-Aldin. 2007. "Determinants of Corporate Dividend Policy in Jordan: An Application of the Tobit Model." *Journal of Economic and Administrative Sciences* 23:2, 44–70.

Al-Yahyaee, Khamis, Toan Pham, and Terry Walter. 2006. "Dividend Policy in the Absence of Taxes." Working Paper, School of Banking and Finance, University of New South Wales.

Anderson, Christopher W. 1999. "Financial Contracting under Extreme Uncertainty: An Analysis of Brazilian Corporate Debentures." *Journal of Financial Economics* 51:1, 45–84.

Bagwell, Laurie S., and John B. Shoven. 1989. "Cash Distributions to Shareholders." *Journal of Economic Perspectives* 3:3, 129–140.

Bailey, Warren, Connie X. Mao, and Kulpatra Sirodom. 2008. "Locals, Foreigners, and Multi-market Trading of Equities: Evidence from Thailand." Working Paper, Cornell University.

Bebczuk, Ricardo N. 2004. "Explaining Dividend Policies in Argentina." Working Paper No. 50, Universidad Nacional de La Plata.

Beim, David O., and Charles Calomiris. 2001. *Emerging Financial Markets*. New York: McGraw-Hill Irwin.

Ben Naceur, Samy, Mohammed Goaied, and Amel Belanes. 2006. "On the Determinants and Dynamics of Dividend Policy." *International Review of Finance* 6:1–2, 1–23.

Bena, Jan, and Jan Hanousek. 2008. "Rent Extraction by Large Shareholders: Evidence Using Dividend Policy in the Czech Republic." *Czech Journal of Economics and Finance* 58:3, 106–130.

Berglöf, Erik, and Anete Pajuste. 2003. "Emerging Owners, Eclipsing Markets? Corporate Governance in Central and Eastern Europe." In *Corporate Governance and Capital Flows in a Global Economy*, ed. Peter K. Cornelius and Bruce Kogut, 276–304. Oxford: Oxford University Press.

Black, Bernard S., Hasung Jang, and Woochan Kim. 2006. "Does Corporate Governance Predict Firms' Market Values? Evidence from Korea." *Journal of Law, Economics, and Organization* 22:2, 366–413.

Brav, Alon, John R. Graham, Campbell R. Harvey, and Roni Michaely. 2005. "Payout Policy in the 21st Century." *Journal of Financial Economics* 77:3, 483–527.

Brav, Alon, and J. B. Heaton. 1998. "Did ERISA's Prudent Man Rule Change the Pricing of Dividend Omitting Firms?" Working Paper, Duke University.

Brockman, Paul, and Dennis Y. Chung. 2001. "Managerial Timing and Corporate Liquidity: Evidence from Actual Share Repurchases." *Journal of Financial Economics* 61:3, 417–448.

Castillo, Augusto, and Keith Jakob. 2006. "The Chilean Ex-Dividend Day." *Global Finance Journal* 17:1, 105–18.

Chang, Shao-Chi, Jung-Ho Lai, and Chen-Hsiang Yu. 2005. "The Intra-Industry Effect of Share Repurchase Deregulation: Evidence from Taiwan." *Review of Pacific Basin Financial Markets and Policies* 8:2, 251–277.

Chiao, Chaoshin, Hsiang-Hsuan Chih, Zi-May Wang, and Ya-Rou Hsu. 2007. "The Order Submission Behaviors Surrounding Open-Market Repurchase Announcements: The Examination of a Missing Link Embedded in the Signaling Hypothesis." Working Paper, National Dong Hwa University, Taiwan.

Christie, William G., and Vikram Nanda. 1994. "Free Cash Flow, Shareholder Value, and the Undistributed Profits Tax of 1936 and 1937." *Journal of Finance* 49:5, 1727–1754.

DeAngelo, Harry, Linda DeAngelo, and Douglas J. Skinner. 2004. "Are Dividends Disappearing? Dividend Concentration and the Consolidation of Earnings." *Journal of Financial Economics* 72:3, 425–456.

Deng, Jianping, Jie Gan, and Jia He. 2007. "Privatization, Large Shareholders' Incentive to Expropriate, and Firm Performance." AFA 2008 New Orleans Meetings Paper.

Denis, David J., and Igor Osobov. 2008. "Why Do Firms Pay Dividends? International Evidence on the Determinants of Dividend Policy." *Journal of Financial Economics* 89:1, 62-82.

De Ridder, Adri. 2006. "Share Repurchases and Firm Behavior." Working Paper, Centre for Banking and Finance. Stockholm, Sweden: Royal Institute of Technology.

Dewenter, Kathryn L., and Vincent A. Warther. 1998. "Dividends, Asymmetric Information, and Agency Conflicts: Evidence from a Comparison of the Dividend Policies of Japanese and U.S. Firms." *Journal of Finance* 53:3, 879–904.

Errunza, Vihang R. 1977. "Gains from Portfolio Diversification into Less Developed Countries' Securities." *Journal of International Business Studies* 8:2, 83–99.

Faccio, Mara, Larry H. P. Lang, and Leslie Young. 2001. "Dividends and Expropriation." *American Economic Review* 91:1, 54–78.

Fama, Eugene F., and Kenneth R. French. 2001. "Disappearing Dividends: Changing Firm Characteristics or Lower Propensity to Pay?" *Journal of Financial Economics* 60:1, 3–43.

Firth, Michael, and Canna S. F. Yeung. 2005. "An Empirical Investigation of Share Buybacks in Hong Kong." *Journal of Emerging Market Finance* 4:3, 207–225.

Glen, Jack D., Yannis Karmokolias, Robert R. Miller, and Sanjay Shah. 1995. "Dividend Policy and Behavior in Emerging Markets: To Pay or Not to Pay?" Discussion Paper No. 26. Washington, DC: International Finance Corporation.

Grullon, Gustavo, and Roni Michaely. 2002. "Dividends, Share Repurchases, and the Substitution Hypothesis." *Journal of Finance* 57:4, 1649–1684.

Gryglewicz, Sebastian. 2004. "Stock Repurchase as an Alternative to Dividend Payout: Evidence from the Warsaw Stock Exchange." Working Paper, Poznan University of Economics.

Gul, Ferdinand A. 1999a. "Government Share Ownership, Investment Opportunity Set and Corporate Policy Choices in China." *Pacific-Basin Finance Journal* 7:2, 157–172.

Gul, Ferdinand A., 1999b. "Growth Opportunities, Capital Structure and Dividend Policies in Japan." *Journal of Corporate Finance* 5:2, 141–168.

Gupta, L. C. 2005. "Corporate Practices Regarding Buyback of Shares and Its Regulation in India." Working Paper, Indian Council of Social Science Research.

Ho, Simon S. M., Kevin C. K. Lam, and Heibatollah Sami. 2004. "The Investment Opportunity Set, Director Ownership, and Corporate Policies: Evidence from an Emerging Market." *Journal of Corporate Finance* 10:3, 383–408.

International Monetary Fund. 2005. "Chapter 4: Corporate Finance in Emerging Markets." In *Global Financial Stability Report*, 92–133. Washington, DC: International Monetary Fund.

International Organization of Securities Commissions (OICV-IOSCO). 2004. *Report of the IOSCO Technical Committee on Stock Repurchase Programs*. Madrid: OICV-IOSCO.

Joh, Sung Wook, and Young Kyung Ko. 2007. "Ownership Structure and Share Repurchases in an Emerging Market: Incentive Alignment or Entrenchment?" Working Paper, Seoul National University.

Jung, Sung-Chang, Yong-Gyo Lee, and John H. Thornton, Jr. 2005. "An Empirical Comparison between Operations of Stabilization Funds and Stock Repurchases in Korea." *Pacific-Basin Finance Journal* 13:3, 319–341.

Kaminsky, Graciela L., Carmen M. Reinhart, and Carlos A. Végh. 2004. "When It Rains, It Pours: Procyclical Capital Flows and Macroeconomic Policies." Working Paper No. 10780, National Bureau of Economic Research.

Kim, Jaemin, Ralf Schremper, and Nikhil Varaiya. 2005. "Open Market Repurchase Regulations: A Cross-Country Examination." *Corporate Finance Review* 9:4, 29–38.

Kim, Woochan, Woojin Kim, and Kap-Sok Kwon. 2007. "Value of Shareholder Activism: Evidence from the Switchers." Law and Economics Working Paper No. 128, University of Texas School of Law.

Kowalewski, Oskar, Ivan Stetsyuk, and Oleksandr Talavera. 2007. "Does Corporate Governance Affect Dividend Policy? Evidence from Poland." Working Paper, Warsaw School of Economics.

Kumar, Jayesh. 2006. "Corporate Governance and Payout Policy in India." *Journal of Emerging Market Finance* 5:1, 15–58.

La Porta, Raphael, Florencio Lopez-de-Silanes, Andrei Shleifer, and Robert W. Vishny. 2000. "Agency Problems and Dividend Policies around the World." *Journal of Finance* 55:1, 1–33.

Lasfer, M. Ameziane. 2000. "The Market Valuation of Share Repurchases in Europe." Working Paper, City University Business School, London.

Lehmann, Alexander, and Ashoka Mody. 2004. "International Dividend Repatriations." Working Paper 04/5, International Monetary Fund.

Lintner, John. 1956. "Distribution of Incomes of Corporations among Dividends, Retained Earnings and Taxes." *American Economic Review* 46:2, 97–113.

Liu, Wei. 2002. "Do Dividends Substitute for Corporate Governance? A Cross-country Dynamic View." Working Paper, University of Indiana, Bloomington.

Mitton, Todd. 2004. "Corporate Governance and Dividend Policy in Emerging Markets." *Emerging Markets Review* 5:4, 409–426.

Morck, Randall, and Bernard Yeung. 2005. "Dividend Taxation and Corporate Governance." *Journal of Economic Perspectives* 19:3, 163–180.

Omran, Mohammed, and John Pointon. 2004. "Dividend Policy, Trading Characteristics and Share Prices: Empirical Evidence from Egyptian Firms." *International Journal of Theoretical and Applied Finance* 7:2, 121–133.

Pallage, Stéphane, and Michel A. Robe. 2003. "On the Welfare Costs of Economic Fluctuations in Developing Countries." *International Economic Review* 44:2, 677–698.

Pandey, I. M. 2001. "Corporate Dividend Policy and Behavior: The Malaysian Experience." Working Paper, Indian Institute of Management, Ahmedabad.

Pistor, Katharina, Yoram Keinan, Jan Kleinheisterkamp, and Mark D. West. 2003. "Innovation in Corporate Law." *Journal of Comparative Economics* 31:4, 676–694.

Price, Richard A., Francisco J. Roman, and Brian R. Rountree. 2007. "Governance Reform and Transparency: The Case of Mexico." Working Paper, Jesse H. Jones Graduate School of Management, Rice University.

Reddy, Y. Subba. 2002. "Dividend Policy of Indian Corporate Firms: An Analysis of Trends and Determinants." National Stock Exchange (NSE) Research Initiative Paper No. 19, Mumbai.

Reddy, Y. Subba, and Subhrendu Rath. 2005. "Disappearing Dividends in Emerging Markets? Evidence from India." *Emerging Markets Finance and Trade* 41:6, 58–82.

Ronapat, Malinee, and Michael Evans. 2005. "Disappearing Dividends in the Thai Capital Market: Changing Firm Characteristics or Lower Propensity to Pay." *Journal of Economic and Social Policy* 10:1, 169–212.

Sabri, Nidal R. 2003. "Using Treasury 'Repurchase' Shares to Stabilize Stock Markets." *International Journal of Business* 8:4, 425–450.

Saito, Richard. 2002. *Share Repurchase Rules and Expropriation of Minority Shareholders: Evidence from Brazil*. Sao Paulo, Brazil: FG Foundation.

Skinner, Douglas J. 2008. "The Evolving Relation between Earnings, Dividends, and Stock Repurchases." *Journal of Financial Economics* 87:3, 582–609.

Smith, Clifford W., and Ross L. Watts. 1992. "The Investment Opportunity Set and Corporate Financing, Dividend, and Compensation Policies." *Journal of Financial Economics* 32:3, 263–292.

Som, Lalita S. 2006. *Stock Market Capitalization and Corporate Governance in India*. New Delhi: Oxford University Press.

Sun, Qian, and Wilson H. S. Tong. 2002. "Malaysia Privatization: A Comprehensive Study." *Financial Management* 31:4, 79–105.

Stulz, René M., and Rohan Williamson. 2003. "Culture, Openness, and Finance." *Journal of Financial Economics* 70:3, 313–349.

Travlos, Nickolaos, Lenos Trigeorgis, and Nikos Vafeas. 2001. "Shareholder Wealth Effects of Dividend Policy Changes in an Emerging Stock Market: The Case of Cyprus." *Multinational Financial Journal* 5:2, 87–112.

Vermaelen, Theo. 2005. "Share Repurchases." *Foundations and Trends in Finance* 1:3, 1–103.

von Eije, J. Henk, and William L. Megginson. 2008. "Dividend Policy and Share Repurchases in the European Union." *Journal of Financial Economics*, 89:2, 347–374.

Wei, Jim Gang, Weiguo Zhang, and Jason ZeZhong Xiao. 2004. "Dividend Payment and Ownership Structure in China." In *Advances in Financial Economics: Corporate Governance*, ed. Mark Hirschey, Kose John, and Anil K. Makhija, 9, 187–219. Amsterdam: JAI Press.

Xu, Xiaonian, and Yan Wang. 1997. "Ownership Structure, Corporate Governance, and Firm Performance: The Case of Chinese Stock Companies." Working Paper No. 1794, World Bank.

Yilmaz, Mustafa Kemal, and Guzhan Gulay. 2006. "Dividend Policies and Price-Volume Reactions to Cash Dividends on the Stock Market: Evidence from the Istanbul Stock Exchange." *Emerging Markets Finance and Trade* 42:4, 19–49.

ABOUT THE AUTHORS

P. C. Kumar is an emeritus professor at the Kogod School of Business, American University. He earned his Ph.D. from Pennsylvania State University in 1975. Kumar's research has been published in *Journal of Finance, Journal of Financial and Quantitative Analysis, Journal of Money, Credit and Banking, Journal of Banking and Finance*, and other academic journals. He has authored a book on the internal sources of development finance. His research interests cover the role of financial institutions and markets in economic development and growth, specifically as applied to emerging markets.

Michel A. Robe is an associate professor of finance at the Kogod School of Business, American University. He received his Ph.D. in financial economics from Carnegie Mellon University in 1995. Before joining American University, Robe taught international finance at the University of Miami and McGill University. His research interests include international financial economics, financial contracting, and the organization of financial markets. His work on market volatility, cross-border financial flows and risk sharing, financial regulation, insider trading, security design, and corporate payout policy has appeared in *Journal of Financial Economics*, *Journal of Financial and Quantitative Analysis*, *International Economic Review*, and other academic journals.

Index

abnormal returns, 42, 168
  cash flow, 151
  dividend change, 157
  insurance, regulated industries, 474
  real estate investment trusts, 475
Act of 1862, 26
adjustment model, 72
agency, 442
  capital costs, 205–206
  catering theory, 224–225
  control, minority shareholders, 62
  cross-country studies, emerging markets, 503–505
  dividend, 424, 426–427
  dividend policy, 448–451
  models, catering theory, 224–225
  shareholders, minority, 62
agency costs, 408, 410, 427
  capital costs, 205–206, 448–449
  cash dividend, 9
  dividend changes, 152–154
  dividend policy, 424, 442, 450
  executive compensation, 454–456
  firm life cycle, 201, 205–206
  free cash flow hypothesis, 145–161, 206
  global role, 155–157
  governance mechanisms, 62
  irrelevance theory, 107–108
  market imperfections, impact, 107–108
  overinvestment, 147–152, 154–155
  risk behavior, 449
  special dividends, 315–316, 318, 322
  stock repurchase, 247–250
  TRA, 470
  utilities, regulated industries, 472–473
agency theory
  dividend policy, 458–459
  free cash flow hypothesis, 450
  model, European, 72
American Revolution, 24–25
American Stock Exchange (AMEX), 208
analytical finance, 97, 110
announcement
  abnormal bond-price reaction, repurchases, 256
  dividend information, relationship, 169
  initiations, price drift, 234
  insurance, regulated industries, 474
  negative share price, repurchases, 247
  non-investment-grade debt, repurchases, 256
  ownership partitioning, 332–333
  period returns, repurchases, 151
  positive returns, repurchases, 247–248
  price drift, initiations, 234

  stock dividends, 332–333
  tender offers, 255
annual aggregate cash distributions, 55–56, 64
arbitrage arguments, 99
asset transfer, special dividends (SDDs), 318
asymmetric information, 163
  catering theory, 223–224
  dividend signaling, 171
  signaling theory, 9
asymmetry theory, stock splits, 368–388
attention hypothesis, stock dividends, 334
average dividend payout ratios, banking, 468

Baker, Farrelly, Edelman followup survey, 366–369
Baker, H. Kent, 366–369
Baker, Wurgler catering theory of dividends, 217–222
Bank holding companies (BHCs), 467, 469
Bank of England, 25
Bank of New York, 25
Bank of North America, 25
Bank of the United States, 25
banking, regulated industries, 477
  BHCs, 467, 469
  CARs, 467–469
  dividend announcements, 468–469
  dividend studies, 463–467
  payout ratios, 468
  quality, 467
  regulatory capital requirements, impact, 464
  Rozeff model, 470
  signaling, 467–469
  TRA, 470
Basel Accord, 477
behavioral explanations, 179–200
  cash dividends, 9
  catering theory, 197
  clientele effects, 194–196
  dividends, 9, 192
  irrelevance, 182–191
  taxes, transaction costs, 196
  theoretical framework, 181
behavioral life cycle (BLC), 180–191, 408–412
behavioral model, 181, 367
bird in hand, 102, 179–180, 190, 472–473
Board of Trade, 28
board structure, corporate governance, 456–457
bond rating, 121
British East India Company, 23–24
British Parliament, 23
Bubble Act, 22, 24–26
bull market, 1990s, 197
Bush administration, 45, 477
buybacks, 11